FUNDAMENTALS OF
ACCOUNTING

F · O · R

DECISION MAKING

FUNDAMENTALS OF ACCOUNTING
F · O · R
DECISION MAKING

Kenneth R. Ferris
Thunderbird, American Graduate School of International Management

Mark E. Haskins
Colgate-Darden Graduate School of Business Administration
University of Virginia

Robert J. Sack
Colgate-Darden Graduate School of Business Administration
University of Virginia

Brandt R. Allen
Colgate-Darden Graduate School of Business Administration
University of Virginia

The McGraw-Hill Companies, Inc.
Primis Custom Publishing

New York ▪ St. Louis ▪ San Francisco ▪ Auckland ▪ Bogotá
Caracas ▪ Lisbon ▪ London ▪ Madrid ▪ Mexico ▪ Milan ▪ Montreal
New Delhi ▪ Paris ▪ San Juan ▪ Singapore ▪ Sydney ▪ Tokyo ▪ Toronto

McGraw-Hill Higher Education
A Division of The **McGraw-Hill** Companies

Previously published under: *Financial Accounting and Reporting, Second Edition,* by Mark E. Haskins, Kenneth R. Ferris, Robert J. Sack, and Brandt R. Allen.

© Richard D. Irwin, Inc., a Times Mirror Higher Education Group, Inc., Company, 1993 and 1997.

FUNDAMENTALS OF ACCOUNTING FOR DECISION MAKING

ISBN 0–07–235860–2

Printed in the United States of America

1 2 3 4 5 6 7 8 9 0 VH/VH 9 0 4 3 2 1 0 9

Editor: Karen Perry
Cover Designer: Maggie Lytle
Printer/Binder: Von Hoffmann Press

To our students, who have sought to know more
and in doing so have challenged us to find
better ways to teach.

ABOUT THE AUTHORS

Kenneth R. Ferris   Kenneth R. Ferris is a Distinguished Professor of World Business at the American Graduate School of International Management (Glendale, Arizona). He received a B.B.A. and an M.B.A. from George Washington University and earned an M.A. and a Ph.D. from Ohio State University. He previously served on the faculties of Northwestern University and Southern Methodist University and has taught at numerous academic institutions in Australia, Japan, and New Zealand. Professor Ferris is the author of nine books and numerous articles and case studies.

Mark E. Haskins   Mr. Haskins is Professor of Business Administration at the Darden Graduate School of Business Administration at the University of Virginia. He received his B.B.A. from the University of Cincinnati and his M.B.A. from Ohio University. He received his Ph.D. in Accounting from Pennsylvania State University.

Mr. Haskins has worked as an auditor for the international accounting firm Arthur Young & Co. He has provided executive education programs for a number of major U.S. corporations domestically and abroad.

Mr. Haskins is coauthor of two other texts titled *Corporate Financial Reporting: Text and Cases,* by Brownlee, Ferris, and Haskins, and *International Financial Reporting and Analysis: A Contextual Emphasis,* by Haskins, Ferris, and Selling.

Robert J. Sack   Mr. Sack is a Professor of Business Administration at the Darden School, the University of Virginia. He joined the Darden School after three years as the chief accountant of the SEC's Enforcement Division and 25 years in public practice as a partner of Touche Ross & Co. where he held a number of positions, including those of National Director of Accounting and Auditing Practice and Director of Professional Standards for Touche Ross International. Mr. Sack is a graduate of Miami University (Ohio).

Mr. Sack has written extensively on the subject of ethics in accounting. For three years he served as managing co-editor of *Accounting Horizons.*

Brandt R. Allen   Brandt R. Allen is the James C. Wheat Professor of Business Administration and Associate Dean for Executive Education at the Darden Graduate Business School, University of Virginia. Before joining the Virginia faculty in 1970, he taught at the Harvard Business School and before that he was a research engineer with the Boeing Company.

He is a well-known author, consultant, and lecturer in both the United States and Europe on the subject of information systems management. His current research focus is on how companies formulate and implement information systems strategy. He is a member of the Conference Board's Council of Information Management Executives. Professor Allen holds a B.S. in mathematics, an M.B.A. from the University of Washington, and a doctorate from Harvard University in control and information systems.

PREFACE

STATEMENT OF PURPOSE

In a past issue of the *Saturday Review,* an article titled "18,000,000 Books Nobody Reads" cited corporate annual reports as very low in interest, clarity, and understandability. This text's primary objective is, to a large extent, to confront this problem by developing future business leaders' financial statement literacy and to do so in a way that incorporates the abilities to (1) understand the nature of business transactions, (2) identify relevant economic events for reporting, (3) determine the most appropriate financial measures for those events, and (4) analyze the effects of those events in firm performance and financial condition. To this end, an underlying theme of the text is that accounting is not divorced from the world it describes or from the behaviors it measures and influences.

Philosophically, we believe that an introductory accounting text, whether used at the undergraduate or graduate level, does not need to explore every nuance of accounting practice and thought. Rather, the most important and predominant contemporary and classical accounting conventions are our foci. In this regard, the goal is to expose and discuss the underlying rationales of those practices and evaluate their effectiveness in providing useful information for decision making. Foremost among the practices investigated are those that purport to portray corporate financial position, operating results, cash flows, manager performance, and financial strength.

Even though the rule orientation of accounting practice cannot be ignored, both the classroom and the boardroom are appropriate places for questioning and debating those rules and conventions. Such scrutiny is crucial because it is important for students to develop an understanding of the management choices that must be made regarding what information to report, how best to report it, when to do so, and where controls are needed to assure reliable and relevant reporting. A critical aspect of these choices, dealt with in this text, is a concern for (1) the characteristics of information that make it most useful for decision making; (2) the characteristics of decision makers that also influence the usefulness of information; and (3) the subsequent behavior of managers, subordinates, and external constituencies that can be expected as a result of implementing certain reporting choices.

There are two reasons for our management/user approach. First, it allows us to deal comprehensively with a complex topic. Second, it helps the student retain a focus on concepts and ideas rather than on procedures. This approach requires considerable discipline on the part of the student, to mentally delegate his or her time to an understanding of business issues and a mastery of the basic financial reporting concepts without becoming too preoccupied with accounting mechanics. Thus, this text is designed primarily for those courses and student groups where the focus is on a balance between the understanding and use of accounting information and its preparation. Provided with a backdrop of contemporary management and financial concerns, students will see that accounting is a significant part of the world it purports to portray rather than an end in itself. On the contrary, students are provided the perspective that accounting information is a critical instrument in presenting a corporation's financial picture to important external constituencies. The raising of issues and concerns springing from this orientation facilitates a focus on substance and also frames students' learning because they have the comfort of a more familiar general business context for thinking about the accounting issue at hand.

KEY FEATURES

Real world based. The authors view accounting as an integral part of corporate decision making and financial analysis. Thus, accounting is not an end but a means to achieving relevant and reliable insights about business conditions, results, and opportunities. This book repeatedly grounds the discussion of accounting issues and methods in contexts of management decision making, financial analysis, management judgments and estimates, behavioral consequences, and/or the political arena, whichever context is most germane. Such an approach poses accounting as a vital, dynamic phenomenon rather than a sterile, procedural set of mechanics. To this end, the text contains *over 100* excerpts from recent annual reports that serve to highlight the realities of the issue at hand and to exemplify the fact that the financial reporting issues presented are pertinent to the day-to-day information concerns faced by real-world managers, lenders, investors, and financial statement users in general.

Holistic business approach. The book's managerial orientation frequently leverages the discussion of a particular topic via linkages with strategic and other functional area concerns typically encountered by managers. For example, receivables issues involve credit and collection policies in addition to the accounting issues. Inventory topics include operations concerns such as JIT and standard costing. In addition, the international aspects germane to many of the financial reporting issues covered in the chapters are also discussed.

Opportunities for student involvement. The end-of-chapter materials provide opportunities for a well-rounded student experience. The assignment questions provide issues for thought and debate where "solutions" are well-reasoned, integrated views. Problems are structured to provide ample opportunities for polishing one's procedural skills as well as for developing a feel for the differences in results when different methods, assumptions, and/or judgments are invoked. Many of the assignments provide real-world settings for exploring the usefulness of accounting information to decision makers who have different perspectives and purposes, come from different environments, and value different outcomes.

Group work and communication skills. Many of the assignments lend themselves to group and/or classroom presentation and write-up. Instructors are presented with materials that provide many of degrees of freedom in this regard.

Ethics and international. Each of the authors have been actively engaged in the development and teaching of ethics materials and courses. Such a perspective is imbedded throughout the text. Moreover, Ferris and Haskins teach international financial reporting courses and provide content material dedicated to that topic throughout each chapter.

Key terms. The language involved in financial reporting encompasses many new terms. Each time a new key term is used in the text, it appears in blue type. In addition, a listing of key terms appears at the end of each chapter, and an extensive glossary appears at the end of the text.

Appendixes. In order to provide instructors a number of degrees of freedom regarding the depth with which to explore a topic, many chapters contain appendixes that provide opportunities for exploring a particular topic in a more detailed manner. It is important to note, however, that a comprehensive, powerful course can be constructed without having to use the appendixes.

ORGANIZATION

This text consists of four major parts and is organized not unlike other texts in its basic sequencing. Do not, however, conclude that it is just like other texts. As has already been pointed out, the orientation taken toward topics, the emphasis placed on certain facets of the topics, and the integration with a larger context make this text distinctive.

Part I. These introductory chapters provide the background for the entire text. In particular, the first chapter's presentation of the Procter & Gamble annual report sets the financial reporting agenda and "creates the need to know." During its discussion, students realize that accounting quickly transcends the necessary but mundane concerns of a green-eye-shaded bookkeeper to encompass those of key managers interested, among other things, in knowing what has been achieved, identifying what remains to be done, monitoring and motivating people better, and efficiently, effectively, and inexpensively raising capital from external sources.

Using generally familiar business contexts, a variety of basic skills are then developed in the remaining Part I chapters. Paramount among the skills developed are (1) the double-entry method of recording transactions; (2) preparation of basic balance sheets and statements of income and owners' equity; (3) familiarity with the language of accounting; and (4) an understanding of some of the fundamental concepts of accounting (e.g., accrual vs. cash, matching, historical costs, materiality) and of the process by which accounting standards are set.

The objective of these three chapters is for students to become comfortable defining a users' information needs, report the most pertinent information in the most useful way, interpret the story reflected by the information, identify the key assumptions underlying the information being reported, and consider the alternative interpretations that would arise with certain changes in some of the key assumptions. Establishing such a dialectical process at a text's outset is important because students must continually consider such an array of issues in order to appreciate and understand the evolutionary nature of contemporary accounting practice.

Part II. The four chapters in this section of the text introduce in more detail the three basic financial statements—the balance sheet, income statement, and statement of cash flows—and provide students with some classical financial analysis tools. All four chapters draw heavily on the concepts, language, and concerns raised in Part I. Moreover, all four chapters integrate the Procter & Gamble annual report presented in Chapter 1 into their discussions as well as utilizing other corporate annual report examples.

An explicit premise running through these chapters is that management has a great deal of influence over the results presented. That is, the financial statements are discussed in such a way as to highlight the fact that they are a part of management's thinking as they make decisions throughout the years. We believe such an orientation not only is valid but also ascribes a great deal of vitality to the statements: They are not merely a sterile codification of numerous transactions whose total implications and results are not known until year-end.

The purpose of dealing so intensely with these financial statements and their analysis at this point in the text is that subsequent chapter topics can then be discussed and debated as to their impact on the three financial statements. Such an objective parallels the manager concerns raised in the chapters and poses very effective learning opportunities for students' recognition of both the key accounting and managerial concerns.

Part III. The chapters in this part are centered on the theme of measuring, reporting, interpreting, and using financial information pertaining to assets, liabilities, and owners' equity. In these chapters students really begin to see clearly and powerfully that accounting simply describes events and circumstances, and those descriptions are a joint product of certain official guidelines, and, more importantly, of the assumptions, actions, and judgments of managers. These chapters consider the financial reporting issues surrounding some of the daily and strategic concerns of managing assets, liabilities, and owners' equity. Moreover, they explore the tension between reporting the "most favorable" versus the "most realistic" picture.

As an example, the text and some of the end-of-chapter materials pertaining to marketable securities bring to light the issues of (1) distinguishing the relative merits of reporting historical costs versus current market values and (2) dealing with the prescriptive nature of FASB rules. Both issues underlie much of financial reporting. In particular, the first issue is often viewed by the uninformed as a shortcoming of financial reporting. We believe students should be sensitive to the pros and cons of reporting costs and current values and should be able to identify situations where one or the other may be more appropriate. In regard to the second issue, students become acutely aware of the volatility that is possible in reported earnings if how things are to be reported is simply left to the discretion of management. They thus realize a need for constraining the discretion available to managers in reporting their companies' financial position and results of operations. This is not to say that the need for management judgments and the consequences of such decisions become less important; on the contrary, a thorough knowledge of official guidelines (constraints) is merely an important prerequisite to identifying viable reporting options, structuring business transactions compatibly with the most desirable ways of reporting them, and factoring into one's decisions the information needs of the interested constituencies.

Besides grounding an accounting issue in the context of a business decision or users' information needs, the chapters also leverage students' understanding of other topics to help in their learning of particular financial reporting topics that may be new to them. For example, anticipating the potentially overwhelming nature of the bonds, leases, and pension topics, the text builds on a thread common to all three topics and familiar to most business students at this point in their education—the present value of a stream of future cash flows. As each of these three topics is introduced via this touchstone, the awesomeness of dealing with the technical aspects of their financial reporting requirements fades. In fact, for most students, the literacy threshold for these three topics, which at the outset seems unachievably distant, becomes reachable with the use of the present value perspective building block already familiar and mastered by most.

Part IV. This final section of the book provides students with an opportunity to consider some of the specific challenges involved in understanding the financial reporting practices of companies as well as some of the nuances inherent in communicating the more qualitative aspects of a company's financial well-being.

The final chapter focuses on some of the interesting challenges and opportunities chief financial officers are likely to encounter as they seek to provide the financial markets with the disclosures that are perceived to be of vital importance in portraying the real depth and breadth of a company's financial health and prospects. Many of the issues are outside the purview of current GAAP but are in many ways tied to efforts to complement, enhance, or clarify the presently required GAAP disclosures.

SUPPLEMENTAL MATERIALS

An *Instructor's Manual* is available to accompany the text. The manual provides "solutions" and suggestions for class discussion. In addition, the manual provides several possible course outlines with pertinent assignments.

Over the years we have benefitted from the ideas and contributions of our colleagues E. R. Brownlee II, C. Ray Smith, and numerous research assistants. Their help has been invaluable.

Kenneth R. Ferris
Mark E. Haskins
Robert J. Sack
Brandt R. Allen

CONTENTS IN BRIEF

CONTENTS

CHAPTER
11

Noncurrent Assets: Fixed Assets, Intangible Assets, and Natural Resources   386

CHAPTER
12

Accounting for Liabilities: Basic Concepts, Payables, Accruals, and Interest-Bearing Debt   423

CHAPTER
13

Leases, Retirement Benefits, and Deferred Income Taxes   470

CHAPTER
14

Owners' Equity   539

PART
IV

Special Considerations in Preparing and Using Accounting Data   583

CHAPTER
15

Communicating Corporate Value   584

Glossary   G1

Index   I1

PART I

Overview of Accounting and Financial Statements

CHAPTER 1

Accounting as the Language of Business

Accounting is a language that people within a firm can use to discuss its projects and progress with one another, and that they can use to tell outsiders what's happening in the firm without giving too many of its secrets to competitors....Natural languages develop grammar and vocabulary without the intervention of standard-setting bodies (with few exceptions, like French). Artificial languages like computer programming languages and the language of accounting seem to benefit from official standards. Standards can be effective even when they are not mandatory: People usually follow a standard because it reduces the cost of communicating with others.[1]

Key Chapter Issues

- Just what is accounting? Is it numbers? Is it words? Is it some combination of the two? When the president of a company reports to shareholders, what is the role of the accounting language as opposed to ordinary business language?
- The idea that accounting is a language suggests an art form rather than a science. What implications does that perspective suggest for management? For financial statement readers?

- What is the difference between an internal management accounting system and an external financial reporting system?
- Accounting communicates information to help people make decisions. What kinds of decisions are at issue?
- What is GAAP? Why is it important? Where does it come from?

[1] F. Black, "Choosing Accounting Rules," *Accounting Horizons*, December 1993, p. 1.

ccounting is a language used by business
people to communicate the financial health
of their enterprise. Like any language, accounting
adheres to certain conventions and concepts that
users of financial statements must understand
to appreciate the story being told. The primary
objective of this book is to help you understand those
concepts and conventions and consequently become
literate and conversant in the language of
accounting.

ACCOUNTING AS A LANGUAGE

Businesspeople use accounting to communicate the results of their company's operations to interested stakeholders both inside and outside the company. It is not enough for a manager to say, at the end of a particular quarter, "We did pretty well." Everyone who has an interest in the company — the management team, the employees, the creditors, the stockholders — will ask for more concrete information. They will want to know, "How were sales? Did margins hold up? What was the bottom line?" Answering such questions requires the use of the language of accounting.

It is important that we explain at the outset what we mean when we use the word **accounting**. When we talk about accounting, as in the sentence "Accounting is the language of business," we mean the numbers that measure the results of a business *and* the explanatory text that provides perspective on the numbers. For example, it may be important to know that sales for the quarter just ended were $653,908, but it is more useful to also know that sales in the same quarter last year were $632,685 and that the increase in sales was due to a 6 percent increase in unit prices offset by a 3 percent decrease in unit volume. Accounting reports typically include raw data (sales for the current quarter), comparative data (sales during a preceding period, or budgeted sales), and explanatory text (**footnotes** or similar commentary). The amount of accounting information — and the mix of data and text — to be included in an accounting report will depend on the kinds of decisions to be made by the users of the report. Accounting information is not generated for its own sake: The cost of an accounting and reporting system is justified only when the reports help people make better decisions.

People inside and outside a company have decisions to make. Senior managers inside a company use accounting information to evaluate the operations of the company and its people, and to make decisions about the company's future. The decisions range from the longest term to the most immediate, including concerns about the company's strategic direction (which business units offer the most potential), resource allocation (which products warrant more advertising dollars), and compensation (which employee teams deserve a financial pat on the back). But operating managers use accounting information also: to articulate their business plans (if we increase market penetration by 3 percent we will need $1,500,000 in additional working capital) and to identify emerging opportunities and problems that need attention and action (overhead costs for May were $45,000 over plan even though production was right on plan).

People outside the company also have decisions to make, and company managers use accounting information to communicate with a variety of interested external stakeholders, including the following:

■ Stockholders, who will decide whether to keep their stock or sell it; and, if they keep it, whether they will vote for incumbent management. Obviously, accounting information is also of interest to potential stockholders, who will decide whether to buy the stock and, if so, at what price.

- Creditors and suppliers, who will decide whether to extend credit and, if they decide to extend credit, the interest rate they will charge.
- Employees and unions, who will evaluate the company's performance as they consider whether they can argue for increased wages and benefits.

As you reflect on this notion of accounting as a medium of communication that provides information to people to help them make decisions, let us direct your thoughts to several implications for managers that flow from that understanding:

1. The complexity and sophistication of the accounting used will vary directly with the nature of the audience addressed. In the same way that couples married for a long time develop a shorthand way of talking to each other, two people operating a partnership can get along quite nicely with a rudimentary accounting system. To manage the company they will need key data on operations, but they will be so close to the business that little interpretive text will be necessary. When their business grows to the point that they need outside financing from a bank or a group of stockholders, the managers will find that those outsiders expect a fairly complete accounting for their investment. Going much further, a multinational company with complex internal operations and a wide range of outside stakeholders will find it necessary to maintain a very comprehensive accounting system to satisfy the needs of the company's diverse constituency. The cost of that increasingly complex accounting and reporting system is part of the price a company pays as it grows in the larger business community.

2. Users of accounting information are interested in both the company's past performance and its future prospects. For example, stockholders want to know what management did with the resources they have been given: Were those resources employed profitably, and have they been preserved? But stockholders also want to know what the company is likely to do in the future: Will the company's earnings increase enough to justify an increase in the stock price? Because of user needs for **stewardship information** and for **prospective information,** accounting tries to communicate both the past and the future. Managers understand that readers of a financial report use that report to measure their stewardship, but they also understand that readers use the reported results from past periods as a base point for projections about the future of the company. The fact that both of those expectations must be met explains much of the complexity of current financial reporting.

3. Business people spend a large part of their working day talking or writing about the business. Some part of that communication is in the form of accounting, and some is in the form of a more generalized business vocabulary. There really isn't any clear dividing line between accounting-as-a-language and the larger business communication system, and it probably isn't important that the dividing line is illusive. It is enough to acknowledge that accounting is a specialized segment of the overall business vocabulary — a specialized segment that has evolved to help business people communicate their companies' financial results.

4. As in any language, the symbols of accounting carry meaning from one person to another only because those people agree on the meaning of the symbols. The symbols and their meaning change over time, when all parties in the communication process agree that the changes make sense. Some of those changes come from usage, as they do with normal language. Unlike public speech, however, the accounting language has several authorities who worry about its effectiveness and have the power to police

it and to amend it when necessary. To effectively use the accounting language, all parties to the communication process need to understand the basic conventions and symbols and to stay current as the language evolves. Users of financial reports, such as bankers or stockholders, use the published company information they receive to make decisions about the company. To make good decisions they must evaluate the accounting information they receive from the company, and to do that they must have a good working understanding of the accounting language. Corporate managers carry the primary burden of telling the company's story. To tell that story most effectively, managers must know how to make the best use of available accounting conventions and, where necessary, develop supplemental communication techniques.

5. Finally, managers often have a vested interest in the decisions that will be made regarding their company. That vested interest has the potential to be a conflict of interest when the decisions turn on the financial story presented by the managers. Every manager has an ethical obligation to be alert to the potential for a conflict of interest and to use accounting in such a way as to describe business results objectively and fairly — regardless of the effect that fair presentation may have on his or her personal well-being.

No language has ever been able to claim perfect communication effectiveness. In the following chapters we will focus on the ways accounting is used in the business world, but we will also try to identify the areas in which accounting conventions remain inadequate.

GENERALLY ACCEPTED ACCOUNTING PRINCIPLES

For intracompany communications, managers can, and usually do, establish accounting rules and conventions for use solely in the company's *internal* reporting system. As a consequence, the reports produced by the internal reporting system can be tailored to the specific informational needs of individual managers. For example, a production manager might need accounting information about the number and cost of units in production, and a sales manager might need information focusing on the selling price and quantities available for sale. Thus the internal reporting system may produce a diverse set of accounting reports, each prepared to satisfy a particular informational need of its internal user. The rules and conventions that guide the internal reporting system can be designed by the managers themselves to suit their specific informational needs. This internal reporting system is commonly called **managerial accounting.**

Although internal accounting reports may vary between companies, *external* accounting reports are more standardized. Because external reports are distributed to a diverse user group, with no naturally common frame of reference, it would be very difficult for the managers of any one company to establish, on their own, a set of reporting conventions for that company's external reports that would automatically ensure understanding by all of those users. It could be argued that the users ought to make the effort to understand each company's individualized accounting approach. The managers could argue that their company is unique and, therefore, they ought to be able to develop an approach to accounting and reporting that is best suited to their circumstances. That approach would require individual users to spend the time to understand the company, its industry, *and* its accounting. The financial community has concluded that it is better for society as a whole if we have one approach to external accounting that all users can understand reasonably well, even if that means that some reporting companies have to alter their preferred approach to fit into the common mold. Although some unique "dialects" are used in highly specialized industries, by and large, external financial reporting adheres to a common body of communication practices mutually accepted and established by the financial community. The rules and conventions that guide the public communication of financial results are referred to as **generally accepted accounting principles** or **GAAP,** and the process is commonly called **financial accounting.**

Most of us encounter financial accounting in the annual and quarterly reports that companies distribute to their external constituencies. Some of those public reports provide a great deal of company-specific information, while others are comparatively spartan. However, all public financial reports provide a set of accounting-based **financial statements** and the related explanatory text, and it is that financial presentation which is of interest to us in this text.

Companies say that their financial statements (and the supporting text) are "prepared in accordance with generally accepted accounting principles" or GAAP. This means that the financial statements meet the standards that the larger community has come to expect for such financial reports. But compliance with GAAP goes beyond meeting a generalized expectation; it also means that the statements meet the requirements of the law. The federal securities laws in the U.S., for example, specify that every company that has publicly traded debt or equity must provide financial reports, on a regular basis, to the holders of those securities, and the courts have determined that those financial reports must be presented in accordance with GAAP. Because of the pervasiveness and the power of the securities market, the GAAP standard that applies to public companies has also become the standard for privately owned companies that issue financial statements to outside parties.

But what is this thing called GAAP? A formal definition describes it as

> a technical term that encompasses the conventions, rules, and procedures necessary to define accepted accounting practice at a particular time. It includes not only broad guidelines of general application but also detailed practices and procedures. Those conventions, rules and procedures provide a standard by which to measure financial presentations.[2]

GAAP is a collection of broad concepts and narrow practices that are generally accepted at a point in time. Together, those concepts and practices become the benchmark for managers as they prepare their company's financial reports. The understanding that GAAP is composed of practices that have become generally accepted is important because it reminds us that the resultant financial statements are to communicate to a diverse, public audience. The notion that the ideas in GAAP are accepted at a point in time is important because it reminds us that GAAP evolves, over time, as new business transactions require new accounting thinking. The statement that GAAP is a collection of concepts and practices is important because it will help us see that accounting is not a codified set of rules that can be memorized but is more a body of common law that needs to be studied as a hierarchy. That GAAP hierarchy includes

- Overall concepts that can be adopted. (For example, because the financial markets do not like surprises, financial reporting tends to be conservative.)
- More specific practices that have been established by standard setters and that can be understood in the context of the overall concepts. (For example, even though we expect great things from our research department, the payoff from such efforts has proven to be uncertain, so we have a specific accounting standard that dictates that research expenditures are charged to expense in the period when they are incurred rather than carried forward into a future period as an asset.)

---

[2] *Codification of Statements on Auditing Statements,* Section 411.02, The American Institute of CPAs (New York, New York, 1994).

- Generally accepted but unwritten procedures and practices that can be analogized from more formally established standards. (We expect great things from our advertising expenditures, too, but because that payoff is also uncertain those expenditures are also charged to expense when incurred rather than deferred until the expected sales are realized.)

While it is important to emphasize the idea that GAAP is a collection of generally accepted practices, it is also important to point out that a number of organizations work hard at molding GAAP according to the public interest. Three institutions in the United States are in the forefront of the effort to push the development of GAAP:

- Under the direction of the U.S. Congress, **the Securities and Exchange Commission** (SEC) administers the laws that regulate U.S. securities markets. Because an efficient securities market requires timely and useful information, the SEC also has the responsibility to establish the form and content of the information that companies are to provide to their public constituencies. The SEC has chosen to specify the required general business disclosures (e.g., description of business risks and opportunities, details of management compensation, and so on) but, for a number of reasons, has delegated to the private sector the establishment of specific accounting standards.

- The **Financial Accounting Standards Board** (FASB) was established in 1973 as the private sector's most recent effort to respond to the SEC's delegation of its standard-setting authority. The FASB is supported by contributions from the major accounting firms and associations, by large corporations, and by the securities industry. Seven independent expert accountants sit on the board, and their efforts are supported by a large expert staff. The FASB issues Statements on Financial Accounting, Technical Bulletins, and Interpretations, all of which establish (or document) provisions of GAAP. The topics on the board's agenda typically include long-standing controversies as well as new, emerging issues.

- The **American Institute of Certified Public Accountants** (AICPA) represents the CPAs who work as independent auditors in public accounting firms as well as the CPAs who work as the accounting officers of large and small companies. The AICPA has a number of committees that consider accounting issues and publish position papers. Those position papers stand as part of GAAP, at least until the FASB is able to consider the subject and issue a more formal, authoritative pronouncement.

In Chapter 2 we will say more about the process of establishing accounting standards and the organizations involved.

The principal focus of this textbook is financial accounting and the most important provisions of GAAP. It should be noted, however, that most companies maintain multiple reporting systems — an internal system for management communications and an external system for communication with outside constituencies. And because some outside constituencies may have special interests (and the power to demand special responses), a company may actually maintain multiple external reporting systems. For example, a company may use a GAAP reporting system for its shareholders and bankers, a separate system following the U.S. Internal Revenue Service Code for its income tax filings, and a third system to present financial information required by applicable regulatory agencies, such as the Office of Thrift Supervision (for savings and loan institutions) or the Federal Energy Regulatory Commission (for public utilities).

The internationalization of the economy has added another dimension to the accounting communications required of most companies. If, for example, a company has debt or equity securities traded on the public exchanges of other countries, it will probably be required to prepare financial reports according to the GAAP rules of those countries as well as in its home country. Each major country has developed its own approach to creating financial accounting standards. Thus, although there is some uniformity, there are also some significant differences in these standards from one country to another. For example, in Germany it has been historically understood that a company has a larger responsibility to its employees and the community than it does to its stockholders. As a consequence, German accounting standards tend to smooth out the peaks and valleys in income so as to present a longer-term, more stable view of company performance. In the United States the stockholders have a more dominant say in the running of the company, and so U.S. accounting standards require more immediate recognition of business events, resulting in more extreme swings in reported results. Such differences are embedded in each country's GAAP and also in their tax and commercial law.

Participants in the international financial markets, however, have become impatient with philosophic arguments that seek to justify GAAP differences across countries and have insisted that the accounting rules be harmonized. They claim that the nationalistic differences in accounting confuse investors and therefore inhibit the flow of international capital. In response to that pressure, the **International Accounting Standards Committee** (IASC) was given a new mandate. The committee had been formed by the accounting professions in the major capitalistic countries but has historically been largely ineffective because each country's committee representative had been inclined to argue in favor of that country's practices. As cross-border securities transactions have increased, the securities regulators from the major countries put great pressure on the IASC to get its act together and to establish a set of accounting principles that would be acceptable across those same borders. Many people said that it couldn't be done, that there were too many deeply vested opinions within the IASC such that any standard that would be acceptable to the majority of countries would be so full of compromises as to be useless. However, the Committee has moved with astonishing speed and effectiveness, and has completed a core set of internationally accepted accounting standards. Many major, non-U.S. international companies have abandoned their home country standards and adopted IASC standards for their public reporting. The list of IASC GAAP adopters is impressive, including Bayer (Germany), Nestle (Switzerland) and Fujitsu (Japan).

There are some major differences between GAAP as it is understood in the U.S. and IASC GAAP. As we prepare this edition of this book, IASC GAAP is not acceptable for financial statements used in the United States. If an international company wants to sell securities in the United States, the SEC insists that its financial statements be re-stated to be in accordance with U.S. GAAP, or at least reconciled to the result that would have been attained if U.S. GAAP had been used. That situation strikes many as jingoistic and, now that there is a body of international standards available, there will be increasing pressure on the SEC to allow international companies to use IASC GAAP statements for their U.S. filings. That will not be an easy decision however: If the German company Seimens is allowed to use IASC GAAP for reporting to shareholders in the U.S., will General Electric petition to use IASC GAAP as well? If all International companies tap the U.S. securities markets using their IASC-based financials to report to their U.S. shareholders, won't investors have to learn two different standards to evaluate alternative investment opportunities? If IASC standards become accepted in the U.S., what role will the FASB play in future standard-setting efforts? It will be very interesting to see how this issue is resolved, and then to think through the implications for users and preparers of financial statements as well as students of accounting.

Before we leave this introduction to GAAP, one final observation is in order: The flexibility in GAAP, even as used in the U.S. is sometimes frustrating to those who expect it to be categorical and rule oriented. It is true that some basic conventions and rules have been established through common usage or pronouncement and must be accepted as they are; however, as with any language, the application of GAAP provides for a surprising amount of latitude in the preparation of financial statements. That flexibility arises as a result of three factors. First, for some transactions, widely diverse accounting approaches had become entrenched as alternative GAAP options long before the SEC or the FASB was established, and those equally acceptable alternative approaches remain in the "language." Second, the financial community continues to develop new business transactions and, until new standards are established, different ways of approaching the accounting for those creative transactions will become accepted in practice. And, third, business transactions are complex and unique, and very often managers develop different interpretations of broadly written financial reporting standards as they try to apply generalized standards to their specific circumstances. This flexibility in GAAP means that there may be more than one acceptable answer to a question. Indeed, it provides an exciting challenge for managers to make the best use of the potential power of the accounting language in communicating the essence of the business they have created.

THE FINANCIAL REPORTING PROCESS: AN OVERVIEW

While it is true that GAAP is important to our thinking because it is the standard by which management measures its financial results, it is not the end objective of our study in this text. The real objective of our study is the financial reporting process — the process management uses to accumulate all of the business transactions during a period, put a value on them, sort them and evaluate them, and produce a GAAP-based financial report. That process is illustrated in Exhibit 1.1. The process of preparing the financial statements really flows through the center of the diagram, subject to the control of management and the influence of the independent auditor. We can see from this illustration that financial statements are fundamentally a summary of all of a company's business transactions tempered by a wide variety of financial judgments made by management. Those transactions and judgments are in turn subject to a company's **internal control structure,** which assures that all transactions and all necessary judgments have been recognized and that they are classified and correctly described in the company's records. A company's accounting system sorts all of the transactions and judgments into similar or related groupings and then aggregates that input in accounts so that the summarized financial statements can be prepared.

As suggested by the top portion of the diagram, the design and maintenance of the internal control structure and the preparation of financial statements are the direct responsibility of corporate management. At the culmination of the accounting process, management evaluates the resulting financial statements to be sure that the end result makes good business sense. That financial statement review begins with the financial management team but should also include operating management (because they know the business best) and top management and the board of directors (because they are ultimately responsible to the stockholders and creditors). To emphasize that responsibility, for example, the New York Stock Exchange insists that all listed companies include in their annual reports a report from top management in which they acknowledge their responsibility for the fairness of the

EXHIBIT 1.1

Overview of the Accounting Communication Process

```
┌────────────────────┐        ┌────────────────────┐        ┌────────────────────┐
│ Management          │        │ Management          │        │ Management          │
│ establishes and     │        │ determines how      │        │ reviews and signs   │
│ monitors control and│        │ GAAP is to be       │        │ off on the financial│
│ reporting system.   │        │ applied.            │        │ statements.         │
└────────────────────┘        └────────────────────┘        └────────────────────┘
```

```
┌─────────────────────────────────────────────┐
│ The internal control structure ensures that  │
│ all transactions and judgments are processed │
│ accurately.                                   │
└─────────────────────────────────────────────┘
```

Quantified transactions	The accounting system	The reporting process	The financial statements
– Sales – Expenditures – Collections – etc.	Quantified transactions and judgments are accumulated in logical groupings and recorded in the accounts.	Basic data are pulled together and appropriate presentation is determined.	After a careful analysis of the resulting financial statements, the final statements are issued to the public.

```
┌──────────────────────┐
│ Quantified           │
│ judgments            │
│ ---------------------│
│ – Valuations         │
│ – Estimates          │
│ – Useful lives       │
│ – etc.               │
└──────────────────────┘
```

```
┌───────────────────────────┐   ┌───────────────────────┐   ┌───────────────────────┐
│ The independent auditor    │   │ The independent        │   │ The independent        │
│ tests the effectiveness of │   │ auditor challenges     │   │ auditor challenges     │
│ the system and examines    │   │ the company's          │   │ the resulting          │
│ the major transactions.    │   │ application of         │   │ financial statements   │
└───────────────────────────┘   │ GAAP.                  │   │ and expresses a        │
                                 └───────────────────────┘   │ professional opinion   │
                                                             │ as to their fairness   │
                                                             │ in accordance with     │
                                                             │ GAAP.                  │
                                                             └───────────────────────┘
```

company's financial statements and assert their discharge of those responsibilities. As more managements see that responsibility more clearly, the reporting practice is spreading to other companies listed on other exchanges.

Although corporate management is responsible for preparing the financial statements and ensuring their overall fairness, the independent auditor is responsible for testing the underlying accounting data and expressing an opinion as to the fairness of the resulting financial statements. As we noted earlier, for a number of reasons, management might have a vested interest in the financial picture that the statements portray and, because of the potential for a serious conflict of interest, the financial community has determined that it is useful to have an independent opinion as to the fairness of those statements. Almost every company, therefore, engages an **independent auditor** to review its financial statements for fairness and consistency with GAAP.

An auditor's examination of a set of financial statements (typically referred to as an **audit**) is conducted according to a set of professional standards referred to as **generally accepted auditing standards (GAAS).** Those standards require the auditor to test the way the system processes routine transactions, to consider the appropriateness of the accounting methods used, and to evaluate the application of GAAP in the company's financial statements. Because an audit relies on test samples of a company's transactions and financial statement accounts, an auditor is typically not held responsible for immaterial errors in the financial statements or for small frauds. But most courts have said that an auditor is responsible for finding material misstatements, whether they result from accounting errors or from management fraud.

Based on their examination, independent auditors issue a report presenting an opinion as to the fairness of the financial statements prepared by management. We will review the content of that report in more detail when we look at the Procter & Gamble financial statements in the next section of this chapter. The most important element of the auditor's report is the **auditor's opinion.** If all goes well, the auditor expresses the opinion that the financial statements fairly present the company's financial condition and results of operations in accordance with generally accepted accounting principles. Obviously, the financial community expects to see such a positive opinion (sometimes referred to as a *clean opinion*) in every company's financial statements. Occasionally, for one reason or another, an auditor finds it necessary to issue an opinion indicating that the financial statements *do not* fairly present the company's financial condition and results of operations in accordance with GAAP. However, the power of the public's expectations is typically so great that most managers work diligently to avoid a financial reporting dispute with their independent auditors.

THE PROCTER & GAMBLE COMPANY — AN ILLUSTRATION

To focus our discussion, and to illustrate how the ideas we have been discussing are applied in practice, we have included at the end of this chapter the "financial results" section from the 1998 annual report to shareholders issued by The Procter & Gamble Company. As do many companies, Procter & Gamble provides a wide range of information in its annual reports, including an overview of the business by the chairman and detailed discussion of operations by management. That commentary is interesting and important, but we want to narrow our focus and look at the way Procter & Gamble manages its financial reporting responsibility. With that objective in mind, we have reproduced here only the financial results section of the company's annual report.

Procter & Gamble's financial results presentation for 1998 includes the following elements:

1. *The Financial Review*, which provides insight on the company and comments on the results reported for the year, looking first at the company as a whole. For example, management comments on the major trends and events of the year and they outline

some of the key factors that influenced the changes in reported results from one year to another. The basic financial statements are presented for the entire company, but in this Financial Review, management tells us about the Company's operations in its various geographic segments. Finally, the Review explains management's approach to several general business problems, including the Company's exposure to exchange rate and commodity price fluctuations, and the systems problems many computers face for the year 2000. All of this discussion is designed to help readers understand the numbers reported in the financial statements that follow.

2. *Responsibility for the Financial Statements and Report of the Independent Auditor,* which provides an affirmation from management of its responsibility for the financial statements, and outlines the steps management took to meet that responsibility. Note that management states that the statements have been prepared in accordance with generally accepted accounting principles, and that the estimates required in the preparation of the statements were based on management's best judgements. The management report also explains the importance of the system of internal control, outlines some of the key features of a system of internal control, and details some of the key features of the Procter & Gamble system. Also on this page is the report from Deloitte & Touche, where they describe the scope of their audit and express their **unqualified opinion,** saying that the Procter & Gamble financial statements "present fairly, in all material aspects, the financial position of the company at June 30, 1998 and June 30,1997, and the results of the operations and cash flows for each of the three years in the period ended June 30, 1998, in conformity with generally accepted accounting principles."

3. The *Consolidated Statement of Earnings,* which show a nice spike in sales in 1998 and a steady increase in operating income from 1996 through 1998. The statement doesn't show it but we can calculate that Procter & Gamble has succeeded in increasing its operating margin in each of the years shown here, from 13.6% in 1996, to 15.3% in 1997, to 16.3% in 1998. Net earnings, after deducting interest and taxes and adding in other income, has grown in each year in absolute terms, but as a percentage of sales the results for 1998 are only 10%, down from a high of 15% in 1997. The earnings statement also shows earnings per share for each year presented. Basic earnings per share is simply the net income for the year divided by the average common shares outstanding during the year. Diluted earnings per share is the net income for the year divided by the sum of the actual shares outstanding and the potential shares which might be outstanding if all convertible securities were converted to common stock. The stock tables in *The Wall Street Journal* report diluted earnings per share for all listed companies. Those tables also report the EPS multiple, which is the diluted earnings per share divided into the current stock price. Stated very simply, an analyst will study a company's income statement, looking for trends, and will develop a forecast of earnings per share for the next year. The analyst then estimates what the EPS multiple will be (based on movements in the market over all, and in the company's industry group) and will calculate an expected sales price for the stock next year. If the current stock price looks attractive compared to that projected price, the analyst issues a "buy" recommendation; if the current price looks less attractive, the analyst may recommend a "hold"or even a "sell" recommendation. Obviously, the company's reported earnings, and the trend in those earnings, is important to the stock price and the company's ability to raise capital.

4. The *Consolidated Balance Sheets* show that cash is down somewhat from the prior year, but machinery and equipment and goodwill (and total assets) are up. Note 2 to the financial statements explains that Procter & Gamble completed a major acquisition this year, which accounts for the jump in goodwill and probably also for the increase in machinery and equipment. In addition to the use of cash, the 1998 acquisition required Procter & Gamble to take on some additional long-term debt, which shows up on the liabilities side of the balance sheet. Interestingly, the shareholders' equity stayed almost the same from 1997 to 1998 even though the company earned more than $3.7 billion this past year. We will see, when we look at the stockholders' equity statement, that Procter & Gamble paid out $1.4 billion in dividends to the shareholders and purchased back some of its stock, paying $1.9 billion. In effect, Procter & Gamble earned $3.7 billion, but paid most of that net income to the shareholders in one form or another, keeping only about $500 million for use in the operations of the company.

5. The *Consolidated Statements of Shareholders' Equity* details the comings and goings in the equity accounts. In addition to the addition of the net earnings for the year and the distribution of those earnings, Procter & Gamble tells us that when they translated the assets and liabilities of its overseas businesses into U.S. dollars, those net assets lost value. GAAP tells Procter & Gamble that they must record that lost dollar value but, because exchange rates go up and down over time, the apparent loss need not go through the income statements. Instead the net translation adjustment goes directly to the equity accounts, as a reduction in shareholders' equity. Those non-income statement charges and credits are included in an equity account called Other Comprehensive Income. The trend in Procter & Gamble's Other Comprehensive Income suggests that it has net investments in countries where the dollar is losing value against the local currency.

6. The *Consolidated Statements of Cash Flows* show us that the company's various operations produced $4.8 billion in cash flows; that the company invested $5.2 billion in an acquisition and in purchases of property and equipment; and that the company borrowed about as much as they paid out to shareholders. The net result of those activities was a reduction in cash of $801 million. That one-year decline in cash ought not be a concern because it is clearly traceable to the one time, major purchase. In the other year displayed here, Procter & Gamble managed to keep its very substantial cash inflows balanced with its cash outflows.

7. *Notes to Consolidated Financial Statements*, which explain the more interesting accounting decisions management made in preparing the financial statements, and expand on the financial presentation in the basic statements. For example, the first paragraph in Note 1 explains that the consolidated financial statements include the assets, liabilities, sales, and expenses of all subsidiaries in which Procter & Gamble has a controlling interest. Where the company has only a 20% to 50% interest, only the net results of the operations of those entities are included in the consolidated financial statements. The third and fourth paragraphs of Note 1 tell us that the company adopted certain new accounting standards during the year, but has not adopted those new standards that have not yet become effective.

The notes also provide us with supplementary detail. Because the basic statements are intended as a general-purpose presentation for a large and diverse audience, they are summarized to a significant degree. Management understands that some readers are interested in more detail in certain areas and thus provides those details in the notes.

For example, the three largest liabilities in the balance sheet appear as single line items. Notes 3 and 4 provide details of the other current and noncurrent liabilities, and the short and long term portion of the debt. Note 2 details a major acquisition, which has been referred to in various places throughout the financial statements themselves. Note 11 provides some detail as to the operations of the company's sub-units. Procter & Gamble states that they manage the company on a geographical basis (as opposed to a product line basis) and so they give details of the operations of the major geographical units, including sales, net earnings, assets employed and capital expenditures.

Finally, the notes tell us what the company is doing in several currently important areas. Because there has been considerable concern about the use of derivatives, the SEC has mandated a set of disclosures, including a statement of company policies regarding the use of derivatives and the off-balance sheet exposure at the current year end. Procter & Gamble complies with that requirement with the information in Note 5. Similarly, almost every company is now subject to some liability for prior mis-use of the environment. In Note 10, Procter & Gamble tells us that they have accrued $66 million to cover the cost of environmental remediation. They also tell us that there is "considerable uncertainty" as to the outcome of all of its contingencies (including possible future claims for environmental problems), but that management believes that the ultimate outcome of any such claims will not be material.

8. *Quarterly Results and Financial Highlights* provides the information we need if we are interested in the trend of results quarter by quarter during the last two years or the trend of results year by year during the last 5 years.

Overall, the annual accounting report contains an enormous quantity of financial information about a company and its operations. We suggest that you take a few moments to familiarize yourself with the general content of the annual financial report of Procter & Gamble, presented in the following pages.

PROCTER & GAMBLE COMPANY ANNUAL REPORT

FINANCIAL REVIEW   The Procter & Gamble Company and Subsidiaries

Results of Operations

The Company achieved record sales, unit volume and net earnings for the year ended June 30, 1998. Basic net earnings per common share increased 13% to $2.74. Worldwide net earnings for the year were $3.78 billion, an 11% increase over the prior year earnings of $3.42 billion.

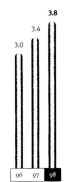

Net Earnings
(Billions of Dollars)

Worldwide net sales for the current year were $37.15 billion, an increase of 4% on worldwide unit volume growth of 6%. The difference between the sales and volume growth rates was primarily due to weaker currencies in Europe and Asia. Excluding these impacts, sales increased 8%.

Worldwide gross margin for the current year was 43.3% compared to 42.7% in the prior year. The current year improvement reflects cost savings, primarily from the Company's ongoing simplification and standardization program, as ongoing cost savings generated by the program exceeded the net cost to fund current year projects.

Worldwide marketing, research and administrative expenses were $10.04 billion compared to $9.77 billion in the prior year. This equates to 27.0% of sales, compared with 27.3% in the prior year. The 3% increase in total spending was primarily due to increased marketing support behind new brands, such as Tampax and Fat Free Pringles, and the expansion of existing brands into new markets.

Operating income grew 10%, primarily reflecting sales growth and cost-control efforts. The Company's net earnings margin increased from 9.5% to 10.2%, the highest level in 57 years.

Interest expense increased 20% to $548 million on increased debt, due mainly to acquisitions. Other income, net, which consists primarily of interest and investment income, contributed $201 million in the current year. In the prior year, other income, net, was $218 million.

The Company's effective tax rate for the year was 33.8% compared to 34.9% in the prior year. The decline reflects the benefits of lower tax rates in Europe, increased research and development tax credits in North America, and continued emphasis on effective tax planning.

In 1997, the Company completed its $2.4 billion restructuring program started in 1993, with annual cost savings in excess of $600 million after tax. The Company is continuing an ongoing program of simplification and standardization, which includes projects to consolidate selected manufacturing facilities, re-engineer manufacturing and distribution processes, redesign organizations, simplify product line-ups and divest non-strategic brands and assets. This program did not have a significant impact on 1998 net earnings, as the aggregate pre-tax cost of projects was offset by gains on sales of non-strategic brands and other assets. The net cost of these activities in 1997 was offset by increased licensing activity in the Health Care sector.

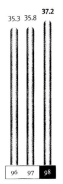

Net Sales
(Billions of Dollars)

1911: First all-vegetable shortening   9

PROCTER & GAMBLE COMPANY ANNUAL REPORT

FINANCIAL REVIEW (CONTINUED)   The Procter & Gamble Company and Subsidiaries

The following provides perspective on the year ended June 30, 1997 versus the prior year:

Worldwide net earnings increased 12% to $3.42 billion in 1997. Net earnings for 1996 were $3.05 billion and included the settlement of the Bankers Trust lawsuit, profit from the sale of the Company's share of a health care joint venture, a reserve for estimated losses on a supply agreement entered into as part of the previous divestiture of the commercial pulp business, and adoption of FASB Statement No. 121 covering recognition of impairment of long-lived assets. If these items had been excluded from 1996 earnings, the growth rate for the year ended June 30, 1997 would have been 13%.

Net Earnings Margin %

8.6%   9.5%   10.2%

96   97   98

Worldwide net sales in 1997 were $35.76 billion, up 1% from the prior year on unit volume growth of 3%. The difference between sales and volume growth rates was primarily due to weaker currencies in Europe and Asia.

Worldwide gross margin increased to 42.7% from 40.7% in 1996, reflecting cost savings from the Company's simplification and standardization efforts and the continuing benefits of the restructuring project initiated in 1993.

Worldwide marketing, research and administrative expenses were 27.3% of sales compared with 27.0% in 1996, primarily due to increases in advertising and research.

Other income, net, was $218 million in 1997. In 1996, other income, net, was $338 million and included a $120 million benefit from reversing the reserve for two interest rate swap contracts following settlement of a lawsuit against Bankers Trust; a $185 million gain on the sale of the Company's 50% share of a health care joint venture to its venture partner; and a $230 million charge to increase the reserve for estimated losses on a supply agreement entered into as part of the previous sale of the Company's commercial pulp business.

Net earnings margin increased to 9.5% in 1997 from 8.6% in 1996, reflecting unit volume growth and continued emphasis on cost control through the Company's simplification and standardization program.

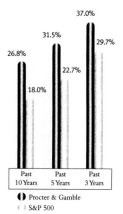

Total Shareholder Return Relative to S&P 500

26.8%   18.0%   31.5%   22.7%   37.0%   29.7%

Past 10 Years   Past 5 Years   Past 3 Years

◑ Procter & Gamble
◑ S&P 500

Financial Condition

Cash flow from operations was $4.89 billion, $5.88 billion and $4.16 billion in 1998, 1997 and 1996, respectively. Operating cash flow provided the primary source of funds to finance operating needs, capital expenditures and the share repurchase programs. Operating cash flow, combined with additional borrowings, provided the primary source of funds to finance current year acquisitions.

Cash and cash equivalents decreased $801 million in the current year to $1.55 billion, primarily due to acquisitions and increased capital expenditures.

Capital expenditures were $2.56 billion in 1998, $2.13 billion in 1997, and $2.18 billion in 1996. Current year expenditures included capacity expansions in the paper and food businesses, primarily in tissue and towel and snacks. Capital expenditures are expected to increase during the upcoming year, reflecting planned capacity increases and technological advances, primarily in the paper and laundry businesses.

1946: First heavy-duty synthetic laundry detergent

PROCTER & GAMBLE COMPANY ANNUAL REPORT

Net cash used for acquisitions completed during 1998 totaled $3.27 billion, the highest level in the Company's history. Acquisitions were largely concentrated in paper businesses, and included Tambrands, Inc. and its global leading brand, Tampax, the Loreto y Peña paper company in Mexico, and the Ssangyong Paper Company in Korea. The Company also increased ownership of various ventures in Asia and Latin America. Current year acquisitions were funded through a combination of existing cash balances and the issuance of debt. Net cash used for acquisition activities in 1997 and 1996 totaled $150 million and $358 million, respectively. The Company continued to divest certain non-strategic brands in 1998 in order to focus organizational resources on the Company's core businesses. The proceeds from these sales, the most significant of which was Duncan Hines, and other asset sales, generated $555 million in cash flow in the current year, compared to $520 million and $402 million in 1997 and 1996, respectively.

The Company initiated a share repurchase program in 1995 which authorized the Company to purchase shares annually to mitigate the dilutive impact of management compensation programs. The Company also initiated discretionary buy-back programs to repurchase additional outstanding shares of up to $1 billion per year during 1997 and 1998, in addition to purchases made under the 1995 program. Current year purchases under the repurchase programs totaled $1.93 billion compared to $1.65 billion in the prior year. The Company has announced plans to increase and accelerate its discretionary share repurchase programs in 1999 beyond its previous annual target of $1 billion.

Operating Cash Flow
(Billions of Dollars)

Common share dividends grew 12% to $1.01 per share in 1998, compared to $.90 and $.80 in 1997 and 1996, respectively. For the coming year, the annual dividend rate will increase to $1.14 per common share, marking the forty-third consecutive year of increased common share dividend payments. Total dividend payments, to both common and preferred shareholders, were $1.46 billion, $1.33 billion and $1.20 billion in 1998, 1997 and 1996, respectively.

Total debt was up $3.06 billion to $8.05 billion, primarily due to the issuance of commercial paper to fund current year acquisitions.

Long-term borrowing available under the Company's shelf registration statement filed in 1995, as amended in July 1997, was $2.0 billion at June 30, 1998. Additionally, the Company has the ability to issue commercial paper at favorable rates.

Net Sales by Geographic Region
(Billions of Dollars)

North America	18.5
Europe, Middle East and Africa	11.8
Asia	3.5
Latin America	2.6
Corporate	0.8

The following pages provide perspective on the Company's geographic operating segments. Geographic segments exclude corporate items, most notably certain financing and employee benefit costs, goodwill amortization, segment eliminations and projects related to the Company's simplification and standardization program.

PROCTER & GAMBLE COMPANY ANNUAL REPORT

FINANCIAL REVIEW (CONTINUED)   The Procter & Gamble Company and Subsidiaries

North America Region

The North America region continued to deliver solid progress, achieving record sales, unit volume and net earnings.

Net sales for the year were $18.46 billion, an increase of 5% from the prior year level of $17.63 billion, on unit volume growth of 4%.

Net earnings for the region were up 10% to $2.47 billion. The region achieved this earnings growth through increased unit volume, a continued focus on cost control through simplification and standardization, and a lower tax rate, primarily related to increased research and development tax credits, partially offset by increased spending on product initiatives. Prior year net earnings were $2.25 billion, which represented a 15% increase over 1996. Net earnings margin for the region was 13.4%, compared to 12.8% and 11.3% in 1997 and 1996, respectively.

The Paper sector led the region's current year volume progress, generating 10% unit volume growth versus the prior year and delivering over half of the region's total unit volume increase. This unit volume growth was achieved behind the strength of the feminine protection business, driven by the Tambrands acquisition; diapers, due to initiative programs; and tissue and towel, as a result of prior year capacity increases. The Paper sector also led the region's profit improvements, driven by volume growth, increased pricing in tissue and towel, and cost reduction from the ongoing simplification and standardization program. In the prior year, operating results were driven by the diaper category, behind the acquisition of baby wipes and the introduction of Pampers Baby-Dry, and by tissue and towel capacity increases.

North America Net Sales (Billions of Dollars)

17.2 17.6 **18.5**
96 97 98

The Laundry and Cleaning sector was also a strong contributor to the region's current year unit volume progress, with a 3% increase over a strong prior year base period. The volume gains were driven by laundry, which also contributed heavily to the sector's earnings progress, and by fabric conditioners.

The Food and Beverage sector achieved 1% unit volume growth in the current year, despite reduced coffee volumes resulting from commodity-based price increases and the sale of Duncan Hines. The snacks category posted the highest increase, behind the launch of Fat Free Pringles. The sector's earnings were negatively impacted by the loss of profit contribution from Duncan Hines, and by investments in new initiatives. In 1997, unit volume growth was led by the snacks category, which achieved double-digit growth behind new production capacity.

Unit volume in the Beauty Care sector grew 2% during the year, led by hair care and deodorants. Net earnings for the sector increased over a strong prior year base, driven by the skin care and personal cleansing and the cosmetics and fragrances categories. Earnings growth declined from the double-digit increases of prior years, due to intense competition in hair care and deodorants, and increased investments in the development of future product initiatives.

North America Net Earnings (Millions of Dollars)

1,953 2,253 **2,474**
96 97 98

1956: First scouring cleanser with effective bleaching

PROCTER & GAMBLE COMPANY ANNUAL REPORT

The Procter & Gamble Company and Subsidiaries

Unit volume in the Health Care sector was down 1%, as volume softness caused by intense competitive activity in oral care was partially offset by improved volume in the pharmaceuticals category. The sector's unit volume posted a 3% decline in 1997 compared to 1996. Earnings declined in 1998, as the sector continued to invest in research and development, primarily in pharmaceuticals, and in marketing support in the highly competitive oral care category. The sector will continue to invest heavily in research and development, with a pipeline for launching new pharmaceutical drugs in the coming years and a renewed focus on future innovations in other health care products.

Europe, Middle East and Africa Region

Record unit volume, sales and earnings in the Europe, Middle East and Africa region were driven by continued expansion into developing markets, increased pricing, cost improvements and lower tax rates.

Net sales grew 2% to $11.84 billion, on 8% unit volume growth. Excluding the effects of unfavorable exchange rates, primarily in Western Europe, sales grew 10%, ahead of volume. During the prior year, sales increased 1% to $11.59 billion, which trailed the 7% unit volume growth rate due to unfavorable exchange rates.

The region's net earnings progress continued in the current year, growing 14% to $1.09 billion. Net earnings in 1997 were $956 million, a 21% increase over 1996. Current year earnings growth was driven by the region's volume growth, continued efforts to reduce cost via simplification and

standardization and lower tax rates, partially offset by negative exchange impacts. The net earnings margin progress also continued in the current year to 9.2%, from 8.3% and 6.9%, in 1997 and 1996, respectively.

Central and Eastern Europe led the region's unit volume growth, with a 25% increase, driven by growth in emerging markets. This follows a 42% growth rate in 1997. Earnings increased as a result of unit volume growth, reduced costs and economies of scale, partially offset by continued investment in new product initiatives and new markets to facilitate future growth.

Middle East and Africa, which includes the region's snack business, increased unit volume 18% over the prior year base period, which also generated a double-digit increase over 1996. Unit volume progress was broadly based across countries and key categories, led by increased snack sales.

Western Europe unit volume increased 2%, reflecting the net impact of the Tambrands acquisition and the divestiture of non-strategic local brands, primarily in health and beauty care. Net earnings increased well above volume growth, due to cost savings, primarily in laundry and cleaning products, and lower tax rates, partially offset by increased spending to promote new brand launches.

Europe, Middle East and Africa Net Sales
(Billions of Dollars)

11.5 11.6 **11.8**

96 97 **98**

Europe, Middle East and Africa Net Earnings
(Millions of Dollars)

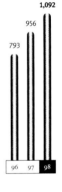

1,092

956

793

96 97 **98**

PROCTER & GAMBLE COMPANY ANNUAL REPORT

FINANCIAL REVIEW (CONTINUED)

The Procter & Gamble Company and Subsidiaries

Asia Region

The Asia region was negatively impacted by a general market contraction caused by the currency and economic crises in Korea and the ASEAN countries (Thailand, Malaysia, Philippines, Indonesia and Singapore) and the continuing economic recession in Japan.

Net sales for the region were $3.45 billion, 3% below the prior year on 4% unit volume growth. Current year volume growth was driven by acquisitions, including Ssangyong, a paper business in Korea, and increased ownership of a venture in China, which more than offset volume declines in the rest of the region. Net sales lagged volume growth as the impact of improved pricing and product mix were more than offset by the impact of unfavorable exchange rate movements. Excluding adverse exchange effects, sales grew 10%, primarily due to pricing aimed at recovering the currency devaluation effects. In the prior year, net sales declined 8% to $3.57 billion on a 7% unit volume decline. Excluding exchange effects in 1997, sales were down 2% versus 1996.

The region's net earnings were $174 million, a 37% decrease from the prior year. Current year earnings were impacted by lower sales, increased investment in new product initiatives and the currency crisis. The prior year net earnings of $275 million represented a 1% increase over 1996. Net earnings margin for the current year was 5.0%, compared to 7.7% in 1997 and 7.0% in 1996. The 1998 margin decline reflects lower sales, exchange impacts and initiative investments.

Greater China's unit volume was up 6% versus the prior year. Volume increases were driven by increased ownership of a joint venture. Net earnings were higher as the impact of increased volume was partially offset by unfavorable sales mix and investment behind new product introductions.

Asia Net Sales
(Billions of Dollars)

3.9

3.6   3.5

96   97   98

In Japan, unit volume was relatively flat, reflecting the continued depressed state of the Japanese economy. Despite the economic troubles, the Company continued to invest in new product initiatives and was successful in increasing market shares during the second half of the year. Net earnings were lower due to unfavorable sales mix, investment in new products and the weakened yen.

The balance of Asia was positively impacted by the acquisition of the Ssangyong Paper Company in Korea. The increased volume in Korea resulting from this acquisition more than offset volume declines brought about by the economic crisis. Earnings, however, declined as a result of the currency crisis.

The Asian markets are expected to remain weak through at least fiscal 1999. Because the Asia region accounted for less than 10% of the Company's total sales and 5% of the Company's total earnings in fiscal 1998, the economic situation is not expected to be significant to the Company's overall growth rate for the coming year. While the region is expected to recover from these difficulties, the depth and duration of the economic effects are still uncertain.

Asia Net Earnings
(Millions of Dollars)

273   275

174

96   97   98

Latin America Region

Latin America continued its positive trends in net sales and net earnings, with current year results being driven by acquisitions and the continued strengthening in Mexico and Venezuela.

Net sales in the region grew 14% to $2.64 billion on 12% unit volume growth, as pricing outpaced the negative impact of currency devaluation. Volume gains resulted from the acquisition of Loreto y Peña, a paper

14   **1961: First successful, mass-marketed disposable diaper**

PROCTER & GAMBLE COMPANY ANNUAL REPORT

The Procter & Gamble Company and Subsidiaries

**Latin America
Net Sales**
(Billions of Dollars)

2.6

2.2   2.3

96   97   98

**Latin America
Net Earnings**
(Millions of Dollars)

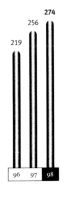

274

256

219

96   97   98

company in Mexico, the buy-out of a paper joint venture in the Southern Cone (Brazil, Argentina, Chile), the prior year acquisition of a laundry and cleaning business in Brazil, and the strengthening of the base business in Mexico, Venezuela and Argentina. In the prior year, sales for the region grew 6% to $2.31 billion, while unit volume was down 2%, reflecting inflation-driven pricing action. In Mexico, the Company's largest operation in the region, business results were strong. Unit volume increased 16%, behind the acquisition of the Loreto y Peña paper company and a general economic recovery in the market.

Net earnings for the region were $274 million, a 7% increase. Current year earnings lagged behind sales growth due to increased investment to support brand expansion in the Southern Cone. Excluding these geographies, the balance of the region's earnings grew in double digits. Prior year net earnings were $256 million, a 17% increase over 1996. Net earnings margin for the current year was 10.4% compared to 11.1% and 10.1% in 1997 and 1996, respectively, reflecting initiative investments.

Prior to January 1, 1998, both Brazil and Peru were highly inflationary economies, and accordingly, the results of the Company's subsidiaries in Brazil and Peru were measured using the United States dollar as their functional currency. Effective January 1, 1998, neither Brazil nor Peru qualified as a highly inflationary economy. The impact of this change was not material.

Hedging and Derivative Financial Instruments

The Company is exposed to market risk, including changes in interest rates, currency exchange rates and commodity prices. To manage the volatility relating to these exposures on a consolidated basis, the Company nets the exposures to take advantage of natural offsets and enters into various derivative transactions for the remaining exposures pursuant to the Company's policies in areas such as counterparty exposure and hedging practices. The financial impacts of these hedging instruments are offset by corresponding changes in the underlying exposures being hedged. The Company does not hold or issue derivative financial instruments for trading purposes. Note 5 to the consolidated financial statements includes a discussion of the Company's accounting policies for financial instruments.

Derivative positions are monitored using techniques including market value, sensitivity analysis and a value at risk model. The tests for interest rate and currency rate exposures discussed below are based on a variance/co-variance value at risk model using a one-year horizon and a 95% confidence level. The model assumes that financial returns are normally distributed and approximates the financial return for options and other non-linear instruments. The model also reflects the impact of correlation and diversification from holding multiple currency and interest rate instruments. Estimates of volatility and correlations of market factors are drawn from the JP Morgan RiskMetrics™ dataset as of June 30, 1998. In cases where data is unavailable in RiskMetrics™, a reasonable approximation is included. The effect of these estimates did not significantly change the total value at risk.

The Company's market risk exposures relative to interest and currency rates, as discussed below, have not changed materially versus the previous reporting period. In addition, the Company is not aware of any facts or circumstances that would significantly impact such exposures in the near-term.

PROCTER & GAMBLE COMPANY ANNUAL REPORT

FINANCIAL REVIEW (CONTINUED)   The Procter & Gamble Company and Subsidiaries

Interest Rate Exposure

Interest rate swaps are used to hedge underlying debt obligations. Certain currency interest rate swaps are designated to hedge the foreign currency exposure of the Company's related foreign net investments.

Based on the Company's overall interest rate exposure as of and during the year ended June 30, 1998, including derivative and other interest rate sensitive instruments, a near-term change in interest rates, within a 95% confidence level based on historical interest rate movements, would not materially affect the consolidated financial position, results of operations or cash flows.

Currency Rate Exposures

The Company manufactures and sells its products in a number of countries throughout the world and, as a result, is exposed to movements in foreign currency exchange rates. The major foreign currency exposures involve the markets in Western Europe, Mexico and Canada. The primary purpose of the Company's foreign currency hedging activities is to protect against the volatility associated with foreign currency purchases of materials and other assets and liabilities created in the normal course of business. Corporate policy prescribes the range of allowable hedging activity. The Company primarily utilizes forward exchange contracts and purchased options with durations of generally less than 12 months.

In addition, the Company enters into foreign currency swaps to hedge intercompany financing transactions, and utilizes purchased foreign currency options with durations of generally less than 18 months and forward exchange contracts to hedge against the effect of exchange rate fluctuations on royalties and foreign source income.

Based on the Company's overall currency rate exposure as of and during the year ended June 30, 1998, including derivative and other foreign currency sensitive instruments, a near-term change in currency rates, within a 95% confidence level based on historical currency rate movements, would not materially affect the consolidated financial position, results of operations or cash flows.

Commodity Price Exposure

Raw materials used by the Company are subject to price volatility caused by weather, supply conditions and other unpredictable factors. The Company uses futures and options contracts, primarily in food and beverage products, to manage the volatility related to certain of these exposures. Gains and losses relating to qualifying hedges of firm commitments or anticipated inventory transactions are deferred in prepaid expenses and are included in the basis of the underlying transactions. Commodity hedging activity is not material to the Company's consolidated financial position, results of operations or cash flows.

Organization 2005

The Company is currently designing Organization 2005, a realignment of the organization structure, work processes and culture to accelerate growth and innovation. While the details are not final, the design will likely include:

- A move from current geographic business units to product-based Global Business Units (GBUs).
- The further strengthening of country-based organizations to provide even greater focus on deep local level consumer and customer knowledge.
- The establishment of centers of excellence for key administrative, logistics and support functions.
- Changes in the culture and reward systems to encourage greater speed, innovation and flexibility.

The nature, timing and implications related to this design change have not yet been determined. The Company expects to finalize plans and to make available further details of the Organization 2005 changes in Fall 1998.

Year 2000

The Company has developed plans to address the possible exposures related to the impact on its computer systems of the Year 2000. Key financial, information and operational systems, including equipment with embedded microprocessors, have been inventoried and assessed, and detailed plans are in place for the required systems modifications or replacements.

1968: First uniformly shaped, stackable potato chip

PROCTER & GAMBLE COMPANY ANNUAL REPORT

The Procter & Gamble Company and Subsidiaries

Progress against these plans is monitored and reported to management and to the Audit Committee of the Board of Directors on a regular basis. Implementation of required changes to critical systems is expected to be completed during fiscal 1999. Testing and certification of critical systems, which includes review of documented remediation work and test results by technical experts, key users and a central project team, is expected to be successfully completed by December 31, 1999. In addition, the Company's Internal Controls organization plans to review the testing and certification process and observe the testing of selected critical systems in each region.

Critical Systems Description

	% of Applications Year 2000 Compliant		
	Actual as of June 1998	Planned December 1998	Planned June 1999
Critical manufacturing, operating and control systems	44%	90%	100%
All other critical systems	56%	100%	100%

Incremental costs, which include contractor costs to modify existing systems and costs of internal resources dedicated to achieving Year 2000 compliance, are charged to expense as incurred. Costs are expected to total approximately $100 million, of which 34% has been spent to date.

The Company is also in contact with suppliers and customers to assess the potential impact on operations if key third parties are not successful in converting their systems in a timely manner. Risk assessment, readiness evaluation, action plans and contingency plans related to these third parties are expected to be completed by December 1998.

The Company's risk management program includes emergency backup and recovery procedures to be followed in the event of failure of a business-critical system. These procedures will be expanded to include specific procedures for potential Year 2000 issues. Contingency plans to protect the business from Year 2000-related interruptions are being developed. These plans will be complete by June 1999 and will include, for example, development of backup procedures, identification of alternate suppliers and possible increases in safety inventory levels.

The Company is taking reasonable steps to prevent major interruptions in the business due to Year 2000 issues. The effect, if any, on the Company's results of operations if the Company, its customers or its suppliers are not fully Year 2000 compliant is not reasonably estimable. The Company believes its global presence and broad-based manufacturing capability help mitigate the risk.

Forward-Looking Statement

The Company has made and will make certain forward-looking statements in the Annual Report and in other contexts relating to volume growth, increases in market shares, Year 2000 compliance, financial goals and cost reduction, among others.

These forward-looking statements represent challenging goals for the Company and are based on certain assumptions and estimates regarding the worldwide economy, technological innovation, competitive activity, pricing, currency movements, product introductions, governmental action and the development of certain markets. Among the key factors necessary to achieve the Company's goals are: (1) the achievement of lower costs and increases in reliability and capacity utilization, resulting from simplification and standardization; (2) the ability to improve results despite high levels of competitive activity and the economic downturn in Asia; (3) the successful implementation of ECR and the ability to maintain key customer relationships in important developed markets; (4) the continuation of substantial growth in significant developing markets such as China, Mexico, Brazil and the countries of Central and Eastern Europe; (5) obtaining successful outcomes in regulatory, tax and legal matters; (6) the ability to continue technological innovation; and (7) the timely resolution of the Year 2000 issue by the Company and its customers and suppliers. If the Company's assumptions and estimates are incorrect or do not come to fruition, or if the Company does not achieve all of these key factors, then the Company's actual performance could vary materially from the forward-looking statements made herein.

1972: First effective dryer-added fabric softener

17

PROCTER & GAMBLE COMPANY ANNUAL REPORT

RESPONSIBILITY FOR THE FINANCIAL STATEMENTS

The Procter & Gamble Company and Subsidiaries

Consolidated financial statements and financial information included in this report are the responsibility of Company management. This includes preparing the statements in accordance with generally accepted accounting principles and necessarily includes estimates based on management's best judgments.

To help insure the accuracy and integrity of Company financial data, management maintains internal controls designed to provide reasonable assurance that transactions are executed as authorized and accurately recorded and that assets are properly safeguarded. These controls are monitored by an ongoing program of internal audits. These audits are supplemented by a self-assessment program that enables individual organizations to evaluate the effectiveness of their controls. Careful selection of employees and appropriate divisions of responsibility are designed to achieve control objectives. The Company's "Worldwide Business Conduct Manual" sets forth management's commitment to conduct its business affairs with the highest ethical standards.

Deloitte & Touche LLP, independent public accountants, have audited and reported on the Company's consolidated financial statements. Their audits were performed in accordance with generally accepted auditing standards.

The Board of Directors, acting through its Audit Committee composed entirely of outside directors, oversees the adequacy of internal controls. The Audit Committee meets periodically with representatives of Deloitte & Touche LLP and internal financial management to review internal control, auditing and financial reporting matters. The independent auditors and the internal auditors also have full and free access to meet privately with the Audit Committee.

John E. Pepper
Chairman and Chief Executive

Erik G. Nelson
Chief Financial Officer

REPORT OF INDEPENDENT ACCOUNTANTS

250 East Fifth Street
Cincinnati, Ohio 45202

To the Board of Directors and Shareholders of The Procter & Gamble Company:

We have audited the accompanying consolidated balance sheets of The Procter & Gamble Company and subsidiaries as of June 30, 1998 and 1997 and the related consolidated statements of earnings, shareholders' equity, and cash flows for each of the three years in the period ended June 30, 1998. These financial statements are the responsibility of the Company's management. Our responsibility is to express an opinion on these financial statements based on our audits.

We conducted our audits in accordance with generally accepted auditing standards. Those standards require that we plan and perform the audits to obtain reasonable assurance about whether the financial statements are free of material misstatement. An audit includes examining, on a test basis, evidence supporting the amounts and disclosures in the financial statements. An audit also includes assessing the accounting principles used and significant estimates made by management, as well as evaluating the overall financial statement presentation. We believe that our audits provide a reasonable basis for our opinion.

In our opinion, the financial statements referred to above present fairly, in all material respects, the financial position of the Company at June 30, 1998 and 1997 and the results of its operations and cash flows for each of the three years in the period ended June 30, 1998, in conformity with generally accepted accounting principles.

July 30, 1998

PROCTER & GAMBLE COMPANY ANNUAL REPORT

CONSOLIDATED STATEMENTS OF EARNINGS   The Procter & Gamble Company and Subsidiaries

Amounts in Millions Except Per Share Amounts	1998	1997	1996
Net Sales	$37,154	$35,764	$35,284
Cost of products sold	21,064	20,510	20,938
Marketing, research and administrative expenses	10,035	9,766	9,531
Operating Income	6,055	5,488	4,815
Interest expense	548	457	484
Other income, net	201	218	338
Earnings Before Income Taxes	5,708	5,249	4,669
Income taxes	1,928	1,834	1,623
Net Earnings	$ 3,780	$ 3,415	$ 3,046
Basic Net Earnings Per Common Share	$ 2.74	$ 2.43	$ 2.14
Diluted Net Earnings Per Common Share	$ 2.56	$ 2.28	$ 2.01
Dividends Per Common Share	$ 1.01	$ .90	$ .80

Years Ended June 30

See accompanying Notes to Consolidated Financial Statements.

1972: First dishwashing liquid with grease-cutting superiority   19

PROCTER & GAMBLE COMPANY ANNUAL REPORT

CONSOLIDATED BALANCE SHEETS   The Procter & Gamble Company and Subsidiaries

	June 30	
Amounts in Millions Except Per Share Amounts	1998	1997
ASSETS		
Current Assets		
Cash and cash equivalents	$ 1,549	$ 2,350
Investment securities	857	760
Accounts receivable	2,781	2,738
Inventories		
Materials and supplies	1,225	1,131
Work in process	343	228
Finished goods	1,716	1,728
Deferred income taxes	595	661
Prepaid expenses and other current assets	1,511	1,190
Total Current Assets	10,577	10,786
Property, Plant and Equipment		
Buildings	3,660	3,409
Machinery and equipment	15,953	14,646
Land	539	570
	20,152	18,625
Accumulated depreciation	(7,972)	(7,249)
Total Property, Plant and Equipment	12,180	11,376
Goodwill and Other Intangible Assets		
Goodwill	7,023	3,915
Trademarks and other intangible assets	1,157	1,085
	8,180	5,000
Accumulated amortization	(1,169)	(1,051)
Total Goodwill and Other Intangible Assets	7,011	3,949
Other Non-Current Assets	1,198	1,433
Total Assets	$30,966	$27,544

See accompanying Notes to Consolidated Financial Statements.

1975: First contour-shaped diaper

PROCTER & GAMBLE COMPANY ANNUAL REPORT

The Procter & Gamble Company and Subsidiaries

Amounts in Millions Except Per Share Amounts	June 30 1998	1997
LIABILITIES AND SHAREHOLDERS' EQUITY		
Current Liabilities		
Accounts payable	$ 2,051	$ 2,203
Accrued and other liabilities	3,942	3,802
Taxes payable	976	944
Debt due within one year	2,281	849
Total Current Liabilities	9,250	7,798
Long-Term Debt	5,765	4,143
Deferred Income Taxes	428	559
Other Non-Current Liabilities	3,287	2,998
Total Liabilities	18,730	15,498
Shareholders' Equity		
Convertible Class A preferred stock,		
stated value $1 per share		
(600 shares authorized)	1,821	1,859
Non-Voting Class B preferred stock,		
stated value $1 per share (200 shares		
authorized; none issued)	–	–
Common stock, stated value $1 per share		
(5,000 shares authorized; shares outstanding:		
1998–1,337.4 and 1997–1,350.8)	1,337	1,351
Additional paid-in capital	907	559
Reserve for employee stock ownership plan debt retirement	(1,616)	(1,634)
Accumulated other comprehensive income	(1,357)	(819)
Retained earnings	11,144	10,730
Total Shareholders' Equity	12,236	12,046
Total Liabilities and Shareholders' Equity	$30,966	$27,544

1978: Didronel, the first global osteoporosis drug

PROCTER & GAMBLE COMPANY ANNUAL REPORT

CONSOLIDATED STATEMENTS OF SHAREHOLDERS' EQUITY   The Procter & Gamble Company and Subsidiaries

Dollars in Millions/Shares in Thousands	Common Shares Outstanding	Common Stock	Preferred Stock	Additional Paid-in Capital	Reserve for ESOP Debt Retirement	Accumulated Other Comprehensive Income	Retained Earnings	Total	Total Comprehensive Income
Balance June 30, 1995	1,373,148	$1,373	$1,913	$129	$(1,734)	$ 65	$ 8,843	$10,589	
Net earnings							3,046	3,046	$3,046
Other comprehensive income:									
Currency translation, net of $80 tax						(483)		(483)	(483)
Other, net of tax						1		1	1
Reclassifications to net earnings						(1)		(1)	(1)
Total comprehensive income									$2,563
Dividends to shareholders:									
Common							(1,099)	(1,099)	
Preferred, net of tax benefit							(103)	(103)	
Treasury purchases	(10,468)	(10)					(422)	(432)	
Employee plan issuances	6,514	6		140				146	
Preferred stock conversions	1,952	2	(27)	25				0	
ESOP debt guarantee reduction					58			58	
Balance June 30, 1996	1,371,146	1,371	1,886	294	(1,676)	(418)	10,265	11,722	
Net earnings							3,415	3,415	$3,415
Other comprehensive income:									
Currency translation, net of $38 tax						(416)		(416)	(416)
Other, net of tax						13		13	13
Reclassifications to net earnings						2		2	2
Total comprehensive income									$3,014
Dividends to shareholders:									
Common							(1,225)	(1,225)	
Preferred, net of tax benefit							(104)	(104)	
Treasury purchases	(30,875)	(31)					(1,621)	(1,652)	
Employee plan issuances	8,801	9		240				249	
Preferred stock conversions	1,771	2	(27)	25				0	
ESOP debt guarantee reduction					42			42	
Balance June 30, 1997	1,350,843	1,351	1,859	559	(1,634)	(819)	10,730	12,046	
Net earnings							3,780	3,780	$3,780
Other comprehensive income:									
Currency translation, net of $25 tax						(537)		(537)	(537)
Other, net of tax						(1)		(1)	(1)
Total comprehensive income									$3,242
Dividends to shareholders:									
Common							(1,358)	(1,358)	
Preferred, net of tax benefit							(104)	(104)	
Treasury purchases	(24,716)	(25)					(1,904)	(1,929)	
Employee plan issuances	8,777	9		312				321	
Preferred stock conversions	2,557	2	(38)	36				0	
ESOP debt guarantee reduction					18			18	
Balance June 30, 1998	1,337,461	$1,337	$1,821	$907	$(1,616)	$(1,357)	$11,144	$12,236	

See accompanying Notes to Consolidated Financial Statements.

22   **1985:** Superior paper-making technology yields stronger, more absorbent paper towels

PROCTER & GAMBLE COMPANY ANNUAL REPORT

CONSOLIDATED STATEMENTS OF CASH FLOWS   The Procter & Gamble Company and Subsidiaries

Amounts in Millions	Years Ended June 30		
	1998	1997	1996
Cash and Cash Equivalents, Beginning of Year	$ 2,350	$ 2,074	$ 2,028
Operating Activities			
Net earnings	3,780	3,415	3,046
Depreciation and amortization	1,598	1,487	1,358
Deferred income taxes	(101)	(26)	328
Change in accounts receivable	42	8	17
Change in inventories	(229)	(71)	202
Change in accounts payable, accrued and other liabilities	(3)	561	(948)
Change in other operating assets and liabilities	(65)	503	(134)
Other	(137)	5	289
Total Operating Activities	4,885	5,882	4,158
Investing Activities			
Capital expenditures	(2,559)	(2,129)	(2,179)
Proceeds from asset sales	555	520	402
Acquisitions	(3,269)	(150)	(358)
Change in investment securities	63	(309)	(331)
Total Investing Activities	(5,210)	(2,068)	(2,466)
Financing Activities			
Dividends to shareholders	(1,462)	(1,329)	(1,202)
Change in short-term debt	1,315	(160)	242
Additions to long-term debt	1,970	224	339
Reductions of long-term debt	(432)	(724)	(619)
Proceeds from stock options	158	134	89
Treasury purchases	(1,929)	(1,652)	(432)
Total Financing Activities	(380)	(3,507)	(1,583)
Effect of Exchange Rate Changes			
on Cash and Cash Equivalents	(96)	(31)	(63)
Change in Cash and Cash Equivalents	(801)	276	46
Cash and Cash Equivalents, End of Year	$ 1,549	$ 2,350	$ 2,074
Supplemental Disclosure			
Cash payments for:			
Interest, net of amount capitalized	$ 536	$ 449	$ 459
Income taxes	2,056	1,380	1,339
Liabilities assumed in acquisitions	808	42	56

See accompanying Notes to Consolidated Financial Statements.

1986: Super-absorbent polymer technology provides unparalleled dryness in a thin diaper   23

PROCTER & GAMBLE COMPANY ANNUAL REPORT

NOTES TO CONSOLIDATED FINANCIAL STATEMENTS

The Procter & Gamble Company and Subsidiaries

Millions of Dollars Except Per Share Amounts

1 | Summary of Significant Accounting Policies

Basis of Presentation: The consolidated financial statements include The Procter & Gamble Company and its controlled subsidiaries (the Company). Investments in companies that are at least 20% to 50% owned, and over which the Company exerts significant influence but does not control the financial and operating decisions, are accounted for by the equity method. These investments are managed as integral parts of the Company's segment operations, and the Company's share of their results is included in net sales for the related segments.

Use of Estimates: Preparation of financial statements in conformity with generally accepted accounting principles requires management to make estimates and assumptions that affect the amounts reported in the consolidated financial statements and accompanying disclosures. These estimates are based on management's best knowledge of current events and actions the Company may undertake in the future. Actual results may ultimately differ from estimates.

Accounting Changes: In 1998, the Company adopted several FASB statements. Statement No. 128, "Earnings per Share," which revises the manner in which earnings per share is calculated, did not impact the Company's previously reported earnings per share. Statement No. 130, "Reporting Comprehensive Income," requires the components of comprehensive income to be disclosed in the financial statements. Statement No. 131, "Disclosures about Segments of an Enterprise and Related Information," requires certain information to be reported about operating segments on a basis consistent with the Company's internal organizational structure. Statement No. 132, "Employers' Disclosures about Pensions and Other Postretirement Benefits," revises the disclosures for pensions and other postretirement benefits and standardizes them into a combined format. Required disclosures have been made and prior years' information has been reclassified for the impact of FASB Statements 130, 131 and 132.

New Pronouncements: In June 1998, the FASB issued Statement No. 133, "Accounting for Derivative Instruments and Hedging Activities," which revises the accounting for derivative financial instruments. In March 1998, the AICPA issued SOP 98-1, "Accounting for the Costs of Computer Software Developed or Obtained for Internal Use," which revises the accounting for software development costs and will require the capitalization of certain costs which the Company has historically expensed. The Company is currently analyzing the impacts of these statements, which are required to be adopted in 2000, and does not expect either statement to have a material impact on the Company's financial position, results of operations or cash flows.

Currency Translation: Financial statements of subsidiaries outside the U.S. generally are measured using the local currency as the functional currency. Adjustments to translate those statements into U.S. dollars are accumulated in a separate component of shareholders' equity. For subsidiaries operating in highly inflationary economies, the U.S. dollar is the functional currency. Remeasurement adjustments for highly inflationary economies and other transactional exchange gains (losses) are reflected in earnings and were $0, $1 and $(28) for 1998, 1997 and 1996, respectively.

Cash Equivalents: Highly liquid investments with maturities of three months or less when purchased are considered cash equivalents.

Inventory Valuation: Inventories are valued at cost, which is not in excess of current market price. Cost is primarily determined by either the average cost or the first-in, first-out method. The replacement cost of last-in, first-out inventories exceeds carrying value by approximately $91 and $122 at June 30, 1998 and 1997, respectively.

Goodwill and Other Intangible Assets: The cost of intangible assets is amortized, principally on a straight-line basis, over the estimated periods benefited, generally 40 years for goodwill and periods ranging from 10 to 40 years for other intangible assets. The realizability of goodwill and other intangibles is evaluated periodically when events or circumstances indicate a possible inability to recover the carrying amount. Such evaluation is based on various analyses, including cash flow and profitability projections that incorporate the impact of existing Company businesses. The analyses necessarily involve significant management judgment to evaluate the capacity of an acquired business to perform within projections. Historically, the Company has generated sufficient returns from acquired businesses to recover the cost of the goodwill and other intangible assets.

1986: First complete shampoo and conditioner in one

PROCTER & GAMBLE COMPANY ANNUAL REPORT

The Procter & Gamble Company and Subsidiaries

Property, Plant and Equipment: Property, plant and equipment are recorded at cost reduced by accumulated depreciation. Depreciation expense is provided based on estimated useful lives using the straight-line method.

Selected Operating Expenses: Research and development costs are charged to earnings as incurred and were $1,546 in 1998, $1,469 in 1997 and $1,399 in 1996. Advertising costs are charged to earnings as incurred and were $3,704 in 1998, $3,466 in 1997 and $3,254 in 1996.

Net Earnings Per Common Share: Net earnings less preferred dividends (net of related tax benefits) are divided by the weighted average number of common shares outstanding during the year to calculate basic net earnings per common share. Diluted net earnings per common share are calculated to give effect to stock options and convertible preferred stock.

Basic and diluted net earnings per share are reconciled as follows:

| | Years Ended June 30 | | |
	1998	1997	1996
Net earnings available to common shareholders	$3,676	$3,311	$2,943
Effect of dilutive securities			
Preferred dividends, net of tax benefit	104	104	103
Preferred dividend impact on funding of ESOP	(25)	(32)	(39)
Diluted net earnings	3,755	3,383	3,007
Basic weighted average common shares outstanding	1,343.4	1,360.3	1,372.6
Effect of dilutive securities			
Conversion of preferred shares	99.8	101.9	103.8
Exercise of stock options	22.3	24.8	19.8
Diluted weighted average common shares outstanding	1,465.5	1,487.0	1,496.2

Stock Split: In July 1997, the Company's board of directors approved a two-for-one stock split that was effective for common and preferred shareholders of record as of August 22, 1997. The financial statements, notes and other references to share and per-share data reflect the stock split for all periods presented.

Fair Values of Financial Instruments: Fair values of cash equivalents, short and long-term investments and short-term debt approximate cost. The estimated fair values of other financial instruments, including debt and risk management instruments, have been determined using available market information and valuation methodologies, primarily discounted cash flow analysis. These estimates require considerable judgment in interpreting market data, and changes in assumptions or estimation methods may significantly affect the fair value estimates.

Major Customer: The Company's largest customer, Wal-Mart Stores, Inc. and its affiliates, accounted for 11% and 10% of consolidated net sales in 1998 and 1997, respectively. These sales occurred primarily in the North America segment.

Reclassifications: Certain reclassifications of prior years' amounts have been made to conform with the current year presentation, primarily related to certain component parts of research and development costs.

2 | Acquisitions

In July 1997, the Company acquired Tambrands, Inc., a company in the feminine protection category, for approximately $1,844 in cash. Other acquisitions in 1998 totaled $1,425 and included the acquisition of paper businesses and increased ownership in various ventures in Latin America and Asia. These acquisitions, all of which were accounted for using the purchase method, resulted in goodwill of $3,335. Acquisitions accounted for as purchases in 1997 and 1996 totaled $150 and $358, respectively.

The following table reflects unaudited pro forma combined results of operations on the basis that the 1998 acquisitions had taken place at the beginning of the year for each of the periods presented:

| | Years Ended June 30 | |
	1998	1997
Pro forma amounts		
Net sales	$37,476	$37,008
Net earnings	3,756	3,409
Net earnings per common share		
Basic	2.72	2.43
Diluted	2.55	2.27

In management's opinion, the unaudited pro forma combined results of operations are not indicative of the actual results that would have occurred under the ownership and management of the Company.

1986: Patented "Wings" technology combined with "Dri-Weave" topsheet creates superior feminine protection   25

PROCTER & GAMBLE COMPANY ANNUAL REPORT

NOTES TO CONSOLIDATED FINANCIAL STATEMENTS (CONTINUED)   The Procter & Gamble Company and Subsidiaries

Millions of Dollars Except Per Share Amounts

3 | Supplemental Balance Sheet Information

	June 30	
	1998	1997
Accrued and Other Liabilities		
Marketing expenses	$1,109	$1,129
Compensation expenses	485	461
Other	2,348	2,212
	3,942	3,802
Other Non-Current Liabilities		
Postretirement benefits	$1,193	$1,300
Pension benefits	843	815
Other	1,251	883
	3,287	2,998

	Currency Translation	Other	Total
Accumulated Other Comprehensive Income			
Balance June 30, 1995	$ 64	$ 1	$ 65
Current period change	(483)	0	(483)
Balance June 30, 1996	(419)	1	(418)
Current period change	(412)	11	(401)
Balance June 30, 1997	(831)	12	(819)
Current period change	(536)	(2)	(538)
Balance June 30, 1998	(1,367)	10	(1,357)

4 | Short-Term and Long-Term Debt

	June 30	
	1998	1997
Short-Term Debt		
U.S. obligations	$1,435	$183
Foreign obligations	560	343
Current portion of long-term debt	286	323
	2,281	849

The weighted average short-term interest rates were 6.2% and 6.9% as of June 30, 1998 and 1997, respectively.

	Average Rate	Maturities	June 30	
			1998	1997
Long-Term Debt				
U.S. notes and debentures	6.96%	1998-2029	$2,897	$2,082
ESOP Series A	8.33%	1998-2004	545	613
ESOP Series B	9.36%	2021	1,000	1,000
U.S. commercial paper			1,207	585
Foreign obligations			402	186
Current portion of long-term debt			(286)	(323)
			5,765	4,143

Long-term weighted average interest rates in the preceding table are as of June 30, 1998 and include the effects of related interest rate swaps discussed in Note 5. Certain commercial paper balances have been classified as long-term debt based on the Company's intent and ability to renew the obligations on a long-term basis. The Company has entered into derivatives that convert certain of these commercial paper obligations into fixed-rate obligations.

The fair value of the long-term debt was $6,412 and $4,509 at June 30, 1998 and 1997, respectively. Long-term debt maturities during the next five years are as follows: 1999–$286; 2000–$387; 2001–$339; 2002–$427 and 2003–$1,141.

5 | Risk Management Activities

The Company is exposed to market risk, including changes in interest rates, currency exchange rates and commodity prices. To manage the volatility relating to these exposures on a consolidated basis, the Company nets the exposures to take advantage of natural offsets and enters into various derivative transactions for the remaining exposures pursuant to the Company's policies in areas such as counterparty exposure and hedging practices. The financial impacts of these hedging instruments are offset by corresponding changes in the underlying exposures being hedged. The Company does not hold or issue derivative financial instruments for trading purposes.

Interest Rate Management

The Company's policy is to manage interest cost using a mix of fixed and variable rate debt. To manage this mix in a cost-efficient manner, the Company enters into interest rate swaps, in which the Company agrees to exchange, at specified intervals, the difference between fixed and variable interest amounts calculated by reference to an agreed-upon notional principal amount. These swaps are designated to hedge underlying debt obligations. For qualifying hedges, the interest rate differential is reflected as an adjustment to interest expense over the life of the swaps.

Certain currency interest rate swaps are designated to hedge the foreign currency exposure of the Company's related foreign net investments. Currency effects of these hedges are reflected in the accumulated other comprehensive income section of shareholders' equity, offsetting a portion of the translation of the net assets.

1989: First North American laundry detergent with activated bleach

PROCTER & GAMBLE COMPANY ANNUAL REPORT

The following table presents information for all interest rate instruments. The notional amount does not necessarily represent amounts exchanged by the parties and, therefore, is not a direct measure of the Company's exposure to credit risk. The fair value approximates the cost to settle the outstanding contracts. The carrying value includes the net amount due to counterparties under swap contracts, currency translation associated with currency interest rate swaps and any marked-to-market value adjustments of instruments.

	June 30	
	1998	1997
Notional amount	$2,149	$1,488
Fair value	$ 7	$ (54)
Carrying value	28	(28)
Unrecognized loss	(21)	(26)

Although derivatives are an important component of the Company's interest rate management program, their incremental effect on interest expense for 1998, 1997 and 1996 was not material.

Currency Rate Management
The Company manufactures and sells its products in a number of countries throughout the world and, as a result, is exposed to movements in foreign currency exchange rates. The major foreign currency exposures involve the markets in Western Europe, Mexico and Canada. The primary purpose of the Company's foreign currency hedging activities is to protect against the volatility associated with foreign currency purchases of materials and other assets and liabilities created in the normal course of business. Corporate policy prescribes the range of allowable hedging activity. The Company primarily utilizes forward exchange contracts and purchased options with durations of generally less than 12 months.

In addition, the Company enters into foreign currency swaps to hedge intercompany financing transactions, and utilizes purchased foreign currency options with durations of generally less than 18 months and forward exchange contracts to hedge against the effect of exchange rate fluctuations on royalties and foreign source income.

Gains and losses related to qualifying hedges of foreign currency firm commitments or anticipated transactions are deferred in prepaid expense and are included in the basis of the underlying transactions. To the extent that a qualifying hedge is terminated or ceases to be effective as a hedge, any deferred gains and losses up to that point continue to be deferred and are included in the basis of the underlying transaction. All other foreign exchange contracts are marked-to-market on a current basis, generally to marketing, research and administration expense. To the extent anticipated transactions are no longer likely to occur, the related hedges are closed with gains or losses charged to earnings on a current basis.

Currency instruments outstanding are as follows:

	June 30	
	1998	1997
Notional amount		
Forward contracts	$3,448	$2,607
Purchased options	1,262	1,643
Currency swaps	217	358
Fair value		
Forward contracts	$ 30	$ (2)
Purchased options	16	38
Currency swaps	8	(1)

The deferred gains and losses on these instruments were not material.

In addition, in order to hedge currency exposures related to the net investments in foreign subsidiaries, the Company utilizes local currency financing entered into by the subsidiaries, and currency interest rate swaps and other foreign currency denominated financing instruments entered into by the parent. Gains and losses on instruments designated as hedges of net investments are offset against the translation effects reflected in shareholders' equity.

Currency interest rate swaps, foreign currency instruments and foreign currency denominated debt that have been designated as hedges of the Company's net investment exposure in certain foreign subsidiaries have notional amounts totaling $1,138 and $936 at June 30, 1998 and 1997, respectively. These hedges resulted in gains of $42 and $63, net of $25 and $38 in tax effects, reflected in shareholders' equity.

PROCTER & GAMBLE COMPANY ANNUAL REPORT

NOTES TO CONSOLIDATED FINANCIAL STATEMENTS (CONTINUED)   The Procter & Gamble Company and Subsidiaries
Millions of Dollars Except Per Share Amounts

Credit Risk

Credit risk arising from the inability of a counterparty to meet the terms of the Company's financial instrument contracts is generally limited to the amounts, if any, by which the counterparty's obligations exceed the obligations of the Company. It is the Company's policy to enter into financial instruments with a diversity of creditworthy counterparties. Therefore, the Company does not expect to incur material credit losses on its risk management or other financial instruments.

6 | Stock Options

The Company has stock-based compensation plans under which stock options are granted annually to key managers and directors at the market price on the date of grant. The grants are fully exercisable after one year and have a ten-year life. In 1998, the Company granted stock options to all eligible employees not covered by the key manager and director plans. These grants, which comprised 8.7 million of the 20.3 million options granted in 1998, are fully exercisable after five years and have a ten-year life. The Company issues stock appreciation rights in countries where stock options have not been approved by local governments.

Pursuant to FASB Statement No. 123, "Accounting for Stock-Based Compensation," the Company has elected to account for its employee stock option plans under APB Opinion No. 25, "Accounting for Stock Issued to Employees." Accordingly, no compensation cost has been recognized for these plans. Had compensation cost for the plans been determined based on the fair value at the grant date consistent with FASB Statement No. 123, the Company's net earnings and earnings per share would have been as follows:

	Years Ended June 30		
	1998	1997	1996
Net earnings			
As reported	$3,780	$3,415	$3,046
Pro forma	3,472	3,305	2,981
Net earnings per common share			
Basic			
As reported	$ 2.74	$ 2.43	$ 2.14
Pro forma	2.51	2.35	2.10
Diluted			
As reported	2.56	2.28	2.01
Pro forma	2.35	2.20	1.97

The fair value of each option grant is estimated on the date of grant using the Binomial option-pricing model with the following weighted average assumptions:

	Years Ended June 30		
	1998	1997	1996
Interest rate	5.6%	6.6%	6.1%
Dividend yield	2%	2%	2%
Expected volatility	26%	22%	20%
Expected life in years	6	6	6

Stock option activity was as follows:

	Options in Thousands		
	1998	1997	1996
Outstanding, July 1	68,514	66,657	63,384
Granted	20,315	10,409	9,605
Exercised	(8,477)	(8,357)	(6,110)
Canceled	(434)	(195)	(222)
Outstanding, June 30	79,918	68,514	66,657
Exercisable	59,610	58,098	57,048
Available for grant	31,558	28,538	24,418
Average price			
Outstanding, beginning of year	$31.00	$24.79	$21.36
Granted	83.26	58.72	40.87
Exercised	18.57	16.02	14.52
Outstanding, end of year	45.58	31.00	24.79
Exercisable, end of year	32.74	26.03	22.09
Weighted average grant date fair value of options	24.56	17.14	10.88

The following table summarizes information about stock options outstanding at June 30, 1998:

	Options Outstanding		
Range of Prices	Number Outstanding (Thousands)	Weighted-Avg Exercise Price	Weighted-Avg Remaining Contractual Life
$ 8 to 30	33,626	$22.69	3.4 years
33 to 46	16,821	37.85	7.1
57 to 71	9,349	60.42	8.5
71 to 85	20,122	83.39	9.5

1990: First tartar control toothpaste

PROCTER & GAMBLE COMPANY ANNUAL REPORT

The Procter & Gamble Company and Subsidiaries

The following table summarizes information about stock options exercisable at June 30, 1998:

Range of Prices	Options Exercisable	
	Number Exercisable (Thousands)	Weighted-Avg Exercise Price
$ 8 to 30	33,626	$22.69
33 to 46	16,821	37.85
57 to 71	9,163	60.24
71 to 85	–	–

7 | Postretirement Benefits

The Company offers various postretirement benefits to its employees.

Defined Contribution Retirement Plans

Within the U.S., the most significant retirement benefit is the defined contribution profit sharing plan funded by an employee stock ownership plan (ESOP) and Company contributions. Annual credits to participants' accounts are based on individual base salaries and years of service, and do not exceed 15% of total participants' annual salaries and wages.

	Years Ended June 30		
	1998	1997	1996
ESOP preferred shares allocated at market value	$235	$247	$200
Company contributions	58	35	75
Benefits earned	293	282	275

Other Retiree Benefits

The Company also provides certain health care and life insurance benefits for substantially all U.S. employees who become eligible for these benefits when they meet minimum age and service requirements. Generally, the health care plans require contributions from retirees and pay a stated percentage of expenses, reduced by deductibles and other coverages. Retiree contributions change annually in line with medical cost trends. These benefits are partially funded by an ESOP, as well as certain other assets contributed by the Company.

Certain other employees, primarily outside the U.S., are covered by local defined benefit pension, health care and life insurance plans.

Summarized information on the Company's postretirement plans is as follows:

	Pension Benefits		Other Retiree Benefits	
	Years Ended June 30			
	1998	1997	1998	1997
Change in Benefit Obligation				
Benefit obligation at beginning of year	$1,991	$1,886	$ 1,460	$ 1,405
Service cost	106	100	42	45
Interest cost	148	131	102	109
Participants' contributions	3	5	11	12
Amendments	21	2	(6)	5
Actuarial loss (gain)	87	54	(71)	(50)
Acquisitions	154	42	1	0
Curtailments	13	0	0	0
Currency exchange	(85)	(117)	(7)	(4)
Benefit payments	(156)	(112)	(67)	(62)
Benefit obligation at end of year	2,282	1,991	1,465	1,460
Change in Plan Assets				
Fair value of plan assets at beginning of year	1,229	1,019	1,828	838
Actual return on plan assets	243	180	803	999
Acquisitions	131	42	0	0
Employer contributions	103	83	37	41
Participants' contributions	3	5	11	12
Currency exchange	(30)	12	(1)	0
Benefit payments	(156)	(112)	(67)	(62)
Fair value of plan assets at end of year	1,523	1,229	2,611	1,828
Funded Status				
Funded status at end of year	(759)	(762)	1,146	368
Unrecognized net actuarial gain	(163)	(95)	(2,354)	(1,691)
Unrecognized transition amount	32	35	0	0
Unrecognized prior service cost	75	43	(21)	(17)
Net amount recognized	(815)	(779)	(1,229)	(1,340)
Prepaid benefit cost	$ 34	$ 52	$ 1	$ 0
Accrued benefit cost	(849)	(831)	(1,230)	(1,340)
Net liability recognized	(815)	(779)	(1,229)	(1,340)

1992: Breakthrough Carezyme technology prevents fuzzing and color fading

29

PROCTER & GAMBLE COMPANY ANNUAL REPORT

NOTES TO CONSOLIDATED FINANCIAL STATEMENTS (CONTINUED)   The Procter & Gamble Company and Subsidiaries
Millions of Dollars Except Per Share Amounts

The Company's stock comprised $2,443 and $1,687 of other retiree plan assets, net of Series B ESOP debt, as of June 30, 1998 and 1997, respectively.

	Pension Benefits		Other Retiree Benefits	
	Years Ended June 30			
	1998	1997	1998	1997
Weighted Average Assumptions				
Discount rate	7.0%	7.2%	6.8%	7.5%
Expected return on plan assets	9%	9%	9%	9%
Rate of compensation increase	5%	5%	–	–
Initial health care cost trend rate*	–	–	8%	9%

*Assumed to decrease gradually to 5% in 2006 and remain at that level thereafter.

	Pension Benefits			Other Retiree Benefits		
	Years Ended June 30					
	1998	1997	1996	1998	1997	1996
Components of Net Periodic Benefit Cost						
Service cost	$ 106	$100	$ 96	$ 42	$ 45	$ 47
Interest cost	148	131	131	102	109	102
Expected return on plan assets	(103)	(87)	(75)	(171)	(138)	(121)
Amortization of prior service cost	7	5	6	(2)	(2)	(2)
Amortization of transition amount	3	0	0	0	0	0
Curtailment loss	12	0	0	0	0	0
Recognized net actuarial gain	0	(7)	(3)	(41)	(18)	(15)
Gross benefit cost	173	142	155	(70)	(4)	11
Dividends on ESOP preferred stock	0	0	0	(78)	(79)	(79)
Net periodic benefit cost	173	142	155	(148)	(83)	(68)

The projected benefit obligation, accumulated benefit obligation and fair value of plan assets for the pension plans with accumulated benefit obligations in excess of plan assets were $1,206, $984 and $155, respectively, as of June 30, 1998, and $1,172, $899 and $158, respectively, as of June 30, 1997.

Assumed health care cost trend rates have a significant effect on the amounts reported for the health care plans. A one-percentage-point change in assumed health care cost trend rates would have the following effects:

	1-Percentage-Point Increase	1-Percentage-Point Decrease
Effect on total of service and interest cost components	$ 26	$ (22)
Effect on postretirement benefit obligation	207	(181)

8 | Employee Stock Ownership Plan

The Company maintains the Procter & Gamble Profit Sharing Trust and Employee Stock Ownership Plan (ESOP) to provide funding for two primary postretirement benefits described in Note 7: a defined contribution profit sharing plan and certain U.S. postretirement health care benefits.

The ESOP borrowed $1,000 in 1989, which has been guaranteed by the Company. The proceeds were used to purchase Series A ESOP Convertible Class A Preferred Stock to fund a portion of the defined contribution plan. Principal and interest requirements are $117 per year, paid by the trust from dividends on the preferred shares and from cash contributions and advances from the Company. The shares are convertible at the option of the holder into one share of the Company's common stock. The liquidation value is equal to the issue price of $13.75 per share.

In 1991, the ESOP borrowed an additional $1,000, also guaranteed by the Company. The proceeds were used to purchase Series B ESOP Convertible Class A Preferred Stock to fund a portion of retiree health care benefits. Debt service requirements are $94 per year, funded by preferred stock dividends and cash contributions from the Company. Each share is convertible at the option of the holder into one share of the Company's common stock. The liquidation value is equal to the issuance price of $26.12 per share.

	Shares in Thousands		
	1998	1997	1996
Shares Outstanding			
Series A	60,635	62,952	64,562
Series B	37,805	38,045	38,204

1992: First penetrating, pro-vitamin formula for hair with superior shine

PROCTER & GAMBLE COMPANY ANNUAL REPORT

The Procter & Gamble Company and Subsidiaries

Shares of the ESOP are allocated at original cost based on debt service requirements, net of advances made by the Company to the trust. The fair value of the Series A shares serves to reduce the Company's cash contribution required to fund the profit sharing plan contributions earned. The Series B shares are considered plan assets of the other retiree benefits plan. Dividends on all preferred shares, net of related tax benefit, are charged to retained earnings. The preferred shares held by the ESOP are considered outstanding from inception for purposes of calculating diluted net earnings per common share.

9 | Income Taxes

Earnings before income taxes consist of the following:

	Years Ended June 30		
	1998	1997	1996
United States	$3,632	$3,232	$3,023
International	2,076	2,017	1,646
	5,708	5,249	4,669

The income tax provision consists of the following:

	Years Ended June 30		
	1998	1997	1996
Current tax expense			
U.S. Federal	$ 996	$ 967	$ 776
International	918	805	413
U.S. State & Local	115	88	106
	2,029	1,860	1,295
Deferred tax expense			
U.S. Federal	51	1	220
International & other	(152)	(27)	108
	(101)	(26)	328
Total	1,928	1,834	1,623

Taxes credited to shareholders' equity for the years ended June 30, 1998 and 1997 were $147 and $97, respectively. Undistributed earnings of foreign subsidiaries that are considered to be reinvested indefinitely were $6,739 at June 30, 1998.

The effective income tax rate was 33.8%, 34.9% and 34.8% in 1998, 1997 and 1996, respectively, compared to the U.S. statutory rate of 35%.

Deferred income tax assets and liabilities are comprised of the following:

	June 30	
	1998	1997
Current deferred tax assets	$ 595	$ 661
Non-current deferred tax assets (liabilities)		
Depreciation	(1,058)	(1,031)
Postretirement benefits	435	475
Loss carryforwards	167	84
Other	28	(87)
	(428)	(559)

Included in the above are total valuation allowances of $177 and $113 in 1998 and 1997, respectively. The valuation allowance increased in 1998 primarily due to the generation of additional net operating loss carryforwards.

10 | Commitments and Contingencies

The Company has purchase commitments for materials, supplies, and property, plant and equipment incidental to the ordinary conduct of business. In the aggregate, such commitments are not at prices in excess of current market.

The Company is subject to various lawsuits and claims with respect to matters such as governmental regulations, income taxes and other actions arising out of the normal course of business. The Company is also subject to contingencies pursuant to environmental laws and regulations that in the future may require the Company to take action to correct the effects on the environment of prior manufacturing and waste disposal practices. Accrued environmental liabilities for remediation and closure costs at June 30, 1998 were $66, and in management's opinion, such accruals are appropriate based on existing facts and circumstances. Current year expenditures were not material.

While the effect on future results of these items is not subject to reasonable estimation because considerable uncertainty exists, in the opinion of management and Company counsel, the ultimate liabilities resulting from such claims will not materially affect the consolidated financial position, results of operations or cash flows of the Company.

1992: Asacol launched for treatment of ulcerative colitis

PROCTER & GAMBLE COMPANY ANNUAL REPORT

NOTES TO CONSOLIDATED FINANCIAL STATEMENTS (CONTINUED)   The Procter & Gamble Company and Subsidiaries
Millions of Dollars Except Per Share Amounts

11 | Segment Information

The Company has adopted FASB Statement No. 131, "Disclosures about Segments of a Business Enterprise and Related Information." The Company is managed in four operating segments: North America, which includes the United States and Canada; Europe, Middle East and Africa; Asia; and Latin America.

Corporate operations include certain financing and employee benefits costs, goodwill amortization, other general corporate income and expense, segment eliminations and projects included in the Company's ongoing simplification and standardization program, which includes costs for consolidation of selected manufacturing facilities, re-engineering of manufacturing and distribution processes, organization redesign and simplified product line-ups, as well as gains and losses on sales of non-strategic brands and assets. Corporate assets include primarily cash, investment securities and goodwill.

		North America	Europe, Middle East and Africa	Asia	Latin America	Corporate	Total
Net Sales	1998	$18,456	$11,835	$3,453	$2,640	$ 770	$37,154
	1997	17,625	11,587	3,573	2,306	673	35,764
	1996	17,230	11,458	3,881	2,173	542	35,284
Net Earnings	1998	2,474	1,092	174	274	(234)	3,780
	1997	2,253	956	275	256	(325)	3,415
	1996	1,953	793	273	219	(192)	3,046
Earnings Before Income Taxes	1998	3,789	1,540	266	329	(216)	5,708
	1997	3,516	1,446	400	326	(439)	5,249
	1996	3,055	1,137	433	236	(192)	4,669
Identifiable Assets	1998	11,063	5,998	2,499	1,519	9,887	30,966
	1997	10,280	5,433	2,726	1,389	7,716	27,544
	1996	10,382	5,853	2,770	1,270	7,455	27,730
Capital Expenditures	1998	1,433	686	266	174	–	2,559
	1997	1,163	547	287	132	–	2,129
	1996	1,080	602	322	175	–	2,179
Depreciation and Amortization	1998	755	374	174	97	198	1,598
	1997	693	405	167	83	139	1,487
	1996	633	380	143	48	154	1,358
Interest Expense	1998	–	–	–	–	548	548
	1997	–	–	–	–	457	457
	1996	–	–	–	–	484	484

Product Net Sales Information
The following is supplemental information on net sales by product groups, aligned as follows:

Laundry and Cleaning – dishcare, fabric conditioners, hard surface cleaners and laundry.

Paper – diapers, feminine protection, incontinence, tissue and towel, and wipes.

Beauty Care – cosmetics and fragrances, deodorants, hair care, and skin care and personal cleansing.

Food and Beverage – coffee, commercial services, juice, peanut butter, shortening and oil, and snacks.

Health Care – gastrointestinal, oral care, pharmaceuticals and respiratory care.

	Laundry and Cleaning	Paper	Beauty Care	Food and Beverage	Health Care	Corporate & Other	Total
1998	$11,099	$10,862	$7,160	$4,376	$2,849	$808	$37,154
1997	10,892	10,101	7,101	4,107	2,895	668	35,764
1996	10,683	10,161	6,916	4,066	2,939	519	35,284

1992: Macrobid launched as a urinary tract anti-infective

PROCTER & GAMBLE COMPANY ANNUAL REPORT

The Procter & Gamble Company and Subsidiaries

12 | Quarterly Results (Unaudited)

		Quarters Ended				Total
		Sept. 30	Dec. 31	Mar. 31	June 30	Year
Net Sales	1997–98	$9,355	$9,641	$8,881	$9,277	$37,154
	1996–97	8,903	9,142	8,771	8,948	35,764
Operating Income	1997–98	1,739	1,688	1,516	1,112	6,055
	1996–97	1,547	1,521	1,383	1,037	5,488
Net Earnings	1997–98	1,087	1,046	961	686	3,780
	1996–97	979	944	881	611	3,415
Basic Net Earnings Per Common Share	1997–98	.79	.76	.69	.50	2.74
	1996–97	.70	.67	.63	.43	2.43
Diluted Net Earnings Per Common Share	1997–98	.73	.71	.65	.47	2.56
	1996–97	.65	.63	.59	.41	2.28

FINANCIAL HIGHLIGHTS
Millions of Dollars Except Per Share Amounts

	1998	1997	1996	1995	1994
Net Sales	37,154	35,764	35,284	33,482	30,385
Operating Income	6,055	5,488	4,815	4,244	3,670
Net Earnings	3,780	3,415	3,046	2,645	2,211
Net Earnings Margin	10.2%	9.5%	8.6%	7.9%	7.3%
Basic Net Earnings Per Common Share	2.74	2.43	2.14	1.85	1.54
Diluted Net Earnings Per Common Share	2.56	2.28	2.01	1.74	1.45
Dividends Per Common Share	1.01	.90	.80	.70	.62
Research and Development Expense	1,546	1,469	1,399	1,304	1,162
Advertising Expense	3,704	3,466	3,254	3,284	2,996
Total Assets	30,966	27,544	27,730	28,125	25,535
Capital Expenditures	2,559	2,129	2,179	2,146	1,841
Long-Term Debt	5,765	4,143	4,670	5,161	4,980
Shareholders' Equity	12,236	12,046	11,722	10,589	8,832

1994: First body wash with puff that cleans and conditions your skin   33

SUMMARY

Accounting is the language of business. Accounting reports are used to convey information about the financial health and performance of companies to various external constituencies such as creditors, lenders, shareholders, public interest groups, employees, and various governmental agencies, all of whom have decisions to make.

The focus of this text is on financial accounting and the generally accepted accounting principles used in preparing quarterly and annual accounting reports. Our goal is to help you become financial statement literate and to be conversant in the language of accounting.

NEW CONCEPTS AND TERMS

Accounting

American Institute of Certified Public Accountants

Audit

Auditor's opinion

Financial accounting

Financial Accounting Standards Board

Financial statements

Footnotes

Generally accepted accounting principles (GAAP)

Generally accepted auditing standards (GAAS)

Independent auditor

Internal control structure

International Accounting Standards Committee (IASC)

Managerial accounting

Prospective information

Securities and Exchange Commission

Stewardship information

Unqualified opinion

ASSIGNMENTS

1.1. Identify five different users of accounting information and discuss briefly the kinds of decisions they must make and the kinds of accounting information they should have in making those decisions.

Assume that the Procter & Gamble financial statements are typical of the statements provided by U.S. companies to their public stockholders. Do those statements meet the information needs you outlined above? To the extent that they do not, why might that be so? Where might users go to find the information needed?

1.2. Assume that you are the chief accounting officer of a major manufacturing company. Identify and describe five principal differences that might exist between your company's managerial accounting reports and its financial accounting reports. Why might those differences exist?

1.3. In your own words, explain what is meant by an internal control structure. You may find it helpful to couch your explanation in the context of a hypothetical company, for example, a rapidly growing manufacturer of electronic components.

1.4. Based on your reading of the report of Procter & Gamble management and the report from the independent auditor, both presented in the chapter, describe in your own words the responsibilities of management and of the auditors for the preparation of the Procter & Gamble financial statements. How are they similar? How are they different? This division of responsibilities has evolved over time. Why might it have evolved as it did?

1.5. Based on your reading of the Procter & Gamble financial statements, identify five measures of performance that you believe to be important and explain why you selected those five. Also identify five measures of Procter & Gamble performance that you believe might be important to a decision to buy Procter & Gamble shares but are not available to you from these financial statements. Why might those measures not be reported in a public financial statement?

1.6. Assume that you will have dinner tomorrow night with an old college friend who is now a successful CPA. Based on your reading of the Procter & Gamble financial statements, identify the 10 most important questions about accounting and the financial reporting process that you would like to pose to your friend. (Try to make those questions as complete as possible. At the conclusion of this course, you ought to go back and see how many of those questions you can answer for yourself.)

CHAPTER 2

There Is More to Accounting Than Meets the Eye

What advantages a merchant derives from double entry bookkeeping! It is among the finest inventions of the human mind; and every good householder should introduce it into his economy.[1]

Key Chapter Issues

- I'm ready to wade into this thing called accounting, but before I set out on this journey, can I get a general road map to help establish a perspective?
- What is the significance of the accounting equation $A = L + OE$? What is the logic behind that algebraic expression?

- What are these tools called the balance sheet, the income statement, and the statement of cash flow? How do we use them? How are they different? How do they relate to each other?
- GAAP is an acronym for Generally Accepted Accounting Principles; where does that general acceptance come from? How would we know when we had achieved it? Who is entitled to proclaim it and interpret it?

---

[1] A quote attributed to J. Wolfgang von Goethe (1749–1832) contained in S. James and R. Parker, *A Dictionary of Business Quotations*, (NY, NY: Simon & Schuster), p. 1.

I n Chapter 1 we set forth the idea that accounting is essentially a communications vehicle and can be compared to a language. We also introduced generally accepted accounting principles (GAAP) as the set of conventions that makes it possible for accounting to communicate to a diverse audience. That discussion pointed out that the word *accounting* means both the numbers included in financial reports and the text that explains and expands on those numerical measures. We looked briefly at the process of preparing financial reports, and we introduced a real-life example we will use throughout the book—the 1998 financial report published by Procter & Gamble Company.

In this chapter we move beyond that introductory discussion to a second level of inquiry. We are still working at a macro level, but we are beginning to get down into more useful detail. This chapter is really three chapters in one: In the first segment we look more deeply into some of the important principles that underlie GAAP, and we consider several institutions that guide the development of the principles, practices, and procedures included within GAAP. In the second segment we explore the basic financial statements in more depth and look at the way those financial statements interrelate. In the final segment, we look at the way Procter & Gamble applied some of the fundamental accounting principles using the company's 1998 financial statements as the vehicle for that discussion.

SOME FUNDAMENTAL QUESTIONS IN ACCOUNTING

The discussion in the introductory chapter was, necessarily, somewhat abstract. However, the process of preparing financial statements for a particular company is never an abstract exercise. Preparing financial statements requires a real person to find specific answers to specific questions. These questions have energized financial people for many years, and the answers that have emerged form the backbone of our present set of generally accepted accounting principles. It is useful at this stage of our inquiry to consider those questions and the answers that are outlined for us in GAAP.

To pursue these questions and their answers, let us create a context. As you think through the following discussion, assume that you have formed a new company to borrow some money to buy an apartment building. Let us assume that you have invested $20,000 of your own money in the company. Let us also assume that the company used your $20,000, borrowed an additional $80,000 from a bank, and then paid $100,000 to buy an existing apartment building. The company's business will be to collect rent from the tenants, pay for maintenance and utilities, pay the principal and interest on the debt, and pay you any profits that may result from the company's operations. As you periodically prepare financial statements to report the status of the company and its success or failure, you will need to address a number of questions.

What Is the Entity Whose Operations Are to Be Covered by This Report?

You could elect to prepare financial statements that reflect only the assets and the activities of the real estate company by itself; alternatively, you could prepare financial statements that report all of your personal assets and activities, which would of course include the assets and activities of the real estate company you just created. What assets and activities should be included in the financial statements, and what should be left out? To make that decision you might ask, "What information does the expected reader of these statements need to know? What information does the reader of these statements have a right to know?" For example, if the bank is entitled to look at only the real estate company to satisfy the $80,000 loan, the financial statements you prepare should cover only that company's activities. However, if the bank has the right to look at the real estate business *and* your personal activities to satisfy the bank loan, it might ask for combined financial statements that cover your own personal activities as well as those of the business.

Following that line of thought, you might also argue that the company's financial statements should include the assets and the activities of your building's tenants—after all, their financial well-being will be crucial to your success and to the bank's ability to collect on its loan. However, the relationship you have with your company is not the same as the relationship your company has with the building's tenants. You control your company, and you can dictate its activities. However, neither you nor your company controls the building's tenants, and they are under no obligation to you or your company except to comply with the terms of the lease. Their assets are not available to you except for the rent they owe. That same thinking directs GAAP. Under GAAP, financial statements include or encompass all of the activities of a particular entity and any other entities that it controls. For example, for various legal reasons, you might want your real estate company to create a subsidiary company and to assign to that subsidiary all of the maintenance work on your building. Regardless of the legal separation of the two companies, the consolidated financial statements of the parent real estate company would include all of its own activities and the activities of the maintenance company. If that maintenance work was instead subcontracted to an independent janitorial firm, your real estate company would not include the activities of that entity in its financial statements. Under GAAP, **consolidated financial statements** typically include the activities of the legal parent company and the activities of all of those other entities that the parent controls. This convention is known as the **entity principle.**

What Measurement Basis Should Be Used in Preparing These Financial Statements?

The simplest measurement basis for the preparation of financial statements is the **cash basis.** The cash basis determines success by comparing the amount of cash on hand at the end of a period against the amount of cash on hand at the beginning of the period. More cash is good; less cash is bad.

Cash-basis accounting is used by some very small companies when there is little difference between a long-range and a short-range view of the business. Cash-basis accounting focuses on cash today and ignores the future cash-generating potential of any other form of asset. For example, in the hypothetical case we are using as our model, a balance sheet prepared on a cash basis of accounting would show no assets (or liabilities) for your company after its purchase of the building; worse, the income statement for the first period would show a loss of $20,000 because of the cash expended for the down payment. The cash basis of accounting is concerned only with *current* cash effects and ignores the possibility of *future* cash effects. Cash-basis accounting, for example, ignores the fact that your company purchased the building because you expected it to earn more cash (in the future) than you initially paid for it, as well as the fact that the building retains that future cash-generating ability. Cash-basis accounting is not considered to be GAAP.

This is not to imply, however, that cash flow information is not useful. It would be very useful to the readers of your company's financial statements to know that all of the company's cash was used for the down payment on the building and that the company would have to borrow money to meet emergency needs. Cash flow information is important to financial statement readers who want a near-term perspective on a company. The financial community has indicated that it wants cash flow information for its near-term decisions, but there has also been a demand for more sophisticated measures of financial status and of operating results.

At the other extreme, you could prepare the financial statements for your real estate business using **fair value accounting.** Under fair value accounting, assets and liabilities are included on a balance sheet at the present value of their expected future cash flows, which is, of course, their current market value. If it is not immediately apparent to you why the market value of an asset should be the present value of its future cash flows, stop a minute and consider the thought process you might follow in a decision to purchase 100 shares of Procter & Gamble stock. You would most likely estimate the dividends you would receive in the future and the increase in share price that might develop during the period you expect to hold the stock. You would then equate those expected future cash flows back to today's equivalent dollar value, using a discount rate equal to the percentage return you expect on a common stock such as Procter & Gamble. If the expected future cash flows, discounted at the rate of return you demand, are more than the current market price of the Procter & Gamble stock, you would buy the stock; alternatively, if the present value of those expected future cash flows is less than the current price of the Procter & Gamble stock, you would look for another investment. That same process describes almost every asset purchase (and sale) decision—including your decision to have your company buy an apartment building for $100,000.

Under fair value accounting, the building you purchased in our example would, at the outset, be valued at $100,000 (assuming you paid fair value for your purchase). If its market value increased to $110,000 by the end of the next accounting period, the balance sheet would reflect that new value, and the $10,000 gain would be included with all of the company's other transactions in the determination of the business's net income for the period. Under this accounting, owners' equity is simply the difference between the aggregate fair value of the assets and that of the debt. Similarly, income (or loss) is simply the difference in the owners' equity at the beginning and at the end of an accounting period. The fair value method has intuitive appeal—it is logical to see the equity of the company as the net fair value of all of its assets and liabilities. However, it is difficult to implement because it is often difficult to obtain fair and accurate values for all assets and liabilities. Fair value accounting is not yet accepted under GAAP.

GAAP requires a middle ground, the **accrual method** of accounting. Accrual accounting assumes that assets *will* generate future cash flows, but because the future is uncertain, a conservative assumption is made that those future cash flows *will be no more* than the assets' original cost. Seldom is a value in excess of the assets' cost ever recognized in the financial statements under U.S. GAAP. This convention is called the **historical cost principle.** However, sometimes we know just enough about the future to be worried. If we know enough about the future to be concerned that the assets might not generate enough cash flow to cover their cost, the original cost values are reduced to the lower, expected future cash flow. Financial people reduce this idea to a shorthand expression: "Assets are carried at the **lower of cost or market.**" This pragmatic modification of the historical cost principle illustrates another accounting axiom: "Never anticipate gains but always anticipate losses."

Accrual accounting is more sophisticated than cash-basis accounting because it assumes that your expenditure to buy the building was made with the reasonable expectation that you would realize a future cash flow benefit from your purchase. But the accrual method is more practical than the fair value method because it ignores "what if" value changes. In fact, under accrual accounting, assets are valued at their *future* cash flows only when the amounts of those future flows are validated by a transaction with a third party. Going back to our model, the building you purchased would continue to be carried on subsequent balance sheets at its historical cost of $100,000 even though a number of qualified appraisers assured you that it *could* be sold for $110,000. Only when the building is actually sold to a third party—when that third party takes on the risks of ownership—will that increase in value be recognized in your company's financial statements.

Assuming that your company adopts accrual accounting, the future benefit inherent in the building would be recorded as an asset with a value of $100,000. A floor buffing machine, purchased today to help keep the halls clean, would also be recorded as an asset—at its purchase price—because you expect the machine to be usable over a period of years. If you purchased a fire insurance policy that provided coverage for the next three years, that policy would also be an asset because you expect that the benefit you will get from that current expenditure will extend over the life of the policy. All of those assets are expected to provide the company with a future value. As we will see later, costs that have been deferred as assets this period will be allocated as expenses against the operations of the future periods that will benefit from their use. Under accrual accounting, an expenditure that benefits the future is recorded as an asset today but will be recognized as an expense in the future when that benefit is realized. Conversely, the money you pay to the janitors to clean the building is a current expense charged against operations of the current period. That expenditure is not an asset because that current cleaning provides no future benefit—the building will have to be cleaned again tomorrow.

Accrual accounting also recognizes the reality of credit in the business world. It measures the cash consequences of a promise given or received when the promise is exchanged, not when the cash actually changes hands. If you sell the building for $110,000 and a third party buys it, promising to pay $110,000 12 months from today, your company would record that promise as an asset (referred to as a *receivable*) at the expected cash flow of $110,000. Similarly, you would remove the building from your balance sheet because it is no longer yours. The liability to the bank remains because you can't pay off the bank loan with a promise—you have to wait until the buyer actually gives you the cash before you can pay off the debt. The difference between the asset value ($110,000) and the debt ($80,000) is the owners' equity. The difference between that equity balance ($30,000) at the end of the period and the equity balance at the beginning ($20,000) is the company's income for the year. That $10,000 gain on the sale is income in that year, even though the cash will not be received until the following year. Accrual accounting assumes that credit transactions will be completed in the ordinary course of business.

Should Your Company's Financial Statements Forecast the Future or Should They Report Only the Past?

Most people who read a financial report are primarily interested in the company's future and are only secondarily interested in its past. Investors and lenders are interested to know what management did with the assets entrusted to its care during the last year, but, more importantly, they want to know whether their investment in the company will bear fruit in the future. With that reader interest in mind, some companies—especially relatively new ones—have prepared financial statements on a prospective basis, outlining the financial results they *expect* to have in the next several years. All projections are by definition uncertain, and most companies have been reluctant to expose themselves to the criticism that would inevitably follow a missed projection. Although prospective-oriented financial statements have a logical appeal, they have not been widely used and are not considered part of GAAP.

GAAP financial statements report a company's historical results based on completed transactions with third parties. Some have described this focus on the past as the **transaction principle.** Under our present financial system, companies publicly report their historical results and usually keep private their expectations about the future. Individual financial statement readers use that historical information and, factoring in their feelings about the future, make their own personal estimates of the company's future results. In effect, the historical financial statements become the basis for those individual's projections of the company's future results. Some people will make that extrapolation more successfully than others—some people are more successful investors than others.

How Should the Company's Ongoing Operations Be Allocated over Time to Prepare Reports for a Specific Period?

Measuring a company's success would be simple if we had only to summarize its operations at the end of its life. The owner's original cash investment would have been fully exploited and converted back to cash. Success would be measured by comparing the amount of cash on hand at the end with the amount of cash that was on hand at the beginning of the company's life. Your company purchased the building because you thought it would produce future cash flows for you. If we could wait 30 years until you were ready to retire, we might accumulate all of the company's cash receipts, including rentals and the proceeds from the final sale of the property; in addition, we would accumulate all of the company's disbursements, including payments to the maintenance people and to the bank for the retirement of the loan. If the receipts exceeded the disbursements by more than $20,000 (your original investment), you could say that the company was successful. If not, the investment was a bad deal. It will be obvious that neither you nor the bank will want to wait 30 years to determine whether the venture was successful. And, consequently, GAAP attempts to deal with the problem of measuring results in those intervening years through a convention known as the **periodic measurement principle.**

Under GAAP, individual business transactions are assessed to determine whether the underlying activities impact the current measurement period, a future measurement period, or a series of future periods. Where the transaction will affect the future, its financial effects are accumulated in the accounts as an asset (or a liability) and, recognized as an expense (or income) in the appropriate subsequent measurement period. In a manufacturing example, if a company produced goods in June and sold them in September, the financial statements for June, July, and August would recognize the cost of those manufactured items as an asset that we call *inventory*. In the September financial statements:

- The income statement would recognize the revenue from the sale, and the balance sheet would recognize the increase in cash or in accounts receivable.
- The income statement would recognize the cost of the merchandise sold, and the balance sheet would recognize the decrease in the inventory asset.
- The income statement would recognize the expected cost of providing for any warranty repairs, and the balance sheet would recognize a liability for those future warranty expenditures.

Note that the income statement for September reflects *all* elements of the sale–the revenue recognition, the cost of the merchandise sold, and the cost of expected future warranty work. Thus, the net income for that month reflects all aspects of the sale transaction.

But let us return to our real estate example. Assume that a tenant signed a three-year lease on a suite in your building and that the lease is cancelable with 60 days' notice. The leasing agent who found the tenant for you earned a $15,000 commission, payable immediately. Under GAAP you would recognize the rent income monthly, as the lease runs its course.

Thus, the rental income is allocated to the calendar periods when it is earned, a convention known as the **allocation principle.** But what should the company do about the commission paid? Under GAAP you would treat that payment as an asset when paid and then allocate it as an expense over the periods when the rent is received. The logic behind this treatment is that the commission payment today will produce benefits in the future as the tenant pays rent. Given that probable future benefit, the commission payment qualifies as an asset. The allocation principle allows us, and in fact requires us, to allocate the impact of an expenditure to the period when the benefit is to be received. Obviously, if there is no probable future benefit from an expenditure today, that expenditure will be treated as an expense today.

Another way of looking at this application of the allocation principle is to say that we want to match all the costs of earning revenue with the recognition of that revenue itself. When we recognize revenue in a certain period, we look backward and forward and record all the expenses that might be associated with that revenue—we match them—and include them in the income statement in the same period. That process of gathering together all the financial effects of a transaction is an application of the **matching principle.** In the real estate example we have been talking about, the largest asset involved in earning the rent revenue is the building itself. GAAP requires that the $100,000 we spent to acquire the building be treated as an asset at the time of the expenditure and that it be allocated to the periods when the building produces rent–lets say 30 years. In effect, we try to match the cost of the building with the rental revenue it produces. This application of the allocation principle is referred to as **depreciation.** Allocation and matching are important requisites to the notion of measuring company results, period by period. It will be apparent that the allocation process requires many estimates by management and a good deal of judgment.

How Conservative (Aggressive) Should I Be When Making the Estimates Required by the Financial Statements?

As you read the preceding discussion, you may have asked what would happen if we subsequently discover that the building has a longer (or shorter) life than 30 years. If it actually has a life of 50 years, you will have allocated too much of the building's cost to the early years and as a result will have reported too little net income in those years. You also may have wondered what would happen if the tenant occupying your suite on a three-year lease moved after the first year. In that case you would have misestimated the life of the commission asset, and you would have allocated too little commission expense to that first year, overstating net income. Estimates are involved in almost every allocation decision that managers make as they prepare GAAP-based financial statements. Because no one (especially investors and lenders) likes unpleasant surprises, most managers adopt a conservative posture as they make those estimates. The logic is that it is better to be conservative about the future so that surprises, if any, are good surprises. This convention is known as the **conservatism principle.**

It should be apparent from the real estate example we discussed that the application of conservatism can create a conflict between future and current results. If the conflict is not immediately apparent to you, stop and think about the choices managers must make as they try to allocate costs between periods. Deciding that an expenditure today has a possible, but not probable future benefit forces the recognition of that expenditure now, as an expense, penalizing operations of the current period. If the hoped-for benefit does materialize in the future, the income statement in that future period will have the benefit of the revenue, but will not have any related expense—the expense will have been recognized in the earlier period. And, of course, the reverse is true.

Consider the following example from the retailing world. In the past, an expenditure for employee training that precede the opening of a new store could justifiably be accounted for as an asset and allocated to expense over some future period after the store was open. In effect, those training costs would be matched with the revenues they are expected to generate. An alternative, more conservative view is to treat those training expenditures as expenses immediately when they are incurred. That posture could be justified by arguing that future sales from the store are uncertain and, until they are realized, the benefits expected from the training are unrealized as well. It used to be that the store manager had to make that allocation decision—future period expense versus current period expense—based on the likelihood that future sales will be sufficient to recover the current training expenditures. However, in 1998, the AICPA's Accounting Standards Executive Committee issued Statement No. 98-5 which forecloses that area of judgment. The new statement concludes that all start up costs should be expensed when incurred, regardless of the future benefit the managers might expect. That new rule, enforcing a very conservative posture on all companies, will be particularly painful to those companies who are in an expansion mode, and opening many new locations every year. Their earnings will be depressed, just at the time they need stockholder support. On the other hand, a stable company, adding only a nominal number of new locations will not be dramatically affected. Before you leave this section of the text, make sure you understand the impact of this new rule, and how that impact might vary between companies.

Do All Assets of My Company Still Have the Potential to Earn Cash Equal to Their Carrying Value Today?

GAAP provides for the fact that allocation estimates will sometimes prove to be wrong and that, now and then, an expenditure that was treated as an asset in one period will subsequently be seen as having no future cash-earning benefit. When that happens, GAAP requires the remaining asset value be charged off as an expense in the period when that discovery is made. (This is another application of the shorthand expression we referred to earlier—assets are carried at the lower-of-cost-or-market value.) Well-managed companies have programs in place to challenge periodically the carrying value of all of their assets to make sure that any declines in estimates of future benefits are recognized as soon as they become apparent. (Incidentally, GAAP does not permit companies to go back and restate prior years' financial statements for incorrect estimates. If hindsight shows that you were too conservative or too liberal, the effect of the adjustment required is recognized only in the financial statements for the period when you realize that your estimate was faulty.)

May I (Must I) Change My Estimates or My Accounting Principles?

Companies occasionally find that, while their assets continue to have value, the future period of benefit that they originally estimated is now seen to be different. Suppose that after 10 years your company decided that the useful economic life of its building was really 50 years rather than 30 years. No accounting would be required at that time because you would simply spread the remaining cost over the remaining (now 40) years. If you concluded that the building life was really only 20 years instead of 30 years, the remaining cost would be allocated over the remaining 10 years. The financial community assumes that financial statements are prepared consistently from one period to the next so that a series of income statements covering a period of years fairly reports the trend in income. The fundamental estimates are not changed year to year but only when required by the facts—a convention we call the **consistency principle.** If significant estimates are changed, GAAP requires that a footnote be included in the financial statements to explain the change and the dollar effect of the change on the future years' income statements.

For many types of economic transactions, a number of alternative accounting methods are available, each producing a very different result. When alternative accounting methods exist, GAAP requires that a company disclose in the footnotes accompanying its financial reports the accounting method that has been selected. Should circumstances change, warranting the use of a different accounting principle, the effect of the change on reported income must be disclosed in the footnotes to permit financial statement users to compare current period results with results from the prior period, which were determined using the prior accounting method—again reflecting the consistency principle.

How Much Detail Must I (May I) Include in These Financial Statements?

The ideal accounting report includes all significant information but excludes trivial or irrelevant details. The financial community (and the courts) have said that financial statements must include all "material information." *Material information* has been defined as information that might influence the decisions of a reasonable person. Managers must ask themselves whether details about their company's financial status would influence the decisions of a potential investor; if so, the information must be included in the basic financial statements or in the related footnotes.

It follows from that understanding that management will, when making accounting estimate decisions, focus its attention principally on those items that might have a material effect on the accounting reports. Immaterial items are given less attention or are ignored. Clearly, careful judgments are required in preparing a set of financial statements, and the responsible manager will exercise that judgment, thinking all the while about the potential readers of the financial statements—investors, creditors, and the public—and their information needs. This convention is known as the **materiality principle.**

THE STANDARD-SETTING PROCESS

The principles outlined in the above set of questions and answers form the basis of GAAP in the United States, and that of many other countries. As we suggested in Chapter 1, however, GAAP is more than a set of principles; GAAP includes a large body of practice and procedure that builds on these principles and enables people to apply the broad principles to specific transactions.

The idea that the principles (and practices and procedures) in GAAP are "generally accepted" suggests that these accounting guidelines emerge from practice as a consensus, and that assessment of GAAP is partly true. Today, however, financial transactions are complex, and the need for timely information from companies is acute. The financial community has decided that it is inappropriate to wait for a consensus to emerge about a new accounting question and has agreed that the emergence of new practices should be led by an authorized standard-setting body. The following discussion outlines the movement toward an institutional approach to the setting of accounting guidelines and the protagonists in that evolution in the U.S..

At the turn of the century the financial community in the U.S. was relatively small. When local businesses borrowed strictly from local banks, personal reputations were more important than financial status in the granting of a loan. Stocks and bonds were investment vehicles only for a small, wealthy, well-acquainted group. To the extent that investments were made outside that group, they were based on personal recommendations of investment bankers. Because communication between creditor and borrower, or between investor and investee, could be direct and personal, financial reporting tended to be tailored and unique, even informal. That informal financial reporting system served the community well for many years, but as the community grew and became more diverse, the need for a more rigorous financial reporting system became apparent.

The need for more formal regulation of the form and content of financial reporting became dramatically apparent with the stock market crash of 1929. The widespread impact of the crash made it clear that a reporting system that relied on personal contact was no longer appropriate. Because the *public* was now seen to be affected by the country's financial system, and more particularly by the financial reporting system, the U.S. Congress passed the Securities Acts of 1933 and 1934 and created the Securities and Exchange Commission (SEC).

The SEC has the responsibility to regulate the various U.S. stock exchanges, the broker-dealers who buy and sell on those exchanges, and mutual funds. The Commission also has the authority to establish the "form and content" of the financial reports required of publicly held companies. Under the Commission's rules, any company that sells stocks or bonds to the public must prepare a financial disclosure package (referred to as a **prospectus**) to give potential investors the information they need to decide whether to buy a company's securities. Every company that has sold securities to the public in the past must, on an ongoing basis, prepare an annual disclosure package (referred to as **Form 10-K**) and quarterly reports (referred to as **Form 10-Q**). Those annual and quarterly reports are designed to help existing investors decide whether they want to retain their investment or to sell, and to help potential investors decide whether they want to buy a company's securities. Those annual and quarterly reports are available from the SEC, either in hard copy or from its world-wide web site. The glossy annual and quarterly reports that companies send to their shareholders include the financial data from the SEC reports as well as additional management commentary.

Although the SEC has the statutory authority to establish the requirements for corporate reporting, it has elected to delegate the development of accounting standards to the private sector. There are probably a number of reasons for that delegation policy. First, the original SEC commissioners concluded that the best accounting rules for the nation's complex financial community would be developed by practitioners with field experience rather than by government employees. Second, the commissioners also concluded that the financial community was more likely to follow rules that it had established for itself than rules set by outsiders, especially a governmental agency. Finally, it became apparent to the commission that enormous pressure was likely to be brought to bear on whoever was responsible for accounting standards. The SEC chose to stand behind the private sector and prod it on rather than face the pressure groups directly.

In response to this prodding, the major certified public accounting (CPA) firms, under the auspices of the American Institute of Certified Public Accountants, began the process of establishing written, standardized, generally accepted accounting principles in 1936. Until 1959, that effort was staffed by senior executives of the leading CPA firms. They were enormously productive at the start, but eventually their deliberations on matters of principle bogged down in debates over firm preference. Apparently, it was difficult for such strongly motivated, visible people to compromise ardently held firm positions. To focus those deliberations on the issues, a new standard-setting body was established in 1959 and staffed with technical experts from each of the large CPA firms. This group, the Accounting Principles Board (APB), was again effective in its early years but was overwhelmed by the "go-go" financial years of the late 1960s. Some people argued that the APB became too technical, too restrictive, and not sufficiently practical. Others argued that the APB became too willing to compromise in the interest of producing timely new standards. In any event, the criticism from the financial community became so strong that the APB lost its standard-setting effectiveness. It was abolished in 1973, and the Financial Accounting Standards Board (FASB) was created to take its place.

Recognizing that the prior standards-setting efforts, relying as they did on the major CPA firms, suffered from a narrow power base, the FASB was designed to appeal to the financial community as a whole. The FASB is funded by voluntary contributions from four different accounting organizations, The Securities Industry Association, The Financial Analysts Association, and from several large corporations. Board members are selected on the basis of their general reputation in the field without regard to their prior affiliation.

The board's procedures require extensive due process. It solicits community advice as it considers its agenda. When a new issue is added to the board's agenda, the FASB staff researches the issue and prepares a discussion memorandum that outlines all of the important points of view that have been expressed. The board solicits written comments in response to every discussion memorandum and often holds public hearings. Based on community input and the board's own deliberations, an exposure draft of a new standard is prepared and circulated for additional comments. After considering public responses to the exposure draft, the board makes final refinements and issues **a statement of financial accounting standards.**

The pronouncements of the board have considerable authority. The SEC considers them to be GAAP for purposes of complying with U.S. securities laws, and CPA firms consider the board's statements to be GAAP for the general-purpose financial statements issued by private companies outside the SEC's jurisdiction.

The board was quite successful in its early years, and has issued more than 130 standards as well as a wide variety of interpretative releases. In more recent years, the board has been subject to increased criticism. Some members of the business community argue that the board has become too concerned with technical accounting questions, and they claim that the cost of complying with the FASB's standards exceeds the benefits to the financial community. That critical assessment is partly true. But it is also true that several of the board's standards have forced companies to recognize liabilities and expenses that were not previously reflected in their financial statements. Part of the criticism of the board is the reaction one might expect whenever more rigorous standards are imposed. Time will tell whether the financial community will continue to support a self-regulated standard-setting process or whether the SEC will be forced to assume that responsibility.

In addition to the pronouncements of the FASB and its predecessors, U.S. GAAP is also established by prevailing accounting practice. In the past, as much as 75 percent of GAAP may have been unwritten precedent. Today, as a result of the work of the FASB, the reverse is true, and probably less than 25 percent of GAAP is based solely on informal, unwritten precedent. Because business is a dynamic process with new financial transactions always being created, no standard-setting agency could ever hope to keep up with the rapid evolution of finance and accounting. When no formal accounting pronouncements exist, new GAAP will continue to be inferred from practices developed by accounting practitioners drawing on the fundamental principles that have historically formed the basis for all GAAP.

THE BASIC FINANCIAL STATEMENTS: AN EXPLORATION

Under generally accepted accounting principles, companies report their financial activities using four basic financial statements:

- The **balance sheet,** also referred to as the **statement of financial position,** presents in summary form the assets a company owned at a particular date, the liabilities the company owed to its lenders and suppliers, and the funds that the owners of the company have invested or left in the company as of that same date.

- The **income statement,** also referred to as the **statement of earnings** or operations, summarizes those transactions that produced revenue for a company as a result of selling products or services during a specific period and those transactions that resulted in expenses for the company during that same period. The difference between the aggregate revenues and aggregate expenses is the net income (or loss) for the company.

- The **statement of owners' equity** summarizes the major transactions that affected the owners' investment in a company, including the company's net income (or loss) and the amount of those earnings that were distributed to the owners during a given period.

- The **statement of cash flows** summarizes the sources of a company's cash funds available for use during a given period and the uses that the company made of those funds.

Under U.S. GAAP, all companies are required to provide a balance sheet, an income statement, and a statement of cash flows as part of their annual report. A statement of owners' equity is also frequently provided, although that information may be presented as part of a company's financial statement footnotes rather than as a separate financial statement. Together, these statements form the nucleus of most accounting reports. We will briefly overview the contents and purpose of each statement now and will consider each one in detail in subsequent chapters.

Balance Sheet

The purpose of the balance sheet is to present, as of a particular point in time, the various resources available for use by a company and the sources the company called upon to fund the acquisition of those resources. These resources are generally referred to as the company's **assets,** and the sources of funding for those resources are either its **liabilities** or its **owners' equity.** As you might surmise, equity is a source of funding provided by its owners. Liabilities, on the other hand, are the sources of funding provided by a company's creditors. In more formal terms:

- *Assets* are tangible or intangible resources, such as cash, property, or patents, that can be measured in dollars, (or some other currency), are owned or controlled by a company, and are expected to provide future economic benefit to the company. The building your real estate company purchased, in our earlier discussions in this chapter, is a classic example of an asset.

- *Liabilities* are the company's obligations to repay money loaned to it, to pay for goods or services it has received, or to fulfill its warranty obligations. Again, the bank debt your real estate company incurred to purchase its building is a good example of a liability.

- *Owners' equity* measures the owners' investment in a company, which may be either in the form of direct investment through the purchase of shares of stock, or indirectly through the retention of the company's earnings. The initial investment you made in your real estate company ($20,000) is an example of direct investment equity. If you choose to leave the company's earnings in the company rather than have them distributed to you, those retained earnings are also an example of owners' equity.

The relationship between the assets (A), liabilities (L), and owners' equity (OE) of a company represents the foundation of accounting. This fundamental relationship may be expressed as

$$A = L + OE$$

In words, the assets of a company at any time always equal the sum of its liabilities and its owners' equity. In more abstract terms, every resource has a source. Not only does this relationship represent the cornerstone of accounting, but also it is the basis of the balance sheet. The balance sheet is like a snapshot presenting the assets of a company juxtaposed against its liabilities and owners' equity as of a particular moment. Over the course of a company's life, a great many transactions will impact the balance sheet accounts. The balance sheet shows the net result of all of those transactions at any date—the net balances in those asset, liability, and owners' equity accounts.

Pictorially, the balance sheet looks like this:

Assets	Liabilities
	Owners' equity

Note that the right and left sides of this box must always be equal. The composition or relative proportions of the right side will vary, however, depending on the sources a company calls upon to fund the acquisition of its assets. In our earlier real estate example, the $100,000 asset equaled the sum of the $80,000 in debt and the $20,000 in equity. If you had put only $10,000 into the company and had borrowed $90,000, the right and left sides of the box would still have been equal, although the relative size of the right-hand boxes would have been different.

Income Statement

Although the balance sheet presents the status of a company's assets, liabilities, and owners' equity *as of* a particular point in time, the income statement presents the results of a series of income-generating transactions *over* a period of time. The income statement reports the revenues earned and the expenses incurred by the company during a given period of operations:

- **Revenues** are the actual or expected cash inflows arising from a company's sales of products or services during a specific period.
- **Expenses** are the **costs** a company incurred in its efforts to generate revenues during that same period.
- **Net income** (or loss) is the excess (or insufficiency) of revenues over expenses; it

represents a summary measure of the overall performance of a company for a given period.

The income statement tells us whether the stockholders are better off as a result of this year's activities, and it helps them understand why they are better off. Did the company sell enough product at the right price? Did management keep expenses under control and in line with the volume of business? What kinds of expenses did we incur this year—were they product related, selling related, or administrative costs?

The relationship between the revenues (R), expenses (E), and net income (NI) of a company may be expressed as

$$R - E = NI$$

and this expression forms the basis of the income statement.

Statement of Owners' Equity

The statement of owners' equity measures both the period-end balance of the owners' investment in a company and the changes in that investment over a period of time. The owners' investment in a company may take several forms: direct investment through the purchase of shares of stock or indirect investment through the retention of some (or all) of the company's earnings for a period.

- **Capital stock** represents the proceeds a company receives from the sale of stock to its shareholders. Sales of stock *between* shareholders do not impact the company's financial statements because those transactions have no direct financial effect on the company.

- **Earnings** (or net income) are the net result of the company's operations for a period— its revenues and expenses. Accounting theory assumes that the company is operated for the benefit of the shareholders, and so the net results of operations (earnings or loss) for a period are added to (or subtracted from) the owners' equity account, pending a decision to distribute some of those earnings to the individual shareholders.

- **Dividends** are the earnings of a company that are paid out to the owners. In a corporation, the owners are not automatically entitled to receive a distribution of the company's earnings; instead, the earnings are paid out to shareholders only when the board of directors believes it will be safe (for the company) to do so. Because the payment of dividends is at the company's discretion, that expenditure of funds is not considered an expense but simply a reduction in equity. Legally, dividends are understood to be a distribution of the earnings of the company, and accounting policy follows that understanding.

- **Retained earnings** are the aggregate of the company's earnings that are retained in the enterprise for future corporate use—that is, those earnings of the company that have not been paid out to its owners as dividends.

The relationship between owners' equity (OE), capital stock (CS), and retained earnings (RE) can be expressed as

$$OE = CS + RE$$

Substituting the net income (NI) and dividends (D) buildup of the retained earnings account for its end-of-period net balance, the statement of owners' equity can be expressed as

$$
\underset{\substack{\text{at the} \\ \text{report} \\ \text{date}}}{\text{OE}} = \underset{\substack{\text{at the} \\ \text{report} \\ \text{date}}}{\text{CS}} + \underset{\substack{\text{for all} \\ \text{periods} \\ \text{from day 1}}}{\text{NI}} - \underset{\substack{\text{for all} \\ \text{periods} \\ \text{from day 1}}}{\text{D}}
$$

Combining this equation for the statement of owners' equity with the overall equation we developed earlier for the balance sheet (A = L + OE), we have

$$
\underset{\substack{\text{at the} \\ \text{report} \\ \text{date}}}{\text{A}} = \underset{\substack{\text{at the} \\ \text{report} \\ \text{date}}}{\text{L}} + \underset{\substack{\text{at the} \\ \text{report} \\ \text{date}}}{\text{CS}} + \underset{\substack{\text{for all} \\ \text{periods} \\ \text{from day 1}}}{\text{NI}} - \underset{\substack{\text{for all} \\ \text{periods} \\ \text{from day 1}}}{\text{D}}
$$

And, finally, combining this equation with the one developed for the income statement (NI = R − E), gives us the following comprehensive set of relationships

$$
\underset{\substack{\text{at the} \\ \text{report} \\ \text{date}}}{\text{A}} = \underset{\substack{\text{at the} \\ \text{report} \\ \text{date}}}{\text{L}} + \underset{\substack{\text{at the} \\ \text{report} \\ \text{date}}}{\text{CS}} + \underset{\substack{\text{for all} \\ \text{periods} \\ \text{from day 1}}}{\text{R}} - \underset{\substack{\text{for all} \\ \text{periods} \\ \text{from day 1}}}{\text{E}} - \underset{\substack{\text{for all} \\ \text{periods} \\ \text{from day 1}}}{\text{D}}
$$

The Interrelationship of the Basic Financial Statements

It is important to stop and consider a key implication of our discussion so far: All business transactions impact the balance sheet in some way. The income statement is only affected by the revenue and expense transactions that flow through the retained earnings account in the balance sheet. The retained earnings account in the balance sheet reflects the sum of all of the revenue and expense transactions since the company's beginning, while the income statement presents the revenue and expense transactions for a particular period.

A balance sheet is a summary of all transactions affecting the company as of a point in time. In theory, we could prepare a balance sheet for this year-end without regard to the balance sheet we prepared at last year-end. But in reality, this year's balance sheet will be an update of the balances from last year: Last year's balance sheet provides the foundation for the construction of this year's balance sheet, and we simply add or subtract from those foundation numbers the effect of transactions during this year. Every balance sheet account will have been affected by some transactions during the year, which will increase or decrease the balance in the account. Generally, shareholders do not care about the detailed transactions that increased or decreased most balance sheet accounts, but they do care about the transactions that affected their equity accounts, in particular the retained earnings account. The income statement is designed to meet that need. With only a few exceptions, an income statement summarizes all of the revenue and expense transactions that increased or decreased the balance in the retained earnings account from last year to this year.

Let's go back to our earlier discussion of your real estate company. You began the company by contributing $20,000 in exchange for all of the company's stock. As a result of that original transaction, the company increased its owners' equity by $20,000 and increased its cash asset by an equal amount. When the company bought the building, making a cash down payment of $20,000 and borrowing the rest of the $100,000 purchase price, the company reduced its cash asset, increased its building asset, and increased its debt liability. In both of those transactions, the accounting equation, A = L + OE, was satisfied, and the balance sheet remained in balance. At the completion of the purchase, the $100,000 building asset is equal to the sum of the $20,000 equity and the $80,000 bank loan. That building purchase has no income effect because the transaction did not result in revenue or expense. If we prepared a set of financial statements immediately after the purchase, the balance sheet would show assets of $100,000, liabilities of $80,000 and owner's equity of $20,000. The income statement would show no transactions. And of course, no income.

But now let's suppose that a tenant rents first floor retail space for $500 a month. When the tenant makes a payment on the lease at the end of the month, the company receives cash of $500 and records rent revenue in an equal amount. Let us also assume that your company employed a janitorial service to keep the retail area clean, spending $100 to have that work performed. As a result of the activities for the month the cash asset account will be increased by $500 and decreased by $100; the same increase and decrease will impact the owners' equity account—retained earnings—because all revenue and expenses accumulate for the benefit (or detriment) of the owners. The balance sheet stays in balance, with a net increase in cash of $400 and an equal net increase in retained earnings. The income statement for that first month will analyze the transactions in the retained earnings account and will show revenue of $500 and expense of $100, for a net income of $400. The rent receipt increased the cash account and the retained earning account, on the balance sheet: In the same way, the maintenance fee reduced the cash account and the retained earnings account, on the balance sheet. Because both of those transactions are revenue and expense transactions, they affect the retained earnings account on the balance sheet—because they are revenue and expense transactions, and because they affect the retained earnings account, they will both appear in the income statement for the period.

Schematically the flow of transactions between the income statement, the statement of owners' equity and the balance sheet can be shown as follows in Exhibit 2.1.

Use our simple real estate example to solidify several important ideas about accounting transactions:

1. *All* of a company's business transactions affect its balance sheet, but only those that have to do with revenue or expense are *also* reflected in the income statement.

2. All revenue and expense transactions impact owners' equity (the retained earnings account), and they also impact some other balance sheet account. That will be so because the balance sheet must always be in balance: Any transaction that impacts the owners' equity account must have an equal impact somewhere else in the balance sheet.

3. A balance sheet as of a current date is connected to an earlier balance sheet as of a prior date by the intervening transactions. The income statement is a summary of the intervening transactions that affected the retained earnings account. The income statement acts as a bridge between a current and an earlier retained earnings balance sheet amount. (Accountants describe this connection by saying that the financial statements *articulate*—they work together.)

EXHIBIT 2.1

Diagrammatic Relationship of the Income Statement and Balance Sheet

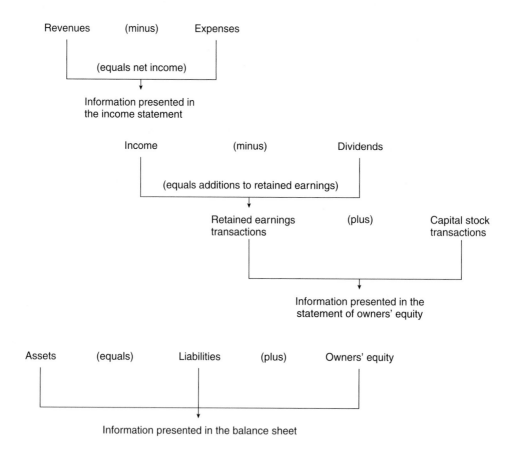

4. The income statement for a period is a summary—a recap—of the revenue and expense transactions that flowed through the retained earnings account during that period. Looking at the balance in the retained earnings account at the end of an accounting period will tell us how much of the company's earnings (if any) have been retained for the use of the business; looking at the change in the retained earnings account from one year to the next would tell us whether the company added anything to the owners' investment during the year. But neither of those numbers will tell us anything about the operations of the company during the current period. The income statement analyzes the revenue and expense transactions during a period and not only summarizes them so that we can determine *whether* the owners are better off as a result of the operations for that period, but also provides the detail so that we know *why* (or why not) they are better off.

In the final equation we developed during our earlier discussion, we had

$$
\underset{\substack{\text{at the} \\ \text{report} \\ \text{date}}}{A} = \underset{\substack{\text{at the} \\ \text{report} \\ \text{date}}}{L} + \underset{\substack{\text{at the} \\ \text{report} \\ \text{date}}}{CS} + \underset{\substack{\text{for all} \\ \text{periods} \\ \text{from day 1}}}{R} - \underset{\substack{\text{for all} \\ \text{periods} \\ \text{from day 1}}}{E} - \underset{\substack{\text{for all} \\ \text{periods} \\ \text{from day 1}}}{D}
$$

We can use this formula to see how the income statement connects the balance sheet for one period with the balance sheet for the next. Let's go back to the real estate company we have been using as our model. At the end of its first month of operations, the company had purchased a building and rented one store. It had received one month's rent of $500 and paid cleaning costs of $100. Let us now assume that we are in the second month of operations and that another retail store has opened, paying additional rent of $600 a month. The maintenance people agree to charge an additional $100 to clean that store, in addition to their charge for the first store. We could present the above formulas for the end of the first month (End of Period 1) and the end of the subsequent month (End of Period 2) as follows:

$$
\underset{\text{EOP1}}{A} = \underset{\text{EOP1}}{L} + \underset{\text{EOP1}}{CS} + \underset{\substack{\text{from day 1} \\ \text{to EOP1}}}{R} - \underset{\substack{\text{from day 1} \\ \text{to EOP1}}}{E} - \underset{\substack{\text{from day 1} \\ \text{to EOP1}}}{D}
$$

and

$$
\underset{\text{EOP2}}{A} = \underset{\text{EOP2}}{L} + \underset{\text{EOP2}}{CS} + \underset{\substack{\text{from day 1} \\ \text{to EOP2}}}{R} - \underset{\substack{\text{from day 1} \\ \text{to EOP2}}}{E} - \underset{\substack{\text{from day 1} \\ \text{to EOP2}}}{D}
$$

The cumulative income statement for the company, for the period from its beginning, would be

$$
\underset{\substack{\text{from day 1} \\ \text{to EOP2}}}{R} - \underset{\substack{\text{from day} \\ \text{to EOP2}}}{E} = \underset{\substack{\text{periods} \\ \text{1 \& 2}}}{NI}
$$

or

$$
\$1,600 - \$300 = \$1,300
$$

But a cumulative income statement doesn't tell much about current operations. The income statement for the most current period, the company's second month, would be

$$
\left[\underset{\substack{\text{from day 1} \\ \text{to EOP2}}}{R} - \underset{\substack{\text{from day 1} \\ \text{to EOP1}}}{R} \right] - \left[\underset{\substack{\text{from day 1} \\ \text{to EOP2}}}{E} - \underset{\substack{\text{from day 1} \\ \text{to EOP1}}}{E} \right] = \underset{\text{period 2}}{NI}
$$

or

$$
\$1,100 - \$200 = \$900
$$

The income statement for that second month will reflect only those transactions that increased the balance in the retained earnings account—in the owners' equity portion of the balance sheet—between the end of month 1 and the end of month 2.

This articulation idea we have been discussing can be shown graphically as in Exhibit 2.2.

EXHIBIT 2.2

Diagrammatic Relationship of the Balance Sheet, the Income Statement, and the Statement of Owners' Equity

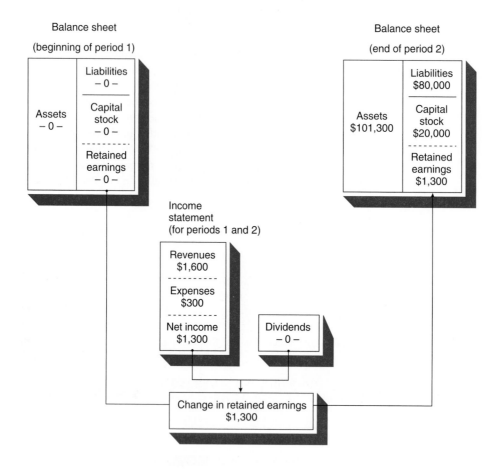

Statement of Cash Flows

The purpose of the statement of cash flows is to explain the change in cash occurring between two successive accounting periods. The cash flows of a company may be conveniently segmented into three categories of interest to financial statement users: cash flows from operations, from investing, and from financing.

Cash flows from operations refers to the net cash flows resulting from the company's principal business activities. In essence, the operating cash flow measures the net income of the company on a cash basis. **Cash flows from investing** refers to buying and selling long-lived assets (e.g., buildings and equipment), making and collecting loans, and acquiring and disposing of another company's debt or equity instruments.

EXHIBIT 2.3

Diagrammatic Relationship of the Basic Financial Statements

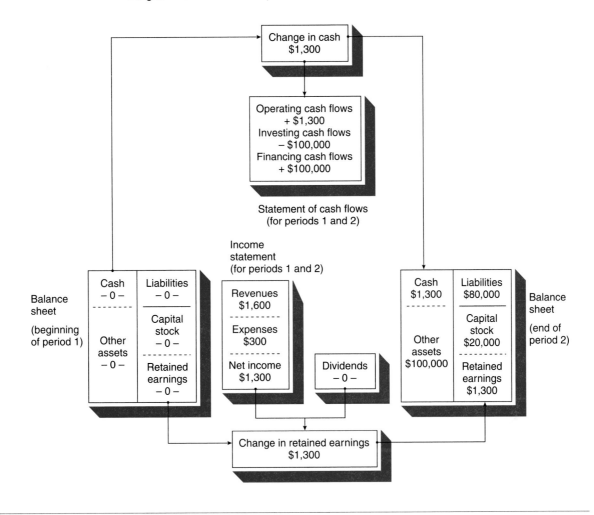

Finally, **cash flows from financing** refers to the activities of a company to obtain funds from existing and new shareholders, provide them a return *on* and a return *of* their investment, and borrow and repay amounts borrowed.

The statement of cash flows is analogous to the income statement: They both summarize the transactions in a balance sheet account that occurred during one period of time. The income statement summarizes the transactions that increased or decreased the retained earnings account, while the statement of cash flows summarizes the transactions that increased or decreased the cash account. Integrating the statement of cash flows into our picture of the financial reporting process yields Exhibit 2.3.

Earlier we described the difference between cash-basis accounting and accrual accounting, but it is worth restating now: The income statement is prepared assuming accrual accounting, while the statement of cash flows is prepared assuming cash-basis accounting. Net income will not be equal to the net change in cash because there are some transactions that impact net income but not cash (for example, sales on credit) and some transactions that impact cash but not income (for example, the purchase of a truck). The two statements measure different things and can (must) be used for different purposes:

- The income statement measures results of operations assuming a credit society and an orderly, normal use of assets—such as equipment and inventory—over time. It helps a reader evaluate the company's performance during the period and make projections about future performance.

- The statement of cash flows outlines the sources and uses of cash during a period. It helps a reader see the company's business strategy and make projections of the company's cash needs in future periods.

In this chapter we have talked about some very important material. To demonstrate the relevance of the ideas we have been discussing, and to put them into a more specific context, we would like to refer you back to the Procter & Gamble financial review that was included at the end of Chapter 1.

First, note that Procter & Gamble's financial statements articulate; that is, the three statements are interrelated. Looking at the balance sheet (pages 26 and 27), we can see that the retained earnings at June 30,1997, was $10,730 million. The Statement of Shareholders' Equity (page 28) shows us that the balance at the end of 1997 was increased by the 1998 net earnings of $3,780 million and was decreased by dividends paid during the year of $1,462 and by the impact of common stock repurchases $1,904. That series of transactions created a new balance in the retained earnings account of $11,144 million, which is included in shareholders' equity in the balance sheet at June 30, 1998. The income added to retained earnings in 1998 is, of course, the income that is reported in the income statement (page 25). The income for 1998, reported in the income statement, connects the balance sheet at the end of 1997 and the balance sheet at the end of 1998.

Also notice that the 1997 balance sheet reports cash of $2,350 million and the 1998 balance sheet reports cash of $1,549 million. The statement of cash flows (page 29) depicts a $801 million decrease in cash as the net of cash provided by operations, cash used for investments, cash used for financing activities, and a small charge to recognize the effect of changes in exchange rates. The change in cash, as analyzed in the statement of cash flows, provides another connection between the balance sheet at June 30, 1997, with the balance sheet at the end of June 30, 1998.

Procter & Gamble's 1998 balance sheet illustrates several other principles we have been discussing. For example, look at the 1998 amount for accounts receivable. You will see that Procter & Gamble reports more than $2.7 billion in amounts due from customers and others. That asset represents cash the company expects to receive in the future as a result of past transactions. Because the company prepares its financial reports on an accrual basis rather than on a cash basis, those transactions were recorded as revenue when the parties agreed to the transaction, and it is not necessary for Procter & Gamble to wait until the cash changes hands to recognize the revenue impact of those transactions. The total amount the company should receive from its customers will be somewhat more than $2.7 billion: Procter & Gamble knows that some of its accounts receivable will prove to be uncollectible and, following the principle of conservatism, management established an allowance for uncollectible accounts, as a contra asset. The summary numbers appearing in the balance sheet are the net of the gross amounts of the receivables due, less the amount that management has set up as the allowance for uncollectible accounts. (Procter & Gamble doesn't tell us what that allowance is, and so it must not be material.)

Some of the other accounting principles we have been discussing are illustrated in the footnotes to the Procter & Gamble financial statements. For example, in Note 1, "Summary of Significant Accounting Policies":

■ The comments under *"Basis of Presentation"* (page 30) explain Procter & Gamble's application of the entity principle. The company includes, in its consolidated financial statements, all of the activities of the parent company, The Procter & Gamble Company, "and its controlled subsidiaries." In other words, if there is a Procter & Gamble subsidiary in Canada that operates a timber and cellulose business, and if Procter & Gamble owns enough of that affiliate's stock to control that business, all of that company's assets and liabilities are added together with those of other controlled companies and those of the parent to form the consolidated balance sheet. Also, that company's sales and expenses would be combined with those of all the other controlled companies to form the consolidated income statement.

■ On the other hand, those companies in which Procter & Gamble owns 20% to 50% of the stock and exerts significant influence but not control are accounted for under the equity method. Procter & Gamble does not include, in its consolidated financial statements, the assets, liabilities, sales, and expenses of those affiliates where it does not have the ability to control the entities; instead, in those situations, Procter & Gamble recognizes in its financial statements only its share of the equity of those ventures (reported as other Non–Current Assets in the balance sheet) and its share of the ventures' earnings (included as a part of net sales of the various segments). The company does not tell us what the financial statements would look like if the affiliates were consolidated, but we can be sure that both assets and liabilities (and sales and expenses) would increase.

■ The comments under *Selected Operating Expenses* (page 31) demonstrate the company's application of the allocation and the conservatism principles. Procter & Gamble has concluded that expenditures for research and development, and for advertising, do not meet the definition of an asset in that the benefit to a future period of an R&D project or a current period's advertising campaign is too uncertain. Instead, those expenditures are charged to expense in the year the service is purchased. Marketing, research, and administrative expenses were $10 billion in 1998, while pre-tax earnings were $5.7 billion. If the company had been able to defer any portion of those marketing or research expenses, there would have been a dollar for dollar increase in pre-tax earnings. To justify that deferral, management would have to have determined that some of those 1998 expenditures would generate revenues in a future year. They could then have recorded those current expenditures as assets this year and carried them forward to allocate them as expenses of that future year. But there is no assurance of any such payoff, and so the advertising and R & D expenditures are treated as expenses in this year.

■ The comments under *Inventories* and *Property, Plant, and Equipment* (pages 30 and 31) illustrate the historical cost principle, the transaction principle, and the principles of matching and allocation. The company's expenditures for raw materials are not charged to expense immediately but are carried forward as assets in the inventory account until the product is manufactured and sold to the wholesale distributor. That is true for the resulting finished goods, too. Those ready-to-deliver products are carried at their aggregate manufacturing cost even though it is a pretty sure thing that they will be sold and that the sales prices will be realized. Until there is a transaction with a third party, the value implied in those finished goods is not recognized in the financial statements.

The costs associated with the inventory are carried as assets until the products are sold. When the products are sold, those related costs are recognized as expenses and matched against the related revenue. Those costs are allocated to an accounting period based on the timing of the related sales transaction. Procter & Gamble's property, plant, and equipment costs are also carried at original cost, but those costs are expensed to future accounting periods based not on related transactions but on the passage of time. The costs of those assets are expensed over time, pro rata, based on management's estimate of the number of periods that will benefit from having those assets at work. The company has $20 billion in assets that will be used up over time (buildings, and machinery and equipment). According to the Statement of Cash Flows, depreciation expense for 1998 was $1.6 billion, which says that the costs of those assets are being expensed over— allocated to—an average life of about 12.5 years.

- Under *Goodwill and Other Intangible Assets* (page 30), Procter & Gamble management illustrates the lower-of-cost-or-market principle. They explain that the company evaluates their intangible assets on a recurring basis to make sure that the investment in those assets will be recovered from the benefits generated from ongoing operations. If it seems likely that the cost of any asset will not be recovered, the carrying value (usually the cost of acquiring the asset) is reduced to its approximate market value. Any such write-down would be an expense in the period when the decline in value is determined.

SUMMARY

Under U.S. GAAP, companies are required to report their financial activities using the basic financial statements: the balance sheet, the income statement, the statement of owners' equity, and the statement of cash flows. Because those statements will be read by a large and diverse group of users, the financial community has said that the financial statements will be prepared in accordance with a set of standards we call GAAP. Those "generally accepted accounting principles" do indeed follow a set of overarching principles, but they are also established in more articulate form by the FASB, an independent standard-setting body supported by the financial community and backed by the SEC.

NEW CONCEPTS AND TERMS

Accrual method	**Consistency principle**
Allocation principle	**Consolidated financial statements**
Assets	**Costs**
Balance sheet	**Dividends**
Capital stock	**Depreciation**
Cash basis	**Earnings**
Cash-basis accounting	**Entity principle**
Cash flows from operations	**Expenses**
Cash flows from investing	**Fair value accounting**
Cash flows from financing	**Form 10-K**
Conservatism principle	**Form 10-Q**

Historical cost principle	**Retained earnings**
Income statement	**Revenues**
Liabilities	**Sales**
Lower-of-cost-or-market value	**Statement of cash flows**
Matching principle	**Statement of earnings**
Materiality principle	**Statement of financial position**
Net income (loss)	**Statement of financial accounting standards**
Owners' equity	**Statement of owners' equity**
Periodic measurement principle	**Transaction principle**
Prospectus	

ASSIGNMENTS

2.1. Using the accounting equation. Applying the basic accounting equation to the Northfield Corporation at two successive year-ends yields the following results:

Year End	Assets	=	Liabilities	+	Equity
1998	$40,000	=	$30,000	+	$10,000
1999	$35,000	=	$20,000	+	$15,000

Required:

Assuming that no dividends were declared and that no additional capital was invested by the owners, what amount would Northfield have reported as its net income or loss for the 1999 year? Please explain your answer in the context of the facts here.

2.2. Accounting concepts. Think about each of the situations described below in the context of the chapter section, "Some Fundamental Questions in Accounting":

a. Disneyland in Anaheim, California, sells coupon books of 20-, 30-, and 40-ride tickets that can be used anytime the park is open. Assume that in January 1999 the amusement park sold $15 million worth of these coupon books. The proceeds were recorded initially as a liability, not as revenue.

b. Disneyland reports on its balance sheet the Anaheim, California, property on which the amusement park is located at its 1955 purchase price.

c. Sky Rider, Inc., specializes in the design and construction of roller coaster rides for amusement parks around the world. Each custom ride takes about two and one-half years to design and build, and the firm typically works on only three or four rides at a time. Nevertheless, the company publishes an annual report with a full income statement detailing its revenues and expenses for each year.

d. Taco Bell, a division of Tricon Inc., owns numerous "taco ranches." The costs to develop each ranch are deferred and reported on the balance sheet as an asset to be written off over the estimated commercially productive lives of the "taco trees."

e. Mac Donald purchased 800 shares of capital stock in PepsiCo, Inc., in January 1998 for $40 per share on the advice of his stockbroker, Ham Berger. Mac then sold one-half of the purchased shares at $38 per share in August of that same year. PepsiCo's annual report, however, reveals that 1.7 billion shares have been outstanding for the last three years. The average book value of the outstanding shares has been $4.50 per share in 1999.

Required:

For each of the above situations, describe the accounting concept or principle that applies as the basis for the accounting followed.

2.3. Procter & Gamble and the accounting equation. Think about the Procter & Gamble financial statements we studied in Chapter 1 and Chapter 2. Assume that the company entered into the transactions listed below.

Required:

Using the three-part box described in this chapter,

Assets	Liabilities
	Owners' equity

describe in your own words how the following six transactions might affect Procter & Gamble's financial statements:

a. The sale of common stock directly to a group of investors for $1 million.

b. The sale of a new issue of bonds directly to investors in the amount of $5 million.

c. Use of the proceeds of the stock sale and the bond sale to retire a $6 million bank debt.

d. The purchase of $100,000 worth of raw materials for the production of toothpaste, paid in cash as demanded by the supplier.

e. The purchase of $250,000 worth of plastic bottles for shampoo, to be paid for within 30 days.

f. Results for the month of January indicating the aggregate net income from all the units of $25 million.

2.4. Accrual versus cash basis accounting. Meredith, Miller, and Associates, Inc., is a management consulting group that was organized for business on August 1, 1998. Greg Meredith and Kate Miller each contributed $20,000 cash for shares of capital stock in the new company. The firm also borrowed $15,000 from a local bank on September 1, 1998; the loan was to be paid in full on August 30, 1999, with interest at the rate of 12 percent annually.

The new company rented office space on September 1, paying two months' rent in advance. The regular monthly rental fees of $600 per month were to be made on the first day of each month beginning on November 1. The company purchased a word-processing system and a fax machine in early August at a total cost of $3,600 cash. The owners estimated that the useful life of the office equipment was three years.

For the five months ended December 31, 1998, the company had rendered $31,000 in consulting services. Of this amount, $19,000 had been collected by year-end. Other costs incurred and paid in cash by year-end included the following:

Utilities	$ 550
Part-time typist	6,000
Miscellaneous office supplies	325

Unpaid bills at year-end included a telephone bill for $75 and wages for the typist of $600.

Required:

You have been retained by the firm of Meredith, Miller, and Associates, Inc., to prepare a set of accounting statements as of December 31, 1998. Using the above information, prepare a balance sheet, an income statement, and a statement of cash flows using the accrual basis of accounting; also prepare an income statement using the cash basis of accounting. On the basis of your findings, be prepared to comment on the performance of the company during its first five months of operation.

2.5. Accounting politics.   Consider the following statements that have been made about accounting and accounting standards:

> "The numbers that accountants report have, or at least are widely thought to have, a *significant* impact on *economic behavior*. Accounting rules therefore affect human behavior. Hence, the process by which they are made is said to be political. It is then only a short step to the assertion that such rules are properly to be made in the political arena, by counting heads and deciding accounting issues by some voting mechanism." [1]

> "The process of setting accounting standards can be described as democratic because like all rule-making bodies the board's right to make rules depends ultimately on the consent of the ruled." [2]

> "The [FASB's] objective must be responsive to many more considerations than accounting theory or our notions of economically useful data....Corporate reporting standards should result in data that are useful for economic decisions *provided that the standard is consistent with the national macroeconomic objectives and the economic programs designed to reach these goals.*" [3]

> "Information cannot be neutral—it cannot therefore be reliable—if it is selected or presented for the purpose of producing some chosen effect on human behavior. It is this quality of neutrality which makes a map reliable; and the essential nature of accounting, I believe, is cartographic. Accounting is financial mapmaking." [4]

> "Some [would say that] the financial phenomena which accountants must report are not independent of the reporting methods selected." [5]

Required:

Prepare a one-page essay explaining your views on the debate described in the above quotes. Your analysis should consider the implications of both sides of the argument, both for the external users of financial statements and for the preparers of that data.

2.6. Current value reporting.   The managers of Property Developments, Inc., were concerned about the depressed price at which the company's stock was trading. It had not gotten much above the $5 range, suggesting that Wall Street thought the company was worth about $5,000,000. The company's net worth (net worth = A – L), according to the most recent financial statements, was about $4,500,000, but everyone knew that the historical cost financial statements seriously understated the value of the company's portfolio of shopping plazas and apartment complexes. It was suggested that the market price of the stock might go up if the value of the company's properties was better understood by a wider audience. PDI management discussed the pros and cons of preparing and publishing current value financial statements for the company. Eventually they agreed that the potential benefit was worth the cost, and the discussion turned to implementation of the idea. An interesting and heated argument ensued as to the definition of *current value* as the term might be used in connection with the preparation of current value financial statements.

The operations manager argued that the properties should be valued at eight times their cash flow, inasmuch as that is the way the company looked at properties they were considering buying.

The construction manager argued that the current value of the properties was the current cost of replacing them, given the inflation that had swept through the construction industry.

The chief financial officer argued that the properties ought to be valued at the price obtained in the sale of comparable properties, inasmuch as that is the way a potential corporate raider would look at the individual properties in a campaign to liquidate the company.

[1,4,5] D. Solomons, "The Politicization of Accounting," *The Journal of Accountancy* (November 1978), pp. 65–72.

[2] *The Structure of Establishing Financial Accounting Standards* (Stamford, Conn.: FAF, April 1977), p. 19.

[3] David M. Hawkins, "Financial Accounting, the Standards Board and Economic Development," one of the 1973–74 Emanuel Saxe Distinguished Lectures in Accounting, published by the Bernard M. Baruch College, City University of New York, April 1975, pp. 7–8.

Required:

Assume that the company is going to prepare current value basis financial statements as a supplement to its GAAP-based, historical cost statements. How should the current values be determined? On the basis of some multiple of current cash flow? On the basis of replacement cost? On the basis of comparable properties' sale prices? Present the rationale for your position.

2.7. Fortunate Corporation finally finds a buyer. Fortunate Corporation had been through very difficult times. Its principal product had been left behind in a consumer style shift, and the company had been forced to get along by manufacturing and selling accessory products. New management had resolved to reduce excess capacity (and operating costs) to maintain the viability of at least some aspects of the company. They put the company's original facility, old Plant #1, on the market, but there were very few inquiries from potential buyers. Then one day, close to the end of the fiscal year, the realtor called to tell them disturbing news: the State Highway Department had announced plans to build a bypass around town and was planning to route the new road right through the center of old Plant #1. The plant and its land were on the books at $10,000,000. Based on the realtor's advice, the company was asking $11,500,000 in its current campaign to dispose of the property. The attorney was able to get a firm commitment from the state that it would buy the property from the company, paying $12,000,000 three years from today in accordance with eminent domain procedures.

Required:

Discuss the application of the notion of lower of cost or market in this situation. How should this situation be reflected in the current year's company financial statements? Why?

2.8. Applications of materiality concept. Consider the application of the idea of materiality in each of the following situations. Assume that for the year ended December 31, 1998, the company has total assets of $10,000,000 and net worth (net worth = A − L) of $3,000,000; sales were $10,000,000 two years ago, $11,000,000 last year, and $12,000,000 this year; net income was $400,000 two years ago, $550,000 last year, and $650,000 this year.

a. Research and development had never been a major expense for the company but had been growing about 5 percent a year. In 1998, it had grown to $500,000. The company had always disclosed in a footnote the amount of R&D expense it had incurred each year but had never included it as a separate line item in the income statement. R&D expenses had always been included in the line item "General and Administrative Expenses."

b. The company's subsidiary in Australia had a fire in its accounting department in mid-December and will not be able to get its financial reports to the home office in accordance with the original schedule for the preparation of the annual report to stockholders. Waiting until the data can be reconstructed and delivered to the home office will mean postponing the usual shareholder meeting for at least a month. In its report to the home office for the 11 months ended November 30, 1998, the subsidiary reported assets of $1,000,000, owners' equity of $300,000, and earnings-to-date of $25,000.

c. Each year the company counted all of the products-in-inventory on hand at all of its locations, priced out those inventory count sheets, and adjusted the balance sheet inventory amount to equal the values indicated by the priced count sheets. That process had been completed in early January, and the inventory account had been adjusted up to $3,000,000. The rest of the work required to pull together the financial statements was almost done, and that was good because the final statements had been promised to the bank early next week. Unfortunately, the inventory control manager called to report an error in the inventory pricing process. It seems that the computer program used to price the count sheets had slipped a decimal point: A product that should have had a value of $5 had been priced at $50. As a result the total inventory was overvalued by $250,000. That error overstated inventory by 8.3 percent, total assets by 2.5 percent, and after-tax income for the year by 19 percent.

d. The financial statements were completed and delivered to the bank and mailed to the shareholders. The manager of the Tucson plant called to say that an accounting employee had disappeared yesterday, and that when people had checked around they found that $10,000 in cash was gone from the plant vault. The employee had been responsible for the plant's payroll and vendor payment system. The plant had processed about $4,000,000 in payroll and $7,000,000 in vendor purchases last year.

Required:

For each of the situations outlined above, explain what you think the company ought to do, giving particular consideration to the concept of materiality. How should the notion of materiality impact the decisions suggested by the above situations?

2.9. Articulated financial statements. Under GAAP, the net earnings for the year less dividends accrued must be equal to the change in net assets (A–L) from the end of last year to the end of the current year. Some have suggested that balance sheets ought to be prepared on a current value basis so as to present a better measure of the shareholders' equity. That idea has been difficult to sell to the financial community because it implies that the income statement would reflect year-to-year changes in value, and those value-driven fluctuations would make it appear that management was not in control of the company. To deal with that concern, it has been suggested that the balance sheet be prepared on a current cost basis and that the income statements ought to be prepared on a historical cost basis. In effect, those commentators are willing to do away with the idea that the balance sheet and the income statement are inextricably linked—that is, they need not be articulated.

Required:

Prepare two short memos, each addressed to the president of Property Developments, Inc. (question 6 above). One memo should argue that the company's balance sheet and income statement could be prepared on different bases, and that they do not need to articulate. The other memo should argue that the statements should be prepared on the same basis and that it is important to preserve the GAAP requirement of articulation.

2.10. Standards for the MD&A. The Securities and Exchange Commission requires (among other things) that companies provide full financial statements to their shareholders every year, as well as a text presentation called "Management Discussion and Analysis" (the MD&A). Procter & Gamble refers to its MD&A as the "Financial Review". The financial statements must be prepared in accordance with GAAP, but there are no standards for the preparation of the MD&A. The SEC's rules for the MD&A simply require management to explain the changes in results from one year to the next, comment on the company's liquidity, and highlight any factor that might make the current statements an inappropriate basis for predicting future trends for the company. Compliance with this requirement has been uneven; some companies have presented quite detailed analytical comparisons of results between years, and some have confined their presentations to simple statements explaining, for instance, that unit sales are up while unit prices have declined. There has been some debate as to whether the SEC (or the FASB) should set more specific standards for the MD&A presentations: more specific standards would obviously enhance the comparability of information between companies, but more specific standards could inhibit the presentation of what is essentially qualitative information.

Required:

Visit your school's library, and select three annual reports from three different companies in the same industry. Read the president's letter and make your own analysis of the companies' results, as reflected in the financial statements. With that general background, study the MD&A presentation in those reports. Based on your assessment of the quality of those MD&A presentations, prepare a one-page letter addressed to the Securities and Exchange Commission, arguing for either greater specificity in the MD&A requirements or continued flexibility in the rules. Your letter should flow logically from the results of your study of the three examples.

2.11. An Accounting Game: The Sheepherders (Part One).* In the high mountains of Chatele, two sheepherders, Deyonne and Batonne, sit arguing their relative positions in life—an argument that has been going on for years. Deyonne says that he has 400 sheep, while Batonne has only 360 sheep. Therefore, Deyonne is much better off. Batonne, on the other hand, argues that he has 30 acres of land while Deyonne has only 20 acres; then too, Deyonne's land was inherited while Batonne had given 35 sheep for 20 acres of land 10 years ago. This year he gave 40 sheep for 10 additional acres of land. Batonne also makes the observation that of Deyonne's sheep 35 belong to another man, and he merely keeps them.

Deyonne counters that he has a large one-room cabin that he built himself. He claims that he has been offered three acres of land for the cabin. Besides these things, he has a plow, which was a gift from a friend and is worth a couple of goats; two carts that were given him in trade for a poor acre of land; and an ox that he acquired for five sheep.

Batonne goes on to say that his wife has orders for five coats to be made of homespun wool and that she will receive 25 goats for them. His wife has 10 goats already, three of which have been received in exchange for one sheep just last year. She has an ox that she acquired in a trade for three sheep. She also has one cart that cost her two sheep. Batonne's two-room cabin, even though smaller in dimension than Deyonne's, should bring him two choice acres of land in trade. Deyonne is reminded by Batonne that he owes Tyrone three sheep for bringing up his lunch each day last year.

Required:

In your opinion, who is wealthier—Deyonne or Batonne?

2.12. An Accounting Game: The Sheepherders (Part Two).† A year has elapsed since you solved Part One of the Sheepherders Game. After studying your solution to Part One, Deyonne and Batonne grudgingly accepted your opinion as to their relative wealths at the end of last year. The passage of time has not diminished their penchant for argument, however. Now they're arguing about who had the largest income for the year just ended.

Deyonne points out that the number of sheep that he personally owns at year-end exceeds his personal holdings at the beginning of the year by 80, whereas Batonne's increase was only 20. Batonne replies that his increase would have been 60 had he not traded 40 sheep during the year for 10 acres of additional land. Besides, Batonne points out that he exchanged 18 sheep during the year for food and clothing items, whereas Deyonne exchanged only seven for such purposes. The food and clothing have been pretty much used up by the end of the year.

Batonne is happy because his wife made five coats during the year (fulfilling the orders she had at the beginning of the year) and received 25 goats for them. She managed to obtain orders for another five coats (again for 25 goats)—orders on which she has not yet begun to work. Deyonne points out that he took to making his own lunches this year; therefore, he does not owe Tyrone anything now. Deyonne was very unhappy one day last year when he discovered that his ox had died of a mysterious illness. Both men are thankful, however, that none of the other animals died or was lost. Except for the matters reported above, Deyonne's and Batonne's holdings at the end of the current year are the same as their holdings at the end of last year.

Required:

How would you, as an outside observer to this argument, define "income?" Given your definition, whose income—Deyonne's or Batonne's—was greater for the past year?

---

* M. Carlson and J. W. Higgins, "A Games Approach to Introducing Accounting," *Accounting Education: Problems and Prospects* (Sarasota, Fla.: American Accounting Association, 1974). Reproduced with permission of the American Accounting Association.

† M. Carlson and J. W. Higgins, "A Games Approach to Introducing Accounting," *Accounting Education: Problems and Prospects* (Sarasota, Fla.: American Accounting Association, 1974). Reproduced with permission of the American Accounting Association.

2.13. Accrual versus cash basis accounting. Apex Machine Tool found itself with an exciting opportunity. A valued customer ordered a special tool and promised to pay $10,000 a year in rent, over a 10-year period, for the use of the tool. Apex ran some numbers and estimated that the tool could be built for $60,000 ($25,000 in material, $10,000 in design cost, and $25,000 in labor and other factory costs), although it was clear that fabrication of the tool would take the better part of a year to complete.

On November 1, 1993, Apex's board of directors approved the project. During the next two months all of the engineering was completed; during January 1994 the steel was ordered and received; the fabrication was completed during the rest of 1994, and the tool was delivered to the customer in December 1994. To finance the purchase of the steel and pay for the cost of the engineering and fabrication, Apex borrowed $60,000 using the rental agreement from the customer as collateral. The bank insisted that the principal on the loan ($60,000) be repaid in equal annual installments of $10,000 beginning December 31, 1995. The bank also insisted on annual interest payments, due December 31 each year, at 10 percent of the average amount of the loan outstanding during the year.

The customer is very happy with the tool but does not expect to have any use for it after the 10-year rental period. Apex plans to take the tool back at the end of the rental period and is sure that it will be good for many more years of useful service. At this time, however, Apex has no other customers in mind for the tool.

Required:

a. Create a time line for the 12 years beginning in 1993 (as illustrated below) and indicate in words where—in which period—the events described above will fall for both a cash basis and an accrual basis.

Cash basis
Accrual basis |———— 1993 ————|———— 1994 ————|———— 1995 ————|

b. Put a label on each of those events, on each side of the line; for example, using the cash basis of accounting, what is the nature of the steel purchase in the early part of 1994? What is the nature of that purchase, using the accrual basis of accounting?

c. Create two sets of income statements for this project, for each of the years 1993, 1994, 1995, 1999, and 2004. One set of statements should use the cash basis of accounting and one set should use the accrual basis.

d. Describe in your own words how the management of Apex might have applied the matching principle and the allocation principle to the above situation, and how its judgments might have been affected by the notion of conservatism.

CHAPTER 3

The Accounting Process

Nowadays, you hear a lot about fancy accounting methods, like lifo and fifo, but back then we were using the ESP *method, which really sped things along when it came time to close those books. It's a pretty basic method: If you can't make your books balance, you take however much they're off by and enter it under the heading* ESP, *which stands for Error Some Place.*[1]

Key Chapter Issues

- I recognize the importance of the accounting equation, but with all of a business's daily transactions, how do we keep the equation in balance?
- How do we get a business event into the accounting system? How do we get that business event through the system and into the financial statements?

- What kinds of business events are recorded in the accounting system and what kinds of events are not? How do we decide which events are recorded and which are not?
- How does the relationship between the balance sheet, the income statement, and the statement of cash flows play out in real life?

---

[1] S. Walton and J Huey, *Sam Walton, Made in America: My Story* (NY: Doubleday Books, 1992), p. 53.

In the first two chapters we compared accounting to a language, and we outlined some of the overarching principles that this language depends upon for its effectiveness as a communications vehicle. In this chapter we want to focus on the accounting process, which gathers the information to be reported and which actually carries the communication to the user. If you were responsible for the six o'clock news you would continually polish your vocabulary and your syntax, but you would also work hard to be sure that your news gathering and your analytical skills were at their best. In the news business, what you have to say really is more important than the way you say it. And so it is with accounting. Managers are concerned that their companies' financial statements comply with GAAP and that the resulting reports communicate effectively. But they also pay a great deal of attention to the underlying accounting process so that what they say in their accounting reports is comprehensive, accurate, and truthful.

The accounting process involves four steps: *measuring* the company's business events; *recording* and storing the quantified measures; sorting through those accumulated, quantified business events and *reporting* the results; and *analyzing* and interpreting those reports. In this chapter we touch briefly on the process of measuring, reporting, and analyzing. We will have more to say about the measurement aspect of the process in subsequent chapters as we discuss the accounting for individual assets and liabilities. And, we will have more to say about reporting and analyzing specifically in the next two chapters and again in the individual asset and liability chapters. The principal focus of this chapter, however, is on the recording process. We have elected to devote considerable attention to the recording process in this early chapter because we believe that a good understanding of that recording process facilitates the subsequent effective use and interpretation of the financial information generated by those processes.

ACCOUNTING INFORMATION SYSTEMS

Measuring

A wide variety of information about an enterprise might be useful to investors and other third parties. However, accounting systems measure, record, and report only those events and transactions that can be objectively measured. For example, it may be quite significant that the president of a company resigned or that a new president has been hired, and a press release describing those events may be given wide distribution. However, because it is difficult to quantify the loss the company has realized as a result of the resignation of a valued leader, or the gain the company will realize as a result of bringing on a new, energetic CEO, neither event would be recorded in the accounting records of the company or reported in the company's financial statements. At the other extreme, severance pay due to the departing CEO or the hiring bonus paid to the new CEO *can* be measured objectively and *will* be recorded in the company's accounts and reflected in its financial statements.

Measurement questions are frequently difficult. Most economic events and transactions (for example, sales of merchandise for cash, purchases of equipment, payment of salaries) can be measured relatively easily. More complex events and transactions (for example, sales on credit terms, expenditures for research and development, the purchase of another business) present more serious measurement problems, as we will see.

Imagine the spectrum of possible business transactions, and their impact on the financial statements, on a continuum that looks like this:

Impact is apparent and measurable	Impact is likely and estimable	Impact is uncertain and unmeasurable

Accounting attempts to deal with all of those events and transactions that are objectively measurable and those that are at least reasonably estimable. For example, at the far left end of the spectrum, the purchase of merchandise is quite routinely recorded at the amount to be paid to a vendor. In the middle of the spectrum, a product recall will be recognized in the financial statements, so long as the cost of the recall can be estimated with a reasonable degree of certainty. Other events and transactions, the financial effects of which cannot be reasonably foreseen or quantified, cannot be recorded in the financial statements and must be explained to those third parties who have an interest in the company using other communication techniques. As an example of an event at the far right end of the spectrum, think about a pharmaceutical company that has just received regulatory permission to market a new, potentially powerful drug; that event will almost certainly be described in press reports and in the president's letter in the annual report to stockholders. But because the financial success of the new product is not known and because its impact cannot now be measured, the event of the new product approval is not recognized in the financial statements. As you can imagine, management depends on its accounting systems to deal with events and transactions on the left side of the continuum and devotes most of its attention to events that fall at the center or the far right side of the spectrum. As management people think about their reporting responsibility, they work hard at making the best estimate they can for the items in the center of the spectrum—which will be recorded in the financial statements based on management's estimated amounts. Management people work hard looking for other ways besides the financial reporting process (using press releases, speeches, analyst presentations, and so forth) to communicate the effect of those events at the right of the spectrum.

Recording

Accounts and the information system. The accounting system of any enterprise is effectively an **information system.** That is, it is a system in which the financial aspects of events and transactions are evaluated, processed, and then reported to various information users. Like all information systems, an accounting system contains files in which the basic data can be stored for future use or processing. In accounting systems, these files are known as **accounts.**

When a business event occurs, the monetary effects of the event are evaluated; if those effects can be measured with a fair degree of accuracy, they are recorded and stored in the appropriate accounts. The accounts are used as storehouses to accumulate the monetary effects of all of the events affecting the entity. Some events will result in increases to an account, others will result in decreases. For example, if we maintained an account for inventory, purchases from suppliers would add to the Inventory account, whereas sales to customers would decrease the Inventory account. At any time, management can look at an account and see how much activity has taken place and can see what the current **balance** in the account is. Going back to our inventory example, management can look on the shelves to see how much product is physically on hand; but to report to our banker how much inventory is on hand, it is more effective to report the cost of that inventory on the shelves. The cost of the inventory on hand will be available in the accounting system, as the balance in the Inventory account.

Each account represents some kind of asset, some type of liability, or a component of owners' equity. In theory, a company could maintain only three accounts: a single asset account, a single liability account, and one owners' equity account. Most companies, however, have many more accounts; the number of accounts needed depends on the complexity of the business and the amount of detail to be presented in the accounting reports. For example, a company may maintain one account labeled "Cash" and accumulate in that account all of the financial effects of events and transactions that impact its cash. On the other hand, many companies maintain individual accounts for different kinds of property and equipment—a separate account for trucks, another for tools, and a third for the factory building. Again, the number of accounts maintained depends on the complexity of the business and on the amount of detail that is to be presented in the basic financial statements.

In manual accounting systems, the accounts are known as **T-accounts,** principally because their format depicts a large "T." The vertical trunk of the "T" divides the account into a left side and a right side. One side is used to accumulate the effects of those transactions that increase the account balance; the other side is used to accumulate the effects of those transactions that decrease the account balance. As we shall see in a later discussion, whether the right side or the left side is used to accumulate increases or decreases depends on the nature of the account. The balance in the account at any time is simply the difference between the total of the increases and the total of the decreases. To prepare a financial report at any particular time, management need only use the balances in each account. A balance sheet is a display of all of the balances in the balance sheet accounts; an income statement is a display of all of the account balances in the income statement accounts.

Computer-based accounting systems also depend on the concept of accounts. The fundamentals of the recording process are the same whether the system is manual or computer based. The monetary amount of each measurable event or transaction is ascribed to the particular account affected; the processing system aggregates all those transactions that affect particular accounts and determines a new balance after each transaction is entered. When the processing for a period is complete, the balances in the accounts are displayed in a financial report. In a computerized system, the accounts no longer have a left side and a right side, rather the increases and decreases are simply entered into the account chronologically. The accounts still act as the repository for the aggregation of transactions, however, and still produce a balance, which is the net result of all of the transactions affecting that account.

It may be helpful to visualize an account as a discrete place where the financial effects of economic events and transactions are accumulated. For example, a simple hypothetical asset account might appear as follows under a manual system and a computerized system:

Manual Accounting System				Computerized Accounting System	
Asset Account				**Asset Account**	
Beginning balance	$10,000			Beginning balance	$10,000
Entry #1	1,000	Entry #2	$ 500	Entry #1	$ 1,000
Entry #3	2,000	Entry #4	1,500	Entry #2	(500)
Entry #6	3,000	Entry #5	2,000	Entry #3	2,000
Ending balance	$12,000			Entry #4	(1,500)
				Entry #5	(2,000)
				Entry #6	3,000
				Ending balance	$12,000

The double-entry system. Understanding that accounts are the repositories where we accumulate and store information, we need to look at the process that actually enters the information into the accounts. But to understand the logic of that entry process, we ought to go back to some basics from the earlier chapters. You will remember that we said that every resource available to the company has a source, and because of that truism, the company's assets always had to be equal to the sum of its liabilities and owners' equity. We stated that basic relationship as

$$A = L + OE$$

An Italian mathematician, Luca Pacioli, developed that equation several centuries ago and invented the double-entry accounting system we use today. His equation holds each business responsible for its assets, and asks, "Where did the funding come from to provide the company's assets?" And perhaps more importantly, it asks, "To whom is management accountable for the protection and employment of those assets?" Going to the accounting process, he reasoned that the best way to be sure that the accounting equation was always in balance was to use a **double-entry accounting system.** Under Pacioli's double-entry system, every time a change was made in one of the accounts represented in the equation, an equal change had to be made in some other account in the equation.

Think of a company's balance sheet as being a delicate balance beam, with a fulcrum at its equal sign and its assets equal to the sum of its liabilities and its equity. If you then think of a business event you would like to enter on that balance beam, you will see that the event must either have an equal effect on each side of the balance beam or have an equal on-and-off effect on one side. To keep the balance beam level, an entered event must either impact both sides equally or have a self-canceling effect on one side.

In accounting, every event is understood to have a double implication because every new resource must have a source, and vice versa. Every accounting event will have two aspects to it: The event will either add equal amounts to both sides of the equation or have a self-canceling effect on one side. In a double-entry accounting system, both aspects of the event are recorded at the same time to be sure that the equation is always in balance. Some accounting events result in an increase in an asset and in a liability; some result in the reverse. Some events result in an increase in an asset and an increase in owners' equity; some result in the reverse. Some events result in an increase in one asset and a decrease in another asset, while others result in an increase in a liability and a decrease in owners' equity.

Consider, for example, a retailer's purchase of $30,000 of merchandise inventory for cash. One asset (inventory) will be increased by $30,000 while another asset (cash) will be decreased by an equal amount. If, however, the retailer purchased the inventory on credit, an asset (inventory) would be increased by $30,000, as would a liability (accounts payable to suppliers). When the retailer pays its suppliers, its liabilities (accounts payable) decrease by $30,000 as do its assets (cash). *All* of the many transactions of even the most complex company are expressed in exactly this manner; an increase or a decrease in one account must, of necessity, result in an equal change in another account, or in a combination of accounts. Regardless of the transaction, the basic accounting equation must always remain in balance.

In a double-entry system, the two aspects of an event are formally entered into the accounts using an **entry.** You can't just say to the system, "Please increase an asset and a liability"; being a system, it will expect something more systematic. Going back to the retailer example we just cited, the entry to purchase the inventory for cash would be written to look something like this:

```
Inventory (A). . . . . . . increase $30,000
       Cash (A). . . . . . .      decrease $30,000
```

We will have more to say later about the actual form of the entry used by most businesspeople.

Accounts represent repositories where the financial effects of a company's economic events and transactions are accumulated; *entries* represent the monetary expression of those events—that is, the input to those accounts. As management thinks through the accounting impact of any business transaction, it usually visualizes the transaction in the form of an entry—which accounts are affected, which accounts are increased, and which are decreased. It is almost always easy to visualize one half of an entry, but sometimes the other half of the entry is more problematic. For example, paying a $10,000 bill for advertising clearly reduces cash, but what should the other side of the entry be? Should another asset, perhaps customer awareness, be increased? Or should retained earning (part of owners' equity) be decreased because the advertising is simply a current period business expense? As you confront accounting questions, you will find it helpful to think through the two sides of each entry in this way. Remember that the accounting equation ($A = L + OE$) must remain in balance. That discipline is the principal advantage of Pacioli's double-entry system.

Thinking through a debit and a credit. As we noted earlier, manual systems use accounts that are divided into a left side and a right side. For reasons that are now lost in time, the left side of those accounts is referred to as the *debit side* and the right side is referred to as the *credit side*. The words *debit* and *credit* are, unfortunately, used in a variety of ways in the business world, as with credit memo or a debit memo. When they are used in an accounting record-keeping context, **debit** and **credit** are simply shorthand ways to refer to the part of an accounting entry that affects the left (debit) side of an account and the right (credit) side of an account, respectively. (Incidentally, when those terms are written, the shorthand is often carried further—debit is usually abbreviated "dr." and credit is usually abbreviated "cr.")

The use of the words *debit* and *credit* gained wide acceptance during the period when manual accounting systems were in place. They continue to be used in accounting discussions today—even in these days of computerized systems when accounts do not have a left or right side but are simply a collection of electronic impulses. Some additional background on the use of these words and some expansion on the way the words are used in the electronic age may be helpful.

Custom has determined that, at least in the United States, balance sheets are prepared with assets on the left side of the balance sheet and the liabilities and owners' equity on the right side (look at the Procter & Gamble balance sheet on pages 26 and 27). From that convention, it followed that the monetary effect of an event that increased an asset was entered on the left side of the asset T-account. The monetary effect of an event that increased a liability or a component of owners' equity account was entered on the right side of the liability and owners' equity T-accounts. We were just considering a retailer's purchase of merchandise inventory by paying cash or by buying on credit; the cash purchase would result in a $30,000 entry to the left side of the inventory account (an increase in that asset) and a $30,000 entry to the right side of the cash account (a decrease in that asset). The purchase on credit would result in a $30,000 entry to the left side of the inventory account (an increase in that asset) and an equal entry to the right side of the accounts payable account (an increase in that liability account).

Building on our earlier discussion of debits and credits, it follows that the entry to the left side of the inventory account is a debit (left-side) entry and the entry to the right side of the cash account or the accounts payable account is a credit (right-side) entry. It will always be so: Increases in assets are left-side entries (debits) while decreases in an asset account are right-side entries (credits). Conversely, an increase in a liability account is a right-side entry (credit) while decreases in liabilities and owners' equity are left-side entries (debits). Finally, because revenues and expenses accrue to the benefit or detriment of the owners, an increase in a revenue account is always a credit entry, while an increase to an expense is always a debit entry. The logic of this system of maintaining accounts—that is, the use of debits and credits—can be more readily seen in the following illustration:

Account

Left	Right
Debit	Credit

The balance sheet accounts can be depicted as follows—think about the way our retailer's purchases impact these accounts and the accounting equation:

Assets			**Liabilities**			**Owners' Equity**	
Dr.	Cr.	=	Dr.	Cr.	+	Dr.	Cr.
increase	decrease		decrease	increase		decrease	increase

Income statement accounts can be depicted in this way:

Revenues			**Expenses**			**Net Income** (an addition to or subtraction from retained earnings)	
Dr.	Cr.	−	Dr.	Cr.	=	Dr.	Cr.
decrease	increase		increase	decrease		decrease (Loss)	increase (Income)

The words *debit* and *credit* are used in the same way in companies in which the accounting system is computerized—the debit entry means an increase in an asset or expense account or a decrease in a liability or owners' equity account, while a credit entry means an increase in a liability or revenue account or an owners' equity account but a decrease in an asset account. The day may come when an increase is referred to simply as an *increase* and a decrease is referred to simply as a *decrease*. Until that day comes, however, it is easier for accountants and businesspeople to adapt to existing conventions and refer to entries with the terms *debits* and *credits*. In this text, we will use both.

Let us summarize what we have been discussing. We have said that every accounting transaction must affect at least two accounts and that the debit side of the transaction must always equal the credit side. We have also stated that accountants and businesspeople analyze a transaction by considering which accounts are affected, in what amounts, and then by thinking through the various debit and credit entries that are required. To record a business event in the company's accounts, an entry is required. Management people use the answers to these questions in the development of that required entry:

1. Is the transaction (or event) complete, and is its effect objectively measurable?
2. What kind of account (asset, liability, or owners' equity) is affected? What specific accounts are affected?

3. Are the affected accounts increased or decreased, and by how much?

4. What are the debit (left-side) and credit (right-side) effects of the transaction according to the rules of double-entry accounting for entering data in the accounts?

When that thinking process is complete, the transaction can be reduced to a written entry so that the information can be processed by the accounting system. A typical entry looks like this:

Debit (Dr.) Account Name (A, L, or OE). . . . . . . (inc./dec.) Amount
Credit (Cr.) Account Name (A, L, or OE) . . . .   (inc./dec.) Amount

Most accounting information systems require a standardized format for their accounting entries to ensure that the system processes all entries properly. Throughout the remainder of this text, we will follow these widely accepted recording rules:

1. The left-side (debit) portion of an entry will be presented first, followed by the right-side (credit) portion which is also slightly indented.

2. The Dr. and Cr. designations will be included, as will the increase (inc.) and decrease (dec.) designation.

3. The full name of the affected account will be used, as will the account classification— asset (A), liability (L), owners' equity (OE), revenue (R), or expense (E).

To illustrate this analytical approach, consider the earlier example in which a retailer purchased merchandise inventory on credit for $30,000. Your responses to the above four questions might appear as follows:

Question	Answer
1. Status of the transaction:	Complete and measurable.
2. Accounts affected:	Asset—Merchandise Inventory (A).
	Liability—Accounts Payable (L).
3. Amounts involved:	Merchandise Inventory increased by $30,000.
	Accounts Payable increased by $30,000.
4. Left-side/right-side effects:	Enter $30,000 on left side of Merchandise Inventory account (a debit) and $30,000 on right side of Accounts Payable account (a credit).

Reduced to entry format, this transaction (and the answers to the four questions) can be summarized as follows:

	Left Side	Right Side
Dr. Merchandise Inventory (A) . . . . (inc.) 30,000		
Cr. Accounts Payable (L)		(inc.) 30,000

As a second illustration, consider a transaction involving the payment of $30,000 by the retailer for the merchandise previously purchased. Following the four steps outlined earlier, this event can be stated as an entry as follows:

Dr. Accounts Payable (L) . . . . (dec.) 30,000
Cr. Cash (A) . . . .   (dec.) 30,000

These two transactions would be reflected in the retailer's T-accounts as follows:

Cash (A)			
Beginning bal. XXX			
	Entry	30,000	

Inventory (A)			
Beginning bal. XXX			
Entry 30,000			

Accounts Payable (L)			
	Entry	30,000	Beginning bal. XXX
			Entry 30,000

Pictorially, these transactions affect the accounting equation as follows:

■ The purchase of inventory:

Assets Inventory + 30,000	Liabilities Accounts Payable + 30,000
	Owners' Equity

■ The payment of the invoice for previously purchased merchandise:

Assets Cash – 30,000	Liabilities Accounts Payable – 30,000
	Owners' Equity

The size of the two halves of the box (depicting the balance sheet) may increase or decrease as transactions are recorded, but the two sides must always remain in balance. Before continuing, think about other transactions that might affect the company and visualize how they would affect the parts of the box.

Processing and Preparing the Financial Statements

After the financial effects of business transactions have been stated as entries for the accounting information system, those entries are then entered into the accounts. This entering process is called **posting,** because the individual entries are posted to the affected accounts.

The process of analyzing business transactions, recognizing the financial effects as entries, and then posting the entries to the T-accounts continues on a day-to-day basis in most companies. At some regular interval (weekly, monthly, quarterly, or annually), the net effect of the individual transactions posted to each account (that is, the **balance** resulting from the increases and decreases) is determined, and the account balances are drawn together into a set of accounting reports. To produce the accounting reports, a number of end-of-period activities must be undertaken, principally to ensure that the accounting information is reliable.

In addition to the entries that have been developed on an ongoing day-to-day basis, some **adjusting entries** may be required as of the end of the period. Company management frequently uses the end of the period as a stimulus to objectively challenge its financial position and ask some of the fundamental questions we discussed in Chapter 2. For example,

■ You will remember that in Chapter 2 we said that a fundamental question had to do with the allocation of the effects of a company's operations over time. More specifically, a chief financial officer (CFO) might ask whether the product development expenses that have been accumulated in an expense account should really be treated as an expense this year or whether there is enough evidence of future payback from that product to justify treating the development expenditures as an asset and allocating the costs over the future years in which the payback will be realized.

■ Another question raised in Chapter 2 asked whether all of the company's assets were likely to produce future cash flows in excess of their carrying values. More specifically, management might ask about the value of inventory reflected in the inventory account. The CFO might ask the operations and marketing people to assess whether there might be a product obsolescence problem or a lower-of-cost-or-market problem that requires a reduction in the balance sheet amount for inventory.

■ And, following up on another question posed in Chapter 2, management might challenge its perception of the lawsuit recently filed against the company. Although an aggressive, defensive posture may be appropriate for the courtroom, management must ask for a conservative estimate of the cost of losing that suit and then consider whether that loss estimate needs to be recognized in the accounts and in the financial statements.

Depending on the answers to such questions, additional entries may be required to adjust the balances in the accounts before the accounting process can be brought to a close for the period.

Another end-of-period activity is the preparation of a **trial balance.** The trial balance is a list of the balances in all of the company's accounts. The trial balance has two uses: (1) It provides an opportunity to examine the aggregated results of the individual entries to see whether the resulting balances make sense as compared to what management expected them to be; and (2) it provides an opportunity to see whether the sum of the accounts with ending debit balances equals the sum of the accounts with ending credit balances. In effect, the trial balance tells us whether our individual entries were in balance and whether we posted the debits and credits correctly. If that review of the trial balance identifies any errors or omissions, they are corrected with further adjusting entries. Depending on the extent of those final corrections, an adjusted trial balance may be prepared to prove that the system is now ready to produce the financial statements. Although the trial balance does not provide any guarantee that we posted the entries to the right accounts, it does provide assurance that the fundamental accounting equation remains in balance.

The next step in the accounting process is the **closing.** In real life, companies maintain individual accounts for all of their revenue accounts and all of their expense accounts, as well as their asset, liability, and owners' equity accounts. At the end of an accounting period, management "closes" the revenue and expense accounts by transferring their balances to the owners' equity retained earnings account, in effect increasing the retained earnings balance by the net income for the period.

The hardware store example we will work through at the end of this chapter will follow that approach, and when you get there you will see that the final entry for the year is the closing entry. If that full-blown process makes sense to you, feel free to follow it through. However, it is clear that the closing process adds several steps to the overall process and you may find it easier to ignore the individual revenue and expense accounts and to think of all revenue transactions as direct additions to retained earnings and all expense transactions as direct deductions from retained earnings. Net income then will be the net result of those additions and deductions from retained earnings *during this current period*. If that approach makes sense to you, you can avoid not only the revenue and expense accounts but also the closing of those accounts to retained earnings. That shortcut approach will be more efficient and should work just as well, given the simplified examples we will be using. But more importantly, it may be easier for you to see how to apply the accounting equation if you visualize every revenue transaction as a direct addition to retained earnings rather than an indirect addition through a subordinate revenue account. Similarly, the impact on the basic equation of an expense transaction may be more clear if you visualize every expense as a direct reduction from retained earnings rather than as an indirect reduction through a subordinate expense account.

To illustrate that idea, consider the following entry, which records cash sales of $50,000 for the month.

```
Dr. Cash (A) . . . . . . . . . . . . . . . . . . . . . . (inc.) 50,000
    Cr. Product Sales (R/RE). . . . . . . . . . . . . . . . . . . .        (inc.) 50,000
```

Note that we have expanded the account classification for the sales side of the entry to indicate that it affects a revenue account (R) and that revenue is really an addition to retained earnings, *(RE)*. Throughout the rest of this chapter we will use that double classification scheme for all entries that affect either revenue or expense. In the rest of the book we will classify income statement accounts as either an R or an E; *we expect you to know that revenues are additions to retained earnings and expenses are deductions from retained earnings.*

If you follow the shorthand approach outlined above, you will enter all revenue and expense transactions directly into retained earnings. You will then prepare the income statement for the year as an analysis of the transactions flowing through the retained earnings account during that year. In contrast to this shorthand approach, the following discussion illustrates how the closing process works and how that process produces an income statement and thereby a retained earnings balance.

At the end of an accounting period, after all of the necessary adjusting entries have been posted, the income statement is prepared using the period-end balances in the revenue and expense accounts. Once that statement is prepared and net income for the period is determined, the revenue and expense accounts are "closed" using an overall entry that zeroes out the balances in the individual revenue and expense accounts and transfers those balances to the retained earnings account. Remembering that a revenue account typically has a right-side balance (a credit balance) and that expense accounts typically have left-side balances (debit balances), a simple company might make the following **closing entry** at the end of a month:

```
Dr. Sales (R) . . . . . . . . . . . . . . . . . . . . . . . . . . . . . . . . (dec.) 14,812
    Cr. Cost of Product Sold (E) . . . . . . . . . . . . . . . . . . .          (dec.) 8,914
    Cr. Selling and Administrative Expenses (E) . . . . . . .          (dec.) 2,414
    Cr. Retained Earnings (OE) . . . . . . . . . . . . . . . . . .          (inc.) 3,484
```

Of course, the net amount transferred to retained earnings ($3,484) is the net income for that period. The revenue and expense accounts are closed out because they are **temporary accounts:** They serve as repositories for transactions that impacted that one accounting period, but they do not (and should not) reflect events that occurred in any prior period. The balance sheet accounts, including the retained earnings account, carry their balances forward to the next period; because they carry a balance forward from year to year and are not closed out at the end of each period, they are called **permanent accounts.** For example, the balance in the inventory account at the end of one accounting period is the beginning balance in that account for the next accounting period. Revenue and expense accounts do not carry their balances over to the next period. Because of the closing entry, the balance in the revenue and expense accounts at the beginning of the next period will have a zero balance and will be ready to begin the accumulation of revenue and expense transactions of that next period.

Let's go back to Procter & Gamble as our reference point. The balance in Procter & Gamble's cash account at June 30, 1998, is $1,549 million. That balance reflects the balance on hand at July 1, 1997, plus or minus the effects of all of the transactions that affected cash during the year. But the balance in the net sales account at June 30, 1988, was $37,154 million, reflecting only those sales that occurred during the year. The accounting system knows to treat the cash account as a carryover account and the net sales account as a this-year-only account because the net sales account at June 30, 1998, was closed to retained earnings. The beginning balance in the net sales account at July 1, 1997, was zero; at June 30, 1988, *before* the closing entry for 1998, it was $37,154 million; at June 30, 1988, *after* the closing entry for 1998, it was again zero. The ending balance in the retained earnings account at June 30, 1988, was $11,144 million; the beginning balance in retained earnings, for the year that will begin on July 1, 1998, is exactly the same.

Whether the shorthand approach or the more complete approach is adopted, an income statement is prepared to summarize the revenue and expense transactions that affected the retained earnings account during the year. Similarly, a statement of cash flows is prepared to summarize the transactions that affected the cash account during the year. Finally, the balance sheet is prepared, drawing on the balances in the various balance sheet accounts.

To prepare the statements, management uses the basic data from the trial balance and presents that data in a way that most meaningfully communicates the company's results. During the preparation of the financial statements, some accounts may be aggregated, but other account balances may have to be disaggregated to determine the amounts for the line items on the statements. In addition, management may decide that for a fair presentation of the company's results, supplemental footnotes are required. In the end, management must satisfy itself that the resulting financial presentation is fair and in accordance with GAAP. This entire process is called the **accounting cycle** and is outlined in Exhibit 3.1.

Before considering an illustration of the accounting cycle, a final word is appropriate. The double-entry accounting system is used throughout the world. While specific account labels may differ, every country has essentially adopted this approach to the recording of financial data. Hence, as you work through this text and encounter financial data from other countries, the differences you may observe will be due to different business conditions or different accounting standards, but they will not be the result of a different accounting process.

EXHIBIT 3.1

The Accounting Cycle

Phase	Information Activity	Time Frame
1. Measuring and recording	Analyze economic transactions. State transactions in accounting language with entries. Post entries to ledger accounts.	During the accounting period
2. Processing: Summarizing, verifying, and aggregating	Prepare trial balance. Prepare adjusting entries Prepare closing entries.	End of period
3. Reporting	Prepare financial statements.	End of period

THE ACCOUNTING PROCESS ILLUSTRATED: BLUE RIDGE HARDWARE CO.

To illustrate the accounting process and the preparation of the basic financial statements, we will trace the business activities of a hypothetical company, Blue Ridge Hardware Co., from its first transaction through the end of its first year of operations. This illustration assumes a manual accounting system because it is easier to see the development of entries and the flow of those entries through the accounts into the final financial statements.

First Year of Operations

The following pages present the basic business transactions that a small retailer might encounter during its first year of operations. The illustration describes the events affecting the business and then outlines the entries required as a result of those transactions. Finally, the accounting process is completed with the preparation of a trial balance and the formal financial statements. For simplicity, all similar transactions that occurred throughout the year have been grouped and only the yearly totals are recorded. For example, transaction no. 5 reflects the total merchandise purchased by the business on account throughout the entire year. On the company's books, however, each individual purchase of merchandise inventory made throughout the year would have been recorded separately and chronologically.

Transaction no. 1. On April 1, 1999, two friends formed the Blue Ridge Hardware Co. and filed for a corporate charter from the state. Each invested $5,000 cash in the new company and received 5,000 shares of stock for the investment. Testing this event against the four-step approach outlined on pages 78 and 79, the transaction is complete and its effect is estimable. The accounts affected are the cash account and the owners' equity account; both will be increased by the amount of cash contributed to the company, and the entry will look like this:

Dr. Cash (A) . . . . (inc.) 10,000
    Cr. Capital Stock (OE) . . . .   (inc.) 10,000

GAAP says that a company may not generate income as a result of transactions with its owners. This receipt of cash increases owners' equity but not retained earnings. It impacts the balance sheet but not the income statement.

Transaction no. 2. Also on April 1, 1999, a three-year lease was signed for the building in which the hardware store is located. The lease called for a monthly rental of $300 and was cancelable by either the lessor or the lessee (Blue Ridge Hardware) with at least 60 days' advance notice.

No entry is needed. This business transaction does not affect the financial resources or obligations of Blue Ridge Hardware. Even though the business signed the lease, the contract is an **executory agreement** that will be consummated over time. Because the lease is readily cancelable by either party, its impact cannot be reasonably estimated and so it will not be recorded in the accounts. As the business uses the building, the monthly lease payments are recorded (see transaction no. 11).

Transaction no. 3. A total of $7,500 was borrowed from a local bank on April 1, 1999. Repayment is to be made over a five-year period, and interest at 12 percent per year is due annually on March 31 on the unpaid balance:

> Dr. Cash (A) . . . . (inc.) 7,500
>   Cr. Bank Loan Payable (L). . . . .   (inc.) 7,500

This receipt of cash is not a revenue item because it must be paid back sometime in the future. Note that the loan carries with it an obligation to pay interest on the borrowed funds. That commitment is not recorded when the loan proceeds are received because (like the lease payments in transaction no. 2) interest accrues over time and is recorded only as time elapses—usually at the end of each accounting period during the adjusting entry process.

Transaction no. 4. During the month of April, store equipment was purchased for $10,000 cash:

> Dr. Store Equipment (A) . . . . (inc.) 10,000
>   Cr. Cash (A). . . . .   (dec.) 10,000

Transaction no. 5. During the year, merchandise inventory in the amount of $57,400 was purchased on credit. Payment was usually due within 30 days of the purchase date:

> Dr. Merchandise Inventory (A) . . . . (inc.) 57,400
>   Cr. Accounts Payable (L) . . . .   (inc.) 57,400

The purchase of equipment in transaction no. 4 is simply an exchange of one asset for another. Similarly, the purchase of inventory in transaction no. 5 is also treated as the acquisition of an asset even though the various suppliers have not yet been paid. The inventory purchase transaction recognizes the payment promise that Blue Ridge Hardware made when it ordered and received the merchandise. The fulfillment of that promise is recognized as a separate, subsequent transaction (see transaction no. 10). The equipment and the inventory are both considered to be assets because they both have continuing value and because both will help the store produce future cash flows from future operations. Because the expense associated with these cash payments will benefit future operations and because we want to match that expense with the related future benefit, we treat the expenditures as assets today and charge them to expense in future transactions (see transactions no. 8 and 15).

Transaction no. 6. During the year, cash sales amounted to $29,800:

```
Dr. Cash (A) . . . . . . . . . . . . . . . . . . . . . . (inc.) 29,800
    Cr. Sales Revenue (R/RE) . . . . . . . . . . . . . . . . . .        (inc.) 29,800
```

Transaction no. 7. During the year, credit sales amounted to $44,700:

```
Dr. Accounts Receivable (A) . . . . . . . . . . (inc.) 44,700
    Cr. Sales Revenue (R/RE) . . . . . . . . . . . . . . . . . .        (inc.) 44,700
```

Both cash sales and credit sales (transactions no. 6 and no. 7) can be considered as revenues for the company because they result from consummated transactions with third-party customers. Note that the credit sales are treated as revenues just as though they had been collected in cash. In both entries, an asset account is increased, as is the revenue (retained earnings) account. The collection of those accounts receivable is treated as a separate transaction affecting only the balance sheet (see transaction no. 9).

Transaction no. 8. The cost of merchandise sold during the year totaled $44,700:

```
Dr. Cost of Merchandise Sold (E/RE). . . . . (inc.) 44,700
    Cr. Merchandise Inventory (A) . . . . . . . . . . . . . . . .        (dec.) 44,700
```

This entry matches the cost of the merchandise sold with the revenue generated by its sale: The difference between the total sales and the cost of merchandise sold is the gross profit from the sales, sometimes called the gross margin. Note that we did not sell all of the merchandise we purchased. Consequently, we have to allocate some of that merchandise purchase to the sales we made this year and some to the sales that will be made in the future. The cost of the merchandise to be sold in the future remains in the inventory asset account while the cost of the merchandise we sold this year is allocated to the cost of sales expense account. How do we make that allocation? That question has been the subject of a great deal of study (and controversy) within the financial community and we will get to it when we study the accounting for inventory in chapter 9.

Transaction no. 9. Collections of cash from accounts receivable (see transaction no. 7) totaled $40,500:

```
Dr. Cash (A) . . . . . . . . . . . . . . . . . . . . . . (inc.) 40,500
    Cr. Accounts Receivable (A). . . . . . . . . . . . . . . . .        (dec.) 40,500
```

Transaction no. 10. Payments for merchandise inventory previously purchased on credit (see transaction no. 5) amounted to $53,600:

```
Dr. Accounts Payable (L) . . . . . . . . . . . . (dec.) 53,600
    Cr. Cash (A). . . . . . . . . . . . . . . . . . . . . . . . . . . .        (dec.) 53,600
```

Transactions no. 9 and 10 are examples of transactions that affect only asset and liability accounts. They represent an exchange of one asset for another or a settlement of a liability using an asset. The revenue or expense aspect of these transactions was recognized earlier when the basic sales and cost of sales entries were recorded. Accrual accounting looks at business events and separates their economic effects from their cash effects.

Transaction no. 11. Cash paid for building rent for the year totaled $3,600:

```
Dr. Rent Expense (E/RE) . . . . . . . . . . . . . (inc.) 3,600
    Cr. Cash (A). . . . . . . . . . . . . . . . . . . . . . . . . . . .        (dec.) 3,600
```

Transaction no. 12. Cash wages paid to employees totaled $14,600. As of March 31, 2000, wages earned by employees but not yet paid were $700:

```
Dr. Wage Expense (E/RE). . . . . . . . . . . . (inc.) 15,300
      Cr. Cash (A). . . . . . . . . . . . . . . . . . . . . . . . . . . . . .      (dec.) 14,600
      Cr. Wages Payable (L). . . . . . . . . . . . . . . . . . . . . .          (inc.) 700
```

Transaction no. 13. Cash paid for utilities amounted to $450. Blue Ridge Hardware estimated that when the March bills were all processed, the company would owe an additional $200 as of March 31, 2000:

```
Dr. Utilities Expense (E/RE) . . . . . . . . . . . . . . (inc.) 650
      Cr. Cash (A). . . . . . . . . . . . . . . . . . . . . . . . . . . . . .      (dec.) 450
      Cr. Utilities Payable (L) . . . . . . . . . . . . . . . . . . . . .       (inc.) 200
```

Transaction no. 14. On March 31, 2000, the interest on the bank loan for the first year was paid:

```
Dr. Interest Expense (E/RE) . . . . . . . . . . . . . . (inc.) 900
      Cr. Cash (A). . . . . . . . . . . . . . . . . . . . . . . . . . . . . .      (dec.) 900
```

Transactions no. 13, 14, and 15 recognize various operating expenses for the current period. These transactions are charged to expenses—that is, they are *not* added to an asset—because they create no measurable future benefit for the store. Note that the expenses are based on what the company estimates they *will owe* up to March 31, 2000, not on what they *have paid.* As a result of the accrual of wages payable and utilities payable, those expenses are charged to operations for the period when the benefit was received, even though the cash will not be paid until the following period.

Transaction no. 15. At year-end the owners estimated that the store equipment had a 10-year life and that one year had passed. Therefore, an adjusting entry was made to allocate $1,000 of the original cost (see transaction no. 4) of the equipment to expense in this first period:

```
Dr. Depreciation Expense (E/RE) . . . . . . . . (inc.) 1,000
      Cr. Accumulated Depreciation (CA) . . . . . . . . . . . .      (inc.) 1,000
```

Some portion of the original cost of the store equipment was used to produce the revenues earned in this period. Under GAAP, the cost of long-lived assets must be allocated to specific accounting periods; the usual way to accomplish this allocation is to estimate the useful life of the asset and to charge a pro rata portion of the cost of that asset to expense each elapsed year. This process of allocation is called depreciation. At times it will be useful to know the original cost of a company's plant and equipment. Therefore, rather than reduce the asset account directly, the annual depreciation allocation is credited to a **contra asset** (CA) account called *Accumulated Depreciation.* This contra account is reported on the balance sheet as a deduction from the store equipment account, thereby preserving the original cost of the equipment and also reporting its net *undepreciated cost.* The undepreciated cost is often referred to as its **book value,** while the cost less depreciation-to-date is referred to as its **net book value.**

Transaction no. 16. Estimated federal and state income taxes paid during the year amounted to $600. At fiscal year-end an additional $2,300 in taxes were due on the income actually earned during the year:

```
Dr. Income Tax Expense (E/RE) . . . . . . . . (inc.) 2,900
   Cr. Cash (A). . . . . . . . . . . . . . . . . . . . . . . . . . . . . .     (dec.)  600
   Cr. Income Taxes Payable (L) . . . . . . . . . . . . . . . .     (inc.) 2,300
```

Transaction no. 17. Cash dividends of $2,000 were declared and paid:

```
Dr. Dividends Declared (COE). . . . . . . . . . (inc.) 2,000
   Cr. Cash (A). . . . . . . . . . . . . . . . . . . . . . . . . . . . .     (dec.) 2,000
```

Repeating an earlier observation, **dividends** are not considered to be an expense of the business but are understood to be distributions of profits to owners. As such, a dividend declaration affects only the balance sheet—a distribution of the income that is added to retained earnings for the year. The Dividends Declared account is a **contra owners' equity** (COE) account, and when the accounts for the year are closed, it is netted to the Retained Earnings account as a partial offset to the earnings for the year.

We can now derive the individual account balances for Blue Ridge Hardware as of March 31, 2000. We will have established a separate account for each specific asset, liability, owners' equity, revenue, and expense account. Together, these accounts form the **chart of accounts** for Blue Ridge Hardware. Because April 1, 1999, was the first day of operations, the beginning balance in each account is $0. Second, we post each entry in the appropriate account and then determine the fiscal year-end balance of each account. The resulting preclosing account balances are shown in Exhibit 3.2.

To verify that the company's accounts are in balance, we can prepare a trial balance using the account balances in Exhibit 3.2. As Exhibit 3.3 reveals, the trial balance for Blue Ridge Hardware is in balance, which tells us that equivalent amounts of debits and credits were posted to the accounts.

The next step in the accounting process involves preparing the income statement, which is followed by preparing the closing entries for the temporary accounts. Finally, we will prepare a balance sheet, a statement of owners' equity, and a statement of cash flows. These final steps in the accounting cycle are illustrated sequentially in Exhibit 3.4 through Exhibit 3.8. Visualize the management of Blue Ridge Hardware as they study the account balances in the trial balance, as they think about the kinds of transactions summarized in each account, and as they decide how the accounts should be displayed in the financial statements. With this simplified example, the process is relatively easy: The income statement is prepared from the revenue and expense accounts or from an analysis of the entries flowing through the retained earnings account during the year. (And the revenue and expense accounts are closed out, ready to start another year.) The balance sheet is prepared using the balances in the asset, liability, and owners' equity accounts at the end of the year. The statement of cash flows is prepared from an analysis of the entries flowing through the cash account during the year. Although this is a simplified example, it demonstrates clearly how the preparation of the financial statements flows directly from the accounting system.

Obviously, the accounting system at Procter & Gamble is much more complex, although it works in much the same way as the system we have described for Blue Ridge Hardware. More importantly, the process of preparing the financial statements from a trial balance is more difficult because there will be many more reporting questions to be addressed. Management must decide which accounts can be combined, which should be presented as separate line items on the statements, and which accounts must be broken down into more detail. The objective of this process is to be sure that the financial statements include enough information to present a fair picture of the company without obscuring reality and without too much detail.

EXHIBIT 3.1

Blue Ridge Hardware Co.
Ledger Accounts
For the Fiscal Year Ended March 31, 2000

Balance Sheet Accounts:

Assets

Cash

4-1-99	0		
(1)	10,000	(4)	10,000
(3)	7,500	(10)	53,600
(6)	29,800	(11)	3,600
(9)	40,500	(12)	14,600
		(13)	450
		(14)	900
		(16)	600
		(17)	2,000
	87,800		85,750
3-31-00	2,050		

Accounts Receivable

4-1-99	0		
(7)	44,700	(9)	40,500
	44,700		40,500
3-31-00	4,200		

Merchandise Inventory

4-1-99	0		
(5)	57,400	(8)	44,700
3-31-00	12,700		

Store Equipment

4-1-99	0		
(4)	10,000		
3-31-00	10,000		

Accumulated Depreciation: Store Equipment

		4-1-99	0
		(15)	1,000
		3-31-00	1,000

= Liabilities

Accounts Payable

		4-1-99	0
(10)	53,600	(5)	57,000
		3-31-00	3,800

Utilities Payable

		4-1-99	0
		(13)	200
		3-31-00	200

Bank Loan Payable

		4-1-99	0
		(3)	7,500
		3-31-00	7,500

Wages Payable

		4-1-99	0
		(12)	700
		3-31-00	700

Income Taxes Payable

		4-1-99	0
		(16)	2,300
		3-31-00	2,300

+ Owners' Equity

Capital Stock

		4-1-99	0
		(1)	10,000
		3-31-00	10,000

Retained Earnings

		4-1-99	0

Dividends Declared

4-1-99	0		
(17)	2,000		
3-31-00	2,000		

Income Statement Accounts:

Sales Revenue

4-1-99	0
(6)	29,800
(7)	44,700
	74,500

Cost of Merchandise Sold

4-1-99	0
(8)	44,700
	44,700

Wage Expense

4-1-99	0
(12)	15,300
	15,300

Income Tax Expense

4-1-99	0
(16)	2,900
	2,900

Interest Expense

4-1-99	0
(14)	900
	900

Rent Expense

4-1-99	0
(11)	3,600
	3,600

Utilities Expense

4-1-99	0
(13)	650
	650

Depreciation Expense

4-1-99	0
(15)	1,000
	1,000

EXHIBIT 3.3

Blue Ridge Hardware Co.
Trial Balance as of
March 31, 2000

Account Title	Debit Balance	Credit Balance
Cash	$ 2,050	
Accounts Receivable	4,200	
Merchandise Inventory	12,700	
Store Equipment	10,000	
Accumulated Depreciation		$1,000
Accounts Payable		3,800
Wages Payable		700
Utilities Payable		200
Income Taxes Payable		2,300
Bank Loan Payable		7,500
Capital Stock		10,000
Retained Earnings		0
Dividends Declared	2,000	
Sales		74,500
Cost of Merchandise Sold	44,700	
Rent Expense	3,600	
Wage Expense	15,300	
Utilities Expense	650	
Income Tax Expense	2,900	
Interest Expense	900	
Depreciation Expense	1,000	
Total	$100,000	$100,000

EXHIBIT 3.4

Blue Ridge Hardware Co.
Income Statement
For the Year Ended March 31, 2000

Net revenues		$74,500
Less: Cost of merchandise sold		(44,700)
Gross margin		29,800
Less: Operating expenses		
Rent expense	$ 3,600	
Wage expense	15,300	
Utilities expense	650	
Depreciation expense	1,000	
		(20,550)
Income from operations		9,250
Less: Interest expense		(900)
Income before taxes		8,350
Less: Federal and state income taxes		(2,900)
Net income		$5,450
Net income per share (10,000 shares outstanding)		$0.545

EXHIBIT 3.5

Blue Ridge Hardware Co.
Closing Entries as of
March 31, 2000

To close the revenue accounts:
Dr. Sales Revenue (R/*RE*) . . . . (dec.)   74,500
  Cr. Retained Earnings (OE) . . . . (inc.)   74,500

To close the expense accounts:
Dr. Retained Earnings (OE). . . . . (dec.)   69,050
  Cr. Cost of Merchandise Sold (E/*RE*) . . . . (dec.)   44,700
  Cr. Rent Expense (E/*RE*) . . . . (dec.)   3,600
  Cr. Wage Expense (E/*RE*) . . . . (dec.)   15,300
  Cr. Utilities Expense (E/*RE*) . . . . (dec.)   650
  Cr. Interest Expense (E/*RE*) . . . . (dec.)   900
  Cr. Depreciation Expense (E/*RE*) . . . . (dec.)   1,000
  Cr. Income Tax Expense (E/*RE*) . . . . (dec.)   2,900

To close the Dividends Declared account:
Dr. Retained Earnings (OE). . . . . (dec.)   2,000
  Cr. Dividends Declared (COE) . . . . (dec.)   2,000

EXHIBIT 3.6

Blue Ridge Hardware Co.
Balance Sheet
As of March 31, 2000

Assets		Equities	
Current assets:		Current liabilities:	
Cash	$ 2,050	Accounts payable	$ 3,800
Accounts receivable	4,200	Wages payable	700
Merchandise inventory	12,700	Utilities payable	200
Total current assets	$18,950	Income tax payable	2,300
		Total current liabilities	$ 7,000
Noncurrent assets:			
Store equipment	10,000	Noncurrent liabilities:	
Less:		Bank loan payable	7,500
Accumulated depreciation	(1,000)	Total liabilities	$14,500
Total noncurrent assets	$ 9,000		
		Owners' equity:	
Total assets	$27,950	Capital stock	10,000
		Retained earnings	3,450
			13,450
		Total liabilities and owners' equity	$27,950

EXHIBIT 3.7

Blue Ridge Hardware Co.
Statement of Owners' Equity
As of March 31, 2000

	Capital Stock		
	Shares	Dollars	Retained Earnings
At April 1, 1999	0	0	0
Stock sales	10,000	$10,000	
Net income for the year			$5,450
Dividends declared			(2,000)
At March 31, 2000	10,000	$10,000	$3,450

EXHIBIT 3.8

Blue Ridge Hardware Co.
Statement of Cash flows
For the year Ended March 31, 2000

Operating activities:	
Net income	$ 5,450
Add: Depreciation on store equipment	1,000
	$6,450
Adjustments for:	
Accounts receivable	$ (4,200)
Merchandise inventory	(12,700)
Accounts payable	3,800
Wages payable	700
Utilities payable	200
Income tax payable	2,300
Cash flow from operating activities	$ (3,450)
Investing activities	
Purchase of store equipment	$(10,000)
Cash flow from investing activities	$(10,000)
Financing activities	
Cash dividends paid	$ (2,000)
Proceeds from bank loan	7,500
Sale of capital stock	10,000
Cash flow from financing activities	$15,500
Increase in cash	$ 2,050
Cash, beginning of year	0
Cash, end of year	$ 2,050

To put you in the mind of the Blue Ridge Hardware owners, study the trial balance and the accounts (Exhibits 3.2 and 3.3) and see how those data were used in creating the financial statements in Exhibits 3.4, 3.6, 3.7, and 3.8. Think about the presentation of these statements, and ask yourself whether you might have made different decisions. (Should we have reported sales in two segments—as cash sales and credit sales? Should we describe our inventory in different categories, such as household items, hardware items, and so forth? Was it necessary to spell out all of the changes in the balance sheet accounts in the determination of cash flow from operations?) And then think about what those financial statements tell you about the operations. To take the process further and ensure that you understand the closing entry process and the linkage between net income and retained earnings, we suggest that you post the journal entries from Exhibit 3.5 to the accounts in Exhibit 3.2. After this posting, all temporary accounts should have a zero ending balance, and the net income of Blue Ridge Hardware will have been transferred to Retained Earnings.

Analysis of Blue Ridge Hardware Co.

Now that the accounting process is complete and the financial reports of Blue Ridge Hardware have been prepared, let us briefly consider what these reports reveal about the enterprise. First, Exhibit 3.4, the income statement, indicates that for the year ended March 31, 2000, Blue Ridge Hardware earned net income of $5,450 on net revenues of $74,500. Because most companies have more expenses than can be justified by the volume of sales during their initial building years, they often lose money during their first year (or years) of operations. With that perspective, it is encouraging that Blue Ridge Hardware achieved a positive net income—its sales volume exceeded its cost of operations. Exhibit 3.7 reveals that, on the basis of these earnings, the enterprise also declared and paid a dividend in the amount of $2,000. And because the full amount of net income for the period was not distributed as a dividend, the owners' investment in the enterprise grew by $3,450. Several important points merit noting. First, the net increase in retained earnings is matched by an equal net increase in the aggregate asset accounts, although it is impossible to find the exact, complementary matching increases. Second, dividends are not reported as an expense of the business on the income statement but instead as a distribution of the company's income to its stockholders. Third, to the extent that the income for the period is not distributed as dividends, it has the same effect as if the owners had invested that amount of new funds in the enterprise.

With respect to the financial condition of the enterprise, Exhibit 3.6, the balance sheet, reveals that at year-end Blue Ridge Hardware has the following:

- Total assets (and aggregate liabilities and, owners' equity) of $27,950.
- Total liabilities of $14,500.
- Owners' equity of $13,450.

The owners' equity, or the company's **net worth,** is the value that would remain if all assets could be converted to cash at their balance sheet values and then used to satisfy all existing liabilities. The liquidation of a company, however, is a rare event, and it is also unlikely that the cash liquidation values of the assets would exactly equal their book value. Consequently, an alternative description of owner's equity or net worth is to say that it is the **net book value** of all assets minus the book value of all liabilities.

The balance sheet also reveals that Blue Ridge Hardware has current assets totaling $18,950, which exceeds not only its total current liabilities of $7,000 but also the sum of current and noncurrent liabilities (that is, $14,500). This indicates that the enterprise is relatively secure in terms of its ability to pay off its outstanding obligations. Finally, Exhibit 3.8, the statement of cash flows, reveals that the enterprise generated a net cash inflow from financing activities in the amount of $15,500 and spent $10,000 in cash on investing activities. An additional $3,450 was spent in support of the company's operations, leaving a net cash balance of $2,050 at year end. To ensure the continued success of the enterprise, it is important for Blue Ridge Hardware to become a net positive generator of cash flows from operations. Clearly, the company will be viable only if the cash flows from operating activities become consistently positive.

SUMMARY

The purpose of this chapter has been to discuss and illustrate the accounting process used in preparing accounting reports. This process involves several distinct activities: analyzing business transactions to assess their financial effect on the assets, liabilities, and owners' equity of an enterprise; recording this analysis in various data files; verifying the accuracy of the recording process; and, finally, preparing and analyzing the financial statements.

Although it is important for you to understand how accounting reports are prepared and how the accounting system operates, our principal goal is to ensure that you understand fully how accounting reports communicate and what they reveal about the operations and financial condition of the enterprise. With that objective in mind, in the chapters that follow we focus not on the process of financial statement preparation but on analyzing important business transactions for the purpose of understanding what information the accounting statements convey.

NEW CONCEPTS AND TERMS

Accounts	Dividends
Accounting cycle	Double-entry accounting system
Adjusting entries	Entry
Balance	Executory agreement
Book value	Information system
Chart of accounts	Net book value
Closing	Net worth
Closing entries	Permanent accounts
Contra asset account	Posting
Contra owners' equity	T-accounts
Credit	Temporary accounts
Debit	Trial balance

ASSIGNMENTS

3.1. Statement preparation. Prill Corporation's December 31, 1999, trial balance contained the following account balances. Prepare an income statement, a balance sheet, and a statement of stockholders' equity for the Prill Corporation as of December 31, 1999.

Accounts Payable: $27,900
Advertising Expense: $5,000
Cash: $1,800
Dividends Paid: $1,000
Income Tax Expense: $6,000
Interest Expense: $2,000
Building (net): $29,700
Depreciation Expense: $1,200
Notes Payable: $6,500
Office Salaries Expense: $19,000
Office Supplies Used: $2,000
Salaries Payable: $500

Accounts Receivable: $19,000
Capital Stock: $60,000
Cost of Goods Sold: $243,000
Sales: $292,000
Income Tax Payable: $3,000
Land: $44,000
Merchandise Inventory: $29,000
Long-Term Debt: $11,000
Notes Receivable: $5,200
Office Supplies Inventory: $1,000
Retained Earnings, 1/1/99: $8,000

3.2. Transaction analysis. For each of the following events note what account should be debited or credited and whether the account is increased or decreased.

Events	Debit	Credit
a. Sold additional shares of capital stock.		
b. Signed a loan to buy delivery truck.		
c. Purchased supplies for cash.		
d. Rendered services and collected cash for those services.		
e. Rendered services to customers who agreed to pay for those services later.		
f. Purchased supplies on account.		
g. Paid utility bill.		
h. Paid office rent.		
i. Collected cash from customers for whom services were previously performed.		
j. Paid interest on the loan.		
k. Used supplies in connection with performing services.		
l. Repaid part of the bank loan principal.		
m. Paid cash dividends to stockholders.		

3.3. Transaction analysis and T-accounts. The following are selected accounts and account balances of the TAP Company on June 30, 1999:

	Balance
Account	**Debit (Credit)**
Cash	$ 125,230
Accounts Receivable	230,520
Office Equipment	358,600
Accumulated Depreciation	(105,400)
Notes Payable	(34,000)
Accounts Payable	(35,000)
Sales Revenue	(478,720)
Sales Discounts	24,000
Gain on Sale of Office Equipment	(4,000)
Inventory	219,340
Purchase Discounts	(2,220)
Cost of Sales	287,232

In addition, the TAP Company entered into the following transactions during the month of July 1999.

July 6	Sold for $7,000 some office equipment that had originally cost $20,000; accumulated depreciation taken to date on the equipment totaled $15,000.
July 7	Sales transactions in the amount of $20,000 were completed, on account, with terms of 2/10, net 30.
July 10	Purchased $10,000 worth of merchandise inventory for cash.
July 15	Purchased a new word processing system costing $40,000, paying $15,000 down and signing a 90-day note, with interest at 10 percent for the balance.
July 16	Received payment of $19,600 for the July 7 sales transactions.
July 19	Completed sales transactions for cash in the amount of $42,000.
July 20	Purchased $26,000 worth of merchandise inventory on account with terms of 2/10, net 30.
July 22	Returned $2,000 worth of defective merchandise from the July 20 purchase for a credit to TAP's account.
July 27	Paid the remaining balance of July 20 purchase less an appropriate discount.

Required:

Analyze and record the above transactions in journal entry form and then determine the July 31 account balances using T-accounts.

3.4. Account analysis. The T-account here depicts a number of transactions that increased and decreased the cash account of Cassidy, Inc., during 1999.

Cash (A)

1-1-99	Balance	–0–	(E)	Paid for store equip.	9,000
(A)	From capital stock	12,500	(F)	Cash sales returned	1,000
(B)	Bank loan	11,500	(G)	Paid mdse. suppliers	55,000
(C)	Cash sales	32,800	(H)	Paid rent	4,800
(D)	Collections of receiv.	43,000	(I)	Paid employees	16,000
			(J)	Paid utilities	600
			(K)	Paid est. income tax	1,000
			(L)	Paid other expenses	900
			(M)	Paid on bank loan—On principal $2,000 interest $600	2,600
			(N)	Paid dividends	2,000
12-31-99	Balance	6,900			

Required:

For each of the identified entries (A through N), prepare a one- or two-sentence explanation of the event that caused the transaction. Be sure that your explanation describes the other account that would have been affected by the entry.

3.5. Event analysis. The accounting records of the Floyd Corporation include the following entries:

(a)	Dr. Accounts Receivable (A)	(inc.) 70,400	
	Cr. Revenue (R)		(inc.) 70,400
(b)	Dr. Cash (A)	(inc.) 78,960	
	Cr. Accounts Receivable (A)		(dec.) 78,960
(c)	Dr. Operating Expenses (E)	(inc.) 720	
	Cr. Supplies on Hand (A)		(dec.) 720
(d)	Dr. Equipment (A)	(inc.) 2,720	
	Cr. Cash (A)		(dec.) 2,720
(e)	Dr. Accounts Payable (L)	(dec.) 2,560	
	Cr. Cash (A)		(dec.) 2,560
(f)	Dr. Notes Payable (L)	(dec.) 20,000	
	Dr. Interest Expense (E)	(inc.) 160	
	Cr. Cash (A)		(dec.) 20,160
(g)	Dr. Dividends (COE)	(inc.) 12,800	
	Cr. Cash (A)		(dec.) 12,800

Required:

For each entry, prepare a one-sentence description of the underlying event.

3.6. Event analysis. The accounting records of Cecil, Inc., include the following entries:

(a)	Dr. Rent Expense (E)	(inc.) 4,500	
	Cr. Prepaid Rent (A)		(dec.) 4,500
(b)	Dr. Unearned Passenger Revenue (L)	(dec.) 27,000	
	Cr. Passenger Revenue (R)		(inc.) 27,000
(c)	Dr. Salaries Expense (E)	(inc.) 4,950	
	Cr. Salaries Payable (L)		(inc.) 4,950
(d)	Dr. Repairs and Maintenance Expense (E)	(inc.) 7,800	
	Cr. Accounts Payable (L)		(inc.) 7,800
(e)	Dr. Repairs and Maintenance Expense (E)	(inc.) 5,550	
	Cr. Spare Parts on Hand (A)		(dec.) 5,550
(f)	Dr. Accounts Receivable (A)	(inc.) 3,800	
	Cr. Office Equipment (A)		(dec.) 3,800
(g)	Dr. Land (A)	(inc.) 24,500	
	Cr. Cash (A)		(dec.) 2,450
	Cr. Notes Payable (L)		(inc.) 22,050
(h)	Dr. Cash (A)	(inc.) 6,900	
	Cr. Accounts Receivable (A)		(dec.) 6,900
(i)	Dr. Cash (A)	(inc.) 12,000	
	Cr. Capital Stock (OE)		(inc.) 12,000

Required:

For each entry, prepare a one-sentence description of the underlying event.

3.7. More complex events and the affected accounts. Consider the following series of events that were part of the activities of the OnTime Manufacturing Company during 1999:

a. On June 30, 1999, the treasurer called the company's banker and asked her to buy a Treasury bill, debiting the company's account. The bill cost $100,000 and carried an interest rate of 10 percent, the interest to be paid at maturity. At December 31, 1999, the company still had the investment.

b. On March 31, 1999, the company bought a lift truck to help move material around in the factory. The truck cost $25,000, but the dealer agreed to finance $20,000 of the purchase price. The company signed a five-year note for $20,000, at 10 percent interest, with interest payable quarterly and principal payable in five equal annual installments.

c. To prepare for a substantial expansion, the company sold $10,000,000 of 10-year, 8 percent bonds on October 1, 1999. An investment banker helped put together the offering document, and an attorney researched the legal aspects of the offering. The total of the professional fees paid to these two firms was $75,000. The bonds require semiannual interest payments and require that the principal be paid in full at maturity.

d. The company owned a piece of land next to its main plant, which they intended to use for the expansion discussed in point (c). During December 1999 the company paid an engineering company $50,000 to make soil tests on the land and paid an architect $50,000 for a preliminary drawing of the anticipated new plant expansion. By the time December 31, 1999, had come, however, the economy had softened substantially, and there was now considerable question as to whether the market was really ready to buy more of the company's products. The expansion plans were put on the back burner for at least a year.

Required:

For each of these events, describe the nature of the accounts that would be affected (asset, liability, owners' equity, revenue or expense) at the date of the event and as of December 31, 1999. In the context of the basic accounting equation, explain the rationale for each answer.

3.8. Transaction analysis: The Bash Company.* The Bash Company, a Charlottesville, Virginia, retailer, was formed on July 1, 1999. During the month of July, the corporation experienced 11 different business transactions. At the end of the month, Bash prepared the following trial balance:

Bash Company
Trial Balance
July 31, 1999

Account	Debit (Left)	Credit (Right)
Cash	$103,000	
Accounts Receivable	6,500	
Allowance for Doubtful Accounts		$ 600
Inventory	10,000	
Equipment (net of $500 depreciation taken to date)	119,500	
Accounts Payable		50,000
Loan Payable (10 annual payments)		120,000
Interest Payable		1,000
Salaries Payable		8,000
Capital Stock		50,000
Retained Earnings		?
	$239,000	$?

Transaction Number	Accounts Affected	Dollar Effect	
		Debit (Left)	Credit (Right)
1			
2			
3			
4			
5			
6			
7			
8			
9			
10			
11			

Required:

Based on the data contained in the trial balance:

a. Fill in the spaces with question marks with the appropriate amounts.

b. Use the above chart to prepare the accounting entries for the 11 transactions that occurred during July. The transactions may be recorded in any order.

Note the following:

1. All sales were on account.

2. All asset purchases were on credit, and no payments were made against these liabilities during the month.

3. No cash was paid for any of the expenses incurred during the month.

4. Because of an unexpected occurrence, one account receivable (totaling $500) was written off during the month.

3.9. Transaction analysis: Denver Wholesale Sporting Goods, Inc.* Below is a partial list of business events entered into by Denver Wholesale Sporting Goods, Inc., during the first fiscal quarter of 1999. Determine how each event, as of the date it occurred, would be recognized, if at all, in the 1999 financial statements. If the event should not be recognized, write NOT RECOGNIZED. If the event should be recognized now for financial-reporting purposes, indicate how (e.g., + or –) and by what dollar amount each of the following financial statement components would be affected (if there is no change in a particular column, leave that space blank): Cash, Net Current Assets (current assets minus current liabilities), Total Assets, Net Assets (total assets minus total liabilities), and Net Income.

M = Million
(Enter + or – and dollar amount or NOT RECOGNIZED)

	Cash	Net Current Assets	Total Assets	Net Assets	Net Income
Sold capital stock for $3M.	+3M	+3M	+3M	+3M	
a. Purchased $8M of merchandise on account.					
b. Sold merchandise for $5M cash (entry for sales only).					
c. Recognized $4M cost of merchandise just sold (entry for cost only).					
d. Borrowed $4M cash, issuing a 90-day, 10% note.					
e. Repaid $4M loan (**d** above) plus $0.1M interest (for 90 days).					
f. Received an order for $3M of merchandise to be shipped next quarter.					
g. Collected a $0.5M account receivable.					
h. Bought equipment for $1M cash.					

i.   Signed a year's rental
      agreement for office
      space for $0.1M a
      month.

      _____ _____ _____ _____ _____

j.   Sold for $0.4M cash a
      long-term stock
      investment that had
      cost $0.5M (in prior
      years, the investment's
      market value fluctuated
      between $0.6M and
      $0.7M).

      _____ _____ _____ _____ _____

k.   Paid cash dividends of
      $0.2M.

      _____ _____ _____ _____ _____

l.   The company has been
      told that its warehouse
      and material-handling
      equipment shown at
      $10M net would cost
      $15M if replaced today.

      _____ _____ _____ _____ _____

m. Paid a $0.3M account
      payable.

      _____ _____ _____ _____ _____

n.   Recognized $0.4M annual
      depreciation on
      equipment.

      _____ _____ _____ _____ _____

o.   Bought a $6M machine,
      paying $2M in cash and
      signing a 10-year note
      for the balance.

      _____ _____ _____ _____ _____

p.   The board of directors
      authorized $10M for
      capital expenditures to
      be made next year.

      _____ _____ _____ _____ _____

q.   Received notice of a
      lawsuit against the
      company for $1M.

      _____ _____ _____ _____ _____

r.   Sold a machine that had a
      book value of $1.5M for
      $2.0M cash.

      _____ _____ _____ _____ _____

s.   Discovered that, because
      of obsolescence,
      inventory that cost
      $0.8M was estimated to
      have a net realizable
      value of only $0.5M.

      _____ _____ _____ _____ _____

t.   An account receivable of
      $0.2M from a sale
      made during 1998 was
      determined to be
      uncollectible.

      _____ _____ _____ _____ _____

3.10. Transaction analysis: Computer Corner, Inc. In the fall of 1998, Gary Reed inherited $100,000. He promptly quit his job, and he and his wife Connie decided to take $75,000 of the inheritance and start their own business. In January 1999, the Reeds opened Computer Corner, Inc., a small retail computer store. At the end of 1999 the trial balance of Computer Corner, Inc. appeared as follows:

Computer Corner, Inc.
Trial Balance
December 31, 1999

Account	Balance (left) Debit	Balance (right) Credit
Cash	$ 23,700	
Accounts Receivable	39,300	
Allowance for Uncollectible Accounts		$ 4,000
Inventory	65,000	
Prepaid Rent	4,000	
Property and Equipment (Net)	22,500	
Accounts Payable		25,000
Salaries Payable		3,500
Interest Payable		3,000
Loan Payable		30,000
Common Stock		75,000
Retained Earnings		14,000
	$154,500	$154,500

The following information pertains to the business during its first year of operation:

1. Signed a five-year lease in January that stipulated a monthly rent of $4,000.

2. Borrowed $30,000 in January from a local bank. The term of the loan was five years and the interest rate was 10 percent.

3. Cash sales for the year totaled $200,000. Credit sales for the year totaled $180,000.

4. One account receivable in the amount of $500 was written off in November as uncollectible.

5. Inventory purchased during the year totaled $280,000. All inventory purchases were on an accounts payable basis.

6. Purchases of property and equipment for the year totaled $25,000 and were paid in cash.

7. Operating expenses for the year included the following:

Supplies	$ 3,500
Utilities	3,000
Insurance	2,000
Salaries	70,000
Advertising	6,500
	$85,000

Included in the Salaries figure was $50,000 attributable to Gary and Connie Reed.

8. The Reeds withdrew $8,000 during the year that was not salary related.

Required:

Based on the information presented in items 1–8 and on the December 31, 1999, trial balance, prepare the journal entries to record the activities of Computer Corner, Inc., for 1999, *including* the initial investment by the owners. Your entries do not need to be recorded in any particular sequence.

3.11. Transaction analysis* Sandy Lawson had been determined to own her own company after completing her MBA. As an accomplished seamstress, she had always had a little business on the side making clothes for friends and specialty stores. The success of the Cabbage Patch dolls convinced her that there was money in stuffed toys. She decided that there was an unexploited niche for a family of animals, each having its own personality.

She took the savings of $7,044 that she had accumulated over the year and, with $263 worth of materials, set out to realize her dreams. Her family was very supportive and lent her $6,000 on a short-term note. She used $3,000 of this to purchase the specialized sewing equipment that she needed to make the animals.

From her years in the clothing business, she managed to find a supplier willing to let her have 90 days credit and invested in an additional $7,364 of materials on 90-day credit terms. Her own car was on its last legs, so she purchased a good secondhand pickup truck for $6,600 that she financed through a bank with a $1,600 deposit. A member of the family had an unused garage where she could set up her equipment. Installation of the equipment cost her $1,053. A year's insurance to cover the equipment cost an additional $1,000. A variety of different supplies necessary to get her operations off the ground absorbed another $963.

By the end of the first six months she had made a substantial payment to her supplier, leaving a balance owed of $3,726 in the account. Sales had gone well and brought in a very welcome and reassuring inflow of cash totaling $12,325. She attributed these sales partly to the advertisement that she had run in a trade magazine, which had cost her $2,442.

Although she had not been able to repay her family or the bank any of the capital that they had lent her, she had paid the family $360 in interest. Wages had totaled $10,697.

While everyone else headed off for New Year's Eve parties, Sandy Lawson sat down at her desk to determine how well her business had done in the first six months of its life. She had worked extremely hard making stuffed toy animals and was proud of the different personalities that she had been able to create. They surrounded her on all sides as she pored over the numbers.

The results, as she figured them, were very pleasing to her. They appear below.

Garland Creations
Income Statement
For the Six Months Just Ended

Revenue		$12,325
Opening inventory	$ 263	
Purchases	7,364	
Wages	10,697	
Prepaid expenses	2,053	
Supplies	963	
Total	21,340	
Less: Closing inventory	16,005	
Cost of goods sold		5,335
Gross margin		6,990
Advertising expenses		2,442
Interest expense		360
Net income		$ 4,188

* This case was prepared by Michael F. van Breda. Copyright 1988 by Michael F. van Breda. Reprinted with permission.

Garland Creations
Balance Sheet
As of the End of the Six Months
Just Ended

Cash	$ 616
Inventory	16,005
Current assets	$16,621
Equipment	3,000
Truck	6,600
Total assets	$26,221
Accounts payable	$ 3,726
Notes payable	6,000
Current liabilities	$ 9,726
Bank loan	5,000
Capital	7,307
Retained earnings	4,188
Total equities	$26,221

Required:

a. Using the description of events in the case and the financial statements provided, replicate the journal entries and the T-accounts Sandy prepared to record the first six months of her business.

b. Where you believe it appropriate, adjust her accounting to better reflect the events. Revise her statements accordingly.

c. Comment on how well the business has done.

3.12. Overview of the accounting cycle* Photovoltaics, Inc., is a Texas-based manufacturer and distributor of photovoltaic solar energy units. The company was founded in 1990 by Arthur Manelas and Harry Linn. Manelas, formerly a research scientist with NASA, had been operating a small photovoltaic manufacturing company in Massachusetts when Linn, a marketing consultant to industry and himself an owner of a solar energy company in Oregon, proposed the joint venture.

The founders planned to take advantage of a major shift in consumer attitudes from fossil fuel energy production to cleaner, cheaper energy generation using wind, water, or sun. The joint venture would merge Linn's marketing experience and access to capital with Manelas' prior manufacturing knowledge and government patent on the photovoltaic unit.

The development of photovoltaic technology had begun in 1954 when scientists at the Bell Laboratories found that crystals of silicon could turn sunlight into electricity. The scientists observed that an electric current was produced when photons, or light energy, would strike silicon atoms, thereby causing electrons to be released. The first application of this technology involved the U.S. space program; NASA used photovoltaic solar cells to power the Vanguard I satellite in 1958.

Today photovoltaic cells are used to power buoys in shipping channels, transmitters on mountain tops, and communication equipment on offshore drilling platforms. In remote locations in Indonesia, Africa, and Australia, where electrical service neither exists nor is cost justified, photovoltaic arrays are used to generate electricity to power such life-sustaining equipment as water pumps and medical refrigerators storing vaccines.

Compared with power generated from such traditional sources as hydroelectric-, coal-, or oil-fueled plants, early photovoltaic arrays were prohibitively expensive (e.g., $2,000 per peak watt). Recent technological advances, however, made the cells so efficient and economical (i.e., $0.185 per peak watt) that they were now competitive with existing alternative energy sources. Elmer B. Kaelin,

---

* This case was prepared by Kenneth R. Ferris. Copyright 1990 by Kenneth R. Ferris.

president of the Potomac Edison Company, warned utility executives that the day was quickly approaching when "homeowners will have every incentive to install solar collectors and pull the plug on the electric company."

Convinced that excellent market opportunities for the solar arrays existed, Linn began preparing a prospectus that could be used to help raise capital to significantly expand Manelas's current operations. The two founders had located a manufacturing facility in Lowell, Massachusetts, that would cost approximately $8 million to acquire and equip with updated production equipment. Based on his prior experience, Linn knew that prospective investors would expect to see the following:

- A statement of financial position classifying the company's assets and equities as they would appear at the preproduction stage.

- A pro forma earnings statement for the first year of operations.

- A pro forma balance sheet as it would appear at the end of the first year of operations.

- A pro forma cash flow statement for the first year of operations.

In anticipation of preparing these reports, Linn collected the following information and arrived at the following projections:

Data related to preproduction transactions

1. Ten million shares of common stock (par value $1) were authorized for sale by the charter of incorporation. Manelas received 500,000 shares in exchange for rights to the photovoltaic patent, and Linn received an equal number of shares after capitalizing the firm with $500,000 in personal funds.

2. Incorporation and attorney's fees amounted to $27,000.

3. The $8 million purchase price of the manufacturing facility and equipment was to be allocated as follows: building—$4.5 million, land—$750,000, and equipment—$2.75 million. In addition, raw materials and partially completed solar units had been purchased on credit from Manelas's original manufacturing company at a cost of $1.3 million. A note, secured by the inventory itself and accruing interest at a rate of 10 percent per annum on the unpaid balance, was issued to Manelas.

Projected data

4. Sales of common stock to independent investors and venture capitalists would total 2.5 million shares. A selling price of $3.25 per share was set, and transaction costs of 1.5 percent of the stock proceeds were projected.

5. Revenues from the sale of solar arrays for the first year were projected to be $480,000, with one-fifth of this amount estimated to be uncollected by year-end. The company had decided to follow a particularly rigid credit policy until operations were well established; hence, no provision for bad debts would be established because no uncollectible accounts were anticipated.

6. Cash purchases of raw materials were estimated at $70,000; the cost of units sold was projected at $215,000.

7. Insurance on the building, equipment, and inventory was expected to cost $2,700 per year.

8. Labor costs were estimated at $72,000; selling and administrative costs were projected at 2 percent of gross sales.

9. The useful life of the acquired assets were estimated as follows:

Building: 20 years
Equipment: 10 years

Linn decided to write the patent off over its legal life of 17 years and the organizational costs (i.e., incorporation and attorney fees) over five years.

10. Salaries to Linn and Manelas were set at $20,000 each for the first year.

11. No principal repayments would be made on the 10 percent notes issued to Manelas during the first year of operations.

12. Income taxes would be calculated as follows:

Income Level	Tax Rate
$0–50,000	15%
50,001–75,000	25
75,001–100,000	34
100,001–335,000	39
335,001–above	34

The company would be required to pay 80 percent of its taxes by year-end.

13. Fifty percent of net income after taxes would be distributed to investors as dividends.

Required:

a. Consider the informational needs of a developing company. Design an efficient accounting system for Photovoltaics, Inc. What accounts would be needed?

b. Prepare the three accounting statements needed for the prospectus.

c. As a prospective investor in the company, what factors would you look for in the accounting statements to help you decide whether to invest in the venture?

3.13. Some unusual applications of accrual accounting

a. The 1994 annual report from CPC International, a large food company, includes the following footnote (dollars in millions):

Restructuring charge

In June 1994 the company recorded a charge of $227 million, $137 million after taxes or $0.92 per common share, to recognize the cost of restructuring. This program compresses into a period from mid-1994 to mid-1996 restructuring activities needed to meet the competitive challenge of increasingly unifying markets throughout the world.

   The majority of the charge relates to the company's European and North American consumer foods business. The restructuring charge and its utilization are summarized below:

$ Millions	Total Charge	Utilized in 1994	To Be Utilized in Future Periods
Employee severance	$102	$ 12	$ 90
Plant and support facilities	114	114	—
Other	11	—	11
Total	$227	$126	$101

The charge is designed to cover the cost of a phased reduction of about 2,600 employees worldwide and the cost of realignment of manufacturing capacity. The realignment will be achieved through a combination of plant closures, specializations, and relocations of production. In total, 24 consumer foods plants and four corn refining plants will be affected by the restructuring.

The time period for completion of the restructuring is from a few months at some sites to two years in instances where alternative production facilities are to be constructed.

At December 31, 1994, $57 million was included in current liabilities and $44 million was included in noncurrent liabilities.

Required:

How would this restructuring program have been recognized in the company's accounts in 1994? What entries might have been made, and what accounts would have been affected? In what ways was the restructuring program not reflected in the 1994 accounts? Explain the rationale the company might have used to support its combination of accounting and disclosure.

b. IBM Corporation describes its exposure for environmental problems with the following footnote in its 1994 annual report (dollars in millions):

In addition, the company continues to participate in environmental assessments and cleanups at a number of locations, including operating facilities, previously owned facilities, and Superfund sites. The company accrues for all known environmental liabilities for remediation cost when a cleanup program becomes probable and costs can be reasonably estimated. Estimated environmental costs associated with postclosure activities, such as the removal and restoration of chemical storage facilities and monitoring, are accrued when the decision is made to close a facility. The amounts accrued, which are undiscounted and do not reflect any insurance recoveries, were $179 million and $77 million at December 31, 1994 and 1993, respectively. The increase in the accrual relates to expected costs of postclosure activities, reassessment of remediation activities at operating facilities, and participation at additional Superfund sites.

The amounts accrued do not cover sites that are in the preliminary stages of investigation where neither the company's percentage of responsibility nor the extent of cleanup required have been identified. Also excluded is the cost of internal environmental protection programs that are primarily preventive in nature. Estimated environmental costs are not expected to materially impact the financial position or results of the company's operations in future periods. However, environmental cleanup periods are protracted in length, and earnings in future periods are subject to changes in environmental remediation regulations.

Required:
How would this environmental exposure have been recognized in the company's accounts in 1994? What entries might have been made, and what accounts would have been affected? In what ways was the environmental exposure not reflected in the 1994 accounts? Explain the rationale the company might have used to support its combination of accounting and disclosure.

PART II

Using and Understanding
the Basic Financial Statements

CHAPTER 4

The Balance Sheet

The importance of the contents of a company's balance sheet cannot be overemphasized. One of the key characteristics that I look for in a potential acquisition is a company whose stock price does not fully reflect the underlying economic value of its operating assets.[1]

Key Chapter Issues

- What is the balance sheet, and what are its principal elements?
- What are the key accounting concepts and conventions underlying the balance sheet?

- What are the principal methods of valuing a company's assets, liabilities, and shareholders' equity?
- What information does a balance sheet convey about a company's financial health?

---

[1] Harold C. Simmons, Chairman of the Board and CEO, Valhi, Inc.

As defined in Chapter 2, the **balance sheet**, or statement of financial position, is an accounting report that summarizes as of a particular date, the assets a company owned, the liabilities it owed, and the owners' investment—their original investment plus that share of prior years' earnings that have been left with the company. The balance sheet may be thought of as a photograph of the financial status and condition of a company.

The balance sheet, like a photograph, depicts the assets and the equities of a company as of a particular date. To appreciate fully the photograph's color, texture, and tone—that is, to understand the complete image in that picture—the financial statement user must understand the specific elements that compose the balance sheet and how these elements are related. That understanding is the focus of this chapter.

THE ELEMENTS OF THE BALANCE SHEET

The principal elements of a company's balance sheet are its assets, liabilities, and shareholders' (or owners') equity. To provide a context for the discussion of these elements, we will refer to Exhibit 4.1, which presents Procter & Gamble's consolidated balance sheet for 1998 with comparative data for 1997. This statement details the year-end balances for each of Procter & Gamble's principal asset accounts, as well as the principal creditor and owner claims on those assets.

We have said that a balance sheet presents a picture of a company's financial status at a given point in time. Theoretically, a balance sheet could be prepared as of any day of the year. Most companies monitor individual elements of their balance sheet on a daily or weekly basis, but normally the complete financial picture is taken only as of a month-end, a quarter-end, or a year-end. Most companies use a calendar year for their accounting reports, but they are not required to do so. In fact, it is often more logical to use a different 12-month period, referred to as a **fiscal year,** ending after a business peak. Many retail companies, for example, use a fiscal year that ends in February or March because December and January are significant trade periods. As an example, Circuit City Stores, Inc., the largest consumer electronics retail chain in the United States, uses a fiscal year ending on the last day of February. Procter & Gamble, on the other hand, uses June 30 as its fiscal year end, perhaps because its consumer products promotion cycle begins anew as school begins in the fall.

Assets: A Company's Resources

A company's assets are the resources that it owns and that provide future economic benefit to the company (that is, can be deployed to generate a profit). Exhibit 4.1 reveals that Procter & Gamble had more than $30,966 million in assets as of June 30, 1998, placing it 101 in the *Fortune* 500 asset rankings. Procter & Gamble's four principal asset categories are:

- Current Assets
- Property, Plant, and Equipment
- Goodwill and Other Intangible Assets
- Other Noncurrent Assets

Procter & Gamble's **current assets** include the assets that the company expects to sell or consume as part of its operations during the next year. These assets include cash and cash equivalents, investment securities, accounts receivable, inventories, deferred income taxes, prepaid expenses and other current assets. The order of presentation of the current assets is intended to inform the reader of the relative liquidity of the assets. Thus, the most liquid current asset is cash, whereas the least liquid is the prepaid expenses. In the U.S. this format of most-to-least liquid is also followed for the asset category as a whole. Thus, the most liquid assets are listed first with the least liquid assets listed last. In other countries, where financial reports are not quite so creditor-oriented, the assets are listed in the order of their importance to the entity, usually beginning with plant and equipment and ending with the current assets. Many European companies follow that practice.

The item **cash and cash equivalents** refers to funds held in corporate bank accounts, cash on hand at various company locations, and cash invested in short-term financial instruments, such as certificates of deposit. **Investment securities,** on the other hand, are temporary, highly marketable investments that Procter & Gamble has in stocks and/or bonds of other companies, such as IBM or AT&T. When a company has a temporary surplus of cash on hand, it may invest these funds in short-term investments to maximize the return on those funds until they are again needed for operations. Because these short-term investments are readily converted to cash, they are frequently aggregated with cash and cash equivalents and called the **liquid assets** of a company. Under GAAP, those securities will be valued at their market price, as of the balance sheet date. Any gain or loss in market value will be an additional element of investment income, along with interest and dividends on those securities.

The item **accounts receivable** represents the amounts owed to Procter & Gamble by its customers who purchased the company's products on credit but had not, as of year-end, paid for those purchases. Accounts receivable are also frequently called **trade receivables** and usually represent sales whose payments are expected in 30, 60, or 90 days after the customer has received the goods and been billed for them. Under GAAP, credit sales are recognized as revenues in the income statement and as accounts receivable on the balance sheet, in the period where the goods are shipped, following the **accrual method;** that is, the sale is recorded because the selling company has completed its part of the sales transaction and expects to be paid. The asset received in exchange for the goods delivered is a promise to be paid, and thus a receivable is recorded by the selling company. In accounting entry form the application of this concept can be illustrated as follows:

Dr. Accounts Receivable (A) . . . . (inc.) $10,000
Cr. Sales (R) . . . .   (inc.) $10,000

At the time of sale, the receivables are recorded at the cash equivalency that Procter & Gamble expects to receive from the credit sale. When companies make an individual sale on credit, they fully expect to collect the cash. Realistically, however, management also knows that some part of the total receivables yet to be collected will prove to be uncollectible. Therefore, an amount reflecting this estimated uncollectible portion, called the **allowance for uncollectible accounts,** is recorded as a contra asset and deducted from the receivable balance reported on the balance sheet. Because management knows that the uncollectible accounts estimate pertains to credit sales already recorded as revenue, the **matching principle** requires that the current period's earnings be charged with an estimate of the cost of that loss, called the **bad debts expense**. Together, these two important concepts can be illustrated with the following single entry:

EXHIBIT 4.1

Procter & Gamble Company and Subsidiaries
Consolidated Balance Sheet
June 30, 1998 and June 30, 1997

Amounts in Millions Except Per Share Amounts	June 30 1998	1997
ASSETS		
Current Assets		
Cash and cash equivalents	$ 1,549	$ 2,350
Investment securities	857	760
Accounts receivable	2,781	2,738
Inventories		
Materials and supplies	1,225	1,131
Work in process	343	228
Finished goods	1,716	1,728
Deferred income taxes	595	661
Prepaid expenses and other current assets	1,511	1,190
Total Current Assets	10,577	10,786
Property, Plant and Equipment		
Buildings	3,660	3,409
Machinery and equipment	15,953	14,646
Land	539	570
	20,152	18,625
Accumulated depreciation	(7,972)	(7,249)
Total Property, Plant and Equipment	12,180	11,376
Goodwill and Other Intangible Assets		
Goodwill	7,023	3,915
Trademarks and other intangible assets	1,157	1,085
	8,180	5,000
Accumulated amortization	(1,169)	(1,051)
Total Goodwill and Other Intangible Assets	7,011	3,949
Other Non-Current Assets	1,198	1,433
Total Assets	$30,966	$27,544

EXHIBIT 4.1 concluded

Procter & Gamble Company and Subsidiaries
Consolidated Balance Sheet
June 30, 1998 and June 30, 1997

	June 30	
Amounts in Millions Except Per Share Amounts	1998	1997
LIABILITIES AND SHAREHOLDERS' EQUITY		
Current Liabilities		
Accounts payable	$ 2,051	$ 2,203
Accrued and other liabilities	3,942	3,802
Taxes payable	976	944
Debt due within one year	2,281	849
Total Current Liabilities	9,250	7,798
Long-Term Debt	5,765	4,143
Deferred Income Taxes	428	559
Other Non-Current Liabilities	3,287	2,998
Total Liabilities	18,730	15,498
Shareholders' Equity		
Convertible Class A preferred stock,		
stated value $1 per share		
(600 shares authorized)	1,821	1,859
Non-Voting Class B preferred stock,		
stated value $1 per share (200 shares		
authorized; none issued)	—	—
Common stock, stated value $1 per share		
(5,000 shares authorized; shares outstanding:		
1998–1,337.4 and 1997–1,350.8)	1,337	1,351
Additional paid-in capital	907	559
Reserve for employee stock ownership plan debt retirement	(1,616)	(1,634)
Accumulated other comprehensive income	(1,357)	(819)
Retained earnings	11,144	10,730
Total Shareholders' Equity	12,236	12,046
Total Liabilities and Shareholders' Equity	$30,966	$27,544

```
Dr. Bad Debts Expense (E) . . . . . . . . . . . (inc.) $2,000
    Cr. Allowance for Uncollectible Accounts (CA). . . . . .        (inc.) $2,000
```

Because Procter & Gamble says that its financial statements are prepared in accordance with GAAP, we can be sure that an **allowance for doubtful accounts** is maintained as a contra asset to the allowance account. Evidently, the amount of the allowance is not material to the balance in the accounts receivable account so the company simply gives us the net amount.

The item **inventories** refers to the aggregate cost of the salable merchandise owned by Procter & Gamble that is available to meet customer demands. The balance sheet tells us that the Inventory account includes amounts for materials (such as cellulose) and supplies (such as cartons) as well as finished goods (such as Luvs disposable diapers, ready for shipment to wholesalers.) Inventory is recorded on the company's books at its cost, namely the price paid to suppliers plus any additional costs incurred to date to convert the inventory materials or supplies into a final salable condition (or its net realizable value, if lower). The difference between the aggregate cost of the finished goods available for sale and the expected sales price represents Procter & Gamble's potential profit, which under GAAP is not recorded in the financial statements until the merchandise has actually been sold.

Deferred income taxes represent the tax benefit Procter & Gamble expects to realize in the future, from some items that were treated as an expense on the income statement in the past but have not yet been taken as a deduction on the company's tax returns. For example, we will see later that the company has recorded $1,193 million in liabilities for post-retirement benefits (such as health care payments) for its current employees and retirees. Those liabilities were recorded when the health care benefits were earned by the employees, with a debit entry to health care expense and a credit entry to the liability. The benefits will not be deductible on the tax return until they are actually paid to the health care provider. Procter & Gamble expects to realize the benefit of those tax deductions when the health care costs are paid, and so they record that tax benefit today, with a debit entry to this asset and a credit entry reducing tax expense.

The final item in the current assets section of the balance sheet is **prepaid expenses.** These assets involve expenditures for the prepayment of such items as rent, insurance, or taxes. Some contractual arrangements (such as rent and insurance) often require payment in advance; in other arrangements, prepayments may earn certain price discounts from suppliers and therefore simply make good business sense. In either case, prepaid expenses represent past cash outflows for which the company expects to receive some future benefit. Following the allocation principle, which we discussed in Chapter 2, that prepayment will be recorded as an asset when the cash disbursement is made, and an appropriate amount will be removed from the asset account and charged to an expense account, year-by-year, as the future benefits are realized.

In sum, looking at Procter & Gamble's balance sheet, Exhibit 4.1, we see that the current assets are:

	1998	1997
Cash and cash equivalents	$ 1,549	$ 2,350
Investment securities	857	760
Accounts receivable (net of allowance)	2,781	2,738
Inventories (total)	3,284	3,087
Deferred Income taxes	595	661
Prepaid expenses and other current assets	1,511	1,190
Total current assets	$10,577	$10,786

Because this group of Procter & Gamble's assets are clearly identified as *current,* by inference the remaining assets are considered *noncurrent.* **Noncurrent assets** are a company's long-lived resources whose consumption or use will take place over more than one accounting period. These assets are frequently segmented into tangible and intangible assets. **Tangible assets,** like property, plant, and equipment, possess identifiable physical characteristics, whereas **intangible assets,** such as goodwill, do not. Nonetheless, both tangible and intangible assets possess revenue-producing characteristics that make them valuable to a company over future periods.

Among Procter & Gamble's noncurrent assets are property, plant, and equipment; goodwill and other intangible assets; and other noncurrent assets. From Exhibit 4.1, these noncurrent assets are detailed as follows:

	1998	1997
Property, Plant, and Equipment, net	$12,180	$11,376
Goodwill and Other Intangible Assets, net	7,011	3,949
Other Noncurrent Assets	1,198	1,433

Property, plant, and equipment, are those long-lived, tangible assets necessary to conduct a company's basic business operations. For a company such as Procter & Gamble, this category includes its manufacturing equipment and facilities, distribution equipment, and facilities and administrative offices. These assets are often called the **fixed assets** of a company. Like inventory, a company's fixed assets are an integral part of its basic operations, but they differ from inventory in two important respects. First, property, plant, and equipment are not owned for the purpose of being sold to customers. Second, these assets are expected to benefit Procter & Gamble's operations for many years. Because of the extended productive life of these assets, the company's cost of property, plant, and equipment is expensed over the assets' expected useful lives rather than totally in the year of acquisition.

The process of allocating a fixed asset's cost over various years is called **depreciation** and is based on the allocation principle discussed in Chapter 2. When an asset is depreciated, a portion of its original cost is charged to expense, and the other side of the accounting entry increases a contra-asset account. As you will remember from the discussion of Blue Ridge Hardware in Chapter 3, many financial statement users want to know the original cost of plant and equipment; hence, the annual depreciation charge is not deducted from the asset account directly but rather is accumulated in a contra-asset (CA) account referred to as Accumulated Depreciation. The contra-asset account is presented on the asset side of the balance sheet but carries a credit balance.

The accounting entry for depreciation expense appears as follows:

```
Dr. Depreciation Expense (E) . . . . . . . . . (inc.) 30,000
    Cr. Accumulated Depreciation (CA). . . . . . . . . . . .      (inc.) 30,000
```

As reported on the balance sheet, **accumulated depreciation** includes not only the current period's charge to expense but also that portion of the asset's cost that has been allocated (that is, expensed) in prior accounting periods. The Accumulated Depreciation account is deducted from the Property, Plant, and Equipment account in reporting the net fixed assets in the balance sheet. The original cost of an asset less the balance in the Accumulated Depreciation account is called the **net book value** or carrying value of the asset. Procter & Gamble tells us that the acquisition cost of its building was $3,660 million, its machinery and equipment was $15,953 million, and its land was $539 million, all as of June 30, 1988. The accumulated depreciation of all of its buildings, machinery and equipment as of that date was $7,972. Note that land is never depreciated because it is assumed that it will not wear out and it will never need to be replaced.

We will have more to say about the accounting for property, plant, and equipment and about the process of depreciation in Chapter 11. At this point, however, it is helpful to emphasize that accounting for depreciation is intended *only* as a process to allocate prior expenditures to future periods. From an economic standpoint, plant and equipment lose *and* gain value over time as a result of a wide variety of factors. As we noted in Chapter 2, U.S. GAAP accounting is based on original costs and thus does not deal with day-to-day, year-to-year changes in *market values*.[2] Hence, the financial statements do not reflect the impact that economic effects might have on the values of a company's plant and equipment. Again, depreciation is not an attempt to recognize a change in market value, but is simply the process of allocating the original cost of an asset over the future periods expected to benefit from that earlier investment.

Intangible assets are those resources owned by the company that can not be physically sited, such as patents, trade names and other proprietary rights. Like other assets, they are recorded at the cost Procter & Gamble paid to acquire them. Procter & Gamble's most important intangible asset is the goodwill it purchased as part of its acquisition of several other companies. Footnote No. 2 in Procter & Gamble's annual report tells us that in 1998 the company paid a total of $3,269 million to acquire Tambrands, Inc. and several paper businesses. Those 1998 acquisitions resulted in the recording of approximately $3,108 million in goodwill. In an accounting context, goodwill is not the value of Procter & Gamble's well regarded reputation, or the value of its various well-known brands. It is only the difference between the amount Procter & Gamble paid to acquire an existing company and the fair value of the individual, identifiable assets that were acquired in that purchase. Like property, plant, and equipment, the cost of goodwill and other intangible assets is normally allocated over the expected useful life of these assets. The process of allocating the cost of an intangible asset over its useful life is called **amortization.**

The final noncurrent asset category is **other noncurrent assets,** which represent an aggregation of miscellaneous assets that are, individually, immaterial in amount.

Liabilities: A Company's Obligations

As defined in Chapter 2, the liabilities of a company are the monetary measures of its obligations to repay money loaned to it, to pay for goods or services it has received, or to fulfill commitments it has made. In essence, a company's liabilities represent claims on its assets. As with assets, it is convenient to aggregate liabilities into current and noncurrent categories, which delineate the expected repayment period for the liability. Thus, **a current liability** is an obligation due during the next operating cycle or the next year, whichever is longer. A **noncurrent liability** is one that will be paid at some future point in time beyond the next year.

Procter & Gamble's balance sheet shows that the company has four principal liability categories:

- Current Liabilities
- Long-Term Debt
- Deferred Income Taxes
- Other Noncurrent Liabilities

---

[2] In some countries, such as the United Kingdom, the balance sheet value of property, plant, and equipment may be adjusted upward to reflect its current market value.

On the balance sheet itself, Procter & Gamble summarizes its current liabilities into four general categories. Those summary numbers are detailed further in Footnotes No. 3 and No. 4. Bringing that footnoted data forward, we can see the company's current liabilities as follows:

	1998	1997
Accounts payable	$2,051	$2,203
Accrued and other liabilities (detailed in note 3)		
Marketing expenses	1,109	1,129
Compensation expenses	485	461
Other	2,348	2,212
Taxes payable	976	944
Debt due within one year (detailed in note 4)		
U.S. obligations	1,435	183
Foreign obligations	560	343
Current portion of long term debt	286	323
Total Current Liabilities	$9,250	$7,798

The basis for the sequencing of these accounts is not as clear-cut as it is on the asset side of the balance sheet. The sequencing within the current liability section and on the entire right side of the balance sheet is primarily intended to reflect the priority standing of the various creditors (i.e., accounts payable are listed before debt due within one year).

Accounts payable or **trade payables** represent the amounts owed to various suppliers for goods and services purchased on credit but not yet paid. The common business practice of giving a purchaser 30 days to pay results in an account receivable for the seller/supplier and an account payable for the buyer/user. **Accrued marketing expenses** represent the amounts due to advertising agencies and similar service companies providing marketing services to Procter & Gamble. **Accrued compensation expenses** refers to the wages and related employee benefits, such as dental and health care, that Procter & Gamble's employees have earned but that the company has not yet paid. **Other accrued expenses** represent those miscellaneous liabilities of the company that are individually immaterial and therefore do not have to be spelled out in detail. Examples might include accrued interest on borrowed funds or accrued utility costs for last month's telephone usage. **Taxes payable** represent Procter & Gamble's estimate of the income taxes that will be owed to federal, state, local, and foreign authorities when the tax returns for the period are completed sometime in 1999. Under accrual accounting, the balance sheet must reflect all obligations owed as of the date of the statement, even if the exact amounts due are not immediately determinable. Thus, the preparation of the 1998 balance sheet may require that some liabilities, such as the 1998 deferred income taxes, be estimated. **Debt due within one year** includes short-term borrowing from banks or other financial institutions—Procter & Gamble tells us that most of its short term borrowings are from U.S. institutions. **Current portion of long-term debt** represent the portion of long-term bank or other borrowings that are due to be paid within the next year. As an example, the principal portion of a 20-year mortgage that is due to be paid in the next 12 months is classified in the current liabilities section of the balance sheet.

Procter & Gamble's noncurrent liabilities fall into three principal categories: long-term debt, other liabilities, and deferred income taxes. According to Footnote No. 4, the **long-term debt** includes notes, debentures and bank loans, and commercial paper. From Footnote No. 3 we know that the other noncurrent liabilities include post-retirement benefits, pension benefits, and "other." Combining the detail from Footnote No.s 3 and 4 with the information from the face of the balance sheet, we can see that the company's long-term obligations are as follows:

	1998	1997
Long–term debt (from Footnote 4)		
U.S. notes and debentures	$2,897	$2,082
ESOP series A loan	545	613
ESOP series B loan	1,000	1,000
U.S. commercial paper	1,207	585
Foreign obligations	402	186
Current portion of long term debt	(286)	(323)
Deferred Income taxes	428	559
Other Non–current liabilities (from note 3)		
Post-retirement benefits	1,193	1,300
Pension benefits	843	815
Other	1,251	883
Total non–current obligations	$9,480	$7,700

Notes and debentures (and **bonds**) are legal terms describing financial instruments issued to financial institutions or sold to investors to raise funds for a company's expansion of its ongoing operations. These legal instruments carry a specified rate of interest (the **coupon rate**) and a specified repayment date (the **maturity date**), which can be a set of serial dates stretching the re-payment of the principle over a number of years, or it can be a single date with the entire principle amount due in a lump sum payment at the end of the term (a **balloon payment**).

Commercial paper is another financial instrument that a company can use to raise money. Commercial paper is usually issued on 30, 60 or 90 day terms, and is sold to money market funds where individual or corporate investors leave excess cash on deposit for short periods. Typically commercial paper carries a relatively low interest rate, in part because it is so short term and in part because it is only sold by very stable, well-known companies who rely on their reputation to borrow in this very transient market place. Procter & Gamble is allowed to treat their commercial paper as long-term debt because they have a credit line with a group of banks, equal to the maximum amount of commercial paper that would ever be outstanding. The understanding is that if Procter & Gamble's reputation should falter, or if the commercial paper market should dry up, the company could always refinance the commercial paper then outstanding by drawing on that line of credit, and taking out an appropriate amount of long-term bank debt. The bank will charge something to maintain that open line of credit but even with that cost, the use of commercial paper saves the company a great deal of interest.

The ESOP series A and B loans are another clever financing tool. The transactions are a bit convoluted, but in short: The company created both a profit sharing plan and a health benefits plan for its employees. The trustees of those plans purchased convertible preferred stock from the company with the expectation that those investments would provide the cash flows necessary to pay benefits to the employees. To purchase those preferred shares, the trustees borrowed the necessary funds from banks, and the company guaranteed those bank debts. Because the transaction was, in substance, a bank borrowing by the company, the bank debt appears in Procter & Gamble's long-term debt. There are two entries as a result of the ESOP transaction—the first is to record the sale of the preferred stock and the receipt of cash, and the second is to recognize the reality of the company's involvement in the bank borrowing.

The entries are as follows:

```
Dr. Cash (A) . . . . . . . . . . . . . . . . . . . . . . . (inc.) XXX
    Cr. Preferred Stock (OE). . . . . . . . . . . . . . . . . . . .        (inc.) XXX
Dr. Reserve for ESOP Debt Retirement (OE)  (inc.) XXX
    Cr. ESOP Debt (L) . . . . . . . . . . . . . . . . . . . . . . . . .        (inc.) XXX
```

The Reserve for the ESOP debt retirement recognizes the fact that Procter & Gamble is obligated to pay dividends on the preferred stock so that the trustees can retire the debt. In effect that reserve acts as an allocation of the company's retained earnings, equal to Procter & Gamble's commitment to pay the ESOP debt. There are some very significant tax advantages to an ESOP and, together with the very real advantages to the employees, these plans can be well worth the effort.

Deferred income taxes on the liability side of the balance sheet represent the tax obligation Procter & Gamble expects to pay in the future, because of deductions that were taken on the income tax return in past years, but were not treated as an expense in the income statement. The classic example of such a timing difference is depreciation: the company has taken the maximum deduction for depreciation on its tax return as might be allowed under the tax code. For its GAAP financial statements, however, Procter & Gamble has calculated its depreciation based on a schedule of lives that is commonly used in the industry. Because the tax deductions in the past have been bigger than the expenses on the books, Procter & Gamble agrees that it will owe some taxes to the IRS after the accelerated tax deductions run out, and there is still some book depreciation to go. We will talk further about deferred taxes, both as assets and as liabilities, when we get to Chapter 13.

The obligations for the **post-retirement benefits** and the **pension benefits** represent the present value of the promises Procter & Gamble has made to its employees regarding the payments that will be made to them after they retire for pension and for health care benefits. The company has funded some of those obligations (in part with the ESOP stock we referred to earlier) but there is still some liability left and it is accrued on the balance sheet.

As we observed in Chapter 1, Procter & Gamble increased both its short term debt and its long-term debt this year, in part, to fund the several major acquisitions it made. It is particularly interesting that most of the increase in debt was in commercial paper and in short-term U.S. obligations. We might expect the company to settle on a longer-term source of funding for those acquisitions as the credit markets in the United States settle down in 1999, and it is clear where interest rates are heading. Or, perhaps the company will plan on an equity offering in the near term to refinance the short-term financing of these 1998 acquisitions.

Shareholders' Equity: The Owners' Investment in a Company

Shareholders' equity refers to the owners' or shareholders' investment in a company. As noted in Chapter 2, the shareholders' investment usually takes two primary forms: the shareholders' purchase of shares of stock from the company and the company's retention of a portion of its earnings.

When a company sells shares of stock, the proceeds are reflected in the **Capital Stock** account. The securities laws of some states permit companies to sell **no-par value stock,** and companies incorporated in those states may include the entire proceeds from a stock sale in a single account designated simply as Capital Stock or **Common Stock.** However, most states in the United States (and indeed most countries) require that a company's capital stock carry a **par value** or **stated value.** The par or stated value of a stock is the **legal value** of a single share of stock and is, in theory, the portion of shareholders' equity that may not legally be paid out as a dividend. That distinction is only theoretical, however, because the par or stated value is established (and can be changed by) the board of directors. Normally, there is no relationship between par value and the fair market value of a stock. For example, although Procter & Gamble issued capital stock with a par value of $1.00, its shares traded on the New York Stock Exchange during 1998 in the range of $62 to $92.

From Exhibit 4.1, Procter & Gamble's owners' equity section on the balance sheet appears as follows:

	1998	1997
Shareholders' Equity		
Convertible Class A preferred stock,		
stated value $1 per share (600 shares authorized)	$ 1,821	$ 1,859
Non–voting Class B preferred stock,		
stated value $1 per share (200 shares authorized;		
none issued)		
Common stock, stated value $1 per share		
(5,000 shares authorized; shares		
outstanding; 1998–1337.4 and 1997–1350.8)	1,337	1,351
Additional paid–in capital	907	559
Reserve for ESOP debt retirement	(1,616)	(1,634)
Accumulated other comprehensive income	(1,357)	(819)
Retained earnings	11,144	10,730
Total Shareholders' Equity	$12,236	$12,046

Because most companies intentionally set a relatively low par or stated value, shares of stock are normally sold at a price in excess of their par or stated value. When this occurs, the excess is reflected in the **Additional Paid-in Capital** account. Thus, the combination of the par value and the capital in excess of par value represents the total contributed capital of a company.

It is instructive to pause here and put this discussion of shareholders' capital in perspective. The distinction between the par value of a stock and the total proceeds received on the sale of the stock is important only for very narrow legal purposes and is of no consequence to company's management. In fact, some companies organized in "par value" states have decided to ignore the distinction in preparing their financial statements and simply present a combined total for capital stock. That aggregate common stock amount represents the amount that the shareholders have paid the company for the stock purchased directly from the company. The discussion of the entity principle in Chapter 2 pointed out that the financial statements reflect only the transactions of the entity, not the transactions of the owners on their own behalf. Therefore, the financial statements reflect purchases of shares by the shareholders directly from the company as well as sales of shares back to the company. However, the company's financial statements do *not* reflect purchases and sales of shares between shareholders and other outsiders.

A company's **charter of incorporation** specifies, among other things, the maximum number of shares of capital stock that can be issued; these are often referred to as the **authorized shares.** When authorized shares are sold to investors, they become **issued shares.** In the United States, companies may repurchase some of their issued shares and retire them or hold them as **treasury stock.** If a company decides to retire and cancel the shares it repurchases, the shares are considered authorized but unissued. That is what Procter

& Gamble does with the shares it has repurchased every year. To record the repurchase and the simultaneous cancellation of shares, the company reduces cash by the amount paid for the stock, and reduces (i) common stock for the par value of the shares retired, and (ii) retained earning for any excess of the purchase price over the par value.

On the other hand, a company may decide to keep the repurchased shares on hand, as issued. If the company does that, the shares are said to be held in the treasury, as **treasury stock.** The entry to record the purchase of treasury stock involves a decrease in cash by the amount paid and an increase in a contra equity account labeled Treasury Stock. Note that the value in the Treasury Stock account will be equal to the total amount the company has paid to reacquire the stock held in the treasury.[3] **Outstanding shares** represent the company's issued shares less any shares held in the treasury.

Remember that capital stock is recorded at the price that the purchasing shareholders paid when they bought the stock directly from the company. Logically, treasury stock is also recorded at the price that the company paid when it reacquired the shares on the open market. Because stock markets tend to fluctuate in response to many factors, there is almost always a difference between the original issue price and the price at which treasury shares are repurchased. Because the GAAP accounting model does not reflect changes in the value of a company's stock from year to year, a company's repurchase of any significant number of shares can result in an anomalous presentation of its owners' equity. For example, Lands End, Inc. reports that, at January 30, 1998, the original issue value of its 40 million common shares outstanding was $26.8 million, or about $.66 per share. However, the balance in the company's treasury stock, contra-equity account was $167.5 million, equal to $18 per share. Obviously, the original issuance of Lands' End stock took place many years ago when the stock price was much lower. Now, however, when any of those shares are repurchased they cost a good deal more. The company still has positive owners' equity because its retained earnings are more than $375 million.

A number of companies purchased substantial amounts of their own stock during major restructurings in the 1980s, and, as a result, their aggregate owners' equity is a nominal balance or even a negative number. It is worth repeating that owners' equity, or net worth, is the difference between the company's assets stated at their book values and the company's liabilities stated at their book values. Owners' equity would be a measure of the fair value of a company *only* if the book value of the assets and the liabilities were also equal to their market values—a coincidence that rarely happens. Therefore, the owners' equity number must be understood to be no more (or less) than a balancing number that forces a company to discipline its accounting process and maintain the A = L + OE equation.

The second principal form of shareholders' equity is the earned capital or retained earnings. The **retained earnings** of a company represent the historical, cumulative portion of net income that has not been paid out to shareholders as dividends, but has been retained in the company to support ongoing operations. Procter & Gamble's financial statements reveal that of the $3,780 million in net income earned in 1998, $1,358 million was paid as dividends to the holders of the common stock and $104 million was paid to the preferred stockholders. Because Procter & Gamble treats its repurchased shares as retired, they deduct the excess-over-par of the shares repurchased this year as a reduction in retained earnings, equal to $1,904 million.

Procter & Gamble reports two other interesting items in the equity section of its balance sheet. First is the "Reserve for employee stock ownership plan debt retirement." This "reserve" was created at the same time as the ESOP trustees took out debt to purchase Procter & Gamble's preferred stock. As discussed in the section above regarding noncurrent debt, the company recorded this reserve at the same time as they recognized their guarantee

---

[3] In some countries, such as France, treasury stock may be accounted for as an asset, usually under the heading "noncurrent investments."

of the ESOP debt. It acts as an allocation of retained earnings, reminding us that the Company has an obligation to pay dividends on the preferred stock, in the years ahead, so that the trustee can make the principle and interest payments on the bank loan.

The second interesting item is something Procter & Gamble calls "Accumulated other comprehensive income." The primary component of this negative number is the adjustment required when the company's international operations are consolidated with the U.S. parent. Roughly half of Procter & Gamble's sales originate outside the United States and about a third of its assets are located outside the U.S. It will be apparent to you that Procter & Gamble cannot combine the accounts of its Japanese subsidiary with those of its U.S. subsidiaries unless it first translates the Japanese accounts from yen to their dollar equivalents. So long as the yen/dollar exchange rate stays the same from year to year, that translation process causes no problem. But if the value of the dollar declines (appreciates) against the yen, the translation process will indicate that a loss (gain) has occurred, even if the Japanese subsidiary has been very profitable.

The financial world has long wondered what to do with that **currency translation adjustment**: few wanted to run the adjustment through the income statement because exchange rates tend to be very volatile and booking those adjustments year to year would make it very difficult to analyze a company's operating performance. It was finally agreed that the translation adjustment would be placed in a separate equity account and accumulated there. That translation adjustment and several other similar items are included in an equity account called **comprehensive income.** The idea is that over a very long time, those adjustments will impact the entity's income, but they do not belong to any specific year's operations. Those adjustments are not income or expense of any particular period, but they will enter into the determination of the entity's "comprehensive income." In 1998, the negative balance in Procter & Gamble's other comprehensive income grew by $538 million, indicating that the company has investments in countries where the foreign currency declined in value against the U.S. dollar.

CONCEPTS AND CONVENTIONS UNDERLYING THE BALANCE SHEET

The measurement and valuation of the various asset and equity accounts on the balance sheet reflect a diverse set of GAAP concepts subject to a variety of management estimates, judgments, and preferences. In Chapters 8–14 we will discuss these issues at length; however, for the moment, let us simply overview the core set of concepts and conventions.

An Overall Balance Sheet Focus

As noted in Chapter 2, the fundamental measurement system used to prepare the balance sheet is the accrual method. Under the accrual method, the financial effects of a transaction are recognized when it occurs without regard to the timing of its cash effects. Thus, the amounts due from customers for product sales that have not yet been paid for (that is, accounts receivable) may be recognized as assets. In addition, the amounts owed for purchases of inventories or other assets (that is, accounts payable) may be reported as liabilities on the balance sheet. Thus, whether or not cash has been received or paid is irrelevant. Assets are recognized on the balance sheet when a company takes possession of, or receives title to an asset, and liabilities are recorded when it has incurred an obligation.

Assets

As noted earlier in this chapter when we discussed Procter & Gamble's various asset accounts, the initial value assigned to each asset on the balance sheet is its acquisition cost, which is assumed to be the fair market value at the time of acquisition. For accounting purposes, *acquisition cost* is defined to encompass more than just the invoice price of an asset. All costs incurred in bringing an asset to its intended, usable condition are considered to be part of its cost. Thus, transportation costs or legal fees associated with acquiring an asset are a part of its cost in addition to the purchase price.

The value of most assets, however, fluctuates over time. In some cases, as with land, the value may increase, whereas with other assets, such as a car, the value will probably fall. Under the historical cost principle, the original acquisition cost of an asset is preserved on the balance sheet. There are a number of reasons for this rigidly observed convention. Most importantly, original cost values represent objective evidence as to the value of an asset, at least at one point in time. Experience has demonstrated that it is often quite difficult (and expensive) to obtain similarly objective, reliable measures at points in time after the original purchase date. An estimated market value established by management for its own company's assets often proves to be optimistic and is, of course, subject to manipulation. In the United States, corporate management has generally been reluctant to estimate market values for assets in part because those estimates have so often proven to be wrong and the management involved has lost credibility. Interestingly, users have also been reluctant to give much credence to estimated values and so there has been no market demand for that information. Therefore, with a few exceptions, GAAP-based financial statements in the United States recognize value changes only when they are validated by a sale in an arm's length transaction to a third party.

The fear of estimated values is a fact in the United States but is not necessarily present in other countries. In many other countries (especially Australia, Italy, and the United Kingdom), periodically appraising the fixed assets of a company and reflecting those appraised values in the company's balance sheet is perfectly acceptable. That asset write-up process has the advantage of quantifying, for the reader of the financial statements, the effect of changes in value on a company. For example, the write-up of assets logically results in an increase in owners' equity; that increase in asset value and that increase in owners' equity could mitigate the anomaly that results when a company buys back its own stock at an aggregate amount greater than the original proceeds received when it was issued. Also, the depreciation of those appraised values increases the company's operating costs and provides a clearer measure of the company's ability to increase its own sales prices in concert with changes in the purchasing value of the local currency. Because those value changes are not reflected in the financial statements of U.S. companies, statement users must (and usually do) make their own adjustments, mentally, as they consider the meaning of those historical cost-based numbers.

What is true for increases in an asset's value, however, is not the case if the value of an asset declines over time. Following the principle of conservatism, any significant decline in the value of an asset must be recorded. That notion is captured in several terms-of-art: accountants say that assets are stated at the **lower of cost or market,** or that financial statements always anticipate losses but never anticipate gains. We have seen that companies estimate the loss they expect to incur in the collection of accounts receivable by setting up an allowance for doubtful accounts. The same thing is required for inventory. Note that in Footnote No. 1, Procter & Gamble states that its "inventory is valued at cost, which is not in excess of current market price." The lower of cost or market idea applies to property and equipment too. Under current accounting, companies are obligated to test the net asset value of all of their noncurrent assets against the cash flow those assets are expected to generate. If the expected cash flow is less than the net book value of the assets, they are to be written down to that **net realizable value.** For example, in 1997 Eli Lilly wrote down the value of the assets connected with its PCS subsidiary. The note describing the write down concluded with these words:

> In the second quarter of 1997, concurrent with PCS' annual planning process, the company determined that PCS' estimated future undiscounted cash flows were below the carrying value of PCS' long-lived assets. Accordingly, during the second quarter of 1997, the company adjusted the carrying value of PCS' long-lived assets, primarily goodwill, to their estimated fair value of approximately $1.5 billion, resulting in a noncash impairment loss of approximately $2.4 billion ($2.21 per share). The estimated fair value was based on anticipated future cash flows discounted at a rate commensurate with the risk involved.

Remember that all noncurrent assets except land are subject to depreciation or amortization—the process by which the costs of those assets are allocated to the operations of individual years. Lilly acquired the PCS business in 1994, so those long-lived assets had been subject to depreciation and amortization for three years. The loss Lilly recorded in 1997 was the difference between the expected cash flow and the undepreciated cost of those assets, or their net book value.

To summarize, then, assets are initially recorded at their acquisition cost. When such values decline due to market externalities or to internal use, the asset values are reduced. When such values increase, with few exceptions (see Chapter 8), no recognition is given in the financial statements. Thus, it may be said that asset values are rarely overstated but may be understated relative to their current fair market value.

Liabilities

The valuation of liabilities on the balance sheet is substantially less complex than the valuation of assets. Theoretically *all* liabilities are valued at the **present value** of the future cash outflows (or other equivalent asset flows) required to satisfy the obligation. The present value of a liability is determined by **discounting** the required future cash outflows using a given rate of interest called the *discount rate* (see Chapter 12). In a word, the discounting process recognizes the time value of money and the fact that a dollar due tomorrow is less costly than a dollar due today. For example, $1,000 due one year from today discounted at 8 percent has a present value of only $925.93.

Although present value is the fundamental valuation approach used for all liabilities, as a practical matter it is rarely used to value short-term liabilities. By definition, short-term liabilities are expected to be satisfied or paid off in the coming year, and there is little difference between the *stated value* of a short-term liability and its present value. Thus, current liabilities are normally reported on the balance sheet at their stated value, or the amount of cash (or other equivalent assets) required to satisfy the obligation at its maturity or due date. Long-term liabilities are also usually presented at their stated value, so long as the required interest on the obligation is equal to the market rate of interest on the date when the debt is incurred. The present value of a liability is determined only once—when the obligation is initially incurred. Unlike assets, liabilities are never revalued on the balance sheet to reflect changes in their underlying market values.

Shareholders' Equity

Although the valuation of assets and liabilities may be defined or explained with reference to specific valuation concepts or methods, the valuation of shareholder or owners' equity is generally not. The valuation of owners' equity on the balance sheet is not an independent process but is the residual valuation that results from subtracting the liabilities from the assets. Capital stock is valued at the amount of assets received in exchange for the stock; treasury stock is valued at its acquisition cost. However, the reported value of retained earnings—the residual earnings after dividends have been paid—depends on the revenues and expenses reflected in the income statement. As you learned from your work in Chapter 3, every revenue and expense decision impacts an asset or a liability, and so the residual of those asset-liability/revenue-expense accounting decisions comes to rest in retained earnings.

The Balance Sheet: International Considerations

Thus far, our discussion of the balance sheet has focused on the format and presentation characteristic of U.S. companies. Not all nations, however, follow the same conventions, concepts, or presentation style. For example, Exhibit 4.2 presents the 1997 consolidated balance sheet of Glaxo Wellcome Plc, a British pharmaceutical company. A cursory review of this exhibit quickly reveals a number of notable differences:

- The order of asset presentation is reversed—fixed assets appear before current assets, thus running from low liquidity to high liquidity.

- The assets and liabilities are commingled, with current liabilities subtracted from current assets to yield net current assets, and then subtracted from total assets; long-term liabilities are then deducted to arrive at the company's net asset position (or "net worth").

- A presentation format of A – L = OE is used, rather than A = L + OE.

- Many terminology differences exist:

U.S.	British
Inventory	Stocks
Accounts receivable	Debtors
Liabilities	Creditors
Capital stock	Called up share capital
Capital in excess of par value	Share premium account

These and other differences may confuse or mislead unwary users of foreign financial statements. They also illustrate the very obvious conclusion that generally accepted accounting practices can and do differ around the world. Throughout the remaining chapters, we will discuss some of these differences.

EXHIBIT 4.2

Glaxo Wellcome Plc
Consolidated Balance Sheet

	Audited at 31.12.97 £m
Fixed assets	
Tangible assets	3,583
Goodwill	—
Investments	52
	3,635
Current assets	
Stocks	855
Debtors	2,285
Equity investments	39
Liquid investments	1,408
Cash at bank	215
	4,802
Creditors: amounts due within one year	
Loans and overdrafts	1,104
Convertible bonds	77
Other creditors	2,705
	3,886
Net current assets	916
Total assets less current liabilities	4,551
Creditors: amounts due after one year	
Loans	1,841
Convertible bonds	—
Other creditors	123
	1,964
Provisions for liabilities and charges	697
Net assets	1,890
Capital and reserves	
Called up share capital	894
Share premium account	805
Goodwill reserves	(4,840)
Other reserves	4,984
Equity shareholders' funds	1,843
Equity minority interests	47
Capital employed	1,890

ANALYZING FINANCIAL STATEMENTS

As we observed in Chapter 1, accounting is a language, a communication device, and therefore not an end in itself. Thus, the presentation of accounting information in a stylized format such as the balance sheet is merely the beginning of the communication process. The recipient of the balance sheet and the other basic financial statements must then use the presented financial data to draw inferences and conclusions about the financial status of a company. Hence, we now focus on the question of how to analyze, evaluate, and interpret balance sheet data.

The analysis of the balance sheet, and of the basic financial statements in general, can occur at various levels of sophistication. At the most fundamental level, an analyst or other financial statement user can review and identify the absolute level of various important account balances. For example, it may be important to note the absolute level of cash on hand. If the level of cash on hand is sufficient to meet a company's most urgent needs (for example, to pay employee salaries and replenish sold inventory), it is unlikely that the company will need to borrow money in the current period to support operations.

In most cases, however, merely identifying the absolute level of various account balances does not provide sufficient information to analyze fully a company's financial position. The absolute level of inventory on hand, for example, informs us only that a company does have some inventory on hand to begin operations in the next period; the absolute level does not tell us whether the available inventory will be sufficient to sustain sales or whether the company will need to purchase or manufacture additional units and, if so, how soon.

To address these more sophisticated questions, it is often useful to construct ratios of various related account balances. For example, to assess the adequacy of existing inventory levels, it is instructive to compare the level of inventory on hand to the level of cost of goods sold in the prior period. This ratio indicates whether the existing inventory is sufficient to cover expected sales, assuming that they are approximately equivalent to the prior period sales.

Ratio analysis is frequently used to gain a more complete understanding of a company's financial stature and condition. Ratios may be investigated both within a given accounting period and across a number of accounting periods. When ratios (or absolute balances) are compared across time periods, particular trends in a company's financial condition or operations may be identified. Not surprisingly, this type of across-period analysis is called **trend analysis.** To facilitate the analysis of financial trends, most companies provide accounting data for at least the current period and the prior period. Moreover, some companies provide summary financial data for as many as 10 years in the annual report: Procter & Gamble provides summary data for 5 years (see page 39). Later in this chapter we will consider some ratio trend data for Procter & Gamble.

Trend analysis is often aided by the use of **common-size financial statements,** in which all amounts are expressed as a percentage of some base financial statement item. For example, a common-size balance sheet might express all asset accounts as a percentage of total assets and all equity accounts as a percentage of total equities. Trend analysis of common-size statements permits the analyst to determine, for example, how the relative composition of total assets or total equities is changing over time.

In addition to comparing a company's performance from one year to the next, it is also instructive to compare the financial results of a given company with those of other companies within the same industry or with industry averages. For example, by comparing the financial results of Procter & Gamble with those of other consumer product companies, an investor may be able to identify which firm presents the best investment opportunity within the industry. Similarly, Standard and Poor's and Moody's investor services, among others, provide industry data to permit comparisons of one company against the average of all companies within a given industry. Use of such data may enable an investor to determine whether a company is outperforming or underperforming the average for that industry. Later in this chapter we will compare Procter & Gamble's balance sheet information to that of the overall consumer products industry and to a variety of industry averages.

Perhaps the most advanced level of financial analysis involves predicting the future financial performance of a company. Most companies prepare projections or **pro forma financial statements** based on assumptions about the future for their own internal planning purposes, but very few companies issue those financial projections publicly. The policy of publishing historic financial statements rather than pro formas is based on two factors. First, actual results almost always turn out differently than the original projections, and few executives have been willing to subject their credibility to the inevitable criticism when actual results are different from the projections. The second factor is economic; if the results are materially different from the pro forma, someone is sure to sue. Even if the projections were prepared in good faith, the company and its management will be forced to devote significant efforts to defend the projections.

Nonetheless, investments should always be made on the basis of expectations about the future, not on the results of the past. Under our present financial system, companies do not publish projections, but independent financial analysts do. They prepare and analyze their own pro forma financial statements for publicly traded companies building on the reported results from the company's financial statements, and using their own carefully developed assumptions about the company's future environment. Using that history and key assumptions about the future, financial analysts develop pro forma financial statements and then render estimates of the analyzed company's future earnings. We will return to this topic in Chapters 5 and 6, where the preparation of pro forma cash flow and income statements will be illustrated.

ANALYZING THE BALANCE SHEET

Ratio analysis is typically utilized to gain an understanding of a company's liquidity, solvency, profitability, and asset management effectiveness. **Liquidity** refers to the likelihood or ability of a company to satisfy its short-term obligations; **solvency** refers to a company's ability to satisfy its long-term obligations. **Profitability,** on the other hand, refers to a company's overall income-generating ability, and **asset management effectiveness** refers to the ability of a company's managers to utilize its assets effectively to produce a return for the company's creditors and owners.

Most profitability ratios are based on income statement accounts; consequently, this topic will be deferred until Chapter 5. The balance sheet, however, is a good source of information regarding a company's liquidity, solvency, and asset management effectiveness. We now turn to some widely accepted indicators of these financial characteristics.

Liquidity

Liquidity is frequently evaluated on the basis of four indicators: (1) the level of cash on hand, (2) the quick ratio, (3) the level of working capital, and (4) the current ratio.

The level of cash (and cash equivalents) on hand is a precise indication of the level of highly liquid resources available for a company's debt repayment or other operating needs. Cash on hand is very measurable and therefore quite certain, but it is also a very conservative measure of liquidity. Only in the most extreme circumstances would a company have to pay all of its bills using only its cash on hand. Hence, a more realistic measure of liquidity is the **quick ratio,** which is calculated as follows:

$$\text{Quick ratio} = \frac{\text{Cash + Marketable securities + Accounts receivable}}{\text{Current liabilities}}$$

The quick ratio examines only the liability coverage provided by the **quick assets**—highly liquid current assets such as cash, cash equivalents, short-term investments, and receivables. Accounts and notes receivables are considered to be quick assets because they can usually be sold to a financial institution or a financial corporation that buys receivables from other companies at a discount (that is, at a price less than the amount to be collected).

A somewhat more general indicator of liquidity that is broader in scope is the level of working capital. Working capital is measured as current assets minus current liabilities. Thus **working capital** is a measure of the net current assets that would be available to support a company's continuing operations *if* all of its current assets could be converted to cash at their balance sheet values and the proceeds were then used to satisfy its current liabilities. The equation is as follows:

$$\text{Working capital = Current assets – Current liabilities}$$

A ratio based on the concept of working capital is the **current ratio,** which is calculated by dividing current assets by current liabilities:

$$\text{Current ratio} = \frac{\text{Current assets}}{\text{Current liabilities}}$$

Both working capital and the current ratio are "coverage" indicators; the former indicates the extent to which current assets cover current liabilities in an *absolute* sense, and the latter indicates the extent of coverage in a *relative* sense. A high current ratio (that is, a substantial amount of working capital) indicates good liquidity, suggesting that a company's currently maturing obligations are likely to be paid on time. A ratio that is too high, however, may suggest an unproductive use of resources because the current assets might be used more effectively by converting them to cash and purchasing, for example, more efficient equipment for the plant.

To illustrate these liquidity measures, let us consider Procter & Gamble's balance sheet for 1998 (see Exhibit 4.1). This balance sheet reveals that, as of June 30, 1998, Procter & Gamble had cash and cash equivalents of more than $1.5 billion on hand, working capital of $1.3 billion, a current ratio of 1.14:1, and a quick ratio of .56:1. The current and quick ratios reveal that for every dollar of current liabilities, Procter & Gamble held $1.14 of current assets and $0.56 of quick assets.

To determine whether these measures indicate high, low, or average liquidity, one can compare them to existing industry averages, to those of a competitor (see Exhibit 4.3), and to the results of prior years. Because Procter & Gamble's balance sheet contains comparative data for 1997, a trend analysis can be easily undertaken.

	1998	1997
Cash and cash equivalents	$1,549 million	$2,350 million
Working capital	1,327 million	2,988 million
Current ratio	1.14:1	1.38:1
Quick ratio	0.56:1	0.75:1

A comparison indicates that Procter & Gamble's liquidity in 1998 declined from that in 1997. The level of cash and cash equivalents decreased by more than $800 million, and the level of working capital decreased by more than $1,661 million. The decline in cash is directly traceable to several major acquisitions. As Footnote No. 2 tells us, Procter & Gamble acquired Tambrands, Inc. "for approximately $1,844 [million] in cash." Other acquisitions in 1988 totaled $1,425 million. Even after these major cash acquisitions, the company presents a strong liquidity position, with a strong current ratio. Procter & Gamble's current ratio is better than that maintained by the household products industry and better than its principle competitor, Colgate–Palmolive (see Exhibit 4.3). It may be that Procter & Gamble had built up its cash reserves in anticipation of this acquisition program, and that its' liquidity measures are now back to a more normal level. In Chapter 6 we will see that there are additional ways to assess a company's liquidity, namely in terms of its operating cash flow.

Solvency

Solvency refers to a company's long-term debt repayment ability and is frequently evaluated on the basis of three indicators: (1) the long-term-debt-to-total assets ratio, (2) the long-term debt-to-owners' equity ratio, and (3) the times-interest-earned ratio. The first two ratios measure the relative *amount* of long-term debt outstanding; the third ratio is a *coverage* ratio of the extent to which debt interest charges are being covered by current earnings.

The concept of solvency and the thrust of these debt-level ratios suggest a negative connotation, as though debt is to be avoided and reduced whenever possible. Debt is not always bad; in fact, it is sometimes healthy. A more positive way to describe a company's debt level is to say that the stockholders' equity is **leveraged;** in effect, a leveraged company supplements its owners' funds with funds from other sources to "lever up" (or "gear up" as they would say in the U.K.) the return to the owners. Before we explore these debt-level ratios, it is appropriate to consider debt at a conceptual level.

The level of debt a company carries—its leverage—is a strategic decision, and that decision is based on the degree of certainty associated with its future cash flows. If the future cash flows are relatively predictable, the company may be able to borrow funds with bank loans or bond issuances at relatively low rates of interest. If a company can borrow money at an after-tax cost that is lower than the cost of its owners' equity funds, that borrowing enables the company to increase its return to its owners. (It may very well be possible to use borrowed funds less expensively than owners' equity funds because interest expense is tax deductible whereas dividends are not.) For example, assume that a company is considering a plant expansion project that is expected to cost $1 million and is expected to earn $100,000 after taxes. If the company is now earning a 10 percent return for its stockholders, that expansion project will not make the company (or its stockholders) any better off. But if the company can borrow 80 percent of those funds at an after-tax cost of 8 percent, the return on the shareholders' investment in this project will grow to 18 percent, as follows:

EXHIBIT 4.3

Financial Ratios for Selected Industries,
Colgate–Palmolive and Procter & Gamble

Industry	Current Ratio	Quick Ratio	Long–Term Debt to Total Assets	Long–Term Debt to Owners' Equity	Times Interest Earned	Asset Turnover	Return on Assets
Panel A: Industry Data							
Airlines	0.8:1	0.8:1	23 percent	98 percent	3.4 times	0.9 times	3.8 percent
Chemicals—general	1.3:1	0.8:1	16 percent	45 percent	8.3 times	1.1 times	8.2 percent
Retail—general	1.7:1	0.8:1	29 percent	97 percent	3.5 times	2.0 times	4.8 percent
Semiconductors	2.3:1	2.0:1	9 percent	13 percent	32 times	1.0 times	11.1 percent
Household products	1.2:1	0.8:1	19 percent	50 percent	9.5 times	1.2 times	10.9 percent

Source: Standard and Poor's Industry Surveys—1996 data

Panel B: Colgate-Palmolive and Procter and Gamble							
Colgate-Palmolive	1.12:1	0.6:1	31 percent	1.07 percent	7.0 times	1.2 times	10.4 percent
Procter & Gamble	1.14:1	0.6:1	19 percent	47 percent	11 times	1.3 times	7.7 percent

Source: 1997 and 1998 annual reports

	Project Funded with Owners' Equity Funds	Project Funded with Borrowed Funds
Cost of project	$1,000,000	$1,000,000
Borrowed funds	0	800,000
Stockholder funds invested	1,000,000	200,000
Expected return on project	100,000	100,000
Interest cost	–0–	64,000
Net return to stockholders	100,000	36,000
Rate of return to stockholders	10%	18%

Leverage is powerful, but it has the power to hurt as well as help. If the project in our example is not as successful as was planned and earns only $50,000 a year, the company will lose money on the $200,000 investment of owners' equity funds. The decision to lever up or lever down is, perhaps, the ultimate expression of management balance. Too little leverage cheats the stockholders of their maximum return; too much leverage raises the risk to the equity holders. Procter & Gamble has adopted a relatively conservative posture, funding 40% of its assets with equity. Colgate–Palmolive, on the other hand, has adopted a more aggressive posture toward debt, and that may explain why the company's return on equity is better than Procter & Gamble's return on equity. Think about why that might be so, and what it might mean to a potential investor who is considering an investment in the consumer/household products industry.

The ratios that follow describe a company's debt exposure, but they should be looked at from two perspectives: Creditors obviously want to maximize their protection, but stockholders look for the best *balance* of debt and equity to ensure the highest return at the least level of risk.

The **debt-to-assets ratio** is a measure of the extent to which a company's assets are financed by creditors and is calculated as follows:[4]

$$\text{Long-term-debt-to-total assets ratio} = \frac{\text{Long-term debt}}{\text{Total assets}}$$

In general, the lower the ratio, the more solvent a company is thought to be. The higher the ratio, the less solvent and the more leveraged (or "geared") a company is considered to be.

A related equation is leverage, generally expressed as a whole number:

$$\text{Leverage} = \frac{\text{Total assets}}{\text{Total owners' equity}}$$

The lower the leverage number is, the more the company has used equity to finance its assets and the lower its exposure to downturns in its business. The higher the number is, the more the company is relying on its creditors for financing, and the more benefits the shareholders derive from those borrowed funds—and the more exposed they are to the risks of the company's business.

The **long-term debt-to-equity ratio** measures the relative composition of a company's long-term capital structure, and is calculated as follows:

$$\text{Long-term-debt-to-equity ratio} = \frac{\text{Long-term debt}}{\text{Owners' equity}}$$

In general, the lower this ratio, the higher the proportion of long-term financing provided by the owners and the more solvent a company is thought to be. Alternatively, the higher this ratio, the more leveraged a company is and the less solvent it is thought to be. In general, creditors like a lower debt-to-equity ratio because they have a prior claim on a company's assets and prefer to have a larger equity cushion beneath them.

A final index of a company's ability to manage its long-term debt is given by the **times-interest-earned ratio,** also known as the interest coverage ratio:

$$\text{Times-interest-earned ratio} = \frac{\text{Net income before income tax + Interest expense}}{\text{Interest expense}}$$

Note that this ratio is calculated using pretax net income because interest is a tax-deductible expense; hence, the numerator is a measure of a company's pretax, pre-interest income. This ratio measures the extent to which a company's earnings during a period cover its interest payments for the same period. In general, the higher the ratio the better, although a high ratio may indicate either high pretax profits or low debt levels. In either case, a high ratio is generally associated with greater solvency and the ability to add new borrowings (that is,

[4] There are several ways to measure a company's use of credit, as you will see in these three ratios. Some analysts compare the company's total liabilities, including such things as accounts payable and accrued taxes, against the total assets. Others achieve the same result, with a little different perspective, by comparing total equity against total assets. Others use only long-term debt in their comparisons against total assets or total equity. There is some logic to the use of total liabilities as the basis for comparison, because "free" credit in the form of accounts payable and accruals is a valid form of capital, and a wise management team will try to make the maximum use of those sources of credit. But there is also some logic in using only long-term debt in the comparison ratios because those other sources of "free" credit are not really dependable–a company could find itself with little or no credit available from its suppliers. In the end, it is up to the analyst to settle on the ratio format that will be most useful in a situation, and perhaps more importantly, to be sure that the ratio format is *consistent* when one company's ratios are compared against another.

increase leverage) in the future. A very low ratio indicates that the company may be missing an opportunity to generate positive marginal returns by not sufficiently leveraging its assets. The times-interest-earned ratio is an income statement-based indicator of solvency.

To illustrate these solvency ratios, consider again information drawn from Procter & Gamble's 1998 financial statements:

	1998	**1997**
Long-term-debt-to-total assets ratio	18.6%	15.0%
Long-term-debt-to-equity ratio	.47:1	.34:1
Times-interest-earned ratio	11.4 times	12.5 times

As compared to 1997, Procter & Gamble's solvency in 1998 declined somewhat. The percentage of assets financed by external borrowings went up to 18.6%, and the ratio of long-term-debt-to-equity went up to almost 50%. We know from the financial statement footnotes that Procter & Gamble spent more than $3 billion on its 1998 acquisitions, some coming from the company's cash reserves and some coming from additional borrowings. Still, the times-interest-earned ratio shows that Procter & Gamble is able to handle the additional debt. The company's long-term-debt-to-assets ratio had been as high as 19% in 1995, but the debt level has been coming down in the intervening years. When we compare Procter & Gamble with Colgate–Palmolive, we can see how conservative Procter & Gamble's financing structure is. In 1997, Colgate's long-term debt was 31% of its total assets, down from about 35% in 1997. Apparently Colgate took on several major acquisitions in 1992 and 1995, and is still working down the related debt. Again, a conservative balance sheet is not necessarily a good thing: It is if you think the economy is headed into rough waters but the lack of leverage could shortchange the stockholders if the economy booms.

Asset Management

Asset management refers to how efficiently a company utilizes its assets. A company with superior asset management usually experiences superior earnings and profitability relative to competitors within its industry. Asset management effectiveness is usually investigated with respect to a company's inventory, receivables, and total assets. Five such indicators are (1) the inventory turnover ratio, (2) the number of days of inventory on hand, (3) the accounts receivable turnover ratio, (4) the average receivable collection period, and (5) the asset turnover ratio.

The quality of a company's inventory management is often revealed by the inventory turnover ratio and the number of days of inventory on hand. The **inventory turnover ratio** measures the number of times that the average level of inventory on hand was sold, or turned, during an accounting period and is calculated as follows:

$$\text{Inventory turnover ratio} = \frac{\text{Cost of goods sold for the period}}{\text{Average inventory held during the period}}$$

In general, the higher the inventory turnover ratio, the more profitable a company is and the more effective the inventory management is thought to be. A high turnover rate also helps to reduce the potential of loss due to product obsolescence or deterioration. If the turnover ratio is too high, however, it may indicate that the company is losing sales opportunities because inventory levels are inadequate. Unfortunately, there is no ideal turnover rate, and to judge the effectiveness of inventory management, it is important to compare this ratio to that of prior periods, to industry averages, or to competitor ratios.

An instructive derivative of the inventory turnover ratio is the **number of days' inventory-on-hand ratio.** This ratio highlights whether inventory levels are appropriate for the current level of sales volume and is calculated as follows:

$$\text{Number of days' inventory on hand} = \frac{365 \text{ days}}{\text{Inventory turnover ratio}}$$

This indicator measures the average number of days required to liquidate the existing stock of inventory based on current sales volume. A high number of day's inventory-on-hand ratio usually reflects an excessive quantity of inventory on hand, suggesting that current production should be curtailed. Alternatively, a very low number of days' inventory-on-hand ratio may also be problematic, indicating an inadequate quantity of inventory on hand and the potential for lost sales or customer complaints. Like the inventory turnover ratio, the number of day's inventory-on-hand ratio has no ideal number.

The quality of receivable management is usually evaluated in the context of the accounts receivable turnover ratio and the average receivable collection period. The **receivable turnover ratio** is a measure of the rate at which a company's accounts and notes receivable are converted to cash. In general, a high ratio indicates excellent receivables management. A low ratio, on the other hand, may indicate serious problems in the sales-receivables-collection cycle. The ratio is calculated as follows:

$$\text{Receivable turnover ratio} = \frac{\text{Net credit sales for the period}}{\text{Average receivable balance for the period}}$$

A derivative of the receivable turnover ratio is the **average receivable collection period,** which measures the average number of days that a receivable is outstanding before the amount is collected. This ratio provides a good indication of the quality of the cash collection policies a company followed relative to the credit terms granted and is calculated like this:

$$\text{Average receivable collection period} = \frac{365 \text{ days}}{\text{Receivable turnover ratio}}$$

A low collection period (in days) not only indicates effective asset management but also provides evidence as to the liquidity of a company's accounts and notes receivable.

These ratios are abstractions, but the impact of the underlying numbers is quite real. It is generally understood that inventory carrying costs are annually at least 20 percent of the value of the inventory. These carrying costs include the cost of the funds invested, the cost of storage and insurance, and the cost of spoilage, which occurs simply because the inventory is on hand. Management must trade off that inventory carrying cost against its need for customer service as it evaluates its inventory turn statistics. The trade-off may not have to be all that painful, however: One major manufacturer found that it was carrying 10 different variations of the same part, each minutely different from the other, because these parts were used on 10 different finished products. The company found that it was able to maintain its customer service levels *and* reduce its inventory levels by redesigning the basic part so that it could be used on all of its finished products, regardless of their variation.

Similarly, accounts receivable have a real cost to the seller, including the cost of the funds invested, the service costs, and the cost of bad debt losses. Typically, bank credit card companies charge the merchant 3 to 4 percent of the amount of a charge sale to cover credit operations costs and provide some measure of profit. Again, management must weigh the cost of its own credit operations against the profit potential of the sale, which might be lost should the customer go somewhere with easier credit policies.

A final indicator of the quality or effectiveness of a company's asset management is given by the **asset turnover ratio.** Unlike the previous four ratios that focus on individual current assets, this ratio examines a company's utilization of its entire asset portfolio. The ratio is calculated as follows:

$$\text{Asset turnover ratio} = \frac{\text{Net sales for the period}}{\text{Average asset balance for the period}}$$

In general, the higher the ratio the better. A high turnover ratio indicates that management is effective in generating revenues from the assets that it has at its disposal. A high turnover rate can also be problematic, however, if the reason for the high turnover is the liquidation of the company's assets. Similarly, a decreasing ratio may not necessarily indicate poor asset utilization if the decline is a result of an increased investment in assets.

To illustrate the asset management ratios, consider again Procter & Gamble's 1998 financial statements:

	1998	1997
Inventory turnover ratio	6.6 times	6.6 times
Number of days' inventory on hand	55.2 days	55.3 days
Receivable turnover ratio	13.5 times	12.8 times
Average receivable collection period	55.2 days	55.3 days
Asset turnover ratio	1.27 imes	1.28 times

Procter & Gamble's asset management position is virtually unchanged from 1997 to 1998, as we might expect for such a large, stable, well run company. Procter & Gamble looks a shade better than the competition: Colgate-Palmolive has an inventory turn of 5.9, an accounts receivable turn of 8.6, and an asset turn of 1.17. According to Standard and Poors, the industry turns its inventory 11.2 times and has an asset turn of 1.2. It may be that Procter & Gamble and Colgate-Palmolive, with their global distribution, have had to maintain larger inventory balances that their more domestic industry peers. They still manage to work their inventory hard, however.

Management Issues

The balance sheet is a powerful analytical tool not only for financial analysts and investors but also for a company's management. Liquidity measures generated from balance sheet data inform management whether the company has sufficient cash (or cash equivalents and other liquid resources) on hand to meet the company's operating needs for the coming period. If the decision is that more liquid resources are needed, solvency measures help management determine the best way to raise the needed funds—by bank borrowing, by the sale of long-term bonds, or by the sale of stock. Asset management indicators, on the other hand, help managers assess the extent to which a firm is operating according to previously established goals or plans. These evaluations are part of what is commonly called the "control function" of management—evaluating the extent to which a company is performing according to strategic plans or budgets. For example, if management has determined that the desired number of days' inventory on hand is 45 (that is, the quantity of inventory on hand is sufficient to cover the next 45 days sales), then a days' inventory-on-hand ratio of 60 indicates that there is excess inventory and the production of new inventory should be slowed. Similarly, if the days' inventory-on-hand falls to 10, management will be alerted that the company may be unable to give prompt, timely service to all of its customers, suggesting that production schedules probably need to be accelerated. Finally, the balance sheet is also an important evaluation instrument for management. By considering such ratios as the asset turnover ratio, the board of directors can assess just how effective the top management of a company was at using the company's resources to produce sales. This information can help the directors decide whether management deserves a bonus or, more importantly, whether the current business strategy should be reconsidered.

SUMMARY

The balance sheet is one of the basic financial statements prepared to communicate a company's financial status and condition. The balance sheet summarizes the assets a company owned, the liabilities it owed, and the accumulated funds that its owners have invested in or left with the company to cover its operating needs.

The balance sheet may be used to investigate a company's liquidity, solvency, leverage, and asset management effectiveness. By itself, the balance sheet reveals very little about the profitability of a company's operations. Hence, the development of a complete understanding of a company's financial health requires considerations beyond the balance sheet, such as an analysis of the income statement, which is the focus of the following chapter.

NEW CONCEPTS AND TERMS

Accounts payable	Cash and cash equivalents
Accounts receivable	Charter of incorporation
Accrual method	Common-size financial statements
Accrued compensation	Common stock
Accrued marketing	Comprehensive income
Accumulated depreciation	Coupon rate
Allowance for uncollectible accounts	Currency translation adjustment
Amortization	Current assets
Asset management effectiveness	Current liability
Asset turnover ratio	Current maturities of long-term debt
Authorized shares	Current ratio
Average receivable collection period	Deferred income taxes
Bad debts expense	Depreciation
Balance sheet	Discounting
Bond	Fiscal year
Capital stock	Fixed assets

Goodwill

Intangible assets

Inventory

Inventory turnover ratio

Issued shares

Legal value

Leverage

Liquid assets

Liquidity

Long-term debt

Long-term-debt-to-equity ratio

Matching principle

Maturity date

Net book value

Net realizable value

No-par value stock

Noncurrent assets

Noncurrent liability

Number of day's inventory-on-hand ratio

Operating cycle

Other assets

Other current liabilities

Other liabilities

Outstanding shares

Paid-in capital in excess of par (stated) value

Par value

Prepaid expenses

Present value

Profitability

Pro forma financial statements

Property, plant, and equipment

Quick assets

Quick ratio

Ratio analysis

Receivable turnover ratio

Retained earnings

Short-term borrowings

Short-term investments

Solvency

Stated value

Tangible assets

Times-interest-earned ratio

Total debt-to-total assets ratio

Trade payables

Trade receivables

Treasury stock

Trend analysis

Working capital

ASSIGNMENTS

4.1. The Balance Sheet. The balance sheet presents a picture of a company's assets, liabilities, and owners' equity as of a point in time. In general, the balance sheet reports items at their historical cost. Consider the typical line items reported in a balance sheet. As the manager of the company publishing the balance sheet, which items would you prefer to report at current market values? As a potential investor in the company, which ones would you like to have information regarding market values? Discuss how the demand for market value information may or may not be consistent with the reporting notions of relevance and reliability.

4.2. Financial Position. Monsanto describes its credit standing with the following words (from the management discussion and analysis segment reviewing the balance sheet):

> **Monsanto Maintains Strong Financial Position**
> Monsanto's financial position remained strong this year, as evidenced by Monsanto's current "A" or better debt rating. Financial resources were adequate to support existing businesses and to fund new business opportunities.

Working capital at year-end was at the same level as that of the prior year-end. Receivables increased primarily as a result of higher fourth quarter sales versus the prior year's fourth quarter sales. The increase in current liabilities principally related to the Agricultural Products restructuring that increased short-term debt.

Total short- and long-term debt at year-end was $258 million higher than that of the prior year-end. The additional long-term debt was used principally for capacity expansions. To maintain adequate financial flexibility and access to debt markets worldwide, Monsanto management intends to maintain an "A" debt rating. Important factors in establishing that rating are the ratio of total debt to total capitalization, which was 35 percent, and the interest coverage ratio, which was 4.8.

Monsanto uses financial markets around the world for its financing needs and has available various short- and medium-term bank credit facilities, which are discussed in the notes to financial statements. These credit facilities provide the financing flexibility to take advantage of investment opportunities that may arise and to satisfy future funding requirements.

In your own words, describe Monsanto's interest in maintaining its "A" rating. Why might they be interested in that rating? What would you expect the company to do to preserve that rating?

4.3. Account identification. With Sears Roebuck and Co. in mind, classify each of the following accounts as either assets, liabilities, or owners' equity:

a. Accounts Payable
b. Prepaid Rent
c. Cash
d. Common Stock
e. Inventory
f. Taxes Payable
g. Land

h. Customer Deposit
i. Patent
j. Accounts Receivable
k. Retained Earnings
l. Pension Obligation
m. Securities Investment

4.4. Financial analysis. Collins Cutlery has a current ratio, based on its June 30, 1999, balance sheet, of 2:1. During the following six months, these independent events took place:

1. Sold an old truck for cash.
2. Declared a cash dividend on common stock.
3. Sold inventory on account (at a profit).
4. Paid off mortgage five years early.
5. Paid cash for a customer list.
6. Temporarily invested cash in government bonds.
7. Purchased inventory for cash.
8. Wrote off an account receivable as uncollectible.
9. Paid the declared cash dividend.
10. Purchased a computer with a two-year promissory note.
11. Collected accounts receivable.
12. Borrowed from bank on a 90-day note.

Required:

For each of the above events, indicate the effect of that event on Collins's working capital and current ratio and its ratio of total debt to equity. Make whatever assumptions you believe necessary to complete this exercise.

4.5. Balance sheet preparation. Presented below are the balance sheet accounts of Global Communications, Inc., as of December 31, 1999:

Accounts payable	$ 4,200	Capital stock, $1 par	$30,000
Accounts receivable	3,000	Discount on bonds payable	1,000
Accumulated depreciation—buildings	5,000	Equipment	18,000
Accumulated depreciation—equipment	3,000	Income taxes payable	3,100
Allowance for uncollectible accounts	500	Inventory—raw material	2,100
Bonds payable (due 2008)	10,000	Inventory—finished goods	5,000
Buildings	20,000	Land	19,000
Cash	4,500	Marketable securities (current asset)	2,000
		Paid-in capital in excess of par value	16,000
		Patent	20,000
		Retained earnings	?
		Wages payable	1,000

Required:

Prepare the December 31, 1999, balance sheet of Global Communications.

4.6. Working with ratios. At lunch one day in the First National Bank's executive dining room, you notice a coworker lunching by himself and studying a set of financial statements. He seems frustrated and is talking to himself. You hear him say, as he picks up his briefcase and leaves, "I do not understand what is going on with this borrower—none of this makes any sense to me." You start to follow him out, when you notice that he has left a scratch sheet behind covered with figures and notes. The bulk of his scratching appears to be a set of ratios. The scratch sheet is as follows:

	This Year	Last Year
Return on owners' equity (net income divided by avg. OE)	22%	19%
Working capital	20,000	5,000
Current ratio	1.25	1.07
Quick ratio	0.5	0.5
Trade receivables, days' sales outstanding	73.00	81.11
Inventory turnover	1.25	1.69
Interest coverage	3.75	4.17
Long-term debt to owners' equity	0.8	0.6
% dividends to owners' equity	22%	19%

Required:

Identify five important issues regarding this borrower this year, which might explain the ratios developed by your frustrated friend.

4.7. Assets at cost or at current value. Pacific Dunlop is an Australian manufacturer of latex products, clothes, and electrical equipment. The company follows normal Australian accounting for its plant and equipment, providing regular revaluations by independent appraisers and by the company officers. The results of that accounting are detailed in the following footnote from its recent financial statements. (The Australian-GAAP based balance sheet reports total property, plant, and equipment of $1,008,197.)

Property, Plant, and Equipment

		Consolidated	
		19X9 ($000)	19X8 ($000)
(a) Freehold land	Independent valuations 31/12/19X7	82,874	91,383
	Officers' valuations 31/12/19X7	608	804
	At cost	15,498	16,537
		98,980	108,724
(b) Freehold buildings	Independent valuations 31/12/19X7	110,452	116,660
	Officers' valuations 31/12/19X7	964	992
	At cost	54,011	52,282
		165,427	169,934
	Less provision for depreciation	16,535	12,005
		148,892	157,929
(c) Leasehold land and buildings	Independent valuations 31/12/19X7	9,661	12,381
	Officers' valuations 31/12/19X7	1,107	1,192
	At cost	17,685	9,963
		28,453	23,536
	Less provision for amortization	4,484	3,445
		23,969	20,091
(d) Plant and equipment	Independent valuations 19X1–19X5		77
	Officers' valuations 19X2–19X4	4,915	4,915
	Deemed value	47	990
	At cost	959,018	902,218
		963,980	908,200
	Less provision for depreciation	427,430	375,464
		536,550	532,736
(e) Leased plant and equipment	At cost	89,664	45,863
	Less provision for amortization	14,776	14,072
		74,888	31,791
(f) Buildings and plant under construction	At cost	124,918	83,489
		1,008,197	934,760

Required:

Comment on the Australian accounting policy, as exemplified in the Pacific Dunlop footnote. Should the accounting profession in the United States permit a similar policy for fixed assets? What would the advantages and disadvantages be for such a policy for U.S. companies? For their financial statement presentation? For their internal management? For their public policy position?

4.8. Foreign currency adjustments. Monsanto, Procter & Gamble, Seagrams, and Snap-On Tools all made the same general statement in their footnotes regarding their policies for the translation of financial statements of subsidiaries that conduct business in currencies other than the U.S. dollar. Monsanto's statement is typical: "Most of Monsanto's non-U.S. entities' financial statements are translated into U.S. dollars using current exchange rates. Unrealized currency adjustments in the Statement of Consolidated Financial Position are accumulated in shareholders' equity."

The accumulated currency adjustment accounts in shareholders' equity for the four companies, at year-end 19X9 and 19X8, were as follows (in millions of dollars):

	Balance in the Account	
	19X9	**19X8**
Monsanto	188	24
Procter & Gamble	44	(63)
Snap-On Tools	(152)	(103)
Seagrams	(13)	(158)

Required:

Assume that the underlying balance sheets of the companies' non-U.S. subsidiaries have not changed significantly. Explain what has happened to cause the changes in the accumulated currency adjustments in each case.

4.9. Balance sheet accounts: Liabilities. Contel Corporation lists the following items in the current liabilities section of the balance sheet. Explain what these items are and why they have to be recorded by Contel as a liability. Why are they current liabilities? Comment on the source of the numbers attributed to those liabilities.

Contel Corporation
Balance Sheet
As of December 31
(in thousands)

	19X9	**19X8**
Liabilities and Stockholders' Equity		
Current liabilities:		
Current maturities of long-term obligations and preferred stock redemptions	$ 194,419	$ 93,640
Interim borrowings	173,073	26,279
Accounts payable	478,579	404,029
Accrued taxes	67,088	166,929
Accrued interest	33,345	35,520
Accrued benefits	53,178	74,444
Advance billings and customer deposits	63,294	77,058
Other	169,429	100,972
	$1,232,405	$978,871

4.10. Leverage. A condensed balance sheet and a condensed income statement for the Lever-Up Corporation for 1999 are as follows:

Condensed Balance Sheet (000 omitted)	12/31/99	Condensed Income Statement (000 omitted)	for the year ended 12/31/99
Current assets	$ 4,500	Sales	$25,000
Fixed assets (net)	9,000	Cost of sales	16,250
Goodwill	2,500	Administrative and selling expenses	6,100
Total assets	$16,000	Interest expense	640
Current liabilities	$ 3,000	Pre-tax income	2,010
8% bonds payable	8,000	Income tax	804
Owners' equity	5,000		
Liabilities and equity	$16,000	Net income	$ 1,206

Lever-Up's sales have been as high as $30,000,000 and as low as $20,000,000 during the last five years, but its interest coverage ratio (profit before taxes and interest divided by interest) has always been in excess of 4.5 during all of those years. The company has maintained an open line of credit with its bank, which would allow it to borrow up to $5,000,000 for a five-year term at 10 percent.

Required:

a. Using the exhibits as a base, prepare at least four different sets of pro forma financial statements to demonstrate the effect of an increase in leverage on the company's return on equity ratio (net income divided by average owners' equity). Two of your pro forma presentations should assume the same sales and operating expenses but different levels of borrowing. As the debt is increased, reduce the level of owners' equity. The other pro forma presentations should assume an increase in debt and increased and decreased levels of sales (assume that cost of sales vary in proportion with sales that the interest expense will be 8% of the year-end debt balance, that the tax expense will be 40% of the pre-tax income and that other expenses are fixed).

b. Prepare a letter to the chairman of the board of Lever-Up, outlining some of the things she might think about as she considers a change in the company's debt/equity structure.

4.11. Treasury stock. The H. J. Heinz Company has 287,400,000 common shares outstanding, and that has been the case for the last several years. The company reported that it had 59,900 shares of its convertible preferred stock outstanding and that it has 33,881,804 shares in its treasury at May 2, 19X9, and that it had 30,437,230 shares in its treasury at May 3, 19X8. The shareholders' equity balance sheet accounts for the company were as follows (thousands of dollars):

	19X9	19X8
Convertible preferred stock	$ 599	$ 757
Common stock	71,850	71,850
Additional capital	152,158	109,665
Retained earnings	2,560,780	2,263,829
Translation adjustments	(73,910)	(89,205)
Total	2,711,477	2,356,896
Treasury shares	(777,548)	(579,658)

Required:

Calculate the per-share values of the preferred stock, the common stock, the total outstanding stock, and the treasury shares, for each year. Why are some values the same each year? Why are some different? Why should there be a difference in the per-share value of the outstanding stock and the treasury stock?

4.12. Analyzing the balance sheet: The comparative balance sheets of United Foods, as of February 28, 19X9 and 19X8, are presented below. Perform a ratio analysis on the company and comment on its solvency, its liquidity, and its return on assets. What advice would you have for United Foods management? (Note that the company earned $5.8 million in 19X9 on sales of $170 million. The company's gross margin was $38.2 million. Note also that in 19X9 the item "other assets" includes an insurance claim receivable for $6.6 million, which is the estimated replacement cost of a processing plant destroyed in a fire. Filing and recording that claim resulted in an after-tax gain of $4.0 million, which is included in net income for 19X9.)

United Foods
Comparative Balance Sheet
As of February 28

	19X9	19X8
Assets		
Cash and cash equivalents	$ 1,367,000	$ 1,103,000
Accounts and notes receivable, less allowance of		
$212,000 and $286,000 for possible losses	16,320,000	15,108,000
Inventories	54,363,000	40,159,000
Prepaid expenses and miscellaneous	3,047,000	2,536,000
Total current assets	75,097,000	58,906,000
Property and equipment		
Land and land improvements	8,185,000	6,693,000
Buildings and leasehold improvements	19,177,000	18,755,000
Machinery, equipment, and improvements	63,929,000	57,902,000
	91,291,000	83,350,000
Less accumulated depreciation and amortization	(37,102,000)	(32,480,000)
Net property and equipment	54,189,000	50,870,000
Other assets	10,887,000	2,164,000
	$140,173,000	$111,940,000

United Foods
Comparative Balance Sheet
As of February 28

	19X9	19X8
Liabilities and Stockholders' Equity		
Current liabilities:		
Accounts payable	$ 12,715,000	$ 6,996,000
Accruals:		
Compensation and related taxes	3,533,000	2,744,000
Pension contributions	876,000	1,455,000
Income taxes	128,000	853,000
Workers compensation insurance	1,074,000	870,000
Miscellaneous	1,263,000	1,730,000
Current maturities of long-term debt	1,034,000	881,000
Total current liabilities	20,623,000	15,529,000
Long-term debt, less current maturities	60,199,000	43,186,000
Deferred income taxes	2,934,000	—
Total liabilities	83,756,000	58,715,000
Commitments and contingencies		
Stockholders' equity		
Preferred stock, $1 par—shares authorized, 10,000,000		
Common stock, Class A, $1 par—shares authorized, 25,000,000; issued 7,642,650 and 7,635,732	7,643,000	7,636,000
Common stock, Class B, $1 par—shares authorized, 10,000,000; issued 7,102,987 and 7,109,905	7,103,000	7,110,000
Additional paid-in capital	8,720,000	8,901,000
Retained earnings	38,335,000	35,269,000
	61,801,000	58,916,000
Treasury stock, at cost, 1,890,004 and 1,991,004 shares	(5,384,000)	(5,691,000)
Total stockholders' equity	56,417,000	53,225,000
	$140,173,000	$111,940,000

4.13. Analyzing the balance sheet: The comparative balance sheets of Tyson Foods at September 30, 19X9 and 19X8, are presented next. Perform a ratio analysis on the company and comment on its liquidity, solvency, and return on assets. Compare the results of your work on the Tyson balance sheet with the results of your work on the United Foods balance sheet (see 4.12.) and comment on the circumstances of the two companies and their apparent strategies. (Note that Tyson earned $120 million in 19X9 on sales of $3.825 billion. Gross margin was $748.5 million.)

Tyson Foods, Inc.
Comparative Balance Sheets
For the Years Ending December 31
(in thousands)

	19X9	19X8
Assets		
Current assets:		
Cash and cash equivalents	$ 16,943	$ 56,490
Accounts receivable	90,839	247,979
Inventories	472,264	408,663
Other current assets	5,812	6,124
Net assets held for sale	—	30,396
Total current assets	585,858	749,652
Property, plant, and equipment, at cost:		
Land	36,945	24,492
Buildings and leasehold improvements	480,691	435,075
Machinery and equipment	876,555	796,166
Land improvements and other	54,057	55,238
Buildings and equipment under construction	50,020	44,291
	1,498,268	1,355,262
Less: Accumulated depreciation	427,152	334,506
Net property, plant, and equipment	1,071,116	1,020,756
Excess of investments over net assets acquired	784,209	745,778
Investments and other assets	59,879	69,894
Total assets	$2,501,062	$2,586,080
Liabilities and Shareholders' Equity		
Current liabilities:		
Current portion of long-term debt	$ 70,058	$ 55,048
Trade accounts payable	203,915	212,001
Accrued salaries and wages	118,947	98,020
Federal and state income taxes payable	8,489	16,714
Accrued interest payable	17,029	6,618
Other current liabilities	64,723	75,747
Current deferred income taxes		5,564
Total current liabilities	483,161	469,712
Long-term debt	950,407	1,319,385
Deferred income taxes	404,506	349,263
Shareholders' equity:		
Common stock ($0.10 par value):		
Class A—Authorized 60,000,000 shares; issued		
34,734,131 shares in 19X9 and 31,574,473 shares		
in 19X8	3,473	3,157
Class B—Authorized 40,000,000 shares; issued		
34,241,259 shares in 19X9 and 34,244,499 shares		
in 19X8	3,424	3,425
Capital in excess of par value	171,021	75,306
Retained earnings	500,268	382,661
	678,186	464,549
Treasury stock—668,587 shares in 19X9 and 1,162,986		
shares in 19X8, at cost	9,343	10,041
Unamortized deferred compensation	5,855	6,788
Total shareholders' equity	662,988	447,720
Total liabilities and shareholders' equity	$2,501,062	$2,586,080

4.14. Balance sheets tell a story.* Presented below are six balance sheets. The balance sheet amounts are expressed as percentages of total assets in order to reflect relative amounts for each account. Each balance sheet represents a different company from a different industry. The industries and companies represented are:

Commercial bank (Sovran Financial Corp.)
Supermarket chain (Albertson's Inc.)
Advertising agency (Interpublic Group)
Discount store chain (Wal-Mart Stores, Inc.)
Electric utility (Pacific Gas & Electric Co.)
Chemical co. (Dow Chemical Co.)

Match the industry with the appropriate column based on your understanding of some of the financial implications of operating in that industry. The identifications often require two or more distinguishing features.

	Year Ended					
	(1) 12/31	(2) 2/2	(3) 12/31	(4) 12/31	(5) 11/31	(6) 12/31
Assets						
Cash and equivalents	11.3	5.1	.3	.5	.2	5.1
Accounts receivable	65.5	2.7	6.9	12.4	2.0	66.0
Inventory	—	27.2	3.1	12.8	52.7	—
Other current assets	—	2.2	3.9	7.4	2.2	7.7
Total current assets	76.8	37.2	14.2	33.1	57.1	78.8
Net plant and equipment	2.2	60.3	74.8	34.5	41.9	7.6
Other assets	21.0	2.5	11.0	32.4	1.0	13.6
Total assets	100%	100%	100%	100%	100%	100%
Liabilities						
Notes payable	15.9	.7	2.9	10.3	.6	3.1
Accounts payable	73.5	23.6	3.8	10.3	21.9	56.3
Accrued taxes	—	1.5	.1	1.2	1.9	2.4
Other current liabilities	.6	4.9	4.3	7.5	8.1	7.7
Total current liabilities	90.0	30.7	11.1	29.3	32.5	69.5
Long-term debt	1.9	11.1	36.6	17.4	18.8	2.1
Other liabilities	1.7	7.9	12.0	7.9	1.4	6.5
Total liabilities	93.6	49.7	59.7	54.6	52.7	78.1
Equity						
Preferred stock	—	—	5.4	—	—	—
Common stock and surplus	1.6	6.5	24.7	12.6	3.6	8.6
Retained earnings	4.8	43.8	10.2	41.5	43.7	18.1
Treasury stock	—	—	—	(8.7)	—	(3.8)
Total equity	6.4	50.3	40.3	45.4	47.3	22.9
Total liabilities and equity	100%	100%	100%	100%	100%	100%

CHAPTER 5

The Income Statement

The income statement, like the balance sheet and the statement of cash flows, presents information that is essentially historical in nature. It describes what has happened, rather than what will happen. Nonetheless, it is probably the single most important source of information for me when I try to evaluate whether our operating units are performing as planned.[1]

Key Chapter Issues

- What is the income statement, and what are its principal elements?
- What are the key accounting concepts and conventions underlying the income statement?
- What are the key principles used in measuring a company's revenues and expenses?

- What information does the income statement convey about a company's financial and operating performance?
- How precise is the net income figure?

[1] Glenn R. Simmons, CEO, Keystone Consolidated Industries, Inc.

A s defined in Chapter 2, the income statement, or statement of earnings, summarizes those transactions during a period that produce revenue for a company as a result of selling a product or service and those transactions during that same period that result in expenses. By summarizing revenues and expenses, the income statement presents a picture of overall profitability of a company's operations.

Some argue that the income statement is the most important of the accounting statements because net income (or, colloquially, "the bottom line") is the basis for so many financial decisions. Management is rewarded or punished in large part depending on whether actual income is or is not equal to planned income. Stock prices rise or fall in large part because the company reports net income higher or lower than the market's expectations. And, because of the market's immediate reaction to the announcement of net income, that bottom-line number is often taken to be the essence of that year's business activity.

Because of the importance of net income, management is often under great pressure as it anticipates the preparation of the income statement for its company. Unfortunately, the normal, healthy pressure for improved *business* results is sometimes translated into pressure for improved *reported* results, as the excerpt from SEC chairman Levitt's speech in Exhibit 5.1 suggests.

Perhaps because the evaluation of both companies and management depends largely on the basis of reported net income, the measurement of income under generally accepted accounting principles (GAAP) has been rigorously defined. Recorded net income does not attempt to measure changes in values of the assets owned by a company, nor does it measure the company's qualitative accomplishments during the year. An accounting system could be designed to capture and report some or all of that type of information. However, faced with a trade-off between the reliability and relevance of presented information, the financial community (including company management) has determined that a reliable measure of income is more important than a broader, perhaps more relevant measure of income.

Financial analysts, for example, have said that they would prefer to have companies quantify only those activities that can be reasonably measured and provide supplementary information about all other activities, such as the value inherent in new products or in the appreciation of a company's assets. Analysts believe that they can evaluate those qualitative developments more objectively on their own.

Most members of management have supported a narrow definition of "income" because they prefer to be measured by a more concrete, more predictable measure of performance. For example, asset appreciation is excluded from the income statement in part because it is so hard to measure, in part because it fluctuates and suggests that a company's results are unstable and in part because those value changes are so completely out of management's control.

Fundamentally, management and analysts know that a living, functioning company is too complex to be represented with a single measure of performance. Procter & Gamble, for example, accomplished much more in 1998 than simply earning $2.74 per share. Thorough financial analysis requires considering all of the numbers in the income statement and asking about their relationships. What is the trend of sales, of expenses, of net income? Does it appear that sales prices are keeping pace with cost increases or are they falling behind? To what degree was income depressed this year as a result of resolving a long-standing problem and therefore clearing the way for increased income in the future? The users of financial statements should also look beyond the income statement and ask about the company's cash flows and the strength of its balance sheet. Finally, to develop a complete picture of a company's results, financial statement users should go beyond the statements and

EXHIBIT 5.1

SEC Chairman Arthur Levitt,
Concerned That The Quality of Corporate Financial Reporting Is Eroding,
Announces Action Plan to Remedy Problem

New York, NY, September 28, 1998 — In a major address on the state of accounting delivered today at New York University, Securities and Exchange Commission Chairman Arthur Levitt expressed concern that the quality of financial reporting in corporate America is eroding and he presented an action plan that calls on the entire financial community to remedy the problem.

Chairman Levitt said, "Increasingly, I have become concerned that the motivation to meet Wall Street earnings expectations may be overriding common sense business practices. Too many corporate managers, auditors, and analysts are participants in a game of nods and winks. In the zeal to satisfy consensus earnings estimates and project a smooth earnings path, wishful thinking may be winning the day over faithful representation."

He added, "As a result, I fear that we are witnessing an erosion in the quality of earnings, and therefore the quality of financial reporting. Managing may be giving way to manipulation; integrity may be losing out to illusion."

Source: SEC web site: Levitt Accounting Speech News–Release, September 28, 1998.

investigate nonfinancial factors, including such things as a company's market share, customer loyalty, and new product development. A wise management provides footnotes and other textual commentaries describing the events of the year and encourages financial statement users to use the income statement only as a starting point for analysis.

Having said all of that, the financial community is occasionally too impatient to study a company in depth and, when pressured for immediate decisions, looks for shortcuts. Net income and earnings per share are the most commonly used shorthand measures of performance, and the income statement maintains its foremost position as *the* vehicle to report a company's financial results. The objective of this chapter is to help you understand the components of the income statement, how it is prepared, and how it can be used.

THE ELEMENTS OF THE INCOME STATEMENT

Terminology and Concepts

When first introduced to the income statement, people often think it strange that such an important topic should be encumbered by so many apparently overlapping and confusing terms. Perhaps the terminology problem can be traced to the attention given to the measurement of income—many people have looked at the subject from diverse viewpoints, and their different perspectives seem to have spawned many different words to express slightly different ideas. On the other hand, perhaps the terminology problem is just a reflection of the inherent complexity of the subject. In any event, the words used are sometimes difficult. Because the topic is so important, it is useful to focus initially on the terminology used in connection with the income statement and to establish a common frame of reference for our subsequent discussions.

Revenues. The senior concept in the income statement, the term **revenues** refers to a company's actual or promised cash inflows resulting from a completed sale of the company's products or the satisfactory delivery of its services. (In some countries, the term *turnover* is used in lieu of *revenues*.) To help you distinguish between a company's revenues and its *cash receipts*, consider the following:

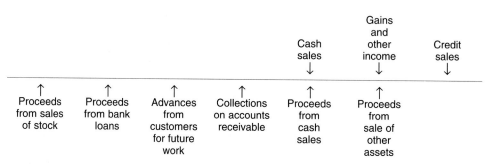

Revenue (a source of income)

Receipts (a source of cash flow)

Proceeds from sales of stock

Proceeds from bank loans

Advances from customers for future work

Collections on accounts receivable

Cash sales — Proceeds from cash sales

Gains and other income — Proceeds from sale of other assets

Credit sales

Cash inflows from the sale of stock or from borrowed money are not revenues but are financing transactions because the entity has continuing responsibilities to the providers of those funds. Cash deposits from a customer in advance of the delivery of a product or service are not revenues, nor will they be recognized as such until the "seller" completes its part of the bargain. In sum, revenues are those actual or expected cash inflows that the company has earned and which it is entitled to retain without qualification. Revenues are part of a company's income stream under accrual accounting. Some revenues also involve the receipt of cash, but others do not. Cash receipts, on the other hand, enter into the determination of a company's cash flows, which is the subject of Chapter 6.

Sales. A legal term, **sales** suggests that the title to property has passed from a seller to a buyer. Most legal sales transactions qualify as revenue, but the accounting world is more interested in the substance of a transaction than in its legal form. Therefore, not all legal sales qualify as revenues for accounting purposes, as we shall see.

Gains and losses. A **gain** is the net revenue a company earned as a result of a business transaction that is not a normal sale of products or delivery of services. For example, a company that sells an excess piece of land that it had purchased earlier for possible expansion will recognize a gain in its income statement to the extent that the sales price of the land is more than the original cost. Conversely, if the sales price is less than the land's cost, the company will recognize a **loss**.

Income. A generic term, **income** usually means revenue from sources other than product sales or from gain-producing transactions, such as interest income or rent income.

Expenses. This term encompasses all actual or expected cash outflows, or cost allocations from prior years' cash outflows, which cannot be justified as an addition to an asset account or a reduction in a liability. To help you distinguish between **expenses** and *cash expenditures*, consider the following chart:

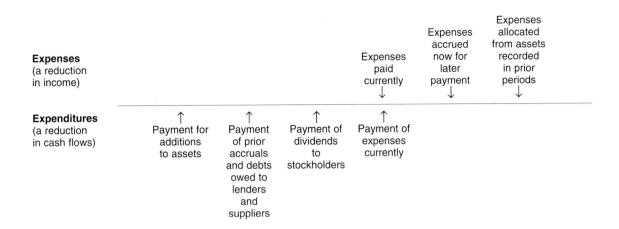

As we said in Chapter 3, an accounting entry to record an expenditure must have two sides; the credit side of an entry to record an expenditure is, of course, a reduction in cash. Whether the debit side is an increase in an expense or an increase in an asset (or a reduction in a liability) depends on a careful analysis of the reason for the expenditure. Principal payments on debt are not expenses because they are simply the repayment of funds provided earlier by a lender. Similarly, expenditures for the reacquisition of some of the company's stock, or dividends paid to the shareholders, are not expenses because they are transactions with the owners. (Remember from our work with Blue Ridge Hardware in Chapter 3 that interest is an expense and, therefore, a deduction from revenues in determining net income, but dividends are not an expense and instead are considered to be a distribution of net income to the shareholders.)[2] An expenditure that creates a future value for the company may be considered an asset. If no measurable future value results from an expenditure, it will be treated as an expense. Most often, an asset created in one year will become an expense in a future year, as with the annual allocation to expense that we call *depreciation*.

Cost. An awkward word, **cost** is best understood when used in conjunction with an explanatory adjective such as material cost, product cost, transportation cost, and so forth. You will hear businesspeople refer to the cost of a new machine, meaning the expenditure required for an asset. Or they will talk about the cost of a transaction, meaning the commission and delivery expenses incurred in connection with making a sale. The ambiguity of the term actually carries over to the traditional terminology used in preparing the income statement. For example, the biggest deduction from revenue in the measurement of net income is referred to as the *cost of goods sold*, which is the total cost of the products removed from inventory and delivered to customers as a result of sales. On the other hand, the other deductions from revenue on the income statement are *selling expenses* and *general and administrative expenses*, which are expenditures that were necessary for the operations of a business during the year.

Net income. The final financial result of all of an entity's operations for the year, **net income** is the difference between total revenues (including product and service revenues, net gains from other transactions, and interest and other income) and the total of the cost of goods sold and operating expenses. The phrases *net income* and *net earnings* are often used interchangeably, and the income statement itself is often referred to as the *earnings statement*. There are a number of intermediate designations on the income statement, such as *income from operations, income before extraordinary items*, and *income before taxes*.

---

[2] Many financial economists consider the inconsistent accounting treatment of dividends and interest charges to be inappropriate. They argue that since interest is the cost of a company's debt financing, and dividends represent the cost of equity financing, the two items should be consistently accounted for. A counterargument, however, relates to tax considerations—in most countries, while interest charges are tax deductible, dividend payments are not.

Consider again the basic accounting equation we studied in Chapter 2:

$$A = L + OE$$

Remember that we said that all changes in owners' equity between one year and the next are reported as either transactions with stockholders or as net income and that all net income items would be presented in the income statement. Conceptually, then,

Last year $A = L + (CS + RE)$
$$\longrightarrow \; = \; \text{This year's income (excluding}$$
This year $A = L + (CS + RE)$ dividend considerations)

Net income is the difference between revenues and expenses for the year, but it can also be seen as that part of the change in owners' equity from one year to the next that can be attributed to transactions with third parties—parties other than the owners.

Profit or loss. This is occasionally a synonym for income. Most often **profit** (or **loss**) is used to describe the income (or loss) effect of an *individual* transaction.

Unfortunately, some of these words are used casually in practice and are often used interchangeably. To understand what meaning is intended, it is important to consider the context in which a word is used and to focus on its meaning in that context.

Revenue and Revenue Recognition: Some Questions and Answers

Income statements always begin with revenue—sales, rent, services, or interest, depending on the nature of the business. Decisions about revenue recognition are among the most important accounting decisions a manager must make. Management is of course concerned about whether the transaction with the customer can count as a sale, but most importantly they worry about which accounting period they should credit with the revenue: should the revenue be included in this quarter, in the next quarter, or should it be deferred until next year. For a simple transaction, for example, a retail sale of merchandise for cash, it is easy to determine which period's income statement should benefit: The revenue is recognized in the period when the merchandise and the cash are exchanged. For more complex transactions, such as the sale of a partially completed building in exchange for cash and a long-term note receivable, it is much more difficult to know whether a sale has really occurred and to decide when the revenue should be recognized. Should the sale be included in the income statement in (1) the period in which the parties agreed to the transaction, (2) the period in which the building is completed, or (3) the period in which the note is finally paid off in cash? Take a moment and think about when revenue should be recognized in the sale of a life insurance policy, the construction of a submarine, or the provision of legal services.

To make those **revenue recognition** decisions—that is, to decide whether a company is entitled to recognize revenue from a transaction in the current period—management must answer three important questions.

Has the buyer accepted substantially all of the risk associated with the product sold (or service provided)? A seller almost always retains some risk related to an item sold as a result of its customer service policies, which provide for product return or repair under warranty. To qualify for revenue recognition at the time of an exchange, the transaction must burden the seller with only ordinary business risks that can be estimated with a reasonable degree of certainty. Almost every consumer product company recognizes revenue when its products are delivered to the customer, and such companies simultaneously recognize an expense and a liability for the estimated warranty services that may be required. If those future expenses cannot be estimated with reasonable accuracy because, for example, it is a very new product and there is not sufficient experience to suggest what the rate of warranty repair will be, the sale itself should not be recorded but should be treated as deferred revenue (a type of liability account). In such a case, the revenue would be deferred until the warranty period on the product expires. The revenue would not be recognized in the income statement when the sale was made, but recognition would be delayed until a subsequent accounting period. That delay in revenue recognition makes good business sense, but it might be painful to a manager who is under pressure from Wall Street to report increased net income.

Have we earned the right to the proceeds from this sale because we have completed our share of the transaction? The seller of a software package such as Lotus Notes™ can answer that question affirmatively when the disks and the manuals are delivered to the customer; in that case the delivery completes the earnings process because Lotus need do nothing more to satisfy the customer. On the other hand, the producer of custom-designed software cannot answer that question affirmatively until the software has been programmed, debugged, and tested successfully on the customer's hardware. Only when all of that has been done can the seller say that the earnings process is complete for that transaction, and only then can the sale be recognized in the seller's income statement. It will not be enough for management to say that they believe the earnings process is complete. Most every company will admit that its long–term future depends on the satisfaction of its customers, and with that in mind, the accounting rules for revenue recognition turn on whether the customer believes the seller has completed the earnings process.

In some very predictable long-term contract situations, the seller may be able to say that the earnings process is complete in phases and, as each phase is completed, recognize a pro rata share of the total expected revenue on the contract and the total expected cost of fulfilling that contract. This accounting convention is referred to as **percentage of completion** accounting (see Chapter 7 for further discussion). Aside from that unique exception, however, sale transactions can be recorded as revenue only when management can objectively affirm that the company's earnings process has been completed.

Can we estimate the collectibility of proceeds from this sale with a reasonable degree of certainty? Under accrual accounting, a seller makes no distinction between cash sales and credit sales on the assumption that collectibility of any resulting receivable is reasonably assured and that any credit loss can be estimated and recorded coincident with recognizing the revenue. However, when the terms of a transaction or the financial status of a buyer raise serious questions about the collectibility of the receivable resulting from the sale, recognition of the revenue should be deferred until that credit question is resolved. In some situations where the collectibility of the receivable is in doubt, the seller may be entitled to recognize revenue on an installment basis; that is, the seller recognizes a pro rata portion of the total expected revenue and a pro rata portion of the total expected cost of the sale as each cash payment is received. The question of collectibility is similar to the first question regarding risk passage—management must be able to estimate reasonably the amount of loss the company will incur as the result of a possible bad debt. If that loss cannot be reasonably estimated based on experience, the recognition of the revenue must be deferred until that uncertainty is resolved.

EXHIBIT 5.2

The Ford Motor Company
Revenue Recognition Policy

Sales are recorded by the company when products are shipped to dealers, except as described below. Estimated costs for approved sales incentive programs normally are recognized as sales reductions at the time of revenue recognition. Estimated costs for sales incentive programs approved subsequent to the time that related sales were recorded are recognized when the programs are approved.

Beginning December 1, 1995, sales through dealers to certain daily rental companies where the daily rental company has an option to require Ford to repurchase vehicles, subject to certain conditions, are recognized over the period of daily rental service in a manner similar to lease accounting. This change in accounting principle was made in accordance with the Emerging Issues Task Force consensus on Issue 95–1, "Revenue Recognition on Sales with a Guaranteed Minimum Residual Value." Ford elected to recognize this change in accounting principle on a prospective basis; the effect on the company's consolidated results of operations was not material. Previously, the company recognized revenue for these vehicles when shipped. The carrying value of these vehicles, included in other current assets, was $2,170 million at December 31, 1997, and $1,803 million at December 31, 1996.

Source: Excerpted from the footnotes to The Ford Motor Company 1997 annual report.

Most companies' sales transactions are straightforward, and the financial statement user can assume that the preceding three questions were asked and answered in a routine fashion. However, when a company's business is complex, the footnotes to the financial statements will describe the revenue recognition policies being followed. For example, in Ford Motor Company's annual report, the company explains that it records a sale when it ships a car to an independent dealer rather than when the car is sold to the ultimate buyer. Ford evidently follows that practice because it is confident that the dealer has assumed all substantive risk at the time of shipment to the dealer. Ford's description of its revenue recognition policy is presented in a footnote, which is reproduced in Exhibit 5.2. Read carefully the comment in the second paragraph of that note. Apparently Ford had been recognizing revenue at the time of delivery for those cars that were shipped to dealers for sale to "certain daily rental companies". But a new accounting rule forced a change in that policy because Ford retained a significant risk on the sale, the risk of a decline in the ultimate residual value of the car.

Occasionally a management group feels pressured to produce increasing net income numbers—the pressure may be from higher-level management or shareholders who want (expect) the company to perform well—and someone in the group will provide an inadequate or incorrect answer to one of the three revenue recognition questions. Unless one of the other members of the group protests, the company's income will be misstated. That misstatement may keep income high for a period and forestall a day of reckoning in the marketplace, but an incorrect answer to a revenue recognition question almost always becomes public, and the human and corporate cost to correct those misstatements is usually very great. Three cases involving misstatement are illustrated in Panel A of Exhibit 5.3. You will note that in several cases, more than one revenue recognition question was asked and more than one wrong answer was given.

EXHIBIT 5.3

Panel A—Revenue Recognition Questions and Answers

Case 1

A manufacturer of designer jeans maintained a policy to sell only to customers whose accounts receivable were current (i.e., only the most recent month's purchases remained unpaid). However, at the end of a particular quarter when sales were below budget, an order came in from a major customer whose account was 90 days past due. At the direction of the CEO, the company recorded the sale in the period when the order was received but held the delivery, setting the jeans aside in the warehouse. The customer was told that the merchandise would be shipped when the account receivable was paid up to a current status. That transaction did *not* qualify for revenue recognition in the period when the order was received because by the manufacturer's own policies, there was a question as to the collectibility of the receivable. Because of its refusal to ship the merchandise, the manufacturer retained all risk on the goods "sold." (Who bore the risk, for example, of a fire in the warehouse or of a dramatic change in styles?) Revenue should have been recognized in the period when the customer's account status was acceptable and when the product was shipped to the customer.

Case 2

A manufacturer of computer equipment maintained a policy to recognize revenue when its products were shipped, pursuant to a valid customer order. So long as the products were on the leading edge of technology, that policy was appropriate because shipment by the manufacturer was the equivalent of customer acceptance. However, there came a time when the competition caught up with the company's products, and customers frequently accepted shipment

subject to testing against a competing product in their own installations. (Had the customer accepted all risk for the equipment shipped?) The company didn't always win those competitions, and many of its shipments were returned. When the business circumstances changed, the company's revenue recognition policies should have changed to recognize revenue only in the period when it had formal customer acceptance in hand. Only then could the company be sure that risk had passed on the "sales" and that collectibility could be estimated with any reasonable degree of certainty.

Case 3

An operator of a computer service bureau also ran a school in which students from disadvantaged neighborhoods were trained on word processors and other computer equipment. The teaching was provided by computer-driven programmed instruction, and the students worked on their programs in labs under the direction of proctors. The tuition was paid periodically by government grants as the students completed phases of the program. The company recognized all of the revenue from the course (less a provision for dropouts) as soon as a student signed up for the course. (Had the company essentially completed its portion of the transaction?) Revenue should *not* have been recognized "up front," when the students signed up for the course, because to complete the earnings process and to ensure their estimates of dropouts, the company had to coach the students through the training and encourage their completion of the course work. Revenue should have been recognized only in the periods when the students completed phases of their course work, and the company completed that phase of its "earnings process."

Panel B—Expense Recognition Questions and Answers

Case 1

A manufacturer of high-tech products was faced with increasing competition and was forced to produce new models of its products before all of the engineering was complete. To meet production schedules, it was necessary to do significant handwork on each unit, which was very expensive. It was decided to send that handwork to a subcontractor because of its cheaper labor rate. Arguing that a failure in tool design caused the production problem and required the handwork, management insisted that the

subcontractor bill the handwork as tooling. The manufacturer accounted for those "tooling charges" as long-term assets and depreciated them against income over five years. (Did the handwork have the potential to earn future cash flows?) The subcontractor agreed to the mislabeled billings because the job was important to its own income. Clearly, the handwork added no new value to the manufacturer and should have been accounted for as part of the current period's cost of sales. The fraud was uncovered when an employee of the subcontractor finally "blew the whistle" on the mislabeled billings.

Case 2

A cable TV company was experiencing much greater growth than it had anticipated. Management was concerned that the growth could not be sustained and so decided to "park" some of its current income for future years. To do so, it set up a reserve account (i.e. a contra asset) and charged current operations with expenses for possible inventory obsolescence. (Were all costs and expenses associated with the current year's revenues appropriately recognized?) In later years, the growth did begin to slow down and eventually slowed disastrously. Rather than recognizing the effect of that slowdown in the income statement, management drew down on that reserve, crediting current income. Those machinations only postponed the inevitable, however, and the company eventually entered bankruptcy. The shareholders sued management because they were misled on the up side and on the down side of the company's business cycle. The shareholders argued that they wanted to know the naked facts about the company's earnings, period by period, and that they had been misled by management's "smoothed" results.

Case 3

A bank had substantial loans outstanding to oil and gas producers at a time when oil prices collapsed. Looking at the collateral behind its loans, the bank realized that under current conditions, the collectibility of those loans was very questionable. Management delayed making any addition to the bank's loan-loss reserve (and taking a current period charge to bad debts expense) because it had some studies suggesting that oil prices would eventually recover. (Were the bank's judgments and estimates sufficiently conservative?) Oil prices did not recover sufficiently, however, and some of the bank's major borrowers eventually collapsed. When that occurred, the bank had to make a major addition to its loan-loss reserve. The shareholders sued, arguing that management knew about the probability of the loan-loss problem much earlier, and, had it accounted for the probable losses conservatively, the shareholders would have had a fairer picture of the bank's operations much earlier.

Expenses and Expense Recognition: Some Questions and Answers

In preparing the income statement, questions concerning the recognition of both revenue and expenses must be addressed. Although the challenges to revenue recognition may be the most dramatic questions posed to management in connection with the preparation of the income statement, measurement of net income is also affected by costs and expenses. And, in fact, management must address similar questions regarding the recognition of expenses.

Have we included in our income statement all of the costs and expenses associated with the revenues we realized during the year? In an accrual accounting system, management's first obligation is to determine whether the revenue to be recognized meets the revenue recognition rules. If so, management's second obligation is to determine what expenses should be matched against that revenue, and to be sure that those expenses are appropriately recognized in the same period as the related revenue. When revenue is recognized in the current period, the *matching principle* requires that all costs and expenses connected with the sale be recognized in the same period. Those costs and expenses to be matched against sales include (1) some prior period costs that have been deferred as an asset as inventory until the period in which the product is sold, (2) current period costs to make the sale, including commissions and freight, and (3) certain future costs, such as the estimated cost of warranty work and estimated losses due to uncollectible receivables. Where the revenue is deferred, to be recognized in a future period, it may be that some current expenditures can be deferred as well. For example, Ford describes the revenue recognition policies (and its treatment of loan origination costs) for its financial services operations as follows:

Revenue Recognition – Financial Services. Revenue from finance receivables is recognized over the term of the receivable using the interest method. Certain loan origination costs are deferred and amortized over the term of the related receivable as a reduction in financing revenue. Revenue from operating leases is recognized as scheduled payments become due.

The costs to be deferred should be directly related to the deferred revenue and, of course, should not exceed the amount of the revenue deferred. The application of the matching principle requires some thought; management must look carefully at the revenue realized during the year and then think carefully about all the past, current, and future expenses that might be connected with those revenue.

As we prepared these financial statements, have our judgments and estimates been appropriately conservative? The decision as to whether an expenditure is an expense of the current year or whether it is an asset to be allocated to expense in future years is sometimes a difficult judgment. Some managers argue that an expenditure has a clear future benefit and should therefore be allocated to future years. Others argue that the benefit is tenuous and the expense should therefore be recognized immediately. For example, some argue logically that an advertising campaign is sure to build product awareness and customer loyalty. Because those benefits will produce future sales, it might be argued that some portion of those advertising expenditures should be treated as an asset and deferred into future periods so that they can be matched against the future sales the campaign generates. However, because those future benefits are uncertain (and because they are difficult to measure), the *principle of conservatism* forces companies to recognize those expenditures as expenses in the period they are incurred.

In practice, management is often tempted to be optimistic. After all, an entrepreneur who has devoted three years to developing a new product must believe strongly in that product to have devoted so much time to it. It naturally follows that the entrepreneur is confident of success and therefore wants to match the costs of that product development with the expected future sales. Determining whether an entity has been appropriately conservative requires an extraordinary amount of objectivity from a responsible management group. It is also possible, however, to be too conservative. An overly conservative approach to the asset/expense decision results in an unduly pessimistic income statement for the current period and an unrealistically profitable picture in subsequent years. As in all key management decisions, the answer is balance: Management must balance its application of the matching principle, which requires the deferral of some expenditures until future periods, with its application of the conservatism principle, which stipulates that the only surprises that should arise in future periods should be good surprises.

Do all of our assets still have the potential to earn future cash flows equal to their current costs? Have we recorded as liabilities all of the future expenditures we are likely to have to make? In addition to our challenge of the income statement, we ought to challenge the balance sheet as well. GAAP requires that an impairment of an asset and the recognition of a liability be recorded—and a charge to expense be recorded as well—when it is probable that an asset has been impaired or a liability has been incurred, and when the amount of the expense can be estimated reasonably. In this context, "probable" is understood to mean that a future event is likely to confirm the impairment or liability incurrence.

Some expenses are probable because they are a natural consequence of a company's activities. For example, a company that sells a consumer product with a warranty will probably incur some warranty expense, and so an estimate of that expense is recorded in the period in which the sales are recorded. Other expenses are probable because of forces outside the company and so are recorded in the period that the outside events become probable. For example, a fashion goods manufacturer knows that its inventory is subject to obsolescence and so analyzes the inventory periodically and records an adjustment to the carrying value of its unsold products when they become unfashionable and difficult to sell.

Some expenses become probable over time as the asset impairment becomes more serious or the threat of a liability becomes more tangible. For example, when a company is sued, its attorneys are not likely to be able to estimate the probability of losing the suit or the possible cost of such a loss. As time goes on, however, they form a clearer picture of the litigation and have a better estimate of winning or losing. At an intermediate stage in the litigation, they may develop an opinion as to the probability of losing the suit, but they still may be a long way from being able to estimate the cost of such a loss. Thus, the company may be required to include a footnote to its financial statements warning of the possibility of such a loss, but the expected future liability is not recognized in the balance sheet, nor is the expense recognized in the income statement. Eventually, a time will come when a settlement is under discussion or when a judgment has been reached and the cost of that lawsuit can be reasonably estimated. At that time, the liability and the expense connected with that lawsuit are recorded in the financial statements.

As you have thought about the three revenue recognition questions and the three expense recognition questions, you have perhaps realized that the critical issues have to do with *timing*. Because the income statement presents the results of operations for a given period of time, all of the critical questions having to do with the preparation of the income statement are timing issues—when, in which period, should an event be recognized? For example, an expenditure for a new roof can be added to the cost of a building and depreciated over the building's remaining life, or it can be charged to maintenance expense at the time of the expenditure. Intellectually, we might debate the nature of the expenditure—whether the new roof is an addition to the building or whether it is simple maintenance—but the practical effect of that debate would be a focus on the timing of the impact of that expenditure on net income. Because an income statement measures results over one period of time, and because income statements for a period of years measure trends of income, the timing of revenue recognition and expense recognition are critical. Management must make those decisions as objectively as possible to produce the fairest measure of results of operation for the period.

To help you review your understanding of expenses and expense recognition, return to Exhibit 5.3 and consider the three cases in panel B. Note the expense questions asked and how they were answered.

REPORTING THE RESULTS OF OPERATIONS: THE PROCTER & GAMBLE COMPANY

Traditionally, income statements are prepared with revenues listed first, followed by various categories of expense deductions, to arrive at a "bottom line," or net income. Income statements may be condensed for brevity, as in the case of Procter & Gamble (see Exhibit 5.4), or expanded for detail, providing many useful subtotals.[3] For example, many companies provide a subtotal after subtracting cost of sales from revenues, which they label **gross margin** or **gross profit.** Comparing gross profit as a percent of sales from year to year

---

[3] Published income statements are almost always comparative, with the results for the current year and at least one, often two, prior years presented. The presentations are consistent, even if classifications in prior years have to be adjusted to conform to the current year's format.

EXHIBIT 5.4

The Procter & Gamble Company
Consolidated Statement of Earnings

Amounts in Millions Except Per Share Amounts	Years Ended June 30		
	1998	1997	1996
Net Sales	$37,154	$35,764	$35,284
Cost of products sold	21,064	20,510	20,938
Marketing, research and administrative expenses	10,035	9,766	9,531
Operating Income	6,055	5,488	4,815
Interest expense	548	457	484
Other income, net	201	218	338
Earnings Before Income Taxes	5,708	5,249	4,669
Income taxes	1,928	1,834	1,623
Net Earnings	$ 3,780	$ 3,415	$ 3,046
Basic Net Earnings Per Common Share	$ 2.74	$ 2.43	$ 2.14
Diluted Net Earnings Per Common Share	$ 2.56	$ 2.28	$ 2.01
Dividends Per Common Share	$ 1.01	$ .90	$ .80

tells the reader whether the company has been able to match increases in costs with increases in sales prices, or whether the company is faced with a cost-price squeeze. Some companies differentiate between **Selling Expenses** and **Administrative Expenses,** because they want the reader to see that any increase in expenses was due to an expansion of sales effort rather than an increase in home office expenses. Procter & Gamble takes a different approach to that disclosure. They show only one line for expenses in the income statement, but in the "Financial Highlights" table (page 39) they tell us what the **Research and Development Expenses** and **Advertising Expenses** have been for each of the past five years. Most companies provide a subtotal labeled **Operating Income,** which shows the results of the business after all operating expenses have been covered, but before the effect of interest, taxes and other non-operating items.

Again, almost every company provides a subtotal labeled **Earnings before taxes,** then subtracts the income tax expense for the year and provides the final total, **Net Earnings.** The detail of the tax expense is almost always provided in a separate footnote (see Procter & Gamble's Footnote No. 9 on page 37). The determination of tax expense, and the make up of the tax footnote is discussed in Chapter 13.

The final data in the Statement of Earnings is **Earnings Per Share.** It is useful to know that the absolute level of Procter & Gamble's earnings increased this year, but absolute earnings can be misleading unless we know whether there was any significant change in the make up of stockholders' equity. Suppose Procter & Gamble had sold a new issue of common stock and had increased its equity by 50%. Even with an increase in absolute earnings in 1998, the original stockholders would be worse off. Similarly, it is misleading to compare Procter & Gamble's net earnings of $3,780 million with Colgate–Palmolive's net earnings of $740 million. Procter & Gamble has 1,343 million shares outstanding whereas Colgate has 295.4 million shares outstanding. Colgate–Palmolive's net earnings are 20% of Procter & Gamble's but Colgate–Palmolive's stockholder base is 22% of Procter & Gamble's numbers. A Procter & Gamble shareholder not only has the benefit of more earnings from the company but, on a pro-rata basis, has to share those earnings with fewer stockholder peers. Because of those comparison problems, GAAP requires every public company to provide a measure called **Basic EPS,** which is simply the weighted average number of common shares outstanding during the year divided into the net earnings for the year. Procter & Gamble's basic EPS of $2.74 tells us that its shareholders are better off than if they had invested in Colgate–Palmolive, because Colgate–Palmolive only earned $2.44 per share.

Because earnings per share numbers provide a basis for comparing one company against another, they are widely used in the stock market. For example, in the last three months of the company's fiscal year, Procter & Gamble's stock traded at about $86 per share. If you bought a share of Procter & Gamble in that time period, you would have paid $86 to gain the right to $2.74 of earnings for the current year. Finance people say that the stock was trading at an **Price/earnings multiple** of 31.4 times, (86/2.74). If we knew that other companies in the industry were trading at an average multiple of 25 times EPS, we might wonder whether the Procter & Gamble stock wasn't rather highly priced. At a multiple of 25, Procter & Gamble's EPS of $2.74 would only justify a stock price of $68.50. But further inquiry would lead us to understand that the stock market has priced Procter & Gamble stock at an above average multiple because the market expects Procter & Gamble's EPS to grow at a faster rate than the industry. Obviously, earning per share and the EPS multiple are very important numbers for both the market and company managers. You might ask yourself why Colgate-Palmolive's multiple is only 27.8 and what Colgate-Palmolive managers might do to convince the market to raise it to 31.4, to equal Procter & Gamble's multiple, and what the impact of that change might be.

When a company has securities outstanding that have some common stock characteristics, such as convertible bonds, options or warrants, a second EPS measure must be provided to reflect the potential dilution to the common stockholders from those securities. To calculate that number, the company adds to the weighted average number of shares actually outstanding, the number of common shares that would be created if the bond (or option, or warrant) were converted. GAAP also requires that the net earnings reported for the year be increased by the after-tax interest expense attributable to those securities. The company then divides the pro forma shares outstanding into the pro forma net earnings. If the resulting number is lower (as it is in Procter & Gamble's case) the income statement must include the result, labeled **Diluted EPS.** In effect, that dual presentation provides the extremes of earnings dilution from the presence of convertible securities: basic EPS assumes that no conversions will take place, while diluted EPS assumes that all possible dilutive conversions will take place. It is up to the reader to form his or her own view as to the likelihood of the conversion, and the resultant dilution. In the case of Procter & Gamble, there is potential dilution to the common stock because the Company issued convertible preferred stock to the trustees of its employee benefit plans: the trustee apparently converts as much of that preferred stock as is necessary to meet the needs of the benefit plans. The Statement of Stockholders Equity (page 28) shows that only about 2 million shares have been converted in each of the last three years. Those conversions are less than .2% of the outstanding shares, so the holder of Procter & Gamble common shares need not be concerned about a large-scale, dilutive conversion any time soon.

The Search for Permanent Earnings

As we have said, the stock market uses historical net earnings numbers to develop a forecast of company's earnings for next year—stock prices are based on prospective earnings and not historical earnings. Part of the analysis required to develop a projection of next year's earnings is to identify those events reflected in the results of this past year that will not impact next year. One of the analyst's most important jobs is the search for **recurring earnings** or **permanent earnings**. We might ask why companies don't present their income statements with a subtotal marked Permanent Earnings and Permanent Earnings Per Share. The analyst community has concluded that they would prefer to determine a company's permanent earnings on their own, based on their own analysis, and have asked only that companies provide some quantified detail about key events during this past year. Companies tell that story, highlighting changes from prior years and identifying items that were unusual this year, in several ways:

- Changes in operating results due to changed business circumstances are discussed generally in the **Management Discussion and Analysis** section of the annual report. In Procter & Gamble's MD&A, the company tells us about the changes in prices, volume and expenses that resulted in the increase in income for 1998. (See Panel A in Exhibit 5-5.)

- **Unusual items** that had a material impact on the year's results may be highlighted in the body of the income statement or they may be discussed in the footnotes. In 1996, American Greetings decided that its investment in its CreateaCard business was not as profitable as they had hoped, and consequently they wrote off $52 million of the original investment, to bring that investment down to the amount of its expected discounted cash flows. Obviously, that write-off distorted American's results for the year and management wanted the readers to know that it should not be considered as part of the company's permanent earnings. Similarly, the company sold two subsidiaries in 1998 and realized a gain on the sales. Management wanted the readers of the financials to know that those gains were not normal, and would not reoccur. Both the loss and the gains were highlighted with a separate line in the income statement and were detailed in a footnote. The footnote gives us the details of the transactions and the dollar amounts, both in absolute terms and in per-share terms (a $.18 per share gain in 1998 and an $.47 per share loss in 1996). With that information, an analyst can make more sense out of the results American Greetings reported in 1996 and 1998. (See Panel B in Exhibit 5-5.)

- **Extraordinary items** are unusual items taken to an extreme. Under GAAP, an extraordinary item must be highlighted in a separate line on the income statement, after taxes. There is to be a preceding line labeled **net earnings before extraordinary items:** there must also to be EPS numbers for the extraordinary item and for earnings before the extraordinary item. Because of the special treatment for these events, including the ability to present on the face of the income statement an EPS number before the extraordinary item, the GAAP rules are very strict as to what does and what does not constitute "extraordinary". To qualify for this special treatment the item must be both unusual and nonrecurring. The American Greetings items discussed above may have been unusual but the company cannot say that they will never again write down the assets of a line of business. (See panel C, of Exhibit 5-5 for an example of the treatment of an extraordinary item—a loss resulting from the early retirement of debt as a part of a corporate reorganization.)

EXHIBIT 5.5

THE SEARCH FOR PERMANENT EARNINGS

Panel A—Procter & Gamble's Management Discussion and Analysis: Results of Operations

The Company achieved record sales, unit volume and net earnings for the year ended June 30, 1998. Basic net earnings per common share increased 13% to $2.74. Worldwide net earnings for the year were $3.78 billion, an 11% increase over the prior year earnings of $3.42 billion.

Worldwide net sales for the current year were $37.15 billion, an increase of 4 % on worldwide unit volume growth of 6% The difference between the sales and volume growth rates was primarily due to weaker currencies in Europe and Asia. Excluding these impacts, sales increased 8 %.

Worldwide gross margin for the current year was 43% compared to 42.7% in the prior year. The current year improvement reflects cost savings, primarily from the Company's ongoing simplification and standardization program, as ongoing cost savings generated by the program exceeded the net cost to fund current year projects.

Worldwide marketing, research and administrative expenses were $10.04 billion compared to $9.77 billion in the prior year. This equates to 27.0% of sales, compared with 27.3% in the prior year. The 3% increase in total spending was primarily due to increased marketing support behind new brands, such as Tampax and Fat Free Pringles, and the expansion of existing brands into new markets.

Operating income grew 10% primarily reflecting sales growth and cost-control efforts. The Company's net earnings margin increased from 9.5% to 10.2%, the highest level in 57 years.

Interest expense increased 20% to $548 million on increased debt, due mainly to acquisitions. Other income, net, which consists primary of interest and investment income, contributed $201 million in the current year. In the prior year, other income, net, was $218 million.

The Company's effective tax rate for the year was 33.8% compared to 34.9% in the prior year. The decline reflects the benefits of lower tax rates in Europe, increased research and development tax credits in North America, and continued emphasis on effective tax planning.

- When a company makes a change in accounting principle, as from one method of depreciation to another, the change must be made retroactively as of the beginning of the year. The entry to recognize the impact of that retroactive change, as of the beginning of the year, will flow through the income statement in an account labeled **Cumulative Effect of a Change in Accounting Principle.** The impact of the change on the current year's operations will be included in the normal operating expense category, but will be explained in a footnote. The cumulative effect of an accounting change is treated just like an extraordinary item: it is highlighted with a separate line entry in the income statement and there is always a preceding line labeled Net Earnings before changes in accounting.

- When a business segment is sold, the revenues and expenses of that unit are pulled out of the company's revenues and expenses and the net result will be presented as a separate line item in the earnings statement, just before net earnings. That line will be labeled **Earnings (loss) from Discontinued Operations.** If there is such a line item, the preceding line, reflecting the results of the rest of the ongoing business, is labeled **Net Earnings From Continuing Operations.**

EXHIBIT 5.5 continued

Panel B—American Greeting's Statement of Income
Years ended February 28 or 29, 1998, 1997 and 1996
(Thousands of dollars, except per share amounts)

	1998	1997	1996
Net sales	$2,198,765	$2,161,089	$2,003,038
Other income	13,349	11,209	8,916
Total revenue	2,212,114	2,172,298	2,011,954
Costs and expenses:			
Material, labor and other production costs	790,688	805,124	762,006
Selling, distribution and marketing	876,822	839,916	770,044
Administrative and general	251,300	242,179	228,544
Non-recurring (gain) charge	(22,125)	—	52,061
Interest	22,992	30,749	24,290
	1,919,677	1,917,968	1,836,945
Income before income taxes	292,437	254,330	175,009
Income taxes	102,353	87,235	59,874
Net income	$ 190,084	$ 167,095	$ 115,135
Earnings per share	$ 2.58	$ 2.23	$ 1.54
Earnings per share—assuming dilution	$ 2.55	$ 2.22	$ 1.53

The Income Statement: International Considerations

As we saw in Chapter 4, the basic concepts, conventions, and presentation format of financial statements may vary from one country to the next, and this is certainly true for the income statement. Exhibit 5.6 presents the consolidated profit and loss account (or income statement) of Glaxo Wellcome Plc, a worldwide pharmaceutical company headquartered in Great Britain. (The letters "Plc" stand for "public limited company," the equivalent of an incorporated company in the United States.) Comparing Glaxo's income statement presentation with that of Procter & Gamble (see Exhibit 5.4) reveals a number of contrasts:

■ Instead of "sales," Glaxo refers to its revenues as "turnover"; similarly, the term "profit" is used in lieu of "income."

■ Glaxo provides little information about its various operating expenses (perhaps to avoid giving confidential information to its competitors), and thus a review of its footnotes (not provided in Exhibit 5.6) for this information would be essential.

EXHIBIT 5.5 concluded

Panel C—The Toro Company
Consolidated Statements of Earnings

	Year Ended	
(Dollars in thousands, except per share data)	October 31 1997	October 31 1996
Net sales	$1,051,204	$930,909
Cost of sales	663,167	589,186
Gross profit	388,037	341,723
Selling, general and administrative expense	315,690	278,284
Earnings from operations	72,347	63,439
Interest expense	19,900	13,590
Other income, net	(7,897)	(10,331)
Earning before income taxes and extraordinary loss	60,344	60,180
Provision for income taxes	23,836	23,771
Net earning before extraordinary loss	36,508	36,409
Extraordinary loss, net of income tax benefit of $1,087	1,663	—
Net earnings	$ 34,845	$ 36,409
Net earnings per share of common stock and common stock equivalent before extraordinary loss	$ 2.93	$ 2.90
Extraordinary loss per share, net of income tax benefit	$ 0.13	—
Net earnings per share of common stock and common stock equivalent	$ 2.80	$ 2.90

Despite these terminology and presentation differences, the revenue and expense recognition practices followed by most British companies in the preparation of the income statement are essentially equivalent to those followed by U.S. companies. This is not to imply that the differences between U.S. and U.K. GAAP are minimal, because in some areas of accounting the accepted practices of the two nations differ dramatically. However, the basic revenue and expense recognition questions that must be addressed by a British company are essentially the same questions addressed by a U.S. company; and the answers are quite often the same.

As a final observation, while Glaxo does provide a presentation of its earnings per ordinary (or common) share, a presentation of EPS is not required in all countries. The IASC, however, recommends the presentation of both basic and diluted EPS; consequently, it is expected that the presentation of EPS data will soon become generally accepted throughout the world.

EXHIBIT 5.6

Glaxo Wellcome Plc
Consolidated Profit and Loss Account

	Audited 12 months to 31 December 1998
	£m
Turnover	7,983
Operating costs	5,300
Trading Profit	2,683
Trading margin	33.6%
Share of profits/ (losses) of joint ventures and associated undertakings	22
Profit on dissolution of joint venture	57
Profit before interest	2,762
Net interest payable	91
Profit on ordinary activities before taxation	2,671
Taxation	815
Tax rate	30.5%
Profit on ordinary activities after taxation	1,856
Minority interests	20
Profit Attributable to Shareholders	1,836
Dividends	1,300
Retained Profit	536
Earnings per Ordinary Share	51.1p

ANALYZING THE INCOME STATEMENT

The principal focus of the income statement is the current operations of a company and thus the overall *profitability* of those operations. An analysis of profitability should proceed at two levels. First, the absolute level of revenues, gross margin, or net income, can be investigated over time (a trend analysis). Second, a series of profitability ratios can be calculated.

As noted in Chapter 4, trend analysis is frequently aided by the use of common-size financial statements. A common-size income statement expresses all statement items as a percentage of gross or net revenues (see Exhibit 5.7).

EXHIBIT 5.7

Blue Ridge Hardware Co.
Income Statement
For the Year Ended March 31, 2000

		Income Statement	Common-Size Statement
Net revenues		$ 74,500	100%
Less: Cost of merchandise sold		(44,700)	60.0
Gross margin		29,800	
Less: Operating expenses			
Rent expense	$ 3,600		4.8
Wage expense	15,300		20.5
Utilities expense	650		0.9
Depreciation expense	1,000		1.3
		(20,550)	
Income from operations		9,250	
Less: Interest expense		(900)	1.2
Income before taxes		8,350	
Less: Federal and state income taxes		(2,900)	3.9
Net income		$ 5,450	7.3

Two widely used profitability ratios are the rate of return on total assets and the rate of return on owners' equity. **The return on total assets** (ROA) measures a company's overall performance or effectiveness in using its available resources to generate income. The ROA is also sometimes called the *return on investment* (ROI) and is calculated as

$$\text{Return on assets} = \frac{\text{Net income after tax}}{\text{Average total assets}}$$

Because net income is generated throughout an accounting period, it would be inappropriate to measure the ROA using the total assets at either the beginning or the end of the period. Both total asset figures represent only a single point in time and may be skewed (either high or low). Hence, in an effort to obtain an assessment of the level of assets available throughout the entire accounting period, an average of the total assets is used in the ROA denominator.

Technically, ROA should be computed using "operating assets" and "operating" income. In most but not all situations, the operating numbers are the same as the totals reported in the financial statements. When making an ROA calculation and comparing one company's results against another, or one year's results against an array of prior years, it is important to be sure that the income and asset measures are determined consistently.

In general, the higher the ROA, the more profitable a company is thought to be. Since there is no ideal measure of ROA, it is important to compare the ROA to that of prior periods, to other competitor companies, and to industry averages.

The **return on owners' equity** (ROE) also measures a company's performance in using its assets to generate income; however, unlike the ROA, this measure relates a company's profitability only to the resources provided by its owners. The ROE is calculated as follows:[4]

$$\text{Return on equity} = \frac{\text{Net income after tax}}{\text{Average owners' equity}}$$

In general, the higher the ROE, the more profitable a company is thought to be.

Other useful profitability indicators are called the *profit margin ratios*. These ratios measure the relative profitability of a company's revenues. For example, the **gross profit margin ratio** is computed as follows:

$$\text{Gross profit margin} = \frac{(\text{Net Sales} - \text{Cost of goods sold})}{\text{Net sales}}$$

The gross profit margin ratio indicates the percentage of each dollar of revenue that is realized as gross profit after deducting the cost of goods or services sold. It represents the profit available to cover a company's other operating expenses, such as selling and administrative expenses, interest, and taxes. It provides an indicator of a company's pricing policies.

The most popular margin ratio is the *net profit margin ratio* or, as it is frequently referred to, the **return on sales** (ROS):

$$\text{Return on sales} = \frac{\text{Net income after tax}}{\text{Net sales}}$$

The ROS indicates the percentage of each dollar of sales revenue that is earned as net income and that may be retained in the company to support future operations or that may be paid to shareholders in the form of a dividend. Again, it is an indicator of a company's pricing policies and practices as well as its ability to control its ongoing expenses.

It is instructive to note that ROS is one of the component ratios that form the ROA ratio:

$$\text{Return on assets} = \text{ROS} \times \text{Asset turnover ratio}$$

$$= \frac{\text{Net income after tax}}{\text{Net sales}} \times \frac{\text{Net sales}}{\text{Average total assets}}$$

$$= \frac{\text{Net income after tax}}{\text{Average total assets}}$$

The asset turnover ratio is a measure of the effectiveness of a company's utilization of available resources to generate sales; it was discussed in Chapter 4.

[4] If a company has both common and preferred stock outstanding, the ROE is usually calculated only for the common stock, as follows:

$$\text{Return on common equity} = \frac{(\text{Net income after tax} - \text{Preferred stock dividends})}{\text{Average common shareholders' equity}}$$

The common shareholders' equity includes the following accounts: Common Stock at Par (or Stated) Value, Paid-in Capital in Excess of Par (or Stated) Value, Retained Earnings, and Treasury Stock.

It is noteworthy that the three profitability indicators, ROA, ROE, and ROS, are closely linked to the financial characteristic of *leverage*, also discussed in Chapter 4. So long as the cost of additional debt does not exceed the return generated from the borrowed funds, each of the profitability indicators should be enhanced. However, as increasing amounts of debt are assumed by a company, these profitability ratios, particularly the ROE, are threatened.

Using Procter & Gamble's consolidated statement of income (see Exhibit 5.4), we can calculate these profitability ratios, and they are as follows:

	1998	1997
Return on assets	12.9%	12.4%
Return on equity	31.1%	28.7%
Gross profit margin	43.3%	42.6%
Return on sales	10.2%	9.5%

Procter & Gamble's profitability improved, year to year. The return on assets grew modestly, but the return on equity improved by a full point and a half. That improvement is no doubt due to the fact that Procter & Gamble borrowed some of the funds necessary to fund its 1998 acquisitions, and those acquisitions earned more than the cost of the borrowed funds. Procter & Gamble benefited from greater leverage in 1998. The gross profit margin grew as did the ROS: Procter & Gamble tells us, in their MD&A, that they have been working to control costs and to simplify and standardize the product line. It appears as though those efforts are bearing fruit.

Management Issues

The income statement is a powerful analytical tool for managers as well as for investors and financial analysts. Just as investors and analysts focus on such profitability indicators as ROA, ROE, ROS, and EPS to help assess the desirability of investing in a particular company, managers likewise use these indicators to help them reach a variety of key decisions. On the one hand, management can use such measures to help identify which operating division or subsidiary would most benefit from further capital investment; and, on the other hand, these same measures can help show which subunits are performing well (that is, according to plan or budget), which are performing poorly, and hence which managers deserve a bonus and which do not. In essence, the profitability indicators can be used in three key management decision-making areas:

- Resource allocation decisions: Where should a company invest its limited economic resources to gain the most benefit?
- Control decisions: Which subunits are performing effectively, and for those subunits that aren't, why aren't they performing effectively?
- Compensation decisions: Which managers have performed most successfully and consequently merit additional compensation (such as a bonus)?

The importance of the income statement to the decision-making role of management also creates a particular accounting dilemma. As noted earlier in the chapter, the income statement (and the balance sheet as well) is significantly impacted by a variety of managerial decisions. For example, management must:

- Select the appropriate revenue recognition method to be used in preparing the income statement.

- Estimate the expected useful life of any depreciable assets and their anticipated salvage value, as well as select the depreciation method to be used.

- Estimate the period's uncollectible accounts receivable expense and the expected sales returns.

These and many other accounting-related inputs to the preparation of the income statement are the responsibility of a company's management team. The dilemma is that those individuals with the greatest responsibility for the accounting decision inputs to the income statement are also those individuals most likely to be impacted by the income statement data in their performance evaluation and compensation. Needless to say, this dilemma should be (and usually is) carefully monitored by the board of directors and the company's independent auditors, both of which retain oversight responsibility for the income statement, in order to ensure that the income data fairly reflects the operations of the company.

Risk and Pro Forma Financial Statements

The analysis of profitability is not an end in itself but is often undertaken as part of a broader assessment of the relative riskiness of a company. In the case of a lending institution evaluating the desirability of lending funds to a company, the principal focus is on default risk, whereas in the case of an investment or brokerage house evaluating the desirability of investing funds in a company, the principal focus is on operational risk.

Default risk refers to the probability that a company will be unable to meet its short-term or long-term obligations. The liquidity and solvency ratios discussed in Chapter 4 provide a good assessment of the probability of default risk.[5] **Operational risk,** on the other hand, refers to the probability that a company will experience unforeseen or unexpected events or factors that will reduce or impair its revenue and earnings streams (and implicitly its cash flow stream). These factors may be economywide (general inflation, recession, or high interest rates), industrywide (increased competition, changes in technology, or raw material/labor constraints), or firm specific (labor disputes, equipment failure, or product safety considerations).

Assessing the operational riskiness of a company involves, in part, developing an understanding of a company's marketplace, its competition, its sensitivity to inflation and interest rate changes, and its ability to respond to new opportunities. By analyzing the resiliency of past operations to prior economic changes, one can formulate assessments of how well (or poorly) current and future operations might respond to future economic changes and opportunities.

The ability to assess operational (and default) risk is tied in part to the ability to generate insightful pro forma financial statements. As discussed in Chapter 4, pro forma financial statements are forecasted financial statements. These forecasts are crucial to lending and investment decisions, for example, because the repayment of debt and the payment of future dividends depend substantially on a company's future profitability.

To illustrate the development of a pro forma income statement, we return to our example of the Blue Ridge Hardware Co. In Chapter 3 we used the transactions of the Blue Ridge Hardware Co. as a basis to prepare financial statements after one year of operations (see Exhibits 3.4, 3.6, and 3.8). The income statement of Blue Ridge Hardware for the year ended March 31, 2000, was presented earlier in Exhibit 5.7.

---

[5] It is important to note that the liquidity and solvency ratios are not independent of the profitability ratios. Indeed, high volatility in current profitability, combined with low liquidity and solvency, may suggest a high degree of default risk.

EXHIBIT 5.8

Blue Ridge Hardware Co.
Pro Forma Income Statement*
For the Year Ended March 31, 2001

Net revenues		$85,675
Less: Cost of merchandise sold		(48,835)
Gross margin		$36,840
Less: Operating expenses		
Rent expense	$ 3,600	
Wage expense	15,300	
Utilities expense	650	
Depreciation expense	1,000	
Advertising expense	2,000	
		(22,550)
Income from operations		14,290
Less: Interest expense		(720)
Income before taxes		13,570
Less: Federal and state income taxes		(4,750)
Net income		$ 8,820

*Assumptions
1. Revenues will increase by 15 percent in response to an advertising campaign costing $2,000.
2. Because of volume purchase discounts, the cost of merchandise sold as a percentage of revenues will decline by 3 percent.
3. All other operating expenses will remain fixed.
4. Income taxes will average 35 percent of pretax income.

As a starting point for preparing a pro forma income statement, it is useful to understand the relationship between the various income statement accounts. One way to do this is to prepare a common-size income statement. Earlier, Exhibit 5.7 presented such a statement for Blue Ridge Hardware for the first year of operations. If multiple periods of data are available, it is best to prepare common-size statements for several periods to determine whether the percentage relationships vary significantly between periods or at various levels of activity.

Since a common-size income statement relates all other account balances to the revenue figure, the most important projection is that of revenues. For illustrative purposes, let us assume that Blue Ridge Hardware is considering an advertising campaign as a means to generate additional future sales. On the basis of discussions with a local advertising agency, Blue Ridge anticipates an expenditure of $2,000 for print advertising to produce a 15 percent growth in sales.

To service the expected increase in customer demand, an additional investment in inventories will be required. However, the cost of merchandise is not expected to increase linearly with sales because volume purchase discounts will be available to lower the overall cost. Thus, the cost of merchandise sold is projected to decline to 57 percent of revenues from the 2000 level of 60 percent. All other outlays for operating expenses are expected to remain fixed in amount because no new employees or store operating hours will be required to handle the expected growth in sales. Further, income taxes are anticipated to remain at 35 percent of pretax income (that is, $2,900/$8,350).

Using these assumptions, it is possible to prepare a pro forma income statement for 2001 to assess the relative impact of the advertising campaign on Blue Ridge Hardware's profitability. Exhibit 5.8 presents a pro forma income statement for the year ended March 31, 2001, which reveals that net income after tax is projected to grow to $8,820, for an increase of $3,370. Thus, if our assumptions are reasonable, it is clear that the profitability of the company is substantially enhanced by the advertising campaign investment. Because advertising may help develop long-term customers, the effects may also have a carryover effect beyond 2001.

Pro formas may also be used to evaluate the desirability of lending money to or investing in a company. In Chapter 6 we will see how the pro forma income statement of Blue Ridge Hardware can be used to construct a pro forma statement of cash flows and a pro forma balance sheet.

SUMMARY

The income statement summarizes transactions that produce revenue for a company as a result of selling a product or service and transactions that result in expenses. It measures the overall profitability of operations and reports the profitability in a number of ways: gross margin, income from continuing operations, net income, and earnings per share.

The measurement of profitability is guided by a number of revenue and expense recognition conventions, principally the accrual principle, the allocation principle, and the matching principle. Evaluating the profitability of operations may be accomplished through a trend analysis of net income or through the calculation of various profitability ratios such as the ROA, ROE, or ROS. It is important to consider pro forma income statements, which can be prepared using reasonable and realistic assumptions of future period activities.

NEW CONCEPTS AND TERMS

Cost	**Gross profit margin ratio**
Cumulative effect of a change in accounting principle	**Income**
	Income from continuing operations
Default risk	**Loss**
Discontinued operations	**Net income**
Earnings per share	**Net income before extraordinary items**
Expenses	**Net income from discontinued operations**
Extraordinary item	**Operational risk**
Gain	**Percentage of completion**
Gross margin	**Permanent earnings**
Gross profit	

Price/earnings multiples	**Revenues**
Profit	**Revenue recognition**
Return on owners' equity	**Sales**
Return on sales	**Unusual item**
Return on total assets	

ASSIGNMENTS

5.1 Revenue Recognition Policy. The Boston Celtics Limited Partnership presents the following footnote in a recent annual report:

> *Revenue and Expense Recognition:* Revenues and expenses are recognized when revenues and the related costs are earned or incurred. Ticket sales and television and radio broadcasting fees generally are recorded as revenues at the time the game to which such proceeds relate is played. Team expenses, principally player and coaches' salaries, related fringe benefits and insurance, and game and playoff expenses, principally National Basketball Association attendance assessments, arena rentals, and travel, are recorded as expense on the same basis. Accordingly, advance ticket sales and advance payments on television and radio broadcasting contracts and payments for team and game expenses not earned or incurred are recorded as deferred game revenues and deferred game expenses, respectively, and amortized ratably as regular season games are played. General and administrative and selling and promotional expenses are charged to operations as incurred.

Comment on the reasoning underlying such policies.

5.2. Transaction analysis: Cash versus accrual basis. Global Enterprises, Inc., began the year with $10,000 cash, some other assets, some vendor payables, and $8,000 in owners' equity. During this current year, Global Enterprises entered into a number of events, including the following:

Event	Income Statement		Cash Balance	
a. Paid utilities of $200.	_____	_____	_____	_____
b. Purchased a $10,000 truck, giving cash and a $9,000 note (interest rate of 8%).	_____	_____	_____	_____
c. Paid dividends of $1,000.	_____	_____	_____	_____
d. Paid consultant $1,500.	_____	_____	_____	_____
e. Sold additional common stock for $6,000 cash.	_____	_____	_____	_____
f. Used $500 of supplies previously purchased.	_____	_____	_____	_____
g. Used truck for 1/10 of useful life.	_____	_____	_____	_____
h. Collected a $75 account receivable.	_____	_____	_____	_____

Required:

Note the effect of each of the preceding events on the company's income statement and its cash balance. For the income statement effects, note the dollar amount and whether the event affected a revenue or an expense. For the cash balance effects, note the dollar amount and whether the cash balance increased or decreased. Where an event has no affect, please note it as such.

5.3. Income measurement. At the beginning of 1999, M. Carlson, the owner and operator of a large agricultural concern, had no inventories on hand. During 1999, however, his company produced 80,000 bushels of corn, 100,000 bushels of soybeans, and 160,000 bushels of barley. Upon completion of the harvest, Carlson sold one-half of each of his crops at the following prices: corn, $4.50 per bushel; soybeans, $3.25 per bushel; and barley, $2 per bushel. At year-end, the remaining half of Carlson's crop was unsold.

To operate the company, Carlson incurred costs during 1999 of $370,000, including $100,000 in depreciation on his buildings and equipment. Moreover, Carlson estimates that his selling and delivery costs on the crops average $0.42 per bushel; these costs are included in his total operating costs given above. Finally, the commodities price quotations reported in the *Wall Street Journal* at year-end revealed that the current market price per bushel for each of the crops was as follows: corn, $5 per bushel; soybeans, $3.47 per bushel; and barley, $2.20 per bushel.

Presented below is the balance sheet for M. Carlson, Inc., as of January 1, 1999:

M. Carlson, Inc.
Balance Sheet
As of January 1, 1999

Assets			Liabilities and Equity	
Cash		$ 75,000	Liabilities	$ -0-
Land		300,000	Owners' equity:	
Buildings and equipment	$750,000		Capital stock	550,000
Less: Accumulated			Retained earnings	225,000
depreciation	(350,000)	400,000		
Total assets		$775,000	Total equities	$775,000

Required:
Prepare an income statement and balance sheet for the company as of December 31, 1999. Prepare a list of the accounting policy decisions that you made in arriving at these statements.

5.4. Income statement concepts. Consider these juxtapositions, each of which suggest some important income statement ideas:

a. Gain versus income

b. Loss versus expense

c. Realized versus recognized

d. Deferred versus prepaid

Required:

Prepare a commentary on each of the above juxtapositions, explaining how the contrasted items are alike and how they are different, and how each of them might be considered in the presentation of the income statement.

5.5. Asset or expense. The King Corporation reported net income of $5,000,000 in 1998, and it appears that 1999 will be similar. During 1999 the company made the following expenditures:

1. $125,000 was spent to resurface the employee parking lot. The resurfacing has to be done about every five years.

2. $250,000 was spent to upgrade the air filtration system in the paint department. The system as it was had worked satisfactorily, but the U.S. Department of Labor had recently promulgated new rules (effective three years from today) that would have required the changes the company made voluntarily.

3. $450,000 was paid to an architect for the design of a new research center. The center was the dream of the prior CEO but has now been shelved because the new officers are more cautious about the future.

4. $300,000 has been spent this year on the development of a new computer-based order entry system. The idea behind the new system is that salespeople in the field will be able to enter orders into the system directly, electronically, so that they can be shipped the very next day. Everyone hopes that the new system will enhance customer service and help stop a sales slide. The system appears to be on track, but another $200,000 will have to be spent before it can be demonstrated that it will work as planned.

5. The company's Texas plant was shut down for about three months this year because of the slow economy. The company struggled to find a way to keep their employees busy so they could keep as many of them as possible. The employees agreed to accept half pay, and the company found maintenance work and training for them. At the end of the period, about 85 percent of the work force was still on the payroll, and when the company went back to work, production resumed without a hitch. The maintenance work done by the employees during this time cost about $500,000; the training time cost the company another $400,000.

Required:

Prepare a one-paragraph memo discussing each of these expenditures, including whether the other side of the entry should be an addition to an asset or an expense charge. Explain your position.

5.6. Revenue recognition. Consider the following unique company situations:

1. The American Health Club sells lifetime memberships costing $1,200, which allow the member unlimited use of any of the company's 100 facilities around the country. The initiation fee may be paid in 24 monthly installments, with a 1 percent interest charge on the unpaid balance.

2. Universal Motors has always offered a limited, 24-month warranty program on its cars, but to counter the incredible competition in the industry, the company has come to the conclusion that they must do something more. With that in mind, they have developed a new program: For a $500 payment at the time of purchase, the customer can buy a five-year warranty that will cover replacement of almost all parts and labor. The purchased warranty expires at the end of five years or when the customer sells the car, whichever occurs first.

3. Community Promotions Corporation sells coupon books that give the holder a 10 percent discount (up to $10) from any of the 25 participating merchants. The buyer of the coupon book pays $50 for the book but obviously can realize up to $250 in benefits. Community Promotions convinces the merchants to participate in the program at no cost, arguing that they will build traffic and have the opportunity for repeat business from the coupon book holders.

4. Household Furnishings Emporium sells appliances and furniture with installment contracts. Those contracts usually carry interest rates of 16 percent or more. When the company has accumulated $200,000 of contracts with a year or more to go, they sell the contracts to a finance company on a nonrecourse basis. The company continues to service the contracts and is paid a service fee, which is based on the cash they collect and turn over to the finance company. If a contract goes bad, Household turns it over to a collection agency and has no further responsibility for it. In January the company sold contracts with a face value of $250,000 and received $265,000 in cash.

5. Neighborhood News, Inc., prints and distributes a weekly newspaper throughout the county. Local merchants order a certain number of the papers each week and pay for them on delivery. The company always takes back any unsold papers, however, and gives the merchant credit.

Required:

For each of these situations, prepare a short memo describing the revenue recognition policy the company ought to follow, explaining the basis for your recommendation.

5.7. Income statement classification. Net income for The Multi Corporation, for the year just ended, is $10,000,000. There is some debate, however, about the presentation of the income statement and the classification of certain events that could be considered material to that net income. In thinking about these items, it is important to know that Multi manufactures and distributes a line of automobile aftermarket accessories, which are sold through Sears and other major retail outlets. The events that follow all occurred or were recognized during the year.

1. A fire destroyed a warehouse in New Jersey. The loss was $2,500,000, half of which was covered by insurance.

2. The company completed a defense contract that produced a $1,250,000 profit. The contract used excess capacity in the plant, and the gross margin went directly to the bottom line. The company hopes to bid on similar contracts but is not sure that there will be a repeat opportunity.

3. An order of seat covers for an East Coast auto parts chain was found to be defective and was returned and scrapped. The loss on the order was $250,000, and the company gave the customer an additional discount of $500,000 on future orders in hopes of protecting the relationship.

4. The company spent $1,000,000 on the development of a catalog, which is to be used to sell parts by direct mail. The catalog probably has a useful life of 24 months. In the first three months of the mail order operations, sales exceeded expectations substantially.

5. To ensure its source of merchandise, the company has made investments in several Pacific Rim supplier companies. An opportunity arose to sell one of those investments at a substantial gain. The company agreed to the sale, received $4,000,000 in cash, realized a $2,000,000 gain, and invested the entire proceeds in a new supplier just beginning business in Mexico.

6. A loan to a manufacturer of car radios was written off this year. In fact, it had been clear for some time that the $1,500,000 note was worthless, but the radio maker was part of a complex of companies, some of whom were important to Multi. Multi's CEO had elected to keep a low profile with regard to the radio maker and had refused to press for payments of principal or interest for fear of alienating the other companies in the group. But now other sources had been found so that the complex was less significant as a supplier, and Multi forced the hand of the radio maker, pushing it into bankruptcy.

Required:

Prepare a paragraph discussing each event, describing how the item should be treated in Multi's income statement for the year just ended. Should the item be classified as unusual, extraordinary, or ordinary? Should the item be carried forward into next year (as an asset) or carried back to last year (as a prior period adjustment)? Be sure to explain the rationale for your decision.

5.8. Balance sheet and income statement ratios. Business analysts often talk about the "DuPont Ratio" (so named because it was developed by financial analysts in the DuPont Corporation many years ago), and by that they mean this interconnection of balance sheet and income statement ratios ("leverage" is assets over equity):

Return on sales $\times$ Asset turnover   = Return on assets
Return on assets $\times$ Leverage   = Return on equity

Let us make some assumptions about two different companies, and state those assumptions in terms of their most important balance sheet and income statement ratios:

Suppose Co. X's financial results depict

2% (ROS) $\times$ 3.4 (Asset turnover)   = 7% (ROA)
7% (ROA) $\times$ 3 (Leverage)   = 21% (ROE)

whereas Co. Y's financials show

$$7\% \text{ (ROS)} \times 1.5 \text{ (Asset turnover)} = 10.5\% \text{ (ROA)}$$
$$10.5\% \text{ (ROA)} \times 2 \text{ (Leverage)} = 21\% \text{ (ROE)}$$

Required:

a. Which company would you rather manage? Why?

b. Which company would you rather invest in? Why?

5.9. Working with income statement ratios. At lunch one day in the executive dining room of the Crest Investment Company, you notice a coworker lunching by herself and studying a set of financial statements. She seems frustrated and is talking to herself. You hear her say as she picks up her briefcase and leaves, "I do not understand what is going on with this company—none of this makes any sense to me." You start to follow her out when you notice that she has left a scratch sheet behind covered with figures; in fact, they appear to be a set of ratios, as follows:

	Last Year	This Year
AVG PRICE/SHARE	$ 5.10	$ 4.80
ROS	8.23%	6.23%
SALES INCREASE	18.30%	−2.00%
GROSS MARGIN	37.50%	35.00%
R&D/SALES	8.17%	6.67%
G&A/SALES	10.62%	12.50%
EFF. TAX RATE	40.00%	42.50%
ASSET TURNOVER	0.95	1.08
ROA	8.68%	5.75%
ROE	20.98%	13.84%

Required:

Identify five important things that may have been going on with this company this year that may explain the ratios developed by your frustrated friend.

5.10. Pro forma income statements. The Quandary Corporation is at a crossroads and must decide whether to expand a new product line or allow its mainline business to work toward liquidation. Income statements for the last three years are as follows:

The Quandary Corporation
Income Statements
(000s omitted)

	Two Years Ago	Last Year	This Year	Next Year	Two Years Out
Sales of old product	$10,000	$8,000	$7,000		
Cost of sales—old product	6,000	5,000	4,550		
Marketing costs—old product	1,500	1,280	1,225		
Depreciation—old product	500	450	400		
Interest—old product	200	180	150		
Contribution—old product	1,800	1,090	675		
Sales—new product	1,000	3,000	4,000		
Cost of sales—new product	750	2,175	2,800		
Marketing costs—new product	200	600	800		
Depreciation—new product	100	110	150		
Interest—new product	50	55	75		
Contribution—new product	(100)	60	175		
Corporate expenses	450	475	500		
Income before taxes	1,250	675	350		
Income taxes	500	270	140		
Net income	$ 750	$ 405	210		
Net assets employed—old prod.	5,000	4,800	4,600		
Net assets employed—new prod.	1,000	1,100	1,500		
Owners' equity	3,600	3,800	3,900		

Required:

Prepare two sets of pro forma income statements for next year and two years out, one set assuming that $10,000,000 is invested in an expansion of the new product line, and one set assuming that the new product line is abandoned. Prepare a memo for the president of Quandary, commenting on the pro forma statements. Your memo should explain the assumptions you made in preparing the pro forma statements and should interpret those statements to help the CEO decide what to do about the new product line.

5.11. Revenue recognition. At the beginning of 1998, John Cornell decided to quit his current job as construction supervisor for Walsh, Inc., a construction company headquartered in Chicago, and formed his own company. When he resigned, he had a written contract to build a custom home in Evanston, Illinois, at a price of $400,000. The full price was payable in cash when the house was completed and available for occupancy.

By year-end 1998, Cornell's new company, Distinctive Homes, Inc., had spent $50,000 for labor, $107,740 for materials, and $3,800 in miscellaneous expenses in connection with construction of the home. Cornell estimated that the project was 70 percent complete at year-end. In addition, construction materials on hand at year-end cost $2,600.

During the year, Distinctive Homes, Inc., had also purchased a small run-down house for $95,000, spent $32,000 fixing it up, and then sold it on November 1, 1998, for $175,000. The buyer paid $25,000 down and signed a note for the remainder of the balance due. The note called for interest payments only, at a rate of 12 percent per year, with a balloon payment for the outstanding balance owed at the end of 2000.

John's wife, Karen, was employed to keep the accounting records for Distinctive Homes, Inc., and on December 31, she prepared the following statement:

Distinctive Homes, Inc.
Where We Stand at Year-End

Assets		Debts and Capital	
Cash	$ 21,000	Accounts payable	$ 44,600
Material on hand	2,600	Owner's investment	242,540
House renovation contract	150,000	Sale of renovated house	175,000
Construction in progress	161,540		
Cost of renovated house	127,000		
Total assets	$462,140	Total debts and capital	$462,140

After reviewing the statement, John and Karen got into a discussion concerning the level of income the company earned during the year. John argued that the entire profit on the sale of the renovated home, along with 70 percent of the expected profit from the construction contract, had been earned. Karen, on the other hand, maintained that the profit on the renovation should be recognized only to the extent of the cash actually collected and that no profit should be recognized on the new home construction until it was completed and available for occupancy.

After discussing the problem at length, John and Karen agreed that there were four possible alternative approaches to measuring the company's income:

1. Report the entire amount of renovation income and a proportionate amount of construction contract income.

2. Report the entire amount of renovation income but none of the construction contract income.

3. Report the renovation income in proportion to the amount of cash received and the construction contract income in proportion to the amount of work completed.

4. Report the renovation income in proportion to the amount of cash received but none of the construction contract income.

Required:

Prepare the balance sheets and income statements that would result under each of the four approaches. Which set of statements do you believe best reflects the results of Distinctive Homes, Inc., for 1998?

5.12. Revenue recognition.   Supercolider, Inc., is an independent research and development laboratory that undertakes contractual research for a variety of corporate and governmental clients. Occasionally, scientists at the laboratory undertake independent research, which, if successful (that is, if it results in new products, designs, or technology), is then marketed by the company.

In January 1996 scientists at Supercolider began work on a number of minor research projects involving high-speed atom smashing. During 1996 costs incurred in these efforts amounted to $363,000. In May 1997 promising results emerged and were reported to the U.S. Department of Energy. Development costs incurred in 1997 through the end of May totaled $204,000.

At this point Supercolider tried to secure a government contract to support the remainder of the research effort. The Department of Energy (DOE) was reluctant, however, to commit substantial sums until further tests had been completed. Nonetheless, to ensure that it retained the first right of refusal, the DOE gave Supercolider a seed grant of $50,000 to help support the continuation of the studies; this grant carried a stipulation that the DOE would retain the right to acquire the results, patents, and copyrights from the research any time on or before December 31, 1998, for $2,400,000.

Further testing proved favorable, although additional development costs incurred in 1997 amounted to $325,000 and to $210,000 in 1998. On December 28, 1998, the DOE exercised its right and agreed to purchase the results, patents, and copyrights from the research. As previously agreed, the DOE paid Supercolider $300,000 immediately, with the remainder of the contract price payable in seven equal annual installments beginning on December 31, 1999, through December 31, 2005. On March 1, 1999, Supercolider delivered all scientific and legal documents, test results, and samples to the DOE offices in Washington, D.C.

Required:

Evaluate the facts of this case and determine when Supercolider, Inc., should recognize the various revenue streams associated with its work on this project. Also determine when Supercolider should recognize the various developmental costs. Be prepared to substantiate your position.

5.13. Financial analysis. Circuit City Stores, Inc., is a premier retail outlet for consumer electronics and major appliances in the United States. Presented below are five years of selected earnings and balance sheet data (years ended February 28 or 29).

	19X9	19X8	19X7	19X6	19X5
Consolidated Summary of Earnings					
(Amount in thousands except per share data)					
Net sales and operating revenues	$2,096,588	$1,721,497	$1,350,425	$1,010,692	$705,490
Cost of sales, buying, and warehousing	1,477,502	1,219,570	961,345	720,187	505,691
Gross profit	619,086	501,927	389,080	290,505	199,799
Selling, general, and administrative expenses	482,229	379,045	291,489	213,816	157,521
Interest expense	8,757	8,382	8,391	5,189	2,257
Total expense	490,986	387,427	299,880	219,005	159,778
Earnings before income taxes	128,100	114,500	89,200	71,500	40,021
Provision for income taxes	50,000	45,025	38,800	36,200	18,000
Net earnings	$ 78,100	$ 69,475	$ 50,400	$ 35,300	$ 22,021
Net earnings per common share:					
Primary and fully diluted	$1.70	$1.52	$1.12	$0.79	$0.50
Number of common shares outstanding at year end	45,860	45,234	44,802	44,380	43,780
Average common shares outstanding—primary	46,068	45,542	44,850	44,500	44,260
Consolidated Summary Balance Sheets					
(Amounts in thousands)					
Current assets	$ 442,208	$ 366,893	$ 265,364	$ 195,482	$135,939
Property and equipment, net	250,006	206,052	155,246	147,213	83,331
Deferred income taxes	6,460	3,023	354	—	1,637
Other assets	14,981	11,513	12,277	18,922	23,029
Total assets	$ 713,655	$ 587,481	$ 433,241	$ 361,617	$243,936
Current liabilities	$ 222,243	$ 192,150	$ 116,218	$ 98,162	$ 82,285
Long-term debt	93,882	94,674	96,676	101,149	40,005
Deferred income taxes	—	—	—	1,392	—
Deferred revenue, deferred credits, and other liabilities	38,244	27,040	18,934	11,643	9,874
Total liabilities	354,369	313,864	231,828	212,346	132,164
Stockholders' equity	359,286	273,617	201,413	149,271	111,772
Total liabilities and stockholders' equity	$ 713,655	$ 587,481	$ 433,241	$ 361,617	$ 243,936
Other Data					
Book value per share of common stock	$ 7.83	$ 6.05	$ 4.50	$ 3.37	$2.54
Cash dividends per share paid on common stock	$ 0.075	$ 0.055	$ 0.0375	$ 0.029	$0.024
Return on average stockholders' equity	24.6%	29.1%	28.7%	27.3%	22.0%
Funded debt to equity ratio	0.26 to 1	0.35 to 1	0.48 to 1	0.68 to 1	0.36 to 1
Number of employees at year-end	13,092	10,481	7,219	5,922	4,554
Number of retail units at year-end	149	122	105	87	69

Required:

Calculate all pertinent ratios. Prepare common-size financial statements. Explain the first four lines in the "other data" section. Overall, how has Circuit City Stores, Inc., been doing?

5.14. Revenue recognition under long-term contracts: Buildmore Construction Company. In June 1996 Buildmore Construction Company (BCC) was employed by the city of Houston, Texas, to assist in constructing its new World Trade Center complex. BCC was to construct the superstructure of a multistory office building as part of the city's downtown redevelopment. The construction agreement called for work to begin no later than August 1996 and required the company to construct the concrete frame for the complex.

Under the terms of the three-year contract, BCC was to receive a total of $10 million in cash payments from the city of Houston, to be paid as follows: 25 percent when the project was 30 percent complete, 25 percent when the project was 60 percent complete, and the remaining 50 percent when the project was fully completed (including all necessary building approvals). The contract, which was of a fixed price variety and hence did not provide for cost overrun recoupment, required that completion estimates be certified by an independent engineering consultant *before* any cash progress payments would be made.

In preparing its bid, BCC had estimated that the total cost to complete the project would be $8.3 million, assuming no cost overruns. Hence, under optimal conditions, the company anticipated a profit of approximately $1.7 million.

During the first year of the contract, BCC incurred actual costs of $2.49 million, and on June 30, 1997, the engineering consulting firm of C. Likert & Associates determined that the project had attained a 30 percent completion level. In the following year, BCC incurred actual costs of $3.1 million. As of June 30, 1998, the firm of C. Likert & Associates determined that the project had attained at least a 60 percent completion level. In their report to the City Authority, however, the consulting engineers noted that BCC might be facing a potential cost overrun situation. In response to this observation, the directors of BCC noted that they had anticipated that a number of economies of scale would arise during the final phases of construction and thereby offset any prior cost overruns.

By May 1999, BCC had completed the remainder of the project. Actual costs incurred during the year to June 30, 1999, amounted to $3.11 million. The firm received a certification for the fully completed work.

Accounting Decision

Prior to issuing the 1997 annual report, the controller's office of BCC determined that the proceeds from the World Trade Center contract would be accounted for using the *completed contract* method. Under this approach, the recognition of income is postponed until essentially all work on the contract has been completed. This method previously had been utilized by the company to account for construction contract income, and it appeared to be a prudent alternative, given the possibility of some cost overrun during the life of the current contract.

Under the completed contract approach, revenues (and thus expenses) are recognized on completion or substantial completion of a contract. In general, a contract is regarded as substantially complete if the remaining costs to complete the project are insignificant in amount. Funds expended under the contract are accounted for in an asset account, Construction in Progress, while progress payments received during the construction phase are accounted for in a Deferred or Unearned Revenue account. Although income is not recognized until completion of the contract, any expected losses should be recognized immediately when identified.

In the process of reaching the decision to use the completed contract method, the controller's office of the Buildmore Construction Company had reviewed *Accounting Research Bulletin No. 45*, "Long-Term Construction Type Contracts." This pronouncement identifies the *percentage of completion* method as the preferred method to account for long-term construction contract income, at least when the estimated costs to complete a contract and the extent of construction progress can be reasonably estimated. Under this method, revenues are recognized in proportion to the amount of construction actually completed in a given period.

Required:

a. Assuming that BCC had no other sources of revenues or expenses, determine the level of profits to be reported for the years ended June 30, 1997, 1998, and 1999, utilizing the following revenue recognition methods:

    (1) Percentage of completion.
    (2) Completed contract.
    (3) Cash basis. (Note: Assume that the City Authority remits cash payments on the same day as work completion certification.)

b. Which set of results (from part a) best reflects the economic performance of the company over the period 1997–1999? What criteria did you apply in the foregoing assessment?

c. What are the advantages and disadvantages of each of the methods from part *a?*

5.15. Revenue and expense recognition: Emergetel. Emergetel manufactures and sells two-way radio equipment used by police and fire departments and similar agencies. Unit sales have held steady over the last several years, but sales prices have been declining because of international competition. Earnings have been depressed, and so has the company's stock price.

California has become the company's most difficult sales territory. Because of the reduction in state and local tax rates in California, agencies responsible for purchasing radio equipment have sought to reduce costs and have turned to less expensive equipment from offshore suppliers. But even more frustrating, Emergetel's remaining California customers have become very demanding, insisting on top performance in very difficult circumstances—in intense urban environments and in rugged, hilly terrain. The Emergetel maintenance staff serving the California area is always the busiest of any in the company.

Harry Smith was assigned sales responsibility for the California territory in late 1989, just after the company lost a bid for a comprehensive new radio system in San Diego. That was a traumatic loss for the company because San Diego had used Emergetel equipment since 1952. The loss of an established customer hurt in three ways: The company lost the sales of the new equipment to be installed; it lost the service revenue on the ongoing maintenance; but perhaps most important, the company lost the opportunity to provide replacement and expansion equipment. Once a customer accepted a major new radio system, it was likely to stay with that supplier for ongoing enhancements. Over the life of a customer relationship, Emergetel estimated that the maintenance and add-on business was worth 10 times the original order.

Smith had worked the state tirelessly, although he had few sales to show for his effort. In late 1998 he came home with a *big* winner. He convinced the State Highway Patrol, the police departments from Los Angeles and the Bay Area, and the State Game and Wildlife Agency to go together and purchase a single radio system from Emergetel that would tie all four agencies' communication systems together. To satisfy the demands of each of those powerful agencies, Smith had promised spectacular performance. To meet the exacting specifications, Emergetel would be forced to redesign its basic equipment and create a "California Special Radio." The engineers estimated that the redesign and tooling involved would take three months and cost $8,000,000. The basic contract totaled $30,000,000. At that price, Emergetel would lose $2,000,000 after covering its direct costs, the design and tooling costs, and an appropriate share of fixed costs. Even so, the long-term potential of the contract was enormous, and Smith was awarded a bonus of $1,000,000, payable in three annual installments, beginning December 31, 1999.

The agencies also signed a combined five-year maintenance contract with Emergetel, providing for a fixed payment of $1,000,000 a quarter beginning March 31, 2000. Based on experience with similar systems, and factoring in the California environment, Emergetel estimated that there would be a 40 percent margin on that business.

The contracts were signed December 30, 1998. Prototype radios were to be delivered for testing by the agencies on March 31, 1999. The operational equipment was to be delivered in three equal stages: July 1999, September 1999, and November 1999. Everything was to be operational by December 30, 1999. The California agencies agreed to pay $6,000,000 on December 30, 1998, and four additional installments of $6,000,000 at the end of each quarter during 1999.

Required:

(Assume that Emergetel uses a calendar year-end for financial reporting purposes and prepares public financial statements every quarter.)

a. How much of the expected $2,000,000 loss on the basic contract should be recognized in Emergetel's quarterly income statements for these periods?

    (1) When the contract is signed. $ _____
    (2) When the radios are delivered. $ _____
    (3) During the term of the maintenance contract. $ _____
    (4) When replacement or expansion radios are sold to the agencies. $ _____
    (5) Other. $ _____

    Explain the rationale for your answers.

b. How much of the $8,000,000 spent for redesign and tooling on the "California Special Radio" should be recognized in Emergetel's quarterly income statements for these periods?

    (1) When the contract is signed. $ _____
    (2) When the radios are delivered. $ _____
    (3) During the term of the maintenance contract. $ _____
    (4) When replacement or expansion radios are sold to the agencies. $ _____
    (5) Other. $ _____

    Explain the rationale for your answers.

c. How much of Smith's $1,000,000 bonus should be recognized in Emergetel's quarterly income statements for these periods?

    (1) When the contract is signed. $ _____
    (2) When the radios are delivered. $ _____
    (3) During the term of the maintenance contract. $ _____
    (4) When replacement or expansion radios are sold to the agencies. $ _____
    (5) Other. $ _____

    Explain the rationale for your answers.

CHAPTER 6

The Statement of Cash Flows

If you are the owner of a business, how rich you feel is determined by the amount of cash going into your bank account (rather than by your accountant's version of profit.)[1]

The cash flow statement is one of the most useful statements companies prepare.[2]

Key Chapter Issues

- What is the statement of cash flows, and what are its principal elements?
- How are statements of cash flows prepared?

- What information does a statement of cash flows convey about a company's health?
- How might future levels of cash flows be projected?

[1] M. Giedroyc, "Tail that Wags the Dog," *Financial Times,* August 15, 1997, p. 10.

[2] J. Hertenstein and S. McKinnon, "Solving the Puzzle of the Cash Flow Statement," *Business Horizons,* January/February 1997, p. 69.

For many years, the principle focus of all financial statement users—creditors, investors, and managers alike—was the accrual-based financial statements, namely the balance sheet and the income statement. These two statements were thought to be not only *necessary* but also *sufficient* to present a complete picture of the financial condition and operations of a company. In recent decades, however, financial statement user preference has shifted from a purely accrual-based information orientation to one that includes *both* accrual and cash flow information.

In recognition of these changing preferences, the FASB in 1987 adopted SFAS No. 95, "Statement of Cash Flows," which specifies the format for a statement of cash flows that is now required in all U.S. published financial statements. The purpose of this chapter is to help students to gain an understanding of the information conveyed by the statement of cash flows and to learn how the statement is prepared and how it can be used and analyzed.

THE STATEMENT OF CASH FLOWS

A Historical Perspective

A noted authority on financial reporting once observed:

> For more than 500 years, until the 1930s, the central focus of financial reporting throughout the world was cash flow and solvency. So I find it somewhat amazing that for the past 50 years, which includes the entire lifespan of the Securities and Exchange Commission and the period of greatest development of external reporting in the United States, the financial community has been obsessed with the income statement and its all-important bottom-line figures—net income and earnings per share.[3]

To help explain the irony suggested by this observation, consider the following. Until the 1920s, the investing public in the United States made relatively few stock investments, and when such stock investments were made, they were typically based on personal contacts and conversations between the investee and the officers of the investor company. In fact, the most common type of financing involved debt between a lending institution and a borrower. Consequently, the principal use of financial statements was to enable creditors to evaluate lending opportunities and to justify the loans that were made; stock investors made relatively little use of such information. Hence, it stands to reason that the financial reporting characteristic of that era focused on liquidity and credit-related information rather than on earnings and investment-related information.

With the advent of a broader public market for stock investments in the late 1920s, the focus of financial statement interest shifted to income and earnings per share. As the level of stock investing increased, the financial community became increasingly interested in earnings and other accrual-based measures. This shift in focus was logical, even if excessive, in that the net income reported by a company is a better predictor of future earnings than is cash flow.[4]

Only after a number of spectacular bankruptcies by companies that had reported positive earnings streams did this earnings fixation begin to subside, with the pendulum swinging back toward a more balanced view. Although some may argue that "cash is king" in financial markets today, it is safe to say that an intelligent reader of financial statements looks at *both* the earnings picture and the cash flow picture.

[3] B.S. Thomas, "The Perils of Ignoring Cash Flow," *Directors and Boards,* Fall 1983, pp. 9–10.

[4] The interested reader is referred to Chapter 3 of *The Modern Theory of Financial Reporting* by L. Brown (Homewood, Ill.: BPI/Irwin, 1987).

The need for information to supplement the accrual-based income statement was first addressed in the United States in 1971 when the predecessor to the FASB, the Accounting Principles Board, required the inclusion of a statement of changes in financial position (SCFP) in published financial statements. (A similar phenomenon occurred in the United Kingdom in 1975 with the advent of the source and application of funds statement.) At that time, businesses were generally given the option of denominating the SCFP in terms of cash or working capital. Virtually all publicly held companies chose the seemingly more sophisticated working capital format for this statement.

The purpose of the SCFP was to explain how a company had funded its activities during the year, with *funds* defined as working capital. However, it did not take long for financial statement users to become disenchanted with the working capital approach to the SCFP because although working capital had a conceptual meaning (current assets minus current liabilities), it did not fully indicate the level of resources available for such normal operating functions as paying for purchases or investments.

This trend of increasing dissatisfaction with the SCFP was, in part, the result of a progressively more widespread call from the investing community for information pertaining to a business enterprise's cash flows. At about this same time, the FASB was also looking into the issue of cash flows. The board's study culminated with the issuance of SFAS No. 95, "Statement of Cash Flows," in November 1987. It was several years later that the British Accounting Standards Board issued its Financial Reporting Standard (FRS) No. 1, requiring publicly held companies to publish a cash flow statement as part of their 1992, and subsequent, annual reports. Likewise, in 1992 the International Accounting Standards Committee (IASC) revised International Accounting Standard (IAS) No. 7 to endorse the presentation of a statement of cash flows in lieu of a statement of changes in financial position (SCFP), operative for 1994 annual reports and thereafter. The formats adopted by both the British and the IASC parallel that detailed for U.S. companies in SFAS No. 95. It is interesting to note, however, that in some countries, like Japan, companies are currently not required to issue a cash flow statement or even a statement tantamount to a SCFP.

SFAS No. 95 requires businesses to include a statement of cash flows when issuing published financial statements. The FASB believes that this requirement will help readers and users of financial statements assess the following:

1. A business's ability to generate future cash flows.
2. A business's ability to meet obligations and pay dividends.
3. The effectiveness with which a business's management has fulfilled its cash stewardship function.

In short, the required cash flow information is intended to aid in determining the amount, timing, and uncertainty of *future* cash flows.

Management Issues

Cash flows represent the most fundamental and prevalent economic events engaged in by businesses. In fact, talk to just about any small business owner, entrepreneur, banker, or chief financial officer and he or she will tell you that the "bottom line" of the income statement has little to do with staying solvent. It is cash planning—specifically, understanding the sources and uses of current and future cash flows—that often makes the difference between corporate success and failure.

Businesses that manage cash effectively benefit in numerous ways. For example, they benefit by having lower financing costs. By accurately forecasting the amount and timing of cash flows, managers minimize their need to borrow, thus lessening their company's interest expense. In addition, improving the amount of cash generated from operations decreases the need to solicit external financing, thus preserving proportionate shareholder value and unused debt capacity.

Cash is also important to external users of management's financial statements. Shareholder and creditor interests are seldom settled by means other than cash. Therefore, cash flow information is very useful in enabling these users to assess a company's ability to (1) generate future positive cash flows from operations, (2) meet its maturing obligations, and (3) pay dividends.

Managers must be cognizant of the fact that accrual accounting often masks a company's underlying cash flows. Under the accrual basis of accounting, revenues are recognized at the time of sale, not when cash is received. Thus, credit sales increase net income but not current cash inflows. The accrual basis of preparing an income statement also reports such noncash expenses as depreciation, amortization, and accrued warranty estimates, which reduce net income and further widen the gulf between it and cash flows. For example, when a business enters into a loan agreement, the loan is reflected as an increase in loans payable on the balance sheet. As the loan is repaid, cash outflows increase and the loan's payable balance decreases. At no time, however, does any record of the cash outflow for the loan repayment appear in the income statement; only the interest expense appears there. For reasons such as this, the management of a business can easily find itself with an income statement that portrays an attractive net income number but without sufficient cash for tomorrow's tax bill, payroll, dividend, or loan payment. To ensure that such payments can be made, and that operations continue in an orderly manner, managers must manage both the timing and amount of cash flows.

THE ELEMENTS OF THE STATEMENT OF CASH FLOWS

The primary objective of the statement of cash flows (SCF) is to explain the change in cash and cash equivalents occurring during a given reporting period. Recall from Chapter 2 that this relationship can be portrayed as in Exhibit 6.1.

For purposes of the SCF, *cash* includes currency on hand and demand deposits and **cash equivalents,** which are short-term, liquid investments (such as U.S. Treasury bills) that are both readily convertible to cash and so close to maturity as to be essentially risk free. Companies must disclose which items are considered to be cash equivalents in their financial statements. Government securities of terms longer than three months, debt securities of terms longer than three months, and equity securities are not considered to be cash equivalents.

Statement Format

The SCF should clearly classify cash flows into one of three principal activities: operating, investing, and financing. **Investing activities** primarily affect the noncurrent asset accounts and include such transactions as making and collecting loans, acquiring and disposing of other entities' debt instruments or equity investments, and buying and selling property, plant, equipment, and other long-lived productive assets. Cash flows from **financing activities** are the results of transactions generally affecting the noncurrent liability and shareholders' equity accounts and include such transactions as obtaining resources from owners and providing them a return *on* and a return *of* their investment and borrowing and repaying

EXHIBIT 6.1

The Relationship between the Statement of Cash Flows
and Consecutive Balance Sheets

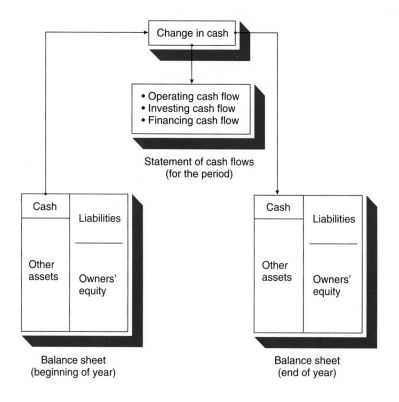

amounts borrowed. Finally, **operating activities** primarily affect the income statement and working capital accounts—in essence, the cash flows from sales of goods or services and cash payments for acquisition of the inputs used to provide the goods or services sold (for example, raw materials and labor). One helpful way to ascertain the appropriate categorization of a given business transaction is to think about the person who might be making the decision to engage in the transaction: Operations people generally make the *operating* decisions, the financial department is likely to be making the *investment* decisions, and the treasurer's office typically makes the *financing* decisions.

Operating activities. In regard to the operating activities section of the SCF, two presentation methods are permissible: the direct method and the indirect method (see Exhibit 6.2). The **direct method** (see Exhibit 6.3) presents major classes of cash receipts and payments. The direct method involves reporting, at a minimum, the **cash flows from operating activities** as the difference between the receipts and payments pertaining to the following separately reported items:

EXHIBIT 6.2

The Statement of Cash Flows:
Direct versus Indirect Methods

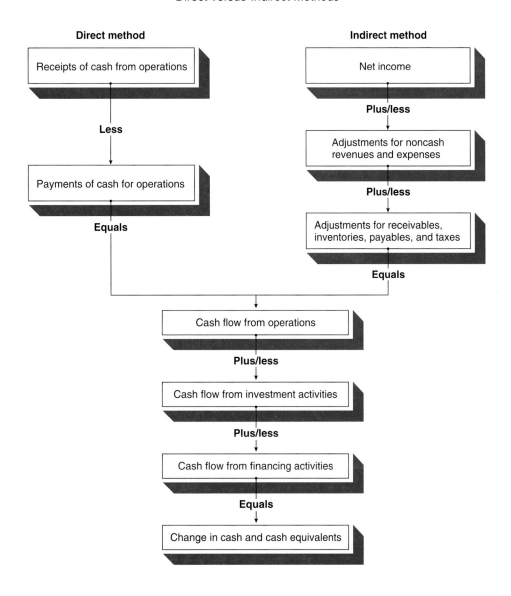

- Cash collected from clients and customers.
- Dividends and interest received.
- Other receipts of operating cash, if any, such as insurance and lawsuit settlements and refunds from suppliers.

EXHIBIT 6.3

Rowe Furniture
Consolidated Statements of Cash Flows

	Year Ended		
	11/30/97 (52 weeks)	12/1/96 (52 weeks)	12/3/95 (53 weeks)
INCREASE (DECREASE) IN CASH			
Cash flows from operating activities:			
Cash received from customers	$142,136	$138,270	$122,918
Cash paid to suppliers and employees	(128,135)	(128,641)	(113,063)
Income taxes paid, net of refunds	(3,781)	(4,013)	(1,911)
Interest paid	(279)	(343)	(388)
Interest received	306	479	232
Other receipts—net	960	1,290	800
Net cash and cash equivalents provided by operating activities	11,207	7,042	8,588
Cash flows from investing activities:			
Proceeds from sale of property and equipment	338	35	6,594
Capital expenditures	(3,261)	(3,856)	(10,686)
Sale (acquisitions) of marketable securities	—	(3)	137
Net cash used in investing activities	(2,923)	(3,824)	(3,955)
Cash flows from financing activities:			
Net borrowings (payments) under line of credit	(1,879)	1,475	(601)
Proceeds from issuance of long-term debt	—	—	200
Payments to reduce long-term debt	(420)	(634)	(455)
Proceeds from issuance of common stock	388	249	122
Dividends paid	(1,308)	(1,075)	(1,090)
Purchase of treasury stock	(6,112)	(1,659)	(2,957)
Net cash used in financing activities	(9,331)	(1,644)	(4,781)
Net increase (decrease) in cash and cash equivalents	(1,047)	1,574	(148)
Cash at beginning of year	1,897	323	471
Cash at end of year	$ 850	$ 1,897	$ 323
RECONCILIATION OF NET EARNINGS TO NET CASH PROVIDED BY OPERATING ACTIVITIES			
Net earnings	$ 6,286	$ 7,052	$ 7,207
Adjustments to reconcile net earnings to net cash provided by operating activities:			
Depreciation and amortization	2,777	2,487	2,175
Provision for deferred compensation	979	1,017	634
Payments made for deferred compensation	(526)	(426)	(449)
Deferred income taxes	(50)	(320)	2,150
Provision for losses on accounts receivable	3,919	490	179
Loss (gain) on disposition of assets	(124)	287	(5,253)
Change in operating assets and liabilities:			
Decrease (increase) in accounts receivable	(1,982)	(4,453)	(2,021)
Decrease (increase) in inventories	(2,071)	63	(1,127)
Decrease (increase) in prepaid expenses	(8)	594	(293)
Decrease (increase) in cash value of life insurance	(120)	(116)	(140)
Decrease (increase) in other assets	(35)	15	320
Increase (decrease) in accounts payable	2,326	(466)	4,080
Increase (decrease) in accrued expenses	(164)	818	1,126
Total adjustments	4,921	(10)	1,381
Net cash provided by operating activities	$ 11,207	$ 7,042	$ 8,588

- Cash payments for wages and other goods and services received.
- Interest paid.
- Taxes paid.
- Other operating cash payments, if any, such as charitable contributions.
- Refunds to customers and lawsuit settlements.

The distinctive feature of the **indirect method** of presenting the SCF is that it reconciles a company's accrual net income with its cash flows from operations. Beginning with net income (see Exhibit 6.4), the reconciliation process converts net income to its cash-basis equivalent by (1) adding back the noncash expenses (such as deferred income taxes, depreciation, and amortization expense) deducted that period in deriving net income, (2) subtracting the noncash revenues (such as undistributed earnings of affiliates) included in the period's net income, and (3) subtracting any gains and adding back any losses incurred on various transactions (such as the sale of a noncurrent asset or the early retirement of long-term debt) that will be reported in the investing and financing sections of the SCF. The first two types of adjustments are designed to eliminate any noncash items that are included in net income under the accrual basis of accounting, whereas the third type of adjustment is designed to avoid the double counting of certain cash flows. For example, if a long-term investment recorded on the books at $100,000 is sold for $120,000, the entire cash inflow of $120,000 should be reported on the SCF as an investing activity. To avoid double counting the $20,000 cash inflow representing the gain on the sale, the $20,000 gain included in accrual net income is subtracted from net income in deriving cash flow from operations in the SCF.

To complete the conversion of the accrual net income figure to the cash flows from operations figure under the indirect method, a final set of adjustments involving the operations-related current asset and current liability accounts is needed. Consider, for example, the fact that the sales figure in Procter & Gamble's income statement (most of which represents credit sales) is equal to this period's cash inflows from sales activities *only if* the year-end accounts receivable balance remains unchanged as compared to the receivable balance at the beginning of the period. This situation is reflected in Scenario 1 of Panel A in Exhibit 6.5. If, during the year, Procter & Gamble collected less than it billed its customers for credit sales, thereby creating an increase in the ending accounts receivable balance, the net income figure in the SCF would need to be reduced by the increase in receivables in order to approximate the period's true cash inflows from sales. Scenario 2 in Panel A of Exhibit 6.5 depicts this situation. Finally, a reduction in the ending receivable balance as compared to the beginning balance indicates that more cash had been collected than is reflected in the current period's sales figure. Thus, the amount of the reduction in the receivable balance should be added to the net income figure on the SCF in order to reflect this higher cash inflow. See, for example, Scenario 3 in Panel A of Exhibit 6.5 and Procter & Gamble's SCF for 1998, 1997, and 1996.

This final set of adjustments needed to derive the cash flow from operations may involve more accounts than the Accounts Receivable account. Consider, for example, the case of inventory. Every period, service businesses accumulate billable time, merchandisers make new purchases, and manufacturers produce additional items. If reported inventory amounts have increased beyond the beginning of period balance (that is, purchases have exceeded sales of inventory), an increased outflow of cash has occurred. Thus, the net increase in inventory must be subtracted from the accrual-based net income to reflect accurately the total cash spent or invested in inventory. On the other hand, if the reported ending inventory amounts have declined relative to their beginning balances, the net decline represents a part

EXHIBIT 6.4

Procter & Gamble
Consolidated Statement of Cash Flows
(in millions)

	Years Ended June 30		
	1998	1997	1996
Cash and Cash Equivalents, Beginning of Year	$ 2,350	$ 2,074	$ 2,028
Operating Activities			
Net earnings	3,780	3,415	3,046
Depreciation and amortization	1,598	1,487	1,358
Deferred income taxes	(101)	(26)	328
Change in accounts receivable	42	8	17
Change in inventories	(229)	(71)	202
Change in accounts payable, accrued and other liabilities	(3)	561	(948)
Change in other operating assets and liabilities	(65)	503	(134)
Other	(137)	5	289
Total Operating Activities	4,885	5,882	4,158
Investing Activities			
Capital expenditures	(2,559)	(2,129)	(2,179)
Proceeds from asset sales	555	520	402
Acquisitions	(3,269)	(150)	(358)
Change in investment securities	63	(309)	(331)
Total Investing Activities	(5,210)	(2,068)	(2,466)
Financing Activities			
Dividends to shareholders	(1,462)	(1,329)	(1,202)
Change in short-term debt	1,315	(160)	242
Additions to long-term debt	1,970	224	339
Reductions of long-term debt	(432)	(724)	(619)
Proceeds from stock options	158	134	89
Treasury purchases	(1,929)	(1,652)	(432)
Total Financing Activities	(380)	(3,507)	(1,583)
Effect of Exchange Rate Changes			
on Cash and Cash Equivalents	(96)	(31)	(63)
Change in Cash and Cash Equivalents	(801)	276	46
Cash and Cash Equivalents, End of Year	$ 1,549	$ 2,350	$ 2,074
Supplemental Disclosure			
Cash payments for:			
Interest, net of amount capitalized	$ 536	$ 449	$ 459
Income taxes	2,056	1,380	1,339
Liabilities assumed in acquisitions	808	42	56

EXHIBIT 6.5

Three Scenarios for Changes in Accounts Receivable and Accrued Wages Payable and Their SCF Reporting

Panel A: Accounts Receivable

Scenario	Accounts Receivable 12/31/99	Credit Sales included in 2000 Net Income	2000 Cash Collections	Accounts Receivable 12/31/00	2000 SCF Net Income Adjustment Related to a Change in Accounts Receivable
1	$10,000	$100,000	$100,000	$10,000	–0–
2	10,000	100,000	95,000	15,000	($5,000)
3	10,000	100,000	102,000	8,000	2,000

Panel B: Accrued Wages Payable

Scenario	Accrued Wages Payable 12/31/99	Wage Expense Deducted in 2000 Net Income	2000 Cash Outflow for Wages	Accrued Wages Payable 12/31/00	2000 SCF Net Income Adjustment related to a Change in Accrued Wages Payable
1	$ 4,000	$ 40,000	$ 40,000	$ 4,000	–0–
2	4,000	40,000	37,000	7,000	$3,000
3	4,000	40,000	43,500	500	(3,500)

---

of the cost of goods sold that is deducted in the income statement but for which no cash was expended this period. This means that the amount of the net decline must be added back to the accrual-based net income number to accurately reflect the actual cash outflows for inventory. Exhibit 6.4 depicts Procter & Gamble's adjustment to reduce accrual net income in 1998 and 1997 for an *increase* in inventories in deriving cash flow from operations.

Similar analyses apply to the accounts payable and to the accrued expenses payable that are a function of purchasing materials, supplies, and labor used in conducting a firm's operations. For example, an increase in accrued expenses payable (such as accrued wages payable) in effect represents a form of cash inflow because the business has not yet expended cash for some of the expenses currently deducted in the income statement (see Panel B in Exhibit 6.5). Alternatively, a decrease in accrued expenses payable in effect signifies an additional cash outflow for expenses booked on the current and/or prior income statement, thus necessitating a reduction in the cash-based net income estimate on the SCF in order to bring it into line with this period's actual cash outflows for expensed items.

It is important to understand fully these current asset and current liability adjustments. A way to facilitate one's understanding of the SCF working capital adjustments is to focus on the more intuitively obvious accounts as was done for accounts receivable and accrued wages payable in Exhibit 6.5. Once you become familiar with how the adjustments for these accounts relate to the SCF, the remaining working capital accounts can be viewed as extensions of the same logic but applied to different balance sheet accounts. Another means to achieve a greater level of understanding of these adjustments is to actually prepare an SCF—an opportunity for which is presented in a subsequent section of this chapter.

It is worth noting that accounts pertaining to the current portion of long-term debt and notes payable are more appropriately considered financing activities than operating activities and are therefore excluded from the conversion of net income to cash flows. Thus, the sum of net income plus all of the adjustments just described (as necessitated by the indirect method of preparing an SCF) results in the amount of cash generated internally by a company, or its *cash flows from operations.* Most companies (like Procter & Gamble) prefer the indirect method of presenting the SCF over the direct method because it provides a link to the income statement and balance sheet, and it is generally less costly to prepare. The FASB, on the other hand, prefers the direct method because it presents a company's major types of cash receipts and payments. As shown in Exhibit 6.2, the cash flows from operations are the same regardless of which method is used. Moreover, if the direct method is used, a reconciliation of net income to cash flow from operations must be presented in a separate schedule as Rowe Furniture does in Exhibit 6.3.

Cash flows from operations is arguably the most important cash flow indicator for users of financial statements because it demonstrates the ability of a company's operations to generate cash for its shareholders, creditors, or future investment. It informs the financial statement reader whether the business's core operations are a net provider or a net user of cash. If the operations of a business use more cash than they provide, cash must then be provided by liquidating investments, seeking further external financing, or decreasing the company's reserves of cash and cash equivalents. If, on the other hand, the operating activities provide cash, as is the case for Procter & Gamble, this additional cash will be available to invest in the business, to repay prior financing, to pay dividends, or merely to increase the cash reserves of the company. In 1998, Procter & Gamble's continuing operations generated a whopping $4.9 billion in cash flows, which was available to finance a variety of firm-related activities.

Investing activities. The next section of the SCF, as shown in Procter & Gamble's SCF (Exhibit 6.4), reports cash flows from investing activities. This section presents the uses and provisions of cash from investments, with the term *investment* used quite broadly. This section details the amounts a company has invested in its own business, equity investments in other firms, and dispositions and purchases of other assets. From Exhibit 6.4, we can see that in 1998 Procter & Gamble invested more than $3.2 billion in new acquisitions; and invested more than $2.55 billion in purchases of property, plant, and equipment. Procter & Gamble's 1998 SCF also reveals that the company received $555 million from the sale of property, plant, and equipment. Overall in 1998, Procter & Gamble's investing activities involved net cash outflows of $5.21 billion.

Financing activities. The final section of an SCF is the cash flow from financing activities. This section details the changes in the capital structure of a company and payments made to provide a return to investors on (and of) their investments in the firm. If cash flows from operations are positive, the company may wish to reduce its debt load, pay dividends, or buy back some of its outstanding shares. These choices must be considered in light of the firm's capital expenditure needs. If, on the other hand, the cash flows from operations are negative, or if they are positive but investing activities used more cash than operations provided (for example, as for Procter & Gamble in 1998 as revealed in Exhibit 6.4), a firm might want to reconsider paying cash dividends; it could be argued that paying dividends under these circumstances involves a partial liquidation of the firm. Given Procter & Gamble's strong history of generating positive cash flows and the modest amount by which its 1998 net cash outflows for investing activities exceeded the cash generated by operations, however, such a consideration was not warranted.

Noncash investing and financing activities. Businesses sometimes engage in **noncash investing and financing activities.** For example, the conversion of debt into owners' equity does not involve any cash inflows or outflows, nor does the acquisition of a piece of equipment financed entirely by the seller. Such noncash activities are either reported in a supplement to the SCF, as in Exhibit 6.4 for Procter & Gamble, or are disclosed elsewhere in the financial statements. Exhibit 6.4 reveals, for example, that Procter & Gamble assumed $808 million in debt for various acquisitions of companies it made during 1998.

PREPARING A STATEMENT OF CASH FLOWS

With the preceding discussion in mind, the best way to gain a full understanding of the SCF is to prepare one. The following simplified example is designed to illustrate the preparation of an indirect method SCF, produced from the comparative income statements (Exhibit 6.6) and balance sheets (Exhibit 6.7) of the Oakencroft Cabinet Company.

In preparing Oakencroft's SCF, it is useful to recall the basic accounting equation regarding assets, liabilities, and owners' equity:

$$A = L + OE \tag{1a}$$

Moreover, it is useful to note that the change in total assets from one period to the next must equal the sum of the changes in the liability and owners' equity accounts over that same period. Thus, Equation (1a) can be restated as

$$\Delta A = \Delta L + \Delta OE \tag{1b}$$

where Δ is interpreted as "the change in." Remember also that assets and liabilities are both composed of current (C) and noncurrent (NC) portions, so Equation (1b) can be restated as

$$\Delta CA + \Delta NCA = \Delta CL + \Delta NCL + \Delta OE \tag{2a}$$

A further breakdown of current assets into their components of cash, accounts receivable, inventories, and prepaid expenses permits a restatement of Equation (2a) as

$$\Delta \text{Cash} + \Delta AR + \Delta \text{Inv} + \Delta \text{Ppd Exp} + \Delta NCA = \Delta CL + \Delta NCL + \Delta OE \tag{2b}$$

Rearranging this equation to isolate the change in cash, we see that

$$\Delta \text{Cash} = \underbrace{\Delta CL - \Delta AR - \Delta \text{Inv} - \Delta \text{Ppd Exp}}_{\text{Operating activities}} \underbrace{- \Delta NCA}_{\substack{\text{Investing} \\ \text{activities}}} \underbrace{+ \Delta NCL + \Delta OE}_{\substack{\text{Financing} \\ \text{activities}}} \tag{3}$$

EXHIBIT 6.6

Oakencroft Cabinet Company
Income Statement
(in thousands of dollars)

	For the Year Ended	
	December 31, 2000	December 31, 1999
Net sales	$ 419,991	$ 341,656
Costs and expenses:		
Cost of sales	(280,746)	(228,681)
Depreciation	(9,033)	(6,843)
Selling, general, and administrative	(85,469)	(65,610)
	(375,248)	(301,134)
Income from operations	44,743	40,522
Interest expense	(1,877)	(1,570)
Other income	2,081	2,807
Earnings before taxes	44,947	41,759
Federal income taxes*	(18,383)	(17,606)
State income taxes	(1,900)	(1,143)
Net income	24,664	23,010
Retained earnings, beginning of year	138,273	121,476
Less: Cash dividends	(6,920)	(6,213)
Retained earnings, end of year	$ 156,017	$ 138,273

*Federal income tax expense included the following:

	2000	1999
Current amount	$18,603	$17,456
Deferred amount	(220)	150
Total	$18,383	$17,606

The dynamics of the statement of cash flows can easily be discerned from this alternative presentation of the accounting equation. For example, if a current liability such as accrued wages payable is increased, the effect is an increase in cash (or a positive cash flow)—in essence, a form of spontaneous financing. If, on the other hand, there is an increase in a current asset account such as Inventory or Prepaid Expenses, cash decreases.

As noted earlier, the starting point for preparing an SCF using the indirect method is the accrual net income for the period. From such a starting point, the net income number must be adjusted for the noncash revenues and expenses that are present in the income statement—primarily depreciation, amortization, deferred taxes,[5] and the undistributed

---

[5] In the United States, a company may prepare its income tax return using different accounting principles than it uses to prepare its financial statements. To the extent that the amount of tax that would be due if the financial statement basis had been used is different from the taxes shown on the tax return, that difference is recorded as *deferred taxes*. Therefore, deferred taxes are different from taxes payable because the deferred taxes become a liability only at some future and uncertain time. Deferred taxes represent a form of interest-free borrowing by the company and are a reconciling item between earnings and cash flow. Taxes currently payable represent the amount of taxes shown on the current tax return, less any prepayments. This topic is discussed in Chapter 13.

EXHIBIT 6.7

Oakencroft Cabinet Company
Balance Sheet
(in thousands of dollars)

	As of		Increase/ Decrease in Account Balance
	December 31, 2000	December 31, 1999	
Assets			
Cash	$ 1,393	$ 2,419	$ (1,026)
Short-term treasury bills	21,172	13,305	7,867
Receivables, less allowances of $3,118 in 2000 and $2,814 in 1999	113,834	103,824	10,010
Inventories:			
Raw materials	19,541	15,305	
Work in process	17,143	14,771	
Finished goods	8,791	5,157	
	45,475	35,233	10,242
Other current assets	5,037	3,229	1,808
Total current assets	$186,911	$158,010	
Property, plant, and equipment:			
Land	3,586	2,842	
Buildings and fixtures	53,082	44,082	
Machinery and equipment	66,978	51,041	
	123,646	97,971	25,675
Less: Accumulated depreciation	50,115	41,082	(9,033)
	73,531	56,889	16,642
Other assets	9,445	18,095	(8,650)
Total assets	$269,887	$232,994	$36,893

earnings of affiliate companies.[6] The 2000 Oakencroft income statement (see Exhibit 6.6) reveals, for example, that $9,033 was deducted as depreciation expense. Because depreciation of property, plant, and equipment requires no cash outlay, the $9,033 must be added back to net income in deriving an estimate of the cash flows from operations. Oakencroft's income statement reveals no other noncash revenues or expenses with the exception of deferred income taxes. From the balance sheet (see Exhibit 6.7), and the income statement footnote, in 2000 there was a decrease in the Deferred Taxes Liability

---

[6] In certain circumstances, a company may include in its own income statement the income of another company that it controls. Those earnings are recognized as they are reported by the other company on the theory that the controlling company could cause those earnings to be remitted to it at any time. Obviously, to the extent that the earnings are not remitted to the parent company in cash, those earnings are an adjustment to accrual earnings to arrive at the operating cash flow. This topic is discussed in Chapter 10.

EXHIBIT 6.7 continued

	As of		Increase/ Decrease in Account Balance
	December 31, 2000	December 31, 1999	
Liabilities			
Notes payable	$ 6,099	$ 3,682	$ 2,417
Current portion of long-term debt	979	1,717	(738)
Accounts payable	20,134	11,033	9,101
Wages payable	15,941	13,144	2,797
Accrued liabilities	10,014	7,478	2,536
Accrued taxes	18,409	14,588	3,821
Total current liabilities	71,576	51,642	
Long-term debt	23,270	24,463	(1,193)
Deferred taxes	9,697	9,917	(220)
Total liabilities	$104,543	$ 86,022	
Stockholders' Equity			
Common stock	$ 10,714	$ 10,443	271
Retained earnings	156,017	138,273	17,744
	166,731	148,716	
Less: Treasury shares	(1,387)	(1,744)	357
Total stockholders' equity	$165,344	$146,972	
Total liabilities and stockholders' equity	$269,887	$232,994	$36,893

account with a commensurate reduction in the total tax expense amount. The overall effect of this change represents an additional cash outlay this period for income taxes owed from an earlier accounting period; that is, the tax expense for this additional amount was recorded in an earlier accounting period but was not paid until this period. Thus, the decrease in deferred tax liabilities in 2000 represents a decrease in operating cash flows this period that was not revealed in the 2000 income statement where only $18,383 was deducted as tax expense. Remembering the relationships from Equation (3), we recognize that this decrease in a liability should, therefore, be subtracted from net income in the operating activities section.

As pointed out earlier, the objective of the SCF is to explain the change in cash and cash equivalents by reporting all of the changes in the noncash accounts. In a sense, this is like trying to define a word without using the word in the definition. In effect, the SCF provides a definition of the change in cash by examining all of the other balance sheet account changes. Thus, the next step in our efforts to develop Oakencroft's SCF (see Exhibit 6.8) is to focus on the adjustments to net income associated with changes in the current asset and current liability operations-related accounts.

From the balance sheet data in Exhibit 6.7, note that accounts receivable increased $10,010 from 1999 to 2000. This means that the company billed its customers for more than

EXHIBIT 6.8

Oakencroft Cabinet Company
Statement of Cash Flows
(in thousands of dollars)

	For the year ended December 31, 2000
Operating activities	
Net income	$24,664
Add: Depreciation and amortization	9,033
Less: Noncash revenues	–0–
Adjustment for deferred taxes, decrease (increase)	(220)
Receivables, decrease (increase)	(10,010)
Inventories, decrease (increase)	(10,242)
Payables, increase (decrease)	14,434
Taxes, increase (decrease)	3,821
Other	(1,808)
	5,008
Cash flow from operating activities	$29,672
Investing activities	
Purchases of property, plant and equipment	(25,675)
Other	8,650
Cash flow from investing activities	($17,025)
Financing activities	
Proceeds from short-term notes payable	2,417
Payments on long-term loans	(1,931)
Sale of stock	271
Reissue of treasury stock	357
Cash dividends paid to stockholders	(6,920)
Cash flow from financing activities	($ 5,806)
Increase (decrease) in cash and cash equivalents	$6,841
Cash and cash equivalents, beginning of year	$15,724
Cash and cash equivalents, end of year	$22,565

it collected from them, which represents sales for which collections have not yet been received. The amount is thus shown as a reduction to net income in the pursuit of converting an accrual-based net income amount to an operating cash flow estimate. With similar logic, the balance sheet data also reveal that accounts payable (along with wages payable and accrued liabilities) increased, indicating that the company was billed for more expenses than it paid; hence, this amount is like a provision of cash and is therefore shown as a positive cash flow. The sum of these items (that is, net income *plus/minus* the noncash revenues and expenses *plus/minus* the changes in working capital accounts) equals the cash flow from operating activities of $29,672.

The investment section of the SCF shows changes in the balance sheet for investments in property, plant, equipment (PP&E), in equity securities from other companies, and in other assets. Note that the balance sheet data indicate that PP&E increased by $25,675. The change in the accumulated depreciation account of $9,033 equals this period's depreciation expense, which has already been placed as an adjusting item in the operating section of Oakencroft's SCF. In the absence of any sales of PP&E during the year, the $25,675 figure equals the cost of *purchases* of PP&E made this year.

It is often helpful to construct a T-account for the PP&E accounts to facilitate these calculations. In this example, the T-accounts are very straightforward:

Property, Plant, and Equipment			Accumulated Depreciation		
1/1/00	97,971			1/1/00	41,082
Purchases	25,675			This year's expense	9,033
12/31/00	$123,646			12/31/00	50,115

If, however, the financial statements had informed readers that PP&E originally costing $10,000 had been sold for $8,000 and the 2000 depreciation expense was $12,033, the reconstruction of the T-accounts would reveal the following:

Property, Plant, and Equipment			Accumulated Depreciation		
1/1/00	97,971			1/1/00	41,082
		Cost of PP&E sold 10,000	Accumulated depreciation on PP&E sold 3,000	This year's expense	12,033
PP&E purchases	35,675				
12/31/00	123,646			12/31/00	50,115

Thus, in this hypothetical scenario where we were given the beginning and ending balances in the PP&E account and the cost of PP&E sold, it is possible to deduce purchases of PP&E totaling $35,675. In addition, it is also possible to determine that $3,000 of depreciation expense had been accumulated over the years for the particular PP&E item sold. In sum, then, the transaction to record the sale would have been as follows:

```
Dr. Cash (A) ........................ (inc.) 8,000
Dr. Accumulated Depreciation (CA) ...... (dec.) 3,000
    Cr. Property, Plant, and Equipment (A) ................. (dec.) 10,000
    Cr. Gain on the sale of Property, Plant, and Equipment (G)... (inc.)   1,000
```

Under this scenario, the SCF would report a $1,000 subtracting adjustment to net income in the operations section and a line item of $8,000 for "proceeds of PP&E sale" in the investing section, as well as another line item of $35,675 for purchases of PP&E. Since in the base case we were not informed of any PP&E sales, we must assume the purchases of PP&E cost $25,675 and depreciation expense was $9,033.

The final section of the SCF, financing activities, shows the net changes in cash flows as a result of payments and proceeds from loans, stock sales and stock repurchases, dividends paid to shareholders, and other financing transactions. Note the increase in short-term notes payable of $2,417. This amount is a provision of cash for the company and is shown as a positive cash flow. In determining the payments on long-term debt ($1,931), both the amounts currently due and those that are noncurrent should be considered. Cash dividends paid to shareholders always represent a use of cash and thus are shown as a negative cash flow.

As a vehicle to verify that the entire change in the retained earnings balance has been accounted for in the SCF, it is useful to reconstruct the changes in this account balance using a T-account. In the following Retained Earnings T-account, note that the net income and dividend figures, both of which now appear in the SCF, fully explain the change in Oakencroft's Retained Earnings account for the period:

Retained Earnings

2000 dividends 6,920	1/1/00	138,273
	2000 net income	24,664
	12/31/00	156,017

The SCF format for reporting these results is shown in Exhibit 6.8. The sum of the three separate sections represents the increase (or decrease) in cash and cash equivalents for the period. When added to the beginning balance of cash and cash equivalents, the resulting sum should equal the ending cash and cash-equivalent balance on the latest balance sheet. If all of the balance sheet changes reflected in Exhibit 6.7 have been included in the SCF, it should balance to the actual change in the cash and cash–equivalent balance ($6,841 for Oakencroft), and the SCF is then complete.

THE STATEMENT OF CASH FLOWS: INTERNATIONAL CONSIDERATIONS

As alluded to earlier, there is a growing global momentum toward accounting standards setters requiring an SCF as part of a company's published annual report. In some countries (such as Germany and Japan) such a financial reporting requirement does not exist. It is interesting to observe, however, that companies in those countries may actually exhibit a preference for publishing such a statement in an attempt to address the perceived information needs of the international investing community. For example, even though German accounting standards do not require an SCF, Hoechst AG (a German chemicals company) chose to present in its 1997 annual report an SCF "reflect[ing] the format recommended by the IAS [No. 7]." Exhibit 6.9 presents Hoechst's SCF, a review of which reveals the similarity in the SCF formats dictated by IAS No. 7 and SFAS No. 95.

It is important to acknowledge the fact that although a non-U.S. company may choose (or may even be required) to publish an SCF, it may be in a form quite different from that required in the United States or that suggested by the IASC. Again consider the German context where an SCF is not required. In Volkswagen's (a German auto maker) 1997 annual report, it presents cash flow-related information (see Exhibit 6.10). Volkswagen and Hoechst may be viewed as competing for the attention, confidence, and resources of the same international audience when they publish their annual reports, yet they do so quite differently in terms of an SCF. As we turn our attention next to analyzing cash flows, users of Volkswagen's cash flow disclosures, for example, must exercise care and caution in making direct comparisons to the cash flow disclosures of a U.S. company or, for that matter, Hoechst.

EXHIBIT 6.9

Hoechst AG
Cash Flow Statement
For Years Ended December 31

	1997 DM m	1996 DM m
Profit before taxes on income	3157	5146
Depreciation of non-current assets	3782	3632
Gain on disposals of non-current assets	− 605	− 1234
Undistributed earnings from equity method investments	− 204	− 134
Net interest expense	1019	780
Income taxes paid	− 965	− 2018
Changes in inventories	− 330	160
Changes in receivables, other assets and deferred income	− 1760	− 162
Proceeds from accounts receivable financing program	530	
Changes in provisions	− 667	− 849
Changes in liabilities excl. corporate debt	− 425	488
Other	− 54	− 149
Cash flows from operating activities	**3478**	**5660**
Capital expenditure on property, plant and equipment and investments in intangible assets	− 3686	− 4021
Acquisitions of businesses and purchases of investments	− 6676	− 2145
Proceeds from disposal of subsidiaries, shareholdings and similar assets	3980	2409
Proceeds from the sale of property, plant and equipment and intangible assets	547	720
Proceeds from the sale of investments	486	311
Proceeds from the sale of marketable securities	85	277
Interest received	332	337
Cash flows from investing activities	**− 4932**	**− 2112**
Capital increases	63	175
Proceeds from long-term corporate debt	498	− 586
Proceeds from short-term corporate debt	3469	− 1163
Dividends paid	− 1047	− 984
Interest paid	− 1306	− 1143
Cash flows from financing activities	**1677**	**− 3701**
Effect of exchange rate changes on cash	7	10
Effect of consolidation changes on cash	− 65	− 89
Changes in cash	**165**	**− 232**
Cash at beginning of year	382	614
at end of year	547	382

ANALYZING CASH FLOWS

By using the relationships depicted in Equation (3), the statement of cash flows itself, and some basic cash flow ratio analysis, financial statement users can increase their understanding of an enterprise and answer questions such as these:

- What is the relationship between cash flows and earnings?
- How are dividends being financed?
- How is debt repayment to be achieved?
- Does the company require outside financing?
- How are the cash flows from operations being used?
- Is management's financial policy reflected in the cash flows?

In Chapters 4 and 5, we saw that financial ratio analysis could be applied to income statement and balance sheet accounts to reveal various insights about a company. Traditional ratio analysis, and even the income statement itself, however, will not provide insights regarding issues such as the timing of cash flows or the effects of operations on liquidity. To obtain this kind of information it is necessary to analyze the information presented in the statement of cash flows.

Cash Flow Ratios

Some useful cash flow ratios are presented in this section.[7] The list is not comprehensive, but it does reveal the relative merit of analyzing the SCF by developing applicable ratios. Each ratio is discussed in light of the Procter & Gamble information presented in Exhibit 6.4. Individually, each ratio gives limited information as of a single point in time, but taken over a period of years and examined in conjunction with other ratios, the cash flow ratios can reveal trends that provide insights about the company and its industry.

Operating funds ratio. Calculated as net income divided by cash flows from operations, the **operating funds ratio** can be used to indicate the portion of operating cash flows provided by net income. Depreciation methods and the management of current asset and current liability accounts are the principal factors highlighted by this ratio because they are the principal adjustments to net income used in calculating the cash flows from operations. This ratio for Procter & Gamble in 1998 was 0.77, indicating that the cash flows from operations were greater than net income and that, on average, there were modest positive adjustments to accrual net income in deriving cash flow from operations. Given the capital-intensive nature of Procter & Gamble's business, there was indeed a large depreciation and amortization expense component ($1,598 million) to the income adjustments made to arrive at the cash flows from operations. Moreover, given the consistent, positive track record of Procter & Gamble's management, one would expect only minor fluctuations in the operations-related current asset or current liability accounts, with only a modest (and most probably positive) impact on cash flows.

---

[7] See D. Giacomino and D.E. Mielke, "Preparation and Use of Cash Flow Statements," *The CPA Journal* (March 1987), pp. 30–35, for a more extensive presentation and discussion of cash flow ratios.

EXHIBIT 6.10

Volkswagen Group
1997 Cash Flow Presentation

	1997	1996
Net earnings	+ 1.361	+ 678
Depreciation and write-up of fixed assets	+ 5.987	+ 4.780
Depreciation and write-up of leasing and rental assets	+ 4.982	+ 4.042
Change in medium and long-term provisions	+ 473	+ 2.294
Other expenses and income not affecting payments	− 627	− 706
Cash flow	**+ 12.181**	**+ 11.088**
Change in short-term provisions	+ 922	+ 2.070
Change in inventories and trade receivables	− 3.798	− 4.973
Change in liabilities (excluding credit liabilities)	+ 1.754	+ 3.199
Other internal financing	**− 1.122**	**+ 296**
Total internal financing	**+ 11.059**	**+ 11.384**
Disposals of fixed assets and leasing and rental assets	+ 2.613	+ 2.182
Additions to tangible fixed assets	− 8.222	− 7.329
Additions to financial assets	− 365	− 311
Additions to leasing and rental assets	− 7.734	− 7.639
Capital investments	**− 13.708**	**− 13.097**
Net cash flow	**− 2.649**	**− 1.713**
Inpayments in respect of capital increase	+ 335	+ 500
Outpayments to stockholders (dividends)	− 325	− 220
Other equity finance	− 156	− 13
Change in financial liabilities	+ 2.916	+ 2.342
Inflow/outflow of funds in respect of financing operations	**+ 2.770**	**+ 2.609**
Change in gross liquidity	**+ 121**	**+ 896**
Gross liquidity at start of period	**+ 17.932**	**+ 17.036**
Gross liquidity at end of period	**+ 18.053**	**+ 17.932**

	Auto-motive	Auto-motive	Financial Services	Financial Services	Volkswagen Group	Volkswagen Group	Change
	31.12.97	31.12.96	31.12.97	31.12.96	31.12.97	31.12.96	
Liquid funds	12,565	12,944	527	184	12,613	13,080	− 467
Securities	3,678	3,311	202	188	3,880	3,499	+ 381
Long-term financial investments	2,160	1,903	−	−	1,560	1,353	+ 207
Gross liquidity	**18,403**	**18,158**	**729**	**372**	**18,053**	**17,932**	**+ 121**
Total third-party borrowings	**− 15,689**	**− 14,950**	**− 31,494**	**− 27,080**	**− 32,990**	**− 30,074**	**− 2,916**
Net liquidity	**+ 2,714**	**+ 3,208**	**− 30,765**	**− 26,708**	**− 14,937**	**− 12,142**	**− 2,795**

Normal operating conditions are likely to yield ratios in the 0.25 to 1.0 range, but not all healthy companies have such ratios, and not all ratios in that range are necessarily good. Different management objectives and different industries tend to be characterized by different "normal" ratio ranges. For example, very high growth periods can result in ratios consistently greater than 1.0 because of the normal increases in receivables and inventories that characterize rapid growth. For example, Northern Telecom Ltd., achieved a 20 percent growth in sales during 1997, and its operating funds ratio for that year was 1.05.

As with all ratios, one must be careful to examine the underlying events reflected by such ratios. A troubled company also may have especially high levels of receivables and inventory, giving rise to a high operating funds ratio. For example, the Grumman Corporation prior to its takeover by Northrop Co., reported a decline in sales but an operating funds ratio of 1.4, reflecting a decline in its cash flow from operations due to a sizeable investment in unsold inventory.

Investment ratio. Calculated as capital expenditures divided by depreciation plus sales of assets, the **investment ratio** reveals the relative level of investment in capital assets and whether a company's productive asset base is expanding or shrinking. The ratio provides some insight regarding management's plans for the future and its analysis of the future economy. In 1998, this ratio for Procter & Gamble was 1.19. The fact that this ratio exceeds 1.0 indicates that Procter & Gamble's management increased the company's relative investment in property, plant, and equipment during the period. Ratio amounts less than 1.0 usually indicate a situation in which the management is, in effect, "harvesting" past investments in capital assets or is not investing in property, plant, and equipment at the same (or faster) rate than these productive assets are being consumed. For example, in the mid 1990s, Woolworth Corporation was forced into a period of retrenchment, as revealed by its 1996 investment ratio of 0.58.

Cash flow adequacy ratio. The **cash flow adequacy ratio** is calculated as the cash flows from operations divided by long-term capital expenditures plus dividends and long-term debt repayment. This ratio helps reveal whether a business is providing sufficient funds through operations to match expenditures for its current capital structure and future asset base. In 1998, Procter & Gamble's cash flow adequacy ratio was 1.09, which indicates that sufficient cash was being generated from operations to provide for the firm's expanded level of long-term investments, dividends, and debt repayment. In general, the closer this ratio is to zero, the greater is a company's dependency on creditors and owners for additional financing to execute plant and equipment expansion programs; the reverse is also true. Because expenditures for these types of items tend to vary from year to year, ratios less than 1.0 are not cause for alarm unless they are consistently below 1.0 for a number of accounting periods. In this regard, Grumman Corporation had a negative cash flow adequacy ratio in 1987, a 0.05 ratio in 1988, and 0.20 in 1989. Clearly, Grumman's ratio trend was in the appropriate direction, but the ratios were so low that it must be concluded that Grumman's management faced a significant challenge to financially service its creditors and shareholders as well as its equipment replacement needs.

Cash sources percentages. This ratio (that is, individual cash flow sources divided by the total sources of cash) for each specific source of cash indicates the degree to which a company provides cash from operations, by external borrowing, or by other means. The 1998 Procter & Gamble cash flow statement shown in Exhibit 6.4 reveals that the total sources of cash (all of the positive cash flow entries) equaled $8,946 million. Individual ratios for each source can be calculated to show the relative importance of a particular activity to the cash flows of the company. For example, 22 percent of Procter & Gamble's cash inflows were provided by long-term borrowings ($1,970 ÷ $8,946), while 6.2 percent was generated by sales of property, plant, and equipment ($555 ÷ $8,946). Such percentages indicate Procter & Gamble's high need for short-term funds, suggesting that cash flow management is primarily a timing issue for Procter & Gamble rather than an inability to generate internally adequate levels of cash flows. Moreover, the 6.2 percent indicates a very low dependence on fixed asset liquidations for cash infusions. It is interesting to note that for 1995, the Woolworth Corporation's sum of these two ratios was 45%, reflecting a relative inability to generate cash flows internally and, consequently, the company's dependency on liquidation of assets and external sources of cash flows to operate.

Dividend payout ratio. Dividends are among the main concerns of a company's shareholders, and, consequently, the amount of cash dividends paid divided by available cash flows from operations is an important indicator for this group. The percentage of cash flow paid to shareholders is an indication of management's commitment to a company's dividend policy as well as high-return projects available to the company for investment. Procter & Gamble's dividend payout ratio in 1998 was 30 percent, a healthy level indicating that 70 percent of its cash flow from operations was available for investing and/or debt repayment purposes. A ratio greater than 100 percent is definitely cause for further investigation because it indicates that the company is paying dividends with funds not provided by the normal operations of the business. Moreover, as this ratio approaches 100 percent, concern should increase as to the ability of a company to maintain such dividend levels and it indicates that less internally generated cash will be available to cover other demands. For example, Grumman Corporation's dividend payout ratio of 78 percent indicates a relatively small amount of internally generated cash available to support the continuing operations of the company's businesses.

Many companies and industries use meaningful cash flow ratios that differ from those noted here. Thus, students are encouraged to consider ratios that are applicable to each industry or situation that they encounter.

Pro Forma Cash Flows

Just as it is instructive to examine various ratios based on the actual reported cash flow components, it is also useful to investigate a company's *expected* cash flows. In Chapter 5 we demonstrated that through the use of reasonable and realistic assumptions, it is possible to prepare forecast or pro forma financial statements. And, just as it is instructive to consider a pro forma income statement, it is useful to examine a pro forma statement of cash flows to anticipate the amount, sources, and uses of subsequent periods' available cash resources.

EXHIBIT 6.11

Blue Ridge Hardware Co.
Pro Forma Statement of Cash Flows
For the Year Ended March 31, 2000

Operating Activities

Net income	$ 8,820
Add: Depreciation on store equipment	1,000
Adjustments for working capital needs:	
Increase in accounts receivable	(1,118)
Increase in merchandise inventory	(635)
Increase in accounts payable	200
Increase in wages payable	–0–
Increase in utilities payable	–0–
Decrease in income tax payable	(1,575)
Cash flow from operating activities	$ 6,692
Investing Activities	$–0–
Financing Activities	
Cash dividends paid	(2,000)
Partial repayment of bank loan	(1,500)
Cash flow for financing activities	$(3,500)
Increase in cash	$ 3,192
Cash, beginning of year	2,050
Cash, end of year	$ 5,242

Using the pro forma income statement for Blue Ridge Hardware Co. (Exhibit 5.8 from Chapter 5) as a starting point, we can develop a pro forma statement of cash flows. To do so, however, requires several additional assumptions that might include the following:

1. The ending balance in accounts receivable increases by 10 percent of the growth in revenues (that is, $0.10 \times \$11,175$).

2. The ending inventory increases by 5 percent of the existing value of goods currently on hand (that is, $0.05 \times \$12,700$).

3. The ending balance of accounts payable increases by $200.

4. Because no new employees need to be hired and operating hours are not extended, the ending balances in wages and utilities payable remain unchanged.

5. Income taxes are paid quarterly; hence, at year-end, only the last quarter's taxes remain unpaid (that is, $0.25 \times \$2,900$).

6. Because all of the equipment and fixtures are new, no asset purchases or replacements are required until 2001.

EXHIBIT 6.12

Blue Ridge Hardware Co.
Pro Forma Balance Sheet
As of March 31, 2000

Assets			Equities		
Current assets:			Current liabilities:		
Cash	$ 5,242		Accounts payable		$ 4,000
Accounts receivable	5,318		Wages payable		700
Merchandise inventory	13,335		Utilities payable		200
Total current assets	$23,895		Income tax payable		725
			Total current liabilities		$ 5,625
Noncurrent assets:					
Store equipment	10,000		Noncurrent liabilities		
Less: Accumulated depreciation	(2,000)		Bank loan payable		6,000
Total noncurrent assets	$ 8,000		Total liabilities		$11,625
			Owners' equity:		
			Capital stock		10,000
			Retained earnings		10,276
					20,276
			Total liabilities and owners'		
Total assets	$31,895		equity		$31,895

7. As required by the loan agreement, one-fifth of the outstanding bank loan is repaid (that is, $0.20 \times \$7,500$).

8. Cash dividends remain at $2,000.

Using these assumptions, along with the Blue Ridge Hardware pro forma income statement from Chapter 5, we can prepare a pro forma statement of cash flows for Blue Ridge Hardware. As revealed in Exhibit 6.11, the cash flows from operating activities are projected to be $6,692 for the year ended March 31, 2000. After paying the cash dividends and the partial loan repayment, the cash balance is projected to increase by $3,192. Such a favorable increase may be viewed by interested parties as a healthy cushion of cash inflows over cash outflows, thus providing a relative amount of comfort regarding the company's ability to generate adequate cash resources in the coming year.

By incorporating the assumptions used in the preparation of the pro forma income statement and the statement of cash flows, it is also possible to prepare a pro forma balance sheet for Blue Ridge Hardware Co. Exhibit 6.12 reveals that if our assumptions hold true, the level of total assets and equities will reach $31,895 by March 31, 2000.

SUMMARY

Informed observers and businesspeople realize that the "bottom line" (that is, net income) has little to do with staying solvent and hence staying in business. Cash planning—specifically, the ability to understand the sources and uses of current and future cash flows—often makes the difference between business success and failure. Firms with excellent products, new equipment, and creative marketing efforts have gone out of business because they mistook earnings profitability for cash solvency.

A balance sheet, an income statement, and a statement of cash flows together provide managers, creditors, and investors alike with important information that is useful in developing a complete understanding of a company's financial status and health. Moreover, as we observed with regard to the balance sheet and income statement, it is possible to construct various ratios from the statement of cash flows that provide insights beyond the absolute level of cash provided or used. It would be quite misleading to suggest that information regarding cash flows is superior to that of earnings in providing a clear and true picture of a company's financial health. *Both* are important; but it is also worth noting the thoughts of one financial writer:

> Though my bottom line is black, I am flat upon my back,
> My cash flows out and customers pay slow.
> The growth of my receivables is almost unbelievable;
> The result is certain—unremitting woe!
> And I hear the banker utter an ominous low mutter,
> "Watch cash flow." [8]

Herbert S. Bailey, Jr., with
apologies to Edgar Allan Poe's
"The Raven"

NEW CONCEPTS AND TERMS

Cash equivalents

Cash flow adequacy ratio

Cash flows from operating activities

Direct method

Dividend payout ratio

Financing activities

Indirect method

Investing activities

Investment ratio

Noncash investing and financing activities

Operating activities

Operating funds ratio

ASSIGNMENTS

6.1. Discuss in general the distinctions between accrual-based accounting and cash-based accounting.

6.2. Why do you think the FASB chose to segregate the statement of cash flows into operating, financing, and investing activity sections? What other categorizations might have merit?

6.3. Discuss the pros and cons of evaluating division managers on a "net cash provided by operations" basis.

---

[8] R. Green, "Are More Chryslers in the Offing?" *Forbes,* February 2, 1981, p. 69.

6.4. Discuss the direct and indirect methods of presenting net cash flows from operating activities. Which do you find most useful? Why?

6.5. Statement of cash flows (indirect method). Presented here are some items involving cash flows taken from the financial records of Tucson Equipment Company for the period ended December 31, 2000:

Net income	$420,000
Payment of dividends	30,000
Ten-year bonds, issued at face value	250,000
Depreciation expense	50,000
Amortization expense	10,000
Beginning cash balance	28,000
Equipment purchased	96,000
Building purchased	114,000
Accounts receivable decrease	4,000
Accounts payable decrease	5,000
Inventories increase	5,000

Required:

Using the facts provided, prepare a statement of cash flows using the indirect method.

6.6. Classification of cash flow items.   Identify whether each of the following is properly classified as an operating, investing, or financing activity in a statement of cash flows. Explain your rationale.

a. Proceeds from sales of two Arizona factories.

b. Interest payments to creditors.

c. Proceeds from issuing shares of stock.

d. Payments to invest in Ford long-term bonds.

e. Payments of dividends to shareholders.

6.7. Account analysis (AICPA adapted).

a. Over the course of the year, a company's accounts receivable declined. In the company's statement of cash flows (operating activities shown using the direct method), the cash collected from customers would be which of the following?

(1) Sales plus accounts receivable at the beginning of the year.

(2) Sales plus the year's net decrease in accounts receivable.

(3) Sales less the year's net decrease in accounts receivable.

(4) The same as sales.

(5) Sales plus accounts receivable at the end of the year.

b. In a statement of cash flows in which the operating activities section is prepared under the indirect method, a gain on the sale of a building should be presented as a (an)

(1) Addition to net income.

(2) Deduction from net income.

(3) Inflow of cash.

(4) Outflow of cash.

c. A company's taxes payable increased during the year. In the company's statement of cash flows in which the operating activities section is prepared under the direct method, the cash paid for taxes would be which of the following?

(1) Tax expense plus taxes payable at the beginning of the year.

(2) Tax expense plus the year's net increase in taxes payable.

(3) The same as tax expense.

(4) Tax expense less the year's net increase in taxes payable.

(5) Tax expense plus taxes payable at the end of the year.

d. A loss on the sale of a warehouse should be presented in a statement of cash flows (using the indirect method for cash flows from operations) as a (an)

(1) Deduction from net income.

(2) Inflow of cash.

(3) Addition to net income.

(4) Outflow of cash.

e. In a statement of cash flows using the indirect method for operating activities, an increase in inventories should be presented as a (an)

(1) Deduction from net income.

(2) Inflow of cash.

(3) Addition to net income.

(4) Outflow of cash.

f. The amortization of an acquired trademark should be presented in a statement of cash flows, using the indirect method for cash flow from operating activities, as a (an)

(1) Financing activity.

(2) Deduction from net income.

(3) Addition to net income.

(4) Investing activity.

6.8. Statement of cash flows (AICPA adapted).

Dalton Corporation's balance sheet as of December 31, 2000 and 1999, and information relating to 2000 activities are presented here.

	December 31,	
	2000	**1999**
Assets		
Cash	$ 15,000	$ 90,000
Short-term investments	200,000	—
Accounts receivable (net)	590,000	440,000
Inventory	600,000	615,000
Long-term investments	310,000	390,000
Property, plant, and equipment	1,800,000	1,100,000
Accumulated depreciation	(500,000)	(500,000)
Goodwill (net)	95,000	105,000
Total assets	$3,110,000	$2,240,000
Liabilities and Stockholders' Equity		
Accounts payable and accrued liabilities	$ 900,000	$850,000
Short-term debt	190,000	—
Common stock, $10 par value	775,000	675,000
Additional paid-in-capital	380,000	300,000
Retained earnings	865,000	415,000
Total liabilities and stockholders' equity	$3,110,000	$2,240,000

Information Relating to 2000 Activities

- Net income was $800,000.
- Cash dividends of $350,000 were declared and paid.
- Equipment costing $450,000 and having a book value of $200,000 was sold for $200,000.
- A long-term investment was sold for $150,000. There were no other transactions affecting long-term investments in 2000.
- 10,000 shares of common stock were issued for $18 a share.
- Short-term investments consist of Treasury bills maturing on June 30, 2001.

(a.) Calculate Dalton's 2000 net cash provided by operating activities.

(b.) Calculate Dalton's 2000 net cash used in investing activities.

(c.) Calculate Dalton's 2000 net cash provided by financing activities.

6.9. Account analysis (AICPA adapted).

Wolfe Hardware Shops, Inc.
Balance sheets

	December 31	
	2000	**1999**
Assets		
Current assets:		
Cash	$ 400,000	$ 250,000
Accounts receivable	990,000	760,000
Merchandise inventory	710,000	400,000
Prepaid expenses	100,000	100,000
Total current assets	2,200,000	1,510,000
Long-term investments	100,000	—
Property, plant, and equipment	1,310,000	800,000
Less: Accumulated depreciation	110,000	80,000
	1,200,000	720,000
Total assets	$3,500,000	$2,230,000
Equities		
Current liabilities:		
Accounts payable	$ 550,000	$ 500,000
Accrued expenses	220,000	200,000
Dividends payable	70,000	—
Total current liabilities	840,000	700,000
Note payable—due in five years	500,000	—
Stockholders' equity:		
Common stock	1,500,000	1,380,000
Retained earnings	660,000	150,000
	2,160,000	1,530,000
Total liabilities and stockholders' equity	$3,500,000	$2,230,000

Wolfe Hardware Shops, Inc.
Income Statements

	Year ended December 31,	
	2000	**1999**
Net credit sales	$8,400,000	$6,000,000
Cost of goods sold	7,000,000	5,200,000
Gross profit	1,400,000	800,000
Expenses (including income taxes)	800,000	420,000
Net income	$ 600,000	$ 380,000

Additional information available included the following:

- All accounts receivable and accounts payable related to trade merchandise. No receivables were written off during 2000.

- The proceeds from the note payable were used to finance a new building.

(a.) Determine Wolfe's cash collected during 2000 from accounts receivable.

(b.) Determine Wolfe's cash payments during 2000 on accounts payable.

(c.) Determine Wolfe's net cash flow from financing activities for 2000.

(d.) Determine Wolfe's net cash flow from investing activities during 2000.

6.10. Cash flow analysis: Monsanto Company.* The Monsanto Company makes and markets high-value chemical and agricultural products, pharmaceuticals, low-calorie sweeteners, industrial process equipment, man-made fibers, plastics, and electronic materials. Monsanto's cash flow statements for a recent three-year period are presented here. Net sales for 19X2, 19X1, and 19X0 were $7,639, $6,879, and $6,747 million, respectively.

Monsanto Company
Statement of Consolidated Cash Flow
(in millions)

	19X2	19X1	19X0
Operating activities:			
Net income (loss)	$436	$ 433	$ (98)
Add: Income tax expense (benefit)	237	203	(170)
Deduct: Extraordinary gain			(30)
Income (loss) before income taxes and extraordinary gain	637	636	(298)
Income tax payments	(229)	(221)	(273)
Items that did not use (provide) cash:			
Depreciation and amortization	679	780	599
Restructuring expense (income)	(32)	(158)	949
Other	37	(9)	(39)
Working-capital changes that provided (used) cash:			
Accounts receivable	(172)	117	2
Inventories	(22)	(2)	(54)
Accounts payable and accrued liabilities	13	(173)	—
Other	(19)	80	41
Nonoperating gains from asset disposals (before tax)	(26)	(90)	(392)
Cash provided by operations	902	960	535
Investing activities:			
Property, plant, and equipment purchases	(505)	(520)	(645)
Acquisition payments for Searle, net of cash acquired of $216			(2,538)
Acquisition and investment payments (other than Searle)	(59)	(29)	(78)
Investment and property disposal proceeds	75	503	1,469
Cash used in investing activities	(489)	(46)	(1,792)
Financing activities:			
Net change in short-term financing	150	33	(108)
Long-term debt proceeds	26	675	415
Long-term debt repayments	(122)	(1,139)	(555)
Searle acquisition financing proceeds			2,754
Short-term debt repayments (Searle acquisition)		(348)	(1,154)
Treasury stock purchases	(339)		(91)
Dividend payments	(212)	(199)	(188)
Other financing activities	33	45	18
Cash (used in) provided by financing activities	(464)	(933)	1,091
Decrease in cash and cash equivalents*	$ (51)	$ (19)	$ (166)

*Includes cash, time deposits, certificates of deposit, and short-term securities.

Required:

a. Historically, one of Monsanto's strong points has been its ability to provide significant cash flow from operations. Although operating income improved in 19X2, cash provided by operations declined. Briefly explain how this happened.

b. Cumulatively, over this three-year period, has Monsanto

   (1) Experienced a net increase or decrease in inventories? How do you know?

   (2) Been able to increase the level of cash provided by operations as a percentage of *total gross cash inflows?* If so, is this increase a sign of good management? Why? If not, is this a sign of bad management? Why?

c. Explain how depreciation and amortization can be the single largest source of cash in 19X2 and 19X1.

d. What might account for the fact that in 19X1 accounts receivable "provided" cash, whereas in 19X2 they "used" cash?

e. As of December 31, 19X2, Monsanto's ending retained earnings balance was $3,282 million. What was Monsanto's December 31, 19X1, retained earnings balance?

6.11. Cash flow statement preparation and interpretation: Compton Computing Systems (A)*
Phillip Brantly, chief financial officer of Compton Computing Systems, sat in his office and considered the company's financial performance for 1999. He had reason to be pleased because just about every measure of financial performance had shown strong improvement for the first three quarters of 1999 and he had no reason to suspect that the last quarter would be any different. However, as he prepared for the final presentation of the 2000 budget to the board of directors, scheduled for December 11, he was uneasy about the economy and how it might affect Compton's financing and capital investment plans for next year. He knew that the board would have detailed discussions of alternative levels of expenditures and contingency financing plans for 2000. Thus, in the two weeks remaining before the meeting, he would need to complete his 1999 projected end-of-year financial statements. Using these statements as a base, he would then be able to determine whether sufficient funds from operations were being generated to portend a favorable cash flow in general through early 2000 and whether the company should proceed with the capital expenditures scheduled for early 2000.

The Company

Compton Computing Systems, headquartered in San Francisco, California, designed, manufactured, and serviced electronic products and systems for measurement and computation applications for general industry use. In addition to a full line of computers and computer-related hardware, Compton also produced and sold an impressive array of electronic test equipment, component parts, and medical test products. Compton's basic business purpose was to provide the capabilities and support needed to help customers worldwide improve their personal and business effectiveness.

The company was founded in 1958 to manufacture electronic measurement devices. It had started research into computers almost at founding and had marketed computers and computer systems since the early 1960s. Emphasis on quality and reliability allowed the company to grow rapidly. An increased need for capital forced the company to go public in 1962, and earnings had been sufficient to pay dividends to stockholders consecutively since 1965.

Through three quarters of 1999, financial performance had been strong. Orders were up 16 percent with net revenue up 25 percent. The fourth quarter, not yet complete, was one of great interest to Brantly. The United States and world economies were having a modest growth year, but predictions of economic slowdown were starting to surface. Many companies began to rethink their outlook for 2000.

Compton's budget for capital expenditures for 2000 had recently been revised and was now predicated on an immediate slowdown in demand for computers and computer systems

---

* This case was prepared by Mark E. Haskins and John B. Bristow. Copyright © 1988 by the Darden Graduate School Foundation, Charlottesville, Virginia. Rev. 11/98. All rights reserved.

domestically and worldwide. In addition, several contingency cost-reduction plans had been readied for implementation if and when revenues started declining. All in all, Brantly believed the company was positioned to withstand a recessionary year.

Preparation for the December Meeting

The 2000 budgetary process at Compton Computing Systems, begun in May 1999, was now complete except for the final approval of the board of directors. What concerned Brantly most was that, through November, indications pointed to a near-record quarter for orders. In fact, Compton's backlog of orders was increasing. National and international economic indicators also showed a strong business environment. The predicted downturn was not yet occurring. A retrenchment at the wrong time in the business cycle would be very costly to the company. Therefore, Brantly intended to go before the board prepared to discuss several alternative capital spending levels. This presentation would require 2000 pro forma financial statements for each of the economic scenarios and comparison with 1999's financial performance. Because actual 1999 financial statements would be unavailable prior to the end of the year, he would have to project those as well.

Brantly had spent most of the day gathering the information he needed to complete the 1999 financial statement projections and had now completed the balance sheets and income statements (presented below). All that remained was to complete the statement of cash flows (SCF) for 1999 by applying the indirect method to his recently completed income statement and comparative balance sheet. He knew from the data he had collected that, in 1999 and 1998, principal payments on the long-term debt had been $49 and $42 million, respectively. He also knew that the company had not disposed of any property or equipment in 1998 but in 1999 had disposed of a building originally costing $18 million, whose book value at the time of the sale was $10 million, for $10 million cash. After reviewing the 1998 SCF, he decided to complete this part of his task before leaving for home that evening.

Required:

Prepare a statement of cash flows for Compton Computing Systems for 1999.

Compton Computing Systems (A)
Consolidated Income Statements
(millions of dollars)

	For the Year Ended December 31		
	Projected 1999	Actual 1998	Actual 1997
Net revenue:			
Equipment	$6,315	$5,622	$5,267
Services	1,775	1,480	1,238
	8,090	7,102	6,505
Cost and expenses:			
Cost of equipment sold	2,723	2,479	2,423
Cost of services	1,062	874	743
Research and development	901	824	685
Marketing and selling	1,612	1,397	1,181
Administration and general	830	748	715
	7,128	6,322	5,747
Earnings before taxes	962	780	758
Provisions for taxes	318	264	269
Net earnings	$ 644	$ 516	$ 489
Notes to financial statements:			
Depreciation	$ 342	$ 321	$ 299

Compton Computing Systems (A)
Consolidated Balance Sheets
(millions of dollars)

	As of December 31		
	Projected 1999	Actual 1998	Actual 1997
Assets			
Cash and cash equivalents	$2,645	$1,372	$1,020
Accounts receivable	1,561	1,344	1,249
Inventories:			
Finished goods	480	427	401
Parts and assemblies	637	554	592
Other current assets	167	117	80
Total current assets	5,490	3,814	3,342
Property, plant, and equipment:			
Land	275	243	230
Buildings and improvements	2,081	1,891	1,653
Equipment	1,761	1,557	1,400
	4,117	3,691	3,283
Less: Accumulated depreciation	1,789	1,455	1,134
	2,328	2,236	2,149
Other assets	315	237	189
Total assets	$8,133	$6,287	$5,680
Liabilities			
Notes payable	$ 240	$229	$ 235
Accounts payable	364	285	268
Accrued wages and benefits	488	395	397
Accrued taxes	229	164	111
Deferred revenues	150	117	100
Other current liabilities	331	230	179
Total current liabilities	1,802	1,420	1,290
Long-term debt	827	110	102
Other liabilities	134	134	92
Deferred taxes	348	249	214
Total liabilities	3,111	1,913	1,698
Stockholders' Equity			
Preferred stock, $1 par	–0–	–0–	–0–
Common stock and paid-in capital in excess of $1 par (less Treasury stock of $68 in 1999, 1998, and 1997)	776	712	780
Retained earnings	4,246	3,662	3,202
Total stockholders' equity	5,022	4,374	3,982
Total liabilities and stockholders' equity	$8,133	$6,287	$5,680

Compton Computing Systems (A)
Statement of Cash Flows
For the Year Ended December 31, 1998
(numbers in parentheses indicate reductions in cash; millions of dollars)

Operations:

Net income	$ 516
Depreciation and amortization	321
Adjustment for deferred revenue	17
Adjustment for deferred taxes	35
	889
Adjustments for:	
Increase in receivables	(95)
Decrease in inventories	12
Increase in accounts payable and other accruals	15
Increase in accrued taxes	53
Increase in other current assets	(37)
Increase in other current liabilities	51
	(1)
Cash flow—operations	888
Investing:	
Payments for additions to property, plant, and equipment	(408)
Increase in other assets	(48)
Cash flow—investing	(456)
Financing:	
Payments on notes payable	(6)
Proceeds from long-term debt	50
Payments on long-term debt	(42)
Increases in other liabilities	42
Repurchase of stock	(68)
Cash dividends paid	(56)
Cash flow—financing	(80)
Increase (decrease) in cash	352
Cash and equivalents—January 1	1,020
Cash and equivalents—December 31	$1,372

6.12. Cash flow statement preparation and industry comparison: Compton Computing Systems (B)* Elizabeth Oakes, an outside director of Compton Computing Systems, sat watching the fog roll in over the Golden Gate Bridge from her office near the Embarcadero. A very familiar sight to her, the fog signaled evening and the close of another day. She had less than a week until the special board meeting at Compton's headquarters.

During the last meeting of the board of directors on December 11, Oakes had listened with great interest to CFO Phillip Brantly present information on the cash flow and cash position of Compton Computing Systems. There had been much debate regarding different economic scenarios and the appropriate management response to the uncertain economy. The meeting had ended with a number of questions unanswered, so the board had agreed to meet three weeks later—January 4—to approve the final 2000 budget for the company. Prior to that meeting, Oakes wanted to review information on other companies, both inside and outside the computing industry to form an opinion on how Compton Computing Systems could respond to the changing economic environment. Her

---

position as senior partner of Oakes, Glass, & Abernathy, a nationally known investment management firm, gave her ready access to financial information on a number of businesses with which to compare Compton. Her intention was to determine what other manufacturing companies had been doing recently regarding capital expenditures and the ways in which those expenditures were being financed. Her staff had provided the names of several suitable companies, and from that list she had chosen two to review that evening.

Background on Compton Computing Systems is found in assignment 6.11.

Preparation for the January 4 Meeting

A trusted member of Oakes' staff had strongly recommended that she study the financial data on Reliant Information Technologies Corporation, a sizeable computer manufacturer competing directly in many of the same markets as Compton. Reliant Information Technologies designed, manufactured, and sold general-purpose computer systems and provided peripheral equipment, software, communications systems, and related products and services, including training and maintenance. Reliant Information Technologies marketed its systems to end users by its own sales force and a variety of third-party sales channels. Since its inception in 1968, it had installed more than 226,000 computer systems worldwide.

Oakes saw that Reliant Information Technologies had not been profitable in 1998. She was interested to determine how the loss would affect Reliant Information Technologies' cash flow from operations and whether the loss might have affected its 1999 capital expenditures relative to those for 1998. Reliant Information Technologies also had just embarked on a cost-reduction and restructuring program similar to the plan for Compton presented by Brantly at the last board meeting. As a part of this restructuring, Reliant Information Technologies had disposed of equipment with a net book value of $3.669 million. The cash purchase price in that amount had been collected in the third quarter of fiscal 1999. Oakes also learned that new long-term loans in the amount of $17.812 million had been subscribed during fiscal 1999.

The other company Oakes chose to study was Red Rock. Red Rock Company was a leading American brewer. In its 115-year history, it had become an increasingly diversified corporation, however, with operations in brewing, ceramics, aluminum, transportation, energy, food products, packaging, and biotechnology. Its ongoing success was based on an uncompromising commitment to quality, dedicated management, technological superiority, and talented employees.

Oakes chose Red Rock for review because it was a diversified, well-managed company that, like Compton, had limited stock distribution. While not nearly as closely held as Red Rock, Compton did have several substantial blocks of stock controlled by a few stockholders. Oakes wondered how this situation might affect dividend distributions, capital expenditures, and cash flows. Red Rock was also conservative regarding its use of debt financing. Compton had a low but increasing, long-term debt-to-equity ratio, and she wondered whether a company could effectively provide cash for expansion without use of significant debt. During 1999 Red Rock had not assumed any new long-term debt and, according to company sources, did not expect to in 2000. Red Rock did receive $25.692 million in cash for selling plant assets with a net book value of that amount.

Oakes, Glass, & Abernathy's files had contained information on both Reliant Information Technologies and Red Rock, but because the 1999 annual statements for both companies had not yet been released, her staff had projected fourth-quarter financials in order to give Oakes annual 1999 financial statements. Before her were the 1998 and 1999 income statements and balance sheets for Reliant Information Technologies and the company's statement of cash flows for 1999, which she had completed. The Red Rock 1998 and 1999 income statements and balance sheets were also on her desk. She knew that, after completing a statement of cash flows for Red Rock, she would need to analyze thoroughly the information she had gathered.

Required:

a. Review the financial statements provided on Compton (from assignment 6.11), Reliant Information Technologies, and Red Rock. Construct a 1999 statement of cash flows for Red Rock. While concentrating on the cash flow statements for the three companies, compare and contrast the companies and discuss the differences and similarities apparent from the financial statements concerning management's cash policies and debt policies, and make generalizations regarding the respective industries.

b. With Reliant Information Technologies having a loss for 1999, why was its cash flow from operations positive? What were the largest *uses* of cash from its statement of cash flows?

c. Why did Red Rock have a decrease in cash in 1999 when the income statement showed a positive net income?

d. How was Red Rock financing increases in investments?

e. What are the similarities and differences in the statements of cash flow of the three companies?

f. Were indications of management's policies and abilities discernible from the financial statements? Explain.

g. Which company was the best prepared to meet a recessionary market? A growing market? Why? What financial information led you to these conclusions?

h. What assumptions and associated limitations arise when you compare and contrast the Reliant Information Technologies and Red Rock statements of cash flow with Compton's?

i. What insights into the operations of a company might be gained by using the direct method that are not readily apparent using the indirect method for the statement of cash flows?

Reliant Information Technologies Corporation

	For the Year Ended December 31	
Consolidated Income Statement (in thousands)	**Projected 1999**	**Actual 1998**
Revenue:		
Equipment	$ 859,455	$ 868,269
Services	414,893	399,690
	1,274,348	1,267,959
Cost and expenses:		
Cost of revenues	608,810	639,574
Depreciation	107,727	92,657
Research and development	159,410	143,076
Marketing expenses	405,005	360,962
Other administrative expenses	53,800	11,000
	1,334,752	1,247,269
Income (loss) from operations	(60,404)	20,690
Other income	2,491	13,175
Interest expense	46,194	30,467
Income before income taxes and equity in net loss of unconsolidated affiliate	(104,107)	3,398
Income tax benefit (provision)	6,987	(945)
Net income before equity in net loss of unconsolidated affiliate	(97,120)	2,453
Equity in net loss of unconsolidated affiliate	(15,189)	(23,433)
Writedown of investment in unconsolidated affiliate	(14,769)	–0–
Net income (loss)	($ 127,078)	($ 20,980)

	As of December 31	
Consolidated Balance Sheet (in thousands)	**Projected 1999**	**Actual 1998**
Assets		
Cash and cash equivalents	$ 136,676	$ 271,537
Marketable equity securities	–0–	30,126
Receivables, less allowance of $25,904 in 1999 and $21,744 in 1998	274,925	260,498
Inventories	189,538	237,585
Other current assets	34,858	23,350
Total current assets	635,997	823,096
Notes receivable	19,481	23,236
Property, plant, and equipment, net	398,944	367,422
Other assets including investment in affiliates	21,062	51,020
Total assets	$1,075,484	$1,264,774
Liabilities and Stockholders' Equity		
Notes payable	$ 38,740	$ 33,451
Accounts payable	103,441	75,536
Other current liabilities	245,369	210,935
Total current liabilities	387,550	319,922
Long-term debt	79,990	240,734
Deferred service revenue	13,378	14,144
Total liabilities	480,918	574,800
Stockholders' equity:		
Common stock	302,639	268,182
Retained earnings	279,749	406,827
Cumulative foreign currency translation adjustment	12,178	14,965
Total stockholders' equity	594,566	689,974
Total liabilities and stockholders' equity	$1,075,484	$1,264,774

Reliant Information Technologies Corporation
Projected Statement of Cash Flows
For the Year Ended December 31, 1999
(numbers in parentheses indicate reductions in cash; thousands of dollars)

Operations:	
Net income	($127,078)
Depreciation	107,727
Other noncash expenses	29,958
Adjustment for deferred taxes	(766)
	9,841
Adjustments for:	
Increase in receivables	(14,427)
Decrease in inventories	48,047
Increase in accounts payable	27,905
Increase in other current assets	(11,508)
Increase in other current liabilities	34,434
	$ 84,451
Cash flow—operations	$ 94,292
Investing:	
Payments for additions to property, plant, and equipment	($142,918)
Proceeds from sale of property, plant, and equipment	3,669
Net sales of marketable equity securities	30,126
Decrease in notes receivable	3,755
Cash flow—investing	($105,368)
Financing:	
Proceeds from notes payable	$ 5,289
Payments on long-term debt	(178,556)
Proceeds from long-term debt	17,812
Proceeds from sale of stock	34,457
Dividends	–0–
Cash flow—financing	($120,998)
Effect of exchange rate changes in cash	(2,787)
Increase (decrease) in cash	(134,861)
Cash and equivalents—January 1	271,537
Cash and equivalents—December 31	$136,676

Red Rock Company
Consolidated Income Statement
(in thousands)

	For the Year Ended	
	Projected December 27, 1999	**Actual December 28, 1998**
Sales	$1,503,805	$1,464,881
Less: Beer excise taxes	153,066	149,951
	1,350,739	1,314,930
Cost and expenses:		
Cost of goods sold	778,943	754,217
Marketing, general and administrative	362,293	336,528
Research and development	21,682	23,443
	1,162,918	1,114,188
Operating income	187,821	200,742
Other (income) expense:		
Interest income	(10,582)	(13,214)
Interest expense	2,604	3,219
Depreciation expense	99,240	91,968
Miscellaneous, net	10,511	8,376
Income before taxes	86,048	110,393
Taxes	37,900	51,000
Net income	$ 48,148	$ 59,393

Red Rock Company
Consolidated Balance Sheet
(thousands of dollars)

	Projected as of December 27, 1999	Actual as of December 28, 1998
Assets		
Cash and cash equivalents	$ 113,454	$ 150,464
Accounts and notes receivable	109,208	99,560
Inventories:		
Finished goods	17,254	18,464
In process	32,881	31,037
Raw materials	64,357	68,409
Packaging materials	40,208	38,632
	154,700	156,542
Prepaid expenses and other current assets	66,591	61,255
Tax prepayments	7,703	5,216
Total current assets	451,656	473,037
Properties, at cost, less accumulated depreciation	975,781	901,172
Excess of cost over net assets of businesses		
acquired, less accumulated amortization	3,356	3,538
Other assets	25,700	18,175
Total assets	$1,456,493	$1,395,922
Liabilities and Stockholders' Equity		
Accounts payable	$ 85,627	$ 75,203
Accrued salaries and benefits	39,132	43,772
Taxes, other than income	26,542	27,840
Income tax liability	9,418	10,759
Other accrued expenses	48,531	43,168
Total current liabilities	209,250	200,742
Accumulated deferred taxes	189,056	181,137
Other liabilities	26,376	17,903
Total liabilities	424,682	399,782
Stockholders' equity:		
Class A common, voting, $1 par	1,260	1,260
Class B common, nonvoting, no par	39,773	34,578
Retaining earnings	1,013,865	983,943
	1,054,898	1,019,781
Less: Class B treasury shares, 10,863,376 in 1999		
and 11,123,876 in 1998	23,087	23,641
Total stockholders' equity	1,031,811	996,140
Total liabilities and stockholders' equity	$1,456,493	$1,395,922

CHAPTER 7

Analyzing and Understanding
Corporate Financial Reports

*Investors, whether novices or veterans, know that decisions
about what and when to buy and sell are based upon
a mix of fear, hopes, hunches, snatches of overheard
conversations, and solid information.…[T]here is no
substitute for information and knowledge…[but] while
financial analysis can provide investors with a clear picture
of a company's operations, it cannot tell them what
individual stock prices will do tomorrow.[1]*

Key Chapter Issues

- How can accounting data be used to develop an understanding of the financial health and performance of a company?
- What is ratio analysis?

- How does accounting information influence the behavior of investors and hence the movement of security prices?
- What special insights are revealed about a company from its statement of cash flows?

---

[1] T. L. O'Glove, *Quality of Earnings* (NY: The Free Press, 1987), pp. 1, xii.

227

In the previous six chapters we focused on developing an understanding of the basic financial statements, the fundamentals of the accounting system that produces those statements, and the institutional environment that surrounds the production of accounting information in general.

In this chapter we attempt to broaden your understanding of accounting information and its uses by considering a number of advanced topics in the analysis of financial statements. To begin, we return to some of the basics of ratio analysis and consider several alternative viewpoints using Procter & Gamble's financial statements. Attention then shifts to the alternative GAAP methods available for use in financial statements and how alternative GAAP impacts ratio analysis and security prices. Finally, we return to the topic of evaluating a company's cash flows and developing pro forma statements from them.

To begin, when a potential investor considers acquiring the shares of a company like Procter & Gamble, a variety of information sources should be consulted. For example, an investor should access the following sources:

- The company's annual and quarterly financial reports.
- Recent articles or news releases appearing in the financial press (such as *Barrons, Business Week, Forbes, Fortune, The Wall Street Journal,* and *The Financial Times*).
- Brokerage firm analyses and reports dealing with the company in particular and its industry in general.
- Investment service firms' reports and analyses (for example, Dun and Bradstreet, Moody's, Standard and Poors, and Value Line).

In this chapter we will consider how these information sources can be used to help an investor reach the very important resource allocation decision: to buy or not to buy.

ASSESSING THE QUALITY OF REPORTED EARNINGS AND FINANCIAL POSITION

Corporate financial reports are the primary means by which companies report their financial condition and performance to interested external parties. In the view of the FASB,

> Financial reporting should provide information that is useful to present and potential investors and creditors and other users in making rational investment, credit, and similar decisions.[2]

Implicit in these uses of financial reports are the concerns of users pertaining to a company's past performance, present condition, and future prospects. The first two of these are the primary focus of the financial statements, related footnotes, management discussion and analysis, and auditor's report. The latter is often the focus of management's letter to shareholders. Quite frankly, though, the assessment of future prospects is best served by users performing their own analysis of company performance and using supplementary third-party commentaries.

Many third-party sources of information about a company are readily available. To illustrate just one of these sources, Exhibit 7.1 presents the Value Line Investment Survey financial evaluation of Procter & Gamble as of July 17, 1998. Not only does this report present abbreviated financial statements and many basic ratios calculated for those statements, but also it presents a brief assessment of the strengths and weaknesses of Procter & Gamble's operations, as well as a prognosis for the future. For example, the Value Line report highlights the following key points:

[2] Financial Accounting Standards Board, *Statement of Financial Accounting Concepts No. 1,* "Objectives of Financial Reporting by Business Enterprises" (Stanford, Conn.: FASB, 1978).

EXHIBIT 7.1

Value Line Investment Survey Report Procter & Gamble

PROCTER & GAMBLE NYSE-PG | RECENT PRICE **92** | P/E RATIO **33.8** (Trailing: 36.8 / Median: 17.0) | RELATIVE P/E RATIO **1.96** | DIV'D YLD **1.1%**

TIMELINESS **3** Lowered 9/19/97	High:	12.9	11.0	17.6	22.8	23.8	27.9	29.4	32.3	44.8	55.5	83.4	94.0			Target Price Range 2001 2002 2003
SAFETY **1** New 7/27/90	Low:	7.5	8.8	10.5	15.4	19.0	22.6	22.6	25.6	30.3	39.7	51.8	77.3			

TECHNICAL **3** Lowered 11/7/97
BETA 1.05 (1.00 = Market)

LEGENDS
— 13.0 x "Cash Flow" p sh
···· Relative Price Strength
2-for-1 split 11/89
2-for-1 split 6/92
2-for-1 split 9/97
Shaded area indicates recession

2001-03 PROJECTIONS

	Price	Gain	Ann'l Total Return
High	90	(Nil)	1%
Low	75	(-20%)	-3%

Insider Decisions

	A	S	O	N	D	J	F	M	A
to Buy	0	0	0	0	0	0	0	0	0
Options	2	0	1	5	0	2	0	0	0
to Sell	6	0	1	10	0	2	0	0	0

Institutional Decisions

	3Q1997	4Q1997	1Q1998
to Buy	306	408	391
to Sell	457	381	417
Hld's(000)	629138	637396	646204

Percent shares traded: 6.0 / 4.0 / 2.0

% TOT. RETURN 6/98

	THIS STOCK	VL ARITH. INDEX
1 yr.	30.6	20.6
3 yr.	166.5	82.1
5 yr.	285.2	127.3

1982	1983	1984	1985	1986	1987	1988	1989	1990	1991	1992	1993	1994	1995	1996	1997	1998	1999	© VALUE LINE PUB., INC.	01-03
9.06	9.39	9.69	10.12	11.47	12.57	14.27	16.51	17.38	19.98	21.63	22.32	22.14	24.35	25.73	26.48	28.00	30.40	Sales per sh A	37.00
.78	.88	.89	.75	.89	1.04	1.26	1.51	1.65	1.96	2.08	2.24	2.37	2.76	3.14	3.55	3.85	4.35	"Cash Flow" per sh	6.05
.58	.64	.65	.48	.53	.57	.75	.89	1.03	1.23	1.31	1.41	1.55	1.86	2.15	2.28	2.55	2.90	Earnings per sh B	4.25
.26	.28	.30	.33	.33	.34	.34	.38	.44	.49	.52	.55	.62	.70	.80	.90	1.00	1.12	Div'ds Decl'd per sh C ■	1.60
.48	.47	.69	.84	.79	.68	.71	.79	.94	1.46	1.41	1.40	1.35	1.56	1.59	1.58	1.75	1.90	Cap'l Spending per sh	2.30
3.15	3.47	3.80	3.94	4.24	4.24	4.68	4.02	4.71	4.25	5.22	4.01	5.03	6.32	7.17	7.54	8.20	9.05	Book Value per sh D	15.40
1323.2	1326.2	1335.9	1339.4	1346.1	1352.2	1354.9	1295.9	1385.2	1352.4	1357.6	1363.5	1369.5	1373.1	1373.1	1350.8	1325.00	1325.00	Common Shs Outst'g E	1325.00
8.5	10.5	10.2	14.6	15.8	18.0	14.4	12.2	16.2	16.7	17.4	17.8	17.5	17.1	19.0	22.6	Bold figures are Value Line estimates		Avg Ann'l P/E Ratio	19.0
.94	.89	.95	1.19	1.07	1.20	1.20	.92	1.20	1.07	1.06	1.05	1.15	1.14	1.19	1.31			Relative P/E Ratio	1.35
5.2%	4.2%	4.5%	4.7%	4.0%	3.3%	3.2%	3.4%	2.6%	2.4%	2.3%	2.2%	2.3%	2.2%	2.0%	1.6%			Avg Ann'l Div'd Yield	1.9%

CAPITAL STRUCTURE as of 3/31/98
Total Debt $7687 mill. Due in 5 Yrs $3260 mill.
LT Debt $5438 mill. LT Interest $415.0 mill.
(Total interest coverage: 12.4x) (31% of Cap'l)
Pension Liability $327.0 mill. in '97 vs. $484.0 mill. in '96.

Pfd Stock $1831 mill. Pfd Div'd $104.0 mill.
(ESOP owns 62,952,000 Class A shares and 38,045,000 Class B shares; each A and B pfd. share is convertible into one common share.) (10% of Cap'l)

Common Stock 1,340,981,583 shs. (59% of Cap'l)
as of 3/31/98 (1467.5 mill. fully dil. shares)

MARKET CAP: $123 billion (Large Cap)

19336	21398	24081	27026	29362	30433	30296	33434	35284	35764	37400	40300	Sales ($mill) A	49000
12.9%	13.1%	12.6%	13.5%	13.3%	14.1%	15.6%	16.2%	17.5%	19.5%	20.0%	20.5%	Operating Margin	23.0%
697.0	767.0	859.0	956.0	1051.0	1140.0	1134.0	1253.0	1358.0	1487.0	1590	1650	Depreciation ($mill)	2000
1020.0	1206.0	1477.0	1773.0	1872.0	2015.0	2211.0	2645.0	3046.0	3415.0	3675	4135	Net Profit ($mill)	6000
37.4%	37.8%	35.7%	34.0%	35.1%	34.0%	33.9%	33.9%	34.8%	34.9%	34.0%	34.0%	Income Tax Rate	34.0%
5.3%	5.6%	6.1%	6.6%	6.4%	6.6%	7.3%	7.9%	8.6%	9.5%	10.0%	10.5%	Net Profit Margin	12.0%
1369.0	1922.0	2227.0	1702.0	1724.0	1688.0	1948.0	2194.0	2982.0	2988.0	4800	6000	Working Cap'l ($mill)	9000
2462.0	3698.0	3588.0	4111.0	5223.0	5174.0	4980.0	5161.0	4670.0	4143.0	5500	6000	Long-Term Debt ($mill)	7000
6337.0	6215.0	7518.0	7736.0	9071.0	7441.0	8832.0	10589	11722	12046	12740	13755	Shr. Equity ($mill)	22100
13.1%	13.8%	15.0%	16.2%	14.3%	17.3%	17.4%	18.0%	19.7%	22.2%	21.0%	22.0%	Return on Total Cap'l	21.5%
16.1%	19.4%	19.6%	22.9%	20.6%	27.1%	25.0%	25.0%	26.0%	28.3%	29.0%	30.0%	Return on Shr. Equity	27.0%
8.6%	13.2%	12.9%	17.8%	15.3%	21.3%	18.3%	18.2%	18.7%	20.5%	20.5%	21.5%	Retained to Com Eq	19.0%
47%	42%	42%	42%	42%	40%	39%	39%	39%	39%	39%	39%	All Div'ds to Net Prof	35%

CURRENT POSITION ($MILL)

	1996	1997	3/31/98
Cash Assets	2520	3110	2306
Receivables	2841	2738	2758
Inventory (LIFO)	3130	3087	3470
Other	2316	1851	2284
Current Assets	10807	10786	10818
Accts Payable	2366	2203	2230
Debt Due	1116	849	2249
Other	4343	4746	4649
Current Liab.	7825	7798	9128

ANNUAL RATES

of change (per sh)	Past 10 Yrs.	Past 5 Yrs.	Est'd '95-'97 to '01-'03
Sales	8.5%	5.5%	6.5%
"Cash Flow"	13.5%	10.5%	11.5%
Earnings	15.0%	12.5%	12.0%
Dividends	9.0%	11.0%	12.0%
Book Value	5.5%	8.0%	14.0%

QUARTERLY SALES ($ mill.) A

Fiscal Year Ends	Sep.30	Dec.31	Mar.31	Jun.30	Full Fiscal Year
1995	8161	8467	8312	8494	33434
1996	9027	9090	8587	8580	35284
1997	8903	9142	8771	8948	35764
1998	9355	9641	8881	9523	37400
1999	10000	10300	9700	10300	40300

EARNINGS PER SHARE A B

Fiscal Year Ends	Sep.30	Dec.31	Mar.31	Jun.30	Full Fiscal Year
1995	.56	.53	.44	.33	1.86
1996	.64	.59	.54	.38	2.15
1997	.65	.63	.59	.41	2.28
1998	.73	.71	.65	.46	2.55
1999	.81	.80	.74	.55	2.90

QUARTERLY DIVIDENDS PAID C ■

Calendar	Mar.31	Jun.30	Sep.30	Dec.31	Full Year
1994	.155	.155	.175	.175	.66
1995	.175	.175	.20	.20	.75
1996	.20	.20	.225	.225	.85
1997	.225	.225	.253	.253	.96
1998	.253	.253			

BUSINESS: The Procter & Gamble Company makes detergents, soaps, toiletries, foods, paper, & industrial products. Brands include: Tide, Cheer, Bold, Oxydol, Era, Crest, Ivory, Zest, Coast, Safeguard, Dawn, Joy, Cascade, Always, Tampax, Downy, Pringles, Bounce, Comet, Head & Shoulders, Prell, Scope, Secret, Bounty, Charmin, Pampers, Luvs, Crisco, Jif, Folger's, Cover Girl, Noxzema, Old Spice, Hawaiian Punch. Foreign oper.: 49% of prof. Has about 103,000 employees, 216,000 stockholders. '97 depr. rate: 8.0%. Est'd plant age: 5 yrs. ESOP controls about 7% of common (and equiv.) shares (1997 ann'l. rpt.). C.E.O.: John Pepper. C.O.O.: Durk Jager. Inc.: Ohio. Addr.: 1 Procter & Gamble Plaza, Cincinnati, Ohio 45202. Tel.: 513-983-1100. Internet: www.pg.com.

Procter & Gamble is trying to rebound from a period in which volume growth has slowed and competitors have capitalized on P&G price increases. The company is upgrading existing brands, increasing capacity and unveiling new products. In August, P&G will ship *Clean Rinse Formula Tide*, a high-margin addition to its *Tide* product line, which already accounts for two-thirds of annual laundry sales (approximately $10 billion). *Bounty*, its bellwether paper product, has become the number one-selling paper towel in Austria and Germany. To help meet the growing European demand, the company will build a $160 million paper towel plant in the U.K., with startup planned for the year 2000. Domestically, an upgraded line of *Pampers*, shipped in May, should help to boost volume growth in the U.S.

Procter & Gamble received some good news in June when the FDA concluded that Olestra, the company's much heralded "fat substitute," does not pose unusual health hazards. The FDA ruling coincides with the summer launch of fat-free *Pringles*. Although we do not expect Olestra-based products to add to the bottom line until the year 2000, the $32 billion snacks market (of which P&G holds only a 2% share) represents a window of opportunity for a company seeking to double sales over the next ten years. **Despite the deceleration in sales growth, Procter & Gamble continues to post double-digit share-net earnings gains.** Margins will probably continue to widen as P&G digests its 1997 acquisition of Tambrands. Improvements in the supply and distribution system throughout the entire company should also help to reduce excess inventory and better anticipate consumer demand. In addition, management's willingness to borrow in order to finance billion-dollar-a-year stock buyback programs should also help keep earnings momentum strong through 1999. **This huge, high-quality company appears to have considerable earnings growth potential over the 3- to 5-year haul.** But there's some risk here. A price surge in recent years, a tripling since early 1995, has put the stock's value above the range we deem probable in 2001-2003.
Luciano Siracusano III   July 17, 1998

(A) Fiscal year ends June 30.
(B) Based on average shares thru '96, diluted thereafter. Excl. nonrecurring gains (losses): '82, $0.01; '83, $0.02; '84, $0.03; '87, $0.03;
'90, $0.09; '93 ($1.95). Next earnings report due late July.
(C) Next div'd meet'g about Oct. 10. Goes ex about Oct 20. Dividend payment dates: Feb.
15, May 15, Aug. 15, Nov. 15. ■ Div'd reinv. plan available.
(D) Incl. intang. In '97: $3949 mill., $2.90/sh.
(E) In mill., adj. for stock splits.

Company's Financial Strength	A++
Stock's Price Stability	85
Price Growth Persistence	100
Earnings Predictability	100

- Procter & Gamble is trying to rebound from a period in which volume growth slowed and competitors capitalized on the company's price increases.

- Procter & Gamble received good news in June: The FDA concluded that Olestra, the company's "fat substitute," did not pose unusual health hazards.

- Despite a deceleration in sales growth, Procter & Gamble continues to post double-digit earnings-per-share gains.

- Procter & Gamble appears to have considerable earnings growth potential over the next 3-to-5 year period.

Note also that in terms of the Value Line investment rating system, Procter & Gamble earned a 1 (highest) on a scale of 1 to 5 in their Safety Ranking System, a 3 (average) in their Timeliness Ranking System, and a Financial Strength Rating of A++.

Because no one knows for certain what a company's future financial results will be, a great deal of emphasis is placed on past and present performance as indicators of the future. In projecting a link between the past and the future, issues falling under the general rubric of the **quality of earnings and financial position** become significant considerations. For example, although the amount of reported earnings is important, so too are the rate of earnings generated on available resources, the stability of earnings, the specific sources of earnings, and the accounting methods used to measure the earnings. Similarly, although it is useful to know the size and variety of asset categories, it is also important to determine their liquidity, operating capacity, and flexibility.

In previous chapters numerous financial ratios were suggested as sources of insight regarding a company's management of the various facets of its operations. For example, in Chapter 4 the accounts receivable turnover ratio was discussed as a means to estimate the rate at which a company's receivables were converted into cash. Chapter 5 presented the return on owners' equity ratio as an indication of the return earned by a company on noncreditor funds. Exhibit 7.2 summarizes the various ratios discussed throughout this text and also introduces a new category of indicators, the *return to investors*.

Return to Investors

For publicly held companies, the **return to investors** is one of the most frequently evaluated areas of company performance. Because investors are often the largest group of stakeholders (both in number and in terms of amount invested) in a company, how well they are rewarded for their investment is of considerable interest and importance. Most indicators of the return to investors are based on current income statement data and, in some cases, on actual stock market price data.

Earnings per share. Perhaps the most often cited measure of shareholder return is a company's **earnings per share,** or EPS. As noted in Chapter 5, EPS represents only those earnings of a company accruing to its voting, or common, shareholders. Thus, in the calculation of EPS, a company's earnings are first reduced for any dividends paid to the preferred shareholders.

EXHIBIT 7.2

Summary of Financial Statement Ratios

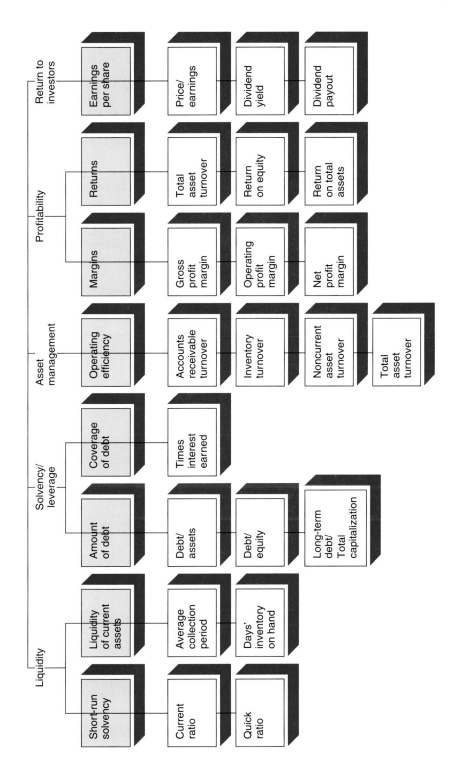

EXHIBIT 7.2 concluded

Summary of Financial Statement Ratios

Liquidity:
  Current ratio = Current assets ÷ Current liabilities
  Quick ratio = (Cash + Marketable securities + Receivables) ÷ Current liabilities
  Average receivable collection period = (Average accounts receivable balance ÷ Net sales) × 365 days
  Average number of days' inventory on hand = (Average inventory balance ÷ Cost of goods sold) × 365 days
Solvency/Leverage:
  Total debt-to-total assets ratio = Total debt ÷ Total assets
  Long-term debt to equity = Long-term debt ÷ Total owners' equity
  Long-term debt to total capitalization ratio = Long-term debt ÷ (Long-term debt + Total owners' equity)
  Times-interest-earned ratio = Net income before interest and income taxes ÷ Interest expense
Asset management:
  Accounts receivable turnover = Net credit sales ÷ Average accounts receivable balance
  Inventory turnover = Cost of goods sold ÷ Average inventory balance
  Noncurrent asset turnover = Net sales ÷ Average noncurrent assets
  Total asset turnover = Net sales ÷ Average total assets
Profitability:
  Gross profit margin = (Net sales − Cost of goods sold) ÷ Net sales
  Operating profit margin = Operating income ÷ Net sales
  Net profit margin = Net income ÷ Net sales
  Return on equity = Net income ÷ Average owners' equity
  Return on total assets = Net income ÷ Average total assets
Return to investors:
  Earnings per share (Net income − preferred stock dividends) ÷ Weighted-average number of common shares outstanding
  Price-earnings ratio = Market price per common share ÷ Basic earnings per share
  Dividend yield = Cash dividend per common share ÷ Market price per common share
  Dividend payout ratio = Cash dividends paid to common stockholders ÷ (Net income − Preferred stock dividends)

The calculation of EPS can be quite complex, often requiring the calculation of two measures, depending on whether a company has other securities outstanding that are convertible into, or exchangeable for, additional shares of common stock. In the simplest case in which a company has only common and nonconvertible preferred stock outstanding, the computation of **basic EPS** is straightforward:

$$\text{Basic EPS} = \frac{\text{Net income} - \text{Preferred dividends}}{\text{Weighted-average number of common shares outstanding}}$$

Note that in the calculation of basic EPS, the divisor is not merely the number of shares outstanding at year-end but rather is an average of the shares outstanding, weighted by the proportion of a given year (or quarter) that the shares were actually in the hands of shareholders.

For a company with securities outstanding that are convertible (for example, convertible bonds or convertible preferred stock) or exchangeable (for example, stock options or warrants) for common stock, the calculation of EPS can be surprisingly difficult. Under these conditions, two calculations may be required—one for basic EPS, as above, and one for diluted EPS.

Diluted EPS is calculated by including in the divisor all potentially dilutive securities that would enable its holder to become a common shareholder:

$$\text{Diluted EPS} = \frac{\text{Net income} - \text{Preferred dividends}}{\text{Weighted-average common shares outstanding} + \text{other potentially dilutive securities}}$$

Other potentially dilutive securities include stock options and warrants whose exercise price is below the average share price for the period; thus, even if such an option or warrant is not exercised (exchanged for common stock) by period-end, it is treated for diluted EPS calculation purposed as if it had been exercised.[3] Similarly, convertible securities such as convertible bonds and convertible preferred stock must be considered in the calculation of diluted EPS so long as these securities are dilutive. No security should be included in the calculation of EPS if its inclusion causes the EPS to increase (referred to as an antidilutive effect). Only those exchangeable or convertible securities causing a dilution of EPS are incorporated in the calculation.

For example, assume the following basic EPS:

$$\text{Basic EPS} = \frac{\$12,000,000 \text{ (net income)} - \$5,000,000 \text{ (convertible preferred dividends)}}{3,500,000 \text{ weighted-average common shares outstanding}}$$
$$= \$2.00$$

If the outstanding convertible preferred stock is assumed to be converted at the beginning of the year into 1 million common shares, the following would be the diluted EPS:

$$\text{Diluted EPS} = \frac{\$12,000,000}{4,500,000 \text{ shares}}$$
$$= \$2.67$$

Because the assumed conversion of the preferred stock had an antidilutive effect (EPS increased to $2.67), it would not be considered in the calculation of diluted EPS. Thus, in this case, basic and diluted EPS will be the same ($2.00 per share).

As this example illustrates, the earnings applicable to common shareholders for each convertible security included in the diluted EPS denominator require an adjustment. For example, if the number of common shares attributable to a convertible preferred stock is used to increase the diluted EPS denominator, the numerator should be increased by the amount of preferred dividends that would no longer be required if the conversion took place. Similarly, if the number of common shares attributable to a convertible bond is used to increase the diluted EPS denominator, the numerator should be increased by the amount of interest on the bonds (net of the related tax effect), that would no longer be paid if conversion took place. The one exception to this involves the exercise of stock options or warrants, which affect only the number of shares outstanding.

[3] When equity contracts such as stock options and warrants are assumed to be exercised for purposes of calculating diluted EPS, the number of shares issued is reduced by a hypothetical repurchase of treasury stock. Thus, if an option to purchase 1,000 common shares at an exercise price of $20 is assumed to be exercised when the average price is $40, the increase in the number of common shares outstanding is only 500, as follows:
- 1,000 shares @ $20 = $20,000
- $20,000 ÷ $40 = 500 shares repurchased as treasury stock
- 1,000 shares issued − 500 shares repurchased = 500 shares

Price-earnings (P/E) ratio. One of the most widely used indicators of a company's investment potential is the price-earnings ratio, or P/E multiple:

$$\text{P/E ratio} = \frac{\text{Market price per common share}}{\text{Basic EPS}}$$

Because the market price of a share of stock is a function of investors' perceptions regarding a company's potential, the same factors that affect those perceptions affect the P/E ratio—factors such as a company's relative investment risk, past earnings record, and growth potential. Many investment houses use the P/E ratio as a criterion to advise their clients about when to buy or sell stocks. A typical rule of thumb followed by some investment advisers is that a company with a low P/E ratio, assuming it is a sound business enterprise, represents a bargain for potential investors *relative to* a company with a higher P/E ratio. Investing solely, or even principally, on the basis of P/E ratios can be a risky investment strategy. P/E ratios are significantly influenced by the level of reported earnings, and, as we will see shortly, it is possible for a company to artificially manage its reported results. Moreover, investing on the basis of P/E ratios ignores the fact that *current* stock prices frequently reflect all publicly available information about a company; thus, it is unlikely that an investor following such a strategy will be able to earn unusual or *abnormal* returns.

At year-end 1998, the P/E ratio for Procter & Gamble was 35; for Colgate-Palmolive it was 37. If we assume that the two companies represent equivalent investment opportunities and that the P/E ratio is an effective means of identifying underpriced stocks, the year-end P/E ratios suggest that Procter & Gamble may have been a better investment opportunity at year-end 1998 than Colgate-Palmolive.

Dividend yield. Some investors are principally interested in the actual level of cash distributed by a company to its shareholders. To these investors, the cash **dividend yield** is an important indicator:

$$\text{Dividend yield} = \frac{\text{Cash dividend per common share}}{\text{Market price per common share}}$$

This measure informs investors of the current cash rate of return on a given common stock, based on its current selling price. During 1998 Procter & Gamble's cash dividend yield was 1.1 percent based on the year-end market price; for Colgate-Palmolive it was 1.2 percent. For an investor interested in current cash income, this measure readily facilitates investment choices.

Dividend payout ratio. A measure of the return actually paid to shareholders is captured in the **cash dividend payout ratio:**

$$\text{Dividend payout ratio} = \frac{\text{Cash dividends to common shareholders}}{\text{Net income} - \text{Preferred dividends}}$$

This ratio measures the percentage of a company's earnings that are actually distributed to its shareholders in the form of cash dividends. From an investor's point of view, a higher dividend payout ratio results in immediate increased cash inflows. On the other hand, from management's perspective, a growth-oriented company would want to maintain minimal payout ratios for the purpose of retaining funds to fuel continued growth, whereas a mature company (such as a utility company) would desire relatively high payout ratios to compensate for the fact that its potential stock appreciation is probably less than that of a growth-oriented company. In both 1997 and 1998 Procter & Gamble's cash dividend payout ratio was approximately 37 percent. These percentages are slightly below the industry average of 41 percent for the same periods.

FINANCIAL STATEMENT ANALYSIS: AN ILLUSTRATION

The topic of financial statement analysis has been a common thread linking the previous three chapters. As Exhibit 7.2 shows, the analysis of financial statements using ratios can be organized into five categories:

1. *Liquidity:* the assessment of a company's ability to meet current short-term obligations as they fall due.
2. *Solvency:* the assessment of a company's long-term debt payment ability.
3. *Asset management:* the assessment of how effectively a company utilizes its available resources.
4. *Profitability:* the assessment of a company's ability to generate revenues in excess of expenses.
5. *Return to investors:* the assessment of the earnings or cash flows accruing to the owners of a company.

Although each of these categories has been covered in detail elsewhere, it is instructive to review the ratios involved using Procter & Gamble's 1998 financial statements.

As Exhibit 7.3 reveals, Procter & Gamble's results for 1998 indicate both positive and negative trends. With respect to liquidity, the current and quick ratios reveal that Procter & Gamble's liquidity declined from 1997 to 1998; on the other hand, the average receivable collection period and average days inventory on hand indicate improved management of these key current assets. With respect to solvency, all ratios except the long-term debt-to - equity ratio suggest an increase in the use of debt financing from 1997 to 1998, and hence a decrease in Procter & Gamble's solvency. The asset management indicators also reveal a mixed picture: accounts receivable and inventory turnover is up, while noncurrent asset and total asset turnover is down. Procter & Gamble's profitability indicators, however, provide a consistent picture of improvement: all five ratios reveal an increase in firm profitability from 1997 to 1998. Finally, with respect to the return-to-investors indicators, Procter & Gamble increased its basic EPS nearly 13 percent in 1998, from $2.43 to $2.74 per share. This improvement, along with a bull stock market environment, helped raise the company's share price $20 per share, from $72 to $92. The stock market's optimism about the company's future prospects can also be seen in its increased price-earnings multiple.

Limitations of Ratio Analysis

Ratio analysis is the most widely used analytical technique for interpreting financial statement data. In spite of its widespread use, however, ratio analysis suffers from certain limitations and is subject to various constraining assumptions.

EXHIBIT 7.3

Procter & Gamble
Financial Statement Ratios

	1998	1997
Liquidity		
Current ratio	1.14:1	1.38:1
Quick ratio	0.56:1	0.75:1
Average receivable collection period	27.1days	27.9 days
Average number of day's inventory on hand	55.2 days	55.0 days
Solvency/leverage		
Total debt-to-total assets ratio	60.1%	56.3%
Long-term debt-to-equity ratio	30.6%	63.9%
Long-term debt-to-total capitalization	43.7%	39.0%
Times-interest-earned ratio	11.4 times	12.5 times
Asset management		
Accounts receivable turnover	13.5 times	13.1 times
Inventory turnover	6.61 times	6.64 times
Noncurrent asset turnover	2.00 times	2.13 times
Total asset turnover	1.27 times	1.30 times
Profitability		
Gross profit margin	43.3%	42.7%
Operating profit margin	16.3%	15.3%
Net profit margin	10.2%	9.6%
Return on equity	31.1%	28.4%
Return on total assets	12.9%	12.4%
Return to investors		
Earnings per share (basic)	$2.74	$2.43
Price/earnings ratio*	35	30
Dividend yield*	1.1%	1.2%
Dividend payout	37.0%	37.0%

*Price = Fourth-quarter closing price.

For example, because a ratio involves *two* financial statement numbers (such as net sales divided by total assets), the analyst must be cautious when inferring a cause if a change in a ratio is observed. Ratio changes may result from a change in either the numerator, the denominator, or both. Thus, when using ratios, the analyst must be prepared to look beyond the ratio itself in an effort to understand the economic event(s) causing the change.

Another concern is that, quite often, changes in financial statement data may be more cosmetic than real. For example, the trend analysis of Procter & Gamble's financial statement data reported in Exhibit 7.3 presupposes consistency in the basic relationships underlying the financial statement numbers. Consequently, any event—be it a real economic event or a cosmetic one—that disturbs an underlying relation will impact the reported ratios.

Although not an exhaustive listing, the following are examples of cosmetic events that will disturb the underlying financial statement relationships and thus must be considered by the astute financial statement user:

1. A structural change in the accounting entity (such as a merger or an acquisition of another company).

2. A change in an accounting method or principle (such as a switch from the LIFO inventory cost flow assumption to FIFO).

3. A change in an accounting estimate (such as an increase in the estimated useful life of a depreciable asset).

4. A change in accounting classification (such as segregating the income or loss on a division recently sold from the income from operations).

These concerns are particularly relevant when accounting data are investigated for trends over a number of accounting periods. The analysis of financial statement data over multiple periods is called **time-series analysis.**

Ratio analysis is most effective when the resulting ratios can be compared against some standard. Frequently, that standard is a similar ratio from a prior period, as in a trend analysis of time-series data. Another useful standard, however, is a ratio from a leading competitor or perhaps the industry in general. Unfortunately, the use of **cross-sectional analysis**—that is, the comparison of a given company's ratios with other companies' data or with industry averages—also involves certain restrictive assumptions, including these:

1. The individual company is assumed to be structurally similar to the competitor or the average of the industry, which is rarely the case.

2. The industry and the company under review are assumed to use a common set of accounting principles and accounting estimates. As we will see shortly, when a company under review uses one set of GAAP and the industry or comparative company uses another set, large cosmetic ratio differences tend to occur.

3. The company under review and the industry are assumed to experience a common set of external influences. A given company, however, may have undergone an unusual economic event (such as a labor strike) having multiple-period implications for its financial data that are not reflected in the industry standard.

Despite these concerns, ratio analysis can be a very powerful analytical tool so long as the analyst recognizes the following important maxim: *Ratios help the financial statement user identify important questions but seldom offer direct answers.* Only by a comprehensive review of the financial statements can answers be obtained.

Horizontal and Vertical Analysis

In addition to ratio analysis, two other types of financial statement analysis are frequently performed—horizontal analysis and vertical analysis. When comparative balance sheets or income statements are presented side by side, the statements can be made more meaningful if the amount of increase or decrease and the percentage change is shown. This type of analysis is known as **horizontal analysis** because the data comparisons are made on a horizontal plane from left to right.

Exhibit 7.4 illustrates a horizontal analysis of Procter & Gamble's income statement. In this two-year comparison, the earlier year (1997) is the base year. The percentage changes are rounded to the nearest tenth of a percent. For Procter & Gamble, it is noteworthy that while 1998 net sales increased by 3.9 percent over 1997 net sales, the cost of products sold increased by only 2.7 percent, suggesting that Procter & Gamble achieved certain production efficiencies through various economies of scale. These economies of scale, along with only a 2.8 percent increase in marketing, research, and administrative expenses, enabled Procter & Gamble to obtain a 10.7 percent growth in 1998 net earnings despite a nearly 20 percent increase in interest expense.

EXHIBIT 7.4

Procter & Gamble
Comparative Income Statements with Horizontal Analysis
For Years Ended June 30, 1998 and 1997
(in millions)

	1998	1997	Amount of Increase (Decrease) during 1998	Percentage Increase (Decrease) during 1998
Net Sales	$37,154	$35,764	$1,390	3.9%
Cost of products sold	21,064	20,510	554	2.7
Marketing, research administrative expenses	10,035	9,766	269	2.8
Operating Income	6,055	5,488	567	10.3
Interest expense	548	457	91	19.9
Other income, net	201	218	(17)	(7.8)
Earnings Before Income Taxes	5,708	5,249	459	8.8
Income taxes	1,928	1,834	94	5.1
Net Earnings	$ 3,780	$ 3,415	$ 365	10.7

In **vertical analysis** three financial statement numbers—total assets, total equities, and net sales—are converted to a base of 100 percent. Each item within the assets and equities on the balance sheet, or each item on the income statement, is then expressed as a percentage of the base number. Since for any given set of financial statements the base numbers represent 100 percent, the restated financial statements are called **common-size statements.**

To illustrate vertical analysis, Exhibit 7.5 presents Procter & Gamble's common-size income statements for 1998 and 1997. An interpretation of vertical statements often parallels the interpretation of horizontal statements. Note that the common-size statements permit both within-period analysis (for example, in 1998 the cost of products sold was approximately 56.7 percent of net sales) and across-period trend analysis (for example, the cost of products sold as a percentage of net sales decreased from 57.4 percent in 1997 to 56.7 percent in 1998, reflecting the economy-of-scale efficiencies noted above). The analysis of common-size statement are often used by analysts and managers alike to help identify the positive and negative trends of a company.

EXHIBIT 7.5

Procter & Gamble
Comparative Common-Size Income Statements
For Years Ended June 30, 1998 and 1997
(in millions)

	1998	Common-Size Percentage	1997	Common-Size Percentage
Net Sales	$ 37,154	100%	$ 35,764	100%
Cost of products sold	21,064	56.7	20,510	57.4
Marketing, research administrative expenses	10,035	27.0	9,766	27.3
Operating Income	6,055	16.3	5,488	15.3
Interest expense	548	1.5	457	1.3
Other income net	201	0.5	218	0.6
Earnings Before Income Taxes	5,708	15.4	5,249	14.7
Income taxes	1,928	5.2	1,834	5.1
Net Earnings	$ 3,780	10.2	$ 3,415	9.6

ACCOUNTING INFORMATION AND STOCK PRICES

As will repeatedly be noted throughout this text, the reporting of earnings and financial position of a company involves both considerable latitude in selecting from an array of generally accepted accounting principles and the inevitable need for management to make numerous valuation estimates and judgments. Given the flexibility available to corporate management in the presentation of financial results, the very human desire to portray their companies in the best light possible, and their awareness of users' concerns about the quality of reported earnings and financial position, it is important to consider the subtle and not-so-subtle items that external users should look for in financial reports as they perform their evaluations of a company.

Consider, for example, the revenue recognition method decision that managers of construction companies must make. Under GAAP, the revenues of such companies may be presented using either the completed contract method or the percentage of completion method. Under the **completed contract method,** management records no revenues until the work to be provided under a multi-period contract is fully completed. Under the **percentage of completion method,** management takes the position that revenue recognition is a function of the portion of work actually completed. Exhibit 7.6 provides a simple illustration contrasting the completed contract and percentage of completion methods for a hypothetical firm. The exhibit reveals that under the completed contract approach, FHAS Corporation would report no earnings in 1997 or 1998 and $1.7 million in earnings in 1999. Under the percentage of completion approach, however, a positive earnings stream ($0.4 million, $0.5 million, and $0.8 million, in 1997, 1998, and 1999, respectively) is reported in each year. The first method defers all earnings until 1999, whereas the second spreads the earnings across the three years as a function of the portion of work actually completed.

EXHIBIT 7.6

Alternative GAAP: Completed
Contract versus Percentage of Completion Methods

In June 1997 FHAS Corporation signed a long-term construction contract to build a shopping center in Houston, Texas. Under the terms of the three-year contract, FHAS would receive a total of $12 million. During 1997, 30 percent of the project was completed at a cost of $3.2 million. In 1998, 40 percent of the project was completed at a cost of $4.3 million; in 1999, the project was completed at a cost of $2.8 million.

Under the completed contract method, FHAS would report earnings as follows:

	1997	1998	1999
Revenues	$–0–	$–0–	$12.0 million
Expenses	–0–	–0–	10.3
Net income	$–0–	$–0–	$ 1.7 million
Return on sales	–0–%	–0–%	14.2%

Under the percentage of completion method, FHAS would report earnings as follows:

	1997	1998	1999
Revenues	$3.6 million	$4.8 million	$3.6 million
Expenses	3.2	4.3	2.8
Net income	$0.4 million	$0.5 million	$0.8 million
Return on sales	11%	10.4%	22.2%

It is clear that although the aggregate results, viewed in their entirety over the three-year period, are equivalent, substantially different impressions are created in any individual year as to the relative success of FHAS Corporation in performing under the contract. It is important to recognize that either the completed contract or the percentage of completion method may be adopted for financial reporting purposes. Moreover, the decision to use one method or the other is exclusively a managerial decision, although the percentage of completion method is preferred by most accountants because it more closely reflects the accrual basis of accounting.

As we see from the data in Exhibit 7.6, the method that a company adopts to report its revenues or expenses may have a significant impact on its actual reported results. Not only will the level of revenues and expenses on the income statement be affected, but so too will the level of reported assets and equities on the balance sheet, along with all the financial ratios calculated using those income statement and balance sheet values. Thus, when analyzing a company's reported performance and financial condition using either absolute figures or ratios, it is important to know just which accounting methods are being used and how those methods are likely to impact the reported values and calculated ratios.

EXHIBIT 7.7

Alternative GAAP and Financial Statement
Analysis: LIFO versus FIFO

Presented below are the income statements and selected financial ratios for two companies that are identical in every respect except with regard to the method of inventory costing and the cost of goods sold:

	FIFO Company	LIFO Company
Net sales	$ 75,000,000	$ 75,000,000
Cost of goods sold	(34,500,000)	(42,300,000)
Gross margin	$ 40,500,000	$ 32,700,000
Other operating expenses	(15,000,000)	(15,000,000)
Net income	$ 25,500,000	$ 17,700,000
Ending inventory	$ 17,250,000	$ 9,450,000
Selected financial ratios:		
Earnings per share	$2.55	$1.77
Current ratio	1.67:1	1.42:1
Working capital	$10.8 m	$5.65 m
Inventory turnover	2:1	4.5:1
Debt-to-equity ratio	1:5.17	1:4.91
Return on assets	10.8%	7.8%
Return on sales	34.0%	23.6%

For example, in Exhibit 7.6, note how the trend in the return on sales ratio dramatically differs for the two methods of reporting revenues.

Exhibit 7.7 provides further evidence of this analytical concern. This exhibit presents the income statement and selected financial indicators for two *economically identical* companies that differ *only* in regard to the accounting method used to value the cost of goods sold and ending inventory. A review of these financial data reveals that because inventory costs are rising, FIFO Company appears to be financially better off than LIFO Company: Earnings and working capital are higher by $7.8 million and $5.15 million, respectively, and the current ratio (liquidity), the debt-to-equity ratio (solvency), and the return on assets and on sales (profitability) are superior. Only the inventory turnover ratio (asset management) appears to be better for LIFO Company.

But are these financial indicators depicting economic reality? Holding the question of taxes aside, the answer is a resounding "No!" The two companies are economically identical in spite of the information revealed by the accounting data and the ratio analysis. If we now add the issue of income taxes and assume that each company uses the same inventory costing method for both tax purposes and for financial statement purposes, our conclusion is even more startling—the LIFO company is actually superior in economic performance because larger cash flows (due to tax savings) are preserved within the company. (LIFO and FIFO are discussed at length in Chapter 9.)

One thing is clear from these illustrations. The use of different financial accounting methods may produce very different impressions about the financial performance of a

EXHIBIT 7.8

Procter & Gamble's Net Jumps 12%, but Shares Fall On Worries About Its Growth Targets

Wall Street Journal; New York; July 31, 1998; By Tara Parker-Pope;

Procter & Gamble Co. posted a 12% jump in profit for its fiscal fourth quarter, but its shares fell 5.1% on worries that the consumer-goods giant will miss future targets because of weak unit sales growth in the U.S. and Europe and continuing troubles in Asia.

For the quarter ended June 30, the Cincinnati maker of Tide detergent and Pampers diapers reported net income of $686 million, or 47 cents a diluted share, up from $611 million, or 41 cents a share, a year earlier, adjusted for a 2-for-1 stock split. Sales climbed 3.7% to $9.28 billion, up from $8.95 billion. Excluding foreign-currency translations, sales would have risen 7%.

The performance matched Wall Street forecasts, but shares slumped after a conference call in which Procter & Gamble warned analysts it may not reach its goal of 10% growth in per-share earnings in the first half of fiscal 1999. Procter & Gamble shares closed at $83.625, down $4.50, in New York Stock Exchange composite trading.

The conference call was "highly cautious," said Paine Webber analyst Andrew Shore, who downgraded Procter & Gamble shares to "neutral" from "attractive." "I've been following this company a long time, and I've never heard them that cautious."

Analysts said the company indicated it still expects to meet annual targets of 11% to 14% growth in per-share earnings.

Procter & Gamble sales volume grew just 3% in the quarter. But excluding Tambrands and other recent acquisitions, sales volume was up only 1%, analysts said. Sales volumes were sluggish around the world, but particularly troublesome in the U.S. and Europe, where competitors have been slow to follow recent Procter & Gamble price increases in detergent, diapers and paper towels. Analysts said Procter & Gamble hinted it may roll back some of its recent price increases, prompting worries about future margin growth.

William H. Steele, an analyst with Buckingham Research Group in San Francisco, downgraded his fiscal 1999 earnings estimates by three cents to $2.83 a diluted share, compared with $2.56 a share for the 1998 fiscal year. "Procter made a veiled reference that they will protect their market shares," he said. Another reason for worries about earnings pressure is that Procter & Gamble is in the midst of one of the most aggressive new-product splurges in its history. New products bode well for the company long-term, analysts said, but mean heightened spending for now.

This, plus the economic troubles in Asia, put analysts in a downbeat mood. "Procter & Gamble goes through these cycles once in a while where it does things that aren't great for shareholders but are great for Procter," said Mr Shore. "It's still one of the finest companies I want someone to own longer-term, but in the near term there is a little too much uncertainty."

For the full year, Procter & Gamble's net rose 11% to $3.78 billion, or $2.56 a diluted share, from $3.42 billion, or $2.28 a diluted share, a year earlier, adjusted for the split. Sales rose 3.9% to $37.15 billion from $35.76 billion. Procter & Gamble Chairman and Chief Executive John E. Pepper said the company delivered "solid results" despite a "challenging economic situation" in Asia. For the year, Asia sales were down 3% to $3.45 billion, and profit for the region fell 37% to $174 million.

Mr. Pepper added that acquisition spending for the fiscal year reached record levels in excess of $3 billion, including Tambrands and paper companies in Mexico and South Korea. "Looking ahead, our focus remains on significantly accelerating sales growth," he said. "Faster, bigger innovation will be the key to both established brands and new products."

company and its management. Of interest to investors and managers, then, is whether these different accounting impressions are also reflected, or even should be reflected, in a company's stock price.

The Efficient Market Hypothesis

Although there is some disagreement over exactly what causes stock prices to move upward and downward, there is little disagreement over the notion that *accounting information* is at least partially responsible for stock price movements. Consider, for example, the news story reported in Exhibit 7.8. This *Wall Street Journal* article reports that Procter & Gamble's 1998 fourth-quarter earnings were up by 12 percent as compared to 1997 fourth-quarter results. Despite the fact that Procter & Gamble's reported performance for 1998 met the expectations of Wall Street forecasters, the company's share price declined 5.1 percent. Analysts and investors were apparently concerned that Procter & Gamble would be unable to meet future earnings projections because of "weak unit sales growth in the U.S. and Europe" and continuing economic problems in Asia.

This article and the resulting share price movement depict the role of accounting information for investors and the stock and bond markets in general. Using the latest accounting results, investors form expectations about the future of companies such as Procter & Gamble and accordingly determine how much they are willing to pay for a share of stock (or a bond) in the company. The negative share price reaction to the Procter & Gamble news indicates that investors' expectations about the future of Procter & Gamble were lowered by the announcement (and hence their unwillingness to pay a higher price for the stock). Notice also how quickly investors responded to the news release—the price of Procter & Gamble's common stock declined by $4.50 very shortly after the story appeared on the Associated Press newswire, and after a related conference call with analysts. The story appeared in the *Wall Street Journal* on the day following the press release by Procter & Gamble.

The relationship between accounting information and stock prices is largely captured by a theory of the functioning of capital markets called the **efficient market hypothesis,** or EMH.[4] The EMH is a widely accepted theory describing how stock and bond prices react to information. In fact, the theory is so well documented that it has been used by the U.S. Supreme Court to describe the behavior of U.S. capital markets. Under the EMH, stock prices are assumed to reflect fully (in terms of price) all publicly available information. When new information (such as the Procter & Gamble earnings announcement) is made public, share prices adjust very quickly to the new information.

Evidence also exists to suggest that the capital markets are not "fooled" by the differences in reported accounting numbers caused by the use of alternative GAAP; that is, sophisticated analysts and investors are apparently able to "see through" the differential accounting effects created by alternative GAAP (e.g. completed contract versus percentage of completion, LIFO versus FIFO, and so on) and are able to properly adjust share prices (by buying or selling) to reflect the true underlying economic value of a company.

An important implication of this theory is that managers of publicly held companies should be unable to manipulate the value of their companies' stock merely by selecting accounting methods that result in the highest level of reported earnings. Because stock prices reflect only *real* economic changes, they will be relatively unaffected by the cosmetic wealth changes associated with alternative GAAP.

Unfortunately, it is sometimes possible to "fool" the stock market and its many investors by disclosing fraudulent financial data. Because share prices are based on all publicly available information, misleading or fraudulent financial information will often cause share prices to adjust inappropriately. The independent public auditor, however, does investigate a company's records to identify any material misstatements, and although not all fraudulent

---

[4] See T. R. Dyckman and D. Morse, *Efficient Capital Markets and Accounting* (Englewood Cliffs, N.J.: Prentice Hall, 1986).

EXHIBIT 7.9

Procter & Gamble
Partial Consolidated Statement of Cash Flow
For Years Ended June 30, 1997 and 1998
(in millions)

	1998	1997	Classification*
Net cash provided by operating activities	$ 4,885	$ 5,882	R
Cash flows—Investing activities			
Capital expenditures	(2,559)	(2,129)	R
Proceeds from asset sales	555	520	R
Acquisitions	(3,269)	(150)	
Change in investment securities	63	(309)	
Net cash used for investing activities	(5,210)	(2,068)	
Cash flows—Financing activities			
Dividends to shareholders	(1,462)	(1,329)	R
Change in short-term debt	1,315	(160)	
Additions to long-term debt	1,970	224	
Reductions of long-term debt	(432)	(724)	R
Proceeds from stock options	158	134	
Treasury stock purchases	(1,929)	(1,652)	R
Net cash used for financing activities	(380)	(3,507)	
Effect of exchange rate changes on cash and cash equivalents	(96)	(31)	
Change in cash and cash equivalents	(801)	276	
Cash and cash equivalents, End of year	$ 1,529	$ 2,350	

*R = Recurring.

acts will be identified, most major errors (be they intentional or not) are identified as part of the annual audit investigation.

One approach used by many professional analysts and investors to evaluate a company's performance *independently* of the particular GAAP used to portray that performance is the analysis of cash flows, to which we now turn.

CASH FLOW ANALYSIS REVISITED

Cash flow is probably one of the most important elements of financial statement analysis. Not only are the reported cash flows invariant to the GAAP methods used to portray accrual net income, but cash is also the only asset without which a company cannot operate. As noted in Chapter 6, U.S. companies presenting audited financial reports are required to present a statement of cash flows.[5] The focus here is the analysis of those reported cash inflows and outflows.

[5] Although the IASC recommends that a statement of cash flows be presented, it is not a required financial statement disclosure in all countries (e.g., Japan).

Exhibit 7.9 presents a partial statement of cash flows for Procter & Gamble for 1997 and 1998. As the exhibit reveals, Procter & Gamble's cash and cash equivalents decreased by $801 million during 1998. Continuing operations provided $4,885 million in cash inflows, financing activities consumed $380 million, and investing activities consumed $5,210 million in cash.

As discussed more thoroughly in prior chapters, an important aspect of financial analysis in general, and cash flow analysis in particular, is the development of pro forma financial statements. An initial step in developing a pro forma statement of cash flows is to identify those cash inflows and outflows that can reasonably be expected to recur in the future. With this in mind, we labeled the various items in Exhibit 7.9 R, for recurring, or left them unlabeled if the items are not expected to be recurring. Admittedly, this decision process is speculative, involving somewhat arbitrary classifications by the financial statement user. But reasonable assertions are possible. For example, the current cash flows from continuing operations *are* likely to be a good estimate of the next period's cash flows from continuing operations, assuming that no material changes in operations occur. Dividends, although discretionary, are considered to be sacrosanct in most firms and thus are quite likely to be paid in the future. Finally, purchases of property, plant, and equipment are usually considered to be recurring because this type of investment is considered necessary for the continued survival and growth of a company such as Procter & Gamble.

Using this classification approach and a few assumptions regarding next period's operations, we can generate a rudimentary assessment of Procter & Gamble's cash flows for 1999. For example, if we assume that similar economic conditions will be experienced in 1999 and therefore that the level of recurring cash flows will remain relatively constant, one baseline estimate of the 1999 cash flows might be as follows:

Procter & Gamble
1999 Pro Forma Cash Flows

Net cash flows from continuing operations	$ 4,885
Net cash used for investing activities*	$(2,004)
Net cash used by financing activities	$(3,823)
Net increase (decrease) in cash and cash equivalents	(942)

*Assumes no new acquisitions or equity investments.

Obviously, this type of analysis depends heavily on the stability of Procter & Gamble's operations and on the classification decisions made by the analyst. As a company releases new information to the public, it is useful to incorporate this new data in any pro forma analysis. In so doing, the projected cash flows are likely to be as accurate as possible given the limited access to available corporate data.

SUMMARY

Almost all kinds of information—about a company specifically or about the economy in general—are likely to have some impact on a company's stock price. This is especially true for accounting information, which is frequently used by investors as a basis to predict future company performance, and, hence, stock value. Some of the specific indicators that investors use to evaluate current performance and to predict future company performance include earnings per share, the price-earnings ratio, dividend yield, and the payout ratio.

When evaluating a company's performance, investors need to consider the effects of alternative accounting methods (for example, LIFO versus FIFO or completed contract versus percentage of completion) on the ratios that they use. Failure to consider these accounting method effects may result in a misallocation of investor resources by overpaying when purchasing a company's shares. One way to examine a company's performance independent of the GAAP used to portray its results is to analyze its cash flows. By examining the financial statements in total and by considering the various trends revealed by ratio analysis, horizontal and vertical analysis, and cash flow analysis, the financial statement user should be able to develop a well-informed assessment of a company and its potential.

NEW CONCEPTS AND TERMS

Antidilutive effect	Efficient market hypothesis
Basic earnings per share	Horizontal analysis
Common-size statements	Percentage of completion method
Completed contract method	Price-earnings ratio
Cross-sectional analysis	Quality of earnings and financial position
Diluted EPS	Return to investors
Dividend payout ratio	Time-series analysis
Dividend yield	Vertical analysis

ASSIGNMENTS

7.1. Calculating earnings per share. Assume that during 1999 FHAS Enterprises has the following securities outstanding:

1. 250,000 shares of common stock with an average market price of $25 per share.

2. Options granted to executives to purchase 4,000 shares of common stock during the next three years at a price of $20 per share.

3. Zero coupon convertible debentures with a maturity value of $10 million, which had been sold at a yield of 12 percent. Each $1,000 face value bond is convertible into 15 shares of common stock.

4. Convertible preferred stock, which had been sold at its par value of $100 to yield 9.5 percent. The preferred stock is convertible into 3 shares of common and 3,000 shares are outstanding.

During 1999, FHAS Enterprises earned $3.2 million after taxes. (Assume that taxes are calculated at 33 percent.)

Required:

Calculate the basic and diluted earnings per share for the company.

7.2. Calculating earnings per share. Edna Lake, Inc., reported the following income data for 1999:

Income before extraordinary items	$174,000
Extraordinary loss (net of income taxes*)	(15,000)
Net income	$159,000

*Effective tax rate = 30 percent.

Throughout 1999 the company had 60,000 shares of common stock outstanding. The stock had traded at an average price of $25 and closed on December 31 at $30 per share. The company also had the following securities outstanding during all of 1999:

Common stock options for the purchase of 8,000 shares at a price of $20 per share.

10 percent convertible bonds, with a face value of $190,000. The bonds had been sold for $200,000 and yielded 9.4 percent. The bonds were convertible into 7,600 shares.

9.2 percent convertible bonds, with a face value of $250,000. The bonds had been sold for $237,500 and yielded 9.7 percent. The bonds were convertible into 10,000 shares.

Required:

a. Using the above data, calculate the basic EPS and the diluted EPS for Edna Lake, Inc., for 1999.

b. Which of the EPS numbers most accurately reflects the company's actual performance during 1999?

7.3. Alternative GAAP: completed contract versus percentage of completion. Thunderbird Construction Company (TCC) was employed to construct a new office facility in downtown Phoenix, Arizona. The three-year project is projected to cost $100 million to complete and is expected to produce gross revenues of $150 million during the three-year period.

In anticipation of the preparation of financial reports covering the project, TCC's controller collected the following financial data (in millions) relating to the project:

	(in millions)		
	1997	**1998**	**1999**
Construction costs incurred	$400	$300	$325
Estimated costs to complete	600	350	—
Progress billings	500	500	500
Collections on billings	—	450	900
Administrative expense	25	25	25

Required:

a. Using the above data, prepare income statements for the company under (1) the completed contract method and (2) the percentage of completion method for each of the three years.

b. Which set of results do you believe most accurately depicts the performance of the company?

7.4. Restating financial statements: inventories.* Presented below are the condensed financial statements for Scott Furniture as of December 31, 1998, and 1999. In the company's 1999 annual report, the following statement appeared:

If first-in, first-out had been in use, inventories would have been $1,960 million, $1,654 million, and $1,388 million higher than reported at December 31, 1999, 1998, and 1997, respectively.

Scott had used the LIFO method since 1980 for both tax and financial reporting purposes.

Required:

a. Assume a tax rate of 35 percent and that Scott had adopted the FIFO method (rather than LIFO) in 1980 and used FIFO through 1999. Restate Scott's balance sheets as of year-end 1998 and 1999 to reflect the use of FIFO.

b. By how much would Scott's net income change in 1998 and 1999 if FIFO were used instead of LIFO?

c. Calculate the following ratios for Scott for 1998 and 1999 under both LIFO and FIFO:
   (1) Current ratio.
   (2) Inventory turnover.
   (3) Average number of days' inventory on hand.
   (4) Total debt-to-equity ratio.

d. Under which method do the ratios look best?

Scott Furniture
Condensed Balance Sheets
As of December 31, 1999 and 1998
(in millions)

	December 31, 1999	December 31, 1998
Assets		
Cash and cash equivalents	$ 104	$ 147
Receivables	912	693
Inventories	1,750	1,670
Land	81	66
Building and equipment (net)	2,928	2,572
Long-term investments	103	85
Other assets and goodwill	220	146
Total	$ 6,098	$ 5,379
Liabilities and Owners' Equity		
Payables and accruals	$ 1,067	$ 790
Income tax payable	198	133
Notes payable	430	404
Deferred income tax	23	(24)
Long-term debt (total)	948	1,011
	$ 2,666	$ 2,314
Owners' Equity		
Common Stock	$ 180	$ 177
Retained earnings	3,252	2,888
Total	$ 6,098	$ 5,379

* 7.4, 7.5, and 7.6 are based on "A What If Exercise," copyright 1982 by the University of Virginia Darden School Foundation, Charlottesville, VA. All rights reserved.

Scott Furniture
Condensed Statement of Income
For the Years Ending December 31, 1999 and 1998
(in millions)

	1999	1998
Sales	$ 8,598	$ 7,613
Cost of goods sold	6,957*	6,172
Other expenses (net)	844	715
Income taxes	232	234
Total expenses	8,033	7,121
Income	$ 565	$ 492
Note:		
Depreciation for year	$ 370	$ 312
Dividends	$ 201	$ 182

*This figure includes depreciation allocable to cost of goods sold.

7.5. Restating financial statements: depreciation.* Scott Furniture's 1999 annual report included the following statement:

> Depreciation is computed principally using accelerated methods…for both income tax and financial reporting purposes.…If the straight-line method had always been in use, "Buildings, machinery, and equipment—net" would have been $504 million, $430 million, and $370 million higher than reported at December 31, 1999, 1998, and 1997, respectively, and depreciation expense for 1999, 1998, and 1997 would have been, respectively, $74 million, $60 million, and $48 million less.

Required:

a. Using the condensed financial statements presented in 7.4 and assuming a 35 percent tax rate, restate Scott's balance sheets for 1998 and 1999 to reflect the use of straight-line (rather than accelerated) depreciation. Assume that the straight-line method is used for financial reporting purposes and that accelerated depreciation is used for tax purposes.

b. By how much would Scott's net income change in 1998 and 1999 as a consequence of using the straight-line method?

c. Calculate the following ratios for Scott in 1998 and 1999 under both depreciation approaches:
  (1) Return on sales.
  (2) Return on total assets.
  (3) Noncurrent asset turnover.
  (4) Total asset turnover.

d. Under which method do the ratios look best?

7.6. Restating financial statements: pooling versus purchase accounting.* In 1985 Scott Furniture acquired the net assets of Erin Corporation by issuing 1,891,678 shares of Scott Furniture stock to the shareholders of Erin. Scott accounted for this transaction as a pooling-of-interests and, accordingly, included in its balance sheet only $32 million (the book value of Erin's net assets in 1985). The transaction was recorded on Scott's books as follows:

> Dr. Net Assets (A). . . . . (inc.) $32.0 million
> Cr. Capital Stock (OE) . . . .   (inc.) $ 3.0 million
> Cr. Retained Earnings (OE) . . . .   (inc.) 29.0 million

At the time of the acquisition, Scott's capital stock was trading on the over-the-counter market at about $50 per share.

Assume that instead of a stock exchange, Scott had sold its shares for $95 million and had used the proceeds to buy Erin's net assets. Assume that the transaction was accounted for as a purchase and that the fair market value of Erin's identifiable net assets equals $32 million.

Required:

a. Restate Scott's 1998 and 1999 financial statements to reflect the use of purchase accounting rather than pooling-of-interests accounting.

b. By how much would Scott's net income in 1998 and 1999 change?

c. Calculate the following ratios for Scott in 1998 and 1999 under both purchase accounting and pooling-of-interests accounting:
   (1) Total debt-to-total assets.
   (2) Book value per share. (Assume that 86.5 million shares are outstanding.)
   (3) Earnings per share.
   (4) Return on equity.

d. Under which method do the ratios look best?

7.7. Alternative GAAP: LIFO versus FIFO. The following information was taken from the 19X9 financial statements of General Electric Company, a major conglomerate with significant product lines in both industrial and consumer markets:

Inventories are valued on a last-in, first-out basis and carry the following balances (in millions) at December 31:

	19X9	19X8
Ending inventory	$3,158	$3,029

If FIFO had been used to value the inventories, they would have been $2,152 million higher than reported at December 31, 19X9 ($2,266 million higher at year-end 19X8). During 19X9, net reductions in inventory levels resulted in liquidations of LIFO bases of $114 million, and in 19X8, $163 million.

Required:

Presented following are the condensed financial statements of General Electric Company. Using this information, answer the following questions:

a. If GE had used FIFO instead of LIFO in all prior years, how would the company's 19X8 and 19X9 financial statements differ? (Ignore any effects on income taxes.)

b. Compare the income tax consequences of GE's use of LIFO rather than FIFO in 19X9.

c. Estimate the total tax savings that GE has received in all prior years as a consequence of using LIFO rather than FIFO. Assume a tax rate of 33 percent.

d. Calculate the following ratios for 19X9 for GE under both FIFO and LIFO:
   (1) Current ratio.
   (2) Quick ratio.
   (3) Inventory turnover.
   (4) Average number of days' inventory on hand.

General Electric Company
Statement of Financial Position
For the Year Ending December 31
(in millions)

	19X9	19X8
Assets:		
Quick assets	$ 7,754	$ 7,327
Inventories	3,158	3,029
Total current assets	$10,912	$10,356
Noncurrent assets	12,376	11,259
Total assets	$23,288	$21,615
Equities:		
Current liabilities	$8,688	$ 8,153
Long-term liabilities	3,162	3,099
Total liabilities	$11,850	$11,252
Owners' equity	11,438	10,363
Total equities	$23,288	$21,615

General Electric Company
Statement of Earnings
For the Years Ended December 31, 19X9, 19X8, and 19X7
(in millions)

	19X9	19X8	19X7
Sales of products and services rendered	$ 26,797	$ 26,500	$ 27,240
Cost of goods sold	(24,248)	(24,095)	(24,793)
Other income and expenses	450	312	167
Provision for income taxes	(975)	(900)	(962)
Net earnings	$ 2,024	$ 1,817	$ 1,652

7.8 Alternative GAAP: leases. MCI is a telecommunications company that leases a substantial quantity of its noncurrent assets. For example, as of March 31, 19X9, MCI had leased more than one-third of its total noncurrent assets, and the obligations associated with those leases represented nearly 50 percent of the company's total long-term debt.

Presented below are condensed balance sheets for MCI as of March 31, 19X9. The company's footnotes revealed the following additional data:

Depreciation of noncurrent assets is calculated using straight-line depreciation, assuming an average useful life of 10 years, unless the lease life is shorter. (No salvage value is assumed.) The value of capitalized leases included in noncurrent assets was as follows (in thousands):

	March 31	
	19X9	19X8
Total capitalized leases	$ 227,582	$ 250,451

At March 31, 19X9, the aggregate minimum rental commitments under noncancelable leases were as follows:

Years Ending March 31,	Capital Leases	Other Leases	Total
2000	$ 57,876,000	$ 16,610,000	$ 74,486,000
2001	50,753,000	15,443,000	66,196,000
2002	42,721,000	14,441,000	57,162,000
2003	35,620,000	12,669,000	48,289,000
2004	24,410,000	10,580,000	34,990,000
2005 and thereafter	17,213,000	49,220,000	66,433,000
Minimum lease payments	228,593,000	$118,963,000	$347,556,000
Less—Amount representing interest	47,388,000		
Present value of future lease payments	$181,205,000		

Interest rates on capital lease obligations on a weighted-average basis approximate 12%.

Required:

Assuming that all "other leases" should be capitalized on the balance sheet, restate MCI's balance sheet as of March 31, 19X9. Calculate the following ratios both before and after restatement:

a. Long-term debt-to-owners' equity.

b. Total debt-to-total assets.

Comment on how the company's bond ratings might be affected following the capitalization of all "other leases."

MCI Communications Corporation
Balance Sheet
As of March 31, 19X9 and 19X8
(in thousands)

	19X9	19X8
Assets:		
Current assets	$228,428	$ 48,946
Noncurrent assets	631,970	417,946
Total assets	$860,398	$466,892
Equities:		
Current liabilities	$185,540	$73,729
Deferred income taxes	34,058	2,409
Long-term debt	400,018	242,707
Owners' equity	240,782	148,047
Total liabilities and owners' equity	$860,398	$466,892

7.9. Financial Analysis: The Income Statement. Presented here are the consolidated statements of income for the Colgate-Palmolive Company. Evaluate the company's operations using ratio analysis and vertical analysis (common-size statements).

Colgate-Palmolive Company
Consolidated Statements of income
(in millions, except per share amount)

	1997	1996	1995
Net sales	$ 9,056.7	$ 8,749.0	$ 8,358.2
Cost of sales	4,461.5	4,451.1	4,353.1
Gross profit	4,595.2	4,297.9	4,005.1
Selling, general and administrative expenses	3,237.0	3,052.1	2,879.6
Provision for restructured operations	—	—	460.5
Other expense (net)	72.4	93.8	96.1
Interest expense (net)	183.5	197.4	205.4
Income before income taxes	1,102.3	954.6	363.5
Provision for income taxes	361.9	319.6	191.5
Net income	$ 740.4	$ 635.0	$ 172.0
Earnings per common share, basic	$ 2.44	$ 2.09	$ 0.52

7.10. Financial Analysis: The Balance Sheet. Presented here are the consolidated balance sheets for the Colgate-Palmolive Company. Evaluate the company's financial condition using ratio analysis and vertical analysis (common-size statements).

Colgate-Palmolive Company
Consolidated Balance Sheets
(in millions, except per share amounts)

	1997	1996
Assets		
Current Assets		
Cash and cash equivalents	$ 183.1	$ 248.2
Marketable securities	22.2	59.6
Receivables (less allowances of 35.8 and 33.8 respectively)	1,037.4	1,064.4
Inventories	728.4	770.7
Other current assets	225.4	229.4
Total current assets	2,196.5	2,372.3
Property, plant and equipment (net)	2,441.0	2,428.9
Goodwill and other intangibles (net)	2,585.3	2,720.4
Other Assets	315.9	379.9
	$7,538.7	$ 7,901.5
Liabilities and Shareholders' Equity		
Current liabilities		
Notes and loans payable	$ 158.4	$ 172.30
Current potion of long-term debt	178.3	110.4
Accounts payable	716.9	751.7
Accrued income taxes	67.0	93.1
Other accruals	838.9	776.8
Total current liabilities	1,959.5	1,904.30
Long-term debt	2,340.3	2,786.80
Deferred income taxes	284.5	234.3
Other liabilities	775.8	942.0

Colgate-Palmolive Company
Consolidated Balance Sheets
(in millions, except per share amounts)

	1997	1996
Shareholders' Equity		
Preferred stock	385.3	392.7
Common stock, $1 par value		
(1 billion shares authorized,		
366.4 million shares issued)	366.4	366.4
Additional paid-in-capital	1,027.4	918.4
Retained earnings	3,138.0	2,731.0
Cumulative translation adjustment	−693.7	−534.7
	4,223.4	3,873.80
Unearned compensation	−364.5	−370.9
Treasury stock, at cost	−1,680.3	−1,468.8
Total shareholders' equity	2,178.6	2,034.1
	$ 7,538.7	$ 7,901.5

7.11. Common-size statements: The case of the unidentified industries.* Analyzing a company's financial statements requires an understanding of the environment in which a firm operates. Many characteristics of this environment are common to all firms in an industry and to some extent influence the financial statements.

Exhibit 1 presents condensed financial statement information for 11 U.S. firms in different industries. Balance sheet and income statement items are expressed as a percentage of total net revenues. To improve the representativeness and "resolution" of these items, they have been calculated as four-year averages instead of annual figures.

The companies represented in the exercise are in the following industries:

- Advertising agency services
- Aircraft manufacturing
- Airline
- Automobile manufacturing
- Brewing
- Computer manufacturing
- Discount retailing
- Grocery store
- Insurance underwriting
- Oil extraction
- Pharmaceutical manufacturing

Required:

Use the data in Exhibit 1 to match the companies with the industries listed above. Variations in SG&A expenses are principally due to differences in the level of advertising. Note also that CFFO stands for cash flow from operations.

---

* This case was prepared by Thomas I Selling. Copyright © 1995. All rights reserved. Reprinted with permission.

EXHIBIT 1

Common-Size Four-Year Average Financial Statements

	1	2	3	4	5	6	7	8	9	10	11
Cash and cash equivalents	0.12	0.01	0.10	0.02	0.12	0.18	2.26	0.05	0.09	0.06	0.01
Net accounts receivable	0.07	0.06	0.20	0.20	0.27	0.73	0.14	0.09	0.12	0.16	0.00
Inventories	0.11	0.06	0.16	0.39	0.13	0.03	0.00	0.01	0.25	0.12	0.10
Total current assets	0.30	0.13	0.46	0.61	0.52	0.94	2.40	0.15	0.46	0.34	0.11
Property, plant, equipment at cost	0.41	0.98	0.28	0.37	0.58	0.24	0.47	1.01	0.59	0.60	0.22
Less: accumulated depreciation	0.19	0.32	0.10	0.14	0.16	0.12	0.19	0.40	0.20	0.79	0.08
Net property, plant, equipment	0.22	0.66	0.18	0.23	0.42	0.12	0.28	0.61	0.39	0.81	0.14
Other assets	0.09	0.14	0.05	0.05	0.01	0.17	0.12	0.15	0.10	0.07	0.49
Total Assets	0.61	0.91	0.69	0.89	0.95	1.23	2.80	0.91	0.95	1.22	0.74
Total current liabilities	0.23	0.14	0.19	0.33	0.35	0.91	1.79	0.26	0.44	0.26	0.11
Long-term debt	0.05	0.25	0.01	0.13	0.03	0.04	0.19	0.24	0.09	0.12	0.06
Other noncurrent liabilities	0.03	0.15	0.04	0.00	0.08	0.04	−0.04	0.19	0.07	0.03	0.03
Total liabilities	0.31	0.54	0.24	0.46	0.46	0.99	1.94	0.69	0.60	0.41	0.20
Owners' equity	0.30	0.38	0.47	0.43	0.49	0.23	0.86	0.22	0.35	0.81	0.54
Total Liabilities and Equity	0.61	0.92	0.71	0.89	0.95	1.22	2.80	0.91	0.95	1.22	0.74
Net Sales or Revenue	1.00	1.00	1.00	1.00	1.00	1.00	1.00	1.00	1.00	1.00	1.00
Cost of goods sold	0.81	0.61	0.61	0.78	0.36	0.58	0.74	0.78	0.75	0.83	0.79
Depreciation expense	0.01	0.05	0.05	0.01	0.05	0.04	0.01	0.07	0.05	0.02	0.01
SG&A expense	0.03	0.20	0.20	0.12	0.07	0.31	0.06	0.10	0.06	0.05	0.16
R&D expense	0.05	0.00	0.04	0.00	0.13	0.00	0.00	0.00	0.04	0.00	0.00
Interest expense	0.00	0.02	0.01	0.01	0.01	0.01	0.04	0.02	0.05	0.01	0.01
Income taxes	0.02	0.05	0.03	0.02	0.13	0.03	0.05	−0.01	0.00	0.06	0.02
Other expense (net)	0.01	0.01	−0.02	0.02	0.19	0.01	0.04	−0.08	0.00	0.01	0.00
Net Income	0.05	0.07	0.08	0.04	0.06	0.02	0.06	−0.04	0.05	0.02	0.01
CFFO/Capital Expenditures	2.11X	2.01X	2.11X	0.93X	1.94X	3.01X	52.33X	0.08X	0.86X	1.44X	3.30X

7.12. Ratio analysis: ratios tell a story.* Financial results vary among companies for a number of reasons. One reason for the variation can be traced to the characteristics of the industries in which the companies work. Some industries require large investments in property, plant, and equipment; others require very little. In some industries, the product-pricing structure allows companies to earn significant profits per sales dollar; in other industries, the product-pricing structure forces a much lower profit margin. In most low-margin industries, however, companies often experience a relatively high volume of product throughput in their businesses. A number of industries are also characterized by lenient credit terms; others sell for cash only.

A second reason for some of the variation in financial results among companies is the result of management policy. Some companies reduce their manufacturing capacity to more closely match their immediate sales prospects; others carry excess capacity to prepare for future expansion. Another policy-related difference is that some companies finance their assets with borrowed funds, but others avoid that leverage and finance their assets with equity.

Of course, one other reason for some of the variation in reported results among companies is the differing competencies of management. Given the same industry characteristics and the same management policies, different companies report different financial results simply because their management staff perform differently.

These differences in industry characteristics, in company policies, and in management performance are reflected in the financial statements and can be highlighted through the use of financial ratios.

Following are balance sheets, in percentage form, and selected ratios computed from fiscal 1997 balance sheets and income statements for 13 companies from the following industries:

1. Airline company.

2. Automobile manufacturer.

3. Pharmaceutical company.

4. Commercial bank.

5. Computer manufacturer.

6. Discount general merchandise store chain.

7. Electric utility.

8. Fast-food chain.

9. Wholesale food distributor.

10. Supermarket chain.

11. Textile manufacturer.

12. Tax services company.

13. Software development company.

These ratios were developed based on the following formulae:

1. Return on sales (ROS) = $\dfrac{\text{Net income before extraordinary items}}{\text{Net sales}}$

2. Asset turnover = $\dfrac{\text{Net sales}}{\text{Average total assets}}$

---

3. Return on assets (ROA) =

$$\frac{\text{Net income}}{\text{Average total assets}}$$

or =

$$\text{ROS} \times \text{Asset turnover}$$

4. Financial leverage =

$$\frac{\text{Liabilities} + \text{Owners' equity}}{\text{Owners' equity}}$$

or =

$$\frac{\text{Total assets}}{\text{Owners' equity}}$$

5. Return on equity (ROE) =

$$\frac{\text{Net income}}{\text{Average total owners' equity}}$$

or =

$$\text{ROA} \times \text{Financial leverage}$$

6. Long-term debt to capital =

$$\frac{\text{LT debt}}{\text{LT debt} + \text{Owners' equity}}$$

7. Current ratio =

$$\frac{\text{Total current assets}}{\text{Total current liabilities}}$$

8. Inventory turnover =

$$\frac{\text{Cost of goods sold}}{\text{Average inventory}}$$

9. Receivables collection =

$$\frac{\text{Average accounts receivable}}{\text{Net sales/365 days}}$$

10. Revenue growth =

$$\frac{\text{This year's net sales} - \text{Last year's net sales}}{\text{Last year's net sales}}$$

11. Gross margin =

$$\frac{\text{Net sales} - \text{Cost of goods sold}}{\text{Net sales}}$$

12. Dividend payout =

$$\frac{\text{Cash dividends}}{\text{Net income}}$$

Required:

Study the common size balance sheet profiles and the financial ratios listed for each of the 13 companies as presented on the next two pages. Your first assignment is to match each column in the exhibit with one of the industries listed previously. Be prepared to give the reasons for your pairings and identify those pieces of data that seem to contradict the pairings you have made.

Ratios Tell a Story

	1	2	3	4	5
Fiscal year-end	Jun-97	Dec-97	Feb-97	Dec-97	Dec-97
Percentage of total:					
Cash and equivalents	62.3	22.6	11.8	12.1	3.5
Receivables	6.8	69.7	3.5	3.4	3.9
Inventory	--	--	19.4	1.8	1.9
Other current assets	3.0	--	2.3	2.3	1.0
Total current assets	72.1	--	37.0	19.6	10.3
Net plant and equipment	10.2	1.6	61.4	65.3	76.6
Financial-service assets	--	--	--	--	--
Goodwill and equity investments	16.3	0.6	--	2.6	--
Other assets	1.4	5.5	1.6	12.5	11.1
Total assets	100.0	100.0	100.0	100.0	100.0
Notes payable	--	2.7	0.5	--	--
Accounts payable	5.0	66.9	16.5	5.5	3.0
Accrued expenses	2.3	0.4	5.8	4.0	1.2
Income taxes	3.2	--	--	1.1	.4
Other current liabilities	14.5	--	1.1	0.4	5.8
Total current liabilities	25.0	--	23.9	11.0	10.4
Long-term debt	--	9.5	12.2	12.9	28.4
Financial-service liability	--	--	--	--	--
Deferred-tax liability	--	--	0.9	4.2	17.6
Other liabilities	--	11.6	4.9	0.6	1.0
Total liabilities	25.0	91.1	41.9	28.7	57.4
Minority interest	--	--	--	--	--
Translation adj. and other	--	--	--	-0.9	--
Preferred stock	6.8	0.1	--	10.3	2.2
Common stock	31.4	8.6	4.1	18.8	9.8
Retained earnings	36.8	0.2	54.5	43.2	30.6
Treasury stock	--	-0.1	-0.5	-0.1	--
Total owners' equity	75.0	8.9	58.1	71.3	42.6
Total liabilities and equity	100.0	100.0	100.0	100.0	100.0
Return on sales	30.4%	9.9%	2.22%	6.41%	10.0%
Asset turnover	.93	0.12	2.63	1.09	0.49
Return on assets	28.3%	1.15%	5.84%	7.00%	4.95%
Leverage	1.38	11.25	1.74	1.66	2.34
Return on equity	39.1%	12.9%	10.2%	11.65%	11.59%
Long-term debt/total capital	--	51.6%	17.4%	15.3%	40.1%
Current ratio	2.87	--	1.55	1.79	.99
Inventory turnover	--	--	10.6	28	10.8
Days receivables outstanding	26	2,195	5	11	29
Revenue growth	31.0%	9.3%	0.5%	7.4%	2.3%
Gross margin	90.4%	--	29.5%	37.9%	--
Dividend payout	0.0%	58.8%	52.3%	24.2%	69.3%

Ratios Tell a Story

6 Oct-97	7 Jan-97	8 Dec-97	9 April-97	10 Dec-97	11 Dec-97	12 Dec-97	13 May-97
14.4	2.2	7.5	35.7	14.7	8.9	4.9	1.7
25.7	2.1	1.1	27.6	1.8	11.1	3.9	18.1
21.3	40.1	2.0	--	1.2	8.3	22.9	28.2
4.5	1.0	2.7	3.4	1.3	3.4	3.7	2.4
65.9	45.4	13.3	66.7	19.0	31.7	35.4	50.4
19.9	51.4	12.4	22.0	80.9	25.6	49.7	21.0
--	--	69.4	--	--	--	--	--
--	--	0.7	4.2	--	36.1	7.3	15.0
14.2	3.2	4.2	7.1	0.1	6.6	7.6	13.6
100.0	100.0	100.0	100.0	100.0	100.0	100.0	100.0
3.9	--	--	14.2	--	3.9	0.9	--
10.0	19.3	4.3	10.2	3.8	12.7	6.5	36.0
13.0	6.1	5.8	6.3	13.7	--	9.9	8.8
4.8	0.8	0.5	6.8	--	3.3	--	--
3.6	1.6	1.3	--	3.0	2.1	6.7	1.9
35.3	27.8	11.9	37.5	20.5	22.0	24.0	46.7
9.9	25.3	2.5	--	14.8	5.2	27.6	5.5
--	--	63.5	--	--	--	--	--
--	1.2	0.4	1.4	10.3	10.9	7.7	3.4
3.8	--	10.4	2.1	7.1	8.8	2.2	--
49.0	54.3	88.7	41.0	52.7	46.9	61.5	55.6
--	2.6	--	6.8	--	4.6	--	--
--	-1.0	-0.4	--	--	--	-1.7	--
--	--	0.2	0.2	--	--	7.5	--
3.7	2.0	2.4	26.2	8.9	20.2	12.8	12.4
47.3	42.1	9.1	35.7	38.4	67.0	19.9	32.0
--	--	--	-9.9	--	-38.7	--	--
51.0	45.7	11.3	59.0	47.3	53.1	38.5	44.4
100.0	100.0	100.0	100.0	100.0	100.0	100.0	100.0
7.27%	2.91%	5.64%	2.48%	8.33%	19.6%	-1.26%	1.74%
1.44	2.72	0.45	1.05	0.96	0.94	1.38	5.96
10.47%	7.92%	2.55%	2.60%	7.99%	18.4%	-1.74%	10.37%
2.01	2.42	9.43	1.80	2.18	2.04	2.55	2.50
21.0%	19.2%	24.1%	4.68%	17.4%	37.5%	-4.44%	25.9%
16.3%	36.9%	18.1%	--	23.8%	8.58%	41.8%	11.0%
1.87	1.64	1.11	1.78	0.93	1.47	1.49	1.08
3.77	5.25	18.0	--	--	5.49	4.81	18.7
65	3	9	81	7	43	17	10
11.6%	12.0%	4.2%	16.5%	12.1%	19.2%	-3.9%	4.9%
33.9%	20.2%	11.4%	66.5%	--	50.1%	14.1%	10.5%
17.0%	15.7%	29.2%	225%	2.0%	44.2%	--	8.7%

7.13. Pro forma financial statements: Hofstedt Oil & Gas Company. The venture capital division of a major U.S. financial institution has elected to fund an investment in an oil and gas exploration and production company that will operate both onshore and offshore in Texas and Louisiana. The initial financing commitment from the bank is for $40 million.

The company's strategic plan calls for an aggressive drilling program to be carried out during 1996. Hofstedt Oil & Gas estimates that it will drill 50 wells at an average cost of $800,000 per well and that 30 of those wells will yield aggregate crude oil reserves of approximately 10 million barrels. The remaining 20 wells are expected to be dry or commercially unproductive. These forecasts were based on the expert opinion of geologists familiar with the properties and were confirmed by petroleum engineers employed directly by the bank.

The company's production plan calls for a maximum exploitation effort to earn the highest financial return. Tom Hofstedt, president of the company, developed the following production scenario:

Year	Number of Barrels to Be Produced	Estimated Selling Price per Barrel	Estimated Lifting Cost Per Barrel
1996	1,000,000	$30	$5
1997	1,500,000	30	5
1998	1,500,000	35	6
1999	2,500,000	40	7
2000	3,500,000	45	8

Hofstedt Oil & Gas is very concerned about the impact of this operation on its financial statements and on the company's stock price. Consequently, any available accounting policy choices loom as very important in the overall evaluation of the investment. As a result, Hofstedt sent a terse memo to the company's controller, the closing line of which stated, "Prepare pro forma statements showing the alternative accounting effects on cash flow, income before tax, and financial position if we elect to use the successful efforts method or the full-cost method."

Required:

For purposes of pro forma statement preparation, assume that the $40 million loan agreement will be repaid as follows: (1) $10 million principal repayment per year to be paid on December 31 beginning on December 31, 1997, and (2) interest payments of 10 percent per year on the balance of the loan outstanding as of the beginning of the year. Ignore income taxes and all other operations. Based on your pro forma cash flows, income statements, and balance sheets for the period 1996 through 2000, what accounting method (successful efforts or full cost) recommendation would you make to Hofstedt, and why?

PART III

Measuring and Reporting Assets and Equities Using Generally Accepted Accounting Principles

CHAPTER 8

Trade Receivables and
Marketable Securities

CHAPTER 9

Inventories and the Cost of
Goods Sold

CHAPTER 10

Active Investments and Business
Combinations

CHAPTER 11

Noncurrent Assets: Fixed Assets,
Intangible Assets, and Natural
Resources

CHAPTER 12

Accounting for Liabilities: Basic
Concepts, Payables, Accruals,
and Interest-Bearing Debt

CHAPTER 13

Leases, Retirement Benefits, and
Deferred Income Taxes

CHAPTER 14

Owners' Equity

CHAPTER 8

Trade Receivables and
Marketable Securities

*Your accounts receivable collection effort will be no
better than the accuracy and timeliness of your
accounting information.*[1]

*Market value accounting has been called a panacea by
some and a placebo by others.*[2]

Key Chapter Issues

- What are accounts receivable and marketable securities?
- At what value should these financial assets be reported on the balance sheet?

- How does the accounting for these assets affect the income statement?
- What management judgments and assumptions are necessary in order to account for these assets?
- What is "mark to market"?

---

[1] S. D. Popell, "Effectively Manage Receivables to Cut Costs," *Harvard Business Review,*
January–February 1981, p. 49.

[2] J. T. Parks, "FASB 115: It's Back to the Future for Market Value Accounting," *Journal of
Accountancy,* September 1993, p. 49.

In the previous chapters, we introduced some of the fundamental concepts involved in preparing and analyzing the three basic financial statements. In a sense, the preceding chapters attempted to demystify the process of constructing a set of financial statements. It is important, however, not to lose sight of the fact that many challenges are inherent in reporting on the financial condition and results of operations for a variety of companies that are engaged in diverse and different activities, have varied histories, and are run by managers with different ideas of how best to achieve certain results—all to the satisfaction of absentee owners who have their own agendas. In light of such circumstances, if the formulation of generally accepted accounting principles seems an imposing task, it is. We must remember that the overall objective of financial reporting is to provide useful information to decision makers. Such an objective necessitates a closer look at the various components making up those three basic financial statements so that you, the user of financial statement information, will be able to comprehend the financial story those statements tell.

Consider the fact that the assets reported on a company's balance sheet may be used in a variety of capacities to benefit the company. For example, one asset, cash, may be used to buy inventories or pay employee salaries. Inventories, another asset, may be sold to produce revenues and, hence, generate new cash inflows. Machinery and equipment may be used to produce new inventory units to sell to customers. Thus, each asset category on the balance sheet effectively serves one or more specialized functions within a company; and each has, as we will see, its own set of accounting challenges.

In this chapter we focus on the accounting for and valuing of trade receivables and marketable securities. Although these two assets differ as to their origin, they have some similar attributes. Both, for example, are **liquid assets;** i.e., they can be readily converted into cash. Both are subject to valuation adjustments for financial reporting purposes—accounts receivable are reported at their net realizable value (that is, the amount of cash flows expected to be realized when they are collected), and marketable securities are generally reported at fair value (that is, the amount of cash obtainable if they were sold).

Our objective in this chapter is to learn how these assets arise, how they are accounted for, how they can be managed and utilized effectively, and how they may be analyzed. We begin with a consideration of trade receivables.

TRADE RECEIVABLES

In Chapter 6 we noted that managing accounts or trade receivables is an important component of the larger concern of managing a company's cash and cash flows. For most businesses, the extension of credit to customers is a normal part of generating sales. Credit sales, however, do not provide immediate cash inflows; indeed, they actually create some uncertainty regarding the timing and amount of expected future cash inflows. Consequently, prior to making a credit sale, management must weigh the cost of the anticipated benefit of increased sales by extending credit to customers who would normally not be willing to purchase goods on a strictly cash basis against the cost associated with the possible uncollectibility of a customer's promised payments of cash.

The accounting entry to record the receipt of a promise to be paid that is generated by a $1,000 credit sale of merchandise is:

Dr. Accounts Receivable (A) . . . . (inc.) 1,000
Cr. Sales (R) . . . . (inc.) 1,000

Notice in this transaction that even though cash is not received, the revenue is still considered to have been earned because the seller's earnings process is assumed to be complete and is therefore recognized in the accounting period in which the sale is made.

When cash is subsequently collected on the account receivable generated by this credit sale, the following transaction is recorded:

Dr. Cash (A) . . . . (inc.) 1,000
    Cr. Accounts Receivable (A) . . . .   (dec.) 1,000

Notice that this cash collection event, by itself, does not affect the company's profitability nor does it change the level of total assets. The cash collection event is merely an exchange of one asset for another, and the accounting entry reflects that fact.

Management Issues

Conventional accounting practice is to use the account title Accounts Receivable or Trade Receivable only for those receivables arising from normal, recurring credit sales of merchandise or services. From a manager's perspective, this practice permits the identification of amounts still to be collected from customers who have already received the goods purchased. Receivables generated by other events, for example by a cash advance to an employee, should not be commingled with the unremitted credit sales still reflected in the Accounts Receivable account. Separate accounts should be created for these other types of receivables to preserve the ease with which the monitoring of credit customer remittances, or lack thereof, may be done.

The primary reason that a company extends credit to customers is to increase sales. From a customer's point of view, credit purchases are preferable to cash purchases, in part because they are convenient and in part because they allow the customer to retain the use of cash for an additional period of time. From the seller's point of view, there is clearly a delay in obtaining the cash associated with having made a credit sale versus a cash sale. One managerial issue for the seller is whether the increase in sales as a result of offering the credit option to prospective buyers more than offsets the cost of granting the credit. Another issue for a company selling goods or services on a credit basis relates to the management of the outstanding receivables. For example, if the Accounts Receivable balance increases during a period when credit sales are relatively stable, a manager should determine whether the increase is due to the collection department's ineffective job or due to more lenient credit terms having been offered to customers.

Besides the administrative costs associated with establishing the credit-granting and cash collection processes, two other costs are associated with extending credit to customers. There is the "time value of money"; a dollar received tomorrow is not worth as much as a dollar received today. Because of this implicit cost of extending credit to customers, managers often offer discounts to credit customers to accelerate cash payments (that is, to induce credit customers to pay prior to the end of the agreed-on credit period).

For example, consider the typical credit sales terms of 2/10, net/30. Translated, these terms mean that if a customer pays for a credit purchase within 10 days of being invoiced, a reduction of 2 percent in the amount due may be taken. If, on the other hand, payment is not remitted within the 10-day discount period, full payment is expected within 30 days. Thus, the key issue is whether the 2 percent discount will be seen as a sufficient inducement for a customer to pay 20 days early. In this case, the answer should be an emphatic "yes" in that the 2 percent savings, when annualized, is equivalent to an opportunity cost of 36 percent annually ($365/20 \times 0.02$). Thus, a credit customer would be well advised to borrow money from a bank, even at the usurious rate of 30 percent annually, to take advantage of such a 2 percent discount offered by a seller.

Upon receipt of a discounted remittance from a credit customer, the seller would record a sales discount as follows:

```
Dr. Cash (A). . . . . . . . . . . . . . . . . . . . . . . . . (inc.) 98
Dr. Sales Discount (CR) . . . . . . . . . . . . . . . . (inc.) 2
    Cr. Accounts Receivable (A) . . . . . . . . . . . . . . . . .          (dec.) 100
```

The sales discount is a contra-revenue (CR) account and would be used in presenting the seller's net sales figure in that period's income statement.

The second cost associated with extending credit to customers pertains to uncollectible receivables. Regardless of the care that managers take to investigate the creditworthiness of customers, some accounts receivable inevitably prove to be uncollectible. Knowing that such circumstances are probable in general (if management knew which specific customers would be the culprits there would be no credit sales made to them), sale prices must be set accordingly. Moreover, as will soon be discussed, sound financial reporting practices dictate that management estimate and record an expense for the estimated uncollectible amount.

Net Realizable Value and Uncollectible Accounts

From a financial reporting perspective, accounts receivable are to be reported in the balance sheet at their **net realizable value** (net collectible amount). The use of net realizable value as a valuation basis for accounts receivable stems, in part, from the fact that receivables are a current asset and financial statement users often compare the level of current assets with the level of current liabilities to assess a company's *liquidity*, or short-term default risk. Hence, to ensure that financial statement users obtain an accurate assessment of liquidity, receivables must be valued at their net realizable or cash collectible amount.

One additional accounts receivable financial reporting concern evolves from the *matching principle.* As mentioned earlier, one of the costs of selling goods on credit is the cost involved in the likely event that not all customers will pay what they owe. Indeed, the experience of virtually all companies indicates that some customers will not pay the amounts owed. In view of this reality, the matching principle dictates that an estimated expense for the cost of extending credit be recorded in the period in which the benefit (that is, the sales revenue) from doing credit business is recorded. Of course, if at the time of a credit sale management knew which specific customer would not pay, the credit sale would not be made. In the face of not knowing in advance which credit customer will default, and in order to achieve the matching principle and report the receivables at their net collectible amount, an *estimate* of their net realizable value that is consistent with prior experience involving customer defaults must be made. In reporting this estimated net realizable amount, the gross amount of the receivables account is reduced by establishing a contra-asset account called the **Allowance for Uncollectible Accounts.** To establish an appropriate allowance amount, managers may use one of two estimation approaches, both involving a historically based percentage: (1) a percentage of the period's credit sales or (2) a percentage of the year-end balance in accounts receivable. It is worth repeating that neither of these approaches identifies *specific* uncollectible accounts, but rather they *estimate* the dollar amount of possible uncollectible accounts.

The first approach to estimating the dollar value of uncollectible accounts is called the **percentage of credit sales** approach and it assumes that a certain proportion of a period's credit sales will never be collected. For example, if credit sales for the year are $1 million and if 3 percent—the company's historical average of uncollected credit sales—is estimated to be the amount that will prove to be uncollectible, the following transaction is recorded at period-end:

Dr. Bad Debt Expense (E) . . . . (inc.) 30,000
   Cr. Allowance for Uncollectible Accounts (CA) . . . .   (inc.) 30,000

Notice the income statement emphasis implicit in this method of estimating the net realizable value of accounts receivables: The $30,000 bad debt expense is derived from a calculation based on the period's credit sales and is thus a direct matching of expenses to related revenues. It is also important to note that a contra-asset account is used for the allowance account. The reason for this is that specific customer accounts have not yet been identified as uncollectible and therefore the Accounts Receivable account, which is an aggregation of *specific* customer receivables, cannot be reduced directly. In essence, the desired goal of reporting receivables in the balance sheet at their net realizable value is achieved by creating a contra-asset account that is netted against gross accounts receivable. For example, PepsiCo's consolidated balance sheet reveals the following presentation for accounts (and notes) receivable:

	(in millions)	
	1997	**1996**
Accounts and notes receivable, less allowance: $125 in 1997 and $166 in 1996	$2,150	$2,276

The contra-asset account serves to reduce the gross receivables amount to an estimated net collectible amount. This contra-asset account balance represents, as of a specific point in time, an amount believed to indicate the amount of outstanding customer accounts that will never be collected. Subsequently, if evidence is obtained that a specific customer account will not be collected (for example, a customer goes bankrupt), that receivable is written off and the receivables account is directly reduced along with a similar reduction in the contra-asset account (in essence, a portion of the contra-asset account's balance is no longer needed). In summary, under the percentage-of-credit-sales method to estimate uncollectible accounts, the balance in the Allowance for Uncollectible Accounts is increased each period by an amount based on a percentage of that period's credit sales (this amount is also the period's bad debt expense to be recorded under this method), and is subsequently decreased by the dollar amount of any *specific* accounts deemed uncollectible and therefore written off.

A second and perhaps more intuitively appealing implementation of the allowance method for estimating the bad debt expense requires an **aging of the outstanding end-of-period accounts receivable.** In recognition of the fact that a large part of a given period's credit sales will already have been collected by period-end, this approach focuses only on those accounts receivable yet to be collected. Under the aging method, outstanding accounts receivable are grouped according to the number of days they are past due. Typical "age" categories for the accounts receivable are: current, 1–30 days overdue, 31–60 days overdue, 61–90 days overdue, and more than 90 days overdue. It is normally the case that as accounts receivable become increasingly overdue, a larger percentage will ultimately prove to be uncollectible. Thus, for each of the increasingly overdue categories, a larger percentage estimate is applied to the respective accounts receivable balance in each category in determining an aggregate estimate of period-end uncollectible receivables.

The aging approach focuses on determining a targeted figure for the period-end balance in the allowance for uncollectible accounts, thus establishing a specific relationship between two balance sheet accounts—the Allowance for Uncollectible Accounts and the Accounts Receivable accounts. The difference between the targeted ending allowance for the Uncollectible Accounts balance and its existing balance is the *adjustment to be made* to the contra-asset account and is the amount recorded as that period's bad debt expense. The transaction recorded under this method is essentially the same as that shown in the percentage-of-credit-sales example, but the amounts are likely to differ.

Note that under either allowance method, specific uncollectible accounts receivable were not identified at the time of recording the bad debt expense estimate and the increase to the contra-asset account. When a specific account receivable is finally identified as uncollectible, it is removed from the books. Under either of the allowance methods, adjusting the books to reflect this writing off of a specific account merely involves reducing the balance in the contra asset Allowance for Uncollectible Accounts (a debit entry) and the balance in the asset Accounts Receivable (a credit entry). Such an entry has no income statement effect, nor does it affect the total assets, the total current assets, or the net realizable value of the accounts receivable remaining on the balance sheet. Indeed, the income statement and the balance sheet effects were anticipated and recognized at the time management recorded the estimate of the uncollectible accounts using either the percentage-of-credit-sales approach or the aging of outstanding receivables approach.

Under either of the allowance methods, if a specific account that has previously been removed from the books (that is, written off) subsequently turns out to be collectible, the prior entry made to reduce the receivable account and the contra-asset account is simply reversed. This transaction increases the balance in both the Accounts Receivable account and the Allowance for Uncollectible Accounts account by the amount now deemed to be collectible. As a final point, it is worth emphasizing that not only is the selection of the estimation method a managerial decision, but so are the percentage estimates that are used. For most firms, the percentage estimates of noncollectibility are based on the firm's actual historical experience and thus tend to be good indicators of future uncollectibility. It is also interesting to note that in some countries, the percentage estimates are prescribed by government statute.

Comprehensive Illustration: Accounting for Receivables

As a comprehensive example of the financial reporting issues for accounts receivables posed thus far, consider the following information pertaining to United Department Stores, Inc. (UDS), for the fiscal year ending January 31, 2000. All amounts are in millions of dollars.

1. For the year, UDS had net sales of $10,512, of which $3,951 were credit sales.

2. The beginning Accounts Receivable balance as of February 1, 1999, was $1,623.5. The beginning balance in the Allowance for Uncollectible Accounts was $36.5.

3. Collections during the year were $3,953.

4. During the year, specific accounts receivable totaling $34.2 were deemed to be uncollectible and were written off (removed from the Accounts Receivable account).

5. Receivables totaling $2.0 that had been previously written off were subsequently deemed to be collectible.

6. As of January 31, 2000, the following aging schedule was prepared for UDS's accounts receivable:

	Amount
Uncollected billings on account:	
Current	$ 62.8
1 to 30 days past due	1,025.2
31 to 60 days past due	356.9
61 to 90 days past due	129.7
Longer than 90 days past due	14.7
Total accounts receivable outstanding	$1,589.3

7. In the judgment of UDS's management and based on past experiences of account collections, the following amounts were anticipated to be uncollectible:

1/4 of 1% of all current accounts:	0.0025 × 62.8	=	$ 0.16
1/2 of 1% of all accounts 1–30 days past due:	0.005 × 1,025.2	=	5.13
2.5% of all accounts 310 days past due:	0.025 × 356.9	=	8.92
10% of all accounts 61–90 days past due:	0.10 × 129.7	=	12.97
50% of all accounts more than 90 days old:	0.50 × 14.7	=	7.35
			$ 34.53

During the year, UDS would have recorded the following sales activity:

```
Dr. Cash (A) . . . . . . . . . . . . . . . . . . . . . . . (inc.) 6,561
Dr. Accounts Receivable (A) . . . . . . . . . . . (inc.) 3,951
    Cr. Sales (R) . . . . . . . . . . . . . . . . . . . . . . . . . . .          (inc.) 10,512
```

(In addition to the above sales entry, an entry would need to be made to adjust the Inventory and Cost of Goods Sold accounts—see Chapter 3.)

During the year, collections of the accounts receivable would be recorded as:

```
Dr. Cash (A) . . . . . . . . . . . . . . . . . . . . . . . (inc.) 3,953
    Cr. Accounts Receivable (A) . . . . . . . . . . . . . . . . .          (dec.) 3,953
```

Next, the transactions recorded during the year to report specific accounts that were written off, as well as to reestablish the specific customer accounts previously written off that were later deemed to be collectible, should be recorded:

```
Dr. Allowance for Uncollectible Accounts (CA). . . . (dec.) 34.2
    Cr. Accounts Receivable (A) . . . . . . . . . . . . . . . . . . . . .          (dec.) 34.2

Dr. Accounts Receivable (A) . . . . . . . . . . . . . . . . . (inc.) 2.0
    Cr. Allowance for Uncollectible Accounts (CA) . . . . . . . . . .          (inc.) 2.0
```

At year-end management must report the net realizable value of the outstanding accounts receivable in its financial statements. In this case UDS uses the aging method; thus, the ending balance in the Allowance for Uncollectible Accounts represents what management believes to be the offset to gross accounts receivables in arriving at their net realizable value. Using the balances in the aging schedule and the percentage estimates given by management, we determine that the ending balance in the contra-asset allowance account should be $34.53. Because the balance in the contra asset account after the previous two transactions were recorded is $4.3 (36.5–34.2+2.0), the expense amount for uncollectible accounts for this period must be $30.23. In essence, the $30.23 (a plug figure) is the amount required to take the balance in the contra asset allowance account to the targeted ending balance of $34.53. The $30.23 is also the amount of the bad debt expense to appear on the current period's income statement. The transaction to record this would be as follows:

Dr. Bad Debt Expense (E). . . . . (inc.) 30.23
Cr. Allowance for Uncollectible accounts (CA). . . . . .   (inc.) 30.23

A reconstruction of the contra asset allowance T-account is helpful in following the flow of these transactions:

Allowance for Uncollectible Accounts

Accounts written-off	34.2	Beginning balance (2/1/99)	36.5
		Restoration of previously written-off accounts	2.0
		Subtotal	4.3
		2000 bad debt expense	30.23
		Targeted ending balance (1/31/00)	34.53

If UDS had used the percentage-of-credit-sales method instead of the aging method, the recorded transactions would remain the same except for the last one involving the Bad Debt Expense account. Assuming that the percentage-of-credit-sales rate used by management was 1 percent, the estimate for uncollectible accounts would be $39.5 ($3,951 credit sales × 0.01). Recall that under the percentage-of-credit-sales approach, this amount is *not* the targeted ending balance for the Allowance for Uncollectible Accounts account but is the amount by which this account is increased. Thus, in this case the year-end balance in the Allowance for Uncollectible Accounts account would become $43.8 ($39.5 + $4.3), and the period's bad debt expense would be $39.5. Take a moment to verify this.

It must be noted that a company that uses the percentage-of-credit-sales method must also carefully evaluate the resulting year-end balance in the Allowance for Uncollectible Accounts account. If sales are flat and that balance continues to increase from period to period, it suggests that the percentage-of-sales rate applied in prior periods is too high and does not reflect the company's real uncollectible accounts experience. If, on the other hand, that balance becomes negative (a debit balance), the percentage-of-sales rate used to estimate uncollectibles has been too low. In either event, management may decide to adjust the percentage factor to a rate more likely to result in increases to the allowance account that, over time, are similar to the amounts subsequently removed from the contra-asset account as specific receivables are found to be uncollectible.

This latter statement is true for both methods. This is so because, consistent with the matching principle, both estimation methods attempt to match the cost of granting credit (the bad debt expense) to the period in which the benefit (the credit sale) was recorded. Thus, the increases and decreases to the Allowance for Uncollectible Accounts account indicate differences between the timing of recording an estimate for anticipated uncollectibles and the actual default of a specific account. Consequently, if the percentage rates used to estimate the future uncollectibles reflect the actual level of uncollectible accounts over a number of periods, the balance in the allowance account should achieve a steady state.

It may be helpful to visualize the operations of the two methods as presented in Exhibit 8.1. Notice that with the percentage-of-credit-sales method, the Allowance for Uncollectible Accounts account is adjusted *by* the calculated amount, whereas with the aging method, the account is adjusted *to* a targeted, calculated amount.

EXHIBIT 8.1

Illustration of Two Methods for Estimating Uncollectible Accounts

Panel A: Percentage-of-Credit-Sales Method

Accounts Receivable		Allowance for Uncollectible Accounts	
Beginning balance			Beginning balance
	Collections and Write-offs		
Credit Sales ----------		Based on percentage of sales	Write-offs
		------------------>	Addition here and as Bad Debt Expense entry
Ending balance			Ending balance

Panel B: Aging of Receivables Method

Accounts Receivable		Allowance for Uncollectible Accounts	
Beginning balance			Beginning balance
	Collections and Write-offs		
Credit Sales			Write-offs
			Plug here for Addition and Bad Debt Expense
Ending balance ----------		Based on aging ---------->	Ending balance

There is one additional means to account for bad debts. The **direct write-off method** is not acceptable in the U.S. (or most other countries) for publicly issued financial statements but is in fact the only acceptable method in the U.S. for tax purposes.[3] Only when evidence is available by which management determines that a *specific* customer's account is uncollectible is a bad debt expense recorded and the Accounts Receivable account balance reduced to the net amount expected to be collected. Under this method, no contra-asset allowance account is ever created, nor is there any attempt to record the bad debt expense amount in the period when the credit sale is made. The entry would be as follows:

Dr. Bad Debt Expense (E) . . . . (inc.) 500
Cr. Accounts Receivable (A) . . . .   (dec.) 500

---

[3] In some countries, the direct write-off method is GAAP.

EXHIBIT 8.2

The Coca-Cola Company and Subsidiaries
Current Assets
(in millions)

	December 31, 1997	December 31, 1996
Current assets:		
Cash and cash equivalents	$ 1,737	$ 1,433
Marketable securities	106	225
	1,843	1,658
Trade accounts receivable, less allowances of $23 in 1997 and $30 in 1996	1,639	1,641
Inventories	959	952
Prepaid expenses and other assets	1,528	1,659
Total current assets	$5,969	$5,910

From a managerial perspective, deciding to write off an account receivable, whether under one of the allowance methods or under the direct write-off method, can be problematic. Managers typically require convincing evidence that a specific account is indeed uncollectible before they delete it from their records. Indirect evidence such as a customer's declaration of bankruptcy or more direct evidence such as correspondence from the customer disputing the amount owed is generally considered to be sufficient evidence to warrant reducing the Accounts Receivable account.[4] In spite of such evidence and despite recording the account write-off, management should continue to attempt to collect any outstanding amount.

Trade Receivable Disclosures

As mentioned earlier, trade receivables appear in the balance sheet in the current assets section and are reported at their net realizable value. Most annual reports present the Trade Receivables account balance *net* of the Allowance for Uncollectible Accounts, with the balance in the allowance account either disclosed beside it or subtracted in the column of reported amounts. Exhibit 8.2, which presents the current asset section of Coca-Cola Corporation's 1997 balance sheet, illustrates this typical method of receivable presentation.

Note that the reader learns from the balance sheet of the amount that Coca-Cola management expects ultimately to collect ($1,639 million), as well as the amount of gross accounts receivable not expected to be collected ($23 million). The sum of these two figures is the amount of gross accounts receivable not yet collected as of year end 1997.

---

[4] As an example of the variability in such management judgments, in an analysis of the bad-debt allowances carried on the 1995 balance sheets by some of the U.S.'s largest drugstore chains, *Drug Topics* (June 24, 1996) reports balances ranging from zero percent of total accounts receivable for Long's Drug Stores to 17 percent for Revco Discount Drug Centers.

EXHIBIT 8.3

General Electric Company
Accounts Receivable Footnote Disclosure
(in millions)

December 31,	1997	1996
Aircraft Engines	$2,118	$1,389
Appliances	479	713
Broadcasting	362	698
Industrial Products and Systems	1,638	1,574
Materials	1,037	1,068
Power Generation	2,206	2,463
Technical Products and Services	787	698
All Other	131	86
Corporate	534	377
	9,292	9,066
Less allowance for losses	(238)	(240)
	$9,054	$8,826

Receivables balances at December 31, 1997 and 1996, before allowance for losses, included $6,125 million and $6,629 million, respectively, from sales of goods and services to customers, and $285 million and $290 million, respectively, from transactions with associated companies.

Current receivables of $303 million at year-end 1997 and $326 million at year-end 1996 arose from sales, principally of aircraft engine goods and services, on open account to various agencies of the U.S. government, which is GE's largest single customer. About 4% of GE's sales of goods and services were to the U.S. government in 1997 (about 5% in 1996 and 1995).

Exhibit 8.3 illustrates another acceptable format for reporting accounts receivable. The balance sheet of General Electric presents only the net realizable value of receivables; the footnotes disclose the balance in the Allowance for Doubtful Accounts account as well as the receivables by lines of business. Such an approach is acceptable, although less common than the approach chosen by Coca-Cola.

Factoring and Pledging

Most companies consider the management of accounts receivable (that is, the efforts undertaken to make sure that payments are promptly received) an important part of their day-to-day operations.[5] However, if a company decides that it does not want to expend the resources necessary to manage the accounts or finds itself short of cash, the company may *factor* its accounts receivable. **Factoring** is a process by which a company can convert its

---

[5] In a recent study of the "hottest jobs in the accounting area," accounts receivable was rated number one in a survey of Chief Financial Officers. See K. Williams, "Where Are the Hot Jobs?," *Management Accounting* (August 1997), p. 14.

receivables into cash by selling them at face value less a service charge for processing the transaction and for the time value of money. Typically, the service charge for factoring receivables is very expensive, from 10 percent to as much as 50 percent or more. How much will be paid to a factor (usually a financial institution) is largely a function of whether the receivables are sold with or without recourse. **With recourse** means that the factor can return a receivable to the company and collect from the company if the receivable turns out to be unpaid as of a certain date. If such an event is likely, the company who has factored its receivables may have to record a liability in anticipation of that event if certain conditions are met. **Without recourse** means that the factor assumes the risk of any losses on collection. In either case, the customer owing the money may or may not be notified that a factor is the ultimate recipient of its payment. Panel A in Exhibit 8.4 typifies corporate disclosures pertaining to the factoring of accounts receivable.

Another way a firm can use accounts receivable to expedite its cash inflows is to pledge them as collateral for a short-term bank loan that may not have been obtainable without the pledge. In **pledging,** a company normally retains title to the accounts receivable but pledges that it will use the proceeds from collection of the receivables to repay the loan. Panel B in Exhibit 8.4 presents Nashua Corporation's disclosures pertaining to the pledging of receivables and inventory against a revolving credit line.

Notes Receivable

Businesses sometimes accept promissory notes from customers in exchange for services or merchandise sold or in place of an outstanding account receivable that a customer is unable to pay according to the original credit terms. A **promissory note** is a legal document that is signed by the customer (*the maker*) promising to pay to the company (*the payee*) a dollar amount (*the principal*) plus interest. The note may become due in total on a stated maturity date or in segments on several dates, at which time(s) the payee receives from the maker the stipulated amount(s) plus any accrued interest.

A promissory note, or note receivable, might be arranged by a seller if a customer is a high credit risk or needs a longer time than usual to pay. Companies often convert overdue accounts receivable to notes receivable so that the amount in question, the new payment date, and an interest charge for the extended payment time may all be formally and specifically stated and agreed to by the customer. Notes receivable classified as current assets are carried in the financial statements at net realizable value, that is, face value, less any allowance for uncollectible accounts. The evaluation process for possible uncollectible notes is exactly the same as for accounts receivable. If the notes receivables are more properly classified as noncurrent, they should be reported at the present value of the expected future cash flows. Later chapters will have more to say about such noncurrent accounts, their valuation, and the concept of present value.

Because promissory notes receivable are negotiable instruments, businesses sometimes sell or pledge notes receivable to a bank (or any other type of factor) to obtain cash prior to the due date of the note. Such transactions are similar to factoring and pledging accounts receivable in that the payee receives the face value of the note less some fee or discount.

EXHIBIT 8.4

Other Accounts Receivable Disclosures

Panel A—Factoring

Cincinnati Milacron, Inc.

In January, 1996, the company entered into a new three year receivables purchase agreement with an independent issuer of receivables-backed commercial paper. This agreement replaced a similar agreement that expired in January, 1996. Under the terms of the new agreement, the company agreed to sell on an ongoing basis and without recourse, an undivided percentage ownership interest in designated pools of accounts receivable. To maintain the balance in the designated pools of accounts receivable sold, the company is obligated to sell undivided percentage interests in new receivables as existing receivables are collected. The agreement permits the sale of up to $75.0 million of undivided interests in accounts receivable through January, 1999.

At December 27, 1997, December 28,1996, and December 30, 1995, the undivided interests in the company's gross accounts receivable that has been sold to the purchasers aggregated $75.0 million, $75.0 million and $69.0 million, respectively. Increases and decreases in the amount sold are reported as operating cash flows in the Consolidated Statement of Cash Flows. Costs related to the sales are included in other costs and expenses-net in the Consolidated Statement of Earnings.

Circuit City Stores, Inc.

In fiscal 1997, the Company adopted SFAS No.125, "Accounting for Transfers and Servicing of Financial Assets and Extinguishments of Liabilities." SFAS No. 125 is effective for transfers and servicing of financial assets and extinguishments of liabilities occurring after December 31, 1996, and is to be applied prospectively. Adoption of SFAS No. 125 did not have a material impact on the Company's financial position, results of operations or liquidity.

The Company enters into securitization transactions, which allow for the sale of credit card receivables to unrelated entities, to finance the consumer revolving credit receivables generated by First North American National Bank, its wholly owned credit card bank subsidiary (the "Bank Subsidiary"). The Company implemented SFAS No. 125 with respect to sales of credit card receivables occurring after December 31, 1996. Proceeds from securitization transactions were $551.1 million for fiscal 1997, $692.3 million for fiscal 1996 and $428.4 million for fiscal 1995.

At February 28 or 29 the following amounts were outstanding:

(Amounts In Thousands)	1997	1996
Securitized receivables	$2,594,651	$1,860,459
Interest retained by Company	(293,586)	(110,459)
Net receivables transferred	$2,301,065	$1,750,000
Net receivables transferred with recourse	$1,317,565	$ 760,000
Program capacity	$2,665,000	$1,910,000

EXHIBIT 8.4 concluded

Other Accounts Receivable Disclosures

The Bank Subsidiary finances its private-label credit card program through a single master trust, through both private placement and the public market. During fiscal 1997, the Bank Subsidiary placed an additional $225 million in the public market for a total program capacity of $1,215 million. The master trust vehicle permits further expansion of the securitization programs to meet future receivables growth. The agreements have no recourse provisions.

In addition, the Bank Subsidiary has an asset securitization program in place for its bank card receivables that allows, as of February 28, 1997, the transfer of up to $1,450 million in receivables. The bank card securitization agreements provide recourse to the Company for any cash flow deficiencies. The Company believes that as of February 28, 1997 no liability existed under these recourse provisions. The finance charges from the transferred receivables are used to fund interest costs, charge-offs, servicing fees and other related costs.

The Bank Subsidiary's servicing revenue, including gains on sales of receivables of $3.7 million for fiscal 1997, totaled $197.0 million for fiscal 1997, $142.9 million for fiscal 1996 and $77.8 million for fiscal 1995. The servicing fees specified in the credit card securitization agreements adequately compensate the Bank Subsidiary for servicing the accounts. Accordingly, no servicing asset or liability has been recorded. Rights recorded for future interest income from serviced assets that exceed the contractually specified servicing fees are carried at fair value and amounted to $3.2 million at February 28, 1997, and are included in net accounts receivable.

Panel B—Pledging

Nashua Corporation

During 1997, the Company negotiated a new secured $18 million line of credit of which $5 million is available exclusively for letters of credit. Borrowings under this facility are collateralized by a security interest in the Company's receivables and inventory. Interest on amounts outstanding under the line of credit is payable at 2 percent above the LIBOR rate which was 6 percent at December 31, 1997. The maturity of this line of credit is April 3, 1999. The agreement contains certain financial covenants with respect to tangible net worth, liquidity and other ratios. In addition, without prior consent of the lenders, the agreement does not allow the payment of dividends and restricts, among other things, the incurrence of additional debt, guarantees, lease arrangements or sale of certain assets. As of December 31, 1997, the Company was in compliance with these covenants. At December 31, 1997, borrowings of $2 million were outstanding under the secured revolving credit facility.

Analyzing Trade Receivables

The level of investment a company might have in receivables at any particular time is affected by many conditions: seasonal, cyclical, or growth changes in sales; the market the company serves; the company's credit and collection policies; and inflation.

The investment in receivables is closely related to the volume of sales for the period immediately preceding a given balance sheet date. If sales during that period were low because of either seasonal or cyclical changes or declining markets, the accounts receivable balance should, all else being equal, be lower than in periods when credit sales were high.

The market a company serves also has a bearing on its receivables balance. In some markets, business cannot be conducted without using credit. Other markets, by custom, require longer or shorter credit terms than usual to facilitate commerce. For example,

Wendy's Corporation requires prompt payment of a percentage of weekly sales from its franchisees, which primarily conduct business with customers on a cash basis. In the recent past, the average receivable collection period for Wendy's, Inc., was about six days. In contrast, many of the credit sales of defense contracting companies are to the U.S. government, which relies on numerous administrative reviews before authorizing payment to its suppliers. Thus, it is not surprising that the financial statements of these contractors reveal collection periods from the various segments of their government contracts ranging from 60 days to more than two years.

A company's credit policy is an important competitive weapon. By allowing more and more potential credit customers to qualify for credit sales, a company's revenues and accounts receivable balances are likely to increase. At the same time, however, the carrying costs and potential losses from uncollectible accounts may also increase. Periods of high interest rates and periods of uncertain business conditions obviously raise the cost of carrying receivables. Thus, a company must weigh the costs of additional sales (increased interest expense and bad debts) against the benefits (increased revenues and increased cash inflows).

Inflation is another factor to be considered in managing a company's investment in receivables. During periods of inflation, the purchasing power of any currency diminishes. Consequently, future collections of receivables represent collections of cheaper dollars. The lost purchasing power of those cheaper dollars is a cost of making credit sales. Indeed, the management of a company domiciled in a hyperinflationary economy, such as has historically been the case in Brazil, seeks to maintain minimal accounts receivable balances.

Many procedures can be used to evaluate the quality of a company's accounts receivable management. Most methods deal with ratio analysis, and the most common index is the average receivable collection period. As discussed in Chapter 4, the average collection period is computed as

$$\text{Average receivable collection period} = \frac{\text{Average accounts receivable balance}}{\text{Total net credit sales/365 days}}$$

The receivable collection period gives an approximate measure of the length of time that a company's accounts receivable have been outstanding.[6] A comparison of this measure with a company's credit terms, with the measure for other firms in the same industry, and with the figures for prior periods indicates a company's efficiency in collecting receivables and its trends in credit management.

Other receivable-related ratios may also be of interest to managers, creditors, and investors; these may include (1) the ratio of accounts receivable that are written off divided by credit sales or by total receivables and (2) the ratio of credit sales to total sales, which reveals how dependent a company is on credit sales. Ratios involving the written-off accounts receivable reveal how correct management has been in determining those customers to which to grant credit, as well as management's effectiveness in collecting those credit sales. In a similar vein, the aging schedule is a good indicator of the quality of the accounts receivables at a particular point in time. (Such information is usually not available to the public but is useful to management.) Frequent preparation of an aging schedule may be crucial to the timely management of credit.

Managers must use such analytical tools to manage their investment in accounts receivable throughout the credit cycle. This cycle, starting with the approval of a credit sale

---

[6] There are different ways to make this calculation. For example, rather than using the average accounts receivable balance, the year-end balance could be used. Another way would be to use credit sales for the fourth quarter divided by 91 days, divided into the year-end balance in accounts receivable. When the amount of "net credit sales" is unknown, it is common to use net sales as a proxy.

and ending with the receipt of cash, is important to a company's continuing operations. Inattention to the details involved throughout the cycle often results in an opportunity cost because cash is needlessly tied up in accounts receivable and, in the worst case, may cause a firm to be critically short of cash.

MARKETABLE SECURITIES

As we have just seen, the management of accounts receivable involves managerial attention to the collection of the promises to pay that a company has received from its customers. In contrast, the management of marketable securities principally involves the managerial concern of how best to invest a company's surplus cash until such funds are needed to support its regular operations.

Fair Value and Its Disclosure

As noted in Chapter 2, one of the long-standing cornerstones of U.S. financial reporting is the historical cost convention. In an attempt to achieve objectivity and reliability in the amounts reported for virtually all assets and liabilities, historical cost (the purchase price paid) has traditionally been the designated reported amount. Unfortunately, historical cost values can quickly become outdated and hence of limited utility. There is, however, another attribute that could be reported—the asset's or liability's **fair value.**[7]

In a recent move toward providing more relevant information, the FASB now requires companies to disclose in their footnotes actual (or estimated if necessary) year-end market value data pertaining to financial instruments, which includes investments in marketable securities.[8] It should be obvious that as stock prices rise or fall, the historical cost of an investment in stocks becomes less relevant as an indicator of the financial wealth represented by those securities. Moreover, as interest rates climb (fall), the market value of bonds declines (rises), thus rendering the price paid for them less relevant as an indicator of their current market value. From an international perspective, it is important to note that the disclosure requirements of *International Accounting Standard* (IAS) No. 32 are similar to U.S. GAAP. A typical U.S. corporate disclosure is presented in Exhibit 8.5, drawn from a recent Perkin-Elmer Corporation annual report. Companies must highlight the investments for which a fair value is not practicable to determine. Companies are also required to describe their means of determining fair value so that readers will have a sense of the reliability and subjectivity of the reported amount.

Mark-to-Market for Certain Investments in Debt and Equity Securities

In ascertaining where to invest corporate cash, managers frequently consider debt and/or equity security investments. Debt securities include such instruments as corporate bonds, government securities, and commercial paper. Equity securities include preferred stock, common stock, and stock options. Generally speaking, such investments are made in

---

[7] For our purposes, we may consider market value as synonymous with fair value. The FASB focuses on fair value because some assets and liabilities do not have active markets in which they are traded, so they do not have a "market value." The term *fair value* is used to embrace the notion of an estimated market price for those assets and liabilities that do not have established markets for their buying and selling. An example is a share of stock in a closely held corporation.

[8] See SFAS No. 107.

EXHIBIT 8.5

Perkin-Elmer Corporation
Fair Value Disclosures

The following methods are used in estimating the fair value of significant financial instruments held or owed by the Company. Cash and short-term investments approximate their carrying amount due to the duration of these instruments. Fair values of minority equity investments and notes receivable are estimated based on quoted market prices, if available, or quoted market prices of financial instruments with similar characteristics. The fair value of debt is based on the current rates offered to the Company for debt of similar remaining maturities. The following table presents the carrying amounts and fair values of the Company's other financial instruments:

(Dollar amounts in millions) At June 30,	Carrying Amount 1997	Fair Value 1997	Carrying Amount 1996	Fair Value 1996
Cash and short-term investments	$ 196.0	$ 196.0	$ 96.6	$ 96.6
Minority equity investments	$ 9.0	$ 9.0	$ 35.6	$ 35.6
Note receivable	$ 7.2	$ 7.2	$ 7.2	$ 7.2
Short-term debt	$ 18.1	$ 18.1	$ 51.1	$ 51.5
Long-term debt	$ 33.6	$ 33.4	$ .9	$ .9

---

securities that have established, broad-based markets that render the investments quite liquid (that is, easily converted to cash) and easily valued at any point in time. For example, any issue of *The Wall Street Journal* provides market price quotes for an extensive variety of such securities.

Prior to 1975, publicly held U.S. companies reported their investments in these types of securities on a cost basis. From 1975 through 1993, publicly held U.S. companies reported their equity security investments in their balance sheets on a lower-of-cost-or-market basis (a practice still embraced by the International Accounting Standards Committee and followed in many countries), while investments in debt securities continued to be reported on a cost basis.[9] However, on December 15, 1993, U.S. GAAP again significantly changed the financial reporting requirements for debt and equity security investments.[10]

Consider for a moment two questions. First, what financial attribute of a debt or equity investment is most relevant to you as an interested observer of companies—a historical cost amount, an amount indicative of the lower of an investment's cost or market value, or the securities' current market value? You probably selected the market value attribute as the most desirable because it can be reliably, objectively determined. Indeed, U.S. GAAP now focuses on fair values (that is, market values).

---

[9] For purposes of this discussion, equity investments are assumed to be passive, that is to say, at a noncontrolling and nonsignificant level, representing less than 20 percent ownership of the investee. Between 1975 and 1993, SFAS No. 12 governed the U.S. accounting for marketable equity securities, and Accounting Research Bulletin No. 43 governed the U.S. accounting for marketable debt securities.

[10] See SFAS No. 115. It is important to note that SFAS No. 115 does not void the disclosure requirements of SFAS No. 107 that were discussed earlier.

The second question to consider is: What are the possible intentions of management regarding investments in these securities? As depicted in Exhibit 8.6, the FASB assumes that limited investments in these securities manifest one of three management intents:

1. **Hold to maturity**—this intent is applicable to debt securities only, and the financial reporting practices germane to such securities are discussed in Chapter 12;
2. Actively **trade** the security in the near term for purposes of generating profits on short-term price differentials; and
3. Make the security **available for sale** when and if deemed appropriate—an intention that is less passive and less long-term than (1) but not as active or short-term as (2).

These three management investment intentions now drive the financial reporting practices for debt and equity security investments under U.S. GAAP. It is also important to observe that at its acquisition, a security must be placed in one of these three categories. Note also from Exhibit 8.6 that, except for trading securities, securities may be reported as either current or noncurrent assets, depending on their intended purpose. Trading securities, by definition, are assumed to be current assets. Last, it is the hold-to-maturity, trading, and available-for-sale classifications that dictate the financial reporting of the security, not the security's designation as a current or noncurrent asset.

Trading securities. The fundamental objective of U.S. GAAP regarding investments classified as **trading securities** is that balance sheets report such investments at market value. As an example, consider the portfolio of securities portrayed in Exhibit 8.7. If a strict cost basis of reporting were followed, the investment account would be reported on the balance sheet at $75,000 as of the end of both Years 1 and 2. If, however, we assume all three securities are appropriately classified as trading securities, the investment account should be shown in the company balance sheet at $80,000 at the end of Year 1 and at $79,500 as of the end of Year 2.

More specifically, the entry to record these securities at their date of *acquisition* would appear as:

```
Dr. Trading security: ABC Corp. Bond (A). . . . . . . . . . . . . . . (inc.) 20,000
Dr. Trading security: 100 shares XT Co. Common stock (A) . . . (inc.) 30,000
Dr. Trading security: 50 shares MN Inc. Preferred stock (A) . . . (inc.) 25,000
    Cr. Cash (A) . . . . . . . . . . . . . . . . . . . . . . . . . . . . . . . . . . . . . . . .   (dec.) 75,000
```

The entry at the end of Year 1 to adjust the balance sheet amount of these securities would be as follows:

```
Dr. Valuation adjustment: ABC Corp. bonds (A). . . . . . (inc.) 1,000
Dr. Valuation adjustment: XT Co. stock (A) . . . . . . . . (inc.) 6,000
    Cr. Valuation adjustment: MN Inc. stock (A) . . . . . . . . . . . . . .   (dec.) 2,000
    Cr. Unrealized holding gain (G) . . . . . . . . . . . . . . . . . . . . . . .   (inc.) 5,000
```

And the entry at the end of Year 2 would be:

```
Dr. Valuation adjustment: XT Co. stock (A) . . . . . . . . (inc.) 2,000
Dr. Unrealized holding loss (Loss) . . . . . . . . . . . . . . . (inc.)   500
    Cr. Valuation adjustment: ABC Corp. bonds (A) . . . . . . . . . . .   (dec.) 1,500
    Cr. Valuation adjustment: MN Inc. stock (A) . . . . . . . . . . . . . .   (dec.) 1,000
```

From this simple example, it is important to note several things. First, the **mark-to-market** process (that is, the recording of market values) is done on an *individual* security basis. This fact provides for a parallelism of market reality and the financial reporting

EXHIBIT 8.6

Financial Reporting of Equity and Debt
Security Investments in the U.S.

Security	Management Intent at Date of Purchase	Balance Sheet Classification	Balance Sheet Valuation	Income Statement Effects*
Debt	Hold-to-maturity	Current asset if maturity date within one year Noncurrent asset if maturity date greater than one year	Amortized cost	• Interest income, including amortization of premium or discount • Realized gains/losses = net sales proceeds – unamortized cost
Debt or equity	Trading (actively trade in near term)	Current asset	Fair value	• Dividend income or interest income, including amortization of premium or discount • Realized gains/losses (which equal the net sales proceeds – latest balance sheet fair value) • Unrealized holding gains/losses
	Available-for-sale (securities not fitting into either of above categories)	Current asset if intent is to sell within one year Noncurrent asset if intent is to not sell within one year	Fair value; owners' equity adjusted for unrealized holding gains/losses	• Dividend income or interest income, including amortization of premium or discount • Realized gain/loss (which equal the net sales proceeds – latest balance sheet fair value ± security's owners' equity accumulated unrealized holding gain/loss balance)

*Realized gains/losses are those transaction-based gains/losses recorded at time of disposition of a security. Unrealized holding gains/losses are those gains/losses periodically recorded prior to disposition of a security.

picture painted for a specific security—reported amounts may rise (XT Co. stock), fall (MN Inc.), or rise and fall (ABC Corp.). Second, information pertaining to a security's original acquisition cost is retained because a valuation adjustment account is used to capture its changes in market value. Third, for a security classified as a trading security, its yearly change in carrying value (that is, the change in reported market value) is recorded as an unrealized holding gain or loss that is then reported in that period's income statement. The rationale for this is that because such securities are regularly traded, their year-end measurement should reflect an "if sold" income statement impact.

EXHIBIT 8.7

Hypothetical Portfolio of Debt and Equity
Security Investment

	Year 1			Year 2		
	Recorded Cost	Market at Year-End	Gain (Loss)	Market at Beginning of Year	Market at Year-End	Gain (Loss)
ABC Corp. bond	$20,000	$21,000	$1,000	$21,000	$19,500	$(1,500)
XT Co. (100 shares of common stock)	30,000	36,000	6,000	36,000	38,000	2,000
MN Inc. (50 shares of preferred stock)	25,000	23,000	(2,000)	23,000	22,000	(1,000)
	$75,000	$80,000	$5,000	$80,000	$79,500	$ (500)

In order to understand how to record the sale of a trading security, consider that during Year 2 the ABC Corp. bond was sold for $20,250 and the XT Co. shares were sold for $37,200. The entry to record the sale would look like this:

```
Dr. Cash (A) . . . . . . . . . . . . . . . . . . . . . . . (inc.) 57,450
    Cr. Realized gain on sale (G) . . . . . . . . . . . . . . . . .    (inc.)    450
    Cr. Valuation adjustment: ABC Corp. bonds (A). . . . .     (dec.)  1,000
    Cr. Valuation adjustment: XT Co. shares (A) . . . . . . .   (dec.)  6,000
    Cr. Trading security: ABC Corp. bond (A) . . . . . . . . .  (dec.) 20,000
    Cr. Trading security: XT Co. shares (A). . . . . . . . . . . (dec.) 30,000
```

Note that the gain on sale is reported as a *realized* gain, meaning that it was created by an actual disposition of the securities, not a year-end revaluation. Note also that the $450 realized gain is equivalent to the change in market value for the two sold securities since last revalued and not since the date of purchase. The total market gain/loss for the investment in the ABC Corp. bond and the XT Co. shares since their acquisition was $7,450 (original cost of $50,000 versus sales proceeds of $57,450). Why wasn't a realized gain of $7,450 recorded at the date of sale? The reason is that $7,000 of the gain had already been reported in Year 1's income statement, albeit as an unrealized holding gain netted against a $2,000 unrealized holding loss on MN Inc. shares.

Available-for-sale securities. Because **available-for-sale securities** are generally purchased with a more long-term intent than trading securities, the *unrealized* gains or losses highlighted by these securities' year-end balance sheet revaluation are reported not in the income statement but rather in the owners' equity (OE) section of the balance sheet as a separate line item.

Consider again the data in Exhibit 8.7 and the sales information presented in the prior section. If the securities shown in Exhibit 8.7 are classified as available for sale, the entry to record their acquisition is the same as shown earlier except for a change in designation from "trading security" to "available-for-sale security." The entry at the end of Year 1 would appear as:

Dr. Valuation adjustment: ABC Corp. bonds (A) . . . (inc.) 1,000
Dr. Valuation adjustment: XT Co. stock (A) . . . . . . (inc.) 6,000
    Cr. Valuation adjustment: MN Inc. stock (A). . . . .   (dec.) 2,000
    Cr. Accumulated unrealized holding gain/loss (OE) . . . . .   (inc.) 5,000

This entry is slightly different from the parallel entry when the securities were classified as trading securities. It is different in that the unrealized gain/loss is reflected (and will be accumulated year-to-year) in an owners' equity account; it is not reported as a yearly income statement amount. At the end of Year 2, the entry would be:

Dr. Valuation adjustment: XT Co. stock (A) . . . . . . (inc.) 2,000
Dr. Accumulated unrealized holding gain/loss
    (OE). . . . . (dec.)   500
    Cr. Valuation adjustment: ABC Corp. bonds (A) . . . .   (dec.) 1,500
    Cr. Valuation adjustment: MN Inc. stock (A) . . . .   (dec.) 1,000

As you may have anticipated, when a security classified as available for sale is sold, the reported *realized* gain/loss will be larger than if it had been classified as a trading security. This has to be the case because the year-to-year market revaluations of an available-for-sale security have not had any prior income statement effect, as is the case for trading securities. Consider again that during Year 2 the ABC bonds were sold for $20,250 and the XT Co. shares were sold for $37,200. Here is the entry to record their sale:

Dr. Cash (A) . . . . (inc.) 57,450
Dr. Accumulated unrealized holding gain/loss
    (OE). . . . . (dec.) 7,000
    Cr. Valuation adjustment: ABC Corp. bonds (A) . . . .   (dec.) 1,000
    Cr. Valuation adjustment: XT Co. shares (A). . . . .   (dec.) 6,000
    Cr. Available-for-sale security: ABC Corp. bonds (A). . . . . . .   (dec.) 20,000
    Cr. Available-for-sale security: XT Co. share (A) . . . .   (dec.) 30,000
    Cr. Realized gain on sale of securities (G) . . . .   (inc.) 7,450

The $7,000 decrease to the OE account is to eliminate that part of the balance in the Accumulated Unrealized Holding Gain/Loss account attributable to the sold securities. Moreover, as can be seen, the realized gain of $7,450 will be reported in the Year 2 income statement, and the gain equals the total income statement income reported when the securities were classified as trading securities; only the timing and labeling differ (all realized in Year 1 and some realized in Year 2 assuming a trading classification). Indeed, it is for these two differences that the classification of securities as trading or available for sale is important. These designations dictate the timing of an income statement effect and the amounts reported on any one income statement. It is therefore incumbent on managers to honestly acknowledge their intentions for a security and to classify it accordingly.

Reclassification of securities. We have just seen the importance of the classification of securities at the time of acquisition. Clearly, a security's classification need not be viewed as epitomizing management's intent forever. If that intent changes, the security should be reclassified at its market value. Consider the reclassification possibilities depicted in Exhibit 8.8, and in particular the four possibilities to and from the trading securities classification.

If a security is to be reclassified from the trading category it should be reported in its new classification at its market value as of the date of reclassification. There is no reversal of any previously recorded income statement unrealized holding gains/losses. Reclassification does, however, necessitate recording in the income statement any unrealized holding gains/losses since the security's last revaluation. Consider the Exhibit 8.7 data and assume that during Year 3, the MN Inc. shares are to be reclassified from the trading to available-

EXHIBIT 8.8

Reclassifications of Investments in Marketable Equity Securities

	Reclassified from:		
Reclassified to:	Hold-to-maturity	Trading	Available-for-sale
Hold-to-maturity	■	A	D
Trading	B	■	B
Available-for-sale	C	A	■

Accounting for gain/loss at reclassification date:

A = Record in income statement only the unrealized holding gain/loss arising since last valuation date.

B = Record in income statement any net unrealized holding gains/losses to date not reflected in prior income statements.

C = Record in owners' equity any net unrealized holding gains/losses to date not reflected in prior income statements.

D = The unrealized holding gain/loss already accumulated in an owners' equity account is amortized over the remaining life of the security as a yield adjustment.

---

for-sale category. At the date of reclassification their market value is $22,750, and through the end of Year 2 $3,000 of unrealized losses have been reported in the income statement. The entry to record the reclassification looks like this:

```
Dr. Available-for-sale security: MN Inc. shares (A). . . (inc.) 22,750
Dr. Valuation adjustment: MN Inc. shares (A). . . . . . . (inc.) 3,000
    Cr. Trading security: MN Inc. shares (A). . . . . . . . . . . . . . . .     (dec.) 25,000
    Cr. Unrealized holding gain on reclassification (G) . . . . . . . . . .     (inc.)   750
```

Assume the same facts except that the MN Inc. shares were classified as available-for-sale at acquisition and are now to be reclassified as trading securities. The entry to accomplish this reclassification would look like this:

```
Dr. Unrealized holding loss on reclassification
    (Loss). . . . . . . . . . . . . . . . . . . . . . . . . . . . . . . . . . (inc.)  2,250
Dr. Trading security: MN Inc. shares (A). . . . . . . . . (inc.) 22,750
Dr. Valuation adjustment: MN Inc. shares (A) . . . . . . (inc.) 3,000
    Cr. Available-for-sale security: MN Inc. shares (A). . . . . . . . . .     (dec.) 25,000
    Cr. Accumulated unrealized holding gain/losses (OE) . . . . . . .     (inc.)  3,000
```

In this latter example the reclassification to a trading security prompts the recording as income the reclassified security's net cumulative unrealized holding gains/losses since acquisition.

Permanent impairments of value. Declines in market value for held-to-maturity or available-for-sale securities that are deemed indicative of permanent value reductions should be reflected in that period's income statement.[11] Up to this point, we have only considered normal market appreciation/depreciation in a security's value. Drawing again on the Exhibit 8.7 data, assume that the XT Co. shares' market value declined to $19,000 during Year 2 because their most profitable overseas division was appropriated by a new, hostile government in that country. The entry to reflect the decline in value as permanent would look like this:

```
Dr. Permanent impairment loss on XT Co. shares  (Loss) . . . (inc.) 11,000
Dr. Accumulated unrealized holding gains/loss
    (OE) . . . . . . . . . . . . . . . . . . . . . . . . . . . . . . . . . . . . . . . . . . (dec.) 6,000
    Cr. Valuation adjustment: XT Co. shares (A) . . . . . . . . . . . . . . . . . . . . .     (dec.)  6,000
    Cr. Available-for-sale security: XT Co. Inc. shares (A) . . . . . . . . . . . . .     (dec.) 11,000
```

In this case it is necessary to eliminate any valuation adjustment balance and accumulated owners' equity unrealized holding gains/losses pertaining to XT Co. because the asset must now be carried at a new cost figure, $19,000, not its original $30,000. The $11,000 loss is recorded and reported in this period's income statement.

Providing informative disclosures. Earlier it was noted that U.S. GAAP has in the case of marketable securities, moved away from historical cost accounting by requiring certain financial statement adjustments for fair value. Exhibit 8.9 presents the fair value disclosures made by General Motors Corporation in its 1997 annual report.

There are a several interesting things to note in GM's disclosure. First, the company details the specific types of assets that it reports as marketable securities. Second, it states that all of its marketable securities are either classified as trading or available-for-sale—none of them are hold-to-maturity. Third, the company informs the reader as to the financial statement disposition of unrealized gains/losses. Fourth, it presents both original cost information as well as the fair (market) value data. Last, the company reports both unrealized as well as realized gain/loss data.

Management Issues

As noted throughout the prior discussion, management's intent regarding its investments in financial instruments is the primary factor determining the mark-to-market accounting for those investments. In particular it should be apparent from the prior discussion that the trading versus available-for-sale classification has certain income statement implications: Holding gains/losses on trading securities are reflected in the income statement whereas those for available-for-sale securities are not. Likewise, management's reclassification and permanent impairment decisions, also have certain income statement implications. Therefore, the flexibility inherent in each of these management decisions presents an opportunity for the managing of net income—an unavoidable phenomenon but one that is hopefully not abused.

There is another issue imbedded in the management of an investment and/or debt portfolio of financial instruments: the level of **financial risk** assumed by having crafted a portfolio of certain instruments (such as stocks, bonds, derivatives) from certain issuers (corporate, governmental), of varying time horizons (short-term, long-term), and perhaps denominated in different currencies (such as dollars, yen, francs). What constitutes an

---

[11] For trading securities, the normal year-end accounting valuation process is sufficient to reflect permanent impairments.

EXHIBIT 8.9

General Motors Corporation
Marketable Securities Disclosure

Marketable securities held by GM are classified as available-for-sale, except for certain mortgage related securities of GMAC, which are classified as trading securities. The aggregate excess of fair value over cost, net of related income taxes, for available-for-sale securities is included as a separate component of stock-holders' equity. The excess of fair value over cost for trading securities is included in income on a current basis. GM determines cost on the specific identification basis.

December 31, 1997	Cost	Fair Value	Unrealized Gains	Unrealized Losses
Type of Security				
Bonds, notes, and other securities				
United States government and governmental agencies and authorities	$ 1,308	$ 1,317	$ 9	$ —
States, municipalities, and political subdivisions	1,576	1,686	121	11
Mortgage-backed securities	110	113	3	—
Other	5,589	5,644	65	10
Total debt securities available for sale	8,583	8,760	198	21
Mortgage-backed securities held for trading purposes	2,063	2,063	—	—
Total debt securities	10,646	10,823	198	21
Equity securities	523	899	416	40
Total investment in securities	$ 11,169	$ 11,722	$ 614	$ 61

December 31, 1996	Cost	Fair Value	Unrealized Gains	Unrealized Losses
Type of Security				
Bonds, notes, and other securities				
United States government and governmental agencies and authorities	$ 1,702	$ 1,705	$ 5	$ 2
States, municipalities, and political subdivisions	1,573	1,648	85	10
Mortgage-backed securities	62	64	2	—
Other	3,410	3,442	40	8
Total debt securities available for sale	6,747	6,859	132	20
Mortgage-backed securities held for trading purposes	697	697	—	—
Total debt securities	7,444	7,556	132	20
Equity securities	328	643	326	11
Total investment in securities	$ 7,772	$ 8,199	$ 458	$ 31

Debt securities totaling $1.2 billion mature within one year, $4.7 billion mature after one through five years, $1.6 billion mature after five years through 10 years, and $3.1 billion mature after 10 years.

Proceeds from sales and maturities of marketable securities totaled $13.6 billion in 1997, $5.7 billion in 1996, and $6.2 billion in 1995. The gross gains and (losses) related to sales of marketable securities were $297 million and $(96) million, $236 million and $(33) million, and $118 million and $(29) million in 1997, 1996, and 1995, respectively.

E X H I B I T   8 . 1 0

Johnson&Johnson
Financial Instrument Risk Disclosures

Derivative Financial Instrument Risk

The Company uses derivative financial instruments to manage the impact of interest rate and foreign exchange rate changes on earnings and cash flows. The Company does not enter into financial instruments for trading or speculative purposes.

The Company has a policy of only entering into contracts with parties that have at least an "A" (or equivalent) credit rating. The conterparties to these contracts are major financial institutions and the Company does not have significant exposure to any one counterparty. Management believes the risk of loss is remote and in any event would be immaterial.

Concentration of Credit Risk

The Company invests its excess cash in both deposits with major banks throughout the world and other high quality short-term liquid money market instruments (commercial paper, government and government agency notes and bills, etc.). The Company has a policy of making investments only with commercial institutions that have at least an "A" (or equivalent) credit ratings These investments generally mature within six months and the Company has not incurred any related losses.

The Company sells a broad range of products in the health care field in most countries of the world. Concentrations of credit risk with respect to trade receivables are limited due to the large number of customers comprising the Company's customer base. Ongoing credit evaluations of customers' base. Ongoing credit evaluations of customers' financial condition are preformed and, generally, no collateral is required. The Company maintains reserves for potential credit losses and such losses, in the aggregate, have not exceeded management's expectations.

---

acceptable level of financial risk for one company may be quite unacceptable to another and shareholders are not without their own risk preferences and perspectives that, in fact, may be congruent with or dissimilar to those of the management running the company whose stock they hold. With the intent of trying to provide a bit more insight into the type and level of risk imbedded in the financial instruments that a company has chosen to become a party to, U.S. companies are required to provide footnote disclosure pertaining to the extent, nature, and terms of the financial instruments' market risk (as well as insights into any concentrated levels of credit risk).[12] Such concerns are also addressed in the recommended disclosures put forth in IAS No. 32 and No. 39. Exhibit 8.10 provides Johnson&Johnson's disclosures in this regard.

Analyzing Marketable Securities

The analysis of marketable securities, like that of accounts receivable, principally relates to the timing and uncertainties regarding the future cash flows represented by the investments. Because marketable securities are highly liquid, they constitute an important potential source of immediate cash inflows, thereby alleviating a company's need to borrow in the short term or to factor receivables. Thus, the larger a company's investment in marketable securities, the larger the available cash reserves at its disposal.

As previously noted, investments in marketable securities are reported at their market value (unless they are classified as hold-to-maturity securities). The reporting of such a value provides a better indicator of the future cash flows likely to be realized from the securities' sale than if the securities were reported at cost or at the lower of cost or market.

---

[12] See SFAS No. 105.

Moreover, the footnote disclosures depicting a company's year-to-year unrealized holding gains/losses on available-for-sale securities may be viewed as providing insights into management's astuteness of having chosen to continue to hold those securities and/or of having bought them in the first place. For example, a simple comparison of the portfolio's yearly appreciation or devaluation, in comparison to pertinent overall market indicators (such as the Dow Jones Industrials average), would indicate buy and hold decisions worse than or better than the market's average.

SUMMARY

Trade receivables and marketable securities are two key assets. Although not considered to be cash equivalents, they are nonetheless both readily convertible into cash. Trade receivables are evidence of a company's revenue production function. Although high receivable balances are not risky in and of themselves, the risk of noncollection of cash is inherent in all promised payments and thus should be closely monitored. Marketable securities represent the investment of cash into corporate securities. These investments are usually quite liquid to permit their easy conversion into cash when needed to support a company's operations.

NEW CONCEPTS AND TERMS

Aging of receivables

Allowance for uncollectible accounts

Available-for-sale securities

Credit sales terms

Direct write-off method

Factoring

Fair value

Financial risk

Hold-to-maturity security

Liquid assets

Mark-to market

Net realizable value

Percentage of credit sales

Pledging

Promissory note

Trading securities

With (without) recourse

ASSIGNMENTS

8.1. Estimating bad debts expense. The trial balance of Sky Company at the end of 2000 included the following account balances:

Account	Debit	Credit
Accounts Receivable	$52,000	
Trade Notes Receivable	10,000	
Marketable Securities	20,000	
Allowance for Uncollectibles	4,000	
Sales		$600,000

The company has *not yet* recorded any bad debt expense for 2000.

Required:

Determine Sky Company's bad debt expense for 2000 assuming the following independent situations:

a. 85 percent of all sales are credit sales and historically, 2 percent of credit sales are never collected.

b. Use of a trade receivables aging schedule provides an estimate of uncollectible accounts of $2,000.

c. The Allowance for Uncollectible Accounts contra-asset account balance is targeted to equal 4 percent of outstanding trade receivables.

8.2. Accounting for bad debts. Consider the following data pertaining to Noble Corp. during 2000:

1. The balance in the Allowance for Doubtful Accounts account at January 1, 2000 was $550,000.

2. During 2000, Noble cleaned up the Accounts Receivable accounts of $790,000 with a write off in that amount.

3. The company received a $60,000 check pertaining to a receivable they had written off in 1999.

4. The desired year-end balance in the Allowance for Doubtful Accounts account was $885,000.

Required:

a. Prepare the journal entries to reflect the data above assuming the following two independent situations:

(1) The allowance method for bad debts.

(2) The direct write-off method for bad debts.

b. What are the pros and cons of each method in light of the matching principle, conservatism principle, and historical cost principle?

8.3. Aging accounts receivables. The following data were taken from the Accounts Receivable account of Horner Products Company as of December 31, 2000:

Receivable Age Classification	Receivable Balances Outstanding	Probability of Noncollection
0–10 days	$200,000	1.0%
11–30 days	120,000	1.5
31–60 days	60,000	3.0
61–90 days	55,000	5.0
91–120 days	22,000	7.5
Over 120 days	4,000	10.0

A prior credit balance of $1,000 existed in the Allowance for Uncollectible Accounts account.

Required:

Determine the amount of bad debt expense to be recorded at year-end 2000 by Horner Products Company.

8.4. Ratio analysis. Presented below are recent summary financial data for the Coca-Cola Co. and PepsiCo. Inc.

	1997	1996
Net sales (in millions):		
Coca-Cola	$ 18,868	$ 18,673
PepsiCo	20,917	20,337
Net trade receivables (in millions):		
Coca-Cola	1,639	1,641
PepsiCo	2,150	2,276

Required:

Using the data presented, calculate the accounts receivable turnover and average number of day's receivable collection period for each company. What is your evaluation of each company's credit management policy?

8.5. Factoring and pledging receivables. Feed and Seed Stores, Inc., was experiencing a temporary shortage of cash. To make it through the next several weeks, the CFO was considering two options. The first was to sell some of the company's accounts receivables to a large, regional factor who agreed to buy as much as $2 million of the company's receivables without recourse at a fee of 15.5 percent of the receivables factored.

The second option was a 60-day loan of an equivalent amount from a local bank, using the outstanding receivables as collateral for the loan. Under this agreement, Feed and Seed would receive 82 percent of the receivables assigned to the bank and would be charged 13 percent annual interest on the outstanding loan.

Required:

Which alternative is better from the company's perspective? Why? What are the entries for each transaction?

8.6. Allowance account analysis. Selling Corporation had always estimated and booked an amount for estimated uncollectible accounts receivable on a *monthly,* 2 percent of credit sales basis. This approach continued through December 2000.

The balance in the Allowance for Doubtful Accounts account was $141,000 at January 1, 2000. During 2000, credit sales totaled $10,000,000; $90,000 of bad debts were written off; and recoveries of accounts previously written off amounted to $18,000. Selling's aging of accounts receivable was prepared for the first time as of December 31, 2000. A summary of the aging is as follows:

Month of Sale	Accounts Receivable as of December 31, 2000	Estimated Percentage Uncollectible
November–December 2000	$1,200,000	1%
July–October	700,000	12
January–June	500,000	30
Prior to January 1, 2000	220,000	80
Total receivable December 31, 2000	$2,620,000	

Based on a review of the accounts in the "Prior to January 1, 2000" aging category, receivables totaling $50,000 were written off on December 31, 2000 (these were included in the $220,000 and represent write-offs in addition to the $90,000 previously written off). In addition, for the year ended December 31, 2000, Selling wanted the Allowance for Doubtful Accounts account to be reported at the amount indicated by the year-end aging analysis of accounts receivable.

Required:

Recreate all the 2000 entries made to the allowance account. What is the December 31, 2000, allowance account balance?

8.7. Accounting for marketable securities. Aspen Mining invests its excess idle cash in marketable equity securities. The following portfolio of stocks as of December 31, 1999, were all purchased in 1999.

	As of December 31, 1999	
	Cost	Market Value
Trading portfolio		
Nella Co.	$ 80,000	$ 72,000
Zen, Inc.	66,000	68,000
Aldon Co.	38,000	36,500
	$ 184,000	$ 176,500
Available-for-sale portfolio		
Leslie, Inc.	$ 36,000	$ 32,500
Diane Properties, Inc.	38,000	36,800
Stillfied Co.	24,000	26,000
	$ 98,000	$ 95,300

During 2000, all Zen, Inc., shares were sold. In addition, all Diane Properties, Inc., shares were transferred to the trading portfolio at a time when their market value equaled $34,000. As of December 31, 2000, the market value of the trading portfolio securities was: Nella, $82,000; Aldon, $39,000; and Diane Properties, $32,000. The remaining securities, composing the available-for-sale portfolio, had market values as of December 31, 2000 of: Leslie, $33,500 and Stillfield, $29,000.

Required:

a. Prepare all necessary 1999 entries pertaining to Aspen Mining's marketable equity security investments. You may ignore the purchase transaction.

b. Prepare all necessary 2000 entries pertaining to Aspen Mining's marketable equity security investments. You may ignore the sales transaction.

8.8. Analyzing marketable securities. Presented below are excerpts from some marketable securities investment footnote disclosures contained in Arden Group, Inc.'s 1997 annual report.

Marketable securities consist of mutual funds, fixed-income securities, preferred stock, common stock, mortgage-backed government securities and collateralized mortgage obligations. Marketable securities are stated at market value as determined by the most recently traded price of each security at the balance sheet date. By policy, the Company invests primarily in high-grade marketable securities. All marketable securities are defined as trading securities or available-for-sale securities under the provisions of Statement of Financial Accounting Standards No. ("SFAS") 115, "Accounting for Certain Investments in Debt and Equity Securities."

Management determines the appropriate classification of its investments in marketable securities at the time of purchase and reevaluates such determination at each balance sheet date. Securities that are bought and held principally for the purpose of selling them in the near term are classified as trading securities and unrealized holding gains and losses are included in earnings. Debt securities for which the Company does not have the intent or ability to hold to maturity and equity securities are classified as available-for-sale. Available-for-sale securities are carried at fair value, with the unrealized gains and losses, net of tax, reported as a separate component of stockholders' equity. The cost of investments sold is determined on the specific identification or the first-in, first-out method. Marketable securities are carried on the balance sheet at their market value.

(In Thousands)	Cost	Unrealized Gain (Loss)	Market Value
As of January 3, 1998:			
Available-for-sale securities:			
Mutual funds	$14,529	$ 843	$15,372
Equity securities	832	(581)	251
Total	$15,361	$ 262	$15,623
As of December 28, 1996:			
Trading securities:			
Mutual funds	$10,997	$ 35	$11,032
Fixed income securities	7,707	(662)	7,045
Equity securities	1,413	114	1,527
Mortgage-backed			
government securities	1,419	7	1,426
Collateralized mortgage			
obligations	328	(2)	326
Total	$21,864	$(508)	$21,356

Realized gains from sale of securities were $ 605,000 and $ 36,000 in 1997 and 1996, respectively.

Required:

a. What is meant by the terms *realized* and *unrealized gain (loss)?*

b. What figure would appear in the asset section of Arden's January 3, 1998, balance sheet for available-for-sale financial instruments?

c. Where in the financial statements would you find Arden's 1997 net unrealized gain of $262?

d. Assume that all of the 1996 year end trading securities were transferred to the available-for-sale category on the first day of the 1997 fiscal year. What would the entry have been?

e. For the 1997 fiscal year, how (if at all), would the $508 unrealized loss be reflected in Arden's statement of cash flows?

8.9. Accounting for receivables.* Suppose that Tentex Company had the following balances in certain of its accounts on December 31, 1999 (in thousands of dollars):

Trade receivables	$350.0	(debit balance)
Allowance for estimated uncollectible accounts	10.2	(credit balance)

and that transactions during 2000 were as follows (in thousands of dollars):

1. Sales on account. $1,585.0

2. Collections on account—$1,549.4 less cash discounts of $27.4.   1,522.0

3. Sales returns (from credit sales).   8.5

4. Accounts written off as uncollectible.   5.4

5. Accounts previously written off now determined to be collectible.   0.7

6. Provision for uncollectible accounts (based on percent of credit sales).   8.0

---

* Problems 8.9, 8.10, and 8.11 Copyright © 1988 by the Darden Graduate Business School Foundation, Charlottesville, VA. All rights reserved.

Required:

Prepare entries for the 2000 transactions. At what figure will Tentex show

a. Net sales in its 2000 income statement?

b. Net trade receivables in its balance sheet of December 31, 2000?

8.10. Accounting for receivables.* Moss Products, Inc., was formed in 1982. Sales have increased on the average of 5 percent per year during its first 14 years of existence, with total sales for 2000 amounting to $350,000. Since incorporation, Moss Products has used the allowance method to account for bad debts. The company's fiscal year is the calendar year.

On January 1, 2000, the company's Allowance for Uncollectible Accounts had a right-side balance of $4,000. During 2000 accounts totaling $3,300 were written off as uncollectible.

Required:

a. What does the January 1, 2000, credit balance of $4,000 in the Allowance for Uncollectible Accounts represent?

b. Since Moss Products wrote off $3,300 in uncollectible accounts during 2000, was the prior year's bad debts estimate overstated? Explain.

c. Prepare the entries to record

   (1) The $3,300 write-off during 2000.

   (2) Moss Products' 2000 bad debts expense assuming these two independent situations: (i) Experience indicates that 1 percent of total annual sales prove uncollectible, and (ii) an aging of the December 31, 2000, accounts receivable indicates that potential uncollectible accounts at year-end total $4,500.

8.11. Credit policy review.* The president, sales manager, and credit manager of Hacket Corporation were discussing the company's present credit policy and possible changes. The sales manager argued that potential sales were being lost to the competition because of Hacket Corporation's tight restrictions on granting credit to consumers. He stated that if credit were extended to a new class of customer, this year's credit sales of $2,500,000 could be increased by at last 20 percent next year with a corresponding increase in uncollectible accounts of only $10,000 over this year's figure of $37,500. With a gross margin on sales of 25 percent, the sales manager continued, the company would certainly come out ahead.

The credit manager, however, believed that a better alternative to easier credit terms would be to accept consumer credit cards like VISA or MasterCard for charge sales. The credit manager said that he had been reading on this topic and he believed this alternative offered the chance to increase sales by 40 percent. The credit card finance charges to Hacket Corporation would amount to 4 percent of the additional sales.

At this point, the president interrupted by saying that he wasn't at all sure that increasing credit sales of any kind was a good thing. In fact, he thought that the $37,500 figure was altogether too high. He wondered whether the company should discontinue offering sales on account.

Required:

a. Determine whether Hacket Corporation would be better off under the sales manager's proposal or the credit manager's proposal.

b. Address the president's suggestion that all credit sales be abolished.

---

* Problems 8.9, 8.10, and 8.11 Copyright © 1988 by the Darden Graduate Business School Foundation, Charlottesville, VA. All rights reserved.

8.12. Accounting for marketable securities. Brownlee Bearings Company has the following securities in its trading portfolio of marketable equity securities on December 31, 2000:

	Cost	Market
2,000 shares of Miller Motors, common	$ 68,500	$ 60,250
10,000 shares of Erving, Inc., common	257,500	257,500
1,000 shares of Magic Ltd., preferred	52,500	56,000
	$378,500	$373,750

All of the securities were purchased in 2000.

In 2001 Brownlee Bearings completed the following securities transactions:

- March 1. Sold 2,000 shares of Miller Motors, common, at $30 per share less fees of $1,500.
- April 1. Bought 1,000 shares of American Steel, common, at $45 per share plus fees of $1,000.
- August 1. Transferred Magic Ltd., preferred, from the trading portfolio to the available-for-sale portfolio when the stock was selling at $50 per share.

Brownlee Bearings Company trading portfolio of marketable equity securities appeared as follows on December 31, 2001:

	Cost	Market
10,000 shares of Erving, Inc., common	$257,500	$291,000
1,000 shares of American Steel, common	46,000	41,000
	$303,500	$332,000

Required:

Prepare the accounting entries for the Brownlee Bearings Company for

a. The 2000 adjusting entry.

b. The sale of Miller Motors stock.

c. The purchase of American Steel stock.

d. The portfolio transfer of Magic Ltd.

e. The 2001 adjusting entry for the trading portfolio of securities.

8.13. Financial statement disclosure: marketable securities.

a. Tub Factory Corporation invested its excess cash in some "hot" stocks during 2000. As of December 31, 2000, the portfolio of trading marketable equity securities consisted of the following common stocks:

		Per Share	
Security	Quantity	Cost	Market
Holden, Inc.	1,000 shares	$ 14	$ 19
Coates Corp.	3,000 shares	27	21
Carey Marine	2,000 shares	36	31

What information should be reported in Tub Factory's December 31, 2000 balance sheet relative to these investments?

b. On December 31, 2001, Tub Factory's portfolio of trading marketable equity securities consisted of the following common stocks:

Security	Quantity	Per Share Cost	Per Share Market
Holden, Inc.	1,000 shares	$ 14	$ 21
Holden, Inc.	2,000 shares	20	21
Lakeshore Company	1,000 shares	17	14
Carey Marine	2,000 shares	36	20

During 2001, Tub Factory sold 3,000 shares of Coates Corp. at a loss of $10,000 and purchased 2,000 more shares of Holden, Inc., and 1,000 shares of Lakeshore Company.

(1) What information should be reported in Tub Factory's December 31, 2001, balance sheet?

(2) What information should be reported to reflect the data in Tub Factory's 2001 income statement?

c. On December 31, 2002, Tub Factory's portfolio of trading marketable equity securities consisted of the following common stocks:

Security	Quantity	Per Share Cost	Per Share Market
Carey Marine	2,000 shares	$ 36	$ 47
Lakeshore Company	500 shares	17	15

During 2002, Tub Factory sold 3,000 shares of Holden, Inc., at a gain of $12,000 and 500 shares of Lakeshore Company at a loss of $2,300.

(1) What information should be reported in Tub Factory's December 31, 2002, balance sheet?

(2) What information should be reported to reflect the above in Tub Factory's 2002 income statement?

8.14. Accounting for bad debts: Omni Products Division. The following two scenarios should be analyzed independently.

Scenario A: The period-end analysis model. The manager of Omni Products Division, Harry Smith, was quite satisfied with all of his section leaders and had developed a high level of trust in their day-to-day decisions. Still, he insisted that he be involved in the critical, long-range judgments. For example, his accounting and control section was efficient and largely trouble-free. However, he carefully monitored the sensitive areas, including the status of collections on accounts receivable, the follow-up on slow-paying customers, and the reasonableness of the ongoing provision for estimated bad debt losses.

Smith's monitoring effort was complicated by the fact that Omni's average sale was less than $1,000 and that the division carried more than 10,000 open customer accounts. He found it difficult to put his hands around the situation because of the amount of detail in the file. To help him monitor the receivables–collections–bad debt situation, he had engaged a consultant some years ago to establish a statistical sampling system. Under the system, the Omni computer section produced a special report each quarter that analyzed the accounts receivable balances based on the dates of the unpaid invoices. This aging report was useful to Smith, helping him identify trends in the status of the receivables.

One of Smith's accounting people tracked a sample of accounts from each aging category and determined which of those sampled accounts were ultimately uncollectible. Based on a simple formula developed by the consultant, the clerk used those findings to calculate a factor for each aging category that would predict what proportion of those accounts would ultimately be uncollectible. The accounting clerk tested the results of the current studies against the numbers developed by the original study and always found that the original numbers were quite valid:

For Every Dollar in the Aging Category	Amount That Will Prove to Be Uncollectible
Current (0–30 days)	$ 0.00
1 month past due (30–60 days)	0.005
2 months past due (60–90 days)	0.05
3–4 months past due (90–150 days)	0.20
5–6 months past due (150–210 days)	0.50

Smith trusted the system and always had the accounting people adjust the period-end allowance for possible bad debts to the amount indicated by the quarterly aging report—the category totals multiplied by the table factors. In the interim months, he had his people record an estimated provision for possible bad debts, but the quarterly financial statements that were sent to the home office always included a revised provision for possible bad debt losses that was simply a plug number from the updated allowance account.

At March 31, 1999, the allowance account was adjusted to $2,658,000, the amount indicated by the aging-analysis process at that date. During the months of April, May, and June, accounts totaling $1,942,000 were turned over to the attorneys and written off. During April and May, Smith had his accounting people book $500,000 a month for possible bad debt losses. The aging of the accounts at June 30, 1999, showed the following:

	(000)
Current	$158,000
1 month past due	43,200
2 months past due	8,240
3–4 months past due	3,650
5–6 months past due	1,840
Total Accounts Receivable balance at June 30, 1999	$214,930

Required:

Determine the amount of the bad debt expense for the month of June 1999.

Scenario B: The percentage-of-credit-sales model. The manager of Omni Products Division, Harry Smith, was quite satisfied with all of his section leaders and had developed a high level of trust in their day-to-day decisions. Still, he insisted that he be involved in the critical, long-range judgments. For example, his accounting and control section was efficient and largely trouble-free. However, he carefully monitored the sensitive areas, including the status of collections on accounts receivable, the follow-up on slow-paying customers, and the reasonableness of the ongoing provision for estimated bad debt losses.

Smith's monitoring effort was complicated by the fact that Omni's average sale was less than $1,000 and that the division carried more than 10,000 open customer accounts. He found it difficult to put his hands around the situation because of the amount of detail in the file. To help him monitor the receivables–collections–bad debt situation, he had engaged a consultant some years ago to establish a statistical sampling system. Following the system, a clerk randomly selected a small number of credit sales each week and followed them through to their conclusion—either collection in cash after varying periods or a write-off because of the buyer's inability to pay. The system was easy to operate, and Smith had been assured that the results of the sample would give a very accurate reflection of the results to be expected from total credit sales. However, because the system required the clerk to follow each sampled credit sale to its conclusion, the results were not always available as quickly as Smith would have liked.

Over the past several years, the results of the system had tracked Smith's expectations, given the state of the economy in each period. The results of the study showed:

Report Dated	For the Year Ended	Average Period until Collection	Percentage of Sales Ultimately Written Off
July 5, 1995	December 31, 1994	14.2 weeks	5.5
July 8, 1996	December 31, 1995	12.4 weeks	4.8
July 7, 1997	December 31, 1996	10.5 weeks	4.6
June 28, 1998	December 31, 1997	9.3 weeks	4.5

Based on the trend through the July 1997 report, Smith had instructed his accounting people to record estimated losses from bad debts for the year ending December 31, 1997, at 4.6 percent of sales, and during the first half of 1998, the division had recorded possible bad debt losses using that 4.6 percent factor. When the June 1998 report came out, Smith was delighted. He had his accounting people reduce the expense for estimated bad debt losses to 4.5 percent of sales, effective with the July 1998 monthly financial statement. They continued with that estimate through the rest of 1998 and through the first six months of 1999. However, as the 1998 spring season wore on, Smith became anxious about the continued use of that low estimate because his customers were experiencing tighter times and the number of day's sales in the receivables balances was growing, suggesting that the trend of prior years was reversing.

The allowance for possible bad debts had a balance of $2,152,000 at December 31, 1998, and through the first six months of 1999, an expense of $3,803,040 had been added to the allowance based on six-month sales of $84,512,000. During that same period of time, accounts totaling $4,203,000 had been turned over to the attorneys for collection and written off. When the results of the statistical study for the year ended December 31, 1998, was completed on July 15, 1999, it confirmed Smith's fears. It showed that credit sales made during the year ended December 31, 1998, took 11.2 weeks to turn to cash and that 4.7 percent of those sales were never collected but were written off. He called a meeting to review this situation with his sales and credit people. He got the sense that the ship had not been run as tightly as he would have liked, and he resolved to understand how that had happened. His immediate concern was the package of financial statements he was to send to the home office the next day for the month of June and the six months ended June 30, 1999. After consulting with his staff, he resolved to add to the allowance for possible bad debts. He instructed his accounting people to increase the six-month expense for possible losses from bad debts to 4.75 percent of sales, taking the effect of the new rate for the expense as a special charge against operations for June.

Required:

Calculate the revised allowance balance as of June 30, 1999.

8.15. Accounting for trade receivables: A. H. Robins Company, Inc.* In mid-January 1985, Dave Bosher, director of corporate accounting for A. H. Robins in Richmond, Virginia, was faced with the task of estimating his company's provision for uncollectible trade receivables for 1984. Mr. Bosher was particularly concerned about the mounting trade receivable balance of one of the company's three major product lines, Caron Fragrances, because he believed that the collectibility of a large portion of this balance was questionable. Customers (several major U.S. retailers) had grown accustomed to taking large unauthorized deductions (referred to by A. H. Robins as "billbacks") on bills from their suppliers in order to widen their otherwise narrow profit margins. In December Mr. Bosher had given the Caron general manager three weeks to "do something about the receivables problem; at least get promises to pay from the major retailers or face a large write-off," but nothing had been done. Therefore, Mr. Bosher was faced with analyzing not only the total outstanding balance in the Caron receivables account, but also with the collectibility of the balance of unauthorized customer deductions. As a consequence of the problem, Mr. Bosher was also prepared to reconsider the company's policies for setting up trade receivables' allowances and writing off bad debts.

---

* Certain case data have been disguised. Copyright © 1985 by the Darden Graduate Business School Foundation, Charlottesville, VA. Rev. 10/88. All rights reserved.

General Company Background

A. H. Robins Company was founded in 1866 as a small apothecary and manufacturing chemist's shop. The company had grown into a multinational corporation engaged primarily in the manufacture and marketing of ethical pharmaceutical products (such as Dimetapp and Reglan), consumer products (Robitussin, Chap Stick lip balm, and Sergeant's pet care products), and Caron Fragrance products (such as Nocturnes). Although sales in 1984 reached a historic high of $632,000,000, the company showed a major loss for the first time. The loss resulted from establishing a $615,000,000 reserve representing an estimate of the minimum costs for compensatory damages and legal expenses arising from the Dalkon Shield litigation. Also during 1984, the Caron trade account receivables grew to $1,600,000, an amount equal to 146 days' sales, and the outstanding billback balance had expanded to $411,902. Consistent with the company's desire to achieve a proper matching of revenues and expenses, recognize losses as early as possible, and reflect economic reality, Dave Bosher believed the time had come to review the company's accounts receivable reserves on all trade receivables.

Accounting for Trade Receivables

Mr. Bosher realized that the company's three major product lines were so diverse with respect to composition and distribution channels that each warranted an individual review of the policy for providing for uncollectible trade receivables. The ethical pharmaceutical product line consisted of pharmaceuticals promoted primarily to physicians, hospitals, and pharmacists; ethical pharmaceuticals were the original products carried by A. H. Robins and accounted for 57 percent of sales and 76 percent of profits. This product line was distributed by A. H. Robins through large wholesalers in the United States and abroad; approximately 88 percent of the sales in this category were to only 410 wholesalers.

Mr. Bosher pointed out that news spread quickly when a particular pharmaceutical wholesaler was in financial trouble, in which case A. H. Robins usually began quickly to monitor the activity in the customer's account closely or, if necessary, terminate Robins's extension of credit. To arrive at a yearly uncollectible receivables provision for the ethical pharmaceutical line, Mr. Bosher set up an allowance based on a review of the individual accounts. Then he prepared an aging schedule of those accounts that he believed posed collection problems. He typically set up an allowance for uncollectibles of 10 percent of the balances that were 1–30 days past due, 25 percent of the balances 31–60 days past due, and 50 percent of the balances over 60 days past due. In some instances, when he had particularly insightful financial information on a customer, he made his own subjective judgment as to the collectibility of the account. Historically, accounts actually going bad and thus necessitating a write-off had been less than 0.2 percent of net sales. The stability of these accounts allowed Mr. Bosher to make his estimates with reasonable confidence.

The distribution system for the consumer products category, which included cough preparations and pharmaceuticals marketed over the counter to the public, was far more complex than for the ethical pharmaceuticals. During 1984 the consumer products line accounted for 39 percent of sales and 23 percent of profits. It was sold not only to major wholesalers but also to thousands of small pharmacies and brokers. Therefore, the individual uncollectible accounts pertaining to consumer products customers were generally either very large or very small, depending on whether the account in trouble was a major wholesaler or one of the numerous "mom and pop" pharmacies. Because the number of accounts was far too many to review individually, Dave Bosher used an allowance method based on a percentage of sales. To date, for the fiscal year ended December 31, 1984, $174,490 in consumer products accounts receivable had been determined to be totally uncollectible.

The Caron Fragrance line, with headquarters and production facilities in France, had become a wholly owned subsidiary of A. H. Robins in 1967. The product line was composed of five fragrances, which were marketed to both male and female upper-income groups. Caron accounted for less than 2 percent of A.H. Robin's sales and in 1984 was just breaking even in profitability. It was distributed in the United States only to major retailers in New York, Atlanta, Miami, Dallas,

Chicago, Los Angeles, and San Francisco; over 80 percent of U.S. Caron sales went to only 35 retail distributors. Mr. Bosher was able to examine the financial standing of each of these customers individually and establish an allowance for bad debts using the same method he used for the ethical pharmaceutical line. For 1984, however, he decided also to use the direct write-off method for billbacks that he deemed uncollectible. Mr. Bosher had already determined that $40,000 in accounts receivable for Caron (not including the billbacks) had actually "gone bad" and were to be written off in 1984 and that the balance in the allowance account should total $59,383.

History of Collections for Trade Receivables

Prior to 1980, responsibility for the collection and accounting for trade receivables at A. H. Robins had been decentralized on a regional basis with separate credit and collections departments for pharmaceuticals, consumer products, and Caron. During those years, customer accounts were reviewed individually in order to derive an allowance for bad debts. In 1980, however, with the number of product lines and accounts growing, the company decided to centralize its receivables function and change its policy to combine an individual review of customer accounts with the percentage-of-sales method of establishing an allowance for bad debts. The company also developed a computerized aging schedule to aid in these computations. Mr. Bosher pointed out that the receivables department currently employed nine people, who spent approximately 40 percent of their time on the Caron accounts.

Since the receivables function had been centralized, Mr. Bosher noticed that the days' sales in trade receivables had shown a gradual improvement for both ethical pharmaceuticals and the consumer products. The receivables for ethical pharmaceuticals had been reduced from 65 days' sales in 1981 to its current balance of 47 days. The consumer products outstanding trade receivables had improved from the equivalent of 91 days' sales in 1982 to 77 days' sales in 1984.

Although centralization had helped the company control collectibility for these two product lines, the same was not true for Caron Fragrances. Here the receivables balance had grown from 73 days' sales in 1981 to 146 days in 1984. More importantly to Mr. Bosher, the disputed-claims portion of the receivables (the billbacks) was 25 percent of the total Caron receivables balance; it ranged from only 1 to 5 percent of the other two product lines. Summary financial data pertinent to the three product lines are shown in Exhibits 1 through 4.

The Billback Dilemma

At the end of 1984, the Caron Fragrance line in the United States had $411,902 in billbacks included in its $1,599,568 of trade receivables (see Exhibit 4). The billback was generated when a retailer made a payment for less than the invoiced amount. In response, A. H. Robins made a new invoice for the unpaid amount and sent it back to the retailer for payment. For example, a $20,000 invoice might be sent to Bloomingdale's, which might remit payment for only $15,000. A. H. Robins would record the original invoice as paid, originate a new invoice (a billback) for the unpaid amount of $5,000, and send it to Bloomingdale's for payment. Almost every Caron invoice had a subsequent billback, and the historical collectibility of these billbacks was considered poor. The history of one typical billback is detailed in Exhibit 5.

A common practice in the United States was for large retailers to take unauthorized deductions on the bills received from their suppliers and attribute the deduction to a promotion allowance, a product demonstration salary, or just an "unidentified deduction." Of the $411,900 in billbacks on Caron, Mr. Bosher decided that $205,000 was attributable to unidentified deductions. The rest Mr. Bosher explained as being more or less the result of a paperwork merry-go-round. Although A. H. Robins had agreements with many of the large retailers to pay for a portion of their promotions or demonstration salaries, the retailers refused to wait for the paperwork to go through to be reimbursed. Instead, they would just deduct the amount they believed they were owed from the goods' invoice amount, which made bookkeeping an extremely difficult task for A. H. Robins. While these practices were rampant in the perfume industry in the United States, they did not occur either with the Caron line in France or with A. H. Robins' other product lines.

EXHIBIT 1

A. H. Robins Company, Inc.
Sales and Receivables Data

	1981	1982	1983	1984
Sales				
Pharmaceuticals	$173,712,923	$128,519,975	$160,077,407	$194,951,564
Consumer products	118,653,484	123,229,687	132,557,961	128,532,000
Caron fragrances	5,132,689	3,860,305	4,899,240	3,993,933
Year-End Trade Receivables				
Pharmaceuticals	$ 30,691,204	$ 17,206,984	$ 20,364,088	$ 25,014,708
Consumer products	7,641,931	30,763,238	28,959,778	27,257,219
Caron fragrances	1,014,773	885,190	1,781,617	1,599,568
Billbacks (included in receivables figures above)				
Pharmaceuticals	$ 552,280	$ 159,908	$ 63,413	$ 218,000
Consumer products	58,932	294,517	1,476,500	1,305,000
Caron fragrances	24,456	319,000	563,097	411,902

Source: Company records.

EXHIBIT 2

A. H. Robins Company, Inc.
Accounts-Receivable Allowance and Write-off Data

	1981	1982	1983
Year-End Balance in Allowance Accounts			
Pharmaceuticals	$ 300,000	$ 203,669	$ 300,000
Consumer products	100,000	241,881	219,000
Caron fragrances	49,516	28,310	60,900
Account-receivable write-offs			
Pharmaceuticals	$ 249,494	$ 278,030	$ 152,283
Consumer products	250,600	474,267	685,671
Caron fragrances	19,991	21,206	100,038

Source: Company records.

Ideally, these large retail customers should have paid their suppliers for the goods received and then billed the suppliers for any agreed-upon shared expenses. Yet, despite the persistence of A. H. Robins' management, the retailers refused to cooperate. In fact, the situation had grown so serious with one retailer that A. H. Robins had stopped shipments for three weeks. In general, however, the Caron product line did not carry enough leverage with the major department stores to use such threats and actions to influence their behavior.

Mr. Bosher's Concern

As Dave Bosher was reviewing the receivables balances for the three product lines for the fiscal year ended December 31, 1984, he wondered what he should do about the mounting billback problem. He also needed a realistic estimate for the corporation's bad debt expense and the receivables allowance balance for 1984.

Required:

a. Recreate the accounting transactions that were made to recognize bad debt expense and accounts receivable write-offs during 1983 for each of the three product lines.

b. What is a reasonable estimate of the bad debt expense for 1984 for ethical pharmaceuticals? Consumer products? Caron fragrances?

Make the appropriate year-end accounting transactions for 1984 and set up t-accounts that show the year-end balance in the allowance accounts.

c. How should Dave Bosher resolve the billback problem with retail customers in the future? How could the accounting information system assist in successfully implementing your suggestions?

EXHIBIT 3a

A. H. Robins Company, Inc.
Example of Accounts Receivable for
Ethical Pharmaceutical Products
as of December 31, 1984
(credit terms 2/10, net 30)

Customer Name	Total Balance Due	Current Items	1–30 Days Past Due	31–60 Days Past Due	Over 60 Days Past Due
1. * Amfak Drug Co.	$ 51,193	—	—	—	$ 51,193
2. * Leigh Laboratories	20,996	$ 4,338	$ 16,658	—	—
3. Edwards Commissary	109,722	—	—	$ 35,802	73,920
4. Central Drug Supply	87,703	—	—	4,618	83,085
5. * Drug Service, Inc.	47,602	—	—	—	47,602
6. Ames Plaza Drugs	59,606	—	—	—	59,606
7. Johnson Drug Co.	56,884	—	—	56,884	—
8. * Armco Pharmac.	31,909	—	—	—	31,909
9. * Northern Medical Supplies	34,634	4,914	5,910	—	22,814
10. Medco Drugs	48,108	4,100	4,008	40,000	—
11. Reeds Drug Supplies	63,498	—	—	—	63,498
12. Remco, Inc.	54,022	—	—	—	54,022
13. Hampton Drug	60,929	—	—	—	60,929
14. * South Bay Drug Co.	36,401	36,401	—	—	—
15. Davis Laboratory Supplies	72,465	—	—	26,082	46,383
16. Ridgefield Drugs, Inc.	18,526	—	18,526	—	—
17. Geer Drug Corp.	49,101	24,312	24,789	—	—
18. Humdico Medical	77,670	18,070	59,600	—	—
19. Albertsons Drugs, Inc.	36,317	8,697	9,402	18,218	—
20. Pharmaceutical Supplies	26,965	—	—	—	26,965
21. * Virginia Drug, Inc.	28,324	—	—	—	28,324
22. Total other accounts (not considered doubtful)	23,942,138	23,942,138			
	$25,014,708	$24,042,970	$138,893	$181,604	$650,245

*See Exhibit 3b for additional financial information.

EXHIBIT 3b

A. H. Robins Company, Inc.
Excerpts from the 1984 Financial Press

Drug Service, Inc., to Post $900,000 Loss, Defaults on Bank Loan

San Jose, Calif.—Drug Service, Inc., said it expects to post a fiscal first-quarter loss of more than $900,000. The company also said it is in default on a $7 million bank loan.

The pharmaceutical wholesaler and distributor said it expects revenue for the quarter ended Sunday of about $3.5 million, down from $11.8 million a year earlier. In the earlier quarter, the company lost $600,000, and stock prices declined dramatically.

Drug Service, Inc. said it had planned to refinance the loan, which came due Sunday, by mortgaging some real estate, but that plan fell through.

Two Former Officers of South Bay Drug Plead Guilty to One Charge

New York—Two former officers of South Bay Drug Co., a small wholesaler for medical supplies and pharmaceuticals that entered bankruptcy law proceedings in December 1984, pleaded guilty in state court here to grand larceny, according to Robert Brams, New York state attorney general.

Rollin H. Need, former president of South Bay Drug Co. and Isaac Comerch, former operations officer, were indicted on charges of conspiracy, fraud, and grand larceny. The conspiracy and fraud charges were dropped when the two pleaded guilty to grand larceny, a spokesman for Mr. Brams said. Charges are still pending against another former officer, Terrence Whitney, who was chief financial officer, the spokesman said.

Mr. Need couldn't be reached for comment on the guilty plea. An attorney for Mr. Comerch said he declined to comment on the case. Mr. Whitney couldn't be reached for comment.

The attorney general said that Messrs. Need and Comerch were ordered to appear in court for sentencing Feb. 2.

Amfak Drug Co. Asks Lenders to Approve Debt Restructuring

Houston—Amfak Drug Co. said it submitted to its lenders a proposal to restructure $1 billion of debt to avert a cash shortage in the first quarter of 1985.

Under the proposal, Amfak Drug Co.'s secured lenders would receive interest and principal payments based on the company's available cash flow until about 1988. Principal payments of about $334 million for Amfak's secured debt are currently due through 1987. Amfak said payments under the debt restructuring would be less than the contracted amounts until 1988. After that, the original payment schedule would resume.

An Amfak spokesman said the company is "optimistic" that the lenders will accept the proposal. If approved, the debt restructuring will become effective Jan. 1. The spokesman said that if lenders don't agree to the proposal, a filing under Chapter 11 of the federal Bankruptcy Code would be considered only as a "last alternative."

Leigh Laboratories Says It May Dismiss up to 100 Employees

Lowell, Mass.—Leigh Laboratories Inc., hurt by slumping demand for its medical equipment, said it may dismiss as many as 100 employees in about 30 days.

The employees, who work at staff positions at the company's headquarters, represent a fraction of Leigh's 8,000 workers. But the layoffs would be the first in about 12 years for Leigh. For the third quarter ended Sept. 31, Leigh's earnings slumped 66 percent, the company's first downturn in quarterly earnings since 1975. For the quarter, Leigh earned 3.2 million, or 12 cents a share, on revenue of $152.7 million.

Leigh said if it isn't able to find alternative work for the 100 employees within 30 days, either at Leigh or at another employer, it would dismiss them with severance pay. Leigh didn't rule out additional layoffs.

Armco Pharmaceuticals Net from Operations Fell 23% in Its 3rd Quarter

Dayton, Ohio—Armco Pharmaceuticals reported a 23 percent drop in earnings from operations for its fiscal third quarter ended May 31.

The company also said its loss for the year ending Aug. 21 will total about $1.9 million, wider than the $1.4 million deficit projected in March.

For fiscal 1983, the wholesaler and distributor of drug products earned $3.1 million, or $1.29 a share. The company blamed its financial condition on the "generally weak industrial economy" and on foreign competition in the pharmaceuticals business.

For the third quarter, Armco Pharmaceuticals posted net income of $432,000, or 18 cents a share, compared with year-earlier profit from continuing operations of $530,000, or 22 cents a share.

Northern Medical Supplies Sets Plan to Close Two Distribution Sites, Cites Rise in Competition

Greenville, S.C.—Northern Medical Supplies said it will close two of its distribution warehouses i   mn   the   Atlantic seaboard region that have been "most directly affected by the surge of imports over the last two years."

Northern Medical Supplies said its warehouse at Rockingham, N.C., which employs 180 people, will be phased out over a period of months.

Operations at its Anderson, S.C., facility, which has 475 employees, are to be reduced in size and eventually will be closed. The final closing date, however, isn't known yet, the company said.

Meanwhile, it said its East Coast distribution facilities will be consolidated at the Pickett facility in Rockingham.

Virginia Drug Company Seeks Buyer

Richmond, Va.—Va. Drug Company, which has filed a request to reorganize under the eye of the U.S. Bankruptcy Court here, is seeking a buyer, its president said yesterday.

James B. Farin, the Va. Drug Company president, said they hope to be bought by Seifer Inc. of Alexandria, Va. However, no written agreement has been made. Farin said Seifer is practically identical to the Richmond-based wholesaler of pharmaceutical drugs.

Va. Drug Co. had operated as many as six distribution outlets about two years ago. When it filed papers in bankruptcy court saying it planned to seek reorganization under Chapter 11, it listed assets of about $6.2 million and debts of about $9.9 million, including notes totaling about $8.5 million from Union Virginia Bank.

EXHIBIT 4

A. H. Robins Company, Inc.
Caron Outstanding Billbacks, December 1984

| | | | Past Due | | | | |
Codes	Outstanding No. of Billbacks	Current	1–30 Days	31–60 Days	61–90 Days	Over 90	Total
51 *	54	$ 6,571.63–	$ 2,154.43–	$ 3,838.88–	$ 1,650.00–	$ 6,268.40–	$ 20,483.34–
52 *	14	4,141.33–	2,965.48–	0.00	64.89–	880.90–	8,052.60–
53 *	60	2,412.67–	9,991.25–	1,210.71–	795.04–	10,953.36–	25,363.03–
54	488	50,283.27	35,072.97	25,031.08	5,947.62	88,635.20	204,970.14
55 *	43	1,791.29–	3,547.82–	2,358.47–	3,280.52–	3,725.40–	14,703.50–
56	18	54.00	278.66	113.10	217.90	643.84	1,307.50
58	92	5,917.00	333.78	843.41	1,212.36	14,184.41	22,490.90
60	1	.00	.00	.00	.00	252.00	252.00
62	119	8,414.87	274.21	3,368.49	14,785.02	19,303.54	46,146.13
64	7	.00	361.45	.00	154.26	469.44	985.15
66	31	1,749.20	744.14	399.08	233.95	582.38	3,708.75
67	6	48.63	.00	203.12	152.27	50.00	454.02
68	140	4,300.00	1,260.35	1,235.00	8,920.63	111,046.19	126,762.17
69	63	487.30	1,145.69	593.57	4,201.89	14,574.00	21,002.45
70	1	0.00	0.00	0.00	2,025.00	0.00	2,025.00
71	1	0.00	0.00	0.00	0.00	157.86	157.86
72	1	0.00	0.00	0.00	0.00	144.50	144.50
73	45	142.03	452.98–	510.75	121.08–	5,386.51	5,465.23
79	26	842.30	80.00	19.20	249.30	14,035.29	15,226.09
Totals	1,210	$60,904.26	$27,534.93	$29,625.68	$38,749.71	$255,087.90	$411,902.48

*A negative billback was generated when a customer made a payment for more than the invoice amount.

Source: Company records.

EXHIBIT 5

A. H. Robins Company, Inc.
History of a Typical Caron Fragrance Billback

Date	Description of Correspondence
2/20/83	Goods shipped to retailer.
3/1/83	Original invoice for $56,702 mailed to retailer (for example, Bloomingdale's).
5/1/83	Past-due notice sent.
7/1/83	Check for $30,000 received by A. H. Robins.
7/15/83	Billback invoice for $26,702 mailed to retailer.
9/1/83	Caron manager called customer regarding billback. Customer will look into outstanding balance.
10/1/83	Received letter from customer saying $26,702 discount taken was attributed to a product promotion booth.
10/15/83	Wrote letter to customer saying only $5,000 was authorized for promotion booth.
11/15/83	Caron manager called customer; customer said they'll take care of the discrepancy.
11/28/83	Received check for $6,000.
12/5/83	Billback #2 generated for $15,702.
1/30/84	Call to customer, who said they were trying to clear up outstanding invoices.
2/15/84	A. H. Robins's credit manager informed customer he was planning a visit to their NY office to clear up all outstanding bills.
3/1/84	Credit manager made NY trip. Customer happened to have billback #2 in their file. They'll check into it.
4/1/84	Received check for $7,000.
4/10/84	Call to customer, who said the balance not paid was for special product advertising.
5/1/84	Billback #3 generated for $6,702. (A. H. Robins allowed $2,000 special promotions discount.)
12/31/84	Billback #3 outstanding. No apparent resolution. Write off?

8.16. Accounting for marketable securities: San Antonio Enterprises.* It was two weeks after the fiscal year ended August 31, 1994, and Joan Compton, the controller of San Antonio Enterprises, was preparing the company's financial statements for the year. Over the past several years, San Antonio Enterprises had been successfully marketing leisure-time products in Texas. Last year, for the first time, the business had produced excess cash, which Joan invested in financial securities. Exhibit 1 details the investment portfolio as of the end of last year.

For the most part, San Antonio's stock investments had not advanced with last year's bull market. Their performance was fairly lackluster, but the decision had been made to hold onto them in the belief that at some point they would climb with the rest of the market. The stock market had slowed near the beginning of this year, and the growth of some of the stocks in San Antonio's portfolio also slowed—in some cases, even reversed.

Looking at the securities' market values as of the end of this year, shown in Exhibit 2, Joan was particularly concerned about the Borden stock. Borden's price had declined sharply during the year, and the current market value was below San Antonio's original purchase price. Joan called her broker, Jeff Fields, to find out what was happening.

E X H I B I T   1

San Antonio Enterprises
Investment Portfolio on August 31, 1993

	Shares	Original Cost	Market Value
Equities			
Trading:			
ICN Pharmaceuticals	2,000	$ 14,000	$ 20,000
Sara Lee	2,000	52,000	40,000
Jefferson Bank	1,000	19,000	21,000
		$ 85,000	$ 81,000
Available for sale:			
Merck	1,000	$ 38,000	$ 32,000
Biocraft	2,000	50,000	58,000
Motorola	1,000	44,000	46,000
Mead	1,000	34,000	39,000
Blockbuster Video	2,000	64,000	54,000
American Cyanamid	1,000	48,000	44,000
Borden	3,000	48,000	36,000
		$326,000	$309,000
Bonds			
Available for sale:			
Ford Motor Company		$120,000	$121,500
Union Carbide		130,000	130,500
Hold to maturity:			
Xerox		100,000	100,750
		$350,000*	$352,750

*The bonds were purchased for an amount equal to their maturity value.

"Well, the company is not expected to meet its projected earnings for the year, their credit rating has fallen from an A+ to a BBB, and they replaced their Chief Financial Officer (CFO) with a CFO from, of all things, the timber industry. I even hear Borden is contemplating selling Elsie the Cow."

"Okay, Jeff, thanks for the information. By the way, did you check the maturity dates on those bonds for me?"

"I sure did, None of your bonds are scheduled to mature this coming year. While I've got you on the line, Joan, I'd like to double-check those trigger prices at which you wanted me to sell some of your stocks: ICN Pharmaceuticals at 14, Sara Lee at 32, and Jefferson Bank Shares at 25. Do you still want these in effect?"

"Yes. By the way, you did sell American Cyanamid before the month ended, didn't you?"

"Sure did. It executed at 100. What a great run it had once American Home Products bid on it. By the way, let me know when you want to sell any of the others."

"Well, my attitude toward the Merck investment has changed. This health care debate in Congress seems like it could go on forever. If Merck inches up another couple of points, sell it. As always, if you have any hot tips, let me know."

"O.K. Anything else?"

"Nope. It's been good talking to you. Thanks for your time, Jeff."

Joan hung up the phone and contemplated the information Jeff had given her. She also decided it was time to study the reports she had seen in the business press (shown in Exhibits 3 and 4). Joan knew that 1993 had been the first year San Antonio Enterprises had adopted a financial reporting rule for investments requiring something called mark-to-market accounting. She knew that she would have to set aside some time to recreate what was done last year in this regard. Joan also knew that her auditor wanted to see the financial statements at the end of the week, so she was determined to finish the books today.

EXHIBIT 2

San Antonio Enterprises
Investment Portfolio Market Values on August 31, 1994

	# Shares	Market Value
Equities		
ICN Pharmaceuticals	2,000	$ 25,500
Sara Lee	2,000	39,000
Jefferson Bank	1,000	23,000
Merck	1,000	34,000
Biocraft	2,000	32,000
Motorola	1,000	51,000
Mead	1,000	50,750
Blockbuster Video	2,000	52,000
Borden	3,000	34,500
		$341,750
Bonds*		
Ford Motor Company		$120,500
Union Carbide		130,100
Xerox		100,200
		$350,800

*No bonds were purchased or sold during 1994.

EXHIBIT 3

San Antonio Enterprises
Information Pertinent to the Borden Investment

Borden Considers Sale or Shutdown Of Dairy Business

BY SUEIN L. HWANG
Staff Reporter of THE WALL STREET JOURNAL

Borden, Inc., under growing pressure from creditors, is considering selling or shutting down its problem-plagued $1.3 billion dairy unit, people close to the company say.

Officials at Borden declined to comment, but people familiar with the situation say the fate of the beleaguered dairy business led the agenda of a board meeting on Tuesday. "Dairy isn't making any progress, and it's a real challenge to management," one executive says. "The [restructuring] plan isn't working."

One of the original cornerstones of the company, the dairy unit remains one of Borden's largest businesses, contributing 25 percent of total sales in 1993. With its familiar mascot Elsie the Cow, the dairy unit is perhaps most closely associated with the Borden name. Until recently, it had also been reasonably profitable, generating about $90 million in 1991.

But at a time when Borden is struggling to revamp its far-flung operations, the dairy unit has become a major headache. The business, which includes milk, cheese, and ice cream, had a loss of $35 million in 1993. Last month, Borden posted weaker-than-expected second-quarter results and said it might not reach its year-end projections. Analysts estimate the dairy unit had a loss of $30 million in the first half of this year.

Yesterday, Moody's Investors Service placed the ratings of $1.9 billion of Borden's long-term debt and commercial paper under review for a possible downgrade. The agency cited weaker-than-expected performance, particularly in the dairy and pasta businesses.

Getting rid of the dairy unit wouldn't be easy. Commodity costs are sky-high, leaving even healthy dairies struggling to eke out a profit. Chief Executive Officer Ervin Shames "is between a rock and a hard place," says John McMillin, an analyst at Prudential Securities Inc. "He can't write off the business without getting shareholders' equity into negative territory."

The problems in the dairy business reflect the turbulence that has plagued Borden in the last few years. After acquiring a number of regional dairies such as Meadow Gold, executives and analysts say the company did little to consolidate them. Last year, Borden finally did attempt a sweeping consolidation of its dairy operations, only to be badly hurt by an attempt to raise prices across the board. "They've changed courses a couple of times and it hasn't quite worked," says Nomi Ghez, an analyst at Goldman, Sachs & Co.

Since the end of 1993, the company has ousted Anthony S. D'Amato as chief executive, put its ailing snack-food unit on the block, and taken a $632 million restructuring charge. Executives say the many changes, which include the recruitment of six new executives into top posts at Borden, have stirred resentment among the old guard—particularly among the insular ranks of the dairy business. "There's been a lot of turnover, and this is a relationship business," says Mr. McMillin.

Source: The Wall Street Journal, August 18, 1994, p. A4. Reprinted by permission of *The Wall Street Journal* © 1994, Dow Jones & Co., Inc. All Rights Reserved Worldwide.

EXHIBIT 4

San Antonio Enterprises
Information Pertinent to the Biocraft Investment

Biocraft Has Come to Terms with the FDA But Analysts Debate Whether to Buy Its Stock

BY JOHN R. DORFMAN AND ELYSE TANOUYE
Staff Reporters of THE WALL STREET JOURNAL

Can Biocraft Laboratories walk away unharmed from a car wreck?

The Fair Lawn, N.J., generic drug maker signed a tough consent agreement in July to settle a dispute with the Food and Drug Administration over manufacturing practices. Now, outside inspectors supervise Biocraft's operations. Proponents say most of Biocraft's troubles are behind it and the stock should rebound from Friday's close of 16 1/8, which was down 57 percent from its 52-week high. But skeptics say a recovery won't be easy, and in this case, the pessimists make some compelling arguments.

A consent decree requiring outside supervision "is not the beginning of recovery," says Hemant Shah, an independent drug analyst with HKS & Co. in Warren, N.J. "What it tells you is that the FDA basically does not trust the company."

Biocraft didn't admit or deny wrongdoing. But tangles of this type can distract managers from running the business, slow down production, harm a company's stature among customers, and make regulators stingy with permission to manufacture more drugs, Mr. Shah says. He predicts Biocraft will only break even in the fiscal year ending next March and will need two years to get back on its feet.

David Saks of Gruntal & Co. disagrees. "The problems are obvious," he says. "They seemingly are being resolved. The company is a low-cost and important supplier of antibiotics." At today's price, Mr. Saks thinks the stock is worth buying even if full recovery is a way off.

Besides, Mr. Saks considers Biocraft takeover bait. "I usually like to see, right smack in my face, strong earnings," he says. "But I feel that the merger mania [in the drug industry] is a new factor. This firm has said that it would seek a strategic alliance or buyout. The CEO is 73 years old and not getting younger. He wants to have his family fortune become liquid."

Each of the dueling analysts boasts a good stock-picking record. In the most recent Wall Street Journal All-Star Analysts Survey, Mr. Saks ranked first for stock picking, Mr. Shah a close second.

Other analysts' opinions are mixed. Jack Lamberton of NatWest Securities calls the stock a buy, projecting fiscal 1997 earnings of $1.18 a share. "Usually consent decrees represent a trough in the fundamentals at any company," he says.

Stephen Buermann of Merrill Lynch considers Biocraft a buy in the long run but not the short run. He guesses the company will be unable to get new drugs approved for a while. Without new drugs, he says, profit margins will be susceptible to erosion. So he pegs this fiscal year's earnings at zero to 10 cents a share.

Bonnie Perkins of Fortaleza Asset Management in Chicago thinks highly of Biocraft's new "state-of-the-art" production facility in Mexico, Mo. But she isn't recommending either a purchase or sale of the stock.

The bears seem to have history on their side, citing slow recoveries by other companies that signed stringent consent orders. Operating under such an agreement "under all circumstances is harmful and expensive," says Neil Sweig of Ladenburg, Thalmann. Sales lost during the supervision period may not be easy to regain, he says.

According to Mr. Shah, Biocraft's revenue is running about 50 percent below normal. Jay T. Snyder, Biocraft's vice president of research and development, won't confirm or deny this figure. (Mr. Snyder is a member of the family that owns about two-thirds of Biocraft stock, and he is the son of the chief executive, Harold Snyder.)

Biocraft's earnings history has been "very spotty," says Mr. Shah. "The most it ever earned was $1.05 [a share] in 1988. It earned 59 cents a share in 1989, 23 cents in 1990, and 27 cents in 1991. It lost 48 cents a share in 1992. It made 42 cents in 1993."

People betting on a merger may care little about the earnings, but a merger isn't a sure thing. According to Mr. Shah, Biocraft has been dangled in front of prospective buyers for about two years, first by Wertheim Schroder and more recently by Goldman Sachs. No takers.

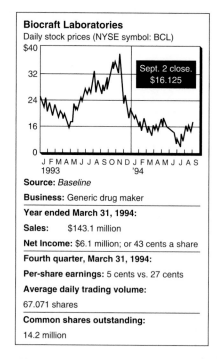

Biocraft Laboratories
Daily stock prices (NYSE symbol: BCL)

Sept. 2 close.
$16.125

J F M A M J J A S O N D J F M A M J J A S
1993   '94

Source: *Baseline*

Business: Generic drug maker

Year ended March 31, 1994:

Sales: $143.1 million

Net Income: $6.1 million; or 43 cents a share

Fourth quarter, March 31, 1994:

Per-share earnings: 5 cents vs. 27 cents

Average daily trading volume:

67.071 shares

Common shares outstanding:

14.2 million

Biocraft's Mr. Snyder won't comment on takeover speculation except to say, "We'll be very successful in the future independently or in partnership with another firm."

Even though Biocraft's stock is down, it isn't cheap. The shares sell for 38 times the past four quarters' earnings and 78 times the average annual earnings for the past five years.

Required:

Make all the judgments and financial statement adjustments necessary for preparing San Antonio's August 31, 1994, year-end balance sheet. Prepare the investments part of that year-end balance sheet.

CHAPTER 9

Inventories and the Cost of Goods Sold

When companies are desperate to stay afloat, inventory fraud is the easiest way to produce instant profits and dress up the balance sheet.[1]

Key Chapter Issues

- What is inventory and what constitutes its cost?
- What are the physical flows versus cost flows for inventory?

- What do the acronyms LIFO, FIFO, LISH, and FISH mean?
- What financial reporting concerns and practices pertain to obsolete inventory?

---

[1] F. Pomerantz, quoted in L. Berton, "Inventory Chicanery Tempts More Firms, Fools More Auditors," *The Wall Street Journal,* December 14, 1992, pp. 1 and A4.

Visualize the items that are on the shelves of your local Kroger or Safeway grocery store. Visualize the millions of gallons of oil in various stages of refinement at Exxon and Texaco sites around the world. Visualize a General Motors or Toyota factory with various types of cars in various stages of assembly. Such images are the images of these companies' inventories—their stock in trade, composed of the goods purchased and/or manufactured to sell to their customers. On the balance sheet, inventories are regarded as current assets because they are expected to be sold and to benefit a business during the next operating cycle. The inventory items sold during a period, and therefore no longer on hand at period-end, are matched against that period's sales revenue and recorded in the income statement as the cost of goods sold. It must be quickly pointed out that in determining the amount to report for the cost of goods sold, however, management is accorded considerable leeway, and the alternative inventory accounting methods available to management can significantly affect both the balance sheet (the reported cost of ending inventory) and the income statement (the reported cost of goods sold attributable to that period).

How does Procter & Gamble, Exxon, General Motors, or Kroger account for its vast and varied inventories? As we will see, the inventory accounting method chosen by management depends on the nature of the industry, certain tax considerations, and a variety of other factors discussed in this chapter. The informed reader is advised to consider both the balance sheet and the income statement effects during the following discussion.

SOME BASIC RELATIONSHIPS: THE COST OF INVENTORY

For all companies, the principal accounting concept involved in valuing inventories is that all goods available for sale during a period must, at year-end, either have been sold or remain in ending inventory. For a *merchandising* business like Wal-Mart, which simply buys goods and sells them as is, this relationship is depicted in Panel A of Exhibit 9.1 and in the following equations:

$$\text{Beginning inventory + Net purchases} \\ = \text{Cost of goods available for sale} \tag{1}$$

$$\text{Cost of goods available for sale} - \text{Cost of goods sold} = \text{Ending inventory} \tag{2}$$

In accounting for a *manufacturing* company's inventory, such as that of Procter & Gamble or General Motors, which transforms raw materials into a final product, the same basic relationship applies, although the process is a bit more complicated and involves a larger number of costs. Manufactured inventories are usually composed of three categories: **raw materials** (RM), which include materials and purchased parts awaiting assembly or manufacture; **work in process** (WIP), which includes partially completed products still in the factory; and **finished goods** (FG), which include fully assembled or manufactured goods available for sale. Each of these three physical categories of inventory must be included in the accounting process.

Raw Materials

The accounting for a manufacturer's raw materials inventory is very similar to accounting for the inventory transactions of a merchandising company. The beginning inventory *plus* net purchases *equals* the raw materials available for use. These raw materials available for

EXHIBIT 9.1

Status of Inventory Items at Year-End

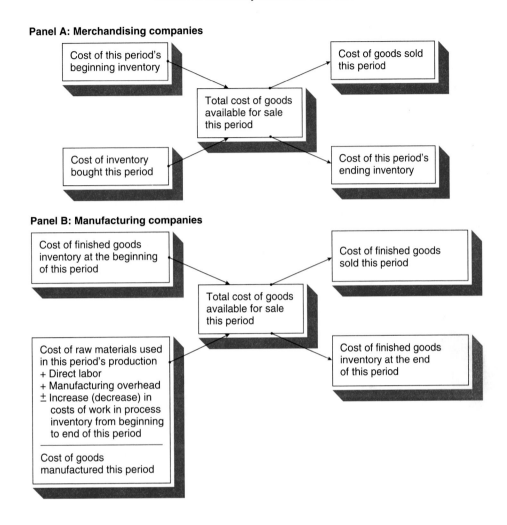

Panel A: Merchandising companies

- Cost of this period's beginning inventory
- Cost of inventory bought this period
- Total cost of goods available for sale this period
- Cost of goods sold this period
- Cost of this period's ending inventory

Panel B: Manufacturing companies

- Cost of finished goods inventory at the beginning of this period
- Cost of raw materials used in this period's production
  + Direct labor
  + Manufacturing overhead
  ± Increase (decrease) in costs of work in process inventory from beginning to end of this period

  Cost of goods manufactured this period
- Total cost of goods available for sale this period
- Cost of finished goods sold this period
- Cost of finished goods inventory at the end of this period

use either remain unused at year-end (and thus in the inventory of unused raw materials at the end of the accounting period) or have been placed in production. This relationship is shown in the following equations:

$$\text{Beginning RM inventory} + \text{Net purchases of RM} = \text{Cost of RM available for use} \qquad (3)$$

$$\text{Cost of RM available for use} - \text{Ending RM inventory} = \text{Cost of RM used} \qquad (4)$$

Work in Process

During the work in process phase of production, the cost of raw materials used, along with the cost of **direct labor** (the labor expended to convert raw materials to finished goods), and all **manufacturing overhead** costs must be assigned to the products being produced. Thus, beginning work in process inventory *plus* the cost of raw materials used during the period *plus* direct labor costs incurred during the period *plus* manufacturing overhead for the period *less* ending work in process inventory *equals* the cost of goods manufactured during the period. These relationships are shown in the following equations:

$$\text{Cost of RM used} + \text{Direct labor cost} + \text{Manufacturing overhead costs} = \text{Total manufacturing costs} \qquad (5)$$

$$\text{Beginning WIP inventory} + \text{Total manufacturing costs} - \text{Ending WIP inventory} = \text{Cost of goods manufactured} \qquad (6)$$

A word about the need and method to assign manufacturing overhead costs to work in process inventories is warranted. *Manufacturing overhead* is a phrase commonly used to describe all factory-related costs, other than raw materials and direct labor, involved in the production of a completed product: electricity, maintenance, supervision, depreciation of machines, and so on. Under U.S. generally accepted accounting principles, inventories must be reported using **full absorption costing**—i.e., all factory costs are considered to be **product costs** and thus need to be assigned to the cost of inventory rather than expensed on the income statement as incurred.[2] The nonfactory-related costs of a manufacturer, such as selling expenses, are called **period costs** and are treated as expenses in the income statement in the period when they are incurred.

As an example, visualize a mattress manufacturing company that uses four raw materials in its production process: fabric, padding, lumber, and springs. To make one mattress, the production supervisor requisitions from the warehouse the appropriate quantity of each raw material (see Panel A, Exhibit 9.2). Once in the factory, the fabric and padding are used by workers to make the outer surface of the mattress. Other workers use the lumber to make the mattress frame. Additional labor is required to mount the springs on the frame and then to cover it with the padded surface. The cost of labor incurred in performing these tasks is considered to be as much a part of the final cost of a completed mattress as the actual materials in it and thus must be added to the inventory account. Manufacturing overhead costs related to these production operations are also incurred. These costs are for items such as equipment maintenance, cleaning supplies, and power, as well as the cost of insurance, taxes, and depreciation pertaining to the factory. A share of these overhead costs are added to the primary product cost (raw materials and direct labor) in order to have a complete (i.e., full) cost for a particular manufactured mattress (see Panel B, Exhibit 9.2) because they are a necessary part of the production process and, consequently, represent part of the total cost of the final product.

Notice in Exhibit 9.2 that the accounting process for manufactured inventories parallels the actual production process. When raw materials sit in a warehouse, their cost sits in the Raw Materials Inventory account. As raw materials and labor start being introduced into the manufacturing process, a Work in Process Inventory account accumulates such costs for the goods in various stages of partial production. Finally, when production is completed on an item, it is physically transferred to a finished goods warehouse or storeroom, and the costs

---

[2] Although full absorption costing of inventories is required by U.S. GAAP, its suitability for operationally managing inventory levels and production processes is often questioned. See for example E. Goldratt, *The Goal* (Great Barrington, MA: North River Press, 1992).

EXHIBIT 9.2

An Illustration of a Manufacturing Process
and Associated Manufacturing Costs

Panel A: Manufacturing Process for One Queen-Sized Mattress

Beginning Warehouse Supply of Raw Materials	Supervisor's Requisition	Production/ Assembly Process	Finished Goods Produced
1,000 yds. fabric	10 yds. ⟶	Covering	
1,000 yds. padding	10 yds. ⟶		One mattress
1,000 board ft. lumber	60 bd. ft. ⟶	Frame	
1,000 springs	40 ⟶	Springs	

Panel B: Inventory Accounts for Queen-Sized Mattress Paralleling Panel A's Manufacturing Process

Beginning Inventory Account of Raw Materials	Additions to Work in Process Inventory Account		Additions to Finished Goods Inventory Account
$3,000 fabric	10 yds. @ $3/yd. ⟶	$ 30	
$2,000 padding	10 yds. @ $2/yd. ⟶	$ 20	
$ 500 lumber	60 bd. ft. @ $0.50/bd. ft. ⟶	$ 30	
$ 800 springs	40 springs @ $0.80/spring ⟶	$ 32	
	Direct labor:		
	Covering (1 hr. @ $25/hr.)	$ 25	
	Frame (1 hr. @ $20/hr.)	$ 20	
	Assembly (1 hr @ $10/hr.)	$ 10	$195
	Manufacturing overhead*		
	Indirect labor	$ 5	
	Supplies	$ 4	
	Utilities	$ 1	
	Depreciation	$ 15	
	Other	$ 3	
		$195	

*The manufacturing overhead amounts are allocations from accumulated indirect cost pools based on some predetermined, estimated relationship (e.g., for every direct labor hour, $5 of depreciation is assigned to the cost of a single mattress). The raw materials and direct labor costs are determined by the actual quantity of materials and labor used in making the one mattress.

accumulated for that finished item are likewise transferred from the Work in Process Inventory account to the Finished Goods Inventory account.

It is worth noting that a challenge arises when a company no longer manufactures only a single product. When it manufactures multiple products, it becomes necessary to determine just how much of the manufacturing overhead costs (such as factory depreciation, equipment maintenance, and supervisors' wages) should be included in the cost of Product A versus Product B. We can readily agree that each of two manufactured products contains a certain quantity of raw material and labor (for example, 40 springs for the deluxe queen mattress versus 15 for a crib-size mattress) and that it took five hours of labor to assemble one queen-size mattress but only two hours of labor to assemble the crib-size mattress. However, no comparable objective and precise assessments are possible for costs such as the factory building's depreciation, equipment maintenance, or supervisors' wages. Similarly, other manufacturing overhead costs such as inspection, warehousing, power, and so on are

EXHIBIT 9.3

Daimler-Benz
Inventory Disclosure

Inventory is valued at the lower of acquisition or manufacturing cost or market, cost being generally determined on the basis of an average or first-in, first-out method (FIFO). Certain of the Group's U.S. businesses'

inventories are valued using the last-in, first-out method (LIFO). Manufacturing costs comprise direct material and labor and applicable manufacturing overheads, including depreciation charges.

not easily quantifiable ingredients of each separate finished model. Exhibit 9.3 presents the inventory footnote (in part) reported by Daimler-Benz in its 1997 annual report wherein the company describes the general factory overhead items included in its inventory valuation.

The fact that there is no objectively measurable means to determine the manufacturing overhead costs incurred by each of two products does not, however, preclude the need to allocate such costs to the final cost of Products A and B for balance sheet reporting purposes. Ideally, the costs not *directly* attributable to inventory units but necessary for their production should be assigned to the finished products by astute managers on a basis reflecting the demands by the various products on those manufacturing resources.[3] For example, manufacturing overhead costs are often allocated to products on the basis of direct labor hours required to produce the product, the machine hours required to produce it, production floor space devoted to the product, the number of production order changes required, or some other measurable allocation basis.

As a simple example of the allocation of factory overhead costs, assume that such costs are expected to total $1 million for the year. Assume further that the number of direct labor hours devoted to each of the two final products has been chosen as the allocation base and that the estimated total number of direct labor hours to produce the volume of products needed to fulfill projected sales is 40,000. These estimates result in an allocation scheme whereby, for every one hour of direct labor incurred in making a particular product, $25 of these manufacturing overhead costs are to be assigned to each finished product ($1 million ÷ 40,000 hours = $25/hour).

The issue of allocating manufacturing overhead costs to various product lines has received increasing attention from corporate managers as the direct material and direct labor cost components of manufactured products have been reduced through various overt cost-cutting measures. At the same time, the use of robotics and other technological innovations in production processes have helped to increase the relative share of overhead costs associated with manufactured products. In spite of the many systematic overhead allocation schemes devised over the years, in the final analysis, they are *all* arbitrary to some degree. Consequently, no single best, theoretically defensible method to allocate manufacturing overhead costs exists. Therefore, even though manufacturing overhead cost allocations are necessary to value a company's ending inventories in the balance sheet, managers must use caution when making strategic operating decisions based, at least in part, on allocated cost information. Given such a situation, it is not surprising that managers are continually

[3] The concept of activity-based costing (ABC) is helpful in this regard. See for example R. Cooper, et. al., *Implementing Activity Based Cost Management: Moving from Analysis to Action* (Montvale, NJ: Institute of Management Accountants, 1992).

searching for more accurate and informative allocation methods to achieve a better matching of expenses to revenues and thus better measures of performance over time.

Finished Goods

At the end of the manufacturing phase, all costs associated with a completed product are transferred from work in process inventory to the finished goods inventory. Accounting for finished goods in a manufacturing firm is again very much like that for a merchandising company. The cost of beginning finished goods (FG) inventory *plus* the cost of goods manufactured (those costs transferred from work in process) *equals* the period's cost of goods available for sale. As of the end of a period, these costs must be attributed to either ending finished goods inventory (unsold goods) or to cost of goods sold. Hence, as depicted in Panel B of Exhibit 9.1, the following relationships exist:

$$\text{Beginning FG inventory} + \text{Cost of goods manufactured} \tag{7}$$
$$= \text{Cost of goods available for sale}$$

$$\text{Cost of goods available for sale} - \text{Cost of goods sold} \tag{8}$$
$$= \text{Ending FG inventory}$$

ACCOUNTING FOR INVENTORY COSTS

So far we have not mentioned the *physical* movement of inventory through a business. Clearly, purchased goods come into a company's facilities, and sold goods leave the premises. The following are pertinent questions that arise when a product is sold: Was that a sale of an item purchased or manufactured yesterday or last month? Does the answer to this question matter?

For a moment, visualize a business that makes and sells a large volume of a single model of chair. All during the year, the company incurs various costs to produce the chairs and to sell the finished product. Assume that you and another customer both arrive at the company's showroom simultaneously. The showroom is full of identical chairs, and both of you select the first chair that you see. Unknown to either of you, the chair you selected was manufactured six months ago, and the one that the other customer chose was manufactured yesterday. Are the actual costs of manufacturing incurred by the company for your chair different than those of the other customer's chair? They *probably* are because of material cost increases or a few more minutes of labor devoted to one or the other of them. Does that fact result in the other customer paying a different price for a chair than you pay? *Probably not.* If the different costs do not result in different sales prices, there is no real need for the company to bother keeping track of the fact that the other customer bought a chair from yesterday's production and you bought one from a prior month's production. But the company does have to record a reduction in the product costs accumulated in the Finished Goods Inventory account and assign them to the Cost of Goods Sold account as a result of its sales to both of you.

Several acceptable methods are used to determine what inventory costs to identify with a particular sale. These cost-flow methods are discussed shortly, and examples of each are presented later. It first must be noted, however, that the *accounting* cost-flow method chosen by management to assign inventory costs to the Cost of Goods Sold account need *not* match the actual *physical* flow of inventory items into and out of a company's warehouse or

EXHIBIT 9.4

Ryan Homes, Inc.
Inventory Method Disclosure: Specific Identification

Inventories

Inventories are stated at the lower of cost or market value. Cost of lots, completed and uncompleted housing units, and land in process of development represent the accumulated actual cost thereof. Field construction supervision salaries and related direct overhead expenses are included in inventory costs. Selling, general, and administrative costs are expensed as incurred. Upon settlement, the cost of the units is expensed on a specific identification basis.

showroom. As satisfying as it may be to know that inventory item no. 59, produced on June 11, 1999, was the item actually sold on August 20, 1999, and its particular cost is the cost deducted from the Finished Goods Inventory account and added to the Cost of Goods Sold account, there are other considerations, providing more valued benefits, that diminish the importance of such a strict tracking of actual inventory items sold. These other considerations are discussed in the following sections.

Specific Identification Method

This cost-flow method is usually reserved for high-value, easily distinguishable items such as cars and jewelry and *does* require individual accounting for each inventory item. Under this approach, the specific costs associated with an inventory item are "attached" to it and remain in the inventory account as long as that item is on hand. The **specific identification method** is the only cost-flow approach that results in the costs flowing from the balance sheet (that is, ending inventory) to the income statement (that is, cost of goods sold) in a sequence exactly matching the product's physical flow from storeroom to customer.

Exhibit 9.4 presents the inventory method footnote from the financial statements of Ryan Homes, Inc., a regional builder of residential dwellings in the mid-Atlantic and southeastern United States. It describes the company's use of the specific identification method and how a company's inventory cost-flow method might be presented in the financial statements. The decision by Ryan Homes to adopt this method appears quite reasonable—the company builds distinctive and expensive homes, which are generally sold one at a time.

The main disadvantage to the specific identification method is that its use is impractical for most types of businesses (such as mass merchandisers and mass manufacturers of homogeneous products) because of the very detailed inventory system required to track each item or each lot of goods purchased or manufactured. On the other hand, the matching of cost of goods sold to the sales revenue of the period perfectly matches the physical flow of specific inventory items, consequently achieving a perfect income statement matching of revenue generated from the item sold with its actual cost.

Average Cost Method

The **average cost method** accounts for inventory costs in a manner that is especially useful when it is impossible (or at least impractical) to attempt to specifically identify the particular units of inventory sold, typically because large volumes of many types of similar products

EXHIBIT 9.5

WLR Foods, Inc.
Inventory Method Disclosure: Average Cost

Inventories of feed, grain, eggs, packaging supplies, processed poultry and meat products are stated at the lower of cost or market as determined by the first-in, first-out valuation method. Live poultry and breeder flocks consist of poultry raised for slaughter and breeders. Poultry raised for slaughter are stated at the lower of average cost or market. Breeders are stated at average cost less accumulated amortization. The cost of breeders are accumulated during their development stage and then amortized into the cost of the eggs produced over the egg production cycle of the breeders.

A summary of inventories at June 27, 1998 and June 28,1997 follows:

Dollars in thousands	1998	1997
Live poultry and breeder flocks	$ 58,947	$ 74,984
Processed poultry and meat products	38,837	53,981
Packaging supplies, parts and other	15,879	17,188
Feed, grain and eggs	14,368	19,398
Total inventories	$128,031	$165,551

are sold. This is the case for such companies as food wholesalers, supermarkets, and retailers in general. For example, WLR Foods, Inc. (see Exhibit 9.5) uses the average cost method for its inventory of live poultry and breeder chickens.

The average cost method is based on the assumption that the cost of the items sold and therefore charged against revenue should be the average unit cost of all the items of a like kind available for sale during the period. The average cost of a particular inventory item (such as a live chicken at a WLR farm) is determined simply by dividing the sum of the different unit costs incurred in raising and processing the chickens during the year by the number of different unit costs represented in that period's chicken raising/processing activity. The resulting unit cost is used to compute both the balance sheet ending inventory cost and the income statement cost of goods sold. The advantages of this approach are that it is very easy to compute and it is very objective in its determination of profits for the period. The disadvantage is that the cost attributed to a single item is not, in reality, a cost that has ever been paid for the item (that is, it is an average).

A refinement of the simple average cost method is the **weighted-average cost method.** Under this method, the calculation of the cost of ending inventory (and cost of goods sold) is accomplished as under the simple average cost method except that the final average cost is weighted by the number of inventory units available at that cost. Where several significantly different costs are incurred in conjunction with significantly different volumes of activity, the weighted-average cost method is generally believed to be preferable to the simple average cost method because it takes into consideration the relative quantity of goods purchased at a given unit cost. Thus, if 100 units of inventory were purchased at $10 each and 1,000 at $14 each, the simple average cost method produces an average unit cost of only $12 (that is, ($10 + $14) ÷ 2), which does not reflect the substantial difference in quantities purchased at the two costs. The weighted-average cost per unit, however, would be $13.64

(that is, $[(100 \times \$10) + (1,000 \times \$14)] \div 1,100$ units), emphasizing the large volume of purchases at the higher cost of $14. The advantages and disadvantages of this method are the same as those for the average cost method.

First-in, First-out (FIFO)

The **first-in, first-out** cost-flow method accounts for inventory under the assumption that the first product physically purchased or manufactured is the first product physically sold. Remember that the actual physical flow of inventory does *not* need to be on a FIFO basis in order for a company to elect to account for its cost flow on a FIFO basis. Thus, under the FIFO method the costs assigned to the Cost of Goods Sold account for the products sold during the period are *not* the most recent costs paid, but they do represent an actual cost incurred for the item at some point in the past. In times of rapid inflation, the cost of goods sold under FIFO is likely to be low relative to a product's current replacement cost and current selling price, and will result in higher net income and thus higher income taxes payable vis-à-vis other inventory cost-flow methods. Because FIFO asserts a cost of goods sold focus, its equivalent for an ending inventory focus is **LISH—last in, still-here.** Thus, ending inventory account balances will approximate the product's current replacement cost, especially if inventory turnover is frequent (that is, if the inventory items are on hand for only a short period of time). In Exhibit 9.5, WLR Foods notes that its inventory of eggs, processed poultry, and meat products are accounted for by the FIFO method, a choice that is intuitively appealing given the perishable nature of the product that this company sells. Panel B in Exhibit 9.6 presents the Swedish company Electrolux's FIFO disclosure. Electrolux is one of the world's largest white goods, floor care products, and industrial laundry companies. In contrast to the perishable goods rationale for WLR Foods' choice of FIFO, Electrolux's products do not provoke a similar conclusion. Nonetheless, all of the company's inventories are accounted for on the FIFO basis.

Last-in, First-out (LIFO)

The **last-in, first-out** cost-flow method accounts for inventory under the assumption that the last product physically purchased or manufactured is the first one physically sold. As a consequence, the focus of ending inventory under LIFO is **first in, still-here (FISH).** Following the reasoning of the FIFO method, this approach means that under LIFO, the cost of the products sold closely approximates the current replacement cost of the product (i.e., the most recent costs incurred in acquiring the item).

For company management, LIFO has advantages and disadvantages just the opposite of those of FIFO. Whereas FIFO presents ending inventory in the balance sheet at an approximation of current **replacement cost** (that is, the most recent cost incurred in acquiring the item), the LIFO method states the ending inventory balance at a mixture of costs incurred in the distant past. In times of high inflation (deflation), the reported ending balance of the inventory account under LIFO can be significantly lower (higher) than under FIFO. On the other hand, FIFO does not report cost of goods sold at the most recent costs; the LIFO method approximates current replacement cost in arriving at the cost reported in the income statement for each product sold (except, as will be discussed later, when the quantity of inventory sold during the period exceeds the quantity acquired during the period). Exhibit 9.7 presents the inventory footnote disclosures from the annual reports of the Willamette Industries and the General Electric Company, both of whom predominantly use LIFO.

EXHIBIT 9.6

Electrolux
Inventory Method Disclosure: FIFO

Inventories are valued at the lower of acquisition cost and market value. Acquisition cost is computed according to the first-in, first-out method (FIFO). Appropriate provisions have been made for obsolescence.

(SEKm)	Group		Parent Company	
	1997	1996	1997	1996
Raw materials	4,126	3,138	142	112
Work in progress	847	2,319	23	23
Finished products	11,481	11,877	317	332
Advances to suppliers	102	213	—	—
Advances from customers	−446	−409	—	—
Total	16,110	17,138	482	467

These disclosures reveal a rich and useful set of inventory-related insights. For example, not all of General Electric's inventories are accounted for using the LIFO method. Indeed, the inventories of General Electric Capital Services (GECS) are accounted for not on a LIFO basis but on FIFO. Moreover, the current cost basis of the inventories that are accounted for on a LIFO basis is either determinable from the information provided (e.g., Willamette) or actually presented (e.g. GE). For Willamette, the cost that would have been reported for ending inventory if current costs had been used would have been $62.7 million higher than the reported 1997 LIFO cost. This difference in ending inventory value, often termed the **LIFO reserve,** also represents the *cumulative* decrease in pretax earnings (a part of owners' equity) through 1997 that Willamette has experienced as a consequence of being on the LIFO method instead of the FIFO method. In other words, if Willamette's inventories would have been higher by this amount, the company's cost of goods sold would have been lower, resulting in $62.7 million higher pretax profits under a current cost method. The portion of this decrease in pretax earnings for just 1997 is the difference between the 1997 cumulative inventory valuation differential and the 1996 cumulative inventory valuation differential, $62.7 million less $46.3 million, or $16.4 million. Given a 34 percent income tax rate for the company in 1997, taxes were $5.6 million less in 1997 than they would have been using a current cost (e.g., FIFO) valuation for those inventory items accounted for under the LIFO method. Thus, in 1997 alone, more than $5.6 million in cash was saved on income taxes by using the LIFO method. Indeed, such tax consequences are a major motivation for companies to adopt the LIFO method.

The GE disclosures present similar information, albeit the current cost vs. LIFO cost differential from 1996 to 1997 is in the opposite direction of Willamette's. This $119 million ($1,098-1,217) decline in the differential is due, as GE notes, to lower inventory quantities on hand at year end and cost decreases. It is interesting to observe that the LIFO reserve differential decreased in each of the three years presented, suggesting that GE is not currently experiencing the tax benefits normally afforded by LIFO.

EXHIBIT 9.7

Inventory Method Disclosure: LIFO

Panel A: Willamette Industries, Inc.

Inventories are valued at the lower of cost or market. Cost is determined on the last-in, first-out (LIFO) method for all major classes of inventory. All other inventories are valued at average cost.

The major components of inventories are as follows:

December 31, (in thousands)	1997	1996
Finished product	$118,046	108,090
Work in progress	7,404	6,182
Raw material	187,912	175,480
Supplies	81,233	76,197
	$394,595	365,949
Valued at:		
LIFO cost	$268,447	249,379
Average cost	126,148	116,570

If current cost rather than LIFO cost had been used by the Company, inventories would have been approximately $62,662 and $46,261 higher in 1997 and 1996 respectively.

Panel B: General Electric

All inventories are stated at the lower of cost or realizable values. Cost for virtually all of GE's U.S. inventories is determined on a last-in, first-out (LIFO) basis. Cost of other GE inventories is primarily determined on a first-in, first-out (FIFO) basis.

GECS inventories consist primarily of finished products held for sale. Cost is primarily determined on a FIFO basis.

December 31 (In millions)	1997	1996
GE		
Raw materials and work in process	$ 3,070	$ 3,028
Finished goods	2,895	2,404
Unbilled shipments	242	258
[Total inventories at current cost]	6,207	5,690
Less revaluation to LIFO	(1,098)	(1,217)
	5,109	4,473
GECS		
Finished goods	786	376
	$ 5,895	$ 4,849

LIFO revaluations decreased $119 million in 1997, compared with decreases of $128 million in 1996 and $87 million in 1995. Included in these changes were decreases of $59 million, $58 million and $88 million in 1997, 1996 and 1995, respectively, that resulted from lower LIFO inventory levels. There were net cost decreases in 1997 and 1996, and no cost change in 1995. As of December 31, 1997, GE is obligated to acquire certain raw materials at market prices through the year 2003 under various take-or-pay or similar arrangements. Annual minimum commitments under these arrangements are insignificant.

It is interesting to consider that from a balance sheet perspective, there is no sound conceptual basis for using LIFO. For example, if a company adopted LIFO in 1985, there simply is no merit to the possibility that its reported 1999 ending inventory figure would contain 1985 costs. Indeed, it is just this possibility that recently prompted the International Accounting Standards Committee to issue a draft proposal seeking to prohibit the use of LIFO for external financial statements. The proposal did gain a modicum of support, but in the end, the proposal was not approved. The committee's revised IAS No. 2 does, however, identify FIFO and weighted average as the preferred inventory cost-flow methods while merely acknowledging LIFO as an allowed alternative.[4] Worldwide, the most prevalent inventory methods are weighted-average and FIFO; LIFO is not available for use in all countries because of its conceptual deficiencies.

A Numerical Illustration

To assist you in understanding the calculations necessary to derive the cost of ending inventory to be presented in the balance sheet and the cost of goods sold for the income statement, we now consider a numerical illustration.

Assume that FHAS Company begins the year with 100 units of an item in inventory and makes the following additions to inventory:

	Quantity	Unit Cost	Total Cost
Beginning inventory:	100 units	@ $1.00	$100.00
Purchase no. 1	110 units	@ $1.10	121.00
Purchase no. 2	120 units	@ $1.25	150.00
Purchase no. 3	115 units	@ $1.50	172.50
Goods available for sale	445 units		$543.50

Assume further that the company sells 300 units for $2 cash per unit and has 145 units left in inventory at year-end. Reported ending inventory and cost of goods sold under the FIFO, LIFO, and weighted-average cost methods would be as follows:

FIFO

Sales (300 units at $2 per unit)			$600.00
Cost of goods available for sale		$543.50	
Less: Cost of goods sold			
100 units at $1.00	$100.00		
110 units at $1.10	121.00		
90 units at $1.25	112.50		
Cost of goods sold		(333.50)	(333.50)
Ending inventory (145 units)			
(115 units at $1.50 + 30 units at $1.25)		$210.00	
Gross profit			$266.50

Weighted-Average

Sales (300 units at $2 per unit)			$600.00
Cost of goods available for sale		$543.50	
Less: Cost of goods sold			
300 units at $1.2213*		(366.39)	(366.39)

[4] In some countries, other inventory valuation methods similar to LIFO are also permitted. For example, in Japan, the HIFO method, or highest-in, first-out, is acceptable. NIFO, or next-in, first-out, is generally not available because most countries base the valuation of inventories on actual, as opposed to replacement costs.

Ending inventory		
(145 units at $1.2213)	$177.11	
Gross profit		$233.61

* $543.50/445 units = $1.2213.

LIFO

Sales (300 units at $2 per unit)			$600.00
Cost of goods available for sale		$543.50	
Less: Cost of goods sold			
115 units at $1.50	$172.50		
120 units at $1.25	150.00		
65 units at $1.10	71.50		
Cost of goods sold		(394.00)	(394.00)
Ending inventory (145 units)			
(100 units at $1.00 + 45 units at $1.10)		$149.50	
Gross profit			$206.00

As these examples indicate, in times of rising costs and stable (or growing) ending inventory quantities, the cost of goods sold is highest using LIFO and lowest using FIFO, with the weighted-average cost method falling between them. The valuation of the units remaining in inventory is highest using FIFO and lowest using LIFO, again with weighted-average cost falling between the two. These characteristics are important when managers are contemplating what picture of their company to portray in the year-end financial statements.

An important part of inventory accounting under the LIFO method is the notion of **inventory layers** and **inventory-layer liquidation.** During a given period, if the inventory purchased or manufactured exceeds the quantities sold, the result is the addition of a "layer" (increment) to the ending inventory balance. Such was the case in the simple numerical example just presented—45 units were added during the period to the beginning inventory level of 100 units. This type of phenomenon is depicted in the 19X2 column in Exhibit 9.8. This 19X2 layer is distinct from the 19X1 layer preceding it in that it reflects an addition of units to ending inventory that will be reported at 19X2 costs. The 19X1 layer, on the other hand, will be costed at 19X1 costs. Together, the sum of the two layers' costs will be reported as the cost of inventory in the 19X2 balance sheet.

In Exhibit 9.8, the 19X2 ending inventory consists of 450 units, composed of a layer of 200 units from 19X1 and a layer of 250 units from 19X2. Both of these LIFO layers will be maintained in inventory through subsequent periods until a net decrease in inventory takes place when period sales exceed the period's production. When this occurs, the prior period's inventory layers are sequentially liquidated. For example, 19X3 witnessed a reduction of the 19X2 layer in the amount of 100 units. The liquidation of a LIFO layer results in the inventory costs of a prior period being used to determine, in part, the current period's cost of goods sold deducted from the current period's revenue. Assuming annual cost increases, the matching of these old (perhaps as much as three or four years) costs with current revenues will result in higher profits than if only current period costs had been used in figuring the current period's cost of goods sold. Note that in Panel B of Exhibit 9.7, General Electric's LIFO-valued inventories for certain products were reduced in 1997, and net income before taxes was increased by $59 million. As a consequence, GE's tax bill, at a 34 percent tax rate, increased $20 million due to this inventory reduction. Such a boost to 1997 earnings was certainly anticipated and orchestrated by GM management as opposed to its being merely "a pleasant surprise." Indeed, many companies are reducing inventory

EXHIBIT 9.8

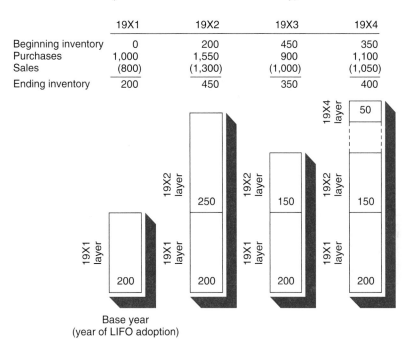

LIFO Layering
(all amounts are units of inventory)

	19X1	19X2	19X3	19X4
Beginning inventory	0	200	450	350
Purchases	1,000	1,550	900	1,100
Sales	(800)	(1,300)	(1,000)	(1,050)
Ending inventory	200	450	350	400

Base year
(year of LIFO adoption)

quantities on hand through outsourcing of production and/or just-in-time production techniques. Lowering inventory levels is often motivated by a desire to reduce the annual carrying costs associated with storing, handling, and insuring large quantities of goods, as well as a desire to garner the capital tied up in goods on hand and to minimize potentially large losses associated with obsolescence.

A prior year's layer, once liquidated, will never be reestablished in subsequent periods. This is true in Exhibit 9.8 for 19X4—a gap exists in the 19X2 layer for that part of the layer liquidated in 19X3, which will never be reestablished.

Inventory Systems: Periodic versus Perpetual

Determining how much of the goods available for sale during a period are still on hand and how much should be charged against income for the period is obviously critical to measuring a company's performance during a period. In addition to the cost-flow method decision, management must also adopt either a perpetual inventory system or a periodic inventory system to record ending inventory costs and cost of goods sold. Under a **periodic system,** the quantity of inventory on hand at any given time must be determined by physically counting the inventory items (usually once a year). The physical count, costed at an appropriate cost (LIFO, FIFO, or average), determines the balance sheet's ending inventory cost. The cost of goods sold for the period can then be determined from the basic relationship of beginning inventory *plus* purchases *minus* the costs attributable to ending inventory quantities. (A periodic system was assumed in the numerical examples above.)

When using a **perpetual system,** management maintains and regularly updates (often daily or, with computer assistance, continuously) an extensive inventory record-keeping system that is able to provide current inventory and cost of goods sold information on a moment's notice (rather than only after a physical count of items on hand). The perpetual system provides a continuous updating of both the Cost of Goods Sold and Ending Inventory account balances. Sound business practice suggests doing an occasional physical count of the inventory on hand to verify the accuracy of a perpetual system.

A final issue involving inventory systems, which will not be discussed at length here, involves the use of standard product costs rather than actual costs. **Standard product costs** are the estimated or projected costs of producing a product. Standard costs are widely used by managers for internal reporting and control purposes, and some companies carry this use over to external financial reporting. Inventory may be costed using standard cost estimates as long as the standard cost of the inventory is not materially different from actual costs. Regardless of whether management decides to use standard costs, decisions are still necessary regarding whether to use a periodic system or a perpetual system and what cost-flow method to adopt.

LOWER OF COST OR MARKET

As has been discussed to this point, the basis of accounting for inventories is historical cost (whether actual or standard), including all costs incurred to bring the goods to a salable condition. Such costs include, but are not limited to, transportation (inbound and/or outbound, depending on the circumstances), handling fees, labor costs, and manufacturing overhead costs. Costs resulting from the marketing and selling activities of a company, even those directly related to a particular product, are normally not included as part of inventory costs.

A departure from the historical cost basis in reporting inventories is necessary when the "market value" of the ending inventory falls below its "cost" (as determined under one of the cost-flow methods). This can occur because of spoilage, obsolescence, or falling market prices for the goods. For example, consider a computer leasing company. Large quantities of computers may be technologically superseded by a newer generation of computers. Inventories of the older generation of computers are not likely to maintain their previous marketability—thus, they decline in market value. This decline in market value should be recognized as an expense of the period in which the reduction in value takes place, and the Inventory account balance should be adjusted to the lower value. Such a reduction represents the application of the **lower-of-cost-or-market principle.** Most companies maintain inventory control systems to help them monitor changing market values and inventory obsolescence.

Certain guidelines pertain to the determination of an inventory's current market value. Because there is no New York Stock Exchange equivalent for all the various items composing different businesses' investments in inventories, specifying a market value can be quite subjective, and thus the need for guidelines exists. To avoid gross manipulations of the lower-of-cost-or-market principle, the accounting profession has defined *market value* as the *replacement cost* of an item. Replacement cost is the cost that a company would incur today to reproduce or reacquire a similar item. Information pertaining to replacement cost is usually compiled from vendor catalogs, engineering estimates, and/or appraisals.

EXHIBIT 9.9

Lower of Cost or Market for Inventory

1   Maximum "market" value
     (Ceiling = Net realizable value (NRV))

2   Replacement cost

3   Minimum "market" value
     (Floor = NRV − Normal profit)

Cost lower than market (chosen from 1, 2, or 3)?

If yes	If no
No inventory adjustment to "market"	Adjust inventory

Replacement cost, as a surrogate for market value, is subject to lower and upper boundaries that should be compared to the recorded historical cost in determining whether a lower-of-cost-or-market adjustment is needed.

The upper boundary (or *ceiling*) has been defined by accounting standard setters as the net realizable value (NRV) of the inventory, that is, the company's selling price of the item less the costs of completing its production and of selling it. The lower boundary (or *floor*) for setting the market value is net realizable value less a normal profit margin. Both boundaries are generalized attempts to keep market value within a reasonable range given the nature of a particular company's inventory and its selling market. As long as replacement cost lies between these two values, it is considered to be a fair approximation of market value. If replacement cost is below the lower boundary, the lower boundary amount is used as the best approximation of market value. Similar considerations apply to the upper boundary. Once a market value is ascertained, inventories should be reported at the lower of their historical cost or market value.

If, for example, a write-down of $1,000 of the inventory's cost is required because its market value has fallen below cost, the following journal entry is made:

Dr. Cost of Goods Sold (E) . . . . (inc.) 1,000
    Cr. Allowance for Decline in the Value of Inventory (CA) . . . .   (inc.) 1,000

Note that the decline in the inventory value is added to the cost of goods sold on the income statement, and an allowance account (a contra-asset account) is reported on the balance sheet as a deduction from the Inventory account. In fact, the allowance account is rarely seen on the balance sheet; most often it is netted out against the balance in the Inventory account.

Some companies avoid the use of an allowance account by crediting the amount of the inventory reduction directly against the Inventory account. In either case, once inventory values have been written down, they cannot be written back up even if the value of the inventory recovers its previously lost value.[5] Exhibit 9.9 summarizes these lower-of-cost-or-market considerations.

FINANCIAL STATEMENT DISCLOSURE

As we have seen in the inventory disclosures contained in earlier exhibits, the general requirements for financial statement disclosure for inventories include the following:

1. A description of the accounting principles a company used in determining reported inventory costs.

2. Reference to any accounting principles or methods of accounting peculiar to the industry in which a company operates.

3. Major categories of inventories.

To maintain interperiod comparability, financial statement readers may assume the consistent application of cost-flow methods from period to period. If, however, a change in inventory accounting method is adopted (such as from FIFO to LIFO), company management is required to disclose the nature of the change and its effect on net income, including, whenever possible, a restatement of prior years' financial statements as if the new method had been in effect during those prior years. The disclosures by Fruit of the Loom, Inc. and Richfood Holding, Inc. (a grocery chain holding company), regarding their changes in inventory accounting methods are presented in Exhibit 9.10.

Note that in April 1990 Richfood Holding changed from FIFO to LIFO for virtually all of its inventory. For the year subsequent to that change, net income was $640,000 less than it would have been had the company remained with FIFO. Such an impact highlights the rising cost nature of this business and points to the fact that ending inventory at April 1991, under the newly adopted LIFO method, is lower than if it had continued to be reported at more recent costs, as the FIFO method would have done. Indeed, the note points to a $1,024,000 difference in ending inventory figures. The note also highlights the fact that prior years' financial statements cannot be restated as if they too had been prepared using the LIFO method. Such a restatement is simply not possible because ending inventory would have to be converted to the "oldest" costs, and it would be purely arbitrary to assume any base prior year start point other than this year—the year of making the change.

On the other hand, Fruit of the Loom, Inc. discloses its change in 1997 from LIFO to FIFO and notes that a retroactive restatement is possible. Such a restatement actually results in the previously reported 1996 earnings being decreased by $4.6 million and the 1995 loss being increased by $.5 million. If additional prior years were reported in Fruit of the Loom's 1997 annual report, they too would be restated because for any previous year-end date, it is possible to determine what ending inventory costs would have been under FIFO. They would simply be those closest to that point in time. Notice that Fruit of the Loom and Richfood both claim that the change in method is prompted by a belief that a better matching of expenses and revenues is achieved by the new method.

---

[5] While under U.S. GAAP the value of inventory may not be written back up even if the inventory recovers in value, in some countries, an upward revaluation is permitted.

EXHIBIT 9.10

Financial Statement Disclosures:
Inventory Method Changes

Panel A: Richfood Holding, Inc., Change to LIFO

1. Inventories

The company values its inventory at the lower of cost or market. Effective April 29, 1990, the company changed its method of determining cost from the first-in, first-out (FIFO) method to the last-in, first-out (LIFO) method for approximately 91 percent of its inventories. Remaining inventories are stated at the lower of cost or market using the FIFO method (see Note 3).

3. Inventories (in thousands)

As a result of the change to the LIFO inventory valuation method for the fiscal year ended April 27, 1991 (see note 1), net earnings decreased by $640, or $0.06 per share. There is no cumulative effect for this change on prior years since the ending inventory as previously reported at April 28, 1990, is the beginning inventory for LIFO purposes. Accordingly, pro forma results of operations for the prior years had LIFO been followed are not determinable. The current replacement cost of LIFO inventories exceeded reported cost by $1,024 at April 27, 1991. The company believes that the use the LIFO method better matches current costs of goods sold with current revenues from inventory sales.

Panel B: Fruit of the Loom, Inc., Change to FIFO

Inventory costs include material, labor and factory overhead. Inventories are stated at the lower of cost (first-in, first-out) or market.

During the fourth quarter of 1997, the Company changed its method of determining the cost of inventories from the LIFO method to the FIFO method as it experienced reduced costs from offshore assembly operations and expects continuing cost reductions. The cost of inventories on a LIFO basis at December 31, 1997 was approximately equal to their replacement cost. Accordingly, the Company believes that the FIFO method will result in a better measurement of operating results. All previously reported results have been restated to reflect the retroactive application of this accounting change as required by generally accepted accounting principles. The accounting change increased the net loss for 1997 by $27,800,000 or $.37 per share. Due principally to the effect of LIFO allowance liquidations, net earnings previously reported for 1996 were reduced by $4,600,000 or $.06 per share, and the net loss previously reported for 1995 increased by $500,000 or $.01 per share.

Management Issues

A variety of inventory issues are of concern to merchandisers and manufacturers alike. One such issue pertains to the physical safeguarding of inventory items. Measures undertaken to prevent employee and/or customer theft often range from patrolling security personnel, to surveillance cameras, to limited access policies, to magnetic alarm strips, and unannounced physical inventory counting. In a related vein are the management concerns for precluding losses due to inventory obsolescence. Thus, we see the dating of perishables (such as food and pharmaceuticals) and the minimization of inventory quantities or the production to order of fashionable items (such as clothes, computers, and music CDs) as companies try to limit their exposure to obsolescence risk.

From a customer service vantage point, managers are concerned with avoiding stock outs. There is nothing quite so frustrating for a customer and a manager than to have a customer respond to a product ad, only to find it out of stock. Managers are fully aware of the customer ill will created by such experiences, and they try to maintain sufficient inventory levels to avoid such events. Carrying inventory, however, is costly. So while managers are trying to avoid stock outs they are also trying to minimize the company's funds tied up in inventory, their investment in warehouse space, and their inventory handling costs. Companies have studied the issue of inventory optimization and have, in many cases, implemented very sophisticated just-in-time (JIT) inventory management systems. Perhaps foremost among the innovators in addressing such concerns are Wal-Mart, American Hospital Supply, and Caterpillar.

Several management concerns are explicitly related to a choice to adopt the LIFO cost-flow method. First, if a U.S. company adopts LIFO for tax purposes, they generally are required by the U.S. Treasury to also use LIFO for externally published income statements. Thus, managers must weigh the cash tax savings that are achievable during periods of rising inventory quantities and costs against the lower earnings reported to shareholders. (The efficient-market hypothesis would assert that financial markets can see through this reporting convention and are not misled or misinformed about the firm's profitability.) Second, once on LIFO for tax purposes, U.S. companies wishing to subsequently switch to some other method must obtain permission to do so from the Internal Revenue Service. One other management LIFO issue pertains to the maintenance of the LIFO layers during periods of increasing costs. If near year-end it appears that a company's LIFO accounting for cost of goods sold will "dip into" a prior year's lower-cost LIFO layer due to this year's unit sales exceeding units purchased or manufactured, management may want to make a year-end purchase of inventory in order to preempt such a "dipping." Clearly, the efficacy of such a purchase, in the absence of any other business reason for it, needs to be considered by managers, if for no other reason than to avoid the additional taxes that are likely to result from a LIFO layer liquidation.

ANALYZING INVENTORIES

Analyzing a company's investment in inventories typically focuses on two questions: Is the investment in inventory likely to produce an adequate return to the company? Is the level of investment in inventory appropriate for anticipated future sales?

With respect to the first question, a widely used financial indicator is the **gross profit margin ratio:**

$$\text{Gross profit margin ratio} = \frac{\text{Gross profit margin}}{\text{Net sales}}$$

This ratio indicates the percentage of each sales dollar that is available to cover a company's period expenses and to provide a return to its owners *after* the cost of goods sold has been deducted. Clearly, the higher this ratio, the more profitable a company's sales of inventory will be. For 1998, Procter & Gamble's gross profit margin ratio is 0.43 [($37,154 − $21,064) ÷ $37,154], which is moderately high when compared to 0.15 for General Motors in 1997. An unacceptably low ratio may indicate several concerns: (1) the company is underpricing its products, or (2) when a product is competitively priced, the cost to manufacture it is too high, perhaps due to inefficiencies in the manufacturing process or in the purchase of raw materials or to the payment of excessively high wages to production employees. The gross profit margin ratio is important to managers because it allows them to determine whether the root of low earnings is attributable to the company's period costs or to its product costs. Likewise, this ratio is important to investors and creditors, enabling them to identify well-managed companies.

With respect to the second question above, two financial ratios are often reviewed: (1) the inventory turnover ratio, and (2) the average days inventory on hand. As discussed in Chapter 7, the **inventory turnover ratio** measures the number of times that the average level (or dollar investment) in inventory was sold, or "turned," during a given accounting period:

$$\text{Inventory turnover ratio} = \frac{\text{Cost of goods sold for the period}}{\text{Average inventory held during the period}}$$

In general, the higher the inventory turnover ratio the better. A relatively high turnover ratio such as Procter & Gamble's 6.6 ($21,064 ÷ 3,185) signals a reduced potential for losses attributable to product obsolescence, which in the case of Procter & Gamble indicates that it is probably incurring minimal costs to maintain an investment in inventory and, simply given the nature of Procter & Gamble's business, a high ratio is to be expected. GM's 1997 inventory turnover ratio is 10.8, indicating a fairly rapid transfer of inventory from GM's books to their dealers. Excessively high turnover ratios may be problematic if the cause is an insufficient investment in inventory. For example, when a company fails to maintain an adequate supply of inventory to meet its customers' needs, it may create order backlogs and customer dissatisfaction, not to mention the possibility of lost sales. On the other hand, a low ratio not warranted by the nature of the company's business may indicate excessive inventory that may not be salable.

The **average number of days' inventory on hand** ratio indicates the average number of days of inventory supplies on hand to meet customer needs, based on recent sales data:

$$\text{Average number of days' inventory on hand} = \frac{365 \text{ days}}{\text{Inventory turnover ratio}}$$

The 1997 average number of days' inventory on hand for Procter & Gamble was 55 days (365 ÷ 6.6), and 34 days for GM. This ratio is important because it reveals whether there is an adequate quantity of inventory on hand or whether there is an excessive quantity; the latter indicates the need to slow or halt production. For both GM and Procter & Gamble, these figures appear acceptable—neither too high to cause worries of slow-moving products nor too low to cause worries of not being able to meet customer orders. (If anything we might wonder why Procter & Gamble's inventory turnover is not higher.) Unfortunately, there is no ideal target for the average number of days' inventory on hand or for the inventory turnover ratio. In fact, these indicators vary substantially among industries and often within the same industry. As a general rule, potential investors, lenders, and managers are well advised to compare these indicators for a given company against the leading firm in that industry.

In conclusion, it is important to note that all of the financial indicators discussed are closely tied to the specific inventory cost-flow assumption utilized by a company. Thus, during a period of rising costs, it would be quite reasonable to expect that a FIFO-accounted company would have a higher gross profit margin ratio but lower inventory turnover ratio than would a LIFO-accounted company. In addition, for cross-company comparisons in which the companies use different cost-flow assumptions, the ending inventory and current period earnings amounts should be adjusted for the LIFO company so that it may be compared more appropriately to the FIFO company. Such adjustments would parallel those described earlier in Exhibit 9.7. A comparison of these three ratios, with and without LIFO, is presented for GM and Procter & Gamble in Exhibit 9.11. In order to determine the

---

EXHIBIT 9.11

1997 Inventory Ratio Analysis with and without LIFO Effects

	Procter & Gamble		General Motors	
	With LIFO	Without LIFO*	With LIFO	Without LIFO*
Gross profit margin ratio	0.43	0.44	0.15	0.16
Inventory turnover ratio	6.6	6.4	10.8	8.9
Average number of days' inventory on hand	55	57	34	41

---

* assumes 34 percent tax rate

"without LIFO" ratios for Procter & Gamble, the following additional information from its footnotes is necessary:

> Inventories are valued at cost which is not in excess of current market price. Cost is primarily determined by either the average cost or the first-in, first-out method. The replacement cost of last-in, first-out inventories exceeds carrying value by approximately $91 and $122 at June 30, 1998 and 1997, respectively.

Note that a significant difference in GM's inventory turnover ratio occurs when the effects of LIFO are deleted from ending inventory and cost of sales. As higher costs are left in inventory and lower costs are assigned to cost of sales (as is the case for adjusting GM to FIFO), inventory turnover does not appear as good. Thus, as seen here, inventory-related financial indicators should be investigated with an eye toward determining the likely impact of the inventory accounting method on the ratios themselves.

SUMMARY

For most nonservice companies, inventories represent a significant current asset. For merchandising companies, inventories may represent the largest single asset category.

Inventories (and cost of goods sold) are usually valued using one of several common cost-flow methods: FIFO, LIFO, or average cost. In addition, the ending inventory must always be evaluated relative to its market (or replacement) value to ensure that the value reported on the balance sheet is not overstated and approximates its net realizable value.

The effective management and utilization of inventory is a hallmark of a well-run company. Thus, analyzing the nature of and investment in inventories is important to investors, creditors, and managers. In addition to reviewing the financial statement disclosure relating to inventories, the financial statement user would be wise to calculate such asset management ratios as the inventory turnover ratio and the average number of days' inventory on hand ratio. These ratios are useful indicators of the quality of a given company's inventory management.

NEW CONCEPTS AND TERMS

Activity-based costing	LIFO reserve
Average cost method	Lower-of-cost-or-market principle
Average number of days' inventory on hand ratio	Manufacturing overhead
	Period costs
Direct labor costs	Periodic inventory system
Finished goods inventory	Perpetual inventory system
First-in, first-out (FIFO)	Product costs
First-in, still-here (FISH)	Raw materials inventory
Gross profit margin ratio	Replacement cost
Inventory layer	Specific identification method
Inventory-layer liquidation	Standard product costs
Inventory turnover ratio	Weighted-average cost method
Last-in, first-out (LIFO)	Work in process inventory
Last-in, still-here (LISH)	

ASSIGNMENTS

9.1. Cost-flow identification. Fill in the blank beside each numbered statement below with one of the inventory cost flow methods discussed in the chapter.

_____ 1. Cost of goods sold is highest for a period wherein inventory purchase costs continuously rose.

_____ 2. The ending inventory is reported at the latest purchase cost.

_____ 3. Achieves best matching of current costs with current revenues in the income statement.

_____ 4. Provides the greatest cash tax savings in a period of rising purchase costs.

_____ 5. Results in the highest ending inventory valuation after a period of steadily declining purchase costs.

9.2. Calculating inventory values. The following cost data from the month of June were taken from the records of The Fertilizer Store:

Beginning inventory:		1,100 lbs. at $ 8	$ 8,800
Purchases:	June 2	2,100 lbs. at $10	21,000
	June 5	600 lbs. at $ 9	5,400
	June 12	1,200 lbs. at $12	14,400
	June 15	800 lbs. at $11	8,800
	June 20	200 lbs. at $10	2,000
			$51,600

June sales totaled $72,000 (4,500 lbs. at $16.00 per lb.), and occurred as follows:

June 10	1,500 lbs.
June 17	2,000 lbs.
June 25	1,000 lbs.

Compute each of the following under LIFO and FIFO, assuming both the periodic and the perpetual systems. In addition, apply the lower-of-cost-or-market principle under the assumption that the year-end market price is $10 per pound.

a. Cost of goods sold.

b. Ending inventory.

c. Gross profit.

9.3. Evaluating inventory errors. Summit Corporation hired a new accountant during June who, it was discovered, had made at least four major mistakes (noted below). Note the June and July financial statement effect of each by completing the table below. Note the effect as: O = overstated, U = understated, and N = no effect. You may ignore taxes and assume that the company uses the periodic inventory system.

Mistake 1. The accountant did not record a $4,000 June credit sale until July. The merchandise was shipped in June and was not included in the June ending inventory. The customer paid for the goods in July.

Mistake 2. The accountant did not record a $6,000 June purchase on account until July when a check was cut to the supplier. The goods were also missed in the June month-end physical count.

Mistake 3. The accountant included $3,000 of obsolete inventory in the June year end inventory count. The obsolete inventory was finally written off in July.

Mistake 4. The accountant treated $10,000 of June manufacturing overhead as a June period cost. In July, all manufacturing costs were properly treated as product costs.

		Total Revenue	Total Expense	Net Income	Total Assets	Total Liabilities	Total Owners' Equity
June	Mistake 1						
	Mistake 2						
	Mistake 3						
	Mistake 4						
July	Mistake 1						
	Mistake 2						
	Mistake 3						
	Mistake 4						

9.4. Calculating cost of goods sold. The following information pertains to Skeen Manufacturing Corporation, a manufacturer of hotel bedroom furniture:

Beginning inventories:	
Raw materials	$ 11,000
Work in process	5,000
Ending inventories:	
Raw materials	16,500
Work in process	6,600
Raw materials used	77,000
Direct labor	55,000
Total manufacturing costs	167,000
Cost of goods available for sale	170,000
Cost of goods sold	159,000
Gross profit	135,000

Required:

Compute the following:

a. Raw materials purchased.

b. Raw materials available for use.

c. Manufacturing overhead.

d. Cost of goods manufactured.

e. Sales.

f. Beginning finished goods inventory.

g. Ending finished goods inventory.

9.5. LIFO vs. FIFO. DFW, Inc., began business on January 1, 19X1, after taking over the business of Dallas–Ft. Worth Partnership. Partnership had been a manufacturer of custom souvenir products. At the time of the takeover, Partnership had on hand 7,500 Dallas Cowboy souvenir pennants valued at $1.35 each.

DFW, Inc., operated as a wholesale manufacturer from 19X1 through 19X6, selling its custom-designed pennants to various retail stores and distributors throughout the Texas area. During that period, the cost to produce and handle the pennants rose steadily, and by the end of 19X5, the cost had increased to $3 per pennant.

During 19X6, however, the price spiral finally broke. A general recession throughout the United States had caused a drop in the cost of labor (unemployment in Texas had exceeded 7 percent) and in the cost of many raw materials. By mid-19X6, the cost to produce a pennant had fallen to approximately $1.35.

Required:

Assume that DFW, Inc., ended 19X6 with 5,000 pennants on hand and that the manufacturer regularly maintained a base stock of at least 5,000 pennants at all times. Based on these facts, indicate whether each of the following statements is true or false, and explain your reasoning.

a. Both LIFO and FIFO would produce exactly the same total reported profit for the period 19X1–19X6.

b. LIFO would show a higher profit for 19X6.

c. FIFO would show a higher profit for 19X1.

d. The inventory of pennants on the balance sheet at year-end 19X3 would be valued higher if LIFO were used.

e. The inventory of pennants on the balance sheet at year-end 19X6 would be $6,750 under both LIFO and FIFO.

f. LIFO would show a lower profit than FIFO for each of the years 19X1 through 19X5.

9.6. LIFO company versus FIFO company. Presented below are the financial statements of two companies that are identical in every respect except the method of valuing their inventories. The method of valuing inventory is LIFO for LIFO Company and FIFO for FIFO Company.

Comparative Income Statements

	FIFO Company	LIFO Company
Sales	$20,000,000	$20,000,000
Less: Cost of sales	9,200,000	11,280,000
Gross profit	$10,800,000	$ 8,720,000
Less: Operating expenses	5,000,000	5,000,000
Net income before tax	$ 5,800,000	$ 3,720,000

Comparative Balance Sheets

	FIFO Company	LIFO Company
Assets		
Cash	$ 3,000,000	$ 3,000,000
Receivables	6,000,000	6,000,000
Inventory	3,800,000	1,720,000
Total current assets	$12,800,000	$10,720,000
Total noncurrent (net)	20,000,000	20,000,000
Total	$32,800,000	$30,720,000
Equities		
Current liabilities	$ 4,200,000	$ 4,200,000
Noncurrent liabilities	9,000,000	9,000,000
Total liabilities	$13,200,000	$13,200,000
Total owners' equity	19,600,000	17,520,000
Total	$32,800,000	$30,720,000

Required:

Using the two sets of financial statements, calculate the following ratios or financial indicators for each firm:

a. Current ratio.

b. Inventory turnover ratio.

c. Average days' inventory on hand.

d. Return on total assets.

e. Total debt to total assets.

f. Long-term debt to owners' equity.

g. Gross margin ratio.

h. Return on sales.

i. Return on owners' equity.

j. Earnings per share (assume 2 million shares outstanding).

Based on the above ratios in part (a)–(j), which company represents

k. The best investment opportunity?

l. The best acquisition opportunity?

m. The best lending opportunity?

9.7. Ratio analysis. Presented below are some recent summary financial data for the Coca-Cola Co. and PepsiCo, Inc.

	1997	1996
Cost of goods sold (in millions):		
Coca-Cola	$6,015	$6,738
PepsiCo	8,525	8,452
Year-end inventory (in millions):		
Coca-Cola	959	952
PepsiCo	732	853

Required:

Using the above data, calculate the inventory turnover and the average number of days' inventory on hand for 1997 for each company. What is your evaluation of each company's inventory management policy?

9.8. Lower of cost or market. Sue Smith was the proprietor of a computer games store. She had recently decided to expand her inventory. To finance the increased inventory, she decided to approach the Wachovia Bank for a loan.

In preparation for a meeting with her accountant to prepare the financial statements that she knew the bank would want, she collected the following information about some of her inventory.

	Computer Game				
	A	B	C	D	E
Cost	$15.00	$15.00	$15.00	$15.00	$15.00
Net realizable value	16.00	17.00	14.00	14.50	14.50
Net realizable value less her normal store profit	14.00	16.00	13.50	14.00	14.00
Replacement cost	16.50	15.50	13.00	14.30	14.75
Quantity in the store	10	8	15	20	15

Required:

For a balance sheet presentation, ascertain the carrying value of this part of Sue's computer games inventory.

9.9. Inventory decisions. Noel Company sells food additives and uses LIFO inventory. One of the company's raw material inventory on January 1, 19X1, consisted of 3,000 lbs. costed at $20 per pound. Purchases and ending inventories in the subsequent years were as follows:

Year	Average Purchase Price per Pound during Year	Costs of Purchases	December 31 Inventory
19X1	25	$384,000	3,600 lbs.
19X2	28	352,000	2,600 lbs.
19X3	30	448,000	4,000 lbs.

Because of temporary scarcities, the raw material is expected to cost $40 per pound in 19X4. Sales for 19X4 are expected to require 7,000 pounds of the raw material. The purchasing agent suggests that the inventory be allowed to decrease to 600 pounds by the end of 19X4 and be replenished to 4,000 pounds in early 19X5. The controller argues that such a policy is foolish. She argues that if inventories are allowed to decrease, the company will pay a very large amount in income taxes (at its current income tax rate of 34 percent). She suggests that the company maintain a 19X4 year-end inventory of 4,000 pounds.

Required:

a. Calculate the cost of goods sold and the dollar value of ending inventory for 19X4 for both scenarios.

	Purchasing Agent	Controller
Cost of goods sold	$ _____	$ _____
Ending inventory	$ _____	$ _____

b. Calculate the tax savings for 19X4 if the advice of the controller is followed rather than that of the purchasing agent.

c. If you were making the decision, what other information might you consider in choosing whose advice to follow?

9.10. Inventory disclosures. Presented below is the inventory footnote taken from a recent Merck & Co., Inc., annual report. When necessary, assume a 40 percent corporate income tax rate.

Merck & Co., Inc. and Subsidiaries
Notes to Financial Statements

Substantially all domestic inventories are valued using the last-in, first-out method (LIFO). Remaining inventories are valued at the lower of first-in, first-out (FIFO) cost or market.

	(in millions)	
Inventories at December 31 consisted of:	19X1	19X0
Finished goods	$359.6	$299.5
Raw materials and work in process	343.0	335.1
Supplies	46.4	41.5
Total (approximate current cost)	749.0	676.1
Reduction to LIFO cost	89.4	96.3
	$659.6	$579.8

Inventories valued at LIFO composed approximately 46 percent and 42 percent of inventories at December 31, 19X1 and 19X0, respectively.

Required:

a. What dollar amount for inventories appears in Merck's December 31, 19X1, balance sheet?

b. If Merck had used current costs for ending inventory valuation rather than those generated by LIFO:

(1) What dollar amount would have appeared for inventories in its December 31, 19X1, balance sheet?

(2) To what extent would its December 31, 19X1, retained earnings balance be different? Higher or lower?

(3) To what extent would its 19X1 net income be different? Higher or lower?

9.11. Inventory disclosures. The 19X2 Reynolds Metals annual report contained the following footnote description of its accounting policies with respect to inventories:

Note A—Significant Accounting Policies

Inventories

Inventories are stated at the lower of cost or market. Cost of inventories of approximately $283 million in 19X2 and $321 million in 19X1 is determined by the last-in, first-out method (LIFO). Remaining inventories of approximately $422 million in 19X2 and $385 million in 19X1 are determined by the average or first-in, first-out (FIFO) methods. If the FIFO method was applied to LIFO inventories, the amount for inventories would increase by approximately $576 million at December 31, 19X2, and $498 million at December 31, 19X1. As a result of LIFO, costs and expenses increased by $78 million in 19X2 and $29 million in 19X1 and decreased by $60 million in 19X0. Included in the total LIFO effect are liquidations of prior year inventories of $26 million in 19X0.

Since certain inventories of the company may be sold at various stages of processing, no practical distinction can be made between finished products, in-process products, and other materials, and therefore inventories are presented as a single classification.

Required:

a. What would the balance sheet inventory amounts have been in 19X2 and 19X1 if all inventories had been reported on a FIFO basis?

b. Please explain the significance of using LIFO for some inventories and FIFO for others. Why do you think Reynolds Metals does this?

c. Explain what happened to Reynolds's inventories in 19X0.

d. Suppose Reynolds had always used FIFO for all inventories and assume the company's 19X2 income tax rate was 34 percent. What difference would it have made in its 19X2 income statement? The balance sheet as of December 31, 19X2? The 19X2 cash flow statement?

9.12. Inventory cost flows: Paragon Electronics, Inc.* One of the first tasks Greg Lemond was assigned on his recent appointment as assistant controller of Paragon Electronics, Inc., involved a review of Paragon's accounting for inventories. One of the specific requests made by Maria Sells, the controller, had been for Lemond to investigate the financial results of two different cost-flow methods: LIFO and weighted average. Paragon uses the periodic FIFO cost-flow method. Lemond contemplated what might be the most informative means to make the appropriate comparisons.

Paragon Electronics, Inc., was a small electronics firm that specialized in the design and production of state-of-the-art electronic systems for advanced Department of Defense projects. Under one particular new project, Paragon had a contract to supply a "package" of subassemblies that were used by a much larger prime contractor (Aero, Inc.) in the production of a new guidance system. Aero, Inc., made all but a select few of the subassemblies used to build the completed guidance system. For those that it did not make, it had chosen a single-source supplier, Paragon, in order to minimize contracting and administrative costs. Paragon manufactured all of the subassemblies contracted to it by Aero, Inc., except the pulsed integrated gyro accelerometer (PIGA). Paragon had found that it would be possible to purchase the PIGA subassemblies from an outside source at a price roughly equivalent to what Paragon's production costs would be. The option of purchasing the PIGAs allowed Paragon to (1) meet its component "package" contract with Aero, Inc., and (2) pursue other contract opportunities using the facilities that would otherwise have been used for PIGA production.

Lemond decided to use the PIGA inventory for his LIFO, FIFO, and weighted-average inventory method comparisons because, for a distinct component not produced internally, he would not have to be concerned with such issues as cost allocations, transfer prices, and so on. He recalled that under the Aero, Inc., contract, Paragon was to supply 500 PIGAs over a six-year period at a price of $950 per unit. Due to production constraints and demands from other programs, Paragon's sole-source supplier would commit to provide only 100 PIGAs a year over a five-year period. The PIGAs would be purchased at the beginning of the year. The unit costs for the PIGAs would increase the first two years due to the market's limited supply but then would decline as competitive sources came on line. Applicable freight and handling costs were included in the purchase price. Relevant selling and general and administrative expenses were expected to be $6,000 a year through 2000 and $2,000 in 2001. For analytical purposes, all purchases and sales between Paragon and its suppliers and customer could be assumed to be on a cash basis.

Lemond noted all of this information and developed a form (shown following) to analyze the PIGA pro forma inventories under the three different cost-flow assumptions. After completing the three relevant versions of this form, Lemond planned to analyze the impact of each of the three methods on each year's balance sheet (see the December 31, 1995, balance sheet), income statement, and cash flow (assuming a 46 percent income tax rate, the same inventory method was used for book and tax purposes, and all taxes are paid currently).

Required:

Perform the analysis Lemond intends to do.

LIFO

Year Total	PIGA Purchases by Paragon Units	Unit Cost	Units Sold to Aero, Inc.	Ending Inventory Units	Unit Cost	Total	Cost of Goods Sold Units	Unit Cost	Total
1996	100	$700	80						
1997	100	800	110						
1998	100	850	92						
1999	100	750	104						
2000	100	650	94						
2001	–0–	N/A	20						

FIFO

1996	100	$700	80
1997	100	800	110
1998	100	850	92
1999	100	750	104
2000	100	650	94
2001	–0–	N/A	20

Weighted Average

1996	100	$700	80
1997	100	800	110
1998	100	850	92
1999	100	750	104
2000	100	650	94
2001	–0–	N/A	20

Paragon Electronics, Inc.
Balance Sheet
For the Year Ending December 31, 1995

Assets		Liabilities & Owners' Equity	
		Liabilities	
Cash	$ 500,000	Account payable	$ 300,000
Accounts receivable	140,000	Accrued expenses	100,000
Inventory	700,000	Current liabilities	400,000
Current assets	$1,340,000	Bond payable	200,000
		Total liabilities	$ 600,000
		Owners' Equity	
Property, plant, and equipment	2,000,000	Retained earnings	$1,140,000
		Common stock	1,600,000
Total assets	$3,340,000	Total equity	$2,740,000
		Total liabilities and owners' equity	$3,340,000

9.13. LIFO valuation—Champion Spark Plug Company.* Champion Spark Plug Company was principally involved in manufacturing, distributing, and marketing spark plugs, windshield wipers, and other automotive components. Through various subsidiaries, however, Champion was also engaged in manufacturing coating application equipment, health care equipment, and cold-drawn steel. Champion made more than 850 types of spark plugs, diesel-starting glow plugs, and related items for a wide array of power-driven devices. Consider the following excerpts from Champion's 1980 annual report:

	(in millions)		
	1980	**1979**	**1978**
Net earnings	$ 36.9	$ 56.9	$ 55.3
Inventory	$261.4	$240.8	$227.1

In 1979 the company adopted the last-in, first-out (LIFO) method of determining costs for substantially all of its U.S. inventories. In prior years, inventory values had been principally computed under the lower-of-cost-or-market, first-in, first-out (FIFO) method. The effect of the change on the operating results for 1979 was to reduce net earnings by $5.8 million, or $0.15 per share.

Inventory balances at December 31, 1980 and 1979, would have been $26.8 million and $10.7 million higher, respectively, if U.S. inventory costs had continued to be determined principally under FIFO rather than LIFO. Net earnings on a primarily FIFO method basis would have been $45.6 million, or $1.19 per share [in 1980] compared to $62.7 million, or $1.64 per share, in 1979.

During 1980, certain inventory balances declined below the levels at the beginning of the year, resulting in a smaller increase in the LIFO reserve than would have occurred if these inventory levels had not declined. Net earnings in 1980 would have been $1.3 million ($0.03 per share) lower had the LIFO reserve addition not been affected by reduced inventories.

It was not practical to determine prior year effects of retroactive LIFO application.

---

* Copyright © 1986 by the Darden Graduate School Foundation, Charlottesville, Virginia. All rights reserved.

Required:

Using the financial information provided, identify the unknowns in the table below. Assume that the effective tax rate for Champion during 1979 and 1980 was 46 percent. (Because the rate was actually a fraction less than 46 percent, any minor "unexplained" differences can be attributed to rounding errors.)

		1980	1979	1978
a.	Inventories on LIFO basis	$ ____	$ ____	NA
b.	Inventories on FIFO basis	$ ____	$ ____	$ ____
c.	Cumulative decrease in pretax earnings resulting from switch to LIFO	$ ____	$ ____	NA
d.	Single-year decrease in pretax earnings resulting from switch to LIFO	$ ____	$ ____	NA
e.	Single-year decrease in after-tax earnings resulting from switch to LIFO	$ ____	$ ____	NA

NA = Not available.

For 1987, Champion's inventory disclosures in the annual report provided the following information:

	(in millions)	
	1987	**1986**
Net earnings	$ 19.1	$ (17.2)
Inventory	$189.9	$174.6

Total inventory costs determined by the LIFO method were $94.3 million at December 31, 1987, and $94.9 million at December 31, 1986. LIFO inventories were $30.9 million and $29.0 million less than estimated current costs at December 31, 1987 and 1986, respectively.

During 1987, 1986, and 1985, certain inventory reductions resulted in liquidations of LIFO inventory quantities. The effect of the reductions was to increase 1987 net earnings by $0.5 million, decrease the 1986 net loss by $0.2 million, and decrease 1985 net earnings by $0.3 million.

In 1986, the company refined its classification of certain costs used in the valuation of domestic inventories. Such reclassifications resulted in a more uniform approach to the valuation of inventories by all domestic operations. The effect of these classification changes was to increase 1986 cost of goods sold by approximately $4.9 million.

Required:

f. What is Champion describing when it talks about "liquidations of LIFO inventory quantities?"

g. Were the reported LIFO inventory dollar balances affected by these liquidations at the end of each of these three years? If so, by what amount? If not, why not? (Note that in 1987 Champion's income tax rate changed from 46 percent to 40 percent.)

9.14. LIFO valuation—Boyd Enterprises.* Boyd Enterprises is a manufacturer of parts used mainly in facsimile equipment and other small office machines. For many years, the company manufactured these parts in several states across the United States. Early in 1989, however, one of the company's principal customers announced its intention to buy machines completely ready for assembly from Japan. The news forced Boyd to close its Texas plant and dispose of its inventories at that location.

---

* This case was prepared by Kenneth R. Ferris and Michael F. van Breda. Copyright 1990 by Michael F. van Breda and Kenneth R. Ferris.

The company's 1989 annual report, which appeared early in 1990, disclosed that the closure of the Texas facility had precipitated a dramatic deterioration in its business accompanied by a significant liquidation of its inventories. The notes to the financial statements made the following facts about its inventories available to shareholders.

Note 1—Summary of Significant Accounting Policies

Inventories are stated at the lower-of-cost-or market value. Cost of inventories is determined by the last-in, first-out method (LIFO), which is less than current cost by $87,609 and $55,952 at December 28, 1988, and December 30, 1989, respectively.

During 1989, inventory quantities were reduced, resulting in a liquidation of LIFO inventory quantities carried at lower costs prevailing in prior years as compared with the 1989 cost of production. As a result, income before taxes was increased by $62,310, equivalent to $2.10 per share after applicable income taxes, of which $26,190 before tax, equivalent to $0.88 per share after applicable income taxes, was reflected in cost of product sold; the balance was included as a reduction of the shutdown/disposal provision (see Note 6).

Note 6—Shutdown Disposal Provision

In the third quarter of 1989, a provision was recorded for the closing of the Texas facilities, which are to be sold or otherwise disposed of. The after-tax provision of $55,595 is equivalent to $2.93 per common share and covers estimated losses on the disposition of property, plant, equipment, inventories, employee severance, and other costs. Net sales of products from these facilities included in consolidated sales totaled $92,465 in 1987, $121,012 in 1988, and $147,554 in 1989.

The note regarding quarterly results told a similar story.

Note 12—Quarterly Results (Unaudited)

During the third and fourth quarters of 1989, inventory quantities were reduced, resulting in a liquidation of LIFO inventory quantities carried at lower costs prevailing in prior years as compared with the cost of 1989 production. As a result, income before taxes was increased by $62,310, equivalent to $2.10 per share after applicable income taxes, of which $36,120 before taxes, equivalent to $1.22 per share after applicable income taxes, was included as a reduction of the shutdown/disposal provision, with the balance reflected in cost of goods sold.

Examination of its situation revealed that in 1986 Boyd had moved from keeping its inventory on a first-in, first-out (FIFO) basis to a LIFO basis. A note to the financial statements at the time described the change.

Note 2—Change in Inventory Valuation Method

In 1986 the company adopted the last-in, first-out (LIFO) method of determining costs for substantially all of its U.S. inventories. In prior years, inventory values were principally computed under the lower-of-cost-or-market, first-in, first-out (FIFO) method.

The effect of the change on the operating results for 1986 was to reduce net earnings after tax by $4,714, or 25 cents per share. The inventory balance at December 31, 1986, would have been $7,365 higher if inventory costs had continued to be determined principally under FIFO rather than LIFO.

It was not practical to determine prior year effects of retroactive LIFO application.

The income statements for the years 1986 through 1989, along with the inventory shown in the balance sheet for each year, appear here. Details of the units purchased each year are also presented.

Boyd Enterprises
Selected Financial Data

	1986	1987	1988	1989
Revenue	$1,058,422	$1,236,091	$1,421,526	$1,277,107
Cost of sales	797,232	958,210	1,085,134	971,550
Gross margin	261,190	277,881	336,392	305,557
Selling and administration	192,775	207,332	209,884	212,567
Loss on write-off (net)	–0–	–0–	–0–	55,595
Income tax	24,629	25,398	45,543	33,476
Net income	43,785	45,151	80,965	3,919
Inventory (per ending balance sheet)	$ 147,304	$ 208,948	$ 232,006	$ 111,904

Required:

Using the 1986 footnote, explain the change in the inventory valuation from FIFO to LIFO. What are the costs and benefits of such an accounting change? Compute the LIFO reserve for each year and show how the company arrived at the effect of $62,310 for the liquidation of LIFO inventory in 1989. Assume an effective tax rate of 36 percent.

Boyd Enterprises
Inventory Summary

	Units	Unit Cost
Opening inventory	60,000	$2.00
Purchases in 1986	103,652	2.00
	293,920	2.10
Sales in 1986	383,920	—
Purchases in 1987	282,220	2.20
	153,450	2.60
Sales in 1987	407,650	—
Purchases in 1988	193,210	2.70
	202,250	2.90
Sales in 1988	386,920	—
Purchases in 1989	196,320	2.90
	82,000	3.00
Sales in 1989	332,580	

CHAPTER 10

Active Investments and Business Combinations

*Marriage is not just spiritual communion and passionate
embraces; marriage is also three-meals-a day and
remembering to carry out the trash.*[1]

Key Chapter Issues

- Why is the accounting required for an active investment different than the accounting required for a passive investment?
- An investor can obviously own any proportion of the outstanding stock of an investee company; how does the accounting vary as that percentage of ownership increases?
- What difference does it make whether a parent company creates a new subsidiary starting with its own capital contribution, or whether the parent acquires the subsidiary from a prior investor?

- If the parent company acquires an interest in another company by paying cash, isn't that the same as if it had bought those assets and liabilities individually?
- What happens if the parent company makes that acquisition using common stock rather than cash?
- The parent company might buy a subsidiary in part to purchase its assets and liabilities but also in part to acquire its reputation. How is the value of that reputation recorded in the acquisition?

[1] J. Brothers, "When Your Husband's Affection Cools," *Good Housekeeping,* May 1972.

I n Chapter 8 we discussed the accounting a company follows when it has a **passive investment** in another company. We said that mark-to-market accounting applies to any situation where the nature of the investment, or the size of the investment, was such that the investor company was just that—an investor. Mark-to-market accounting applies to situations where the investor company *is not* in a position to exercise any significant amount of influence over the activities of the investee company (typically because the investor's ownership is in bonds or preferred stock or because the investor owns less than 20 percent of the investee's common stock). This chapter discusses the accounting for **active investments**—those investments where the investor company owns more than 20 percent of the (voting) common stock of another company and, as a result, is able to exercise a significant degree of influence over the policies and operations of that investee company.

Active investments are those intercompany relationships where—as the opening quote from Dr. Joyce Brothers suggests—the two companies work together day-to-day for their common good.

First, however, this chapter looks at the nature of intercorporate investments and explores why the accounting for an active investment in another company might be different than the accounting required for a passive investment. Building on that understanding of intercorporate investing, the chapter then discusses the accounting to be followed when one company has an active investment in another company, focusing primarily on situations where the investee company was started by the investor company. Finally, the chapter looks at the accounting to be followed when the investor company gains a significant ownership interest in an investee company, acquiring that interest from a prior owner.

THE NATURE OF
INTERCORPORATE INVESTMENTS

There are many reasons why one company might make an investment in another. The simplest reason for such an investment is to earn a return on the funds invested. But an investor company might also invest in another so that the investee can grow (expand its distribution network, for example) and become a larger customer for the investor's products. Or the reverse could be true: The investor could make an investment in an investee company to help the investee company develop its capabilities (a natural resource, for example) and thereby become a more reliable supplier to the investor. Where the objective of the investment is exclusively to earn a financial return, or where the objective is a combination of earning a return and supporting the investee, the investor company can pick from a range of investment vehicles. The investment can be in the form of an informal cash advance, a formal loan, or a purchase of the investee's bonds, preferred stock, or common stock. Most often those investments will be passive investments because the investor usually must accept the decisions of investee management; if the investor is not happy with those decisions, the only recourse it usually has is to sell the investment.

Under normal circumstances, neither the making of a loan to an investee company nor the ownership of a company's bonds or preferred stock gives the investor any power or influence over the investee's operations. The only investment vehicle that gives the investor any voice in the activities of the investee is an investment in common stock. The distinguishing characteristic of an investment in common stock is the right it conveys to elect members of the investee's board of directors and, through the board, to influence decisions of the investee's management. It is that characteristic, the ability to vote for the board of directors and the ability to influence investee management, that is the focus of this chapter. Here we are interested only in investments in common stock and, further, only in situations where the size of that investment is large enough that the investor's wishes must, at the very least, be given serious consideration by investee management. The discussion in this chapter assumes that both the *investor* and the *investee* are corporations and not individuals; further, the discussion assumes that the companies are commercial corporations and not mutual funds or other financial institutions. Mutual fund accounting and the accounting for banks and insurance companies are both unique and beyond our inquiry here.

An investor company can own any amount of the common stock of the investee, and the degree of influence the investor exercises will vary directly with the percentage of the investee's stock it owns. The most common investor–investee common stock relationship is a parent–subsidiary relationship. In those situations, the investor owns such a large percentage of stock that it is able to control completely the activities of the investee. When two companies are in such a close-knit relationship, the investor company is usually referred to as the **parent** and the investee as the **subsidiary.**

It is theoretically possible for a company to conduct all of its business through a single legal corporate entity. Only the smallest companies operate in that form, however. Most business entities of any size are composed of a parent corporation that owns the stock of various subsidiary corporations, which in turn might own the stock of still other sub-subsidiary corporations. For tax or legal reasons it may be important for the entity to conduct its business in one particular state, or in another country, in the form of a separate corporation. For risk protection purposes, it may also be advisable to legally isolate certain aspects of the overall business in a separate subsidiary corporation.

From an accounting standpoint, the legal corporate structure is usually invisible. As readers of the Procter & Gamble annual report, or even as investors, we will never know how many separate companies make up the Procter & Gamble network. In accounting, a substance-over-form perspective is adopted wherein if the parent company owns a controlling interest in the common stock of a subsidiary, the two legal entities are viewed as one business entity and their financial results are presented in *consolidated* financial statements. That position is based on the understanding that a controlling shareholder can cause its subsidiary to do whatever the parent wishes. Because of its controlling stock ownership, a parent company can cause the subsidiary to pay dividends on command, transfer products at arbitrary prices, or even dissolve itself—subject only to certain legal protections for any minority shareholders. In other countries, the legal status of a corporation is more sacred than in the United States and there are many more restrictions on the actions a parent can cause a subsidiary to undertake. Nonetheless, even in the most legally oriented societies, it has become clear that the relationships between parent and subsidiary companies are so close (and non–arm's length in nature) that it is necessary to see them as parts of one larger, single entity; thus, we focus on the financial results of the entity as a whole rather than on its parts.

In addition to the intercompany investments between a legal parent and its wholly owned subsidiaries, the investor company might have investments in other entities where the size of the investment is significant but not controlling. As noted earlier, where the investor owns a controlling interest in the common stock of another company, there is a parent–subsidiary relationship. Where the investor owns enough common stock to be able to *influence* but not *control* the policies and activities of the investee company, the two companies are said to be **affiliates.**

The Significance of the Size of an Investment

It may be helpful to think of the different levels of investment one company might make in another as points along a spectrum:

Investor Ownership
of Investee Common Stock Outstanding

1% |——————————————————————————————————| 100%

It should be apparent that the management of an investee company is likely to be more sensitive to the wishes of an investor with an investment at the right side of the continuum than at the left. In fact, an investor that owns 100 percent of the common stock of an investee will be in a position to completely direct the activities of the investee company just as though the investee company was a branch of the investor. On the other hand, an investor that owns an investment at the far left of the continuum should not be accorded any more deference than any other investor. In between those two extremes are situations where the investor can exercise varying degrees of influence over the investee, based on the various degrees of ownership of common stock.

Looking across the spectrum, there are obviously many different stock ownership positions an investor company could have, and, conceptually, it would be nice to account for each specific intercompany investment according to the substance of the relationship that exists between the investor and investee. In reality, however, three different forms of accounting have evolved and every intercorporate investment will be accounted for using one of these three forms. The three forms of accounting for intercorporate investments in common stock are as follows:

- Where the nature of the investment or the size of the investment is such that the investor is only a passive investor, the investment is accounted for using mark-to-market accounting as described in Chapter 8. Typically, that accounting is followed where the investment is in the form of bonds or preferred stock, or where the investor owns less than 20 percent of the investee's common stock.

- Where the investor owns enough common stock of the investee company to be able to exercise *significant influence* over the activities of the investee but is not in a position to *control* the investee, the investment is accounted for using **equity accounting** (described in the next section of this chapter). In practice, equity accounting is used where the investor owns more than 20 percent but less than 50 percent of the common stock of the investee.

- Where the investor owns enough of the investee's common stock to be able to *control* the activities of the investee company, consolidation accounting is used (described in the final section of this chapter). Typically, **consolidation accounting** is used when the investor owns more than 50 percent of the common stock of the investee company.[2]

Referring back to the continuum presented earlier, the ownership positions and the accounting required can be visualized this way:

---

[2] In general practice, a parent *may not use* consolidation accounting unless it owns more than 50 percent of the voting stock of the subsidiary; that rule has also been applied in the reverse, in that consolidation *has been required* whenever the parent owns more than 50 percent of the subsidiary's voting stock. However, in recent years it has been apparent that there are many ways for one company to control another beyond the ownership of a certain amount of voting stock. The Financial Accounting Standards Board has been studying the rules for consolidation accounting to see if there might be other ways to identify control situations.

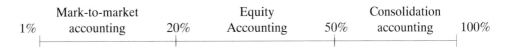

Investor Ownership
of Investee Common Stock Outstanding

	Mark-to-market		Equity		Consolidation	
1%	accounting	20%	Accounting	50%	accounting	100%

EQUITY ACCOUNTING

When the investor owns from 20 percent to 50 percent of the common stock of the investee, the investor must follow the provisions of equity accounting for that investment. The logic behind equity accounting goes something like this: Because the investor's ownership of a significant block of the investee's stock gives it the power to exercise significant influence over the operations of the investee company, the investor should be held accountable for the exercise of that power. Under equity accounting, the investor records its initial investment at the amount it paid to acquire the stock. That accounting is the same as for any other asset. But as time passes, equity accounting differs from ordinary asset accounting in that each year, as the investee reports its income or loss, the investor is obligated to recognize in its own income statement, its proportionate share of the investee's net income or loss. When the investor records its share of the investee's net income, it also increases its own income and its own retained earnings. To keep its balance sheet in balance, the investor must also increase its Investment in Affiliate asset account by the same amount.

Let's create an example to illustrate these ideas. Assume that Johnson Paper Company joins with two other paper companies to build a wood pulp plant in Georgia. Each company agrees to purchase one-third of the output of the pulp plant for their further use in the manufacture of fine papers. The pulp plant will be owned and operated by a new company (let's call it Woodland, Inc.), which in turn will be owned by the three investor companies. Each of the investors puts in $1 million and is given 100,000 shares of stock in Woodland, Inc. Under the terms of their agreement, each investor company is entitled to elect two directors to Woodland's board of directors. Each investor can be said to have significant influence over the operations of the investee company, Woodland, but none will be able to control it.

Johnson would record its initial investment with the following entry:

> Dr. Investment in Woodland (A) . . . . . . (inc.) 1,000,000
>   Cr. Cash (A) . . . . (dec.) 1,000,000

Notice that Johnson's investment account on this first day in the life of Woodland, Inc., is exactly equal to its proportionate share of Woodland's owners' equity account. But let's take the example forward. In its first year of operations, Woodland borrows additional funds from a bank and constructs the pulp plant. Because it is not yet in production, Woodland reports a loss of $600,000 in that first year. Using equity accounting, Johnson would record its share of that loss with the following entry:

> Dr. Loss on equity investment (Loss) . . . . (inc.) 200,000
>   Cr. Investment in Woodland (A) . . . . (dec.) 200,000

Notice that this entry reduces Johnson's investment account to $800,000 so that it is exactly equal to its one-third share of Woodland's net equity—the sum of Woodland's common stock ($3,000,000) and retained earnings (a negative $600,000). That investment–equity relationship is the objective of the equity accounting method.

Johnson's management might try to argue that the company should not have to record that $200,000 loss; after all, the loss was recorded by a separate legal entity and there is no reason to believe that Johnson's investment in that entity is impaired in any way. They might argue that the value of the investment has grown now that the plant is almost complete and will soon be producing low-cost, high-quality raw material for Johnson's future benefit. However, the proponents of equity accounting would reply that the legal separation between Johnson Paper and Woodland is superficial. Johnson has at least an implicit obligation to Woodland (and its banker) because of its significant involvement in the new company and specifically because of its ability to influence the operations of the new company. Therefore, the accounting for the investment should ignore the legal separation between Johnson and Woodland and focus on the substance of the relationship. Equity accounting proponents would also argue that Johnson could have built this plant on its own but chose to share its cost and its potential with two other investors. If Johnson had built the plant on its own it would have incurred the start-up costs on its own. In this scenario, Johnson shares Woodland's losses with two other parties, and the one-third sharing of the initial loss is exactly the result produced for Johnson with equity accounting. If you have been following this discussion so far, and you have accepted the idea that Johnson must record its share of Woodland's loss, you might be thinking that Johnson must also record its share of Woodland's asset (the building) and the bank loan. Hold on to that idea—we will address the balance sheet aspects of equity accounting very soon.

When Woodland begins operations, it will begin to earn profits. Assume that in its second year of operations Woodland's net income is $300,000. Under equity accounting, Johnson would record the following entry:

```
Dr. Investment in Woodland (A). . . . . . . (inc.) 100,000
    Cr. Income on equity investment (Gain) . . . . . . . . .      (inc.) 100,000
```

The theory behind this entry is that Johnson was in a position to exercise significant influence over Woodland, including its cost controls and its pricing policies. As a result of that ability to influence Woodland's operations, Johnson recognizes the results of those operations—or more correctly, its share of those operations. Further, the logic of equity accounting is based on the understanding that Johnson could have influenced its two other partners to cause Woodland to pay its earnings out as dividends. Johnson chose not to exert that pressure and so, in effect, agreed to invest its share of Woodland's earnings back into the company.

Suppose Woodland reports the following results in years 1, 2 and 3:

Year 1:	Net Loss of $600,000
Year 2:	Net Income of $300,000
Year 3:	Net Income of $450,000

In Year 3, Johnson would make an entry similar to the one it made for Year 2, increasing its investment account and recognizing its share of Woodland's income for the year. But suppose that the board of directors agrees to a dividend payout in Year 3 of $0.30 per share. Johnson would make the following entry to record that dividend:

```
Dr. Cash (A) . . . . . . . . . . . . . . . . . . . . . . (inc.) 30,000
    Cr. Investment in Woodland (A) . . . . . . . . . . . . . .      (dec.) 30,000
```

As you think about the flow of these entries, you will see that equity accounting requires Johnson to account for its investment in Woodland on the accrual basis: Earnings from the investment are recorded when they are earned, not when the cash is paid out. That accounting is consistent with the notion that Johnson's 33 percent ownership of Woodland gives it the ability to influence the operations of Woodland. Because Johnson can influence Woodland's success or failure, it should recognize its share of that success or failure. Further, Johnson can influence the timing of Woodland's dividend payout, and so equity accounting treats the payout of the investee's earnings as being subject to Johnson's choice. Under equity accounting, Johnson treats the receipt of Woodland dividends as a partial liquidation of its investment in Woodland. The dividend is, in effect, a return *of* its investment as opposed to a return *on* its investment. Finally, notice that after three years of operations, Johnson's investment account is exactly equal to its one-third share of Woodland's net equity.

	Woodland's Equity Accounts	Johnson's Investment Account
Initial investment	$3,000,000	$1,000,000
First year's loss	−600,000	−200,000
Second year's income	300,000	100,000
Third year's income	450,000	150,000
Dividends paid	−90,000	−30,000
Balance at the end of the third year	$3,060,000	$1,020,000

Equity accounting requires the investor to maintain an investment account that reflects increases and decreases in its share of the equity of the investee, and it requires the investor to report that share of equity as an asset in its balance sheet. Similarly, equity accounting requires the investor to report its share of the investee's earnings or loss in its income statement.

GAAP in the United States requires the equity investor to report that investment and that income (loss) as single-line entries in the investor's financial statements. U.S. GAAP does not permit an investor to report its share of the investee's individual assets and liabilities, nor its share of the investee's sales and expenses. That restriction is odd because the underlying theory of equity accounting would seem to support a proportionate consolidation by the investor of its share of the investee's assets and liabilities and its revenues and expenses. After all, if an investor can exercise significant influence over the investee's net assets, it ought to be able to exercise significant influence over the investee's individual assets and liabilities as well. Similarly, if the investor has a large enough investment to influence the investee's net income, it would seem logical to assume that the investor has significant influence over its sales and expenses. But that so-called **proportional consolidation** approach—where the investor records and reports its share of each of the investee's assets and liabilities and its share of the investee's sales and expenses—is not GAAP in the United States.

International Accounting Standards for equity accounting are almost identical to U.S. GAAP where the investor company has significant influence over the investee. However, International Standards distinguish between equity accounting situations and **joint ventures.** Where there is a contractual agreement among the investors as to the management of the investee, the IAS guidelines refer to that situation as a joint venture and they require the investors to use proportional consolidation: the investors would report their share of the investee's revenues and costs and their share of the investee's assets and liabilities. In the

EXHIBIT 10.1

Occidental Petroleum Company
Equity Method Disclosures

From the Balance Sheet:

	Assets at December 31	
In millions, except share amounts	**1997**	**1996**
Current Assets		
Cash and cash equivalents	$ 113	$ 258
Trade receivables, net of reserves of $24 in both 1997 and 1996	603	626
Receivables from joint ventures, partnerships and other	210	131
Inventories	604	582
Prepaid expenses and other	386	313
Total current assets	1,916	1,910
Long-Term Receivables, Net	153	153
Equity Investments (Notes 1 and 15)	921	985
Property, Plant And Equipment, At Cost		
Oil and gas operations	9,039	8,554
Chemical operations	6,077	5,893
Corporate and other	1,441	1,439
	16,557	15,886
Accumulated depreciation, depletion, and amortization	(7,967)	(7,690)
	8,590	8,196
Other Assets	470	416
Net Assets Of Discontinued Operations	3,232	3,321
	$15,282	$14,981

United States, an investment in a joint venture is accounted for using equity accounting, just as in any other "significant influence" situation. So, with our example of the Johnson Paper Company investment in the Woodland paper mill, the investors would use equity accounting if they followed U.S. GAAP, but they would use proportionate consolidation if they followed IASC GAAP.

The application of equity accounting (as practiced in the United States) is illustrated in the extracts from the 1997 annual report of Occidental Petroleum, Inc., presented in Exhibit 10.1. Note that in its income statement, Occidental reports only its proportionate share of the net income of its equity-accounting affiliates, not its share of their sales and expenses. Similarly, Occidental's balance sheet reports only the company's share of the net assets of its 20 to 50 percent owned equity-accounting affiliates.

The two shaded sentences in Occidental's footnote illustrate several interesting points about equity accounting:

■ The Company tells us that the market value of its investment in Canadian Oxy was $910 million compared to the equity accounting-based book value of only $263 million.

EXHIBIT 10.1 continued

From the Income Statement:

| | Net Income For the years ended December 31 | | |
	1997	1996	1995
Revenues			
Net sales and operating revenues			
Oil and gas operations	$3,667	$3,680	$3,019
Chemical operations	4,349	4,307	5,370
	8,016	7,987	8,389
Interest, dividends and other income	88	244	105
Gains on disposition of assets, net	(4)	11	45
Income from equity investments (Note 15)	1	70	94
	8,101	8,312	8,633
Costs and Other Deductions			
Cost of sales	5,060	5,060	5,492
Selling, general administrative and other			
operating expenses	1,002	933	996
Depreciation, depletion and amortization of assets	822	761	768
Environmental remediation	136	100	21
Exploration expense	119	120	106
Interest and debt expense, net	434	482	579
	7,573	7,456	7,962
Income (Loss) from Continuing Operations before Taxes	528	856	671
Provision for domestic and foreign income and			
other taxes	311	342	313
Income (Loss) from Continuing Operations	217	514	358
Discontinued operations, net	(607)	184	153
Extraordinary gain (loss), net	—	(30)	—
Net Income (Loss)	$ (390)	$ 668	$ 511
Earnings (Loss) Applicable to Common Stock	$ (478)	$ 575	$ 418
Basic Earnings Per Common Share			
Income (loss) from continuing operations	$ .39	$ 1.30	$ .83
Discontinued operations, net	(1.82)	.56	.48
Extraordinary gain (loss), net	—	(.09)	—
Basic Earnings (loss) Per Common Share	$ (1.43)	$ 1.77	$ 1.31
Diluted Earnings (Loss) Per Common Share	$ (1.43)	$ 1.73	$ 1.31

EXHIBIT 10.1 concluded

Note 15: Investments

Investments in companies,other than oil and gas exploration and production companies, in which Occidental has a voting stock interest of at least 20 percent, but not more than 50 percent, and certain partnerships are accounted for on the equity method. At December 31, 1997, Occidental's equity investments consisted primarily of a pipeline in the Dutch sector of the North Sea, an investment of approximately 30 percent in the common shares of CanadianOxy and various chemical partnerships and joint ventures. Equity investments paid dividends of $50 million, $48 million and $34 million to Occidental in 1997, 1996 and 1995, respectively. Cumulative undistributed earnings since acquisition, in the amount of $204 million, of 50-percent-or-less-owned companies have been accounted for by Occidental under the equity method.

At December 31, 1997 and 1996, Occidental's investment in equity investees exceeded the historical underlying equity in net assets by approximately $226 million and $258 million, respectively, which is being amortized into income over periods not exceeding 40 years. The aggregate market value of the investment in CanadianOxy, based on the quoted market price for CanadianOxy common shares, was $910 million at December 31, 1997, compared with an aggregate book value of $263 million.

Occidental and its subsidiaries' purchases from certain chemical partnerships were $232 million, $183 million and $192 million in 1997, 1996 and 1995, respectively. Occidental and its subsidiaries' sales to certain chemical partnerships were $328 million, $245 million and $263 million, in 1997, 1996 and 1995, respectively.

The following table presents Occidental's proportional interest in the summarized financial information of its equity method investments (in millions):

For the years ended December 31	1997	1996	1995
Revenues	$ 959	$ 849	$764
Costs and expenses	958	779	670
Net income	$ 1	$ 70	$ 94

Balance at December 31,	1997	1996
Current assets	$ 297	$ 257
Noncurrent assets	$1,564	$1,108
Current liabilities	$ 252	$ 156
Noncurrent liabilities	$1,113	$ 657
Stockholders' equity	$ 496	$ 552

If Occidental had held an investment of less than 20%, classified as a passive investment, that market value would have been recorded on Occidental's balance sheet and the increase in market value would have been recorded in owners' equity for the year. Under equity accounting, the investor only increases its investment account for its share of the undistributed earnings of the investee, and the investor ignores the market value of that investment under the assumption that it is a long term investment and not for sale.

■ The company says that its investment in its affiliates exceeded its share of the underlying equity reported by those companies by $226 million. That difference arises because Occidental purchased an interest in one or more of those companies on the open market and paid more than the book value of the stock for that acquisition. In the Johnson Paper example used earlier, the investors were all in on the project at the start, and their original investments were exactly equal to their original share of the investee's equity; equity accounting kept that relationship in place year by year. In Occidental's case, some of those investments were made after the investee company was under way, and Occidental was forced to pay a premium over the investee's historical book value to purchase that investment. GAAP requires any such excess , generally called goodwill, to be amortized over a period not in excess of 40 years. Occidental will reduce its share of the earnings reported by those equity companies to reflect that amortization. We will have more to say about that excess purchase price amortization later.

CONSOLIDATION ACCOUNTING

When an investor company owns more than 50 percent of the common stock of an investee, the investor must use consolidation accounting for that investment. Consolidation accounting assumes that the investor (the parent) can do more than just influence the activities of the investee and can in fact control the investee. An investor company will need to be sensitive to the legal rights of the investee's other shareholders—if any—but it is typically true that ownership of 50 percent or more of the stock of a company gives the investor the right to elect all of the members of the board of directors and to determine the policies and operations of the investee. Following on that understanding, GAAP requires any company that owns 50 percent or more of the stock of another company to use **consolidation accounting;** that is, the investor will present only consolidated financial statements, combining the investee's assets, liabilities, sales, and expenses with its own.

When A Subsidiary Is Created by the Parent Company

Referring to the Johnson Paper example, assume that Johnson put up all of the $3,000,000 equity that was required to fund the beginning of Woodland, Inc., and thus was the sole shareholder. Johnson Paper is therefore the parent company and Woodland is its subsidiary. Also assume that Woodland is in the third year of operations and that it has reported these results during that three-year period:

Year 1:	Net loss of $600,000
Year 2:	Net income of $300,000
Year 3:	Net income of $450,000
Year 3:	Dividends of $90,000

With a 100 percent ownership, Johnson's investment in Woodland at the end of the third year would be $3,060,000. Woodland would have common stock equal to $3,000,000 and retained earnings of $60,000, for a total equity of $3,060,000. Because Johnson controls Woodland, consolidation accounting argues that we ought to look beyond the legal separation of the two companies and see them as a single entity. The proponents of consolidation accounting are impatient with the idea that Johnson would only reflect an Investment in Woodland account on its balance sheet and instead insist on knowing what that investment represents in the way of specific assets, liabilities, revenues, and expenses. For example, assume the detailed balance sheets of Woodland and Johnson as of the end of Year 3 are as presented in the first two columns of this table:

Balance Sheets at the End of Year Three
(000 omitted)

	Johnson Paper	Woodland, Inc.	Consolidated Johnson Paper
Cash	$ 1,000	$ 500	$ 1,500
Accounts receivable	2,500	800	3,300
Inventory	2,800	900	3,700
Net property	5,200	3,400	8,600
Investment in Woodland	3,060	—	—
Total assets	14,560	5,600	17,100
Accounts payable	1,200	290	1,490
Long-term debt	300	2,250	2,550
Total liabilities	1,500	2,540	4,040
Net assets	$13,060	$3,060	$13,060
The equivalent net equity is represented by:			
Common stock	$ 8,000	$3,000	$8,000
Retained earnings	5,060	60	5,060
Total Equity	$13,060	$3,060	$13,060

Because Johnson has control over Woodland, when Johnson issues financial statements to its shareholders or its creditors, it must issue consolidated financial statements; no shareholder or creditor would be interested in the statements of the parent alone because everyone understands that the parent's operations are only part of the overall story. *In this situation, where the parent company founded the wholly-owned subsidiary,* consolidation accounting simply combines the assets and liabilities of the two entities, eliminating the parent's investment account and the subsidiary's owners' equity accounts. The parent's investment and the subsidiary's owners' equity accounts are eliminated to avoid double-counting: if they were not eliminated, the consolidated balance sheet would show an investment in the subsidiary and the outstanding stock of the subsidiary. Consolidation accounting ignores the parent's investment and the subsidiary's equity: consolidation accounting assumes that the parent directly owns the subsidiary's cash and inventory, and so forth.

Developing the consolidated income statement for Johnson is more complex than developing the balance sheet because there may be significant intercompany transactions between the two companies. Assume, for example, that all of Woodland's sales are made to Johnson. The income statements of the two companies separately and the consolidated income statement for the third year of operations might look like this:

Income Statements for Year Three
(000 omitted)

	Johnson Paper	Woodland, Inc.	Consolidated Johnson Paper
Sales	$28,750	$6,000	$28,750
Cost of sales	14,500	3,800	12,300*
Gross profit	14,250	2,200	16,450
Expenses and taxes	9,400	1,700	11,100
Earnings of Woodland	500	—	—
Net income	$ 5,350	$ 500	$ 5,350

* Consolidated cost of sales is calculated this way: Johnson's costs of $14,500 less the $6,000 of material it purchased from Woodland, plus Woodland's $3,800 cost of manufacturing those materials, all of which equals the consolidated cost of sales of $12,300.

The consolidated income statement would include all of the transactions the two companies had with outsiders but would eliminate all intercompany transactions that took place between the two companies. Hence, consolidated sales include only the sales with Johnson's outside customers and do not include the sales Woodland made to its parent. The consolidated costs of sales include the costs Johnson paid to outsiders and the net cost of manufacturing the raw material it purchased from Woodland. The consolidated statements look beyond the legal division between the two companies and ignore any transactions between them; the consolidated statements look only for those transactions that took place with entities *outside* the corporate group.

When A Subsidiary Is Acquired Rather Than Created

Most parent-subsidiary relationships exist because the parent created the subsidiary for an explicit purpose, as in the Johnson Paper/Woodland example and as in the case of General Motors creating its wholly-owned subsidiary GMAC. In those situations, the parent's investment in the subsidiary will always be equal to the subsidiary's net assets at their book value. Such subsidiary relationships are the most common intercompany relationship, but they are not the ones that get the most attention. Most arguments about the accounting for intercompany relationships occur because the parent did not create the subsidiary but instead acquired it from someone else. The distinctive feature of those acquired-subsidiary situations is that the seller usually demands a price in excess of the book value of the net assets of the company to be sold, and so the purchasing company's original investment will be in excess of the acquired company's recorded net assets.[3] It is very rare that an investor is able to acquire a company by paying a price exactly equal to the book value of the

---

[3] Think about the conversations an investor-company team might have as they evaluate a proposed acquisition of an existing company. As you visualize their conversations, it may be helpful to remember the accounting equation, A = L + OE or alternatively, A − L = OE. In words, net assets must be equal to owners' equity. A negotiating team in an acquisition may talk about buying the shareholders' equity in the investee, or they may talk about buying the investee's net assets. They are, of course, talking about the same acquisition but looking at it from a different perspective. Incidentally, an investor may occasionally decide that it is not interested in the investee's legal corporate entity (perhaps the investee is saddled with substantial litigation) and conclude that they are only interested in the actual assets owned by the investee company. It is possible to buy all of the assets of a company, just as it is possible to purchase an individual asset owned by another company. The accounting for any such basket purchase of assets is the same as the accounting accorded the purchase of an individual asset. It may be necessary to allocate the total purchase price over all the individual assets acquired, and if so, the allocation process described in the next section would apply. If such a basket purchase is made, the company from whom the assets were acquired continues to exist, with its previous shareholders.

acquiree's net assets. Usually the seller demands a premium, arguing that the potential of the target company is greater than that indicated by the net book values reported on its balance sheet.

Accounting for that excess purchase price almost always raises questions and inspires spirited discussion. As a result of the heated debates on this subject, two methods of accounting for an acquired subsidiary have developed. The most prevalent method is the purchase method, which is discussed next. The alternative method, the pooling-of-interests method, is discussed in the following section.

The Purchase Method of Accounting for Subsidiary Acquisitions

Under the **purchase method** of accounting for the acquisition of a subsidiary, the acquiring company records its investment at the price it pays to acquire the stock of the new subsidiary, just as it would record the cost of any asset. And, consolidation accounting will be applied just as if the subsidiary had been created from scratch, with a few extra steps, as follows:

1. First the parent determines the fair market values for all of the identifiable assets owned and liabilities owed by its new subsidiary and asks the subsidiary to record those fair values in its accounts. Said another way, the parent will ask the subsidiary to replace the cost it had recorded for its assets and liabilities with a new cost—the cost the parent paid to acquire the subsidiary-as-a-whole. For instance, suppose you had created the Woodlands company to build a pulp plant, putting in an investment of $3 million. You might have borrowed $2 million more and spent $5 million to build the plant. If you are successful in getting the plant up and running, the fair value of that property might be more than its original cost to you because of your efforts in making it operational. Lets assume that the fair value of the operating plant is now $5.5 million. If we decide to buy your shares in Woodland, we would pay you $3.5 million, and after the purchase we would ask our new subsidiary to change the "cost" of the plant from $5 million to $5.5 million: that $5.5 million in assets, less the $2 million in debt, would result in an equity that is equal to our cost. Consolidation accounting could then proceed exactly as described earlier.

2. Everyone hopes that the fair values of the subsidiary's individual assets and the fair value of the individual liabilities will net out to exactly equal the total purchase price paid by the parent. But that is rarely the case. If the net of the fair value of the subsidiary's assets and its liabilities is less than the parent's purchase price, that excess will be treated as a new asset for the subsidiary—GAAP calls that asset **goodwill.** The logic behind that designation is that "goodwill" is the price the parent paid for the unseen assets acquired in the transaction, most likely the relationships between the subsidiary and its customers, its employees, and its suppliers.

3. In the rare situation where the purchase price is less than the net fair value of the assets acquired, the shortfall is often referred to as **negative goodwill.** That implied negative goodwill is allocated as a pro rata reduction in the fair market value of the new subsidiary's property, plant, and equipment.

Let's create a new example to illustrate the accounting required for an investee where the parent purchases the investee rather than creates it. Assume that a major computer company decides that it has been late in recognizing the value of the Internet and decides to catch up by acquiring a company that has developed state-of-the-art software for use on the Internet.

The software company (let's call it NetWorld) has relatively little in the way of assets, but does have great promise. The computer company (let's call it Power Computer) offers to exchange a new issue of preferred stock for the 100,000 common shares held by NetWorld's stockholders. (An investor may use any form of consideration that is acceptable to the investee shareholders who are selling: cash, notes, bonds, preferred stock, or common stock.) The cost of the acquisition is measured by the market value of the consideration given. Let us assume that Power's investment bankers determine that the new issue of Power preferred stock will have a market value of $10 per share. If the NetWorld stockholders accept the exchange offer, Power would have paid $1 million for the acquisition.

The entry Power Computer would make to record that acquisition would look like this:

Dr. Investment in NetWorld (A) . . . . (inc.) 1,000,000
    Cr. Preferred stock (OE) . . . .   (inc.) 1,000,000

Let us also assume that the balance sheets of the two companies just prior to the exchange are as depicted in the first two columns of the following table, and the fair values of the assets and liabilities of NetWorld are as depicted in the third column. You will see that we have added $250 million in Goodwill to NetWorld's asset to make its new net asset total equal the price Power Computer paid to acquire the stock. If we were to prepare a consolidated balance sheet immediately after the acquisition, it would appear as in the last column of the table.

Balance Sheets at Date of NetWorld Acquisition
(000 omitted)

	Power Computer	NetWorld (Historical Cost)	NetWorld (Fair Value)	Consolidated Power
Cash	$ 1,550	$ 500	$ 500	$ 2,050
Accounts receivable	1,500	800	800	2,300
Inventory	1,800	600	600	2,400
Computer equipment, net of accumulated depreciation	2,200	750	800	3,000
Software, net	1,200	150	400	1,600
Other property, net	4,300	300	300	4,600
Other assets	500	50	50	550
Investment in NetWorld	1,000	—	—	—
Goodwill	—	—	250	250
Total assets	14,050	3,150	3,700	16,750
Accounts payable	1,900	450	450	2,350
Long-term debt	3,500	2,250	2,250	5,750
Total liabilities	5,400	2,700	2,700	8,100
Net assets	8,650	450	1,000	8,650
The equivalent net equity is represented by:				
Preferred stock	1,000	—		1,000
Common stock	2,850	100		2,850
Retained earnings	4,800	350		4,800
Total equity	$ 8,650	$ 450		$ 8,650

Note that the consolidated balance sheet treats this purchase accounting transaction just as though Power had paid $1,000,000 and acquired NetWorld's individual assets and liabilities in a basket transaction. There is no investment account but instead the consolidated balance sheet includes the NetWorld assets and liabilities (including some goodwill) that Power obtained in exchange for its $1,000,000 purchase price.

The goodwill in that consolidated balance sheet is calculated as follows:

Total NetWorld purchase price	$1,000,000
NetWorld's net assets acquired (at historic costs)	450,000
Additional fair market values acquired, not recognized in Net World's recorded historic costs:	
Computer equipment	50,000
Software	250,000
Total identifiable assets	$ 750,000
Goodwill present at NetWorld	$ 250,000

If we assume that the transaction took place on June 30, 2000, the consolidated income statement for the two companies at December 31, 2000, might look like this:

Income Statements for 2000
(000 omitted)

	Power Computer		NetWorld		Consolidated Power
	Jan to June	July to Dec	Jan to June	July to Dec	2000
Sales	$7,900	$8,300	$1,500	$2,000	$18,200
Cost of sales	4,000	4,500	1,100	1,300	9,800
Gross margin	3,900	3,800	400	700	8,400
Selling expenses	750	850	300	400	2,000
Administrative expenses	400	480	100	125	1,005
Depreciation	200	225	50	75	500
Extra depreciation and amortization	—	—	—	27	27
Interest	100	120	100	125	345
Taxes	950	900	—	—	1,850
Total expenses	2,400	2,575	550	752	5,727
Net income	$1,500	$1,225	$ (150)	$ (52)	$ 2,673

Note that the consolidated income statement includes the earnings (loss) of NetWorld for only the last six months of the year—since the date of the acquisition. Note also that there will be additional depreciation and amortization in the consolidated financial statements to expense a portion of the new values that were recognized in the acquisition. The extra charge assumes that NetWorld's computer and software assets had an average remaining life of 10 years; as a result, $15,000 ($30,000 annually, but half that for this six-month period) of the extra value allocated to NetWorld's property was charged as additional depreciation in the consolidated financial statements. The extra expense also assumes that Power management decided that the goodwill they acquired with their purchase of the NetWorld stock had a life of 10 years; as a consequence, the consolidated income statement reflects an amortization expense of $12,500 ($25,000 for the full year, but half that for this six-month period).[4]

---

[4] GAAP in the United States sets a maximum life of 40 years for goodwill, and many companies use that maximum. In Japan, the maximum is 5 years. The International Accounting Standards Committee, which is working to establish one set of standards for use throughout the world, has said that the maximum life for goodwill should be 20 years. In the interest of harmonization, the FASB is considering the adoption of a similar rule.

The consolidated financial statements covering the period when the acquisition occurred will include a footnote describing the acquisition and explaining how the acquisition impacted the statements for the year. The footnote will usually include a pro forma table that shows what consolidated income would have been had the acquisition taken place at the first of the year. The example from the 1997 annual report of The Toro Company, detailed in Exhibit 10.2, illustrates the disclosures required when a new subsidiary has been acquired and the purchase method is used.

The income statement in Toro's 1997 annual report provides this data (in millions):

	1997	1996
Net sales	$1,051.2	$930.9
Net earnings, before extraordinary item	36.5	36.4

Toro's Statements of Earnings, as reported to the shareholders for 1997 and 1996, depicts an increase in sales, with 1997 sales reaching $1 billion. However, the acquisition footnote tells us that the purchase of the Hardie Group took place on December 1, 1996 so we know that the results reported for 1996 only included the Hardie Group for one month. The results for 1997 include the results of the Hardie Group for 12 months. The pro-forma sales numbers suggest that year-to-year sales actually decreased by $9 million.

The reported net earnings before extraordinary items for 1997 and 1996 (including only one month of Hardie's operations) showed very little movement, year to year. However, had the acquisition taken place at the beginning of 1996, net earnings year-to-year would have increased by more than $4 million, suggesting that there was real benefit from the acquisition. Actually, there should be no difference between the 1997 net earnings in the financial statements and the pro forma net earnings in the footnote, because both numbers include Hardie operations for 12 months. There is a slight difference because of "certain other adjustments" as Toro explains in the footnote. But, as we might expect, there is a big difference between the 1996 net earnings reported in the financial statements and the pro forma numbers in the footnote. Toro explains that the lower pro forma numbers are due in part to the assumed charges for goodwill amortization and interest expense as if those expenses had been charged for the entire year rather than one month. But also, the pro forma net earnings numbers reflect the results of Hardie's operations for the full 12 months. Because of the magnitude of the difference between the reported numbers and the pro forma numbers we can conclude that the Hardie Group lost money in 1996. Because the pro forma net earnings show an increase from 1996 to 1997, we have to conclude that Toro was able to improve the Hardie operations in 1997. However, we might wonder why Toro would have paid $118 million for a company who had such disappointing results in the year of the acquisition—there must be more to the new acquisition than is reflected in the financial statements.

EXHIBIT 10.2

The Toro Company
Acquisition Accounting Disclosures:
Purchase Method

Business Acquisitions

Effective December 1, 1996 the company acquired the James Hardie Irrigation Group (Hardie) from James Hardie Industries Limited (JHI Limited) for $118,030,000 based on estimated, unaudited aggregate shareholders' equity of Hardie on December 1, 1996, subject to further adjustment based on final audit results.

Based on the financial statements of Hardie as of the acquisition date, shareholders' equity at the acquisition date was approximately $10,545,000 less than the estimated equity used as the closing date purchase price, and this $10,545,000 is to be returned from JHI Limited to the company. In addition, under the procedures established in the purchase agreement, the company and JHI Limited have entered into an arbitration process related to the valuation of assets, accounting methods applied, estimates used and other items. The resolution of these matters may result in an additional reduction of the purchase price.

The acquisition is accounted for using the purchase accounting method and, accordingly, the initial purchase price of $118,030,000 has been allocated based on the estimated fair values of assets acquired and liabilities assumed on the date of acquisition. The excess of the purchase price over the estimated fair value of net tangible assets acquired has been recorded as goodwill and is being amortized on a straight-line basis over 20 years. Any additional reductions in the purchase price, as a result of resolution of the objections discussed in the preceding paragraph, will result in a reduction of goodwill. The related effect of these adjustments on the Consolidated Statement of Earnings of the company is not expected to be material.

The following unaudited pro forma information presents a summary of consolidated results of operations of the company and Hardie as if the acquisition had occurred at the beginning of fiscal 1996, with pro forma adjustments to give effect to amortization of goodwill, interest expense on acquisition debt and certain other adjustments, together with the related income tax effects.

	Year Ended	
(Dollars in thousands, except per share data)	October 31 1997	October 31 1996
Net sales	$1,065,370	$1,074,783
Net earnings before extraordinary loss	$ 34,811	$ 30,423
Extraordinary loss, net of income tax benefit	1,663	—
Net earnings	$ 33,148	$ 30,423

The Pooling-of-Interests Method of Accounting for Subsidiary Acquisitions

The purchase method of accounting is quite logical because it records the net assets acquired (that is, the investee's assets and liabilities) at their fair value. Some managers, however, object to purchase accounting because it combines the assets of the investee company at their fair market value with the assets of the investor company, which are stated at their historic cost. Some managers also object to the inclusion of an intangible asset labeled *goodwill* on their balance sheet. They apparently believe that readers of the statements discount the value of such an intangible asset. Finally, on a more pragmatic note, some managers object to the purchase method because the higher asset values, including the newly recognized goodwill, result in increased amortization and depreciation expenses, depressing future consolidated earnings.

Because of such objections, the **pooling-of-interests method** (or *merger accounting* as it is called in most European countries) takes an entirely different approach to the accounting for an acquired subsidiary. It may be used only in those very special situations where the parent acquires control of a target subsidiary by exchanging its own common stock for the common stock of the target company. A few other complex rules determine whether an acquisition qualifies for use of the pooling method, but primarily, the parent must use its common stock as consideration for the transaction.

The theory behind the pooling method is that the shareholders have simply pooled their interests in the two companies, and there has been no purchase of any assets. Because the owners have pooled their interests, there was no arm's-length transaction between them, and so it has not been possible to determine any new asset values. Because there was no purchase transaction, and because it has not been possible to determine any new asset values, the two companies bring only their historical costs to the consolidation. The parent company values its new investment at the historical cost of the new subsidiary's net assets—the historical cost of the subsidiary's assets less the historical costs of its liabilities.[5] Therefore, using pooling accounting, the consolidation of the two companies' balance sheets is simply a matter of adding the two individual companies' assets and liabilities together, eliminating the parent's Investment in Subsidiary account and the subsidiary's owners' equity. No current values are recognized. The end result is just as though the parent created the subsidiary at its very beginning.

Let's return to the example of Power Computer and NetWorld that was used earlier. Instead of issuing preferred stock in the acquisition of NetWorld, assume Power issues common stock because it wants to use the pooling method. Power would make the following entry to record the exchange of its common stock for the common stock of NetWorld:

```
Dr. Investment in NetWorld (A) . . . . . . . . (inc.) 450,000
     Cr. Common stock (OE) . . . . . . . . . . . . . . . . . . . . .        (inc.) 450,000
```

Note that the stock Power issued is valued at the historical cost of the net assets of NetWorld. It is important to understand that the real exchange of value involved in the transaction must be the same—the NetWorld shareholders will not be content to accept common stock from Power worth anything less than $1,000,000. To make the deal acceptable, Power must issue enough shares of its common stock so as to give the NetWorld shareholders the same value as they would have received with the preferred stock. If we assume that Power's stock trades at $20 per share, Power will issue 50,000 shares of its common stock in this transaction. Pooling accounting, however, ignores all current values involved in the transaction and records the Power stock issued at the historical-cost value of the net assets received from NetWorld—in this case at $9.00 a share ($450,000/50,000 shares). Pooling accounting assumes that the Power and the NetWorld shareholders have always been together, and there has been no purchase and no new valuation.

---

[5] Remembering that A = L + OE and A − L = OE, it should be apparent that the historic cost of the subsidiary's net assets is the same as the subsidiary's historical cost of its equity.

Because this is a common stock transaction, Power would not have issued the preferred stock as it did in our earlier purchase accounting transaction but rather would have issued common stock. We can assume, however, that all of the other asset and liability balances are the same as they were in that earlier example. If Power issued common stock as consideration for the transaction, and if Power used the pooling method to account for the transaction, the consolidated balance sheet just after the transaction would look like this:

Balance Sheets at Date of NetWorld Acquisition
(000 omitted)

	Power Computer	NetWorld (Historical Cost)	NetWorld (Fair Value)	Consolidated Power
Cash	$ 1,550	$ 500	$ 500	$ 2,050
Accounts receivable	1,500	800	800	2,300
Inventory	1,800	600	600	2,400
Computer equipment, net of accumulated depreciation	2,200	750	800	2,950
Software, net	1,200	150	400	1,350
Other property, net	4,300	300	300	4,600
Other assets	500	50	50	550
Investment in NetWorld	450	—	—	—
Goodwill	—	—	—	—
Total assets	13,500	3,150	3,450	16,200
Accounts payable	1,900	450	450	2,350
Long-term debt	3,500	2,250	2,250	5,750
Total liabilities	5,400	2,700	2,700	8,100
Net assets	8,100	450	750	8,100
The equivalent net equity is represented by common stock:				
Prior issuances	2,850	100		2,850
New issuance	450	—		450
Retained earnings	4,800	350		4,800
Total equity	$ 8,100	$ 450		$ 8,100

Notice that under pooling accounting, the parent's investment exactly equals the net original asset value of the subsidiary—under pooling accounting we ignore the real value of the consideration given. As a result, the consolidation is quite simple. Power's investment account and the equivalent NetWorld owners' equity accounts are eliminated; the remaining assets, liabilities, and owners' equity accounts simply are added across.[6] Notice also that the pooling method ignores any difference between the fair market values of NetWorld's assets and their historical costs; the consolidated balance sheet is prepared by combining the historical costs from both companies. Finally, notice that pooling ignores any goodwill that might have been implied in the transaction.

---

[6] Most likely, the parent will make one further adjustment to the historical values as recorded in the two companies' balance sheets as the consolidation is prepared. Because this is a pooling-of-interests, it is assumed that the two companies have been together since the beginning. Given that assumption, the consolidated retained earnings should be the sum of the retained earnings originally reported by the two companies; the consolidated common stock amount is therefore simply a plug figure to balance the consolidated balance sheet. The only restriction is that the parent's common stock account must not go below the par value of the shares outstanding. Assuming that limitation is not a factor in this case, the final consolidated equity presentation would look like this:

Common stock	$2,950
Retained earnings	5,150
Total equity	$8,100

The other significant difference between the purchase method and the pooling interests method arises in the preparation of the income statement. Remember that the pooling method argues that the two shareholder groups have simply merged their ownership interests and that no purchase has taken place. Building on that theoretical foundation, the pooling method ignores the transaction date and assumes that the companies have been together forever. Therefore, when the consolidated income statement is prepared, the sales, costs, and expenses reported by the two companies for the *entire* year are added together as though the acquisition had taken place at the beginning of the year. In fact, when the consolidated annual report is prepared, *all* of the income statements presented for a three-year period, a five-year period, or a 10-year period, will be combined in exactly the same way. Pooling accounting assumes that the two companies have been together from the beginning of their corporate lives. Assuming that the acquisition took place on June 30, 2000, the consolidated income statement for Power Computer for 2000 would look like this:

Income Statements for the 2000 Year
(000 omitted)

	Power Computer		Networld		Consolidated Power
	Jan to June	July to Dec	Jan to June	July to Dec	2000
Sales	$7,900	$8,300	$1,500	$2,000	$19,700
Cost of sales	4,000	4,500	1,100	1,300	10,900
Gross margin	3,900	3,800	400	700	8,800
Selling expenses	750	850	300	400	2,300
Administrative expenses	400	480	100	125	1,105
Depreciation	200	225	50	75	550
Extra depreciation and amortization	—	—	—	—	—
Interest	100	120	100	125	445
Taxes	950	900	—	—	1,850
Total expenses	2,400	2,575	550	725	6,250
Net income	$1,500	$1,225	$ (150)	$ (25)	$ 2,550

Notice that the results of the two companies for the entire year have been combined in the consolidated income statement. Note also that there is no additional depreciation or amortization because there was no recognition of the current values inherent in NetWorld's assets and liabilities.

In the year of the acquisition, the footnotes to the financial statements will provide the details of the transaction and will describe the impact the acquisition had on the consolidated income statement. To illustrate that disclosure, consider a classic pooling case—the merger of AT&T with McCaw Cellular Communications in 1994. Exhibit 10.3 shows a footnote from AT&T describing its acquisition of McCaw, using the pooling method. At the time of this merger, AT&T's shares traded at about $55, indicating that AT&T management thought that McCaw was worth $10.8 billion. Because of the start-up losses it had incurred setting up its cellular network, McCaw had reported losses in all prior years. The company reported a negative net equity of $37.0 million in its balance sheet just prior to the acquisition. If purchase accounting had been used for this transaction, we can assume that *all* of AT&T's purchase price would have been allocated to additional asset values at McCaw and that a substantial amount of goodwill would have been recorded. It is easy to understand why AT&T might have wanted this transaction to be accounted for as a pooling: not only did the company avoid the recognition of a very large amount of goodwill on the consolidated balance sheet, it avoided the future income charges from the depreciation of the extra asset values that would have been recorded and the amortization of that goodwill. If AT&T had been required to amortize $10 billion in additional assets over the maximum of 40 years, the annual cost would have been $250 million, approaching 10% of net income. But note that the combined entity is almost sure to show increased net income, as McCaw moves out of its start up operations. Because the income statements under pooling accounting are restated for all years presented, they will show the evolution of McCaw as though it was an AT&T accomplishment.

Although the pooling method is firmly entrenched in U.S. GAAP, its conceptual underpinnings are obviously weak. No one really believes that the shareholders of McCaw Cellular and AT&T pooled their equity interests and marched forward together into the wireless future. Using a more recent example, it is hard to think of Daimler-Benz and Chrysler, who merged in a pooling in 1998, as having been together from their very beginnings. The pooling method really has appeal only because of the accounting burdens that accompany the use of the purchase method.

There is some evidence that an acquisition-minded company will pay more if the transaction can be accorded pooling treatment, simply to avoid the amortization of goodwill which would result from the use of purchase accounting. And many negotiations are tortured as the parties try to find an agreement that will give the sellers the return they expect, but still preserve the form of the transaction so as to allow the purchaser to use pooling accounting.

As a result of all of the problems presented by the pooling method, and because the International Accounting Standards Committee has adopted rules that call for a very narrow definition of poolings (a merger of equals), the FASB has decided to re-think the accounting for business combinations. As this edition of this text goes to press, it appears that the FASB is prepared to narrow (if not eliminate) the use of pooling accounting effective January, 2001, and to require the amortization of goodwill (from purchase accounting transactions) over 20 years.

Minority Interests

As discussed previously, consolidation accounting is relatively straightforward when a parent owns 100 percent of the stock of the subsidiary. Consolidation accounting can be a bit more complicated, however, when the parent owns less than 100 percent of the common stock of the subsidiary. The basic process is as presented earlier, but now the parent cannot say that it owns all of the net assets of the subsidiary or that it earned all of the subsidiary's net income. The portion of the subsidiary's net assets owned by the other stockholders—in effect their share of the subsidiary's equity—is reflected in the consolidated balance sheet as a separate line item just after the liabilities, labeled **minority interest.** In the consolidated income statement, the minority owners' share of the earnings of the subsidiary is included as a single expense item, positioned just before income taxes and referred to as **minority interest in earnings of subsidiaries.** Thus, in both the consolidated balance sheet and the consolidated income statement, all of the assets, liabilities, and the sales and expenses of the subsidiary are combined with those of the parent, with these additional minority interest lines subtracting out the net assets and net income ascribable to the minority shareholders.

EXHIBIT 10.3

AT&T and Subsidiaries
Acquisition Accounting Disclosures:
Pooling Method

Merger with McCaw Cellular Communications, Inc. (McCaw)

On September 19, 1994, AT&T merged with McCaw. As a result, 197.5 million shares of McCaw common stock were converted into shares of AT&T common stock at an exchange ratio of one share of AT&T common stock for each McCaw share. In addition, AT&T assumed 11.3 million McCaw stock options, which were converted into AT&T stock options at the same exchange ratio, resulting in 11.3 million additional AT&T stock options at an average exercise price of $27.43. The merger was accounted for as a pooling of interests,

and the consolidated financial statements were restated for all periods prior to the merger to include the accounts and operations of McCaw. Intercompany transactions prior to 1994 were not eliminated due to immateriality. Merger-related expenses of $246 million incurred in 1994 ($187 million net of taxes) were reported as selling, general, and administrative expenses. Certain reclassifications were made to McCaw's accounts to conform to AT&T's presentation. Premerger operating results of the companies in the current presentation were:

Dollars in millions	Nine Months Ended September 30, 1994	Year Ended December 31, 1993	1992
Sales and revenues			
AT&T	$52,178	$67,156	$64,904
McCaw	2,062	2,195	1,743
Eliminations	(256)	—	—
Total	$53,984	$69,351	$66,647
Net income (loss)			
AT&T	$ 3,431	$ (3,794)	$ 3,807
McCaw	34	(2,112)*	(365)
Eliminations	(93)	—	—
Total	$ 3,372	$ (5,906)	$ 3,442

*Includes a charge of $45 million previously reported as an extraordinary item for the early redemption of debt.

The Essence of Consolidation Accounting

A large publicly held company can have thousands of subsidiaries, and the system required to gather the data from all of those entities and to keep track of their intercompany transactions can be extraordinarily complex. In reality, however, the process is quite simple: The preparation of consolidated financial statements for a multinational company is, by and large, a scaled-up version of the Johnson Paper and the Power Computer examples we have been discussing. The essence of consolidation accounting, whether practiced by Procter & Gamble or the fictitious Johnson Paper or Power Computer, is this:

- The legal structure of the entities is ignored and the accounting follows the substance of the relationship. Where the parent controls a subsidiary as a result of the parent's ownership of 50 percent or more of the subsidiary's common stock, the consolidated financial statements include all of the parent's assets and liabilities, combined with all of the subsidiary's assets and liabilities. Similarly, the two companies' sales and expenses are combined.

- Consolidation requires that all intercompany transactions be eliminated. Because they are intercompany transactions, they should not be included in the consolidated financial statements. Because they are intercompany transactions, each transaction in one company has a mirror image in the other. The effect of the transaction must be eliminated from each company's accounts to avoid double counting in the consolidation.

- Where the parent owns less than 100 percent of the subsidiary, any minority interest in the subsidiary's net assets is shown in the consolidated balance sheet as a credit balance; technically, the minority interest is neither debt nor owners' equity—it is simply a balancing account needed to preserve the fundamental accounting equation $A = L + OE$. Any minority interest in the profit of the subsidiary is included in the consolidated income statement as a subtraction from the consolidated income.

- Where the parent acquires its interest in the subsidiary from an earlier owner, the accounting is determined by the form of the consideration given. Where the transaction fails to meet the tests for pooling accounting, purchase accounting must be used. Under purchase accounting, the purchase price paid by the parent is allocated to the subsidiary's assets and liabilities in proportion to their individual fair values. Where there is excess purchase price that cannot be allocated to specific assets or liabilities, the remaining purchase price must be allocated to goodwill. The consolidated balance sheet reports the accounts of the newly acquired subsidiary at the current cost of the individual assets and liabilities acquired as a result of the purchase of the subsidiary's stock. The consolidated income statements will include the results of the two companies only from the date of acquisition; those consolidated income statements must include additional expense charges to cover the depreciation of the new asset values recognized and the amortization of any goodwill recorded.

- Where the parent acquires its interest in the subsidiary from an earlier owner, using common stock as the medium of exchange, it may be possible to use pooling accounting. Under pooling accounting, the common stock given up in the exchange will be valued at the historical cost of the net assets acquired. It is not necessary to allocate the "purchase price" because there has been no purchase, and it is not necessary to recognize any goodwill. The consolidated balance sheet reports the assets and liabilities of the subsidiary at their original historical costs. Because there are no new asset values, there are no additional charges for depreciation or amortization. The income statements for the combined companies will include the operations of each company as of the beginning of each year presented, just as though the two companies had been together from the beginning of their respective lives.

TAXATION ISSUES

Under current U.S. tax law, two companies may file a consolidated tax return only when both are U.S. companies and only when the parent owns more than 80 percent of the subsidiary. There is no such thing as equity accounting under tax law, and so in every other intercompany investment situation, each company involved in the relationship will be obligated to file a separate tax return and pay tax on its own earnings. For example, where Company A owns 75 percent of the stock of Company B, both of those companies will file tax returns and both will pay tax on their net income as determined by their own stand-alone books. This is true even though Company A controls Company B and has a great deal to say about how much income Company B earns. To reduce the potential for double taxation, however, tax law allows for a *dividend-received deduction.* A company that owns less than 20 percent of another may deduct from its taxable income up to 70 percent of the dividends it receives from that other company. When an investor owns between 20 percent and 80 percent of an investee company, it is entitled to deduct up to 80 percent of all dividends received from that investee. Notice that a company that is an investor but owns less than 80 percent of the investee will not be taxed on the investee's reported earnings, only on the dividends the investee pays—when and if they are paid. Even then, the dividend-received deduction substantially reduces the tax that would otherwise be due on that dividend distribution.

In situations where the investor owns more than 20 percent but less than 80 percent of the investee's stock, or where the parent owns 100% of a foreign subsidiary, there will likely be a significant difference in the income the investor recognizes for its financial reports and the income it recognizes in its tax returns, assuming that the investee does not pay out all of its earnings as dividends. The investor should accrue a liability for the taxes it will have to pay when the earnings it recognized under the equity method, or under consolidation accounting for foreign subsidiaries, are eventually distributed in the form of dividends. Every year that accrued liability should be adjusted to recognize the tax that will be due as a result of any additional income reported but not distributed by the subsidiary. The tax expense that should be accrued against that currently recognized income will be reduced by (1) the expected dividend-received credit and (2) the possibility that the earnings that have been retained by the investee will be permanently invested or distributed to the investor in a tax-free manner. Occidental explains their decision to *not* accrue taxes on their subsidiary's earnings in Exhibit 10.4.

When an investor company acquires an investee, management has to decide whether the transaction is a pooling or a purchase for accounting purposes, and that decision will sometimes drive the structure of the transaction. If it is desirable that the transaction be accorded pooling accounting, it will have to be a stock for stock transaction and other criteria will also have to be met. Management will also have to decide how to structure the transaction for tax purposes, depending on the needs of the parties to the negotiations. The tax rules for mergers and acquisitions are very complex, but they can be summarized this way:

- If an investor company acquires the stock of an investee company from the investee's shareholders and gives some form of equity such as common stock or preferred stock, the transaction is tax free to all parties.[7] The investee shareholders pay no tax until they sell the securities they received from the investor. The investee company continues to

---

[7] Technically, these transactions are not tax free but are tax deferred. The selling shareholders will not be obligated for any tax in a sale so long as they exchange one security for another; their cost for the new security is the same as their cost basis in the security they gave up. They will pay a tax when they sell any of the new securities, and the taxable gain will be the difference between the original cost basis and the current proceeds. In the same way, the investee company may avoid taxes on the gain suggested by the price paid by the investor; but when the investor causes the investee to sell any assets, that taxable gain on that sale will be calculated as the difference between the investee's original historical costs and the current proceeds—and that will be so whether the transaction is a purchase or a pooling for accounting purposes.

EXHIBIT 10.4

Occidental Petroleum Company
Disclosure of Tax Status of International Subsidiaries

From the deferred tax footnote:

A deferred tax liability of approximately $80 million at December 31, 1997 has not been recognized for temporary differences related to Occidental's investment in certain foreign subsidiaries primarily as a result of unremitted earnings of consolidated subsidiaries, as it is Occidental's intention, generally, to reinvest such earnings permanently.

---

calculate its tax depreciation (and its gains and losses on asset sales) using its historical costs, and that depreciation is used in its own tax return or the consolidated return of the investee and investor. That is true whether the investor uses equity accounting for financial reporting purposes or consolidates the investee using purchase accounting or pooling accounting. Because this is a tax-free transaction to the investee company, neither the investor company nor the investee company gets any tax benefit from any new asset values that might otherwise have been implied in the purchase price. Obviously, this form of transaction is attractive to the selling investee shareholders but less so to the investor.

- If an investor acquires the stock of an investee company from the investee's shareholders and gives cash or notes, the investee shareholders pay tax on the capital gain they have realized—the difference between the value per share they received and the cost basis of the shares they held. Nonetheless, because this was a transaction between the investee shareholders and the investor company, the transaction is tax free to the investee company. The investee company continues to calculate its tax depreciation (and its gains and losses on asset sales) using its historical costs, and that depreciation will be used in the investee's tax return if the company files its own tax return, or it will be passed to the investor's consolidated tax return if the investor owns 80 percent or more of the investee. This is true whether the investor uses equity accounting for financial reporting purposes or consolidates the investee using purchase accounting or pooling accounting. As before, so long as the investee company is not subject to any tax on a gain in the transaction, neither the investor company nor the investee company gets any tax benefit from any new asset values that might otherwise have been implied in the purchase price.

- If an investor buys assets and liabilities directly from the original investee company and puts them into a newly created investee company, the new investee company (and, indirectly, the investor) may claim tax-deductible depreciation on all of the new asset values implied in the acquisition purchase price, including any goodwill. But of course the original investee company, which is now a shell, has an obligation to pay a tax on the gain implied in those new asset values.

- In the earlier example where the investor buys the investee stock directly from the investee stockholders, it may be possible to obtain the tax benefit of the new values implied in the acquisition purchase price, but only as a result of a special tax election:

The investor may elect to have the transaction treated as though it had purchased assets and liabilities directly from the company, thereby claiming depreciation on the new, purchase price–based asset values and similarly claiming a deduction for the amortization of the goodwill. However, to make that election, the investor would also have to agree to have its investee subsidiary pay the tax today on the gain implied in those new values. Only in a very unusual situation would the future benefit of those extra deductions be worth paying out the tax on the gain today.

In most situations, where purchase accounting is used for a consolidated subsidiary there will be significant differences between the tax bases of the assets and the new cost bases that are used for financial reporting in the consolidation. Those differences require deferred tax accounting, as described in Chapter 13.

OTHER MANAGEMENT CONSIDERATIONS

Segment Data and Deconsolidations

During the 1960s and 1970s, conglomerates were popular with Wall Street on the theory that a diversified company could protect a shareholder in the same way as a diversified portfolio might (that is, via risk diversification). Companies in cyclical industries sought investees in countercyclical businesses to balance their aggregate income stream. However, some conglomerates became so complex that it became difficult to evaluate how their assets were employed or what the sources of their revenues were. Accounting standard setters have attempted to deal with that problem by insisting that consolidated companies report supplemental, summarized line-of-business information. (See, for example, page 38, in Chapter 1, which presents line-of-business information for Procter & Gamble).

Even with the availability of line-of-business information, conglomerate companies have fallen out of favor with the investment community, in part because market analysts have become specialized by industry and no single analyst can follow a company as complex as, say, General Electric. Moreover, the more attractive components of a conglomerate were often ignored by the market, causing the stock price of such companies to languish. Given those problems, there has been a move to deconglomerate. Coca-Cola Company, for example, put most of its bottling business into one investee company and then sold 51 percent of the voting stock in that company (called Coca-Cola Enterprises, or CCE) to the public.

During the focus-on-the-core-business period of the 1990's, other companies have gone farther and have actually spun off their diversified businesses. PepsiCo spun off its restaurant and snack food businesses and AT&T spun off its computer operations and its equipment businesses. Accounting for a spin off program is much less complex than an acquisition program. A spin off—that is, distributing a subsidiary's stock to the parent's stockholders as a special dividend—is very straightforward: the parent passes the subsidiary's assets and its liabilities to the new spun off company, at the parent's book value. The theory for that accounting is that there has been no arms-length transaction between third parties. On the other hand, if a subsidiary is sold to another company, the selling parent compares the proceeds received with the net book value of the subsidiary sold, and then recognizes a gain or loss on the transaction. In each case, the subsidiary's book value numbers are determined by the original accounting the parent used when the subsidiary was acquired. If the subsidiary was acquired in a pooling transaction, the book values of the subsidiary's assets and liabilities will be based on its own original cost. If the subsidiary was acquired in a purchase transaction, the book value of the subsidiary's assets and liabilities will be the fair values determined when the purchase took place.

Push-Down Accounting

In the examples we used to demonstrate the effects of purchase accounting, we assumed that the subsidiary was asked by its new parent to change its asset and liability values to reflect the values at the date of the aquisition—including any goodwill that was implicit in the purchase price. But, it is not necessary that those new values be pushed down to the subsidiary. For one reason or another the subsidiary may retain its historical costs

Occasionally, a subsidiary will be obligated to prepare financial statements covering only its own operations, either for a regulatory filing or to demonstrate compliance with a contract. When those separate financial statements of the subsidiary are required, they must include disclosures indicating the degree of control exercised by the parent. But that caution aside, the accounting world has debated what asset values ought to be used for those separate statements: Should the subsidiary's historical costs be used, or should the new costs paid by the parent and attributable to the subsidiary be used? A theory called **push-down accounting** has come to the fore; its proponents argue that the parent's costs for the subsidiary ought to be pushed down to take the place of the subsidiary's historical costs. They argue that the old costs are irrelevant because the subsidiary is now being run by new, different owners, and those new owners have different expectations for the subsidiary. The new owners measure success or failure of the new subsidiary against the investment they made, and that investment ought to be seen as the new cost basis for the subsidiary. In those situations where there has been a substantial change in ownership in a transaction that qualifies for purchase accounting, push-down accounting is GAAP for any separate financial statements subsequently required for the subsidiary.

This discussion also raises an interesting management accounting issue. If the subsidiary is to be measured by how well it does against the new costs implied in the acquisition price, should not the managers of the subsidiary be measured against those new costs as well? Even if it is not necessary to publish separate financial statements for the subsidiary, it makes sense to push the values from the purchase down into the subsidiary's accounts so that measures such as return on assets, return on equity, and other ratios are prepared using the costs that the parent understands to be embedded in the subsidiary. In fact, it makes sense to do that whether the acquisition was accounted for as a pooling or as a purchase. The values implied by the consideration given up by the parent ought to be used in measuring the performance of the subsidiary management regardless of the accounting used.

SUMMARY

In today's complex business community, it is quite common to find that companies invest in each other. These long-term intercorporate investments are undertaken for a variety of reasons, such as to gain control over a major competitor or supplier, to diversify business risk, and to produce additional income and cash flows.

The financial reporting of these investments is largely dictated by the extent of the investor's stockholdings in the investee. When a relatively small (less than 20 percent of the outstanding shares) amount of stock is owned, the investor most commonly reports its investment using mark-to-market accounting. When the size of the investment is sufficient to influence the operating activities of the investee (usually 20 to 50 percent stockholding), equity accounting is most likely to be used. Finally, when an investor gains control of an investee (that is, its stockholding exceeds 50 percent of the outstanding voting shares), the financial results of the two companies must be reported on a consolidated basis. Such investments may be accounted for using the purchase method or, under certain circumstance, the pooling-of-interests method.

NEW CONCEPTS AND TERMS

Active investment

Affiliates

Consolidation accounting

Cumulative Translation Adjustment account

Current rate method

Economic exposure

Equity accounting

Foreign exchange risk

Functional currency

Goodwill

Minority interest

Minority interest in earnings of subsidiaries

Negative goodwill

Parent company

Passive investment

Pooling-of-interests method

Proportional consolidation

Purchase method

Push-down accounting

Subsidiary company

Transaction exposure

Translation exposure

Accounting for Foreign Operations

There appears to be a fairly well-established pattern of evolution for most business enterprises: After successfully establishing a local market, the enterprise then seeks out other new markets. Thus, it is not at all surprising to find that most mature, successful U.S. companies have expanded their area of operations beyond the borders of the United States. When a company does establish operations outside the United States, a question arises: How best to financially portray those foreign operations.

Essentially, there are two choices. First, the company may prepare financial statements for its foreign operations (that is, subsidiary, affiliate, or division) using the generally accepted accounting principles of the host foreign country, expressing those statements in the currency (such as the dollar in Canada, the yen in Japan, or the peso in Mexico) of the host country. Second, the company may prepare financial statements for its foreign operations using U.S. GAAP and translating the value of those foreign operations into U.S. dollars.

Because of the diversity in GAAP among countries, the FASB has determined that the second option is the most informative one for U.S. analysts, creditors, and investors, and it is required for companies issuing publicly traded securities on U.S. exchanges. Consequently, in this appendix we focus on how such companies translate their foreign operations into U.S. equivalents and how that information can be used to understand the foreign activities of a company.

Foreign Exchange Risk

In prior chapters we discussed the various types of *risk* that companies face as part of their normal business operations. The three principal types of risk are operating risk, default risk, and financial risk. When a company maintains foreign operations, however, it is also subject to a fourth type of risk—**foreign exchange risk.** This type of risk occurs because the exchange rates between the U.S. dollar and foreign currencies are rarely stable, creating value changes in international operations.

Foreign exchange risk is usually thought to result from three elements: translation exposure, transaction exposure, and economic exposure. **Translation exposure** occurs as a result of the need to translate (or convert) the financial statements of a foreign division or subsidiary into U.S. dollars in order to prepare consolidated financial statements for the

entire company. This type of exposure is solely the result of the *consolidation process* and, consequently, is sometimes referred to as *accounting exposure.* **Transaction exposure** occurs during the normal course of international business transactions when a lag occurs between the date on which a contract is signed or goods delivered and the date of payment. This type of exposure has real cash flow consequences if the exchange rate changes between the date the transaction occurs and the date the currency exchange occurs. **Economic exposure** is a prospective concept focusing on the impact of exchange rate fluctuations on the future operations of a foreign division or subsidiary. As exchange rates change, the competitive position of companies operating in that country change: As the local currency strengthens, exports are easier, and vice versa.

Translation of Foreign Operations

Current U.S. GAAP stipulates that the translation of foreign operations should be undertaken using a "functional currency" approach. A company's (or subsidiary's) **functional currency** is defined to be the currency of the primary economic environment in which it operates. Thus, a subsidiary that does business exclusively or principally in Japan has a functional currency of the yen. Moreover, the foreign subsidiary's accounts should be determined (or redetermined, as the case may be) using U.S. GAAP and initially reported in terms of its functional currency. The foreign subsidiary's financial statements thus prepared are then *translated* into U.S. dollars using the **current rate method.** Under this approach, the subsidiary's income statement is converted into U.S. dollars using the average exchange rate for the period, and its balance sheet is converted at the exchange rate existing on the date of the translation (for example, December 31).

Gains and losses due to translation (or accounting) exposure are accumulated into an owners' equity account, the **Cumulative Translation Adjustment** account, and have no effect on net income. As we said in Chapter 5, the Cumulative Translation Adjustment account is usually one of the principle components of Comprehensive Other Income. A company's presentation of Comprehensive Other Income gathers up all transactions that impact the equity accounts but are not included in Net Earnings. See, for example, Procter & Gamble's treatment of currency translation, and its presentation of Total Comprehensive Income, on page 28. Gains and losses due to transaction exposure are reported as a separate line item on a company's income statement.

Exhibit 10A.1 illustrates the translation process for FHAS, Inc., a company which operates in the United States and in another country where the currency is the fictitious zlot. Note that since the exchange rate of the U.S. dollar declined relative to the zlot (or, alternatively, the zlot increased in value relative to the U.S. dollar), the value of FHAS's subsidiary's net assets and operations increased over the 2000 fiscal year. As a consequence, the prior accumulation in the Translation Adjustment account, representing an exchange loss, was eliminated, ultimately ending the period in a gain position. This gain remains unreported until the subsidiary is sold or its operations discontinued.

The translation process illustrated in Exhibit 10A.1 was accomplished using a few basic conventions:

1. Assets and liabilities on the balance sheet are translated at the end-of-period exchange rate.

2. Owners' equity (in this case, common stock and retained earnings) is translated at the exchange rate in effect when the account balance was created.

EXHIBIT 10A.1

FHAS, Inc.
Translation of Foreign Financial Statements

FHAS, Inc., is a U.S. corporation with a foreign subsidiary operating principally in one other country. The foreign subsidiary, hereafter called Pty. Limited, was founded in 1980 and had a cumulative translation adjustment of $(10,780) as of January 1, 2000. The exchange rates between the zlot and the U.S. dollar in 2000 were as follows:

January 1:	.75	(1Z = $0.75 U.S.)
December 31:	.78	(1Z = $0.78 U.S.)
Average:	.76	

Pty. Limited
Statement of Income
December 31, 2000

	Local Country Zlots (Functional Currency)	Exchange Rate	U.S. Dollars
Sales	Z1,148,000	.76	$872,480
Costs and expenses:			
Cost of sales	Z 588,000	.76	$446,880
Depreciation	56,700	.76	43,092
General and administrative	101,500	.76	77,140
Interest	35,000	.76	26,600
	Z 781,200		$593,712
Net income before taxes	366,800		278,768
Income taxes	186,200	.76	141,512
Net income	Z 180,600		$137,256

3. The income statement is translated at the average exchange rate for the period.

4. Dividends are translated at the actual exchange rate at the time of payment.

Take a moment to review the income statement and balance sheet in Exhibit 10A.1 and consider the reconciliation of the ending balance in the Retained Earnings and Cumulative Translation Adjustment accounts.

As a consequence of the translation process, financial statement users are able to view, in a single set of financial statements, all of a company's operations—both foreign and domestic—using a consistent set of accounting methods (U.S. GAAP). Thus, the process of determining whether a company's overall performance has increased (or declined) is made easier. Note that the process of translating the various accounts of a foreign subsidiary into their U.S. dollar equivalents is a necessary step *preceding* the consolidation of those accounts with the U.S. parent. Once the translation process is complete, the consolidation process as described in Chapter 10 can be undertaken.

EXHIBIT 10A.1 concluded

Pty. Limited
Balance Sheet

	Beginning-of-Year			End-of-Year		
	Local Country Ƶ	Exchange Rate	United States $	Local Country Ƶ	Exchange Rate	United States $
Assets						
Cash	Ƶ 28,000	.75	$ 21,000	Ƶ 63,000	.78	$ 49,140
Accounts receivable	84,000	.75	63,000	103,600	.78	80,808
Inventory	98,000	.75	73,500	140,000	.78	109,200
Property, plant, and equipment (net)	476,700	.75	357,525	462,000	.78	360,360
Total assets	Ƶ686,700		$515,025	Ƶ768,600		$599,508
Liabilities						
Accounts payable	Ƶ 84,700	.75	63,525	Ƶ 56,000	.78	43,680
Long-term debt	350,000	.75	262,500	280,000	.78	218,400
Total liabilities	Ƶ434,700		$326,025	Ƶ336,000		$262,080
Stockholders' equity:						
Common stock	Ƶ 42,000	H*	$ 25,830	Ƶ 42,000	H*	$ 25,830
Retained earnings	210,000	H*	173,950	390,600		311,206
Cumulative translation adjustment	—		(10,780)	—		392
Total equity	Ƶ252,000		$189,000	Ƶ432,600		$337,428
Total liabilities and equity	Ƶ686,700		$515,025	Ƶ768,600		$599,508

Reconciliation of ending balance in retained earnings:

	U.S. dollars
Retained earnings, 1/1/2000	$173,950
Net income (translated)	137,256
Retained earnings, 12/31/2000	$311,206

Reconciliation of Cumulative Translation Adjustment account:

Balance, 1/1/2000	$ (10,780)
Adjustment for beginning net assets, with increase in exchange rate from $0.75 to $0.78: Ƶ252,000 × $0.03	7,560
Adjustment for net income, with increase in exchange rate from average of $0.76 to $0.78: Ƶ180,600 × $0.02	3,612
Balance, 12/31/2000	$ 392

*Refers to the historic exchange rate in effect when the account balance was created.

ASSIGNMENTS

10.1. Accounting for intercorporate investments: the equity method. In January 2000 Contran Corp. acquired a 40 percent ownership interest in the National Lock Company, paying $3.5 million. During the year, National Lock declared (and paid) its usual dividends totaling $240,000. Following a year-end audit by its independent auditors, National Lock released its 2000 earnings report, which showed earnings of $850,000 for the year.

Bill Montgomery, controller for Contran, considered this information and how it should be reflected in Contran's 2000 financial statements. With some concern, he also noted that as of December 31, 2000, Contran's original investment was now worth only $3.25 million according to National Lock's quoted share prices in the over-the-counter market. He was confident, however, that the market price decline was only temporary, and he expected a full recovery in 2001.

Required:

How should Contran value its investment in National Lock at year-end 2000? Assume that National reported a *loss* of $300,000 for 2000. How would Contran's valuation of National Lock change?

10.2. Applying the equity method—a further example. On October 1, 2000, Westover Corporation purchased 35 percent of the outstanding common stock of Graydon Corporation for $500,000. For the quarter ending December 31, 2000 Graydon Corporation declared and paid a dividend totaling $80,000. For the same quarter, Graydon Corporation reported net income of $160,000, even though net income for the year was only $10,000.

Required:

a. Prepare Westover's 2000 entries for its investment in Graydon Corporation.

b. What line item(s) and amount(s) will appear on Westover's 2000 balance sheet, income statement, and statement of cash flows related to its investment in Graydon?

10.3. Accounts affected by purchase accounting. On January 1, 2000, Acquiror issued stock to Acquiree's stockholders for all of Acquiree's outstanding shares. The market value of Acquiror's stock involved in that exchange was $40,000. At that time, the appraised value of Acquiree's net assets was equal to its recorded book value except for the PP&E which was appraised at $54,000.

December 31, 1999
Preacquisition
Balance Sheets

	Acquiror	Acquiree
Cash	$ 6,000	$ 1,000
Accts. Receivable	14,000	8,000
Inventory	22,000	12,000
PP&E (net)	80,000	50,000
Other Assets	4,000	2,000
	$126,000	$73,000
Accts. Payable	$ 10,000	$ 2,500
Other Current Liab.	10,000	1,500
Bonds Payable	24,000	35,000
Common Stock	50,000	25,000
Retained Earnings	32,000	9,000
	$126,000	$73,000

Required:

Prepare two consolidated balance sheets as of January 1, 2000 using:

a. The purchase method.

b. The pooling-of-interests method.

10.4. Purchase accounting.* The statements of financial position of Company P and Company Q and the fair value of Company Q's assets at December 31, 2000, were as follows (in thousands of dollars):

	Historical Costs		Company Q Fair Value
	Company P	Company Q	
Assets:			
Cash	$1,100	$ 50	$ 50
Trade receivables	500	225	225
Inventories	1,000	125	175
Property, plant, and equipment (net)	2,500	250	450
	5,100	650	900
Deduct liabilities	750	100	100
Net assets	$4,350	$550	800
Stockholders' equity:			
Capital stock (no par)	3,000	200	
Retained earnings	1,350	350	
	$4,350	$550	

Market value per share at 12/31/00 was $200 for Company P's stock and $400 for Company Q's.

Required:

The management of Company P was considering several approaches to the acquisition of Company Q.

Approach 1. If, as of December 31, 2000, Company P negotiated to purchase the assets and assumed the liabilities of Company Q for $800,000 cash:

a. What entry(ies) would Company P make? Company Q?

b. How would the statements of financial position look for Company P and Company Q after these entries had been made?

c. What entry(ies) would Company P and Company Q make, and how would the financial statements look afterward, if the purchase price was $900,000 in cash?

Approach 2. If, as of December 31, 2000, Company P negotiated to purchase all of Company Q's assets and assumed all of Company Q's liabilities, as in Approach 1, but instead of cash payment, the purchase price was 4,000 shares of Company P stock:

d. What entry(ies) would Company P make? Company Q?

e. How would the statements of financial position look for Company P and Company Q after these entries were made?

f. What entry(ies) should Company P and Company Q make, and how would the financial statements look afterward, if the purchase price were paid to Company Q by issuance of 4,500 shares of Company P's stock?

Approach 3. If, as of December 31, 2000, Company P negotiated to purchase from the stockholders of Company Q their 2,000 shares for $400 cash per share (Company Q was to become a subsidiary of Company P):

g. What entry(ies) would Company P make? Company Q?

h. How would the consolidated statement of financial position for Companies P and Q look at December 31, 2000?

i. What entry(ies) would Company P and Company Q make, and how would the consolidated statement of financial position look afterward, if the price paid for each Company Q share was $450?

Approach 4. If, as of December 31, 2000, Company P negotiated with the stockholders of Company Q to issue 4,000 shares of its voting common stock in exchange for the 2,000 shares of outstanding Company Q's stock (Company Q was to become a subsidiary of Company P):

j. What entry(ies) would Company P make? Company Q?

k. How would the consolidated statement of financial position of Company P and Company Q look at December 31, 2000? (Assume the pooling method is not permissable here.)

l. What entry(ies) would Company P and Company Q make, and how would the consolidated statement of financial position look afterward, if Company P were to exchange 4,500 shares of its stock for all of the 2,000 shares of Company Q?

10.5. Contrasting the equity method and the mark-to-market method.* The balance sheet of DAE Corporation at December 31, 2000, shows a long-term investment in the common stock of Wallace Corporation of $350,000. The investment was purchased by DAE in January 1997, and the following information pertaining to Wallace Corporation is available:

Year	Income or (Loss)	Dividends Paid
1997	($30,000)	-0-
1998	120,000	$50,000
1999	150,000	60,000
2000	200,000	80,000

Market value of the investment in Wallace Corporation at December 31, 2000, was $350,000.

Required:

a. Assuming that DAE Corporation's investment is classified as available for sale and that it represents a 10 percent interest in Wallace, determine how much DAE paid for Wallace's stock in January 1997.

b. Assuming that DAE Corporation's investment represents a 25 percent interest in Wallace Corporation, determine how much DAE paid for Wallace's stock in January 1997.

10.6. Contrasting Pooling-of-Interests and Purchase Accounting.* Preacquisition balance sheets of Al and Syd corporations are shown below:

	Preacquisition Balance Sheets (in thousands)	
	Al Corporation	Syd Corporation
Assets		
Cash	$ 8,000	$ 2,500
Marketable securities	5,000	3,500
Accounts receivable (net)	7,500	5,000
Inventories (LIFO)	19,000	9,500
Fixed assets (net)	38,000	23,000
Other assets	4,500	1,500
Total assets	$82,000	$45,000
Liabilities and Stockholders' Equity		
Accounts payable	$ 9,500	$ 7,500
Other current liabilities	4,000	3,000
Bonds payable	11,000	—
Other long-term debt	7,500	12,500
Common stock ($10 par)	12,000	—
Common stock ($5 par)	—	6,000
Capital in excess of par	7,000	2,000
Retained earnings	31,000	14,000
Total liabilities and stockholders' equity	$82,000	$45,000

Subsequent to a six-month period of intense negotiating, Al Corporation agreed to purchase all of the outstanding common stock of Syd Corporation at a price of $29.4 million. In arriving at this price, Al Corporation placed the following fair market values on Syd Corporation's assets:

Asset	Fair Market Value (thousands)
Cash	$ 2,500
Marketable securities	4,500
Accounts receivable (net)	3,500
Inventories	13,000
Fixed assets (net)	28,000
Other assets	0
Total	$51,500

According to the terms of the agreement, Al Corporation was to issue one share of its common stock in exchange for each share of Syd Corporation's outstanding common stock. Subsequent to the exchange of common stock, Syd Corporation was to become a wholly owned subsidiary of Al Corporation. The current market price of Al Corporation's common stock was $24.50 per share.

Required:

Al Corporation expects to be able to account for its acquisition of Syd Corporation using the pooling-of-interests method. There is, however, some question about a possible violation of one of

---

the numerous pooling criteria. You have been asked by Al Corporation's management to prepare a consolidated balance sheet to reflect the acquisition of Syd Corporation under both the pooling-of-interests and the purchase methods of accounting.

10.7. Application of the pooling-of-interests method of accounting.* On November 9, 2000, Shea & Shea Corporation merged with Garbo Associates by an exchange of one share of Shea & Shea for one share of Garbo. Shea & Shea issued 1,891,678 of its shares and accounted for the transaction using the pooling-of-interests rather than the purchase method. In accounting for the issue of 1,891,678 shares, Shea & Shea increased its no-par common stock account by $3,300,000.

Garbo's net assets on November 9, 2000, can be approximated as follows:

Capital stock (1,891,678 shares)			$3.3 million
Retained earnings at 12/31/99		$25.5	
Net income 1/1/00 to 11/9/00 (313 days)			
313/365 of $6.2	$5.3		
Less dividends from 1/1/00 to 11/9/00	(2.1)	3.2	
			$28.7 million
Garbo's estimated owners' equity (net assets)			$32.0 million

For purposes of the questions to follow, assume that the market value of Shea & Shea stock at November 9, 2000, was $50 a share, or a total of $94.6 million for the 1,891,678 shares issued in the exchange.

Required:

a. What entry did Shea & Shea make to record the acquisition of Garbo? Why?

b. What difference(s) would it have made if Shea & Shea had treated the transaction under the purchase method rather than the pooling-of-interests method?

c. If you had been a Garbo stockholder, are there any reasons that you would have preferred one share of Shea & Shea stock for each Garbo share you owned rather than $50 in cash?

d. If you were a part of Shea & Shea's management, are there any reasons you would have preferred treating the share-for-share exchange under the pooling-of-interests method rather than under the purchase method?

10.8. Application of consolidation accounting. Joann Jones was the plant manager of World Wide Incorporated's (WWI) California assembly plant. She was pulling together the material for the company's year-end reporting package to send to World Wide's home office. Her systems people gave her the following data pertaining to the suppliers her plant had used during the year:

	Actual Invoice Cost		
Suppliers	**Beginning Inventory**	**Purchases**	**Ending Inventory**
WWI subsidiaries:			
Arizona	$25,000	$175,000	$20,000
Northeast	15,000	125,000	18,000
Southwest	12,000	250,000	10,000
Outside contractors:			
National	14,000	85,000	12,000
Amalgamated	8,000	62,000	6,500

World Wide's home office told Jones that the Arizona plant had experienced a 25 percent profit rate during the last several years, Northwest had experienced a 20 percent rate, and Southwest had experienced a 15 percent rate.

Required:

Calculate for Jones the value of her plant's ending inventory and the materials cost component of the cost of goods sold for the year.

10.9. Consolidated vs. unconsolidated reporting. "Why me?" thought Connie Likert. "My first day on the job at the bank and instead of getting a company with a nice single set of financial statements, I get five separate sets of statements that supposedly fit together."

Likert had just started as a new credit analyst for the First National Bank of Bruceton Mills, having just completed an MBA degree with a major in finance at the local university. From the loan officer responsible for this client, Likert learned the following information about each of the four companies associated with UFS Corporation and about UFS Corporation itself.

UFS Corporation. UFS Corporation is a manufacturing company whose principal products are microwave ovens, refrigerators, and conventional ovens. The company has had a long history (more than 50 years) of selling high-quality, high-priced home appliances; however, recent reductions in the price of competitor products forced UFS to consider ways to provide assistance to its customers to help them buy its products. As a consequence, UFS started its own finance subsidiary, the UFS Acceptance Corporation, to assist customers in financing their purchases.

UFS Corporation is also associated with three other companies. It holds an 80 percent interest in Scrub-All, a company that makes automatic dishwashers. UFS purchased this interest in Scrub-All because the company's product line complemented its own items, and the products were of a quality that UFS would have had difficulty duplicating. Further, to ensure a steady supply of chrome parts for its appliances, UFS obtained a 10 percent interest in the common stock of Acme Chrome Company. Well over 50 percent of Acme's sales were attributed to purchases by UFS and Scrub-All. Further, to compete in the low-end market for various appliances, UFS Corporation formed a joint venture with Whirlwind Products Co. to produce such appliances.

UFS Acceptance Corporation. Created nearly five years ago, UFS Acceptance Corporation is a wholly owned subsidiary that purchases consumer notes from its parent, UFS Corporation. UFS Acceptance borrows funds from several banking institutions on a medium- and long-term basis and uses the margins between the short-term interest rates on the consumer notes and the rates on its medium- and long-term liabilities to cover its overhead costs. The parent company guarantees all of the borrowings of UFS Acceptance Corporation.

Scrub-All Company. With an ownership interest of 80 percent of the common stock of Scrub-All, UFS Corporation controls the tactical and strategic policies of Scrub-All Company through an interlocking board of directors. Scrub-All, like UFS, sold its consumer notes to UFS Acceptance Corporation. The family that originally started Scrub-All still holds a 20 percent ownership interest in the common stock of the company.

Acme Chrome Company. To guarantee a steady supply of chrome parts and a quality cadre of people who could work with the engineers of UFS in the design of new parts, UFS purchased a 10 percent interest in Acme Chrome Company. Over the years, a strong relationship had developed between UFS and Acme. For example, Acme schedules the production runs of its other customers around the production needs of UFS and Scrub-All.

Spotless Appliance Company. Both UFS Corporation and Whirlwind Products Company (an otherwise unrelated company) contributed half of the funds necessary to start Spotless Appliance Company. Spotless Appliance Company makes low-end appliance models that are sold under the Spotless trade name or are labeled with various department store names. The board of directors of Spotless Appliance Company consists of an equal number of members voted in by each of UFS Corporation and Whirlwind Products Company and three members from outside either of the respective companies. Any debt of Spotless is guaranteed by both UFS Corporation and Whirlwind Products Company.

Kirk Tennant, the loan officer responsible for UFS, provided Likert with the financial statements of the five companies (presented on the following pages) and asked her to answer some basic credit review questions concerning an expansion loan application that had been received from UFS management. Before Likert could complete the credit review, she identified the following questions that needed to be answered so that she could understand the relationship between the various companies.

Required:

a. Why are the investments in Acme Chrome and Spotless Appliance Companies shown on the UFS Corporation balance sheet while the investments in Scrub-All and UFS Acceptance Corporation are omitted?

b. What is meant by the carrying value "at equity" for the investment in Spotless Appliance Company?

c. Why is the investment in Acme Chrome Company shown "at cost"?

d. Explain the Goodwill account. What other name is sometimes used instead of goodwill, and to what company is this account related?

e. What is meant by "minority interest," and to what company is this account related? Is this a liability or an equity account?

f. What are UFS Corporation's current ratio, debt-to-equity ratio, and debt-to-asset ratio? Are these ratios at an acceptable level?

g. How would the balance sheet of UFS Corporation appear if Spotless Appliance Company were consolidated? Would you recommend consolidation for Spotless?

h. How would the ratios calculated in part (f) differ after the consolidation of Spotless Appliance? Can an argument be made for consolidating Acme Chrome Company?

i. How would the balance sheet of the parent company appear without including any of the consolidated subsidiaries? Which balance sheet would you use to make this credit decision?

UFS Corporation
Consolidated Statement of Financial Position
December 31, 2000

Assets	
Current assets	$ 37,500,000
Notes receivable	58,000,000
Investment in stock of Spotless Appliance at equity (50%)	1,750,000
Investment in stock of Acme Chrome Company (10%) at cost*	5,600,000
Other assets	101,500,000
Goodwill	3,200,000
Total assets	$207,550,000
Liabilities and Stockholders' Equity	
Current liabilities	$31,500,000
Long-term liabilities	102,100,000
Minority interest	7,500,000
Common stock	15,000,000
Retained earnings	51,450,000
Total liabilities and stockholders' equity	$207,550,000

*Cost approximates market value.

UFS Acceptance Corporation
Statement of Financial Position
December 31, 2000

Assets

Current assets	$ 8,000,000
Notes receivable	58,000,000
Other assets	6,500,000
Total assets	$72,500,000

Liabilities and Stockholders' Equity

Current liabilities*	$5,000,000
Long-term debt	47,100,000
Common stock ($1 par)	10,000,000
Retained earnings	10,400,000
Total liabilities and equities	$72,500,000

*$3,000,000 of the current liabilities is a promissory
note to UFS Corporation. UFS Corporation accounts
for this as a long-term receivable in other assets.

Scrub-All Company
Statement of Financial Position
December 31, 2000

Assets

Current assets	$16,400,000
Other assets	52,600,000
Total assets	$69,000,000

Liabilities and Stockholders' Equity

Current liabilities	$13,350,000
Long-term liabilities	18,150,000
Common stock	12,000,000
Retained earnings	25,500,000
Total liabilities and stockholders' equity	$69,000,000

Acme Chrome Company
Statement of Financial Position
December 31, 2000

Assets

Current assets	$14,750,000
Other assets	36,250,000
Total assets	$51,000,000

Liabilities and Stockholders' Equity

Current liabilities	$5,000,000
Long-term liabilities	15,000,000
Capital stock	18,750,000
Retained earnings	12,250,000
Total liabilities and stockholders' equity	$51,000,000

Spotless Appliance Company
Statement of Financial Position
December 31, 2000

Assets	
Current assets	$ 8,500,000
Other assets	16,000,000
Total assets	$24,500,000
Liabilities and Stockholders' Equity	
Current liabilities	$ 3,000,000
Long-term debt	18,000,000
Common stock ($1 par)	6,000,000
Retained earnings	(2,500,000)
Total liabilities and equities	$24,500,000

10.10. Purchase vs. pooling. Steady Growth, Inc. (SGI), began business in 1974 as part of an effort to popularize natural foods, a subject that was of passionate interest to its founders. The founding group was part counterculture and part agricultural engineer. It successfully developed a line of alternative, organic fertilizers and pesticides. Sales grew modestly but steadily and by 1981 had reached $25 million a year. SGI produced 30 different items, all sold under the Steady Growth trade name. Organic farmers marketed their products explaining that they used only Steady Growth products; natural food stores specifically advertised products as "grown the Steady Growth way." To provide funds for its own growth and to share the benefits of the business, SGI sold stock in 1982 to the natural food wholesale and retail community. The founding group retained about 60 percent of the stock, but the publicly held shares traded occasionally on the Pacific Coast Exchange at prices that approximated SGI's book value per share, about $20.

In early 1999 the press was full of stories about chemical contamination of apples and other fruit crops. Overnight, the general public became interested in organically grown produce, and SGI found itself swamped with orders. As the spring planting season began, SGI's inventory was completely sold out, and production capacity for the year was committed by orders taken in March. SGI management looked at its order books and decided that the company might be ready finally to move into the really "big time." They worked with a team of financial advisers and developed a plan for a management-led leveraged buyout. They arranged to borrow the requisite funds and proposed a cash repurchase of all the stock in the hands of the public at $30 a share.

But SGI was not the only company to notice the public interest in natural foods. Enormous, Inc., a large food chain, notified SGI's board of directors that it would be interested in acquiring the company. Later SGI's board received a similar proposal from an international chemical concern. A spirited bidding war ensued. After several weeks of intense negotiations, SGI's board agreed to recommend to the shareholders that they tender their stock to Enormous in a share-for-share exchange. Enormous's shares were actively traded, and on the day of the announcement the market price of its stock was $40 a share.

The exchange was completed on September 30, 1999, and SGI became a wholly owned subsidiary of Enormous. Some of the founders of SGI took their newfound wealth and left to pursue other interests. Some stayed on, in part because of the salary promised by Enormous and in part because they still believed in the need to promote the cause of natural foods. Enormous sent in a team of transitional managers to help get SGI into the mainstream. As part of their initial review, the Enormous team members determined that the book value of SGI's assets and liabilities equaled their market values, with a few exceptions: SGI's land had appreciated to a current market value of $4,500,000, and the equipment (which had all been handmade) had a current value of $6,000,000. On the other hand, SGI had been rather lenient with its credit policies, and the Enormous staff determined that an additional doubtful account allowance of $500,000 was required. The transitional team also noted that SGI had paid $1,250,000 for a 15 percent interest in a fruit drink business, which was now worth only $1,000,000. SGI had been committed to the fruit drink company, but as part of the planning for the leveraged buyout, management had decided to sell the investment and had transferred the asset to the current category. Finally, SGI's original funding had been in the form of a government-subsidized loan, which had carried a 5 percent interest rate. Because of the low interest rate, the present value of the loan was now only $17,500,000.

The trade name Steady Growth was registered to SGI and was now an Enormous asset. Unfortunately, none of the industry experts on the transitional team was able to put a market value on that asset.

Required:

a. Using the preacquisition historical data presented next, prepare consolidated balance sheets for Enormous as of September 30, 1999, giving effect to the acquisition of SGI. Prepare one balance sheet assuming that the purchase method was used in the acquisition and one assuming the pooling-of-interests method was used.

b. What consolidated earnings will Enormous report in its interim report for the nine months ended September 30, 1999?

   (1) Under the purchase method?

   (2) Under the pooling-of-interests method?

c. When will the extra $500,000 allowance for doubtful accounts appear as a provision in an income statement under the pooling-of-interests method? Under the purchase method?

d. At what amount did you record SGI's appreciated land? At what amount did you record Enormous' appreciated long-term investments? Did you treat them the same? If not, why not?

e. At what amount did you record the stock issued to the SGI shareholders? Did you record the stock issued at the same amount for both the purchase and pooling-of-interests methods? If so, why? If not, what happened to the difference?

f. Outline the pros and cons that might be presented in arguments for or against the pooling-of-interests and purchase methods of accounting in this situation.

Enormous, Inc.
Preconsolidated Balance sheet
September 30, 1999
(millions)

	Preacquisition Historical Data	
	Enormous	**SGI**
Current assets		
Cash	$ 31.0	$ 2.0
Accounts receivable	15.0	4.5
Inventories	27.0	0.5
Investments		1.0
Total current assets	73.0	8.0
Fixed assets (net of accumulated depreciation)		
Machinery and equipment	25.0	5.0
Buildings	112.0	18.0
Trucks	54.0	0.5
Land	19.0	2.5
Net fixed assets	210.0	26.0
Equity investments (market value $12)	12.0	
Goodwill	2.0	
Total assets	$ 297.0	$ 34.0
Current liabilities		
Accounts payable	$ 25.0	$ 6.0
Accrued expenses	12.0	3.5
Total current liabilities	37.0	9.5
Mortgages and loans payable	165.0	18.0
Owners' equity		
Common stock		
Retained earnings	95.0	6.5
Total owners' equity		
Total liabilities and equity	$ 297.0	$ 34.0
Earnings, 1/1/99 to 9/30/99	$ 3.02	$ 2.78
Shares outstanding	3,250,000	325,000
Market price per share of common stock	$40	$20

10.11. Purchase vs. pooling. Subsequent to an unsuccessful hostile takeover attempt, Alliance Corporation entered into friendly negotiations for the acquisition of Felker Corporation. Following two months of discussions, Alliance Corporation agreed to purchase all of the outstanding common stock of Felker Corporation at a price of $36 million. In arriving at this price, Alliance Corporation placed the following fair market values on Felker Corporation's assets at the time of acquisition:

Felker's Assets	Fair Market Values ($ thousands)
Cash	$ 1,300
Marketable securities	1,800
Accounts receivable (net)	1,900
Inventories	10,700
Fixed assets (net)	21,400
Patents	5,500
Other assets	-0-
Goodwill	-0-
Total	$42,600

According to the terms of the agreement, Alliance Corporation was to issue two shares of its common stock in exchange for each share of Felker Corporation's outstanding common stock. Subsequent to the acquisition, Felker was to become a wholly owned subsidiary of Alliance. The market price of Alliance Corporation's common stock at the time of the acquisition was $45 per share.

Required:

Alliance Corporation expects to be able to account for its acquisition of Felker Corporation using the pooling-of-interests method. The resulting consolidated balance sheet under this method follows. Also shown is Felker Corporation's preacquisition balance sheet. Using these two balance sheets and the information provided above, prepare the preacquisition balance sheet for Alliance Corporation and the consolidated balance sheet, assuming the acquisition is accounted for using the purchase method.

	Preacquisition Balance Sheets ($ thousands)		Consolidated Balance Sheets ($ thousands)	
	Alliance Corp.	Felker Corp.	Purchase Method	Pooling-of-Interests Method
Assets				
Cash	_____	$ 1,300	_____	$ 4,800
Marketable securities	_____	1,500	_____	3,900
Accounts receivable (net)	_____	2,100	_____	7,300
Inventories	_____	11,800	_____	35,500
Fixed assets (net)	_____	18,600	_____	60,000
Patents	_____	1,700	_____	5,700
Other assets	_____	500	_____	2,800
Goodwill	_____	1,500	_____	1,500
Total	$_____	$39,000	$_____	$121,500
Liabilities and Stockholders' Equity				
Accounts payable	_____	$ 2,700	_____	$ 11,200
Other current liabilities	_____	1,400	_____	4,400
Long-term debt	_____	8,000	_____	28,000
Common stock (no par)	_____	1,400	_____	20,100
Retained earnings	_____	25,500	_____	57,800
Total	$_____	$39,000	$_____	$121,500

CHAPTER 11

Noncurrent Assets: Fixed Assets, Intangible Assets, and Natural Resources

As CEO of a capital-intensive company, I can assure you that the management of our noncurrent asset base is critical to our long-term success. The accelerating pace of technology, coupled with rapidly evolving markets, requires that we "get it right" on the front end, maintain peak performance of equipment throughout its useful life, and look beyond our customers' current requirements to invest in capital assets meeting tomorrow's customer needs.[1]

Key Chapter Issues

- What are fixed assets, and how are they valued on the balance sheet?
- Why, and how, is the cost of fixed assets allocated to the various periods benefiting from those assets?

- What are intangible assets and natural resources, and how are they accounted for on the balance sheet and the income statement?
- What special management issues arise regarding the accounting for noncurrent assets?

[1] Ronald J. Simmons, CEO, WFC, Inc.

Noncurrent assets represent the principal long-term revenue-producing assets of most companies. In the case of a manufacturing company, the fixed assets (or property, plant, and equipment) are used to manufacture the products that are ultimately sold to customers. In the case of a computer software development company, a copyright on a computer software package provides the company with the monopolistic right to the earnings stream associated with the sale of the package. In the case of an oil and gas company, the oil and gas properties or leaseholds the company owns provide it with access to new salable reserves.

The focus of this chapter is on the analysis and financial reporting issues pertaining to these three types of noncurrent assets. Two important financial reporting questions characterize the financial management of these assets: What cost should be assigned to the asset (that is, capitalized to the balance sheet)? How should the asset's cost systematically be expensed (matched) against the revenues produced by the asset?

FIXED ASSETS AND DEPRECIATION

Fixed assets are long-lived tangible assets owned by a company for the purpose of deriving a benefit from their *use* rather than from their resale. Fixed assets include such *property, plant, and equipment* (PP&E) as buildings; land used or held as factory and office locations (not depreciable); land improvements such as landscaping and parking lots; machinery and equipment; office furniture and fixtures; and vehicles.

The primary financial reporting issues associated with these assets are the following:

1. Determining the cost to be recorded in the balance sheet at the time of acquisition (the **capitalization** issue).

2. Determining the income statement depreciation expense to be reported (the **allocation** issue). In this regard, decisions must be made regarding the preferred depreciation method, the estimated useful life of the asset, and its estimated salvage value.

3. Distinguishing between those fixed asset–related expenditures made subsequent to the initial acquisition (such as repairs and improvements) that should be expensed when incurred and those that should be capitalized (added to the asset's reported balance sheet value) and subsequently depreciated over future periods.

4. Determining if, and when, the revenue-generating capacity of such long-lived assets has diminished as a consequence of factors other than normal day-to-day use, and whether a write-down of the balance sheet value of the assets should be recorded in the company's financial statements.

5. Accounting for the sale or other disposition of an asset.

Determining Original Cost: The Capitalization Issue

Fixed assets are initially reported in the balance sheet at their original cost (that is, the outlay of cash or cash equivalents at the date of purchase). The original acquisition cost of a fixed asset includes *all* costs incurred in getting the asset ready for its intended use. For example, surveying costs, title searches, the costs of clearing unwanted trees and buildings, and the costs of soil and water tests are all a part of the land's original cost. In addition, when a company contracts with another party to construct a new building, all construction-related costs incurred are part of its original cost. In this regard, architect's fees, inspection costs,

EXHIBIT 11.1

Determining the Cost of an Asset

Omar Corporation paid $200,000 for a tract of land that had an old gas station on it. The gas station was razed at a cost of $10,000, and a new warehouse was constructed at a cost of $250,000. In addition, several other costs were incurred:

Legal fees (for the purchase of the land)	$ 5,000
Architect's fees	22,000
Interest on construction loan	18,000

Omar Corporation should record two assets as follows:

Dr. Land (A) . . . . . . (inc.) $215,000
  Cr. Cash (A) . . . . (dec.) $215,000

(The value of the land is determined as follows: $200,000 + $10,000 + $5,000 = $215,000.)

Dr. Building (A). . . . (inc.) $290,000
  Cr. Cash (A) . . . . (dec.) $290,000

(The value of the building is determined as follows: $250,000 + $22,000 + $18,000 = $290,000.)
    It is important to distinguish between the land and the building because only the building will be depreciated. The land will not be depreciated but will continue to be reported at its original cost until sold.

payments to the contractor, and interest on the construction loan are all properly included in the building's original cost. In the case of machinery and equipment, original cost includes purchase price, freight in, and the cost of initial setup and installation. An example regarding these items is presented in Exhibit 11.1.

As an incentive to purchase and promptly pay for a particular piece of equipment, sellers often offer discounts to potential purchasers. When a cash discount is received on the purchase of equipment (or any other asset, for that matter), the equipment's cost should be reported net of the discount. Another means to attract potential buyers involves various seller-sponsored financing plans. For example, a buyer's recorded cost when fixed assets are bought on an installment payment plan is not the sum of the total payments to be made but rather the *present value* of the installment obligation (that is, today's cash-equivalent purchase price) as of the date of purchase. (Present value will be discussed in Chapter 12.) Fixed assets also may be acquired by issuing capital stock. In this case, the cash-equivalent value of the issued stock, as of the date of the transaction, is used to cost the assets. Sometimes an old asset is traded in on a new one (for example, a used truck for a new one). In such an arrangement the market value of the old asset plus the cash paid for the new one is the cost of the new asset to be reported on the balance sheet.

It is important to note that a popular means by which corporate managers may obtain property is to lease it under a long-term, noncancelable lease. If the lease meets certain criteria, generally accepted accounting principles stipulate the recording of a leasehold right as an asset and a lease obligation as a liability. Under these circumstances, the leased asset would be depreciated in the same way as any other fixed asset owned by the company, except that the depreciation period may be limited by the lease term. A more detailed description of lease accounting is provided in Chapter 13.

Depreciation: The Allocation Issue

The purpose of recording depreciation is to reflect the "using up" of the productive capacity of a company's PP&E and to match this cost of doing business with the revenues that the PP&E helped generate. The process of recording depreciation is nothing more than allocating the depreciable cost (that is, original cost less estimated salvage value) of a company's PP&E to the accounting periods during which the PP&E is used. (A word of caution: Sometimes the business use of the term *property, plant, and equipment* is meant to include the land owned by a company on which its plant, offices, loading terminals, and so forth are built. In such circumstances, even though the gross dollar amount reported for PP&E on the balance sheet may include the cost of land, such costs are *not* depreciable. In such circumstances, land is not viewed as being "used up" and therefore is not depreciated.)

The periodic amount of PP&E cost allocated to the income statement is called *depreciation expense* and serves to reduce the net income of the period. In determining a given period's depreciation expense, corporate managers must assess the useful lives and salvage values of the PP&E items, as well as select a systematic method to allocate the costs of the PP&E items over their respective estimated useful lives. These three management decisions (useful life, salvage value, and depreciation method) involve considerable discretion and judgment and may frequently have a significant financial effect on a company's earnings. Each of these decisions is discussed at length in the following sections. It is important to remember that it is possible that a PP&E item that has been fully depreciated in the accounting records may still be an integral part of a company's operations and/or may be sold to another company at a significant price. It is also important to note that **net book value** (that is, original cost less accumulated depreciation) does not approximate an asset's fair market value, nor is it intended to.

Useful life. In estimating the useful lives of various PP&E components, managers must consider the manner in which the assets are expected to be used and maintained. Generally, useful lives are established based on the assumption that normal repairs and maintenance will be made to keep the assets in good operating condition. In situations in which maintenance programs deviate from what is considered normal, estimated useful lives should be adjusted accordingly.

The two primary factors that managers should consider when estimating the useful lives of their PP&E are physical life and technological life. **Physical life** refers to the length of time an asset can reasonably be expected to last before it physically wears out. When physical life is influenced more by the passage of time than by use (as for a building) or when it is difficult to assess the level of usage, useful life is usually expressed in terms of years. When physical life is influenced more by use (as for a machine or a vehicle) than by the passage of time, useful life is often expressed in terms of expected output (such as units produced or miles driven).

For many PP&E items, the concept of technological life has a greater relevance to managers in estimating useful life than does physical life. **Technological life** refers to the length of time an asset can reasonably be expected to generate economic benefits before it becomes obsolete. Two types of obsolescence must be considered: product obsolescence and process obsolescence. **Product obsolescence** pertains to the market lives of the products that are produced by the PP&E. For example, auto manufacturers normally depreciate tooling costs over two or three years because of the product obsolescence brought about by frequent model changes even though the physical life of the tooling equipment may be many more years. **Process obsolescence** pertains to the PP&E item itself becoming obsolete because of subsequent technological improvements. For example, the useful lives of computer equipment have generally been set with the expectation that process obsolescence would occur prior to the time the equipment was physically worn out.

It is important to note that this discussion of estimating useful lives of PP&E pertains solely to financial reporting. As discussed in a later section of this chapter, a country's tax code often specifies useful-life rules for income tax purposes.

Depreciation methods. For financial reporting purposes, corporate management has a choice of several generally accepted methods for allocating the depreciable cost of PP&E over an asset's estimated useful life. The common element among these alternatives is that they each result in a systematic process of cost allocation.

1. **Straight-line method**—The annual depreciation expense is determined by dividing the *depreciable cost* of an asset by its estimated life. The *depreciable cost* is the original cost less the estimated salvage value; hence,

   Annual depreciation expense = (1/n) (Cost − Salvage value)

   where n = estimated life in years

   For example, consider an asset with an original cost of $8,000, an estimated salvage value of $500 (and thus a depreciable cost of $7,500) and an estimated useful life of five years. Under straight-line depreciation, the depreciable cost of $7,500 is divided by 5 to give an annual depreciation figure of $1,500 for each of the five years of the asset's estimated useful life.

2. **Double-declining-balance method**—This method requires the calculation of the straight-line percentage rate (1/n), which is then doubled and applied each year to the PP&E's decreasing *net book value* (that is, the recorded cost less depreciation taken to date). The amount of depreciation taken to date for a particular asset is often referred to as the asset's **accumulated depreciation.** Salvage value is ignored in determining net book value, but the recording of depreciation expense should stop when the asset's net book value equals its salvage value. Hence,

   Annual depreciation expense = (2/n) (Net book value)

   Consider again an asset with an original cost of $8,000, salvage value of $500, and an estimated life of five years. The straight-line percentage rate is 20 percent (1/5 years) and the double-declining-balance rate is 40 percent (2/5). Thus, under the declining-balance method, depreciation is 40 percent of $8,000, or $3,200 for the first year; 40 percent of $4,800 ($8,000 less $3,200), or $1,920, for the second year; 40 percent of $2,880 ($8,000 less $5,120), or $1,152, for the third year. In the final two years, the depreciation calculation will often be converted to a straight-line basis. When the accumulated depreciation recorded for this asset reaches $7,500, its depreciation expensing stops.

3. **Sum-of-the-years' digits method**—Just as the double-declining-balance method results in the recording of larger depreciation expense amounts in the early years of an asset's life (referred to as an *acceleration of depreciation*), so also does the sum-of-the-years' digits (SYD) method.

   Under this method, declining fractions are applied to the asset's *depreciable cost.* The denominator of the fraction is the sum of the digits of the years of useful life (SYD = n(n + 1)/2). The numerator is the number of years of useful life remaining, including the present year. The only rationale behind the mechanics of the SYD method is that it is systematic and results in higher depreciation expense amounts earlier in an asset's life than under the straight-line method.

   Consider again an asset costing $8,000 with an estimated salvage value of $500, a depreciable cost of $7,500, and an estimated life of five years. The sum of the years' digits (1, 2, 3, 4, and 5) is 15. Hence, depreciation expense for the first year is 5/15ths of

$7,500, or $2,500; for the second year, it is 4/15ths of $7,500, or $2,000; for the third year it is 3/15ths of $7,500, or $1,500, and so on.

4. **Physical-unit methods.**

a. **Machine-hour method**—The number of hours a machine is to be used during its useful life is often a better basis for determining depreciation expense than the mere passage of time. Under the machine-hour method, depreciation expense is determined according to the number of hours the asset is actually used during an accounting period relative to the total number of hours it can ultimately be used (that is, the usage or productivity rate):

Annual depreciation expense =
$$\frac{\text{Actual machine hours used in this period}}{\text{Total estimated machine hours}} \times (\text{Cost} - \text{Salvage value})$$

Referring again to the asset with a cost of $8,000, an estimated salvage of $500, and a depreciable cost of $7,500, its estimated lifetime hours are 15,000 and the hours actually used during the first year are 1,800. The depreciable cost of $7,500 divided by the total hours of 15,000 yields $0.50 to be allocated to each hour of use. Depreciation expense for the first year on this machine is therefore $900 (1,800 times $0.50 per hour of use).

b. **Units-of-production method**—This method is conceptually similar to the machine-hour method except that an estimate is made of the number of units to be produced by a machine during its useful life. Depreciation expense for a period is then determined according to the number of units actually produced during the period relative to the estimated lifetime potential of the machine.

Again using the example of an asset with a cost of $8,000 and an estimated salvage value of $500, assume that its projected units of production are 25,000. The asset's depreciable cost of $7,500 divided by 25,000 units yields $0.30 depreciation expense per unit produced. Thus, if in its first year of use, 5,000 units are produced, the depreciation expense for that year is $1,500.

The double-declining-balance and sum-of-the-years' digits methods are often referred to as **accelerated methods of depreciation.** The phenomenon captured by accelerated depreciation methods is that more depreciation expense is recorded in the early years of an asset's life as compared to the amount that would be recorded under the straight-line method. Rationales frequently given for using accelerated methods include (1) an asset is more useful to management when newer because it is more efficient; and (2) repairs and maintenance costs complement an asset's yearly accelerated depreciation in deriving a year-by-year cost of owning and using the asset; that is, repair and maintenance expenses are normally greater in later years when the accelerated depreciation expense amount has lessened. This latter notion may be more clearly understood through the following graphic representation:

EXHIBIT 11.2

A Comparison of Depreciation Methods*

		Depreciation Method			
Year	Straight-Line	Double-Declining-Balance	Sum-of-the-Years' Digits	Machine-Hour	Units-of-Production
1	$1,500	$3,200	$2,500	$ 900	$1,500
2	1,500	1,920	2,000	1,500	1,650
3	1,500	1,152	1,500	1,600	1,950
4	1,500	614	1,000	3,000	1,950
5	1,500	614	500	500	450
	$7,500	$7,500	$7,500	$7,500	$7,500

*Assumptions: A machine with an original cost of $8,000 is estimated to have a useful life of five years and an estimated salvage value of $500; the machine is assumed to be operated for the following number of hours, producing the following number of units:

Year	Hours Operated	Units Produced
1	1,800	5,000
2	3,000	5,500
3	3,200	6,500
4	6,000	6,500
5	1,000	1,500
	15,000	25,000

Exhibit 11.2 summarizes the results of the five depreciation method examples. Note the variability across the different methods for any given year. In spite of this variability, however, the *total* depreciation expense reported over the life of an asset must be the same under each of the methods. Thus, it can be seen that the financial reporting of depreciation is fundamentally a decision concerning the *timing* as to when an asset's cost is systematically allocated to the income statement in the form of depreciation expense.

The accounting entry to record the annual depreciation expense on an asset appears as follows:

```
Dr. Depreciation Expense (E) . . . . . . . . . . (inc.) 4,000
    Cr. Accumulated Depreciation (CA). . . . . . . . . . . .      (inc.) 4,000
```

Note that the cost basis of the asset is preserved in the PP&E account because the credit entry is to a contra-asset account. Using this approach, the balance sheet will reveal not only the original cost of the asset but also its total depreciation taken to date and its remaining undepreciated cost. From this information, it is possible to make rough estimates of the age of a company's assets—the larger the net book value relative to the original cost of the PP&E, the newer (on average) are the company's assets.

EXHIBIT 11.3

Depreciation-Method and Asset-Life Disclosures

Panel A—Snap-On-Tools Corporation

Property and equipment

Land, buildings, machinery, and equipment are carried at original cost. Depreciation and amortization are provided for primarily by using accelerated depreciation methods on all property acquired prior to December 31 in the current year. For financial statement purposes, the company adopted the straight-line depreciation method for all property acquired after December 30. The company believes the new method will more accurately reflect its financial results by better matching costs of new property over the useful lives of these assets. In addition, the new method more closely conforms with that prevalent in the industry.

The estimated service lives of property and equipment are as follows:

Buildings and improvements	5 to 45 years
Machinery and equipment	3 to 15 years
Furniture and fixtures	3 to 15 years
Transportation vehicles	2 to 5 years

Panel B—Ace Hardware Corp.

Depreciation expense is computed on both straight-line and accelerated methods based on estimated useful lives as follows:

	Useful Life (Years)	Principal Depreciation method
Buildings and improvements	10–40	Straight line
Warehouse equipment	5–10	Sum of years
Office equipment	3–10	Various
Manufacturing equipment	3–20	Straight line
Transportation equipment	3–7	Straight line

Panel C—Kmart Corporation

Depreciation

The company computes depreciation on owned property principally on the straight-line method for financial statement purposes and on accelerated methods for income tax purposes. Most store properties are leased and improvements are amortized over the term of the lease but not more than 25 years. Other annual rates used in computing depreciation for financial statement purposes are 2% to 4% for buildings, 10% to 14% for store fixtures, and 5% to 33% for other fixtures and equipment.

Presented in Exhibit 11.3 are the financial statement disclosures of three companies pertaining to their choices of asset lives and depreciation methods. In reviewing those examples, consider the impact of the different lives and methods on the companies' reported depreciation expense and depreciable fixed assets. In particular, note that for machinery and equipment, Snap-On-Tools Corporation generally uses shorter estimated lives than Kmart Corporation and uses mostly accelerated depreciation methods rather than the straight-line method. Clearly, Snap-On-Tools Corporation records a larger depreciation expense deduction sooner than Kmart, all other things being equal. Also note that Ace Hardware Corp., which has somewhat different asset lives than the other two companies, uses a variety of depreciation methods and has five categories of PP&E versus four and three for Snap-On-Tools and Kmart, respectively. Such variations between companies highlight some of the latitude left to management as they decide how best to depreciate their assets.

Capitalizing depreciation. The depreciation allocated to each accounting period may be charged, in part, against net income as a period expense (as has already been discussed) and, in part, to work-in-process inventory as manufacturing overhead (see Chapter 9). To the extent that the depreciation costs are incurred "under the factory roof" (that is, are a part of the costs of manufacturing a product), management should capitalize them as a product cost by increasing the Work-in-Process Inventory account instead of recording depreciation expense on the income statement. If added to Work-in-Process Inventory, the depreciation will become a deduction in the income statement only when the finished goods with which it is associated are sold and an accounting entry for the cost of goods sold is made.

Changes in Depreciation Accounting Policy

During the course of depreciating either a particular asset or an entire array of fixed assets, corporate managers may decide to modify or adjust their initial estimates and decisions underlying the calculation of depreciation. For example, a change in the depreciation method from the double-declining-balance method to the straight-line method might be undertaken because other similar companies are predominantly using the straight-line method. In this case, the decision to change depreciation methods is probably motivated by management's desire to appear to be using the industry-preferred method, as well as a desire to improve the firm's within-industry comparative financial standing. When such a change in accounting method is made, its cumulative effect is recorded on a net-of-taxes basis in the current financial statements, and all subsequent financial statements reflect the use of the new method.

To illustrate such a change, consider again the data presented in Exhibit 11.2. Assume, for example, that in Year 3 a change from the double-declining-balance method (DDB) to the straight-line method is to be made. Through the end of Year 2, depreciation totaling $5,120 has been taken under the DDB method, whereas if the straight-line method had been used, only $3,000 in depreciation deductions would have been recorded. Thus, at the beginning of Year 3, an entry to restate the depreciation account balances would be needed as follows:

```
Dr. Accumulated Depreciation (CA) . . . . . . . . . . . . . . . . . . . . . (dec.) 2,120*
     Cr. Cumulative Effect of Change in Accounting Method (Income) . . . . . . . .     (inc.) 2,120
*($5,120 − $3,000 = $2,120)
```

The account Cumulative Effect of Change in Accounting Method is reported on the company's Year 3 income statement and thus will increase the period's net income. Because of the unusual nature of this account, it is separately and prominently disclosed on the income statement if material in amount. In addition to the above entry to reflect the change in depreciation method, the regular Year 3 depreciation expense under the new method also needs to be recorded:

```
Dr. Depreciation Expense (E) . . . . . . . . . . . (inc.) 1,500
     Cr. Accumulated Depreciation (CA). . . . . . . . . . . . .     (inc.) 1,500
```

Another depreciation-related change often made by corporate managers involves the estimated useful life of an asset or a group of assets. This type of change involves a change in an *estimate* rather than in a *method* and is usually dealt with on a prospective, or future, basis. For example, if in Year 3 management decided that the expected useful life of an asset being depreciated was really eight years instead of five, no accounting entry would be required to restate the previous years' depreciation deductions. Instead, all future depreciation calculations would be based on a remaining estimated life of six rather than three years. Thus, an estimate change such as this does not affect prior published financial statements but only future reported results.

When accounting method or estimate changes are undertaken by management, the effect of the change on the current financial statements must be described in the company's

EXHIBIT 11.3

Changes in Depreciation Methods and Estimates

Panel A—AT&T

Accounting Change

Effective the beginning of the year, for certain network equipment, AT&T changed its method of depreciation from straight-line to sum-of-the-years' digits, shortened the estimated depreciable lives, and decreased the estimated net salvage. These changes were implemented to better match revenues and expenses because of rapid technological changes occurring in response to customer requirements and competition. The new depreciation method was applied retroactively to all digital circuit, digital operator services, and radio equipment. Other network equipment, principally lightguide cable and central office buildings, continues to be depreciated on a straight-line basis. The changes in estimates of depreciable lives and net salvage were made prospectively. The effect of these changes was to decrease net income by approximately $393 million or $0.36 per share. The cumulative prior years' effect of the change in depreciation method was not material.

Panel B—Owens-Corning Fiberglas Corporation

Depreciation of Plant and Equipment

During the year, the company completed a review of its fixed asset lives. The company determined that as a result of actions taken to increase its preventative maintenance and programs initiated with its equipment suppliers to increase the quality of their products, actual lives for certain asset categories were generally longer than the useful lives for depreciation purposes. Therefore, the company extended the estimated useful lives of certain categories of plant and equipment. The effect of this change in estimate reduced depreciation expense for the year by $14 million and increased income before cumulative effect of accounting change by $8 million ($0.19 per share).

footnotes. Exhibit 11.4 presents such footnote disclosures made by two prominent corporations—AT&T and Owens-Corning Fiberglas Corporation. Note in Panel A that AT&T changed three things—depreciation method, estimated useful lives, and estimated salvage value. All three changes had the combined effect of decreasing net income by almost $400 million. AT&T mentions that the portion of this decrease attributable to the cumulative effect of just the change in depreciation method is not material and thus not reported separately in the note or in the income statement. On the other hand, the financial effect of Owens-Corning's change is to increase pretax earnings by $8 million. The change made by Owens-Corning, however, did not involve a change in depreciation method but only in estimated useful lives, and even though material, it is thus not required to be shown separately in the income statement. It is important to note that although Owens-Corning's pretax earnings increased due to this accounting change, there was no increase in the company's operating cash flows, nor was there any increase in the operating efficiency of the company (the same can be said for AT&T).

Depreciation Myths

A number of myths exist concerning depreciation. One myth states that for financial reporting purposes, depreciation expense reflects the decline in the market value of the depreciable asset and that the asset's net book value approximates the asset's current fair market value. On the contrary, the recording of depreciation is a process of cost allocation, not of valuation. Accordingly, depreciation expense is not intended to equal the change in an asset's market value, nor is its net book value intended to reflect the market value of the asset at the end of any period.

A second depreciation myth is that the depreciation accounting process provides the means for replacement of the asset at the end of its useful life. On the contrary, the costs allocated to depreciation expense are costs *already incurred,* not some budgeted amount for a future period's purchase of a replacement asset. In fact, the recording of depreciation is not even premised on a belief that the asset will be replaced when it wears out.

Another myth is that depreciation provides cash. As discussed in Chapter 6, the statement of cash flows usually lists net income first among the sources of operating cash flows. To adjust this figure to a cash-based net income approximation, depreciation is added back. The sum of net income plus depreciation and other pertinent items is then labeled *cash flow from operations.* As a consequence of this separate listing of depreciation in the statement of cash flows, some financial statement readers have been led to the false conclusion that depreciation provides cash. This is *not so*! Depreciation is a noncash expense that is recognized under the accrual basis of accounting but in no way constitutes a cash inflow. Depreciation does, however, reduce the taxable net income amount reported on a company's tax return and thus lowers the amount of taxes to be paid. So to the extent that depreciation reduces the cash outflow for taxes otherwise due, it can be thought of as having an indirect cash flow benefit.

Tax Depreciation in the U.S.

In 1986, the U.S. Congress passed the Tax Reform Act of 1986—the second time in 5 years and the fourth time in 25 years that the tax rules concerning depreciable assets had undergone revision.[2] Each successive piece of legislation sought to restrict the diversity of depreciation practices employed for similar assets (for example, to standardize the estimated useful life of similar assets) and reflected a particular fiscal policy of the U.S. government at the time of passage (such as the use of shorter estimated asset lives as an attempt to stimulate increased corporate investment in capital assets). Under rules put in place by the 1986 Tax Reform Act, the **Modified Accelerated Cost Recovery System** (MACRS) is the only accelerated depreciation method acceptable for tax purposes; straight-line, machine-hours, and units-of-production methods are also still acceptable methods.

MACRS defines nine classifications of fixed asset lives and uses the term *cost recovery* in place of the term *depreciation:*

MACRS Classification	Asset Description
3-year property	Race horses and some special-use tools
5-year property	Autos, trucks, R&D equipment, certain technological equipment, computers, office machinery
7-year property	Office furniture, railroad track and rolling stock, some agricultural structures, and other unclassified property
10-year property	Vessels, barges, and tugs
15-year property	Communications equipment and water treatment facilities
20-year property	Some real property, sewage treatment facilities, and general-use agricultural buildings
27.5-year property	Residential real property
39-year property	Most building and plant facilities
50-year property	Railroad gradings and tunnel bores

[2] For assets put in service before 1962, IRS *Bulletin F* rules apply. For assets placed in service after 1962 and before 1971, managers may choose general depreciation rules or the Class Life System (CLS). After 1971 but before 1981, the taxpayer may choose from the Asset Depreciation Range (ADR) System or the general depreciation rules. In 1981 the Economic Recovery Tax Act of 1981 inaugurated the use of the Accelerated Cost Recovery System (ACRS), which applies to all assets placed in service between 1981 and 1986. Assets placed in service after 1986 are subject to MACRS.

Under MACRS, the cost of 3-year, 5-year, 7-year, and 10-year property may be recovered using the double-declining-balance method over 3, 5, 7, and 10 years, respectively. The cost of 15-year and 20-year property may be recovered using the 150 percent-declining-balance method over 15 and 20 years; the costs of 27.5-year, 39-year, and 50-year property are to be recovered using only the straight-line method. When using MACRS, estimated salvage value is *not* considered.

For tax purposes, all asset classes except the 27.5-year, 39-year, and 50-year classes must also conform to the **half-year convention.** An asset is said to have been put in service or disposed of at the mid-point of the year regardless of the date actually placed in service or disposed of, thereby allowing one-half of a year's depreciation in the year in which the asset is placed in service and one-half year's depreciation in the year in which the asset is disposed of. Moreover, for those classes of assets using one of the declining-balance methods, a switch to the straight-line method is permitted at the time during an asset's life when the prospective annual straight-line depreciation amount, recalculated using the net book value and remaining life as of that instant, exceeds that year's declining-balance method amount.

For new and used assets placed into service after December 31, 1986, the current tax law requires the use of MACRS as the only accelerated method. Companies must continue to use previously adopted tax depreciation methods on all fixed assets put into service prior to 1987. Those methods might include ACRS, sum-of-the-years' digits, various declining-balance methods, or other methods previously acceptable to the IRS.

Financial reporting and tax depreciation. The depreciation expense that a company records for external financial reporting is usually not the same amount as is reported on its income tax return. This may occur for a variety of legitimate reasons. For example, a company may choose to use the straight-line method of depreciation for its external financial statements but the MACRS method (as required by the IRS) for its income tax return.

For external financial statements, corporate managers typically adopt depreciation methods that result in a total depreciation expense for the year that indicates the cost of utilizing their fixed assets for the period while also striving to maximize reported net income. For tax return purposes, management should use the method that gives them the greatest tax savings. As a result, many corporate managers choose accelerated methods of depreciation and the shorter IRS lives for income tax return purposes but the straight-line method and longer estimated useful lives for financial reporting purposes. In such cases, the income tax actually owed (per the tax return) is not the same amount as the income tax due based on the income reported in the published annual report. In general, the tax liability (per the tax return), tax expense (per the accounting records), and related difference are recorded in an accounting entry such as the following:[3]

```
Dr. Income Tax Expense (E). . . . . . . . . . . . . (inc.) 120
     Cr. Income Taxes Payable (L). . . . . . . . . . . . . . . .        (inc.) 100
     Cr. Deferred Income Taxes (L) . . . . . . . . . . . . . . .        (inc.)  20
```

A detailed discussion of the Deferred Income Taxes account noted in this entry is left until Chapter 13. For now, it is important only to recognize the need for such an account in order to reconcile the difference between the tax expense and the tax liability accounts. In this illustration, the deferred income tax account is classified as a liability because the account presumably will be reduced in later years when the depreciation deducted on the income tax return becomes less than the depreciation expense reported in the published income statement.

---

[3] In some countries (such as Germany, Japan, and Sweden), the amount of depreciation expense deducted for tax purposes is limited to the depreciation charge taken for financial reporting (or book) purposes. As a consequence, no deferred income taxes result because the depreciation deductions for book and tax purposes are equivalent.

EXHIBIT 11.5

Pacific Gas & Electric Co.
Financial Reporting versus Tax-Return Depreciation

Depreciation

For financial reporting purposes, depreciation of plant in service is computed using a

straight-line remaining life method. For federal income tax purposes, the most liberal depreciation methods allowed by the Internal Revenue Code generally are used.

Exhibit 11.5 presents the depreciation disclosures of the Pacific Gas & Electric Company (PG&E) that highlight the differences in financial reporting and tax return depreciation. To illustrate the effect of such differences, we assume that PG&E purchased a piece of production equipment costing $100,000 that is classified under MACRS as five-year property. Assume further that PG&E's chief financial officer has decided to use straight-line depreciation for financial reporting purposes and estimates that the equipment will be used for eight years and will have a salvage value of $20,000 at the end of the eighth year. If the corporation uses a half-year convention for both tax and financial reporting purposes, the depreciation schedules for tax and financial reporting purposes will be as follows:

Year	MACRS Tax-Return Depreciation Expense	Financial Reporting Depreciation Expense
1	$ 20,000	$ 5,000
2	32,000	10,000
3	19,200	10,000
4	11,520	10,000
5	11,520*	10,000
6	5,760	10,000
7	0	10,000
8	0	10,000
9	0	5,000
Total	$100,000	$80,000

*Beginning in Year 5, the straight-line method over the asset's remaining years (1.5) provides a depreciation amount greater than that from the continued use of the double-declining-balance method; thus, Year 5's allowable depreciation switches to a straight-line amount.

In Year 1, PG&E will show depreciation expense of $5,000 in its income statement but will deduct $20,000 in its tax return for cost recovery under MACRS. This procedure will cause income on the company's tax return to be $15,000 less than its accounting income and, at a 34 percent tax rate, will defer $5,100 in taxes to subsequent years. In its income statement, PG&E will show its tax expense based on its income statement profit and, as a result, will recognize a deferred tax liability of $5,100 in its balance sheet.

Two additional aspects of this example are important to note. First, capital investment decisions involving net present value and internal rate of return techniques employing the cash flows resulting from depreciation-generated tax savings should be based on tax return depreciation deductions, not those reported for financial reporting purposes (these topics are usually part of a managerial finance course). Second, as noted earlier, MACRS ignores the salvage value of an asset, and this permits greater tax return depreciation deductions over the life of an asset than would otherwise be taken in the published income statement. On the other hand, the IRS has reduced the amount of flexibility available to a company preparing its tax return by eliminating those decisions relating to the length of an asset's life, the expected salvage value, and effectively, the method of depreciation.

Repairs, Maintenance, and Betterments

Costs incurred for the purpose of maintaining the existing service level of PP&E are classified as *repairs and maintenance* and should be treated by managers as expenses of the period in which they are incurred. Costs incurred to improve an asset beyond its original service potential are viewed as *betterments* and should be capitalized rather than expensed. Capitalizing betterments increases an asset's book value because these costs are added to the asset's original recorded cost. The capitalized cost is subsequently expensed over future periods as an additional component of depreciation. The first part of Phelps Dodge Corporation's PP&E footnote (see Panel B, Exhibit 11.8) makes this distinction.

Distinguishing between an ordinary repair or maintenance expenditure and an asset betterment expenditure is difficult in many instances. For both financial accounting and income tax purposes (in this area, financial reporting and tax guidelines are the same), management's rationale for a particular expenditure and the nature of the asset alteration itself are important factors in determining whether the expenditure is properly recorded as a repair/maintenance expense item or as a betterment item. For example, replacing a roof on a production plant after 2 years is probably a repair item to be expensed, whereas replacing a roof after 20 years is probably best treated as a betterment item to be capitalized on the balance sheet. Similarly, servicing the engines of a fleet of trucks every 5,000 miles represents a normal maintenance expense, but rebuilding the engines after 100,000 miles of use represents a betterment expenditure because the life of the asset has been extended.

The reporting of these asset-related expenditures should attempt to reflect the intended purpose of the expenditure. For financial reporting purposes, managers generally argue for capitalizing such expenditures in order to keep current reported profits as high as possible (by reducing the current level of deductions against net income). For tax purposes, however, the greatest benefit is achieved by expensing as many of these PP&E-related expenditures in the current period as is permitted. Once again, this situation presents another instance about which there may be disagreements between corporate management and tax authorities as to what constitutes a repair/maintenance and what constitutes a betterment. It does stand to reason, however, that the logic applied to a particular expenditure would lead to a single classification that should be used for both tax and financial reporting purposes.

Impairment

A long-standing concern regarding the reporting and valuation of long-lived assets has been the recognition and timing of asset impairments. Because assets are valuable to an company by virtue of their revenue-producing capacity, an **impairment** occurs whenever that revenue-generating ability is reduced. Consider, for example, a real estate development company holding land whose market value has fallen below its original cost. If this decline in value is not expected to recover in the foreseeable future, it is reasonable to conclude that the land's future revenue-producing capacity for the company has been impaired; and

E X H I B I T 1 1 . 6

Asset Impairment Disclosures

Panel A—Coca-Cola Enterprises, Inc.

Impairment of Long-Lived Assets

In the event that facts and circumstances indicate that the cost of franchise assets or other assets may be impaired, an evaluation of recoverability would be performed. If an evaluation is required, the estimated future undiscounted cash flows associated with the asset would be compared to the asset's carrying amount to determine if a write-down to market value or discounted cash flow value is required.

Panel B—Stone Container Corporation

Goodwill

Goodwill is amortized on a straight-line basis over 40 years and is recorded net of accumulated amortization of approximately $129 million. The company assesses at each balance sheet date whether there has been a permanent impairment in the value of goodwill. This is accomplished by determining whether projected undiscounted future cash flows from operations exceed the net book value of goodwill as of the assessment date. Such projections reflect price, volume, and cost assumptions. Additional factors considered by management in the preparation of the projections and in assessing the value of goodwill include the effects of obsolescence, demand, competition, and other pertinent economic factors and trends and prospects that may have an impact on the value or remaining useful life of goodwill.

consequently, a write-down (that is, a loss) on the carrying value of the land should be recorded on the company's financial statements.

Regrettably, it is often quite difficult to unequivocally conclude that an asset's revenue-generating ability has declined or, alternatively, in the context of our real estate example above, that the drop in real estate prices is anything but temporary. To help resolve this issue, the FASB has developed criteria for financial statement preparers to help identify when an asset impairment has definitively occurred, and consequently, when a loss should be recorded. The accounting entry to record an impairment might appear as follows:

```
Dr. Loss on Asset Impairment (Loss) . . . . . . . . (inc.) 2,000,000
     Cr. Property, Plant, and Equipment (A) . . . . . . . . . . . . . . .      (dec.) 2,000,000
```

The FASB concluded that all long-lived assets (including identifiable intangibles and goodwill) should be reviewed for possible revaluation whenever events or changes in circumstances indicate that the carrying amount of the assets may not be fully recoverable. Examples of such events or changes in circumstances may include the following:

- A significant decline in the market value of an asset.
- A significant change in the extent or manner in which an asset is used.
- A significant adverse change in the business climate that affects the value of an asset.
- An accumulation of capitalized costs significantly in excess of the amount originally expected to acquire or construct the asset.
- A forecast suggesting that the use of the asset will be associated with continuing losses.

If any of these events or circumstances are present, the company should estimate the future cash flows expected to result from the use of the asset and its eventual disposition. If the sum

EXHIBIT 11.7

Chiron Corporation
Consolidated Statement of Operations
(in thousands, except per share data)

	Year Ended December 31	
	1997	1996
Income (loss) from operations	75,207	90,263
Gain on sale of noncurrent assets	18,597	—
Gain on sale of interest in affiliated company	—	12,226
Interest expense	(33,257)	(30,934)
Other income, net	16,348	7,190
Income (loss) from continuing operations before income taxes	76,895	78,745
Provision for income taxes	26,057	22,142
Income (loss) from continuing operations	50,838	56,603
Discontinued operations (Note 3):		
Income (loss) from discontinued operations	5,224	(1,458)
Gain on disposal of discontinued operations	15,157	—
Net income (loss)	$ 71,219	$ 55,145
Earnings per common share:		
Income (loss) from continuing operations	$ 0.29	$ 0.33
Net income (loss)	$ 0.41	$ 0.33
Earnings per common share—assuming dilution:		
Income (loss) from continuing operations	$ 0.29	$ 0.32
Net income (loss)	$ 0.40	$ 0.31

of the *undiscounted* future net cash flows is less than its carrying value, an impairment loss should be immediately recorded. Panel A of Exhibit 11.6 illustrates a general statement regarding impairment as disclosed by Coca-Cola Enterprises, Inc. Panel B presents the goodwill impairment policy of the Stone Container Corporation.

Accounting for the Sale or Disposition of an Asset

When a PP&E item is sold or otherwise disposed of, both the original cost and the associated accumulated depreciation must be removed from the books. If the proceeds from the disposal exceed the asset's net book value, a gain is recognized. If the proceeds are less than the net book value, a loss is recognized. For example, if a machine with an original cost of $90,000 and accumulated depreciation of $70,000 is sold for $30,000 cash, the entry to record the sale is as follows:

```
Dr. Cash (A) . . . . . . . . . . . . . . . . . . . . . . . (inc.) 30,000
Dr. Accumulated Depreciation (CA) . . . . . (dec.) 70,000
    Cr. Machine (A) . . . . . . . . . . . . . . . . . . . . . . . . .          (dec.) 90,000
    Cr. Gain on Sale (Gain) . . . . . . . . . . . . . . . . . . . .          (inc.)  10,000
```

EXHIBIT 11.7 concluded

Chiron Corporation
Consolidated Statement of Cash Flows
(in thousands)

	Year Ended December 31	
	1997	1996
Cash flows from operating activities:		
Net income (loss)	$ 71,219	$ 55,145
Adjustments to reconcile net income (loss) to net cash provided by (used in) operating activities:		
Depreciation and amortization	102,589	105,080
Impairment loss on long-lived assets	31,300	—
Gain on sale of noncurrent assets	(18,597)	—
Gain on sale of equity securities and interest in affiliated company	(5,541)	(12,226)
Write-off of purchased in-process technologies	—	—
Write-off of property, plant, equipment and leasehold improvements	4,291	5,031
Reserves	30,046	16,895
Changes in estimated liabilities	(17,596)	—
Deferred income taxes	(20,556)	6,972
Tax benefits from employee stock plans	17,923	1,398
Undistributed earnings of affiliates	(14,473)	(6,841)
Other, net	11,614	17,393
Changes, excluding effect of acquisitions, to:		
Accounts receivable	(12,974)	(75,825)
Inventories	(40,635)	(48,545)
Other current assets	8,355	(20,187)
Accounts payable and accrued expenses	(2,062)	11,427
Current portion of unearned revenue	(5,907)	(1,162)
Other current liabilities	5,890	1,921
Other noncurrent liabilities	4,626	6,253
Net cash provided by (used in) operating activities	149,512	62,729
Cash flows from investing activities:		
Purchases of investments in marketable debt securities	(219,522)	(55,008)
Proceeds from sale and maturity of investments in marketable debt securities	120,306	143,922
Businesses acquired, net of cash acquired	—	(374)
Capital expenditures	(77,524)	(120,162)
Proceeds from sale of assets	29,928	—
Proceeds from sale of equity securities and interest in affiliated company	5,596	14,000
Purchases of investments in equity securities and affiliated companies	(10,942)	(130,308)
Increase in other assets	(16,804)	(43,351)
Net cash used in investing activities	(168,962)	(191,281)
Cash flows from financing activities:		
Net borrowings (payments) under line of credit arrangements	—	(12,606)
Proceeds from issuance of short-term debt	20,589	100,000
Proceeds from issuance of common stock	61,502	44,597
Proceeds from capital contribution from Novartis	—	—
Repayment of notes payable and capital leases	(32,272)	(9,643)
Net cash provided by financing activities	49,819	122,348
Net increase (decrease) in cash and cash equivalents	30,369	(6,204)
Cash and cash equivalents at beginning of the year	68,114	74,318
Cash and cash equivalents at end of the year	$ 98,483	$ 68,114

The $10,000 gain on sale appears in the income statement covering the period in which the sale was made. Consistent with the reporting of gains from the sale of inventory, the gain on the sale of PP&E is reported in the period in which the sales event takes place rather than in the period in which the asset's market value appreciated above its net book value. (This latter possibility, as discussed in Chapter 8, is the approach followed for marketable equity securities classified as trading securities.) The principal difference between these two approaches relates to the degree of objectivity present in attempts to assess when the appreciation in asset value occurred. In the absence of a market mechanism, like the stock market, to establish appreciated value objectively, GAAP relies on the occurrence of an actual sale transaction as a signal to record value appreciation (that is, a gain on sale).

In contrast to a gain on the sale of inventory, which is considered to be operations related, the gain (or loss) on the sale of PP&E is considered to be a nonoperating event because it is assumed that the company is not in the business of selling its PP&E. Thus, in the statement of cash flows (Chapter 6) and in the income statement (Chapter 5), PP&E sales are reported, but not as part of continuing operations. Exhibit 11.7 depicts the fact that Chiron Corporation reported gains from sales of PP&E as a separate (nonoperating) line item in its income statement and statement of cash flows (see shaded areas). Moreover, in order to report the total proceeds from such sales, which would include amounts recognized as gains, the operating cash flows section in Chiron's statement of cash flows shows an adjustment for the gains, and the total proceeds are then shown in the investing activities section.

Financial Statement Presentation and Disclosure

In the balance sheet, PP&E are shown in the noncurrent asset section. Land is reported at its original cost, whereas buildings, machinery, vehicles, and equipment are shown at original cost less the portion of that cost previously allocated as depreciation.

The annual expense for depreciation may or may not be shown in the body of the income statement. If it is not reported separately in the income statement, the amount expensed may be found in the notes to financial statements or as a line item in the statement of cash flows. The notes to the financial statements include substantial information regarding a company's fixed assets, depreciation policies, and related expenditures. Complete examples of the typical financial statement disclosures for PP&E are presented in Exhibit 11.8.

Managerial Issues

The property, plant, and equipment purchase decision is one of the most important decisions a manager makes because of the size of the investment and the long-term nature of the asset and related financing. A number of financial considerations that parallel some of this chapter's earlier discussions are involved in such purchase decisions. If the decision to buy a piece of equipment is determined, in part, on the asset's estimated net present value or internal rate of return (two very common capital budgeting techniques), then the asset's estimated useful life, periodic tax depreciation amount, salvage value, initial cost, and gains or losses on disposal of the assets being replaced are important factors to be considered. These factors are important because they influence the amount and timing of the cash flows generated by the particular asset under consideration and, thus, are an integral part in calculating the asset's net present value.

Some observers of corporate financial reporting have sarcastically observed that corporate accounting departments have become the best-performing profit centers for many companies—a comment that reflects the bottom-line impact attributable to the various

EXHIBIT 11.8

Fixed Asset Disclosures

Panel A—Stone Container Corp.

Property, Plant, Equipment, and Depreciation

Property, plant, and equipment are stated at cost. Expenditures for maintenance and repairs are charged to income as incurred. Additions, improvements, and major replacements are capitalized. The cost and accumulated depreciation related to assets sold or retired are removed from the accounts, and any gain or loss is credited or charged to income.

For financial reporting purposes, depreciation is provided on the straight-line method over the estimated useful lives of depreciable assets, or over the duration of the leases for capitalized leases, based on the following annual rates:

Type of Asset	Rates
Machinery and equipment	5% to 33%
Buildings and leasehold improvements	2% to 7%
Land improvements	4% to 7%

Effective the beginning of the year, the company changed its estimates of the useful lives of certain machinery and equipment at its paper mills. Mill asset depreciation lives that previously averaged 16 years were increased to an average of 20 years, while mill asset depreciation lives that previously averaged 10–12 years were increased to an average of 14–16 years. These changes were made to better reflect the estimated periods during which such assets will remain in service. The change had the effect of reducing depreciation expense by $39.8 million and increasing net income by $20.2 million, or $0.34 per common share.

Panel B—Phelps Dodge Corp.

Property, Plant, and Equipment

Property, plant, and equipment are carried at cost. Cost of significant assets includes capitalized interest incurred during the construction and development period. Expenditures for replacements and betterments are capitalized; maintenance and repair expenditures are charged to operations as incurred.

The principal depreciation methods used are the units of production method for mining, smelting, and refining operations and, for other operations, the straight-line method based upon the estimated lives of specific classes or groups of depreciable assets. Upon disposal of assets depreciated on a group basis, cost less salvage is charged to accumulated depreciation.

Values for mining properties represent mainly acquisition costs or pre-1932 engineering valuations. Depletion of mines is computed on the basis of an overall unit rate applied to the pounds of principal products sold from mine production.

Mine exploration costs and development costs to maintain production of operating mines are charged to operations as incurred. Mine development expenditures at new mines and major development expenditures at operating mines that are expected to benefit future production are capitalized and amortized on the units of production method over the estimated commercially recoverable minerals.

financial reporting alternatives available under GAAP. Recall from Chapter 9, for example, the discussion of how net income could be significantly influenced by management's choice of LIFO versus FIFO for purposes of valuing ending inventory and the cost of goods sold. A similar concern exists with regard to fixed assets: Management's choice of depreciation method, expected useful life, and anticipated salvage value can have a material, direct effect on the company's bottom line. Recall our earlier example involving Owens-Corning, which increased its net income by more than $8 million through discretionary PP&E accounting policy decisions. Although managers do have this flexibility available to them under GAAP, changes in accounting methods and estimates must be documented in the published financial statements. Such changes should be infrequent to avoid the appearance of overt earnings management.

Other, less critical management concerns include reducing the clerical costs associated with the accounting for fixed assets. In this regard, most companies, as a matter of policy, set a lower limit (for example, $500) for capitalizing assets. The purchase of any item costing less than this amount is expensed. This policy reduces the number of items that must be depreciated on a periodic basis even though many of those assets expensed will be used for more than one year. Because of the immateriality of these small dollar items, they do not affect the overall accuracy of the financial statements.

Another clerical-saving policy involves depreciating assets for a half-year in the year of acquisition and in the final year of their planned life rather than using the actual fractional parts of the year. Many companies adopt a half-year depreciation convention for the year of acquisition. Under this convention, capitalized property is depreciated on a six-month basis for the first year regardless of when it was acquired. A similar convention is normally adopted for the year of disposition if the asset is not fully depreciated at the time of disposition. Fortunately, in the U.S. the IRS recognizes the validity of this convention.

Time and money also can be saved by using similar policies for both accounting and tax purposes when possible. Adopting the same depreciation method for general accounting as that used for tax purposes, for example, minimizes the amount of work required to maintain two sets of records. Managers still must ensure, however, that fixed asset costs are allocated for accounting purposes in a rational and systematic manner. Managers also should be concerned with preserving cash flows to the company through well-planned tax depreciation policies.

INTANGIBLE ASSETS

Accounting for assets such as inventories and property, plant, and equipment seems relatively straightforward because these items are tangible in nature and their revenue-producing potential as assets is readily apparent. In contrast, the accounting for an intangible asset may not be so readily apparent because such assets do not physically produce goods or services. The term **intangible asset** refers to "certain long-lived legal rights and competitive advantages developed or acquired by a business enterprise"[4] exemplified by such items as patents, trademarks, and franchises. In the following section we will focus on such questions as: What cost should be assigned to a trademark on the balance sheet? Should a trademark be depreciated? If so, what is its useful life?

The financial reporting for most intangible assets is similar to that for fixed tangible assets such as property, plant, and equipment. At the date of acquisition, an intangible asset's cost must be determined and recorded at the fair market value of the consideration given up or the item acquired, whichever is more clearly determinable. When payment is noncash, every effort should be made to determine the market value of the noncash payment. If that is not possible, then the corporate manager should attempt to determine the market value of the intangible asset received. The consideration given (or the value of the asset received) becomes the basis for recording the asset—in effect, its recorded cost.

Consider, for example, the purchase of a franchise agreement for a combination of cash and capital stock. At the time of purchase, the capital stock has a market value of $250,000; hence, the accounting entry to record the acquisition of the franchise appears as follows:

```
Dr. Franchise (A). . . . . . . . . . . . . . . . . (inc.) 300,000
    Cr. Cash (A). . . . . . . . . . . . . . . . . . . . . . . . . . .   (dec.)  50,000
    Cr. Capital Stock (OE) . . . . . . . . . . . . . . . . . . . .   (inc.) 250,000
```

---

[4] *1998 GAAP Guide* (New York: Harcourt Brace & Company, 1998), p. 23.04.

Over its useful economic life, the intangible asset's recorded cost must be allocated to the periods benefited. GAAP assumes that the economic utility of an intangible asset declines (is used up) over its life, and therefore the total cost should be systematically allocated as a period expense against the income of the company. This process, which is similar to the depreciation of fixed assets, is referred to as **amortization.** The period of time over which the recording of amortization takes place depends on the estimated economic life of the asset and varies from case to case. Generally accepted accounting principles provide the following insights:

> The recorded costs of intangible assets should be amortized by systematic charges to income over the periods estimated to be benefited....The cost of each type of intangible should be amortized on the basis of the estimated life of that specific asset....The period of amortization should not, however, exceed 40 years.[5]

Amortization of an intangible asset normally relies on the straight-line method over the estimated economic life of the asset unless an alternative method can be shown to comply more closely with the "using up" of the asset. By convention, amortization expense usually results in a direct reduction to the intangible asset account rather than an increase to a contra-asset allowance account as is done for depreciation charges related to property, plant, and equipment. In the previous franchise example, if the contractual term of the franchise agreement was 10 years, the accounting entry to record each year's amortization expense is as follows:

```
Dr. Franchise Amortization Expense (E). . . (inc.) 30,000
    Cr. Franchise (A) . . . . . . . . . . . . . . . . . . . . . . . . .        (dec.) 30,000
```

As with any asset, when intangible assets are disposed of, sold, or exchanged, they must be removed from the accounts, and any gain or loss must be recorded at that time. Continuing with the previous example, assume that after eight years the franchise is sold for a cash payment of $80,000. The entry appears as follows:

```
Dr. Cash (A) . . . . . . . . . . . . . . . . . . . . . . (inc.) 80,000
    Cr. Franchise (A) . . . . . . . . . . . . . . . . . . . . . . . . .        (dec.) 60,000
    Cr. Gain on Sale of Franchise (Gain) . . . . . . . . . . .        (inc.)  20,000
```

A Taxonomy for Intangible Assets

Intangible assets may differ from one another in several ways. Depending on these key dimensions, the accounting for the intangible asset under consideration may differ from that just described for the franchise example.

From a financial reporting perspective, managers must consider three key characteristics of intangibles. The first characteristic is *identifiability and separability:* Can the intangible asset be considered separately and distinctly from the other assets of the company? The usual test for separate identity is to determine whether the asset can be sold individually (as can a patent) or is so intertwined with the company that it cannot be separated (as is customer goodwill). The second issue pertains to the *manner of acquisition:* Was the intangible asset developed internally (like a proprietary manufacturing process) or was it

[5] Accounting Principles Board, *Opinion No. 17* "Intangible Assets" (APB, 1970), par. 9.

E X H I B I T   1 1 . 9

A Classification Taxonomy for Intangible Assets

	Asset specifically identifiable and separable	Asset not specifically identifiable and separable
Internally developed	• R&D costs • Costs specifically attached to development of proprietary products or processes **Expense** I	II • Customer relations • Quality reputation **Expense**

Externally developed	III
	
	• Costs of obtaining a
	  - patent
	  - copyright
	  - trademark or tradename
	  - franchise
	• Organization costs
	• Beneficial contracts
	• Government concessions
	
	Capitalize
		IV
		
		• Excess purchase price paid on acquisition of another company (goodwill)
		
		Capitalize

Method of acquisition

purchased externally (like a franchise or an exclusive license)? A final issue pertains to the expected *period of benefit:* What is the economic life of the intangible asset? For some intangible assets, such as patents and franchises, the maximum economic life is legally or contractually determined. For others, such as trademarks, the economic life is not easily determined because of the potential for continual legal renewals and extensions. Moreover, the useful life of an intangible asset, like a trademark or patent, may be affected by product or process obsolescence, competitors' actions, and changes in technology. The only guidelines available to managers of U.S. companies in choosing an appropriate useful life is that the period selected should not be longer than the intangible's legal life, if it has one, and it cannot exceed 40 years in any case.

Exhibit 11.9 presents a summary of these dimensions with a taxonomy for a variety of intangible assets that distinguishes between those that are specifically identifiable and separable and those that are not and between those assets developed internally and those acquired externally.

Accounting Guidelines

Internally developed intangibles. The costs associated with internally developed intangible assets that are not specifically identifiable and separable are expensed against income in the period incurred. Stated in the language of current financial reporting standards, costs "...inherent in a continuing business and related to the enterprise as a whole—such as [customer] goodwill—should be deducted from income when incurred."[6] On the other hand, internally incurred costs associated with identifiable and separable intangible assets are expensed unless they are incurred under contract to an outside party. A classic example are R&D expenses incurred under a contractual agreement for the benefit of another entity. These expenses should be capitalized as an inventory-type item (that is, one held for sale) as opposed to a depreciable asset (one held for internal production).

On the other hand, consider the issue of in-house research and development costs. Prior to 1975, accounting convention was to capitalize R&D expenses, based on the observation that such expenses were investments in the products and operations of the future and were thus a cost of bringing those future assets to a usable condition. However, because of practical realities (less than 1 in 10 new product ideas ever go to market, and the ability to predict which one will be successful is highly uncertain), capitalizing R&D expenditures seldom achieved the ultimate matching of revenues and expenses it sought to achieve.

A recent case highlights the nontrivial issue of accounting for R&D expenditures. During the 1980s, Glaxo-Wellcome spent and expensed more than $80 million on R&D that ultimately led to the AIDS drug AZT. As the R&D was being incurred, management did not know whether the outcome would result in an effective, marketable AIDS drug. All expenditures therefore were expensed, as were another $700 million of R&D on other diseases that produced nothing of significance. On the day that the U.S. Food and Drug Administration approved AZT, it became a valuable asset that was not, and could not, be reported on the balance sheet. In setting the retail price for AZT, however, Glaxo-Wellcome managers asked this question: What is the cost of the product? Various stakeholders in the pricing decision argued for quite different points of view. Some argued that only the $80 million specifically associated with the AZT product development should be considered; others argued that AZT pricing had to be sufficient to recover the entire R&D budget of $780 million. Still others argued that the price should be merely the cost involved in manufacturing the drug. This debate illustrates the divergent views that exist as to whether R&D should be considered part of a product's cost, and, if so, whether only direct R&D costs or both direct and indirect costs be considered. Financial reporting practice does not help management in this case because it requires the conservative "solution" of treating R&D expenditures as a period cost rather than a product cost. In so doing, GAAP emphasizes objectivity over subjectivity and conservatism over optimism, resulting in a decoupling of accounting policy from strategic management decisions.

Externally developed intangibles. The consideration paid to external parties for control of specifically identifiable and separable intangible assets (Exhibit 11.9, Quadrant III) should be capitalized and systematically amortized over the economic life of the asset (but not to exceed 40 years). Examples include government concessions (such as licenses to develop a country's resources), beneficial contracts for goods or services below market rates, and trademarks.

Patents, for example, are exclusive legal rights to products registered with the U.S. Patent Office; they recognize the holder's right to use, manufacture, dispose of, and control in every way the patented product or process without hindrance from others. Patents have a legal life of 17 years, but their economic life may be much shorter because of technological

---

[6] Accounting Principles Board, *Opinion No. 17.*

EXHIBIT 11.10

Intangible Asset Disclosures

Panel A—Chiron Corporation

Intangible assets consist primarily of purchased technologies, goodwill, and patents, and are amortized on a straight-line basis over their estimated useful lives, ranging from 3 to 17 years.

In accordance with Statement of Financial Accounting Standard No. 121, "Accounting for the Impairment of Long-Lived Assets," the company reviews, as circumstances dictate, the carrying amount of its intangible assets. Recoverability is determined by comparing the projected undiscounted net cash flows of the long-lived assets against their respective carrying amounts. The amount of impairment, if any, is measured based on the excess of the carrying value over the fair value.

Panel B—McDonnell Douglas Corp.

Intangible Assets

Intangible assets consist of capitalized computer software and the unamortized balances of the excess of the cost of acquired companies (or significant interests therein) over the values assigned to net tangible assets. The latter amounts have been assigned to government programs, computer software, leaseholds, and goodwill. These intangibles are being amortized over 3 to 10 years, except goodwill, which has various periods up to 40 years.

Panel C—Polaroid Corp.

Patents and Trademarks

Patents and trademarks are valued at $1.

Panel D—Air Products, Inc.

Patents

Expenses related to the development of patents are deducted from income as they occur. Patents acquired from other companies are recorded at their purchase price and charged to income over the remaining life of the patent.

---

obsolescence. Similarly, *copyrights* are legal rights of protection given to the creators of published materials. U.S. copyright law has recently been changed so that copyrights now extend protection for the life of the creator plus 50 years, or if the copyright is held by a corporation (deemed to have an indeterminate life), 75 years from the date of first publication. *Franchises* are the rights granted by one company to another to use a specific designation in their business; use can be limited in term by contract or be renewable indefinitely to create essentially an indeterminate life. If a franchise is renewable indefinitely, it should be amortized over a period not to exceed 40 years. *Trademarks* are registered claims of ownership to names, symbols, slogans, or other devices providing distinctive identity of a product. Although they have no legally limited life, trademarks often have limited economic life. If an estimate of the economic life can be made, it should be used as the term for amortization of the asset. If no estimate of economic life can be made, the asset should be amortized over a period not to exceed 40 years. As noted in Exhibit 11.9 (Quadrant III), the costs of obtaining a patent, copyright, franchise, or trademark should be capitalized as intangible assets. It is important to note that the costs of producing an asset (for example, a feature motion picture) should be reported as an asset separate from the costs incurred in obtaining the copyright on the film.

Exhibit 11.10 presents several corporate disclosures for intangible assets representing different approaches to amortization. Note in particular McDonnell Douglas's statement as to the variety of intangible assets reported in its balance sheet and to the fact that they are being amortized over 3 to 10 years. Chiron Corporation, on the other hand, chooses to amortize somewhat similar items over 3 to 17 years. Air Products' disclosure points out that internally incurred costs leading to a patent are expensed whereas externally incurred costs

E X H I B I T   1 1 . 1 1

Dresser Industries' Disclosure for Bredero
Price Holding Acquisition

The company acquired all the outstanding stock of Bredero Price Holding B.V., a Netherlands corporation, from Koninklijke Begemann Groep N.V. for approximately $161.5 million in cash. Bredero Price is a multinational company that provides pipe coating for both onshore and offshore markets.

The company also acquired TK Valve & Manufacturing, Inc., from Sooner Pipe & Supply Corporation, Tulsa, Oklahoma, for approximately $143.5 million in cash. TK

Valve supplies ball valves for the oil and gas production and transmission industry.

The purchase price exceeded the fair value of the net assets acquired by approximately $122 million for Bredero Price and approximately $92 million for TK Valve. Both acquisitions were accounted for as purchases. The resulting goodwill is being amortized on a straight-line basis over 40 years.

---

associated with acquisition of a patent are capitalized. Last, note how Polaroid Corp. reports the patents on all of its very valuable, highly lucrative proprietary products and processes— at $1. Because the bulk of such costs were internally incurred, and because the patent filing costs were probably immaterial relative to the asset's value, all such costs were expensed. In order to draw the reader's attention to their patented propriety processes and products, however, Polaroid chooses to report them, albeit at the unique cost figure of $1.

Goodwill: Special considerations. As has already been mentioned, costs associated with internally created goodwill (such as public service expenditures, employee development, charitable contributions, customer service expenses, and so on) are not capitalized. They are expensed in the period in which they are incurred. As discussed in Chapter 10, the acquisition of another business, however, often creates the need to identify and record a goodwill intangible asset pertaining to the acquired company (Exhibit 11.9, Quadrant IV). Consider for a moment the fact that the only reason Dresser Industries' management was willing to pay in excess of $122 million more for Bredero Price Holding B.V. than the fair market value of Bredero's net assets was the customer loyalty, managerial talent, sound reputation, and so on already built up by Bredero Price (Exhibit 11.11). Although Bredero Price was never permitted to record an intangible asset for such goodwill-related factors, the external acquisition of Bredero Price by Dresser Industries was an event that justified Dresser's recording of Bredero's goodwill. In essence, a marketplace valuation of that goodwill had been made and confirmed via the payment of a price for Bredero Price in excess of Bredero's net assets' appraised fair market value. This premium paid was recorded as goodwill on Dresser's books. In the U.S., such goodwill is assumed to be of indeterminate life but, by convention, is amortized over a life not to exceed 40 years.

Beginning in 1994, goodwill became tax-deductible in the United States over an amortizable life of 15 years. When a company's estimated amortizable life of goodwill for accounting purposes (usually 40 years) differs from that assumed for tax purposes, the effect of this difference is captured in the deferred income tax account. (There will be more on this topic in Chapter 13.)

NATURAL RESOURCES

Natural resources include such assets as timber, oil, gas, iron ore, coal, and uranium. Like intangible assets, natural resources may be either internally or externally developed. When these assets are externally developed, they are reported on the balance sheet at their acquisition cost less any depletion taken subsequent to acquisition. Alternatively, when they are internally developed, several valuation approaches may be adopted.

The two principal valuation alternatives that exist for companies in the extractive industries are the full cost method and the successful efforts method. Under the **full cost method,** *all* costs associated with the exploration for and development of natural resources are capitalized to the natural resource accounts on the balance sheet. There is little disagreement over this method *except* when unsuccessful exploration activities are involved. Under the full cost method, the costs of unsuccessful exploration activities are also capitalized to the balance sheet under the philosophy that the development of new resource reserves is a speculative activity involving some inherent failure. In contrast, under the **successful efforts method,** only the costs associated with successful exploration and development activity are capitalized to the balance sheet accounts. The costs of any unsuccessful activity are expensed against net income.

Both the full cost and the successful efforts methods are generally accepted, and thus both are available for use by managers of natural resource companies in the extractive industries. In practice, however, only small resource companies tend to use the full cost method, whereas larger companies tend to prefer the successful efforts method (see panels A, B, and C, Exhibit 11.12), which is also the method of choice among most preparers of financial statements. Under both methods, however, the costs capitalized to the balance sheet are subject to certain constraints in a manner similar to the effect that the lower-of-cost-or-market method has on inventory. In the event that the current market value of a company's reserves of natural resources declines substantially, it may become necessary to write down the value of the capitalized balance sheet values. Thus, just as the lower-of-cost-or-market method prevents the overstatement of inventories, this "ceiling test" similarly constrains the value of natural resources on the balance sheet.

Natural resource companies not involved in the extractive industries, such as a timber company, usually capitalize all of their initial expenditures while expensing their ongoing maintenance and development costs. Except in those cases involving forest fires, which destroy substantial portions of a company's timber reserves, the initial capitalized cost is carried on the balance sheet until the reserves are harvested (see Panel D, Exhibit 11.12).

Depletion

Depletion refers to the periodic expensing of the capitalized natural resource cost. Unlike depreciation, there is only one generally accepted depletion approach, the units-of-production method, which is conceptually and procedurally similar to the units-of-production method of depreciation sometimes used by companies for machinery and equipment. The first step is to estimate the number of units—barrels of crude oil, tons of ore, or board feet of timber—in a well, mine, or tract of forest. Next, a depletion rate per unit must be determined. For example, if the estimated number of tons of ore in a mine was 200,000 and the mine's original cost (less estimated residual value) was $820,000, the depletion rate per ton would be $4.10. Last, the depletion expense for the year is figured. So if during the first year 22,000 tons were taken out, the depletion expense for the year would be 22,000 times $4.10, or $90,200. The accounting entry follows:

EXHIBIT 11.12

Natural Resource Disclosures

Panel A—Homestake Mining Co.

Exploration costs, including those incurred through partnerships and joint ventures, are charged to operations in the year incurred.

Preoperating and development costs relating to new mines and major programs at existing mines are capitalized. Ordinary mine development costs to maintain production and underground equipment acquisitions are charged to operations as incurred.

Depreciation, depletion, and amortization of mining properties, mine development costs, and major plant facilities are computed principally by the units-of-production method (based on estimated proven and probable ore reserves). Proven and probable ore reserves reflect estimated quantities of commercially recoverable reserves that the company believes can be recovered in the future from known mineral deposits. Such estimates are based on current and projected costs and product prices.

Panel B—Amoco Corporation

Costs Incurred in Oil and Gas Producing Activities

The corporation follows the successful efforts method of accounting. Costs of property acquisitions, successful exploratory wells, all development costs (including CO_2 and certain other injected materials in enhanced recovery projects), and support equipment and facilities are capitalized. Unsuccessful exploratory wells are expensed when determined to be nonproductive. Production costs, overhead, and all exploration costs other than exploratory drilling are charged against income as incurred.

Depreciation, Depletion, and Amortization

Depletion of the cost of producing oil and gas properties, amortization of related intangible drilling and development costs, and depreciation of tangible lease and well equipment are computed on the units-of-production method.

The portion of costs of unproved oil and gas properties estimated to be nonproductive is amortized over projected holding periods.

Panel C—Mobil Corp.

Oil and Gas Accounting Method

Mobil follows the "successful efforts" method of accounting prescribed by Financial Accounting Standard (FAS) 19, Financial Accounting and Reporting by Oil and Gas Producing Companies.

Exploration and Mineral Rights (Leases)

Direct acquisition costs of unproved mineral rights (leases) are capitalized and then amortized in the manner stated below. Payments made in lieu of drilling on nonproducing leaseholds are charged to expense currently.

Geological, Geophysical and Intangible Drilling Costs

Geological and geophysical costs are charged to expense as incurred. Intangible drilling costs of all development wells and of exploratory wells that result in additions to proved reserves are capitalized.

Depreciation, Depletion, and Amortization

Annual charges to income for depreciation and the estimated cost for restoration and removal of major producing facilities are computed on a straight-line basis over the useful lives of the various classes of properties or, where appropriate for producing properties, on a unit-of-production basis by individual fields.

Costs of producing properties are generally accumulated by field. Depletion of these costs and amortization of capitalized intangible drilling costs are calculated on a unit-of-production basis.

Capitalized acquisition costs of significant unproved mineral rights and unamortized costs of significant developed properties are assessed periodically on a property-by-property basis to determine whether their values have been impaired; where impairment is indicated, a loss is recognized.

Capitalized acquisition costs of other unproved mineral rights are amortized over the expected holding period. When a mineral right is surrendered, any unamortized cost is charged to expense. When a property is determined to contain proved reserves, the mineral right then becomes subject to depletion on a unit-of-production basis.

Panel D—Stone Container Corp.

Timberlands

Timberlands are stated at cost less accumulated cost of timber harvested. The company amortized its private fee timber costs over the total fiber that will be available during the estimated growth cycle. Cost of nonfee timber harvested is determined on the basis of timber removal rates and the estimated volume of recoverable timber. The company capitalizes interest costs related to premerchantable timber.

Dr. Depletion Expense (E). . . . . (inc.) 90,200
   Cr. Allowance for Depletion (CA). . . . .   (inc.) 90,200

The Allowance for Depletion account is conceptually similar to the Accumulated Depreciation account. The depletion example above is referred to as *cost depletion,* and it is generally used for financial reporting purposes. U.S. tax law allows another method, referred to as *percentage depletion.* This method is not permissible for financial reporting purposes because it is not based on the asset's cost basis. Under percentage depletion, depletion expense for a period is figured by multiplying the gross income generated by the natural resource asset that period by a percentage rate legislated in the tax law (for example, 22 percent). Over the asset's life, for tax purposes, the accumulated depletion amount can exceed the cost of the resource, whereas for accounting purposes, the accumulated depletion cannot exceed the original cost of the resource less its estimated residual value. The difference between the two depletion methods results in a permanent difference between tax accounting and financial accounting. As will be explained in Chapter 13, no deferred taxes are recognized for such permanent differences.

INTERNATIONAL CONSIDERATIONS

Fixed assets. The accounting for noncurrent assets can vary dramatically from one country to the next. While U.S. GAAP rigidly adheres to the historical cost concept as the basis for valuing these assets, many countries permit, and some even require, a departure from the historical cost principle. Italy, for example, periodically passes legislation that requires publicly held companies to revalue their noncurrent assets using governmentally approved price indexes. This process insures that all Italian companies consistently restate their balance sheet values to reflect the effects of inflation in that country. In yet other countries, such as Australia and the United Kingdom, revaluation of noncurrent assets is not required but is widely practiced.

Consider for example, Exhibit 11.13, which presents the asset revaluation disclosures of Foster's Brewing Group Limited, a global beer and wine company, headquartered in Australia. This exhibit reveals that Foster's revalues its property, plant and equipment at least every three years. The revaluations are provided in some cases by licensed independent appraisers and in others by the company's directors. The exhibit also reveals that the depreciation expense taken on the revalued property is based on the adjusted amounts, not historical cost. Proponents of revaluation argue that the process results in a more fairly stated balance sheet presentation of a company's net worth,[7] and that since depreciation is based upon revalued amounts, the reported net income more accurately reflects a company's true (inflation-adjusted) earnings. The accounting entry for the revaluation of PP&E might appear as follows:

Dr. PP&E (A). . . . . (inc.) $10,000
   Cr. Asset Revaluation Reserve (OE) . . . .   (inc.) $10,000

Intangible assets. Considerable diversity also exists around the world in the accounting for intangible assets. While under U.S. GAAP all intangible assets must be amortized against net income, in some countries (such as France), amortization is not required where the value of an intangible asset can be shown to be increasing or where the end of the useful economic life of the asset cannot be foreseen. With respect to research and development expenditures, U.S. GAAP requires that most of these expenditures be expensed in the period in which they

---

[7] Revaluation proponents suggest that the balance sheet values of companies using U.S. GAAP are inherently conservatively biased, possibly to the extent of being misleading.

EXHIBIT 11.13

Asset Revaluation Disclosures: Foster's Brewing Group Limited

Panel A—Statement of Accounting Policies

Property, Plant and Equipment

Plant and equipment is depreciated by the Group so that the assets are written off over their estimated useful economic lives, using reducing balance or straight line methods as appropriate. Lease premiums and leasehold improvements are written off over the period of the lease or estimated useful economic life, whichever is the shorter. Freehold buildings used in the production of income and which are to be retained are depreciated at rates which vary with the circumstances.

Property, plant and equipment shown at valuation has been revalued on an existing use basis. It is the Group's policy to undertake valuations of property, plant and equipment on a regular basis, at intervals not exceeding three years. The last valuation was in 1996.

Panel B—Notes to Financial Statements

Note 10 Property, plant and equipment

	1997	1996	1997	1996
	FBG Limited		Consolidated	
	$m	$m	$m	$m
Land, buildings and improvements				
Freehold				
at directors' valuation 1996			594.6	598.8
accumulated depreciation			(6.5)	—
at cost			127.8	—
accumulated depreciation			(0.5)	—
Leasehold				
at directors' valuation 1996	4.0	4.2	51.3	51.6
accumulated depreciation	(0.5)	—	(1.9)	—
at cost	0.1	—	4.1	—
accumulated depreciation			(0.1)	—
Vineyard improvements				
at directors' valuation 1996			67.2	67.2
accumulated depreciation			(1.2)	—
at cost			4.8	—
accumulated depreciation			(0.1)	—
projects in progress at cost			15.4	4.6
	3.6	4.2	854.9	722.2
Plant and equipment				
at directors' valuation 1996	15.9	15.9	690.5	692.8
accumulated depreciation	(1.2)	—	(50.1)	—
at cost	1.2	—	142.7	—
accumulated depreciation			(9.9)	—
under finance lease			6.6	9.3
accumulated amortization			(1.8)	(1.0)
projects in progress at cost			66.3	107.0
	15.9	15.9	844.3	808.1
	19.5	20.1	1,699.2	1,530.3

are incurred. In other countries (such as Brazil), capitalization of R&D outlays is permitted, in large measure as an incentive to companies to invest in the development of new products. Finally, as noted in Chapter 10, while goodwill is capitalized to the balance sheet under U.S. GAAP, in other countries (such as Sweden and the Netherlands) it is more commonly expensed in total in the year of acquisition by reducing shareholders' equity; that accounting entry might appear as follows:

```
Dr. Retained Earnings (OE) . . . . . . . . . (dec.) $50,000
    Cr. Goodwill (A) . . . . . . . . . . . . . . . . . . . . . . . . . . .    (dec.) $50,000
```

The charge-to-equity treatment of goodwill avoids the "drag" on future corporate income that results from the periodic amortization of goodwill. Even in countries that require the capitalization of goodwill, there is considerable diversity in the allowable amortizable life, as the following data reveal:

Country	Maximum Amortizable Life (in Years)
Australia	20
Canada	40
Germany	5
Italy	10
Japan	5
United States	40

SUMMARY

Noncurrent assets are the principal long-term revenue-producing assets of most companies. Because of the significant dollar investment in these assets, the accounting methods adopted for them may have a material impact on both a company's balance sheet and income statement. Although the initial cash outflow to acquire these assets affects the statement of cash flows, the periodic amortization of intangibles, the depreciation of fixed assets, and the depletion of natural resources do not affect it; amortization, depreciation, and depletion expenses are added back to net income to adjust the accrual operating results for these noncash expenses to arrive at the cash flows from operations.

When evaluating the performance of a company or its management, it is important to consider how effectively the noncurrent assets were utilized. Such ratios as the asset turnover ratio and the return on noncurrent assets, as discussed in Chapter 4, are instructive indicators in this regard.

NEW CONCEPTS AND TERMS

Accelerated methods of depreciation	**Capitalization**
Accumulated depreciation	**Depletion**
Allocation	**Double-declining-balance method**
Amortization	**Fixed assets**

Full cost method	Physical life
Half-year convention	Process obsolescence
Impairment	Product obsolescence
Intangible asset	Straight-line method
Machine-hour method	Successful efforts method
Modified Accelerated Cost Recovery System	Sum-of-the-years' digits method
Net book value	Technological life
	Units-of-production method

ASSIGNMENTS

11.1. Estimating depreciation and book value. Equipment costing $29,000, with a scrap value of $3,000, was purchased on January 1, 1998, by Global Communications, Inc. The estimated useful life of the equipment was four years and it was expected to generate 80,000 finished units of production. Units actually produced were 14,000 in 1998 and 20,000 in 1999. Complete the following table.

	Depreciation Expense		Net Book Value	
Depreciation Method	1998	1999	12/31/98	12/31/99
Straight line				
Sum-of-the-years' digits				
Double-declining balance				
Units of production				

11.2. Income statement preparation. Ottawa Oil Corporation paid $4,000,000 for land with proven oil reserves. The company spent another $300,000 building roads and water run off ponds. The petroleum engineers were certain of at least 1 million barrels of oil and perhaps as many as 1.5 million. In 10 to 12 years, when the wells dry up, the derricks will be dismantled at a cost estimated to be equivalent to the land's then market value.

A record of other capital expenditures made during the year, exclusive of the $300,000 costs previously mentioned, is as follows:

Asset	Estimated Service Life	Cost	
Field office building	20 years	$400,000	20,000
Derricks	12 years	700,000	
Miscellaneous equipment	7 years	200,000	

The miscellaneous equipment (comprised of trailers, trucks, and crude oil assaying equipment) is movable to other sites.

During the oil field's first full year of operation, Ottawa experienced the following:

Barrels of oil extracted and sold at $15 per barrel	200,000
Field labor and other operating costs (exclusive of depreciation and depletion)	$800,000
Selling and administrative expenses	$100,000

Required:

Prepare an income statement for the first full year of the oil field's operations. (Assume every well dug, struck oil.)

11.3. Accounting for the sale of an asset. On January 1, 1994, Home Computing Consulting Corporation purchased a number of pieces of new equipment, including a new, state-of-the-art printer. The printer cost $8,000 and was expected to last 8 years. Home used the double-declining-balance method of depreciation for both financial reporting and tax purposes. By December 1998, the home computing consulting business had begun to slow down. The company found itself with underutilized employees and equipment. Near the end of 1998, the company sold the printer in exchange for a $1,000 note receivable that required three annual payments of $333. The original estimated salvage value was zero.

Required:

a. What entry(ies) should Home make regarding the printer for the year ended December 31, 1998?

b. What entry(ies) should Home make regarding the printer for the year ended December 31, 1998, if the note is agreed on in principle in 1998 but not signed until early January 1999?

11.4. Repair and maintenance expense. During 1998, Cemex S.A. made the following expenditures relating to plant, machinery and equipment:

■ Overhaul of several machines at a cost of $50,000 to improve efficiency in production over their remaining five-year useful lives. The overhaul was completed on December 31, 1998.

■ Regularly scheduled repairs at a cost of $25,000.

■ A broken cooling pump on a machine was replaced at a cost of $4,000.

Required:

What amount should be expensed as repairs and maintenance in 1998?

11.5. Estimating depletion expense. In January 1998, Craig Mining Corporation purchased a mine for $5 million with ore reserves estimated at 2,600,000 tons. The property has an estimated value of $500,000 as a landfill after the ore has been extracted. Craig incurred $1.2 million of development costs preparing the property for its mining operation. During 1998, 300,000 tons were removed and 250,000 tons were sold.

Required:

For the year ended December 31, 1998, Craig should include what amount of depletion in its cost of goods sold? Explain.

11.6. Accounting for intangible assets. Global Enterprises, Inc., had a balance sheet loaded with intangible assets. During 1999 four additional decisions were required regarding various intangible asset-related expenditures.

Required:

a. Should the legal fees incurred in successfully defending a copyrighted song be capitalized? Explain.

b. Should the costs of creating customer goodwill be capitalized? Explain.

c. Should the purchase of a customer list be capitalized and expensed? Explain.

d. Should the legal fees incurred by a company in a successful defense of its CEO against a discrimination suit be capitalized? Explain.

11.7. Accounting for asset exchanges. On September 1, 1998, Ruane, Inc., exchanged several excess lap top computers it owned for a used tractor suitable for its landscaping needs. Ruane bought the lap tops in 1996 for $18,000. As of September 1, 1998, the lap tops had a book value of $7,000 and a fair market value of $5,000. Ruane gave $3,000 in cash in addition to the lap tops as part of this transaction. The previous owner of the tractor had been advertising it for sale at $10,000.

Required:

At what amount should the tractor be recorded in Ruane's books?

11.8. Capitalization policy. On January 2, 1999, Keystone Plc. replaced its truck and dolley system of moving product around its factory with a computerized conveyor system. The following information was available on that date:

Purchase price of new conveyor	$100,000
Book value of trucks and dolleys	4,000
Fair value of trucks and dolleys	10,000
Installation cost of new conveyor (primarily Keystone labor)	6,000

The small fleet of trucks and dolleys was sold for $10,000.

Required:

The new conveyor should be recorded at what amount?

11.9. Depreciation policy. USX Corporation provided the following footnote in a recent set of financial statements detailing its depreciation policies.

> *Property, plant, and equipment*—Except for oil and gas producing properties, depreciation is generally computed on the straight-line method based upon the estimated lives of the assets. The corporation's method of computing depreciation of steel assets modifies straight-line depreciation based on the level of production. The modification ranges from a minimum of 80 percent at a production level of 50 percent of capacity and below, to a maximum of 130 percent for a 100 percent production level. No modification is made at the 85 percent production level, considered the normal long-range level.
>
> Depletion of the cost of mineral properties, other than oil and gas, is based on rates that are expected to amortize the cost over the estimated tonnage of minerals to be removed.
>
> Depreciation and depletion of oil and gas producing properties are computed at rates applied to the units of production on the basis of proved oil and gas reserves as determined by the corporation's geologists and engineers.
>
> When a plant or major facility within a plant is sold or otherwise disposed of by the corporation, any gain or loss is reflected in income. Proceeds from the sale of other facilities depreciated on a group basis are credited to the depreciation reserve. When facilities depreciated on an individual basis are sold, the difference between the selling price and the remaining undepreciated value is reflected in income.

Required:

a. In your own words, explain USX's depreciation policy for steel assets.

b. What rationale would support USX's depreciation policy?

11.10. Accounting for fixed assets. Kraft, Inc., included the following footnote in one of its recent annual reports:

> Properties are stated at cost. Depreciation is determined on a straight-line basis over estimated useful lives. For certain machinery and equipment, depreciation is determined on a composite basis over estimated group lives. The estimated useful lives are principally 10 to 40 years for buildings and improvements and 2 to 25 years for machinery and equipment.
>
> On routine disposals of depreciable assets accounted for on a composite basis, the gross book value less the proceeds or salvage value is charged to accumulated depreciation. On all other sales or retirements of property, plant, and equipment, gain or loss is recognized. Expenditures for maintenance and repairs are charged to expense.

Required:

a. What does Kraft mean when it refers to depreciation "being determined on a composite basis"? Why might management have chosen this approach?

b. Do gains/losses on routine disposals of depreciable assets accounted for on a composite basis affect current period income? Explain.

c. Do gains/losses on all other sales or retirements of property, plant, and equipment affect current period net income? Explain.

11.11. Analyzing income statement data. The top part of a recent Pioneer income statement is as follows:

	(In thousands)		
	19X9	**19X8**	**19X7**
Net sales	$874,871	$839,878	$884,726
Operating costs and expenses:			
Cost of goods sold	$399,464	$416,640	$426,768
Research and development	54,484	49,866	45,618
Selling	195,046	185,206	189,598
General and administrative	79,507	70,786	55,781
Restructuring and early retirement	—	—	12,913
Provision for plant closings	4,176	1,912	5,643
Loss on discontinued business	27,269	—	—
	$759,946	$724,410	$736,321
Operating income	$114,925	$115,468	$148,405

The top part of Pioneer's most recent cash flow statement is as follows:

	(in thousands)		
	19X9	19X8	19X7
Cash flows from operating activities			
Net income	$ 65,128	$ 53,939	$ 73,753
Noncash expenses included in net income:			
Depreciation	46,890	44,709	36,648
Amortization	3,023	2,924	3,055
Loss on disposal of property and equipment	7,044	4,962	6,919
Other	1,698	2,625	6,028
Foreign currency exchange losses	3,737	4,362	4,196
Change in assets and liabilities net of effects from purchase of subsidiaries:			
(Increase) in receivables	(17,343)	(16,995)	(36,272)
(Increase) decrease in inventories	41,427	22,655	(21,915)
Increase (decrease) in accounts payable and accrued expenses	26,614	(718)	22,281
Increase (decrease) in income taxes payable	11,102	(31,639)	4,137
Other prepaids, deferrals and accruals, net	(4,151)	10,153	(6,881)
Net cash provided by operating activities	$185,169	$ 96,977	$ 91,949
Cash flows from investing activities			
Purchase of property and equipment	$ (67,841)	$(72,768)	$(93,576)
Proceeds from sale of property and equipment	7,362	4,434	5,477
Purchase of subsidiaries, net of cash and cash equivalents acquired	(6,159)	—	(7,271)
Other	(4,390)	132	(1,059)
Net cash (used in) investing activities	$ (71,028)	$(68,202)	$(96,429)

On the 19X9 and 19X8 balance sheets, Pioneer included the following:

(in thousands) Assets	19X9	19X8
Property and equipment	$ 46,457	$ 43,638
Buildings	237,298	214,368
Machinery and equipment	290,558	262,930
Construction in progress	12,451	27,008
	$586,764	$547,944
Less accumulated depreciation	201,285	170,781
	$385,479	$377,163

Required:

a. The cash flow statement shows $46.89 million for depreciation for 19X9, yet this figure does not seem to appear on the consolidated statements of income. Please explain.

b. This $46.89 million of depreciation does not seem to explain the change in the accumulated depreciation figures that exists between the 19X8 and 19X9 balance sheets. Please explain; use figures as necessary.

c. The purchase of property and equipment shown on the cash flow statement of $67.84 million in 19X9 does not agree with the change in the property, plant, and equipment figures between the 19X8 and 19X9 balance sheets. Please explain; use figures as necessary.

11.12. Accounting for goodwill.   In May 1994, the Swiss pharmaceutical company Roche Holdings Ltd. acquired Syntex Corporation (a U.S. company) for $5.3 billion. And one month later, Sandoz Ltd., another Swiss pharmaceutical company, offered $3.7 billion for Gerber Products Co.

According to analysts familiar with the two transactions, the purchases were motivated by two factors. First, a strong Swiss franc relative to the U.S. dollar made the acquisition of Syntex and Gerber appear relatively inexpensive despite the high U.S. dollar price tag. Second, a dramatic change in International Accounting Standards Committee (IASC) guidelines with respect to the accounting for goodwill would become effective at year-end 1994. (Goodwill refers to the amount paid for a company in excess of its fair market value. For example, Roche's offer price exceeded Syntex's fair market value by approximately $3.0 billion, and Sandoz's offer for Gerber exceeded that company's fair market value by about $2.0 billion.)

Prior to 1995, most European companies had a choice as to how they accounted for goodwill: They could either capitalize goodwill to the balance sheet and then amortize it against earnings, or they could write the goodwill off in total against existing shareholders' equity. Most European firms, including Roche and Sandoz, chose the latter method. Beginning in 1995, the charge-to-equity method would no longer be available for many European companies as part of the IASC's harmonization efforts.

Required:

a. What is the advantage of the charge-off method of accounting for goodwill to companies like Roche and Sandoz? Why would they prefer it to the alternative of capitalizing and amortizing goodwill?

b. How do U.S. companies account for goodwill?

c. Which method do you prefer, and why?

11.13. Fixed assets and natural resources.   Near the end of 1996, Andrew and Michael Miller formed the Salem Coal Company. According to the charter of incorporation, the purpose of the new business was to "locate, develop, extract, and transport" coal reserves in the state of West Virginia. The company remained closely held until January 1998, at which time a small public offering of common shares was held. According to the prospectus, the funds raised through the public offering would be used to acquire coal reserves and removal and transportation equipment and to construct miscellaneous facilities for the administration of the company's coal operations.

Approximately $4 million was raised through the offering and was dispersed during 1998 as follows:

1. In February, the Salem Coal Company paid $2.35 million for a tract of land in Grant District (Preston County) containing estimated coal reserves of 3.5 million tons. Following extraction and reclamation, it was anticipated that the land would have a resale value of $280,000 for agricultural purposes. In addition, the purchase price included a $50,000 reclamation bond that would be refunded if the reclamation work met certain standards established by the West Virginia Department of Natural Resources.

2. The following equipment was purchased:

Quantity	Item	Estimated Useful Life	Per Unit Price
1	Bulldozer	15 years	$195,000
1	Earthmover with dragline and stripping bucket	10 years	425,000
3	Dump trucks	5 years	75,000

PART III   Measuring and Reporting Assets and Equities Using GAAP

The scrap value of the equipment at retirement was anticipated to be nominal. Signed checks for the equipment were delivered to the vendors on March 1.

3. A storage facility was constructed on the site at a cost of $150,000. It was anticipated that it would not be economically feasible to remove the building from the land after coal operations had terminated. In addition, it was uncertain whether the facilities might have alternative uses to subsequent landowners. Construction was completed by mid-May.

During May and June 1998, the company spent an additional $200,000 to prepare the site for operations. Finally, by mid-June, extraction operations began. By the end of 1998, 700,000 tons of coal had been mined and sold to the Monongahela Power Company at an average price of $15 per delivered ton.

Operating expenses (exclusive of depreciation and depletion) and selling and administrative expenses incurred in connection with the mining operations totaled $550,000.

Required:

a. Before financial statements can be prepared for the year ended December 31, 1998, a number of accounting policy decisions must be made. Prepare a list of those policy decisions and describe what accounting methods you would adopt and why. Assume that these decisions are to be made for financial reporting purposes only.

b. On the basis of your policy selections in part (a), prepare an income statement and a partial balance sheet as of December 31, 1998. Assume an average tax rate of 34 percent.

CHAPTER 12

Accounting for Liabilities: Basic Concepts, Payables, Accruals, and Interest-Bearing Debt

Many companies are beginning to examine the notion that they ultimately will be responsible for the costs of recycling and final disposition of their products, a responsibility variously labeled life-cycle assessment, take-back principle, or cradle-to-grave responsibility. The related notion of full cost accounting requires companies to gather all of the costs related to a product, including the environmental costs, and apply them to both products and divisions.[1]

Key Chapter Issues

- When does an obligation become a liability and how are liabilities valued?
- What obligations are not recognized in financial statements and why?
- Why are some liabilities recorded at present value when others are not?
- Which liabilities are only estimated as opposed to being measured and why?

- What are contingent liabilities and how are they described in the financial statements?
- What are the special problems of valuing interest-bearing debt?
- What are derivatives and how are they recorded or described?

---

[1] Marc Epstein, "Environmentally Responsible Corporations," *Management Accounting,* April 1994, p. 74.

As discussed in previous chapters, assets are the tangible and intangible resources owned or controlled by an entity. They represent the uses of cash and other funds of the firm. The sources of these funds are the entity's liabilities and owners' equity. Thus, when one looks at the assets on the balance sheet and wonders, "Where did the money for these assets come from?" the answer is that part came from the owners—the owners' equity—and the rest came from creditors—the liabilities. Creditors are any parties to which an entity owes money or other consideration and may include lenders, suppliers, employees, or governmental agencies (such as the IRS). For many corporations, creditors are the largest source of funding. For example, as of June 30, 1998, more than 60% of Procter & Gamble's assets were funded by creditors: banks and other lenders which lent the company money, suppliers who sold product to the company on credit, and others.

Corporate liabilities present a number of accounting and valuation problems. Some liabilities are current and must be paid within a few days; others may extend 50 years or more. Some are for definite amounts that can be established from invoices, employment agreements, tax filings, and other documents; others, such as the provisions for anticipated warranty expenses, pensions, lawsuits, and deferred taxes, can only be estimated.

The purpose of this chapter is to consider the questions "What liabilities does a company have?" and "How should those liabilities be valued?" The three types of liabilities that present the most difficult valuation issues are saved for Chapter 13; these include leases, pensions, and deferred income taxes. As we shall see in this chapter, in theory, *all* liabilities should be reported at the present value of their related cash outflows. In reality, however, only some obligations are actually valued in this way. Students unfamiliar with the concept of present value, or the calculation of discounted cash flows, are urged to review Appendix A of this chapter before proceeding.

CONCEPTUAL OVERVIEW

Every entity has a variety of **obligations;** only some of these are recognized in the financial statements as liabilities. Obligations are recognized as liabilities when they can be determined with reasonable precision, cannot be avoided, and are created by an event that has already occurred. Obligations that do *not* meet these three tests include, for example, a signed, binding contract to purchase certain products when the goods have not been received or a lawsuit for which damages have not yet been assessed.

As a general rule, short-term liabilities are recorded at their face amount (such as the amount printed on a bank note or an invoice), and long-term liabilities are recorded at their **present value** (that is, the value *today* of receiving—or paying—a given future sum of money). Although the conventional practice is to ignore present values on relatively short-term items such as accounts payable and accrued expenses payable (because the difference between the present value and face value of such a claim is usually insignificant), some current liabilities (such as the current portion of a mortgage payable) are nevertheless reported at their present values. Conversely, most long-term liabilities are carried at their present values, but a few are not, as shown in Exhibit 12.1.

CURRENT LIABILITIES: PAYABLES AND ACCRUALS

Current liabilities are those obligations to be repaid during the next year or during the next operating cycle (if longer than a year in length). All other liabilities are noncurrent.

Accounts payable are the normally recurring obligations of a business for the purchase of materials, parts, fuel, and other items used in manufacturing or for purchases of merchandise to be resold, as in retailing. These liabilities are the easiest to value because an

EXHIBIT 12.1

A Taxonomy of Liabilities

	Current liabilities	Noncurrent liabilities
Valued at face amounts	Accounts payable Accrued expenses Income taxes payable Dividends payable Unearned revenue Warranty obligations	Unearned revenue Warranty obligations

Valued at present value	Loans payable
	Current portion:
	   Notes payable
	   Bonds payable
	   Leases payable
		Loans payable
		Notes payable
		Bonds payable
		Leases payable
		Pension obligations

Shown at some other value	Deferred taxes	Deferred taxes Other liablities

invoice or electronic transmission from the supplier provides the exchange price, and a receiving report from within the company indicates proper receipt of the item(s). About the only accounting policy issue a business entity faces here is whether to record the payable at its *gross* or *net* value.

If the merchandise is purchased for $10,000 and the payment terms are 2/10, net 30, the firm may pay the net amount ($9,800) within 10 days (that is, net of the 2 percent discount), or it must pay the gross amount of $10,000 within 30 days. The transaction to record the cash disbursement is relatively straightforward, but how should the company record the liability originally? Companies typically choose one accounting policy and follow it for all such purchases, even if they sometimes take the discount but do not at other times. If a company chooses to use the gross method (that is, all purchases are initially recorded at the gross amount), when a discount is taken, the amount is recorded in the Purchase Discount account and appears on the income statement as miscellaneous revenue or as a reduction to the cost of sales. If, on the other hand, the net method is used (that is, all purchases are initially recorded at the net amount), when a discount is missed because the entity did not pay on time, an expense entry to an account such as Purchase Discounts Lost or Interest Expense is generated. The latter is the most common policy in large firms. It is typically called the "sore thumb" choice because any discounts lost are highlighted.

Using the example just discussed, the transactions would be recorded as follows:

Gross method

At the time of purchase:

```
       Dr. Inventory (A) . . . . . . . . . . . . . . . . . . . . (inc.) 10,000
           Cr. Accounts Payable (L) . . . . . . . . . . . . . . . . . . . .      (inc.) 10,000
```

If the discount is taken:

```
Dr. Accounts Payable (L) . . . . . . . . . . . . (dec.) 10,000
    Cr. Cash (A). . . . . . . . . . . . . . . . . . . . . . . . . . . . . .      (dec.) 9,800
    Cr. Purchase Discounts (R) . . . . . . . . . . . . . . . . .      (inc.)   200
```

If the discount is not taken, the liability is satisfied by a cash payment of $10,000.

Net method

At the time of purchase:

```
Dr. Inventory (A. . . . . . . . . . . . . . . . . . . . . (inc.) 9,800
    Cr. Accounts Payable (L) . . . . . . . . . . . . . . . . . . . .      (inc.) 9.800
```

If the discount is taken, as is assumed by this method, the liability is satisfied by a payment of $9,800. If the discount is not taken, the entry looks like this:

```
Dr. Accounts Payable (L) . . . . . . . . . . . . . (dec.) 9,800
Dr. Interest Expense (E) . . . . . . . . . . . . . . . (inc.)  200
    Cr. Cash (A). . . . . . . . . . . . . . . . . . . . . . . . . . . . . .      (dec.) 10,000
```

Accrued expenses payable usually includes the obligations to employees for wages earned but not paid, the employer's portion of any salary or wage taxes due the government, and any amounts accrued for interest or rent expense. For example, if a company owes $15,000 for computer rental charges but payment is not due for another 10 days, the amount would be accrued by the following entry:

```
Dr. Computer Rental Expense (E) . . . . . . . (inc.) 15,000
    Cr. Accrued Expenses Payable (L) . . . . . . . . . . . . .      (inc.) 15,000
```

Payables and accruals, including current income taxes payable and dividends payable, are valued at their face amounts, not at their present value. The time and trouble to determine their present value is generally not worth the effort for such a slight difference in value (and it would be needlessly confusing to many readers of financial statements). For example, the present value of the $15,000 of accrued computer rentals due in 10 days is $14,959.02, assuming a discount rate of 10 percent. The purist might argue that this amount should be recorded as the liability, with the difference of $40.98 recorded as interest expense. Fortunately for both the readers of financial statements and the preparers, this practice is not followed unless the amounts are material.

Unearned revenue (or deferred income) is another current liability not usually reported at its present value; rather, it is shown at the amount received less whatever has been taken into income (earned) to date. For example, when an airline sells a ticket for $1,000 cash 30 days in advance of a scheduled flight, the transaction is recorded as follows:

```
Dr. Cash (A) . . . . . . . . . . . . . . . . . . . . . . . . (inc.) 1,000
    Cr. Unearned Revenue (L) . . . . . . . . . . . . . . . . . . .      (inc.) 1,000
```

Because the service has not yet been rendered, the revenue has not been earned and thus cannot be recognized. When the passenger actually takes the flight and the airline receives the flight coupon, the transaction is recorded as follows:

```
Dr. Unearned Revenue (L). . . . . . . . . . . . . (dec.) 1,000
    Cr. Revenue (R) . . . . . . . . . . . . . . . . . . . . . . . . . . . .      (inc.) 1,000
```

EXHIBIT 12.2

Procter & Gamble
Current Liabilities Section
As of June 30, 1998 and June 30, 1997
(in millions)

	1998	1997
Current Liabilities		
Accounts payable	$2,051	$2,203
Accrued and other liabilities	3,942	3,802
Taxes payable	976	944
Debt due within one year	2,281	849
Total Current Liabilities	9,250	7,798

Warranty obligations arise when a company sells a product and agrees to repair it and/or provide certain other services if the product fails. An automobile manufacturer, for example, may guarantee free repairs for four years or 60,000 miles, whichever comes first (it also may provide a loaner car while the repairs are being made). The accounting challenge for such obligations is one of *matching*. The sale is recorded when the buyer takes delivery of the car, but the repairs may not occur until some time far into the future. To match the expenses with the related revenues and avoid overstating income at the time of sale, the warranty costs associated with each car sale are estimated. These estimates are based on historical analysis, engineering assessments, and management judgment. At the time of sale or at the end of the sale's accounting period, an entry to record the expected warranty obligation is made:

```
Dr. Warranty Expense (E). . . . . . . . . . . . . . . (inc.) 500
    Cr. Estimated Warranty Obligation (L). . . . . . . . . . .        (inc.) 500
```

When a cash payment is made by a dealer for warranty services provided to a customer, the following entry is made:

```
Dr. Estimated Warranty Obligation (L) . . . . . . (dec.) 100
    Cr. Cash (A). . . . . . . . . . . . . . . . . . . . . . . . . . . . . .        (dec.) 100
```

Note that this accrual-oriented method to account for warranties has the effect of reflecting the *total* estimated warranty obligation and the *total* estimated warranty costs at the time of the sale. Hence, there will be no income statement impact in future periods for this particular car when warranty repairs are actually made. From time to time, adjustments are necessary to the estimating procedures to ensure that the total outstanding warranty obligation is a reasonable approximation of the total warranty costs yet to be incurred.

Exhibit 12.2, taken from Procter & Gamble's 1998 annual report, illustrates a typical format for reporting current liabilities. With the exception of the Debt due within one year account, each of the current liabilities is shown at its actual or face amount without considering its present value. Debt due within one year *is* shown at present value because only the principal portion is included, not the interest. Procter & Gamble's footnotes provide further information about these current obligations—for example, the composition of the accrued and other liabilities and the taxes payable to federal, state, or foreign taxation authorities.

LOANS, BILLS, NOTES, AND BONDS

Loans and securities are two basic types of interest-bearing obligations. *Loans* are monetary agreements between two parties. The parties negotiate and sign an agreement that sets forth the terms and conditions of the loan. Loans may be of a short duration or may extend for many years. Although almost anyone can borrow or lend money, commercial banks are typically the primary source of business loans for short and intermediate-term borrowing (that is, up to five years). Life insurance companies, on the other hand, have been the traditional source of business loans with maturities of 10 or more years.

Debt in the form of *securities* includes bills, certificates, notes, and bonds. For these obligations, the borrower formalizes the terms and conditions of the loan in a document, which is then sold. The most common type of bill is a T-bill, or U.S. Treasury bill—a short-term U.S. government debt obligation. The most common type of certificate is the **certificate of deposit,** or CD—an obligation of a commercial bank. Notes and bonds are the most common form of intermediate and long-term debt securities issued by *corporations.* Bills, certificates, and, in some cases, notes, are short-term obligations with maturities of less than a year. The maturity period for notes is usually 1 to 10 years, and for bonds, usually more than 10 years.

Current Loans Payable

Loans, notes, certificates, bills, and other current interest-bearing debt (which will henceforth be called *current loans payable*) are recorded at their present value. For example, suppose a company borrows $100,000 for six months at 10 percent with interest payable monthly. Essentially, the company receives $100,000 upon signing the loan agreement and agrees to pay a total of $5,000 ($833.33 per month) in interest over six months and a lump sum representing the repayment of the principal of $100,000 in six months. Thus, the cash flows for this loan appear as follows:

	Cash Flow at End of Month							Total
	Now	1	2	3	4	5	6	
Loan proceeds	100,000							
Interest payments		(833)	(833)	(833)	(833)	(833)	(833)	(5,000)
Principal repayment							(100,000)	(100,000)

This agreement calls for the company to repay $105,000 in total, but accounting practice for short-term loans (and long-term ones, for that matter) is to record this stream of cash outflows at their discounted or *present value.*[2] Thus, the entry to record the loan at its inception looks like this:

Dr. Cash (A) . . . . (inc.) 100,000
  Cr. Loan Payable (L). . . . . (inc.) 100,000

---

[2] A financial calculator can be used to verify that the present value of the six monthly interest payments of $833, plus the principal payment of $100,000 in the sixth month, is indeed $100,000 when the interest rate is 10 percent (that is, FV = −100,000, PMT = −833, N = 6, I = 0.833, 10%/12).

Each month an entry for the accrued interest is also necessary:

> Dr. Interest Expense (E). . . . . (inc.) 833
> Cr. Loan Interest Payable (L) . . . .   (inc.) 833

When the interest is paid, the Loan Interest Payable account is decreased.

A complication with some short-term loans is that they are often issued on a discounted basis, as if the interest were prepaid. For example, a company may agree to pay $100,000 in six months and receive only $95,000 now. Convention is to record this note at $100,000, with the difference going to a contra-liability (CL) account. Thus, the transaction would be recorded as follows:

> Dr. Cash (A) . . . . (inc.) 95,000
> Dr. Discount on Notes Payable (CL) . . . . . . (inc.) 5,000
> Cr. Notes Payable (L) . . . .   (inc.) 100,000

Of course, this note is stated at its present value ($95,000), but the rate is not quite 10 percent (the effective interest rate is 10.53 percent). Each month an entry is made for the accrual of the prepaid interest:

> Dr. Interest Expense (E). . . . . (inc.) 833
> Cr. Discount on Notes Payable (CL) . . . .   (dec.) 833

After six months the contra-liability account will be zero, and the net liability (that is, Notes Payable less Discount on Notes Payable) will reflect the note's maturity value of $100,000.

Sometimes a company may sign a note when it does not know the implicit interest rate; perhaps it knows only the actual payments to be made over time. (For example, the notes could be in exchange for a special, one-of-a-kind machine for which the buyer does not know the market value.) Conventional practice is to discount the payments at an interest rate that matches the risk characteristics of the note. For example, if the note is noncancelable, a low-risk debt rate such as the prime rate or the company's incremental borrowing rate may be used.

Bonds, Notes, and Loans: Long-Term Debt

The term **bond** refers to a variety of long-term obligations evidenced by a document that may be sold or traded. The entity issuing a bond is the borrower, and the buyer of those bonds is the lender. **Debentures,** for example, are general obligation bonds issued by a company. **Mortgage bonds** and **revenue bonds** are examples of bonds in which particular corporate assets are pledged as security for the debt.

Bond liabilities are recorded at their present value in a manner similar to that used for current loans payable. The present value of the combined interest and principal payments on a bond is the same as the principal outstanding on the bond when discounting is done at the effective interest rate on the bond. (If this concept is not clear, refer to Appendix 12A for examples and an explanation.)

If bonds are issued or sold at their face amount, the accounting is straightforward. For example, assume that a company issues $50 million of 11 percent, 20-year debentures with annual interest payments. The entry to record the initial borrowing looks like this:

> Dr. Cash (A) . . . . (inc.) 50,000,000
> Cr. Bonds Payable (L) . . . .   (inc.) 50,000,000

This entry assumes that the company sold the bonds itself and thus incurred no transaction costs. In reality, most companies hire a bond underwriter to place or sell debt securities and thus incur certain transaction fees when debt securities are sold.

When the annual interest payment is made, the following entry is recorded:

Dr. Interest Expense (E) . . . . (inc.) 5,500,000
    Cr. Cash (A) . . . . (dec.) 5,500,000

The cash payment is calculated by multiplying the stated borrowing rate (or coupon rate) of 11 percent times the maturity value of $50 million.

Assuming that the bonds are retired on the maturity date, we make the following entry:

Dr. Bonds Payable (L) . . . . (dec.) 50,000,000
    Cr. Cash (A) . . . . (dec.) 50,000,000

Like discounted notes, bonds present accounting problems because the amount printed on the face of a bond certificate may not be what the issuing company (the borrower) ultimately receives in cash, and from the buyers' perspective, it may not be what the purchaser (the lender) ultimately has to pay. Bonds often sell at a **premium** or **discount** when first issued because of interest rate changes in the bond market between the time the bonds are priced (and the certificates printed) and the time customers actually buy them. Most corporate bonds issued in the United States come to market at a slight discount because it is psychologically easier to sell a security at a discount than at a premium.

From the bond buyer's perspective, money is lent when the bonds are purchased. In exchange for cash the buyer receives a promise of a stream of cash flows (the annuity interest payments) over the life of the bond plus a terminal cash flow payment (the lump-sum principal repayment) at the **maturity date.** The value of these cash flows depends upon the interest rate, or **yield rate,** used to discount them. Interest (yield) rates change continually due to market forces such as world political conditions, the general health of the economy, inflation, and investor expectations, to name just a few.

For example, a $1,000, 20-year, 11 percent, annual interest payment bond may come to market when the yield rate for that class and risk of bond has just increased to $11\frac{1}{8}$ percent. Because of the rise in interest rates, the bond will actually sell for only $990.13, or a discount of $9.87.[3] Suppose an entire issue of these bonds with a face value of $50 million were sold in the market and brought the issuing firm $49,506,333. Note that 11 percent bonds pay $5.5 million per year in interest (the coupon amount), and $50 million (the **maturity value**) is to be repaid at the end of the 20th year. The present value of these payments at 11 percent is, of course, $50 million, whereas at $11\frac{1}{8}$ percent, the **effective rate,** the present value is only $49,506,333, which is the amount of cash that the bond-issuing company can expect to receive if the bonds are sold to yield $11\frac{1}{8}$ percent. The difference between the face amount of $50 million and the selling price of $49,506,333 is the *bond discount,* which must be amortized over the 20-year life of the debt. The following is the accounting challenge in a situation like this:

1. To show the bond liability at its present value, not its face amount.
2. To show the annual interest expense at the effective rate ($11\frac{1}{8}$ percent), not the stated or **coupon rate** (11 percent).

---

[3] To verify this number using a financial calculator, the keying is FV = 1,000, PMT = 110 (that is, 11% × $1,000), N = 20, I = 11.125 (11⅛%).

The transaction to record the sale of bonds for this example is:

```
Dr. Cash (A). . . . . . . . . . . . . . . . . . . (inc.) 49,506,333
Dr. Bond Discount (CL) . . . . . . . . . . . . (inc.)   493,667
    Cr. Bonds Payable (L) . . . . . . . . . . . . . . . . . . . . . .        (inc.) 50,000,000
```

Thus, the bonds would be recorded initially on the balance sheet at $49,506,333, the present value at the time of issuance. At the end of each year, two transactions are required: one to record the interest paid on the bonds and the second to amortize the bond discount. Bond discounts (or premiums) are typically amortized over the life of a bond using the **effective interest method** rather than straight-line amortization. To facilitate the preparation of the two transactions, the borrower usually prepares a bond amortization schedule similar to that in Exhibit 12.3. This schedule adjusts the actual interest expense, based on $11\frac{1}{8}$ percent on $49,506,333 in the first year, by amortizing the bond discount of $493,667. The key to Exhibit 12.3 is that the total yearly interest expense (column 2) is always $11\frac{1}{8}$ percent (the effective rate) of the outstanding net liability (column 5). Of course, the net liability is also equivalent to the present value of the future payments (cash interest to be paid plus the principal) discounted at $11\frac{1}{8}$ percent.

Another way to think about this is that in terms of face amounts, $50 million is being borrowed for 20 years on which $5.5 million per year (or $110 million in total) of interest will be paid in cash. In fact, however, only $49,506,333 is borrowed, although a full $50 million will be repaid in 20 years. The difference of $493,667 represents additional interest, and, thus, the total interest expense paid over the life of the debt is $110,493,667. By spreading the $493,667 over 20 years (as revealed in column 3 of Exhibit 12.3), the borrower's income statement shows an interest expense equal to $11\frac{1}{8}$ percent of the bond value as reported on the company's balance sheet (*not* 11 percent of $50 million).

The entries at the end of Year 1 for this bond would be recorded as follows:

```
Dr. Interest Expense (E) . . . . . . . . . . . (inc.) 5,500,000
    Cr. Cash (A) . . . . . . . . . . . . . . . . . . . . . . . . . . . . .        (dec.) 5,500,000
```

and

```
Dr. Interest Expense (E) . . . . . . . . . . . . . . (inc.) 7,580
    Cr. Bond Discount (CL). . . . . . . . . . . . . . . . . . . . .        (dec.) 7,580
```

The two separate entries can also be combined into one:

```
Dr. Interest Expense (E) . . . . . . . . . . . (inc.) 5,507,580
    Cr. Cash (A) . . . . . . . . . . . . . . . . . . . . . . . . . . . . .        (dec.) 5,500,000
    Cr. Bond Discount (CL). . . . . . . . . . . . . . . . . . . . .        (dec.)      7,580
```

The income statement reflects total interest expense of $5,507,580 for Year 1. Note that this expense is exactly $11\frac{1}{8}$ percent of the outstanding bond liability ($11\frac{1}{8}$ percent $\times$ $49,506,333 = \$5,507,580$).

For financial statement purposes, the details of each bond issue should be disclosed in the footnotes and should reveal the aggregate present value of all bond liabilities and the aggregate principal payments to be made for each over the next five years. Bond liabilities are shown in the balance sheet net of any premium or discount. On the balance sheet, the current principal obligation is classified as a current liability; the remainder is included under noncurrent liabilities. Thus, for the bonds under discussion here, at the end of Year 1, the balance sheet shows nothing related to these bonds under current liabilities (because no

EXHIBIT 12.3

Amortization of a Bond Discount

Year	(1) Coupon Interest (11.0%)	(2) Effective Interest (11.125%)	(3) Discount Amortization (2-1)	(4) Unamortized Discount (4-3)	(5) Present Value of Bond ($50,000,000-4)
				$493,667	$49,506,333
1	$ 5,500,000⁺	$ 5,507,580*	$ 7,580	$486,087	$49,513,913
2	5,500,000	5,508,423	8,423	477,664	49,522,336
3	5,500,000	5,509,360	9,360	468,304	49,531,695
4	5,500,000	5,510,401	10,401	457,904	49,542,096
5	5,500,000	5,511,558	11,558	446,345	49,553,655
6	5,500,000	5,512,844	12,844	433,501	49,566,499
7	5,500,000	5,514,273	14,273	419,228	49,580,722
8	5,500,000	5,515,861	15,861	403,367	49,596,663
9	5,500,000	5,517,625	17,625	385,742	49,614,258
10	5,500,000	5,519,586	19,586	366,156	49,633,844
11	5,500,000	5,521,765	21,765	344,391	49,655,604
12	5,500,000	5,524,187	24,187	320,204	49,679,796
13	5,500,000	5,526,877	26,877	293,327	49,706,673
14	5,500,000	5,529,867	29,867	263,459	47,736,541
15	5,500,000	5,533,190	33,190	230,269	49,769,731
16	5,500,000	5,536,883	36,883	193,387	49,806,631
17	5,500,000	5,540,986	40,986	152,401	49,847,599
18	5,500,000	5,545,545	45,545	106,855	49,893,145
19	5,500,000	5,550,612	50,612	56,243	49,943,757
20	5,500,000	5,556,243	56,243	–0–	50,000,000
Total	$110,000,000	$110,493,667	$493,667		

⁺ ($50,000,000 × 11%)
* ($49,506,333 × 11.125%)

principal repayments are to be made in Year 2 and the accrued interest was paid in cash). The balance sheet reports $49,513,913 under noncurrent liabilities reflecting the *net* bond liability:

Bonds payable	$50,000,000
Less: Unamortized bond discount	486,087
Bonds payable (net)	$49,513,913

Although rare, bonds are also sometimes sold at a premium. It is more difficult to sell securities at a premium for psychological reasons. Consequently, bond issuers usually err on the discount side when setting the interest rate to be printed on their bonds. When market interest rates are lower than a bond's coupon (stated) rate, however, a bond premium results. Conceptually, accounting for bond premiums is the reverse of accounting for bond discounts. Suppose, for example, that the $50 million in bonds actually sell for $50,501,800, resulting in an effective yield of only $10^{7}/_{8}$ percent.[4] The transaction for the issuer at the time of sale looks like this:

```
Dr. Cash (A) . . . . . . . . . . . . . . . . . . (inc.) 50,501,800
    Cr. Bonds Payable (L) . . . . . . . . . . . . . . . . . . . . . .      (inc.) 50,000,000
    Cr. Bond Premium (L). . . . . . . . . . . . . . . . . . . . . . .      (inc.)    501,800
```

When the first interest payment is made at the end of Year 1, the two transactions necessary to record the interest payment and the amortization of the premium are as follows:

```
Dr. Interest Expense (E) . . . . . . . . . . . (inc.) 5,500,000
    Cr. Cash (A) . . . . . . . . . . . . . . . . . . . . . . . . . . . .    (dec.) 5,500,000
```

and

```
Dr. Bond Premium (L) . . . . . . . . . . . . . . . (dec.) 7,928
    Cr. Interest Expense (E) . . . . . . . . . . . . . . . . . . . . .      (dec.) 7,928
```

These two separate entries can be combined into a single one as follows:

```
Dr. Interest Expense (E) . . . . . . . . . . . (inc.) 5,492,072
Dr. Bond Premium (L) . . . . . . . . . . . . . . (dec.)   7,928
    Cr. Cash (A) . . . . . . . . . . . . . . . . . . . . . . . . . . . .    (dec.) 5,500,000
```

Note that the premium is amortized in a manner similar to that illustrated in Exhibit 12.3, except that the effect is to reduce the effective interest expense, not to raise it.

Early Debt Retirement

If a company chooses to retire its debt early (that is, prior to its scheduled maturity date as printed on the bond certificate) by exercising call provisions or purchasing its debt securities in the open market, accounting practice requires that any gain or loss from the extinguishment of debt retirement be recognized in the current income statement as an extraordinary item.[5] For example, suppose that the $50 million in 11 percent bonds, sold at a premium, were retired after one year by repurchase of the bonds for an aggregate of $52 million. Because the net book value of the bonds after one year is $50,493,872 ($50,501,800 − 7,928), the *seller* records a loss of $1,506,128:

```
Dr. Loss on Early Retirement (Loss) . . (inc.)  1,506,128
Dr. Bonds Payable (L) . . . . . . . . . . . (dec.) 50,000,000
Dr. Bond Premium (L) . . . . . . . . . . . . (dec.)   493,872
    Cr. Cash (A) . . . . . . . . . . . . . . . . . . . . . . . . . . . .    (dec.) 52,000,000
```

The costs incurred to actually issue the bonds such as for underwriting, engraving, printing, and registration should be capitalized and amortized over the life of the bonds; amortization should be based on the effective interest method. Often, however, these transaction costs are expensed on a straight line basis because they are immaterial in amount.

---

[4] To determine the present value of these bonds using a financial calculator, the keying is FV = −50,000,000, PMT = −5,500,000, N = 20, I = 10.875.

[5] Early retirement of debt is a common occurrence. At first glance, it may seem inappropriate to treat the associated gains or losses as *extraordinary;* however, generally accepted accounting practice is to do just that to prevent corporations from attempting to "manage earnings" by retiring selected bonds as needed to raise or lower reported accounting income.

Financial Disclosure

As the business activities of American corporations become more global and as borrowing arrangements become more complex, the valuation of short- and long-term debt becomes ever more important. Accordingly, the footnote disclosures for these debts have become more extensive.[6] Johnson & Johnson's 1997 annual report provides an illuminating example. Johnson & Johnson lists just one line in their balance sheet for long-term debt, $1,126 million for 1997, although the details are explained fully in a company footnote, which has been reproduced as Exhibit 12.4. Note that the company has borrowings with maturities ranging from 1 year to 27 years and denominated in U.S. dollars, Eurodollars ($ dollar denominated notes issued in the European market), Euros (the single European currency), Italian Lira, Deutsche Marks, Swiss Francs, and notes linked to a currency index. The weighted average effective interest rate for all of the company's long-term debt was 6.96% in 1997, although the rates varied considerably from one issue to another. In the case of borrowings denominated in currencies other than the U.S. dollar, the effective rate can be influenced by exchange rates, and all of these rates are affected by the maturity of the debt issue as well as the rates in effect at the issue date. Perhaps the most interesting issues are the first two: $300 million of 8.72% debentures due in 2024, and $250 million of 6.73% debentures due in 2023. How could two debt issues with similar maturity dates have such dramatically different interest rates? Either they were issued at very different times when rates had changed considerably, or one issue has special features that the other lacks.

Consider also Exhibit 12.5, which was taken from the 1996 annual report of Sun Microsystems. It illustrates the required disclosures for both short-term borrowings and long-term debt, and the "fair values" of those financial instruments. Beginning in 1992, U.S. GAAP required the disclosure of fair values not just for debt and equity securities owned, but also for long-term debt outstanding. Sometimes such fair values present puzzles for financial analysts, and there's one in the Sun footnote. Note that in 1995, the 10.55%, $76,452 thousand senior notes had a fair value of $78,918 thousand, or 3.23% over the debt's carrying amount. Presumably, interest rates declined since the notes were originally issued so the fair value was greater than its carrying value. During fiscal 1996 almost half of those notes were repaid, resulting in a carrying amount of $38,400 at year end. Note also that the fair value of the remaining notes, $39,855, is 3.79% greater than its carrying amount. This increase in fair value over carrying value suggests interest rates fell during the year. However, the reverse situation seems to have occurred with the 10.18% mortgage notes. These notes were valued at 12% above their carrying value on June 30, 1995, and only 8% above the carrying amount the following year. If interest rates were falling shouldn't the mortgage loan behave the same way as the senior notes? Ordinarily yes, but there's also another factor at work: maturity. If the mortgage loan is close to maturity (and the senior notes are not) then this sort of phenomenon will occur. Even if interest rates are declining, the excess of the fair value over the carrying value will approach zero as the security reaches its maturity date.

---

[6] Liability footnote disclosures found in other countries tend to be less detailed than those found in U.S. corporate annual reports. Moreover, debt valuation practices also differ around the world. For example, the International Accounting Standards Committee permits liabilities to be valued at either present value or face/settlement value. Despite the many merits of using the present value approach, many countries (e.g., Japan) do use the settlement value as the basis to value all liabilities.

EXHIBIT 12.4

Footnote Disclosure for Johnson & Johnson Borrowings

Borrowings

The components of long-term debt are as follows:

(Dollars in Millions)	1997	Eff. Rate	1996	Eff. Rate
8.72% Debentures due 2024	$ 300	8.72%	300	8.72%
6.73% Debentures due 2023	250	6.73	250	6.73
7⅜% Eurodollar Notes due 1997	–	–	200	7.43
7⅜% Eurodollar Notes due 2002	199	7.49	199	7.49
8.25% Eurodollar Notes due 2004	199	8.37	199	8.37
9% European Currency Unit Notes due 1997[1]	–	–	186	6.84
11¼% Italian Lire Notes due 1998[1]	115	4.88	132	4.84
5% Deutsche Mark Notes due 2001[3]	101	1.98	114	1.98
5⅜% Swiss Franc Notes due 1997[1]	–	–	112	4.64
4½% Currency Indexed Notes due 1998[1]	72	5.26	67	5.12
8.18% to 8.25% Medium Term notes due 1998	65	8.23	65	8.23
Industrial Revenue Bonds	57	5.77	61	5.62
Other, principally international	36	–	32	–
	1,394	6.96 [2]	1,917	6.80 [2]
Less current portion	268		507	
	$1,126		$1,410	

[1] The principal amounts of these debt issues include the effect of foreign currency movements. Such debt was converted to fixed or floating rate U.S. dollar liabilities via interest rate and currency swaps. Unrealized currency gains (losses) on currency swaps are not included in the basis of the related debt transactions and are classified in the balance sheet as other assets (liabilities).

[2] Weighted average effective rate.

[3] Represents 5% Deutsche Mark notes due 2001 issued by a Japanese subsidiary and converted to a 1.98% fixed rate yen note via an interest rate and currency swap.

The Company has access to substantial sources of funds at numerous banks worldwide. Total unused credit available to the Company approximates $3.2 billion, including $1.2 billion of credit commitments with various worldwide banks, $800 million of which will expire on October 2 ,1998 and $400 million on October 6, 2002. Borrowings under the credit line agreements will bear interest based on either bids provided by the banks, the prime rate or London Interbank Offered Rates (LIBOR), plus applicable margins.

The Company's shelf registration filed with the Securities and Exchange Commission enables the Company to issue up to $2.59 billion of unsecured debt securities, and warrants to purchase debt securities, under its medium term note (MTN) program. No MTN's were issued during 1997. At December 28, 1997, the Company had $2.29 billion remaining on its shelf registration. The Company did not issue any long-term public debt in 1997.

Short-term borrowings and current portion of long-term debt amounted to $714 million at the end of 1997. These borrowings are composed of $115 million equivalent of 11.25% Italian Lire notes, $72 million 4.5% currency indexed notes, $65 million MTN's and $462 million of local borrowings, principally by international subsidiaries.

Aggregate maturities of long-term obligations for each of the next five years commencing in 1998 are:

(Dollars in Millions)	1998	1999	2000	2001	2002	After 2002
	$268	$18	$6	$105	$203	$794

EXHIBIT 12.5

Sun Microsystems
Footnote Disclosure for Debt and the Fair Value
of Financial Instruments

The fair value of the Company's borrowing arrangements and other financial instruments is as follows:

	At June 30, 1996	
	Asset (Liability)	
(in thousands)	Carrying amount	Fair value
10.55% senior notes	$(38,400)	$(39,855)
10.18% mortgage loan	(40,000)	(43,230)
Forward foreign exchange contracts	1,877	1,877
Foreign currency option contracts	–	3,094
Short-term borrowings	(49,161)	(49,161)
Other interest rate swap agreements, net	–	260

	At June 30, 1995	
	Asset (Liability)	
(in thousands)	Carrying amount	Fair value
10.55% senior notes	$(76,452)	$(78,918)
10.18% mortgage loan	(40,000)	(44,485)
Forward foreign exchange contracts	(2,227)	(2,227)
Foreign currency option contracts	–	413
Short-term borrowings	(50,786)	(50,786)
Other interest rate swap agreements, net	–	(802)

The fair value of long-term debt is estimated based on current interest rates available to the Company for debt instruments with similar terms, degree of risk, and remaining maturities. The estimated fair value of forward foreign exchange contracts is based on the estimated amount at which they could be settled based on market exchange rates. The fair value of foreign currency option contracts and interest rate swap agreements is obtained from dealer quotes and represents the estimated amount the Company would receive or pay to terminate the agreements.

CONTINGENT LIABILITIES

What happens when there is only the possibility of a liability, such as in the case of a lawsuit or, in more recent times, for environmental liabilities? Lawsuits against corporations and partnerships can be huge with much contingent on a judgment, settlement, petition, or judicial finding. For example, the Price Waterhouse accounting firm was sued for $11 billion by the liquidators of the failed BCCI bank. Similarly, costs to clean up the known hazardous waste sites in the United States are estimated to run into the hundreds of billions of dollars. The accounting challenge here is to determine when and how these potential obligations are to be recognized.

A contingent liability is generally defined as

> an existing condition, situation, or set of circumstances involving uncertainty as to possible…loss…to an enterprise that will ultimately be resolved when one or more future events occur or fail to occur. Resolution of the uncertainty may confirm the…impairment of an asset or incurrence of a liability.

Contingent liabilities are usually not reported on the balance sheet. However, an expense entry and offsetting liability must be recorded when both of the following conditions are met:

1. It is probable that an asset has been impaired or a liability has been incurred at the date of the financial statements.

2. The amount of the loss can be reasonably estimated.[7]

Whether or not a contingent liability is recognized, the circumstances surrounding the potential obligation must be disclosed, the possible losses described, and any amounts accrued identified. Exhibit 12.6 contains selected paragraphs from footnote Q, "Commitments and Contingent Liabilities," in the 1997 annual report of Dow Chemical. It provides a number of interesting illustrations of these requirements. The first paragraph discloses the charges taken by Dow Corning, a 50 percent owned, unconsolidated subsidiary of Dow Chemical, related to breast implant litigation. Note that Dow Corning's total pretax charge over the two years was $1,681 million and that this was net of expected insurance recoveries, on a present value basis (at least the 1993 portion was). Disclosing contingent liabilities net of estimated recoveries and at present value have been controversial issues for some time.

The next two paragraphs describe Dow's accounting for the subsidiary through 1995. By then, Dow had effectively written off its investment in the subsidiary. The company also discusses the likely impact of related litigation, and reports that "it is possible" that these other claims could have a materially adverse impact on Dow, but that the amount cannot be estimated. Finally, the company discusses its pending breast implant litigation and other significant lawsuits but concludes that the likelihood of a material loss is remote.

During the 1970s, a series of environmental catastrophes (such as the Love Canal crisis in Niagara, New York) brought the problem of hazardous wastes to public attention. The U.S. Congress reacted to the problem by passing the Resource Conservation and Recovery Act (RCRA) in 1976 and the Comprehensive Environmental Response, Compensation, and Liability Act (CERCLA) in 1980. With this legislation began the Superfund National Priorities List—a list of designated locations having hazardous waste problems. Currently there are over 1,200 waste sites on the list, with another 30,000 potential locations under review as Superfund candidates.

Under CERCLA, entities suspected of having contaminated a given site are identified as *potentially responsible parties,* or PRPs. Whenever possible, the Environmental Protection Agency (EPA) compels PRPs to clean up sites they created or contributed to creating. If the EPA is unable to identify PRPs for a given site, the agency will itself pay for site cleanup using Superfund Trust funds authorized by Congress. In many instances businesses are identified as the PRPs for a site, and thus issues arise as to the appropriate accounting and reporting that should be adopted.

---

[7] Source: SFAS No. 5, "Accounting for Contingencies," (Financial Accounting Standards Board: Norwalk, CT, 1975), para. 8.

EXHIBIT 12.6

The Dow Chemical Company
Footnote Disclosure for Commitments and
Contingent Liabilities

Q Commitments and Contingent Liabilities

In January 1994, Dow Corning Corporation (Dow Corning), in which the Company is a 50 percent shareholder, announced a pretax charge of $640 ($415 after tax) for the fourth quarter of 1993. In January 1995, Dow Corning announced a pretax charge of $241 ($152 after tax) for the fourth quarter of 1994. These charges included Dow Corning's best estimate of its potential liability for breast implant litigation based on a global Breast Implant Litigation Settlement Agreement (the Settlement Agreement); litigation and claims outside the Settlement Agreement; and provisions for legal, administrative and research costs related to breast implants. The charges for 1993 and 1994 included pretax amounts of $1,240 and $441, less expected insurance recoveries of $600 and $200, respectively. The 1993 amounts reported by Dow Corning were determined on a present value basis. On an undiscounted basis, the estimated liability noted above for 1993 was $2,300 less expected insurance recoveries of $1,200.

As a result of the Dow Corning actions, the Company recorded its 50 percent share of the charges, net of tax benefits available to Dow. The impact on net income was a charge of $192 for 1993 and $70 for 1994.

Dow Corning reported an after tax net loss of $167 for the second quarter of 1995 as a result of a $221 after tax charge taken to reflect a change in accounting method from the present value basis noted above to an undiscounted basis resulting from the uncertainties associated with its voluntary filing for protection under Chapter 11 of the U.S. Bankruptcy Code on May 15, 1995. As a result of such loss and Chapter 11 filing, the Company recognized a pretax charge against income of $330 for the second quarter of 1995, fully reserved its investment in Dow Corning and is not recognizing its 50 percent share of equity earnings while Dow Corning remains in Chapter 11.

On September 1, 1994, Judge Sam C. Pointer, Jr. of the U.S. District Court for the Northern District of Alabama approved the Settlement Agreement, pursuant to which plaintiffs choosing to participate in the Settlement Agreement released the Company from liability. The Company was not a participant in the Settlement Agreement nor was it required to contribute to the settlement. On October 7, 1995, Judge Pointer issued an order which concluded that the Settlement Agreement was not workable in its then-current form because the funds committed to it by industry participants were inadequate. The order provided that plaintiffs who had previously agreed to participate in the Settlement Agreement could opt out after November 30, 1995.

The Company's maximum exposure for breast implant product liability claims against Dow Corning is limited to its investment in Dow Corning which, after the second quarter of 1995 charge noted above, is zero. As a result, any future charges by Dow Corning related to such claims or as a result of the Chapter 11 proceeding would not have an adverse impact on the Company's consolidated financial statements.

The Company is separately named as a defendant in more than 13,000 breast implant product liability cases. In these situations, plaintiffs have alleged that the Company should be liable for Dow Corning's alleged torts based on the Company's 50 percent stock ownership in Dow Corning and that the Company should be liable by virtue of alleged "direct participation" by the Company or its agents in Dow Corning's breast implant business. These latter, direct participation claims include counts sounding in strict liability, fraud, aiding and abetting, conspiracy, concert of action and negligence.

Judge Pointer was appointed by the Federal Judicial Panel on Multidistrict Litigation to oversee all of the product liability cases involving silicone breast implants filed in the U.S. federal courts. Initially, in a ruling issued on December 1, 1993, Judge Pointer granted the Company's motion for summary judgement, finding that there was no basis on which a jury could conclude that the Company was liable for any claimed defects in the breast implants manufactured by Dow Corning. In an interlocutory opinion issued on April 25, 1995, Judge Pointer affirmed his earlier ruling as to plaintiffs' corporate control claims but vacated that ruling as to plaintiffs' direct participation claims.

It is the opinion of the Company's management that the possibility is remote that plaintiffs will prevail on the theory that the Company should be liable in the breast implant litigation because of its shareholder relationship with Dow Corning. The Company's management believes that there is no merit to plaintiffs' claims that the Company is liable for alleged defects in Dow Corning's silicone products because of the Company's alleged direct participation in the development of those products, and the Company intends to contest those claims vigorously. Management believes that the possibility is remote that a resolution of plaintiffs' direct participation claims, including the vigorous defense against those claims, would have a material adverse impact on the Company's financial position or cash flows. Nevertheless, in light of Judge Pointer's April 25, 1995, ruling, it its possible that a resolution of plaintiffs' direct participation claims, including the vigorous defense against those claims, could have a material adverse impact on the Company's net income for a particular period, although it its impossible at this time to estimate the range or amount of any such impact.

Numerous lawsuits have been brought against the Company and other chemical companies alleging that the manufacture, distribution of use of pesticides containing dibromochloropropane (DBCP) has caused, among other things, property damage, including contamination of groundwater. To date, there have been no verdicts or judgements against the Company in connection with these allegations. It is the opinion of the Company's management that the possibility is remote that the resolution of such lawsuits will have a material adverse impact on the Company's consolidated financial statements.

EXHIBIT 12.6 concluded

The Dow Chemical Company
Footnote Disclosure for Commitments and
Contingent Liabilities

Accruals for environmental matters are recorded when it is probable that a liability has been incurred and the amount of the liability can be reasonably estimated, based on current law and existing technologies. The Company had accrued $283 at December 31, 1997, for environmental matters, including $11 for the remediation of Superfund sites. This is management's best estimate of the costs for remediation and restoration with respect to environmental matters for which the Company has accrued liabilities, although the ultimate cost with respect to these particular matters could range up to twice that amount. Inherent uncertainties exist in these estimates primarily due to unknown conditions, changing governmental regulations and legal standards regarding liability, and evolving technologies for handling site remediation and restoration. It is the opinion of the Company's management that the possibility is remote that costs in excess of those accrued or disclosed will have a material adverse impact on the Company's consolidated financial statements.

In addition to the breast implant, DBCP and environmental remediation matters, the Company is party to a number of other claims and lawsuits arising out of the normal course of business with respect to commercial matters, including product liability, governmental regulation and other actions. Certain of these actions purport to be class actions and seek damages in very large amounts. All such claims are being contested.

Dow has an active risk management program consisting of numerous insurance policies secured from many carriers at various times. These policies provide coverage which will be utilized to minimize the impact, if any, of the contingencies described above.

Except for the possible effect on the Company's net income for breast implant litigation described above, it is the opinion of the Company's management that the possibility is remote that the aggregate of all claims and lawsuits will have a material adverse impact on the Company's consolidated financial statements.

A Canadian subsidiary has entered into two 20-year agreements, which expire in 1998 and 2004, to purchase ethylene. The purchase price is determined on a cost-of-service basis which, in addition to covering all operating expenses and debt service costs, provides the owner of the manufacturing plants with a specified return on capital. Total purchases under the agreements were $199, $221 and $204 in 1997, 1996 and 1995, respectively.

At December 31, 1997, the Company had various outstanding commitments for take or pay and throughput agreements, including the Canadian subsidiary's ethylene contracts, for terms extending from one to 20 years. In general, such commitments were at prices not in excess of current market prices

Fixed and Determinable Portion of Take of Pay and Throughput Obligations

1998	$ 215
1999	179
2000	168
2001	157
2002	148
2003 through expiration of contracts	1,270
Total	$2,137

In addition to the take or pay obligations at December 31, 1997, the Company had outstanding purchase commitments which range from one to 18 years for steam, electrical power, materials, property, and other items used in the normal course of business of approximately $178. In general, such commitments were at prices not in excess of current market prices. The Company also had outstanding direct and indirect commitments for construction performance and lease payment guarantees and other obligations of $226.

From a contingent liability perspective, if an environmental contingency loss is "probable" and can be reasonably estimated, a loss reflecting the expected cost to restore the environment and settle any related litigation (such as health claims) must be accrued on the company's financial statements. Alternatively, if the loss is only "reasonably probable" or "remote," no disclosure is required.

The tenth paragraph of Exhibit 12.6 describes what Dow Chemical's management concluded about its own Superfund liability; obviously, they decided the loss both was probable and could be estimated (at $283 million) although they also conclude that the possible costs could be twice as much. Dow does not identify whether this amount is net of expected recoveries or at present value; however, in 1993 the Emerging Issues Task Force (EITF) of the FASB and later the SEC ruled that environmental liabilities should be reduced by expected recoveries only when the claim for recovery is probable of realization. Discounting of environmental obligations is permitted only if the amounts and timing of the cash payments for cleanup are reliably determinable, and only on a site-by-site basis. It seems likely that Dow's accrued liability is not a net figure and is not discounted.

The EITF also concluded that not all costs associated with environmental contingencies need to be deducted from current earnings. Consider, for example, the situation of a property owner who acquires a building in which asbestos fibers have been used as insulation. Various federal, state, and local laws now require the removal or containment of "dangerous asbestos." The EITF determined that the costs incurred to treat or remove asbestos (within a reasonable period of time after a property with a known asbestos problem is acquired) *should* be capitalized as part of the cost of the acquired property as a betterment. The EITF also determined that while, in general, environmental contamination treatment costs should be charged to expense, some costs may be capitalized if they are recoverable, as indicated by the following criteria:

1. The costs extend the life, increase the capacity, or improve the safety or efficiency of property owned by the company.

2. The costs mitigate or prevent environmental contamination that has yet to occur and that otherwise may result from future operations or activities.

3. The costs are incurred in preparing the property for sale.

The costs of complying with today's and tomorrow's environmental regulations and society's expectations pose interesting questions for accountants. These issues will take on greater importance in the years to come. For example, in the summer of 1995, Shell Oil agreed to abort their planned dumping of the Brent Spar oil-storage rig in the North Atlantic after protests instigated by Greenpeace. Whatever the merits of the case, whether dumping or salvage on land was environmentally better, the cost differential was £36 million. Over 200 rigs in the North Sea must be salvaged eventually. How should the owners of those rigs provide for this teardown cost, and when? And what about the costs for recycling old automobiles, railroad cars, chemical plants, office towers, and shipyards? When should they be recorded as liabilities? Where should the costs of those liabilities be charged? Are we miscosting products and services by not including these costs? It doesn't take long to appreciate the seriousness of this issue.

DERIVATIVES AND OTHER OFF-BALANCE-SHEET RISKS

Another set of corporate obligations not considered formal liabilities under U.S. GAAP are repurchase agreements, letters of credit, interest swaps, forward purchase agreements for securities or commodities, options, and variations of these types of transactions. These agreements are termed **financial instruments** if they impose an obligation or right to exchange cash or some other financial instrument under potentially unfavorable terms. A simple example of a financial instrument might be a repurchase agreement or "repo." In this situation, Company X might sell a package of securities to Company Y, subject to an agreement whereby Y sells them back at the same price one year later. This is rather common. A corporation with temporarily surplus funds might buy some bonds from a brokerage firm. During the period of the agreement the corporation earns interest on the bonds but risks no loss of principal because under the terms of the repo it will resell the bonds to the brokerage firm for what it paid for them. Brokerage firms like these agreements because they usually include a provision that permits substitution of one bond for another of comparable risk, maturity, yield, and so on. This is how brokerage firms keep a large inventory of bonds available for sale to their customers: The bonds out on repo can be sold and replaced with a similar bond. It's a win-win proposition: The company earns interest on the bonds with no principal risk, and the brokerage gets a large inventory of bonds without putting up any cash.

This simple repo raises serious accounting issues for both parties. Both face the possibility of a significant loss. The brokerage firm could suffer a major loss if the value of the bonds declined—this is the **market risk.** The corporation faces a **credit risk** because the brokerage firm may not be around to honor the agreement, and, consequently, the corporation faces the same market risk as the brokerage firm because it may be left holding worthless bonds.

Financial instruments are considered to constitute **off-balance-sheet risk** "if the risk of loss, even if remote, exceeds the amount recognized, if any, in the financial statements."[8] The repo is a good example of just such a situation. During the period when the repo is outstanding, the balance sheet does not reflect the possibility that the brokerage firm could suffer a big principal loss, a loss far greater than any fee income recognized on the sale of the bonds. In the same vein, the corporation could suffer a big principal loss—far greater than any interest income earned on those bonds during the period of the repo agreement. The matter is important because the amount of off-balance-sheet risk assumed by U.S. corporations, under this definition, is huge. For example, in 1994 many people first heard of *derivatives* when Orange County, California, discovered it had lost $1.7 billion on a $7.5 billion investment pool and a number of corporations reported big losses from derivatives, losses that surprised both shareholders and corporation directors. Similarly, in 1998 the hedge fund Long-Term Capital Management lost $4.4 billion, almost all of its capital, in just a few weeks. $3 billion of those losses came on just two kinds of derivatives: interest-rate swaps and long-term stock options. In fact, derivatives and derivative contracts are not new. They have been routinely used by corporations to help manage risk for decades.

Derivative financial instruments are off-balance-sheet options, forwards, futures, swaps, and similar agreements that provide the owner with a benefit or loss based on the underlying value of an asset or index. The instrument or contract "derives" its value from some other asset or index. A simple example of a derivative financial instrument might be the following. Imagine two people debating who has the best terms on a home mortgage. Each thinks the other has the better deal: "I think you will be better off next year because you've got a fixed rate and I think rates are rising." The other person may disagree: "Actually, I think you're better off with a variable rate because my big concern is that rates will drop." (Assume that both parties pay the same interest rate now and have the same principal outstanding.) All that's missing is for someone to say, "Well, if that's the way you feel, then let's agree to pay each other's interest payments for a year." They may not know what to call it, but they have just created a derivative financial instrument.

The corporate version of this neighborhood vignette is an *interest rate swap* wherein Company X, with outstanding debt at a fixed rate, is able to enter into a contract with some other party, say Company Y, whereby Y pays a fixed rate of interest to X over the period of the agreement and, in return, X agrees to pay Y a variable rate of interest linked to some index like a bank lending rate. The effect of the agreement is to transform X's fixed-rate debt

[8] J. R. Williams, *Miller's Comprehensive GAAP Guide* (New York: Harcourt Brace Jovanovich, 1995).

into a variable rate. In fact, Company X will receive a series of fixed payments from Y and will give Y a series of payments linked to some index. The derivative is like an off-balance-sheet receivable to X from Y—and an off-balance-sheet payable from X to Y.

The agreements are "off balance sheet" because the contracts are written in such a way, and the rates negotiated in such a way, that little or no funds change hands when the contracts are signed. Said another way, one can purchase an interest rate swap for zero cost today. Yet that swap may obligate the firm to future payments and receipts which, if circumstances change, could mean large loses for the company. The off-balance sheet agreement, which had no original cost, and zero market value on the day of signing, could take on a very large value, positive or negative, soon after.

Appendix 12B describes off-balance-sheet risks and derivatives in more detail and illustrates the required accounting and footnote disclosures under GAAP, with examples drawn from several current annual reports. But for our purposes here, a summary explanation is sufficient. Information on all financial instruments with off-balance-sheet risk (as just defined) must be disclosed in the footnotes and must include

- The contractual amounts.
- The nature of the agreement.
- The terms and conditions.
- The market and credit risk.
- The cash requirements and the related accounting policies.

Additional disclosure requirements for derivatives used for trading purposes (i.e. speculation) require fair value reporting as well as disclosure of trading gains and losses by class of activity. Ordinarily, accounting for trading and speculative activities using financial instruments requires that they be marked to market and that unrealized gains and losses be included in income. Derivatives not used for trading, such as hedging, require a different accounting and another set of disclosures that focus on the reasons for using hedges, descriptions of the types of derivatives used, and the risks being hedged.

Many of the most common derivatives, such as interest rate swaps, when used to hedge as opposed to trading, qualify for **hedge accounting** (explained in Appendix 12B); accordingly, these instruments are recorded at cost and are amortized over the life of the instrument. Changing interest rates or price levels are recognized each period as actual receipts and payments are made under the swap. As a consequence of hedge accounting, the gains or losses on the swap or hedging instrument are recognized at the same time as the losses or gains on the asset or liability being hedged. For example, if an interest rate swap is used to hedge interest rate risk on the company's outstanding debt, say by transforming variable-rate debt to fixed, then if interest rates rise, the gain from the swap should offset the rising interest expense on the debt. If interest rates fall, a loss on the swap will offset the declining interest expense on the original debt.

It can become quite complex, but not all companies use every type of derivative. Understanding what is happening with derivatives does require careful study of footnotes. Exhibit 12.7 is an example of the disclosure made by Dresser Industries in its 1994 annual report. In January 1994, Dresser acquired Baroid Corporation and its $150 million, 8 percent senior notes, which Dresser subsequently guaranteed. To hedge their risk as they saw it, they entered into a three-year reverse swap arrangement as described in the footnote. It works like this:

E X H I B I T   1 2 . 7

Dresser Industries
Footnote Disclosure of Derivatives

Baroid entered into a three year reverse interest rate swap beginning May 7, 1993 and ending May 7, 1996. Under terms of the swap agreement, the Company receives a fixed interest payment of 4.9% and pays six-month LIBOR for the prior six months on $150 million. The effect of the reverse interest rate swap is to convert the first three years of the 8% Senior Notes from a fixed rate obligation to a floating rate obligation (composed of a fixed payment of 3.1% plus a floating payment based on six-month LIBOR for the prior six months). If on the date to set the interest rate, six-month LIBOR is less than 4.9%, the Company pays an effective floating rate of less than 8.0% and conversely if six-month LIBOR is greater than 4.9% the Company pays an effective floating rate greater than 8.0%. The effect of the swap is accrued monthly based upon current LIBOR estimates. The swap agreement increased interest expense $1.0 million in 1994 and decreased interest expense $1.2 million in 1993.

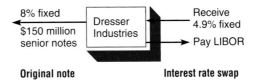

Look carefully at the wording—it's not a misprint. The effect of the swap together with the outstanding notes is such that Dresser has converted its 8 percent fixed-rate notes into a 3.1 percent fixed-rate note plus a trailing six-month variable London Interbank Offered Rate (LIBOR) as follows, all based on the $150 million face amount:

Original note	Pay 8% fixed
Swap	Receive 4.9% fixed Pay LIBOR (6-month trailing)
Net of the above	Pay 3.1% fixed Pay LIBOR (6-month trailing)

Exhibit 12.8 presents a portion of the risk management footnote from Procter & Gamble's 1998 annual report, particularly the segment related to interest rate swaps and currency interest rate swaps. Note that the company says these activities are intended to manage their exposure to market risks, not for trading (speculation). The company had interest rate swaps and currency interest rate swaps on a notional amount totalling $2,149 million as of June 30, 1998. "Notional amount" means the base number used in the swap contract: one million dollars, five million; ten million; whatever was used for that specific swap contract. The carrying value (amortized cost) of these swaps taken together was only $28 million while the fair value was only $7 million. To put this in simple terms, during 1998 Procter & Gamble incurred interest expenses of $548 million (reading from the income statement). The company bought or wrote a number of swap contracts to hedge their exposure to interest rate changes. In total, the net cost of these contracts was $28 million and

EXHIBIT 12.8

The Procter & Gamble Company and Subsidiaries
Footnote Disclosures for Risk Management Activities

Risk Management Activities

The Company is exposed to market risk, including changes in interest rates, currency exchange rates and commodity prices. To manage the volatility relating to these exposures on a consolidated basis, the Company nets the exposures to take advantage of natural offsets and enters into various derivative transactions for the remaining exposures pursuant to the Company's policies in areas such as counterparty exposure and hedging instruments are offset by corresponding changes in the underlying exposures being hedged. The Company does not hold or issue derivative financial instruments for trading purposes.

Interest rate management

The Company's policy is to manage interest cost using a mix of fixed and variable rate debt. To manage this mix in a cost-efficient manner, the Company enters into interest rate swaps, in which the Company agrees to exchange, at specified intervals, the difference between fixed and variable interest amounts calculated by reference to an agreed-upon notional principal amount. These swaps are designated to hedge underlying debt obligations. For qualifying hedges, the interest rate differential is reflected as an adjustment to interest expense over the life of the swaps.

Certain currency interest rate swaps are designated to hedge the foreign currency exposure of the Company's related foreign net investments. Currency effects of these hedges are reflected in the accumulated other comprehensive income section of shareholders' equity, offsetting a portion of the translation of the net assets.

The following table presents information for all interest rate instruments. The notional amount does not necessarily represent amounts exchanged by the parties and, therefore, is not a direct measure of the Company's exposure to credit risk. The fair value approximates the cost to settle the outstanding contracts. The carrying value includes the net amount due to counterparties under swap contracts, currency translation associated with currency interest rate swaps and any marked-to-market value adjustments of instruments.

	June 30	
	1998	**1997**
Notional amount	$2,149	$1,488
Fair value	$ 7	$ (54)
Carrying value	28	(28)
Unrecognized loss	(21)	(26)

Although derivatives are an important component of the Company's interest rate management program, their incremental effect on interest expense for 1998, 1997 and 1996 was not material.

the fair value only $7 million even though the base amounts, or notional values, of these contracts exceeded $2 billion. The last sentence in the footnote admits that, in spite of their efforts in buying and selling interest rate swaps, the overall impact on interest expense was negligible. Perhaps that's good news. If a company was able to substantially increase or decrease its interest expense through derivative transactions during a period when interest rates were reasonably flat, one might wonder whether the objective was hedging or trading.

It is important to remember that a swap is a contract or agreement all by itself that is technically, and legally, independent of the loan agreement it seeks to modify. The swaps appear in the balance sheet as current assets or current liabilities even though the terms of the swap might extend several years. Presumably this is because the swaps can be and are resold as market conditions change. The swaps can be netted on the balance sheet because both the pay and receive sides are from and to the same party. If hedge accounting conditions are satisfied, the swap is recorded at cost and is amortized over its life. If not, it is considered a trading security and is recorded at fair value. Remember, even though the carrying amount of a derivative like a swap may be modest, it can bring substantial loss (or gain) to its holder.

For example, in 1994 Procter and Gamble announced the loss of $157 million on just two derivative contracts. Using interest rate swaps in an effort to save 75 basis points (0.75 percent) on $200 million of debt, or $1.5 million saved each year for five years (0.3 percent of Procter and Gamble's total yearly interest expense) the company found itself on the wrong end of rising interest rates in 1993 and 1994, and eventually was locked into paying 14.12 percent *above* commercial paper rates for almost five years! Procter and Gamble's 1994 annual report remarked soberly, "Leveraged options can magnify the impact of interest rate changes." Indeed they can!

MANAGEMENT CONSIDERATIONS

In earlier chapters we discussed the need to manage the components of working capital so as to minimize the amount of idle cash. We also observed that an important aspect of management's job was to balance:

- The need to maintain an adequate working capital position (to be able to pay bills when they come due) against the cost of maintaining that liquid position.
- The need for inventory (to be able to fill orders promptly) against the cost of carrying that inventory.
- The need to extend credit (to be able to expand sales) against the cost of carrying those receivables.

This chapter's discussion of the liability side of the balance sheet has noted that the source of some of the costs involved in maintaining too liquid a position, namely tying up funds in cash, in inventory, or in receivables, could alternatively be used to reduce interest-carrying debt. To the extent that management can reduce the cost of that debt, it also reduces the cost of carrying working capital and thereby makes the balancing job easier and less critical.

Management can reduce some of the cost of carrying inventory by slowing down payments to suppliers. But suppliers are important stakeholders in the company, and an extended payment program is likely to cost the company in the long run. For example, suppliers may decide to cover their own costs of carrying a receivable due from a company by raising their prices. Or they may simply decide not to do business with the company at any price. Worse, an extended payout program may force the supplier into an illiquid position or even cause bankruptcy, resulting in the loss of a critical resource for the company. Clearly, the management of payables requires delicate balancing.

Liabilities need to be managed in much the same way as a company's assets to produce the greatest return on the shareholders' funds as is practical and consistent with the company's long-term goals and ethical values. Even the interest-bearing liabilities need to be managed for the benefit of shareholders. If a company earns 10 percent after tax on its assets, and shareholders expect a 20 percent return on their investment, it would appear to be foolish to borrow money for an expansion if borrowing costs are 12 percent. But interest on debt is tax deductible, whereas the dividends paid to stockholders are not. Therefore, the cost of a loan in this situation is really only 8 percent if we assume a 35 percent tax rate. With that perspective, borrowing makes sense because shareholders earn the extra 2 percent on the newly acquired assets *without* investing any more capital.

In theory, a company could borrow all of its funds and provide an infinite rate of return to its shareholders. It stands to reason, however, that no creditor would lend on that basis. Lenders require some equity protection for their risk, and as that protection decreases, their risk rises; and accordingly, they will charge more for their lendings. Most managements today carefully manage their company's leverage ratio to operate with the least amount of shareholder capital, consistent with the most cost advantageous credit rating from their borrowers. Managing that relationship requires careful attention to the credit markets and to the attitudes of the company's credit suppliers.

Payables and accruals require only minor amounts of management's attention; typically they are driven by the purchase of assets or the incurring of wage or operating costs. The key decision is almost always, "Should we recognize this event as an asset (or a cost), and at what value?" The liability side of the transaction is usually quite simple. However, many liabilities require serious management attention as to whether, in fact, a liability exists, and if so, at what value. One of the toughest accounting tasks managers face is to define all of a company's liabilities. Stock options, promised pension benefits, lawsuits brought against the firm, forward contracts for the purchase or delivery of a product or service, and environmental cleanup obligations are all common examples of the nature of the task.

Debt placements or sales raise another set of issues. Thoughtful managers must consider a host of factors before obligating the organization to a particular form of debt. Should it be short- or long-term? Denominated in what currency? Collateralized by what assets or contracts? Hedged by what kinds of financial instruments? Good borrowing decisions require a keen understanding of risk management. Obviously one does not want to borrow long-term and invest short-term, thereby running the sort of risk that the U.S. savings and loan companies faced in the 1980s. U.S. companies with substantial overseas sales often borrow from the same markets into which they sell so as to match their risks of changes in exchange rates. They may also hedge their borrowing to manage interest, exchange rates, or both.

Derivatives themselves are another thorny issue for managers. They are essential elements for any company facing market price risks or risks of currency exchange or interest rate fluctuations; but how can management ensure that derivatives are not being abused or that the business has not taken on another, undetected risk without management knowledge? Finally, there is the issue of what can be explained to the shareholders and the other readers of financial statements.

SUMMARY

Liabilities are the short- and long-term obligations of a company, usually involving the repayment of cash. In this chapter we learned that most current liabilities are valued at their face value, whereas most long-term liabilities are valued at their present value. The present value of a liability represents the amount of cash (or other assets) necessary to satisfy a liability *today,* as opposed to its maturity date in the future.

Understanding the extent of obligations that are present in a company is important. If a company has borrowed too much, it may face a high degree of *default risk* for nonpayment of its obligations. On the other hand, for most companies, borrowing some level of funds is usually advantageous so long as the company is able to produce a return on the borrowed funds that exceeds the cost of borrowing.

NEW CONCEPTS AND TERMS

Accounts payable	Futures
Accrued expenses payable	Gross method
Annuity	Hedge accounting
Bond	Market risk
Call option	Maturity date
Certificate of deposit	Maturity value
Compound interest	Mortgage bond
Contingent liability	Net method
Coupon rate	Obligations
Credit risk	Off-balance-sheet risk
Current liabilities	Options
Debenture	Premium
Derivative financial instruments	Put option
Discount	Present value
Discounted value	Revenue bond
Effective interest method	Time value of money
Effective rate	Unearned revenue
Face amount	Value at risk
Financial instrument	Warranty obligation
Forward	Yield rate

The Time Value of Money

One of the most important and pervasive concepts in business is the **time value of money.** We take it for granted, for example, that when we deposit a sum of money in a bank or savings institution, we will receive *interest* on those deposited funds. In effect, the deposited funds have an income-producing feature—the time value of money. By allowing a bank or savings institution to use the funds, perhaps to loan them to someone else, we receive a fee (interest income).

Even when funds are not deposited in a financial institution, they are assumed to have a time value of money. For example, some automobile manufacturers advertise that a customer may buy their product, pay for the purchase over 48 months, but incur no interest charges. Realistically, it is improbable that any manufacturer is able to finance its customers' purchases over extended periods without charging some interest costs; in any case, such practice makes very little business sense. In most cases in which zero interest is advertised, the manufacturer has added an *implicit* cost of financing the purchase over time into the consumer's purchase price. When this occurs, the consumer is faced with an accounting dilemma, namely to determine the true cost of the item versus the implicit cost of paying for the purchase over 36, 48, or 60 months.

To illustrate, suppose that on December 31, 1997, Cavalier Company purchased a new delivery van from a local truck dealer, Keller Auto & Truck Company. According to the agreement between the two companies, Cavalier will pay Keller $20,000 on December 31, 1999—two years hence—and issues a non-interest-bearing note in that amount. On the basis of recent conversations with a loan officer at a bank, executives at Cavalier are aware that they could have borrowed the $20,000 for the two-year period at 10 percent interest. Thus, the accounting dilemma is to answer the following questions: What amount did Cavalier pay for the van? At what value should Cavalier's note payable be shown on the company's December 31, 1997, balance sheet?

Both questions can be answered by determining the cash equivalent value of the Cavalier note on December 31, 1997. Obviously, this figure is less than the $20,000 to be paid on December 31, 1999, because of the time value of money. If Cavalier had borrowed $1 from its banker at 10 percent, it would become $1.10 at the end of one year, and this $1.10 would become $1.21 at the end of a second year (if interest is compounded annually).[1] Thus, the problem is to determine the value of the Cavalier note *exclusive* of the time value of money. To accomplish this, we must look to present value concepts for help.

---

[1] The concept of **compound interest** is based on the assumption that interest earned on a savings deposit in the current period will be left on deposit so that in subsequent periods, interest will be earned not only on the original deposit but also on the interest on deposit from prior periods.

Present value or **discounted value** refers to *today's* value of receiving (or paying) a given sum of money in the future. For example, if we are able to deposit $1 in a bank today and interest is compounded annually at 10 percent, the value of our deposit will be $1.10 at the end of one year. The value to be received at the end of one year is known as the *future value* and, computationally, is given by the following equation:

$$F_{n,i} = (1 + i)^n$$

where $F_{n,i}$ is the future (compounded) value of $1 at interest rate i for n periods. Thus,

$$F_{1,0.10} = (1 + 0.10)^1 = 1.10$$

To understand the concept of present value, it is a simple matter to consider merely the reverse (or inverse) of the concept of *future value.* For example, if we are to receive $1.10 in one year, and if interest is calculated at 10 percent annually, what is the value of that payment today? Using the equation for present value computations,

$$P_{n,i} = \frac{1}{(1 + i)^n}$$

we can readily determine that the present value of receiving $1 in one year at 10 percent interest is 0.90909. To determine the present value (PV) of receiving $1.10 in one year, it is a simple matter to multiply the two figures together:

$$PV = \$1.10 \ (0.09090) = \$1$$

Thus, the present value today of receiving $1.10 in one year at 10 percent interest is $1.

With these concepts in mind, we can now approach the problem of determining the cash equivalent value of the Cavalier note. The present value of Cavalier's $20,000 so-called non-interest-bearing, two-year note should bear the same relationship to $20,000 as $1 does to $1.21. Hence,

$$\$PV/\$20,000 = \$1.00/\$1.21$$
$$\$PV = \$20,000 \times (\$1.00/\$1.21)$$
$$\$PV = \$20,000 \times 0.82645$$

Thus, the present value factor for 10 percent compounded annually for two years is 0.82645. Therefore, $20,000 times 0.82645 is $16,529, the figure at which the note payable (and the van) should be shown on Cavalier's December 31, 1997, balance sheet.

To verify this figure, consider the perspective of Cavalier's banker. If the bank lent Cavalier the $16,529.00 on December 31, 1997, at 10 percent interest, the compounded amount owed one year later, at December 31, 1998, would become $18,181.90 ($16,529 $\times$ 1.10) and two years later, at December 31, 1999, would become $20,000 ($18,181.90 $\times$ 1.10). Thus, $16,529.00 at December 31, 1997, is equivalent, at 10 percent interest compounded annually, to $20,000 two years later. Stated alternatively, $16,529.00 is the present value of $20,000 in two years at 10 percent interest compounded annually. Generalized factors for determining the present value of a single, lump sum amount are given in Exhibit 12A.1.

EXHIBIT 12A.1

Present Value of $1 Received at End of Period Indicated
$$PV = 1/(1 + i)^n$$

End of Period	2%	4%	6%	8%	10%	12%	14%	16%	18%	20%	25%	30%
1	0.98	0.96	0.94	0.93	0.91	0.89	0.88	0.86	0.85	0.83	0.80	0.77
2	0.96	0.92	0.89	0.86	0.83	0.80	0.77	0.75	0.71	0.70	0.64	0.59
3	0.94	0.89	0.84	0.79	0.75	0.71	0.67	0.64	0.61	0.58	0.51	0.46
4	0.93	0.86	0.79	0.73	0.68	0.63	0.59	0.55	0.52	0.48	0.41	0.35
5	0.90	0.82	0.75	0.68	0.62	0.57	0.52	0.47	0.44	0.40	0.33	0.27
6	0.89	0.79	0.71	0.63	0.56	0.51	0.46	0.41	0.37	0.34	0.26	0.20
7	0.87	0.76	0.66	0.59	0.51	0.45	0.40	0.36	0.31	0.28	0.21	0.16
8	0.85	0.73	0.63	0.54	0.47	0.41	0.35	0.30	0.27	0.23	0.17	0.12
9	0.84	0.70	0.59	0.50	0.42	0.36	0.31	0.26	0.22	0.19	0.13	0.10
10	0.82	0.68	0.56	0.46	0.39	0.32	0.27	0.23	0.19	0.16	0.11	0.07
11	0.81	0.65	0.52	0.43	0.35	0.29	0.23	0.20	0.16	0.14	0.09	0.06
12	0.79	0.63	0.50	0.40	0.32	0.26	0.21	0.17	0.14	0.11	0.07	0.04
13	0.77	0.60	0.47	0.37	0.29	0.23	0.18	0.14	0.12	0.09	0.05	0.03
14	0.76	0.58	0.44	0.34	0.26	0.20	0.16	0.13	0.10	0.08	0.04	0.03
15	0.74	0.55	0.42	0.31	0.24	0.18	0.14	0.11	0.08	0.07	0.04	0.02
20	0.67	0.45	0.31	0.22	0.15	0.10	0.07	0.05	0.04	0.03	0.01	0.01
25	0.61	0.37	0.23	0.15	0.09	0.06	0.04	0.03	0.02	0.01	*	*
30	0.55	0.31	0.17	0.10	0.06	0.03	0.02	0.01	0.01	*	*	*
35	0.50	0.25	0.13	0.07	0.04	0.02	0.01	0.01	*	*	*	*
40	0.45	0.21	0.10	0.05	0.02	0.01	*	*	*	*	*	*

Present Value of an Annuity

The Cavalier Company illustration is an example of determining the present value of a future lump sum to be paid (or received). Let us assume that it is necessary to know the present value, at 6 percent annually, of three year-end payments of $8,000 each. Such a uniform amount payable (or receivable) each period for a stated number of periods is called an **annuity.** One way to find the present value of an annuity of $8,000 for three years is to compute the present value of each payment and then sum the three present value amounts:

End of Period	Present Value Factor (Exhibit 12A.1)	Present Value of $8,000 Payable
1	0.94	$ 7,520
2	0.89	7,120
3	0.84	6,720
	2.67	$21,360

A more expeditious way of determining the present value of this annuity is to use a table of present value annuity factors, factors that are merely successive sums of present value, single payment factors. Exhibit 12A.2 shows a factor of 2.67 for three years at 6 percent; this factor multiplied by the $8,000 annuity amount results in the present value figure of $21,360.

EXHIBIT 12A.2

Present Value of $1 Received at End of Each Period Indicated
$$PV = 1/i\,[1-1/(1 + i\,)^n]$$

End of Period	2%	4%	6%	8%	10%	12%	14%	16%	18%	20%	25%	30%
1	0.98	0.96	0.94	0.93	0.91	0.89	0.88	0.86	0.85	0.83	0.80	0.77
2	1.94	1.88	1.83	1.79	1.74	1.69	1.65	1.61	1.56	1.53	1.44	1.36
3	2.88	2.77	2.67	2.58	2.49	2.40	2.32	2.25	2.17	2.11	1.95	1.82
4	3.81	3.63	3.46	3.31	3.17	3.03	2.91	2.80	2.69	2.59	2.36	2.17
5	4.71	4.45	4.21	3.99	3.79	3.60	3.43	3.27	3.13	2.99	2.69	2.44
6	5.60	5.24	4.92	4.62	4.35	4.11	3.89	3.68	3.50	3.33	2.95	2.64
7	6.47	6.00	5.58	5.21	4.86	4.56	4.29	4.04	3.81	3.61	3.16	2.80
8	7.32	6.76	6.21	5.75	5.33	4.97	4.64	4.34	4.08	3.84	3.33	2.92
9	8.16	7.43	6.80	6.25	5.75	5.33	4.96	4.60	4.30	4.03	3.46	3.02
10	8.98	8.11	7.36	6.71	6.14	5.65	5.22	4.83	4.49	4.19	3.57	3.09
11	9.79	8.76	7.88	7.14	6.49	5.94	5.45	5.03	4.65	4.33	3.66	3.15
12	10.58	9.39	8.38	7.54	6.81	6.20	5.66	5.20	4.79	4.44	3.73	3.19
13	11.35	9.99	8.85	7.91	7.10	6.43	5.84	5.34	4.91	4.53	3.78	3.22
14	12.11	10.57	9.29	8.25	7.36	6.63	6.00	5.47	5.01	4.61	3.82	3.25
15	12.85	11.12	9.71	8.56	7.60	6.81	6.14	5.58	5.09	4.68	3.86	3.27
20	16.35	13.59	11.47	9.82	8.51	7.47	6.62	5.93	5.35	4.87	3.95	3.32
25	19.52	15.62	12.78	10.68	9.08	7.85	6.88	6.09	5.47	4.95	3.99	3.33
30	22.40	17.30	13.76	11.26	9.43	8.06	7.01	6.18	5.52	4.98	4.00	3.33
35	25.00	18.67	14.49	11.65	9.64	8.18	7.07	6.21	5.54	4.99	4.00	3.33
40	27.36	19.80	15.04	11.92	9.78	8.25	7.11	6.23	5.55	5.00	4.00	3.33

To verify this calculation, let us again assume the perspective of a lender. If a financial institution lent $21,360 repayable in three annual installments of $8,000 each, the debtor would record the receipt of $21,360 in cash and the associated liability for the same amount. At the end of each year, however, a $8,000 cash disbursement must be made to the bank, for a total outflow of $24,000 over the life of the loan. Clearly, each of the $8,000 payments contains amounts applicable to (1) the interest required by the bank in exchange for foregoing the use of the $21,360 loaned to the debtor and (2) the repayment of the loan principal. The following table depicts the annual parts of each payment attributable to interest and principal:

Year	Loan Principal at Beginning of Year	Portion of $8,000 Applied to	
		Interest at 6%	Principal Repayment
1	$21,360.00	$1,281.60	$ 6,718.40
2	14,641.60	878.50	7,121.50
3	7,520.10	451.20	7,548.80
		$2,611.30	$21,388.70*

*Not precisely equal to $21,360 due to rounding.

Present value annuity factors are appropriate to use when the stream of cash flows are equal amounts and occur at the end of a constant sequence of periods. It is worth noting again that the Exhibit 12A.2 factors are merely the successive sums of the factors from Exhibit 12A.1.

An Illustration

Assume that Cavalier Company wanted to raise $10 million by issuing bonds payable due five years from the date of issue, with 8 percent interest payable annually. As a simplification, assume further that the net proceeds the company receives from the issuance of the bonds is the full $10 million. What liability should Cavalier report on its balance sheet?

The company will pay $14 million over the five-year period, but the present value, at 8 percent, is only $10 million:

Year	Interest at End of Year (Millions)	Principal at End of year	Factor at 8% (Exhibit 12A.1)	Present Value Amount (Millions)*
1	$0.8	—	0.93	$0.744
2	0.8	—	0.86	0.688
3	0.8	—	0.79	0.632
4	0.8	—	0.73	0.548
5	0.8	—	0.68	0.544
		10.0	0.68	6.800
				$9.992

*A shorter way to do this problem would be to use an Exhibit 12A.2 factor: 3.99 (8 percent; 5 years) times $0.8 million annual interest cash outflows, which equals $3,192,000, and this plus $6,800,000, the present value of the single $10 million principal amount ($10 million times Exhibit 12A.1 factor of 0.68), gives $9,992,000.

Note that debt issued at a yield rate equal to its coupon rate will be sold at an amount equal to its face value.

Now assume that two years after these bonds were issued, an investor wanted to buy $100,000 of the bonds at a price that would yield a 10 percent return. How much should the investor pay?

Graphically, the cash flows of such an investment involve an annuity stream of $8,000 in annual interest inflows (or 8 percent of $100,000) and a one-time principal receipt of $100,000. Using an effective interest rate of 10 percent, the investor should pay $95,000 (or $94,920 rounded off):

Cash Flows at End of Year			Exhibit 12A.1 Factors at 10%	Present Value Amount
1	2	3		
$8,000			0.91	$ 7,280.00
	$8,000		0.83	6,640.00
		$ 8,000	0.75	6,000.00
		100,000	0.75	75,000.00
				$94,920.00

Note that the appropriate present value interest factors were selected using the real (or effective) rate of interest (10 percent) on the bonds, not the coupon or stated rate of interest (8 percent). Even though the bonds carry a stated rate of 8 percent, the price at which the bonds may be bought (or sold) will fluctuate to enable the investor to earn a fair (market) rate of return.

Derivatives and Other Off-Balance-Sheet Risks

This appendix describes off-balance-sheet financial instruments and each of the four basic kinds of derivatives. We also describe the accounting and disclosures that are required under U.S. GAAP together with examples from recent annual reports.

Financial instruments, including derivatives, have become very important tools for many corporations and for the financial community in general. The number of derivative contracts has grown dramatically, involving trillions of dollars, and they are steadily growing in their complexity as well. Unfortunately, they are not well understood by either investors or creditors.

Off-Balance Sheet Risk

As defined in Chapter 12, certain financial agreements expose an entity to substantial risk and yet do not appear as such in the balance sheet. Examples of such off-balance-sheet risks include:

- Obligations arising from financial instruments sold short.
- Receivables sold with recourse.
- Repurchase agreements.
- Options.
- Loan commitments.
- Interest rate caps and floors.
- Financial guarantees.
- Letters of credit.
- Interest rate swaps.
- Currency swaps.
- Financial futures contracts (hedges and nonhedges).
- Financial forward contracts (hedges and nonhedges).

Some of these agreements are conditional, like an option; others are unconditional, as with a forward or futures contract. Note that some off-balance-sheet financial instruments are associated with a balance sheet liability, such as an interest rate swap. Some are associated with an asset, such as a repurchase (or repo) agreement tied to securities owned; and some are associated with neither an asset nor a liability, such as a forward interest agreement.

Derivatives

Derivatives are a subset of these off-balance-sheet risks. There are four important types of derivatives, each with many variations:

1. Financial futures contracts
2. Options
3. Interest rate swaps
4. Financial forward contracts

Futures

Futures contracts were the first derivatives, and they have been used for generations. In the classic agricultural future, a farmer enters into an agreement to sell a certain quantity (and prescribed quality) of a commodity at a certain price and at a certain time, usually at the end of the harvest. It might be to deliver 10,000 bushels of number 2 yellow corn for $2.74 per bushel at the Cargill elevator in Omaha, Nebraska. This agreement or futures contract can be resold to someone else. There is a market for corn and one for corn futures. Commodity exchanges in the United States routinely trade futures in corn, wheat, oats, cattle, hogs, and dozens of other products. The important thing to understand about a futures contract is that it is an unconditional agreement to sell; it is not like an option. In addition to commodities, futures can be used for securities as well. Security exchanges trade U.S. Treasury futures, currency futures, and futures based on certain other financial instruments. The commodities and financial futures exchanges, and the futures contracts that they trade, permit companies to hedge against changes in the price of corn or oil, the prices of Japanese yen and German marks. And, of course, some entities buy and sell futures contracts on speculation rather than to hedge a business price risk.

U.S. accounting rules require that all futures contracts be marked to market and, if the futures contract is a hedge (that is, an attempt to offset or eliminate some type of risk exposure), any gains or losses on the contract be deferred until gains or losses on the hedged item are realized. If the futures contract is not a hedge, any gains or losses should be recognized each period, such as quarterly for most publicly traded U.S. companies.

Options

Options are conditional contracts concerning the sale or purchase of a currency or commodity at some time in the future. A **call option** permits the holder to purchase a certain security or commodity at some given date. For example, an individual, called the holder, may have the right, but not an obligation, to purchase a thousand shares of Intel Corporation stock at $120 per share on, or prior to, a certain date, say, six months from today. Such an agreement requires two parties: the purchaser or holder of the call option and the issuer or writer of the option, who has the contractual obligation to sell those shares of stock in six months if the holder so demands.

A **put option** works much the same way, but in reverse: The owner or holder has the right to sell a particular security or commodity for a set price at some time in the future—and the issuer or writer of the put option is then obligated to buy at that price if so instructed by the holder. The Wall Street expression "He can really *put* it to you" captures the essence of a put option. It enables you to force someone to buy a security at a price above market value.

Accounting for options purchased is somewhat more complex than for futures because a futures contract is a binding agreement while an option is a right, not an obligation. In general, options are marked to market unless they are designated hedges, in which case the mark-to-market adjustment is deferred. Because the premium paid for an option includes both intrinsic value and time value, the two elements are separated. The time value is amortized over the life of the option; the intrinsic value, if any, is recorded as an asset and marked-to-market at the end of each accounting period.[1]

Interest Rate Swaps

Interest rate swaps have already been described in the text. The 1998 Procter & Gamble annual report illustrated the disclosure required by U.S. GAAP for such transactions. Interest rate swaps are typically used to provide a degree of protection against a feared change in interest rates, but they actually exchange one risk for another. Interest rate floors and caps can be thought of as variations of the basic interest rate swap from a fixed rate to a variable one. When the variable rate is capped, floored, or both, there is less risk; accordingly, there is an additional cost either in a fee paid or in some other fashion. Caps and floors can also be added to an existing variable rate instrument. The important point here is that these contracts are like side agreements. Their effect is to modify a company's risk position in some fashion. The exact effect depends upon future events.

Forwards

Forwards are a type of financial futures contract. The financial futures market trades standardized amount contracts with standard time periods, such as $1 million for 12 months. Forwards are customized or tailored financial futures contracts that can be used by the buyer to hedge a specific risk over a specific time period, such as the purchase of DM 6.3 million (deutsche marks) on September 20.

Hedge Accounting

Organizations such as brokerage firms, swap dealers, investment companies, hedge funds, and pension funds are, by definition, traders and must account for financial instruments on a mark-to-market basis. However, firms that use derivatives as hedges to reduce their exposure to changing interest rates or commodity price changes, for example, may qualify for **hedge accounting.** The general idea behind hedge accounting is one of matching: Gains or losses on the hedge should be recognized in the same time period as the loss or gain on the hedged item—that is, the debt instrument or commodity. For example, if a hedge transaction is undertaken so as to reduce the exposure of the firm to a steep drop in the value of a commodity, then unrealized gains on the hedge may be recognized only to the extent of a corresponding write-down in the carrying value of the inventory item—that is, the commodity itself. Beyond that, all unrealized gains or losses are deferred until the hedge is terminated or the hedged item is expensed.

Interest rate swaps are treated in a similar fashion: Since the underlying debt item, a note or bond outstanding, is not marked to market, it is not appropriate to realize gains or losses on the swap contract used to hedge that interest rate exposure. Accordingly, the interest

---

[1] Accounting for options sold is beyond the scope of this appendix.

expense for a given period on an interest rate swap is the net of the interest received and the interest paid on the swap. This offsets the interest expense on the underlying debt. The resulting net expense is at the revised or transformed interest rate. In other words, if the original debt item was at a variable rate and the swap transformed the debt into a fixed rate of 7 percent, then hedge accounting will result in a combined or net interest expense for the period of 7 percent, if it's a perfect swap. If the swap was to transform fixed-rate debt to a variable rate, then the resulting interest expense will be at that variable rate.

Under hedge accounting, the swap itself is recorded at cost. It is then amortized over the life of the swap. Most interest rate swaps have little or no cost. They are typically carried as a current asset, even if they have a lifetime greater than one year.

It is inappropriate to recognize gains or losses on the value of a swap except if the underlying asset or liability being hedged is adjusted. Unrealized gains or losses do appear in the footnote disclosures, however.

There are three conditions for the use of hedge accounting; each instrument must be examined on a case-by-case basis. The requirements are these:

1. *Risk.* The item being hedged must expose the company to a real risk.

2. *Reduced exposure.* The hedge must reduce the exposure to that risk. Hedges are often created using a basis other than the exact asset or index of the item being hedged; this is called *cross-hedging.* The firm must be able to establish that the hedge actually reduces exposure to risk associated with the underlying asset or liability.

3. *Purpose of hedging.* The hedge must be so identified from the start. The firm cannot designate an instrument as a hedge after the fact.

Required Disclosures

The requirements for financial disclosure of financial instruments with off-balance-sheet risk include the following:[2]

- The face or contract amount (or the notional amount if there is no face or contract amount).

- The nature and terms, including, at a minimum, a discussion of credit and market risk, cash requirements of the instrument, and the related accounting policies.

With certain exceptions, the following must also be disclosed for each class of off-balance-sheet risk:[3]

- The maximum amount of accounting loss that would be incurred if any party failed to perform completely according to the terms of the financial instrument with off-balance-sheet risk, even if this is a remote possibility, and the collateral or other security for the amount due, if any, was absolutely worthless (in other words, a worst-case scenario).

- The entity's policy for determining the amount of collateral or other security required to support financial instruments subject to credit risk, information about the entity's access to that collateral or other security, and the nature and a brief description of the collateral or other security (in other words, an entity's policy for requiring security and a brief description of the security supporting financial instruments with off-balance-sheet risk of accounting loss).

[2] J. R. Williams, *Miller's Comprehensive GAAP Guide* (New York: Harcourt Brace Jovanovich, 1995).

[3] Williams, *Miller's Comprehensive GAAP Guide.*

Specifically excluded from this requirement are most insurance contracts, unconditional purchase obligations, pensions, stock options, leases, and certain other items.

U.S. GAAP also requires disclosure of the fair values of financial instruments using quoted market prices or estimates based on market prices. If fair values are not practicable to estimate, that must be explained; the details of the instrument must be disclosed as well.

If a firm owns derivatives used for trading, the following disclosure must be made:

1. The average and end-of-period amounts of fair value, distinguishing between assets and liabilities.

2. The net gains or losses (often referred to as net trading revenues) arising from derivative financial instruments trading activities during the period, disaggregated by class, business activity, risk, or another category consistent with management of those activities and when those net trading gains and losses are reported in the income statement.[4]

Derivatives used for hedging require the following disclosures:

1. A description of the entity's objectives for holding or issuing the derivative financial instrument, the context needed to understand those objectives, and the entity's strategies for achieving those objectives.

2. A description of how the derivative financial instruments are reported in the financial statements, including

   a. Policies for recognizing and measuring the derivative financial instruments held or issued.

   b. When recognized, and where those instruments are reported in the statement of financial position and income statement.

3. For derivative financial instruments that are held or issued for the purpose of hedging anticipated transactions:

   a. A description of the anticipated transactions for which risks are hedged with derivative financial instruments, including the period of time until the anticipated transactions are expected to occur.

   b. A description of the classes of derivative financial instruments used to hedge the anticipated transactions.

   c. The amount of hedging gains and losses explicitly deferred.

   d. A description of the transactions or other events that result in the recognition of earnings of gains or losses deferred by hedge accounting.[5]

The FASB has urged, but has not required, that firms disclose even more information about their derivatives and other financial instruments, including information about interest rates, commodity prices, foreign exchange, or whatever risks were germane to the firm. In particular, the FASB urged disclosing the hypothetical impact of large (±100 or 200 basis points) shifts in interest rates or comparable movements in commodities prices or value at risk from derivatives and other financial instruments. **Value at risk** is the expected loss from adverse market movements at a specified probability and specific time frame. For example, value at risk simulation models might be used to state that the net value of a pool of financial

---

[4] Williams, *Miller's Comprehensive GAAP Guide.*

[5] Williams, *Miller's Comprehensive GAAP Guide.*

EXHIBIT 12B.1

United Technologies Corporation
Disclosure of Foreign Exchange Contracts and Financial Instruments

Foreign Exchange

The Corporation conducts business in many different currencies and, accordingly, is subject to the inherent risks associated with foreign exchange rate movements. The financial position and results of operations of substantially all of the Corporation's foreign subsidiaries are measured using the local currency as the functional currency. The aggregate effects of translating the financial statements of these subsidiaries are deferred as a separate component of shareowners' equity. The Corporation had foreign currency net assets in more than forty currencies, aggregating $1.4 billion and $1.8 billion at December 31, 1997 and 1996, including Canadian dollar net assets of $420 million and $460 million, respectively. The Corporation's net assets in the Asia Pacific region were $441 million and $524 million at December 31, 1997 and 1996, respectively.

At December 31, 1996, the Corporation had $139 million notional principal amount of outstanding currency swap contracts, to hedge its foreign net assets, which were terminated in 1997.

Foreign currency commitment and transaction exposures are managed at the operating unit level as an integral part of the business and residual exposures that cannot be offset to an insignificant amount are hedged. These hedges are executed by authorized management at the operating units and are scheduled to mature coincident with the timing of the underlying foreign currency commitments and transactions. Hedged items include foreign currency denominated receivables and payables on the balance sheet, firm purchase orders and firm sales commitments.

At December 31, the Corporation had the following amounts related to foreign exchange contracts hedging foreign currency transactions and firm commitments:

in millions of dollars	1997	1996
Notional amount:		
Buy contracts	$1,747	$1,928
Sell contracts	1,062	780
Gains and losses explicitly deferred as a result of hedging firm commitment:		
Gains deferred	$ 14	$ 14
Losses deferred	(69)	(14)
	$ (55)	$ –

The deferred gains and losses are expected to be recognized in earnings over the next two years, as these transactions are realized, along with the offsetting gains and losses on the underlying commitments.

---

instruments could be expected to change by no more than a certain percent on 95 out of a 100 trading days in response to either interest rate or currency exchange rates.

Examples

Probably the best way to understand what these requirements mean in practice is to examine some representative corporate disclosures. Exhibit 12.B.1 is the disclosure footnote for foreign exchange contracts from the United Technologies Corporation 1997 annual report. The company reports that it has current hedges, probably currency futures and options,

---

EXHIBIT 12B.1 continued

United Technologies Corporation
Disclosure of Foreign Exchange Contracts and Financial Instruments

13. Financial Instruments

The Corporation operates internationally and, in the normal course of business, is exposed to fluctuations in interest rates and currency values. These fluctuations can increase the costs of financing, investing and operating the business. The Corporation manages this risk to acceptable limits through the use of derivatives to create offsetting positions in foreign currency markets. The Corporation views derivative financial instruments as risk management tools and is not party to any leveraged derivatives.

The notional amounts of derivative contracts do not represent the amounts exchanged by the parties, and thus are not a measure of the exposure of the Corporation through its use of derivatives. The amounts exchanged by the parties are normally based on the notional amounts and other terms of the derivatives, which relate to exchange rates. The value of derivatives is derived from those underlying parameters and changes in the relevant rates.

By nature, all financial instruments involve market and credit risk. The Corporation enters into derivative financial instruments with major investment grade financial institutions. The Corporation has policies to monitor its credit risks of counterparties to derivative financial instruments. Pursuant to these policies the Corporation periodically determines the fair value of its derivative instruments in order to identity its credit exposure. The Corporation diversifies the counterparties used as a means to limit counterparty exposure and concentration of risk. Credit risk is assessed prior to entering into transactions and periodically thereafter. The Corporation does not anticipate nonperformance by any of these counterparties.

The fair value of a financial instrument is the amount at which the instrument could be exchanged in a current transaction between willing parties, other than in a forced or liquidation sale. Significant differences can arise between the fair value and carrying amount of financial instruments at historic cost.

---

covering $1.7 billion of sales contracts. Because they are hedges, any gains and losses are deferred until the hedged item is recognized. Total net deferred losses under these agreements netted to zero in 1996 and a net $55 million loss is 1997. Because these losses are deferred, they do not appear in either the balance sheet or the income statement. These "losses" are merely the difference between the cost of the hedge and its fair value at December 31, 1997. Several items in the company's discussion of financial instruments are noteworthy. In the first paragraph the company explains why it uses derivatives. The next paragraph provides an explanation of "notional amounts." In the third paragraph, the company indicates that it tries to limit the number of derivative transactions with any one party.

Exhibit 12.B.2, from the 1997 annual report of Corn Products International illustrates the disclosures for commodities. The company had a total of $154 million in open contracts, almost half to be completed before March 31, 1998. As of December 31, 1997, the company reports that on the futures contracts held, there was a $5.3 million difference between contract amount and market rates. Also in the previous year, the company moved to sell their positions in some futures contracts when prices moved contrary to expectations. That move triggered a $40 million loss. Yet remember that the contracts themselves were probably being carried at very small amounts. Like an iceberg, it's what's below the surface that can do real harm.

EXHIBIT 12B.1 concluded

United Technologies Corporation
Disclosure of Foreign Exchange Contracts and Financial Instruments

The carrying amounts and fair values of financial instruments are as follows:

	December 31, 1997		December 31, 1996	
in millions of dollars	Carrying Amount	Fair Value	Carrying Amount	Fair Value
Financial assets:				
Long-term receivables	$ 91	$ 89	$ 118	$ 118
Customer financing assets	117	117	136	133
Financial liabilities:				
Short-term borrowings	217	217	251	250
Long-term debt	1,087	1,260	1,169	1,339
Foreign exchange contracts:				
In a receivable position	21	20	24	29
In a payable position	97	69	29	(1)

The following methods and assumptions were used to estimate the fair value of financial instruments:

Cash, Cash Equivalents and Short-Term Borrowings

The carrying amount approximates fair value because of the short maturity of those instruments.

Long-term Receivables and Customer Financing Assets

The fair values are based on quoted market prices for those or similar instruments. When quoted market prices are not available, an approximation of fair value is based upon projected cash flows discounted at an estimated current market rate of interest.

Debt

The fair values are estimated based on quoted market prices for the same or similar issues or on the current rates offered to the Corporation for debt of the same remaining maturities.

Foreign Exchange Contracts

The fair values are estimated based on the amount that the Corporation would receive or pay to terminate the agreements at the reporting date.

Financing Commitments

The Corporation had outstanding financing commitments totaling approximately $934 million and $1,553 million at December 31, 1997 and 1996. Risks associated with changes in interest rates are negated by the fact that interest rates are variable during the commitment term and are set at the date of funding based on current market conditions, the fair value of the underlying collateral and the credit worthiness of the customers. As a result, the fair value of these financings is expected to equal the amounts funded. The fair value of the commitment itself is not readily determinable and is not considered significant. Additional information pertaining to these commitments is included in note 4.

EXHIBIT 12B.2

Corn Products International, Inc.
Disclosure of Financial Instruments

Note 10 Financial Instruments

Fair value of financial instruments

The carrying values of cash equivalents, accounts receivable, accounts payable and debt approximate fair values.

Commodities

At December 31, 1997, the Company had open corn commodity futures contracts of $154 million. Contracts open for delivery beyond March 31, 1998, amounted to $88 million, of which $59 million is due in May, 1998, $28

million is due in July, 1998, and $1 million in December, 1998. At December 31, 1997, the price of corn under these contracts was $5.3 million above market quotations of the same date.

During the fourth quarter of 1996, the Company recognized a loss of $40 million for certain liquidated corn futures. These futures had been designed to protect anticipated firm-priced business against an expected run-up in corn prices. When corn prices instead fell sharply and the business as anticipated did not materialize, the Company liquidated the futures contracts.

ASSIGNMENTS

12.1. Purchase discounts.   Olympic Distributors of Seattle, Washington, distributes general hardware items to more than a thousand retail customers in the Northwest. Olympic's management manages its cash flow carefully and almost always takes the purchase discounts offered by its suppliers. Recently, many manufacturers have reduced their discounts or have changed the terms and conditions. Occasionally, Olympic has lost discounts by choosing to pay later. Naomi Herring, Olympic's accounts payable supervisor, set out to bring some order to the process. The company has a long-standing revolving loan agreement with a local bank whereby the effective interest rate is one point over prime; thus, Olympic is currently paying 9.5 percent on its short-term borrowing. In the past three years, that cost has been as high as 14 percent and as low as 8.5 percent.

Herring rummaged through the pile of invoices on her desk, noting the different purchase discounts, terms, and conditions given by various vendors. Most fell into one of three categories:

1. 1/10 days, net 30.

2. 2/10 days, net 30.

3. Net 30 days, 2 percent monthly finance charge on balances over 30 days.

Required:

a. Prepare a table with interest rates from 10 to 20 percent, indicating for each of the three types of conditions whether Olympic should take the discounts for prompt payment or not.

b. How would you explain to a new employee why the typical 2/10, net 30 terms and conditions are really a good deal for a company paying (or earning) 12 percent on its money?

12.2. Bond valuation. MTF, Inc., was a manufacturer of electronic components for facsimile equipment. The company financed the expansion of its production facilities by issuing $10 million, 10-year bonds carrying a coupon rate of 8 percent, with interest payable annually on December 31.

The bonds had been issued on January 1, and at the time of the issuance, the market rate of interest on similar risk-rated instruments was 6 percent. Hence, the bonds were sold into the market at a price reflecting an effective yield of 6 percent.

Two years later, the market rate of interest on comparable debt instruments had climbed to a record high level of 12 percent. The CEO of MTF, Inc., realized that this might be an opportune time to repurchase the bonds, particularly because an unexpected surplus of cash made the outstanding debt no longer necessary.

	Present Value of $1 to Be Received at the End of Year			Present Value of $1 to Be Received at the End of Each Year for Years		
	6%	8%	12%	6%	8%	12%
1	0.9434	0.9259	0.8930	0.9434	0.9259	0.8930
2	0.8900	0.8573	0.7970	1.8334	1.7833	1.6900
3	0.8396	0.7938	0.7120	2.6730	2.5771	2.4020
8	0.6274	0.5403	0.4040	6.2098	5.7466	4.9680
9	0.5919	0.5002	0.3610	6.8017	6.2469	5.3280
10	0.5584	0.4632	0.3220	7.3601	6.7101	5.6500

Required:

Using the present value data in the table, calculate the following:

a. The proceeds received by the company at initial issuance.

b. The interest expense to be reported in each of the two years that the bonds were outstanding.

c. The amount of cash needed to retire the debt after two years, assuming a yield rate of 12 percent.

d. Evaluate the merits of retiring the bonds early. Do you agree with the CEO?

12.3. Accounting for zero-coupon debentures. In December 1990, Alza Corp. of Palo Alto, California, offered for sale $750 million of zero-coupon debentures. The bonds were offered for sale at $221.87 for each $1,000 face amount. Alza, a pharmaceutical products maker, expected to receive $166.4 million from the debt sale.

Required:

How would Alza Corp. account for the proceeds from the sale of bonds? Why would Alza want to sell zero-coupon bonds? Why would anyone buy them?

12.4. Debt retirement. In March 1987, Continental Airlines sold $350 million of aircraft bonds. The bonds took their name from the fact that Continental had secured the debt with a pool of 53 airplanes and 55 engines, initially valued at $467 million.

By 1990, however, Continental was experiencing serious financial difficulties and lacked sufficient cash flows to continue operations. Consequently, with bondholder approval, Continental removed some of the planes from the pool and sold them to raise cash to support operations. After taking the airplanes from the asset pool, Continental was required (within a reasonable period of time) either to replenish the pool or to retire some of the bonds. Continental chose the latter option, and in late 1990 went into the market and repurchased $167 million (face value) of its aircraft bonds at a price of $0.58 on the dollar.

Required:

a. Assuming that Continental initially issued the aircraft bonds at par value, how would the company account for the debt repurchase?

b. Was the decision to retire the debt a good one?

12.5. Accounting for long-term bonds. On March 1, 1996, Proctor Company sold $10,000,000 principal amount of its 8 percent bonds. The maturity date of the bonds was March 1, 2016 and interest was due semiannually each September first and March first. The sale of the bonds netted $10,400,000.

Required:

a. Did the buyers of the bonds make a mistake in paying more than the face amount for the bonds? Explain.

b. What specific accounts and amounts pertaining to the bonds would appear on Proctor's balance sheet at December 31, 2005, and on its 2005 income statement?

c. Assuming the bonds are allowed to mature in 20 years, the total interest expense for Proctor, related to those bonds, would total what amount?

12.6. Issuing bonds at a discount. Hopewell, Inc., issued $5,000,000 face value of its 10 percent bonds on January 1, 1996. The bonds matured in 10 years, and interest was payable semiannually. Hopewell, Inc. netted $4,800,000 from the issue.

Required:

a. What is the entry for the January 1, 1996 bond issue?

b. What are the 1996 semiannual journal entries?

c. What is the December 31, 2005 journal entry, assuming the bonds have matured then?

12.7. Amortization of debt discount. In October 1989, Sun Microsystems, Inc., sold $135 million of 6⅜ percent convertible subordinated debentures due October 15, 1999. They were sold at 84.9 percent of face value, with an effective annual yield to maturity of 8.67 percent. Interest is to be paid semiannually beginning April 1990. As of June 30, 1991, the debentures were valued at $117,013 on Sun's balance sheet.

Required:

Assuming no early retirements or conversions, what will these debentures be valued at on June 30, 1992?

12.8. Accounting for warranties. Signal Communications provides certain warranties for its products. As of January 1, 1996, the Provision for Estimated Warranty Costs account stood at $72,500. Warranty costs were estimated to be 0.5 percent of sales. Prepare entries related to warranties for the years 1996, 1997, and 1998 using the following:

	Sales (Millions)	Actual Warranty Costs
1996	$6.5	$53,200
1997	7.9	49,800
1998	5.8	61,100

Required:

a. What will appear on the income statements for each of these three years relating to warranties?

b. What will be the amount in the Provision for Estimated Warranty costs account at December 31, 1998?

12.9. Mortgages. A mortgage is a type of loan that is secured by property. Suppose a company acquired a building financed with a 20-year, 9½ percent mortgage with level payments to be made monthly. An amount of $20 million was to be borrowed under this mortgage.

Required:

a. What would the payments be?

b. How would the mortgage appear in the company's balance sheet after the third year?

Suppose that after three years the building is refinanced with a new 20-year mortgage; this time the rate is 8 percent. The amount of the new loan is to be the exact principal amount of the loan it replaces.

c. What difference would it make in the monthly payments?

d. What transactions would be made to repay the old loan and consummate the new one? Explain.

12.10. Accounting for mortgages in the United Kingdom. Most home mortgages in the United Kingdom are of a variable-rate type. At the time the mortgage is issued, a monthly payment is determined by the bank or building society holding the mortgage. As interest rates change, the monthly payment typically remains constant (at least during the early years) while the principal is adjusted to account for the change in interest rates. The following is an example to see how this might work.

Suppose one had a £100,000, 20-year mortgage established when interest rates were 10 percent. Monthly payments would be £965. Now suppose the following:

Month	Interest Rate Percentage
1	10
2	11
3	12
4	11
5	10
6	9

Required:

At the end of six months, what is the outstanding principal on this mortgage? How much interest has been paid?

12.11. The making of a derivative. Global United, Inc., was concerned about declining interest rates and its exposure on a $100 million, 71/2 percent fixed rate note. The note had three years to run and could not be called. The LIBOR was then 6 percent. Global wished to hedge against any further decline in interest rates and so approached Gotham Bank in hopes of securing an interest rate swap on their $100 million note.

Gotham responded by informing Global that three-year, fixed-to-variable swaps on LIBOR were then paying 7 percent. In other words, Global would receive 7 percent over the three-year period and would pay LIBOR, then at 6 percent, based on a three-month trailing rate. It would look like this to Global:

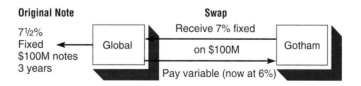

Global responded by asking, "But how do we make that swap fit our situation, we're not paying 7 percent!" Gotham's answer was to scale up the notional amount to

$$(7.5/7) \times 100 = 107 \text{ million.}$$

Eventually they agreed to do the swap at 110 million:

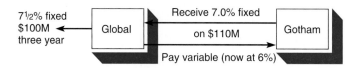

Required:

Let's look at three scenarios:

1. Status quo—no change in interest rates.

2. Rising LIBOR. At the end of the first quarter, LIBOR has moved to 6.25 percent and Global must pay 6.25% × 110/4 million or $1,718,750. Rates keep rising 25 basis points per quarter.

3. Rates fall. LIBOR at the end of quarter 1 is 5.75 percent and then the first quarter's payment to Gotham is $1,581,250. Rates will continue to drop 25 basis points a quarter.

For each scenario:

a. What are the cash flows?

b. What accounting should Global make at the time the derivative is executed? At the end of each quarter?

c. What is the fair value at the end of each quarter?

d. What alternative accounting should be considered for such swaps?

e. Assume Gotham owns the other side of this swap. What entries should they make?

12.12. Contingencies. The following appeared in Philip Morris Companies Inc. 1994 annual report in the footnote titled Contingencies:

> In May 1994, an action was filed in Mississippi state court against the leading United States cigarette manufacturers and others, including the Company, by the Attorney General of Mississippi seeking reimbursement of Medicaid and other expenditures by the State of Mississippi claimed to have been made to treat smoking-related diseases. Plaintiff also seeks an injunction barring defendants from selling or encouraging the sale of cigarettes to minors. In June 1994, defendants removed the case to the United States District Court for the Southern District of Mississippi. In that same month, plaintiff moved to remand the case back to state court. Plaintiff's motion was granted on August 17, 1994 and the case remanded to state Chancery Court. In September 1994, the plaintiff moved to strike defendants' challenges to the sufficiency of the complaint and the subject matter jurisdiction of the Chancery Court. Also in September 1994, defendants moved to transfer the case from the Chancery Court to the Circuit Court. In October 1994, defendants moved for judgment on the pleadings. All three motions are presently pending. In December 1994, the Governor of the State of Mississippi filed an amicus brief in support of defendants' motions.
>
> In August 1994, an action was filed in Minnesota state court against the leading United States cigarette manufacturers and others, including the Company, by the Attorney General of Minnesota and Blue Cross and Blue Shield of Minnesota seeking reimbursement of Medicaid and other expenditures by the plaintiffs claimed to have been made to treat smoking-related diseases. Plaintiffs assert causes of action of negligent performance of a voluntary undertaking, violation of Minnesota antitrust laws, violation of consumer protection statutes, restitution, and conspiracy.

These are 2 of 13 cases in which significant developments occurred in 1994. Are these liabilities? How should they be reported? Why?

12.13. Borrowings. The following footnote appeared in the 1990 annual report of Bausch & Lomb, Inc.:

> The terms of a revolving credit and term loan agreement provide for a 364-day revolving credit line with a six-month term loan provision thereafter, under which the company may borrow up to $100,000,000. A commitment fee at a rate of .05 percent is charged on the unused portion. For any six-month period during the year the agreement includes a provision that allows the company to increase its borrowings up to an additional $150,000,000. A commitment fee of $62,500 per year is paid under this provision. The interest rate for total borrowings under the agreement is the prime rate or, at the company's option, a mutually acceptable market rate. At December 19, 1990, this revolving credit and term loan agreement supported $100,000,000 of unsecured promissory notes that have been classified as long-term debt. While the company intends to refinance these obligations, the level of the outstanding debt may fluctuate from time to time.

What business event has occurred? Bausch & Lomb's fiscal year ended December 29, 1990. What would you expect on its 1990 balance sheet and on the 1990 income statement related to this footnote?

12.14. Financial Instrument Disclosures. The following is found in the 1997 annual report of PepsiCo.

Note 10—Long-term Debt

	1997	1996
Long-term Debt		
Commercial paper (5.4%)	$ —	$1,176
Notes due 1998—2011 (6.5% and 6.4%)	2,643	3,111
Various foreign currency debt, due 1998—2001		
(5.2% and 5.5%)	809	1,448
Zero coupon notes, $1.0 billion due 1998—2012		
(10.5% and 7.9%)	480	930
Euro notes due 1998—1999		
(5.8% and 5.5%)	500	700
Other, due 1998—2020 (7.5% and 7.1%)	514	809
	$4,946	$8,174

The interest rates in the above table include the effects of associated interest rate and currency swaps at year-end 1997 and 1996. See Note 11 for a discussion of PepsiCo's use of interest rate and currency swaps, its management of the inherent credit risk and fair value information related to debt and interest rate and currency swaps.

The following table indicates the notional amount and weighted average interest rates, by category, of interest rate swaps outstanding at year-end 1997 and 1996, respectively. The weighted average variable interest rates that PepsiCo pays, which are primarily indexed to either commercial paper or LIBOR rates, are based on rates as of the respective balance sheet date and are subject to change. Terms of interest rate swaps match the terms of the debt they modify. The swaps terminate at various dates through 2011.

	1997	1996
Receive fixed-pay variable		
Notional amount	**$2,584**	$3,976
Weighted average receive rate	**6.8%**	6.6%
Weighted average pay rate	**5.8%**	5.5%
Receive variable-pay variable		
Notional amount	**$ 250**	$ 552
Weighted average receive rate	**5.7%**	5.5%
Weighted average pay rate	**5.8%**	5.7%
Receive variable-pay fixed		
Notional amount	**$ 215**	$ 215
Weighted average receive rate	**5.9%**	5.6%
Weighted average pay rate	**8.2%**	8.2%

At year-end 1997, approximately 77% of total debt was exposed to variable interest rates, compared to 74% in 1996. In addition to variable rate long-term debt, all debt with maturities of less that one year is categorized as a variable for purposes of this measure.

PepiCo enters into currency swaps to hedge its currency exposure on certain non-U.S. dollar denominated debt. At year-end 1997, the aggregate carrying amount of the debt was $629 million and the payables under related currency swaps were $104 million, resulting in a net effective U.S. dollar liability of $733 million with a weighted average interest rate of 5.8%, including the effects of related interest rate swaps. At year-end 1996, the carrying amount of this debt aggregates $1.8 billion and the receivables and payables under related currency swaps aggregate $54 million and $59 million, respectively, resulting in a net effective U.S. dollar liability of $1.8 billion with a weighted average interest rate of 5.6%, including the effects of related interest rate swaps.

At year-end 1997 and 1996, PepsiCo's unused revolving credit facilities covering potential borrowings aggregate $2.75 billion and $3.5 billion, respectively. The 1997 facilities expire in 2002. These credit facilities exist largely to support the issuances of short-term borrowings and are available for general corporate purposes.

At year-end 1997 and 1996, $2.1 billion and $3.5 billion, respectively, of short-term borrowings were classified as long-term debt, reflecting PepsiCo's intent and ability, through the existence of the unused credit facilities, to refinance these borrowings.

The annual maturities of long-term debt through 2002 are: 1998—$2.1 billion, 1999—$939 million, 2000—$746 million, 2001—$353 million and 2002—$330 million.

Note 11—Financial Instruments

Derivative Instruments

PepsiCo's policy prohibits the use of derivative instruments for trading purposes and PepsiCo has procedures in place to monitor and control their use.

PepsiCo's use of derivative instruments is primarily limited to interest rate and currency swaps, which are entered into with the objective of reducing borrowing costs. PepsiCo enters into interest rate and currency swaps to effectively change the interest rate and currency of specific debt issuances. These swaps are entered into concurrently with the issuance of the debt they are intended to modify. The notional amount, interest payment and maturity dates of the swaps match the principal, interest payment and maturity dates of the related debt. Accordingly, any market risk or opportunity associated with these swaps is offset by the opposite market impact on the related debt. PepsiCo's credit risk related to interest rate and currency swaps is considered low because they are entered into only with strong credit-worthy counterparties, are generally settled on a net basis and are of relatively short duration. See Note 10 for the notional amounts, related interest rates and maturities of the interest rate and currency swaps. See Management's Discussion and Analysis—Market Risk beginning on page 13.

Fair Value

Carrying amounts and fair values of PepsiCo's financial instrument.

	1997		1996
	Carrying Amount	Fair Value	Carrying Amount
Assets			
Cash and cash equivalents	$1,928	$1,928	$ 307
Short-term investments	$ 955	$ 955	$ 289
Other assets (noncurrent investments)	$ 15	$ 15	$ 15
Liabilities			
Debt			
Long-term debt	$4,946	$5,161	$8,174
Debt-related derivative instruments			
Open contracts in asset position	(28)	(22)	(91)
Open contracts in liability position	107	109	62
Net debt	$5,025	$5,248	$8,145

The carrying amounts in the above table are included in the Consolidated Balance Sheet under the indicated captions,except for debt-related derivative instruments (interest rate and current swaps), which are included in the appropriate current or noncurrent asset or liability caption. Short-term investments consist primarily of debt securities and have been classified as held-to-maturity. Noncurrent investments mature at various dates through 2000.

Because of the short maturity of cash equivalents and short-term investments, the carrying amounts approximate fair value. The fair value of noncurrent investments is based upon market quotes. The fair value of debt and debt-related derivative instruments was estimated using market quotes and calculated based on market rates.

Explain the table in footnote 10 that begins "Receive fixed-pay variable." What are these items? Can you tell if PepsiCo is losing or gaining with these instruments?

Leases, Retirement Benefits, and Deferred Income Taxes

*It was a matter of equity that current taxpayers not have to
foot the bill for future retirement costs.*[1]

Key Chapter Issues

- When does a lease become, in substance, a purchase of assets with a built-in financing program?
- How should leased assets be valued on the balance sheet?
- How should the pension obligations of a company appear in the financial statements?
- Are the investments set aside to pay pensions and other retirement benefits corporate assets, or do they belong to the pensioners?

- Should companies recognize an expense today for employees that might not retire for 30 years or might not even live to retire?
- On the matter of income taxes, why is it that the income tax expense in the income statement is almost never what the company actually must pay?
- Why can some companies defer paying taxes indefinitely while others cannot?
- How can a company have both deferred tax assets and deferred tax liabilities at the same time?

---

[1] "The Whitman Effect," *The New York Times,* July 9, 1995, p. 14 (section 4).

I n the previous chapter we considered the valuation processes for current and noncurrent liabilities in general. In this chapter we consider three unique liabilities that frequently arise in the financial statements of publicly held companies: leases, retirement benefits, and deferred income taxes.

Deferred taxes do not depend on present-value concepts for their measurement, while the other two items do. Our focus in this chapter is similar to that of Chapter 12; namely, we consider two questions: "Do these obligations exist?" "If so, how should they be valued on the financial statements?"

LEASES

Leasing of assets is a common activity for many corporations, governmental agencies, and not-for-profit entities. It is used by large organizations and small ones, by the financially strong as well as the weak. Some types of leases result in the reporting of both assets and liabilities on the balance sheet, but others do not. Just about any kind of asset can be leased—computers, copy machines, vehicles, aircraft, naval vessels, buildings, and manufacturing equipment, to name just a few.

Companies lease assets for many reasons. They use leases, for example, as a form of financing that permits a company to acquire an asset without the immediate cash consequences of purchasing it. Moreover, companies with weak credit ratings sometimes find borrowing money difficult. Thus, for these companies, leasing may be the only way to obtain the assets they need to carry on their business. Financially healthy companies, on the other hand, often lease simply because they have better alternatives for investing their cash. Sometimes the decision to lease an asset is driven by tax considerations. Finally, many companies lease assets because they find the ancillary services provided by leasing companies to be attractive. Leasing specialists often become experts at purchasing, installing, and maintaining the assets that they lease. They frequently make it easy to upgrade an asset and thereby obtain access to the latest available technology. Moreover, these leasing specialists often tailor the lease payments to the particular cash flow circumstances of the lessee.

As one might expect, there are some drawbacks to leasing. The interest rate implicit in the lease payments is frequently somewhat higher than long-term borrowing rates. In addition, lessees often face restrictions as to how an asset can be used. For example, if a purchased computer becomes redundant or is no longer needed, it can be sold, whereas with a leased computer, the lessee may be unable to cancel the lease without incurring a costly penalty.

From an accounting perspective, there are two types of leases. **Operating leases** are nothing more than short-term rental agreements. For example, a grocery store (the *lessee*) may lease a new delivery vehicle from an auto dealership (the *lessor*) for one year. Accounting for such a lease is simple: Each month, an entry is made for the lease expense, which is deducted from revenues in the income statement. No lease asset or lease liability appears on the balance sheet. Since the company has use of the asset without having to purchase it, this type of arrangement is often referred to as **off-balance-sheet financing.**

Other leases are simply long-term purchase agreements structured as leases; essentially, they are installment purchases. The grocery store, for example, might sign a noncancelable agreement to lease a delivery vehicle for four years at amounts sufficient to cover the cost of the vehicle, interest, and administrative costs and with an option to purchase the vehicle for a nominal sum at the end of the lease period. The substance of this type of lease agreement is clear: The company has acquired an asset and has incurred a liability. Except for legal distinctions, it is equivalent to borrowing the money and buying the asset outright. Leases of this type are called **capital leases** and appear as both assets and liabilities on the lessee's balance sheet. The periodic lease payments are discounted (see Appendix 12A) at either the interest rate implicit in the lease or the lessee's incremental borrowing rate, whichever is lower, and this present value amount is used to value both the leased asset and the lease liability on the lessee's balance sheet. Note that the amount used to value the leased asset and lease liability is *not* necessarily the same as its market value. This is an important point. A company may lease an asset for, say, ten years and it may qualify as a capital lease, but the lease agreement is for only ten years! After the tenth year, the lessor may go on to release that asset to yet another company. The asset might have a substantial residual value. In such situations the market value of the asset at the time the lease was signed is irrelevant; what is relevant is the present value of the lease payments.

For many years executives, accountants, leasing companies, and the Internal Revenue Service have considered which lease arrangements constitute a capital lease and thus necessitate disclosure on the balance sheet. In general, for U.S. GAAP, capital leases are leases whose terms meet *any one* of the following four tests:

1. Ownership is transferred to the lessee by the end of the lease (the *ownership test*).

2. The lease contains an option to purchase the asset at a bargain price (the *alternative ownership test*).

3. The lease term is equal to 75 percent or more of the remaining estimated economic life of the asset (the *economic life test*).

4. The present value of the minimum lease payments (excluding any "executory" costs for insurance, maintenance, taxes, and the like) equals or exceeds 90 percent of the fair market value of the asset (the *value test*).

If none of these conditions is met, the lease agreement is considered to be an *operating lease.*[2]

Accounting for Capital Leases

Terminology is critical to any discussion of leases. There are capital-lease *assets* and capital-lease *liabilities* and, of course, lease interest *expense* for *lessees* and lease *revenues* for *lessors*. The agreement itself is called the **lease.** From a **lessee's** perspective, the accounting issues related to capital leases involve measuring the lease liability and asset, the cost of financing (interest expense), and the cost of the use of the asset (amortization expense). The related accounting issues for a **lessor,** the owner of the asset, pertain to the valuation of the lease asset and the amount of lease revenue.

The following example will be used to illustrate lease accounting for a lessee.[3]

Suppose American Airlines decides to acquire the use of a new Boeing 737 valued at $125 million. Because of its current cash position, the airline does not want to purchase the aircraft outright. Instead, it decides to approach several insurance companies that might be interested in purchasing the aircraft and then leasing it to American. Assume that the best

[2] Some leases clearly fall in the middle, but no one has created any "middle ground" accounting rules. Many computer leases fit this description in that they run for most of the technological life of an asset and are noncancelable, but the leasing company (the lessor) keeps the asset, and the deal is structured so that the lessor will actually lose money unless it can release or sell the asset at a good price at the end of the initial lease term.

[3] The accounting for lessors is discussed in Appendix 13A, "Leases in Detail."

terms are available from Prudential Insurance Co. for a 10-year, quarterly installment, level payment, full-payout lease, with a quarterly payment of $4,479,871. Assume further that the airline's bank borrowing rate is 9½ percent, that the lease transfers ownership of the 737 to the airline after the last payment, and that the airline is to perform all maintenance and repairs and is responsible for insuring the aircraft.

From the lessee's point of view, the agreement should be considered a capital lease. It meets both the ownership and the valuation tests of the capital-lease decision rules. The interest rate implicit in the lease is 8 percent (2 percent per quarter), which can be derived by simple present value techniques.[4] Because the implicit rate is lower than the company's incremental borrowing rate (that is, 9½ percent per year), the lease payments are discounted at the 2 percent quarterly rate. The present value of the capital-lease liability and the capital-lease asset is $125 million; hence, American Airlines would record the lease at signing as follows:

        Dr. Leased Aircraft (A) . . . . (inc.) 125,000,000
             Cr. Capital Lease (L). . . . .   (inc.) 125,000,000

The lease liability will be amortized using an interest amortization schedule similar to a mortgage payment table that separates the lease payments into two parts, principal repayment and interest expense. The interest amortization schedule for the American Airlines/Prudential lease is shown in Exhibit 13A.1 in Appendix 13A to this chapter. The following entry illustrates how the quarterly lease payment at the beginning of the second quarter would be recorded:

        Dr. Capital Lease (L) . . . . (dec.) 2,069,468
        Dr. Interest Expense (E) . . . . (inc.) 2,410,403
             Cr. Cash (A) . . . .   (dec.) 4,479,871

The leased asset also must be depreciated following the asset-depreciation policies that American Airlines uses for similar assets.

Assuming that American Airlines depreciates the leased asset on a straight-line basis over 12 years (or 48 quarters), the quarterly depreciation expense would be $2,604,167 ($125,000,000/48), and the accounting entry would look like this:

        Dr. Depreciation Expense (E) . . . . (inc.) 2,604,167
             Cr. Accumulated Depreciation (CA). . . . .   (inc.) 2,604,167

Capitalized leases for buildings and equipment are ordinarily included with other property, plant, and equipment, net of accumulated depreciation, in the balance sheet. In classified balance sheets, the next year's principal reduction is shown as a current liability, and the noncurrent liabilities section includes the capital-lease liabilities less any current portion.

As can be seen in Exhibit 13.1 (Panel A), AMR Corporation, the parent company of American Airlines, listed its flight equipment acquired with capital leases separately from its other fixed assets. The capital-lease liability appeared, in part, as a current liability and the remainder as noncurrent. Thus, as of December 31, 1997, AMR Corporation valued its equipment and property under capital leases at $2,086 million; the liability outstanding on these leases was $1,764 million ($135 million current and $1,629 million long term).

---

[4] Using a financial calculator, this can be easily derived. Because lease payments are made at the beginning of a period, set the calculator to *begin*. (The default option on many popular financial calculators assumes that cash flows occur at the end of a period.) Then, enter PV = 125,000,000, N = 40, and obtain PMT = –4,479,871.05—or a quarterly payment of $4.48 million.

EXHIBIT 13.1

AMR Corporation
Lease Disclosures

Panel A: Partial balance sheet

	December 31,	
(in millions)	1997	1996
Equipment and Property		
Flight equipment, at cost	13,002	13,107
Less accumulated depreciation	4,459	3,922
	8,543	9,185
Purchase deposits for flight equipment	754	
Other equipment and property, at cost	4,158	3,982
Less accumulated depreciation	2,284	2,100
	1,874	1,882
	11,171	11,067
Equipment and Property Under Capital Leases		
Flight equipment	2,980	2,998
Other equipment and property	274	261
	3,254	3,259
Less accumulated amortization	1,168	1,021
	2,086	2,238
Current Liabilities		
Accounts payable	$ 1,021	$ 1,068
Accrued salaries and wages	897	823
Accrued liabilities	1,123	1,232
Air traffic liability	2,044	1,889
Current maturities of long-term debt	397	424
Current obligations under capital leases	135	130
Total current liabilities	5,617	5,566
Long-Term Debt, Less Current Maturities	2,260	2,752
Obligations Under Capital Leases, Less Current Obligations	1,629	1,790
Other Liabilities and Credits		
Deferred income taxes	1,105	743
Deferred gains	610	647
Postretirement benefits	1,579	1,530
Other liabilities and deferred credits	1,899	1,801
	5,193	4,721

EXHIBIT 13.1 concluded

Panel B: Footnote

4. Leases

AMR's subsidiaries lease various types of equipment and property, including aircraft, passenger terminals, equipment and various other facilities. The future minimum lease payments required under capital leases, together with the present value of net minimum lease payments, and future minimum lease payments required under operating leases that have initial or remaining non-cancelable lease terms in excess of one year as of December 31, 1997, were (in millions):

Year Ending December 31,	Capital Leases	Operating Leases
1998	$ 255	$ 1,011
1999	250	985
2000	315	935
2001	297	931
2002	247	887
2003 and subsequent	1,206	13,366
	2,570[1]	$18,115[2]
Less amount representing interest	806	
Present value of net minimum lease payments	$1,764	

[1] Future minimum payments required under capital leases include $192 million guaranteed by AMR relating to special facility revenue bonds issued by municipalities.

[2] Future minimum payments required under operating leases include $6.2 billion guaranteed by AMR relating to special facility revenue bonds issued by municipalities.

At December 31, 1997, the Company had 186 jet aircraft and 44 turboprop aircraft under operating leases, and 82 jet aircraft and 63 turboprop aircraft under capital leases. The aircraft leases can generally be renewed at rates based on fair market value at the end of the lease term for one to five years. Most aircraft leases have purchase options at or near the end of the lease term at fair market value, but generally not to exceed a stated percentage of the defined lessor's cost of the aircraft at a predetermined fixed amount.

During 1996, American made prepayments totaling $565 million on cancelable operating leases it had on 12 of its Boeing 767-300 aircraft. Upon the expiration of the amended leases, American can purchase the aircraft for a nominal amount. As a result, the aircraft are recorded as flight equipment under capital leases.

Rent expense, excluding landing fees, was $1.2 billion for 1997 and 1996 and $1.3 billion for 1995.

Footnote 4 (Panel B of Exhibit 13.1) includes additional details of these leases and also describes other flight equipment under operating leases. It shows that most of the lease payments for both capital and operating leases are deferred into the next century. It is interesting that so much of AMR's leases are operating as opposed to capital leases. Some of AMR's operating leases are for 10 years, with renewal provisions for another 10 to 12 years; yet they are cancelable upon 30 days notice! This cancellation clause certainly keeps the leases from meeting the test for capitalization of a lease; but one has to wonder what penalties or fees are associated with the cancellation. It raises the basic question about leases: Is the substance of this transaction a purchase with long-term financing or is it a short-term rental? With the airliner market as soft as it was in the mid-1990s, would Boeing build and rent 12 planes under leases with such short cancellation periods unless they were protected in some fashion? And if Boeing is protected, then isn't AMR bearing the risk of ownership?

In many countries (Switzerland and India, for example), leases are not capitalized; instead, all leases are treated like operating leases. This could represent a significant off-balance-sheet asset and liability for many companies reporting in other countries. The International Accounting Standards Committee's Revised *IAS No. 17* does deal with classifying a lease as a finance lease (equivalent to the U.S. notion of a capital lease) or operating lease. Indeed, the IASC and U.S. criteria are similar except that the IASC is not as specific as U.S. GAAP. For example, where U.S. GAAP stipulates the existence of a capital lease if the lease term is greater than or equal to 75 percent of the asset's useful life, the IASC's guidelines are if "the lease term is for the major part of the useful life of the asset." Clearly, such a criterion is more susceptible to alternative interpretation than the more precise, albeit arbitrary, U.S. notion of 75 percent.

In summary, at the inception of a capital lease, the present value of the future lease payments is the value assigned to the capital-lease liability (net of any executory costs). Lease payments are discounted at the lessee's incremental borrowing rate unless the rate implicit in a lease is at a lower rate; then the implicit rate is used. The capital-lease asset is also valued at the present value of the lease payments. From that moment on, the two figures are rarely the same. Assets acquired under capital leases are depreciated using the straight-line or some accelerated method as if the assets were owned. Capital-lease liabilities are amortized using the effective interest method as if they were bonds.

Financial Disclosures for Capital Leases

At a minimum, the footnotes to a lessee's financial statements must show the following information for all capital leases:

1. The gross (undiscounted) lease payments.
2. The gross lease payments for each of the next five years and the total lease commitment (reduced by imputed interest).
3. The minimum rentals to be received under noncancelable subleases.
4. The total contingent rentals this year (leases based on something other than the simple passage of time).

For example, Exhibit 13.2 contains the lease footnote from Tricon Inc.'s (KFC, Taco Bell, and Pizza Hut restaurants) 1997 annual report. The present value of these lease obligations, $140 million, would be included in the balance sheet as a liability; the rest ($127 million) is interest. Note that most leases are of the operating type and do not appear as liabilities.

Lessors follow rules similar to those for lease capitalization so long as there are no uncertainties as to the amounts to be received or any question as to their collectibility. Lease assets and liabilities for lessors must be shown separately on the balance sheet, and there are substantial footnote disclosure requirements as well. The accounting followed by lessors is discussed in Appendix 13A, "Leases in Detail."

Management Issues

Most large leases are carefully structured to meet the needs and constraints of both the lessee and the lessor. Often there is considerable negotiation or even competitive bidding. One of

---

E X H I B I T   1 3 . 2

Tricon, Inc.
Lease Disclosures

Leases

We have non-cancelable commitments under both capital and long-term operating leases, primarily for Company restaurants. Capital and operating lease commitments expire at various dates through 2067 and, in many cases, provide for rent escalations and renewal options. Most leases require payment of related executory costs, which include property taxes, maintenance and insurance.

Future minimum commitments and sublease receivables under non-cancelable leases are set forth below:

| | Commitments | | Sublease Receivables | |
	Capital	Operating	Direct Financing	Operating
1998	$ 26	$ 253	$ 3	$12
1999	24	219	2	11
2000	23	190	2	9
2001	21	170	2	8
2002	20	152	2	7
Later Years	153	801	15	38
	$267	$1,785	$26	$85

At year-end 1997, the present value of minimum payments under capital leases was $140 million, after deducting $127 million representing imputed interest.

The details of rental expense and income are set forth below:

	1997	1996	1995
Rental expense			
Minimum	$317	$312	$309
Contingent	30	32	27
	$347	$344	$336
Minimum rental income	$ 19	$ 16	$ 8

Contingent rentals are based on sales in excess of levels stipulated in the lease agreements.

---

the first considerations is often one of accounting: "Will this be a capital lease?" No doubt many leases have been designed so as to skirt the accounting requirements for capitalization. Some leases tailor the payment amounts and dates to the expected cash availability of the lessee (or cash requirements of the lessor). Issues related to terminating or extending a lease may receive more attention than anything else. Lessees want to protect themselves against surprises; lessors want the same protection. For example, one of the biggest concerns in equipment leasing is the threat of technological obsolescence. Some companies lease computers to protect themselves against the risk, although they, in fact, pay a premium for this protection one way or the other.

RETIREMENT BENEFITS

Of all the obligations of a corporation (or a government), pensions and other retirement benefits probably present some of the most complex accounting issues. The size of the private U.S. pension system is enormous. Perhaps one-half of the full-time U.S. workforce is covered by private pension plans, with thousands of billions of dollars being managed by pension-fund administrators. One private pension fund, TIAA-CREF, had more than $220 billion of invested pension assets. Some major corporations today have more pensioners than employees! Almost everyone has a stake in the pension system: current employees and retirees, corporate executives, investment managers and advisers, unions, government officials, the IRS, accountants and actuaries, shareholders, lenders, and even the Financial Accounting Standards Board.

As one might expect, one must learn a unique vocabulary before understanding the subject of pensions. In simple terms, a **pension** is a promise to pay certain benefits to employees as specified in an agreement (the plan). The terms *contribution* and its derivatives appear frequently in any discussion of pensions. Unfortunately, *contribution* can refer either to the amounts paid into the plan or to the amounts paid out of the plan to the pensioner. In regard to payments to a plan, *contributory* pension plans are those to which employees may be required to contribute. *Noncontributory* plans are those in which the employer makes all the payments. On the payout side, regardless of who makes the actual contributions, defined-contribution and defined-benefit plans are the two most common types of pension plans.

Defined-Contribution Pension Plans

Under a **defined-contribution plan** an employer promises to pay a specific amount per month (or quarter or year) to an employee's union or to an independent pension-fund administrator on behalf of an employee. The retirement plans for college professors are a good example.

Many U.S. colleges and universities pay a set percentage of a professor's salary each month to TIAA-CREF, a pension organization founded just for this purpose. If the professor moves from one university to another, the new employer begins paying to TIAA-CREF (assuming the new employer also uses TIAA-CREF for this purpose, and many universities do). TIAA-CREF invests the money and keeps track of the contributions made on behalf of each professor and the related earnings on those contributions. Upon retirement, the faculty member then begins receiving a monthly pension check based on his or her accumulated pension account balance. The college or university really has no pension liability to the professors beyond making those monthly payments. A professor's retirement benefits are purely a function of the total contributions he or she earns over the years from various employers, plus the earnings on those funds. Thus, the more contributions made and the better the earnings record of the invested contributions, the larger the professor's retirement income.

Accounting for defined-contribution pension funds is a simple task. Each month, the employer makes an entry to record the pension expense and the accrued pension liability. Within a few days or weeks, the liability is satisfied by a check written to the pension fund.

Defined-Benefit Pension Plans

As the name suggests, **defined-benefit plans** are pension plans that specify the *future* amount an employee will receive on retirement. The amount is usually a function of the

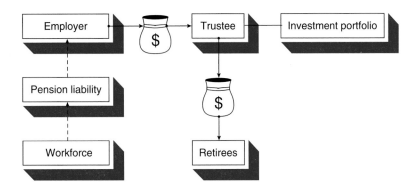

EXHIBIT 13.3

Money Flow for Defined-Benefit Pension Plans

employee's age, years of service, and salary level. Companies must estimate the *current* cost of these future pension benefits and record this cost as its pension expense for the current year. The offsetting entry is a current pension liability. Ordinarily, the company then eliminates this pension liability by paying cash (called *funding*) to an independent, third-party trustee. The trustee invests these funds and pays the retirees when they become eligible. This process is illustrated in Exhibit 13.3.

The assets of a pension fund appear on the books of the pension trustee, not on the books of the employer. It is important to understand that the trustee is only the agent of the employer. *The employer's obligation remains even after it has made the payments to the trustee.* If the trustee makes poor investments and runs out of money, the employer is still obligated to pay the pensions for the committed retirement benefits.

Ideally, the trustee should have just enough funds to satisfy the terms of the pension agreement. Occasionally, however, a fund becomes overfunded and an employer may either stop contributing to the fund for a while or may request that the trustee return the excess funds.

It is important to note that in the United States, corporations are *not* required to provide pensions to their employees. However, if they choose to do so, there are laws that prescribe how pensions are to be administered. The Employee Retirement Income and Security Act of 1974 (**ERISA**) is such a law. Moreover, tax regulations prescribe how much pension cost can be deducted for income tax purposes (usually it is the amount actually paid in cash by the company to the trustee). And, of course, generally accepted accounting practices specify how such costs are to be expensed, how liabilities are to be valued, and what supplemental information is to be disclosed in the footnotes.

Pension Expense

U.S. GAAP for defined-benefit pension plans requires that the cost of pension benefits be recognized during the period in which those benefits are earned. For example, suppose that a particular pension plan promised an employee a monthly pension of 1.5 percent of her salary at retirement for each year of service to a company. Consequently, if the employee worked 30 years prior to retirement, she would receive a monthly pension equal to 45 percent of her monthly salary at retirement. Assuming that she worked from 1999 to 2029, she would begin receiving her pension payments in 2030. Clearly, however, some portion of the payments received in 2030 were earned in 1999. Consequently, the cost of that portion of her expected pension benefit, adjusted for various estimates, including the present value, must be recognized as pension expense in 1999!

A typical pension expense entry recorded by an employer while its future retirees are currently working would appear as follows:

```
Dr. Pension Expense (E). . . . . . . . . . . . . (inc.) 10,000
    Cr. Accrued Pension Liability (L). . . . . . . . . . . . . .     (inc.) 10,000
```

The liability disappears when the pension liability is funded (that is, when cash is paid to the pension trustee):

```
Dr. Accrued Pension Liability (L). . . . . . . (dec.) 10,000
    Cr. Cash (A). . . . . . . . . . . . . . . . . . . . . . . . . . . . .     (dec.) 10,000
```

If the pension liability is not funded, the accrued pension liability remains on the books. If it is funded at an amount higher than the accrued pension liability, an asset account, Prepaid Pension Cost, is created.

As you might expect, the accounting for defined-benefit pension plans requires considerable estimating: How many employees will qualify for pensions? How long will they work? How many will live to retirement age? What salaries will they be receiving? How long will they live while retired? How much will the trustee earn on the funds? What must the company pay now to satisfy all of its future obligations? If the pension fund is underfunded, how should the company "catch up"?

For many years, defined-benefit pension obligations were considered to be economic obligations but not accounting liabilities. This is still the case in many countries today. It was argued that an employer did not legally have a liability to an employee *until* that employee actually reached retirement age—and then the only liability was to make one month's benefit payment! If the retiree lived another month, another month's benefit payment was due, and so on. How could pension promises made to employees with many years still to work be considered accounting liabilities when no one could know what future salary levels would be?

For example, Toyota Motor Corporation, a company with ¥13,854 billion in assets, recognized a pension liability at fiscal year end 1998 in the amount of ¥379,085 million (or about $3.3 billion). In its footnotes, the company explained that this was the amount required to satisfy all employee pension claims assuming that all workers terminated their employment as of that date. Obviously, the company's future obligation would be considerably higher than $3.3 billion depending upon how long employees remained with the company and their future salary levels. Just how large the future liability will be was not estimated.

In view of the history of this issue, U.S. pension accounting represents a compromise. Employers must record as an expense the current cost of pension benefits earned by employees, but estimates of the total pension obligation are relegated to the footnotes, and the emphasis is on the projected benefits at current salary levels. Only under a special circumstance, when the total pension obligation significantly exceeds total pension plan assets, is the pension obligation recorded as a balance sheet liability. Such a liability would be in addition to any yearly accrued pension liability amount arising from a particular year's underfunding of pension expense.

Financial Disclosures for Pensions

Because of the importance of pensions and the complexity presented by their accounting, U.S. GAAP requires extensive footnote disclosure. Three items—pension expense, projected benefit obligation, and the plan assets at fair value—deserve special attention in these disclosures. We have already discussed the concept of pension expense. The **projected benefit obligation,** or PBO, is the present value of all future pension benefits earned by employees as of a particular date. Of course, it must reflect expected mortality, future wage levels, and some of the other assumptions we have already mentioned. The term **plan assets at fair value** refers to the market value of the investment portfolio held by the pension trustee as of the employer company's balance sheet date.

Exhibit 13.4 illustrates typical employer company pension disclosures. It is taken from the 1997 annual report of Bestfoods. The total pension expense (net periodic pension cost) for 1997 was $10 million, consisting of $19 million current service cost, $37 million interest cost on pension liabilities, $200 million actual return on plan assets and $154 million of other adjustments. These calculations are explained more fully in Appendix 13B. The actual return on plan assets in 1997 was double the amount for 1996. This was, in part, due to the strong U.S. stock market in 1997.

The footnote also shows the funded status of the plan. The PBO for Bestfoods U.S. plans was $539 million ($537 for plans where assets exceeded accumulated benefits and $2 million in the other plans) as of December 31, 1997, and $553 million the previous year. The total assets in the hands of the trustees of Bestfoods' U.S. plans were $803 million as of December 31, 1998, which was $58 million higher than the previous year. Plan assets are increased by the amount earned in any year plus the cash payments (funding) received from the company less the amounts paid to the beneficiaries.

For example, if we assume Bestfoods funded its 1997 pension cost ($10 million) then pension trustees' account would appear as:

Fund Assets

Beginning Balance	650		
Net Earned	200	57	Paid to beneficiaries
Received from Company	10		
Ending Balance	803		

It is important to note that neither the PBO nor the plan assets appear on an employer's balance sheet. U.S. GAAP requires the recording of a portion of the PBO as a pension liability on the balance sheet *only* when the PBO is "significantly underfunded." The test used to decide how much of the pension obligation should be recorded as a liability is based on a fourth figure, the **accumulated benefits obligation,** or ABO. The ABO is the present value of all pension benefits earned based on *current* salary levels. Thus, it is the same as the PBO but without the projection of future salary increases. A pension liability is recognized on the balance sheet only to the extent to which the ABO exceeds the plan assets:

Accumulated benefits obligation
Less: Plan assets and book reserves

Minimum pension liability

E X H I B I T 1 3 . 4

Bestfoods
Pension Disclosures

Pension plans

The Company and its subsidiaries have a number of non-contributory defined benefit pension plans covering substantially all U.S. employees, including certain employees in foreign countries. Plans for most salaried employees provide pay related benefits based on years of service. Plans for hourly employees generally provide benefits based on flat-dollar amounts and years of service. The Company's general funding policy is to provide contributions within the limits of deductibility under current tax regulations. Certain foreign countries allow income tax deductions without regard to contribution levels, and the Company's policy in those countries is to make the contribution required by the terms of the plan. Domestic plan assets consist primarily of common stock, real estate, corporate debt securities, and short-term investment funds. Approximately $100 million (12%) of the domestic qualified plan assets are invested in the Company's common stock.

The components of net periodic pension cost are as follows:

U.S. Plans

$ Millions	1997	1996	1995
Service cost	$ 19	$ 20	$ 15
Interest cost on projected benefit obligation	37	36	36
Actual return on plan assets	(200)	(95)	(106)
Net amortization and deferral	154	53	67
Net periodic pension cost	$ 10	$ 14	$ 12

Non-U.S. Plans

$ Millions	1997	1996	1995
Service cost	$ 17	$ 18	$ 16
Interest cost on projected benefit obligation	41	42	41
Actual return on plan assets	(48)	(25)	(28)
Net amortization and deferral	19	4	9
Net periodic pension cost	$ 29	$ 39	$ 38

If the minimum pension liability must be recognized, the entry reduces owners' equity unless the minimum liability arises because of changes in the plan that increase benefit levels and for certain other technical reasons. When this is the cause of the minimum liability, an asset account called the **Unfunded Pension Cost** is created.

In summary, if a minimum pension liability arises as a consequence of an increase in pension benefits, the following entry is made:

Dr. Unfunded Pension Cost (A) . . . . (inc.) XX
Cr. Pension Liability (L). . . . .   (inc.) XX

EXHIBIT 13.4 concluded

The funded status for the Company's major pension plans is as follows:

U.S. Plans

$ Millions	Assets exceed accumulated benefits		Accumulated benefits exceed assets	
	1997	1996	1997	1996
Actuarial present value of benefit obligation:				
Vested	$(468)	$(452)	$ (2)	$(14)
Nonvested	(10)	(18)	–	4
Accumulated benefit obligation	(478)	(470)	(2)	(10)
Effect of projected future compensation levels	(59)	(61)	–	(12)
Projected benefit obligation	(537)	(531)	(2)	(22)
Plan assets at fair value	803	645	–	5
Plan assets in excess of (less than) projected benefit obligation	266	114	(2)	(17)
Unrecognized net loss (gain)	(255)	(60)	(1)	–
Unrecognized prior service cost	20	14	–	11
Unrecognized net transition obligation	3	8	–	(2)
Post September 30 contributions	–	1	–	–
(Accrued) prepaid pension cost at December 31	$ 34	$ 77	$ (3)	$ (8)

The 1997 balances reflect the reduction of $14.1 million for restructuring activities and the net transfer of $11.5 million accrued pension costs to Corn Products International.

But if a minimum pension liability results as a consequence of underfunding, the entry is as follows:

```
Dr. Unfunded Pension Cost (COE) . . . . . . . . . (inc.) XX
    Cr. Pension Liability (L). . . . . . . . . . . . . . . . . . . . . .          (inc.) XX
```

The test for the minimum pension liability is made each time financial statements are prepared. If a new minimum pension liability is applicable, the old entry is reversed and a new entry is made as just explained. Bestfoods did not face the Unfunded Pension Cost requirement because their plan assets exceeded the ABO. Book reserves, sometimes called current pension liability, result when pension expense of the form

```
Dr. Pension Expense (E). . . . . . . . . . . . . . . . (inc.) XX
    Cr. Pension Liability (L). . . . . . . . . . . . . . . . . . . . . .          (inc.) XX
```

EXHIBIT 13.5

SYSCO Corporation
Pension Disclosures

EMPLOYEE BENEFIT PLANS

SYSCO has defined benefit and defined contribution retirement plans for its employees. Also, the company contributes to various multi-employer plans under collective bargaining agreements.

The defined contribution 401(k) plan provides that under certain circumstances the company may make matching contributions of up to 50% of the first 6% of a participant's compensation. SYSCO's contribution to this plan was $5,660,000 in 1998, $4,975,000 in 1997 and $4,629,000 in 1996. The defined benefit pension plans pay benefits to employees at retirement using formulas based on a participant's years of service and compensation.

The funded status of the defined benefit plans is as follows:

	June 27, 1998	June 28, 1997
Assets available for benefits	$287,482,000	$247,783,000
Projected benefit obligation		
Vested	(244,050,000)	(182,005,000)
Nonvested	(17,938,000)	(12,696,000)
Total accumulated benefit obligation	(261,988,000)	(194,701,000)
Effect of projected future compensation increases	(45,164,000)	(30,203,000)
Total actuarial projected benefit obligation	(307,152,000)	(224,904,000)
Assets (less than) in excess of projected obligation	$ (19,670,000)	$ 22,879,000
Consisting of:		
Amounts to be offset against (charged to) future pension costs		
Remaining assets in excess of obligation existing at adoption of SFAS 87 in 1986	$ 5,598,000	$ 6,777,000
Unrecognized actuarial (loss) gain due to differences in assumptions and actual experience	(15,977,000)	8,974,000
Unrecognized prior service cost	6,262,000	7,199,000
Accrued pension costs	(15,553,000)	(71,000)
	$ (19,670,000)	$ 22,879,000

The projected unit credit method was used to determine the actuarial present value of the accumulated benefit obligation and the projected benefit obligation. The discount rate used was 7.25% in 1998, 8.0% in 1997 and 7.75% in 1996 and the rate of increase in future compensation levels used was 5.5% in each year. The expected long-term rate of return on assets was 10.5% in 1998 and 9.0% in 1997 and 1996. The plans invest primarily in marketable securities and time deposits.

Net pension costs were as follows:

	1998	1997	1996
Defined benefit plans			
Benefits earned during the year	$ 23,144,000	$ 20,599,000	$ 19,885,000
Interest accrued on benefits earned in prior years	19,372,000	16,412,000	13,812,000
Actual return on plan assets	(48,932,000)	(34,477,000)	(31,865,000)
Net amortization and deferral	21,317,00	14,744,000	16,999,000
Net pension costs from defined benefit plans	14,901,000	17,278,000	18,831,000
Defined contribution plans	5,660,000	4,975,000	4,629,000
Multi-employer pension plans	19,633,000	18,427,000	16,560,000
Net pension costs	$ 40,194,000	$ 40,680,000	$ 40,020,000

results in a liability that is not fully funded. It is really a situation of "expensed but not funded." This means that for purposes of testing for the minimum pension liability, a particular pension plan can be in one of three states at any moment:

- Overfunded—plan assets exceed ABO.

- Underfunded—it has been necessary to record an entry for Unfunded Pension Cost.

- Underfunded but recognized—ABO exceeds plan assets but ABO is less than the sum of plan assets and book reserves.

SYSCO Corporation's footnote disclosure from its 1998 annual report is shown in Exhibit 13.5. It illustrates all of these points concerning the accounting for pensions. The company operates three different types of pension plans. The defined benefit plans had total assets of $287.5 million as of June 27, 1998. The ABO at that date was $262.0 million (of which $244 million was vested) and the PBO was $307.2 million. This means that if the company terminated the defined benefit pension plans as of the end of fiscal 1998 (June 27, 1998), the assets ($287.5 million) should be sufficient to satisfy the pension obligations ($262.0 million including the nonvested part). However, assuming the plans continue and employee salary levels increase, thus triggering higher pension benefits, the PBO is no doubt a better measure of SYSCO's future pension obligation. As of June 27, 1998, the PBO exceeded the assets by $19.7 million, or about 7%. Note that in the previous year, assets exceeded the PBO by a similar amount.

OTHER RETIREMENT BENEFITS

In addition to the accounting for pensions, corporations must also accrue the expected cost of providing any promised retiree health care, life insurance, and other postretirement benefits. In general, the accounting is similar to that for pensions. Moreover, the employer's obligation for these benefits must be fully recognized by the date the employee became eligible for the benefits, and the accrual period must begin at the employee's hire date.

In the case of health care benefits, corporations must estimate participation rates for their workforce, retirement ages, per capita claims costs by age, health care cost trends, and Medicare reimbursement rates, as well as the sorts of assumptions required in pension accounting: Employee turnover, dependency status, mortality, and the rates of return on plan assets. What makes health care estimating different than that for pension costing is the sensitivity of some of the assumptions. For example, vested pension benefits become corporate obligations even if the employee changes jobs, but most corporate postemployment health benefit programs are restricted to employees who work right up to normal retirement. So estimates of employee turnover are particularly important, as are estimates of dependency, because most plans extend benefits to a spouse and other dependents. Even the age of expected retirement is key because of the copayments or coverage available through other health plans or Medicare. Finally, health care costs are especially sensitive to estimates of longevity. Because of such sensitivity, SFAS No. 106 requires that companies disclose the impact on current health care costs and the accumulated postretirement benefit (APB) for health care benefits of a 1 percentage point increase in the cost of health care cost trends.

The required disclosure for postretirement benefits other than for pensions is illustrated in Exhibit 13.6, taken from the 1997 annual report of General Electric (GE) Company. The current cost for GE's retiree health and life insurance plans in 1997 was $455 million, mostly for health care. That cost appears as an expense in the income statement, although GE

E X H I B I T 1 3 . 6

General Electric Corporation
Costs for Retiree Health and Life Plans

Retiree Health and Life Benefits

GE and its affiliates sponsor a number of retiree health and life insurance benefit plans. Principal retiree benefit plans are discussed below; other such plans are not significant individually or in the aggregate.

Principal retiree benefit plans generally provide health and life insurance benefits to employees who retire under the GE Pension Plan with 10 or more years of service. Retirees share in the cost of their health care benefits. Benefit provisions are subject to collective bargaining. At the end of 1997, these plans covered approximately 250,000 retirees and dependents. Details of cost for principal retiree benefit plans follow.

Cost of retiree benefit plans

(In millions)	1997	1996	1995
Retiree health plans			
Service cost for benefits earned	$ 90	$ 77	$ 73
Interest cost on benefit obligation	183	166	189
Amortization	13	—	(12)
Special early retirement cost	152	—	—
Retiree health plan cost	438	243	250
Retiree life plans			
Service cost for benefits earned	17	16	13
Interest cost on benefit obligation	116	106	108
Actual return on plan assets	(343)	(225)	(329)
Unrecognized portion of return	206	93	206
Amortization	8	12	1
Special early retirement cost	13	—	—
Retiree life plan cost (income)	17	2	(1)
Total cost	**$455**	**$245**	**$249**

Funding policy for retiree health benefits is generally to pay covered expenses as they are incurred. GE funds retiree life insurance benefits at its discretion and within limits imposed by tax laws.

Funded status of retiree benefit plans

December 31 (In millions)	1997	1996
Market-related value of assets	$1,621	$1,487
Accumulated postretirement benefit obligation	4,775	3,954

The market-related value of assets of retiree life plans recognizes market appreciation or depreciation in the portfolio over five years, a method that reduces the short-term impact of market fluctuations.

Plan assets are held in trust and consist mainly of common stock and fixed-income investments. GE common stock represented about 4% and 3% of trust assets at year-end 1997 and 1996, respectively.

EXHIBIT 13.6 concluded

An analysis of amounts shown in the Statement of Financial Position is presented below.

Retiree benefit liability/asset

December 31 (In millions)	Health Plans		Life Plans	
	1997	**1996**	**1997**	**1996**
Accumulated postretirement benefit obligation				
Retirees and dependents	**$2,445**	$1,889	**$ 1,417**	$ 1,305
Employees eligible to retire	**104**	86	**45**	45
Other employees	**549**	440	**215**	189
	3,098	2,415	**1,677**	1,539
Add (deduct) unamortized balances				
Experience (losses) gains	**(423)**	(195)	**127**	(41)
Plan amendments	**(171)**	157	**55**	109
Current value of trust assets	**—**	—	**(1,917)**	(1,682)
Retiree benefit liability (prepaid asset)	**$2,504**	$2,377	**$ (58)**	$ (75)

Actuarial assumptions and techniques used to determine costs and benefit obligations for principal retiree benefit plans are shown below.

Actuarial assumptions

December 31	1997	1996
Discount rate	**7.0%**	7.5%
Compensation increases	**4.5**	4.5
Health care cost trends (a)	**7.8**	8.0
Return on assets for the year	**9.5**	9.5

(a) Gradually declining to 5.0% after 2002.

Increasing the health care cost trend rates by one percentage point would not have had a material effect on the December 31, 1997, accumulated postretirement benefit obligation or the annual cost of retiree health plans.

Experience gains and losses, as well as the effects of changes in actuarial assumptions and plan provisions, are amortized over employees' average future service period.

does not necessarily fund this expense. Note that the PBO for retiree health and life plans, $4.775 billion, greatly exceeds the plan assets of $1.621 billion.

Accounting for postretirement health care and related benefits is prescribed by SFAS No. 106, which became effective in 1991. In that year GE recorded a $1.8 billion charge reflecting this accounting change, which lowered reported earnings per share by $2.07, about the size of the annual dividend. Obviously it made a big difference in reported results, although GE did not fund this provision. As of December 31, 1997, it remained on GE's balance sheet as a liability. Clearly, SFAS No. 106 is a change that was long overdue. Corporations have been promising health care benefits to retirees for decades. With rising health care costs and no government takeover of health care plans, the magnitudes of these corporate obligations have become very large.

Management Issues

Pensions present a wealth of management issues, not the least of which is the decision of whether to have a pension plan at all. ERISA does not require a business to offer a pension plan to its employees, but if one is offered, ERISA does prescribe rules as to eligibility, vesting, funding, termination insurance, fiduciary standards, disclosure, and reporting. Faced with large numbers of pensioners or pensioners-to-be and smaller workforces, companies have been struggling to curtail their expensive retirement benefits, such as health care programs and pensions, without demoralizing the existing employees.

Other than the issues of benefits and changes to benefits, the biggest pension and retirement benefits decision for many companies is the one of funding or fund recoveries. Firms with "overfunded" plans have been recovering assets from their plan trustees or have simply stopped further funding of pension costs. Firms driven by the concepts of "shareholder value" and "economic value-added" often look at every asset, every cost, and every employee questioning: "What's the value proposition for this item?" As a consequence, pension plans have become targets for cash recoveries.

DEFERRED INCOME TAXES

Income taxes represent one of the largest obligations arising from operations that a company must satisfy. Some of these taxes must be paid currently; others may be postponed for many years. This section focuses on those income taxes that, because of the particular provisions of the U.S. Internal Revenue Code, may be postponed until some future date.

Because of differences between U.S. GAAP and tax accounting, the amounts due to the taxing authorities for a given period are not necessarily what should be reported as income tax expense of that period. The accounting issue behind deferred taxes is one of matching: Income tax expense is the periodic cost associated with particular revenue and expense items recognized in that accounting period's financial statements. This cost, however, is independent of when those particular revenue and expense items are recognized for income tax return purposes. If revenues and expenses are recorded in this year's income statement, the related income tax expense should also appear in this year's income statement *even* if the recognition of those revenues and expenses (and their associated income tax liability) can be deferred until some later date for tax purposes. This process is called **interperiod tax allocation;** it is really just another form of accrual accounting. It recognizes business events (in this case, the income tax expense) at some moment more appropriate than simply when the tax bill appears or must be paid in cash. Without interperiod tax accounting, a company's

EXHIBIT 13.7

Common Business Events Associated with
Deferred Income Taxes

Event	Prevalent Accounting Treatment	Prevalent Tax Treatment
Depreciation of long-term assets	Straight-line method	Accelerated methods
Installment sales	Immediate recognition	Recognized when cash is received
Bad debt expense	Estimated and recognized in the period corresponding with the actual credit sale	Recognized when written off
Warranty expense	Estimated and recognized in the period of product sale	Recognized when paid
Environmental cost	Estimated and accrued	Recognized when paid
Retiree health cost	Estimated and accrued	Recognized when paid

operating results can fluctuate wildly because of tax accounting conventions, even if the basic operations of the business are stable.

Almost all business events have the potential to be recognized at different times for tax purposes than for accounting purposes, but the most common accounting-tax differences leading to deferred income taxes are those listed in Exhibit 13.7. In the following illustration, we will use depreciation accounting to demonstrate the role of interperiod tax allocation.

An Illustration: Sample Company

Ideally, in published financial statements, the cost of an asset is assigned to various years in whatever manner best reflects the use of the asset over its lifetime. Tax accounting also expenses that same cost over the asset's life but often with different amounts being charged to different years. One often hears the expression that "U.S. companies keep two sets of books". What this means is simply that U.S. tax rules are often different from U.S. GAAP. Moreover, companies have much different objectives when reporting income to the IRS than when reporting income to owners and potential shareholders. Thus, in the case of depreciation, although both tax and accounting statements reflect the same *total* depreciation expense over the life of an asset, the tax depreciation is typically accelerated or "front loaded" while the accounting depreciation is usually flat or straight-line.

Imagine that a company purchases an asset costing $1,000 which, because of special tax incentives, can be depreciated for tax purposes over only two years (50 percent each year) and which, for accounting purposes, can be depreciated over four years (25 percent per year). For simplicity, assume that the company is subject to a 40 percent tax rate. The differences between the accounting depreciation and tax depreciation deductions are as follows:

	Year 1	Year 2	Year 3	Year 4
Accounting depreciation	$ 250	$ 250	$250	$250
Tax depreciation	500	500	–0–	–0–
Difference	(250)	(250)	250	250
Tax impact of difference at 40 percent	($100)	($100)	$100	$100

In essence, $250 *more* tax depreciation will be taken in Years 1 and 2 and $250 *less* tax depreciation will be taken in Years 3 and 4. Take a moment and consider the implications of these differences. The taxes actually due in Years 1 and 2 will be $100 *lower;* in Years 3 and 4, the actual taxes due will be $100 *higher* than will be reflected in the accounting income statements. In total, however, over the four-year period, the amount of taxes will be the same under either system. If this were the only accounting-tax difference that the company had, the accounting income tax *expense* in Years 1 and 2 would simply be the taxes actually due plus $100. In Years 3 and 4, this process would be reversed—the accounting income tax *expense* would be the taxes actually due minus $100.

Exhibit 13.8 illustrates the effect of these accounting-tax differences, as well as the use of interperiod tax allocation to account for these differences. In this example, we assume that revenues for each period are $1,000 and that all other expenses other than depreciation total $400 per year. Note that the income tax *liability* (per the tax return) for each of the first two years would be only $40 and then would increase to $240 per year for the next two years. On the accounting income statement, the total income tax *expense* is adjusted to eliminate what would otherwise be a distortion caused by the special tax depreciation allowances. The additional $100 of income tax *expense* in Years 1 and 2 increases the Deferred Tax Liability account. Note that this account builds up in Years 1 and 2 and then reverses in Years 3 and 4 when the total income tax *liability* is higher than the total income tax *expense.* Also note that the events that gave rise to this situation were the purchase of an asset and the decision to use different accounting and tax depreciation schedules.

The use of a Deferred Tax Liability account on the balance sheet eliminates the distortion that would otherwise occur if the current tax liability (per the tax return) were considered to be the income tax expense for the year. Deferred tax accounting makes the total income tax expense in the income statement conform to the accounting treatment used for depreciation in that statement.

The Deferred Tax Liability account at the end of Years 1, 2, and 3 is a liability in the sense that someday income taxes will be payable *in excess of what the accounting statements would otherwise suggest.* In simple terms, Sample Company temporarily avoided $100 of income tax payments in Year 1 because it used a more rapid method of depreciation for tax reporting than was used for accounting purposes. Someday that advantage will reverse; the fast depreciation write-offs will run out with straight-line depreciation continuing in the accounting records. At that time, the tax return will reflect higher taxable income than the accounting statements, and the tax bills coming into the company will be far higher than what would be predicted from the figure for income before tax on the accounting income statement. Like a buffer, the Deferred Tax Liability account is used to prevent such distortions. Expenses are credited to this account when temporary tax advantages lower taxable income, and when the differences reverse, the buffer is reduced.

EXHIBIT 13.8

Sample Company
Deferred Income Taxes

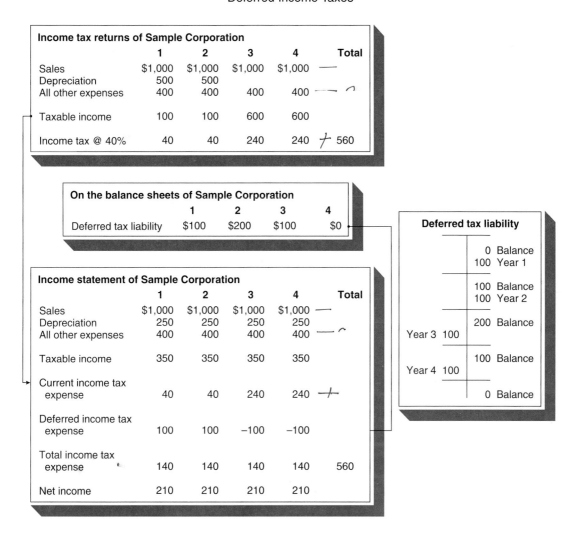

Income tax returns of Sample Corporation

	1	2	3	4	Total
Sales	$1,000	$1,000	$1,000	$1,000	—
Depreciation	500	500			
All other expenses	400	400	400	400	—
Taxable income	100	100	600	600	
Income tax @ 40%	40	40	240	240	560

On the balance sheets of Sample Corporation

	1	2	3	4
Deferred tax liability	$100	$200	$100	$0

Income statement of Sample Corporation

	1	2	3	4	Total
Sales	$1,000	$1,000	$1,000	$1,000	—
Depreciation	250	250	250	250	
All other expenses	400	400	400	400	—
Taxable income	350	350	350	350	
Current income tax expense	40	40	240	240	
Deferred income tax expense	100	100	−100	−100	
Total income tax expense	140	140	140	140	560
Net income	210	210	210	210	

Deferred tax liability

	0 Balance
	100 Year 1
	100 Balance
	100 Year 2
	200 Balance
Year 3 100	
	100 Balance
Year 4 100	
	0 Balance

Temporary and Permanent Differences

Temporary differences. Interperiod tax allocation is used when tax returns and the accounting reports reflect **temporary differences,** as with depreciation. By definition, temporary differences always reverse themselves at some point. Tax depreciation may exceed accounting depreciation for a while for any particular asset, but eventually the reverse will occur, and by the end of the life of the asset, the sum of the differences (positives and negatives) will always be zero. Accordingly, the deferred tax liability associated with this asset may increase for a few years on the balance sheet, but then it will decline and eventually become zero.

Even though the temporary difference that triggered the deferred tax liability (or asset if the account has a debit balance) will always reverse itself for any particular item having a temporary difference, it is possible for an account such as the Deferred Tax Liability to keep increasing *in total,* for example, if a business is growing and more assets are being acquired.

Permanent differences. Depreciation differences between tax and accounting statements illustrate a temporary difference because for any given asset, the total difference over time is zero. **Permanent differences,** on the other hand, arise when an item is included for accounting purposes but will never appear in the determination of taxable income (or vice versa). For example, interest on municipal bonds is a revenue item for accounting purposes but is not taxable in the U.S.—it represents a permanent difference in the income reported to the IRS versus the income reported to shareholders. Deferred taxes are never calculated for permanent differences; they are simply ignored in the interperiod tax allocation process.

Events that lead to temporary differences. Temporary accounting differences may arise as a result of two types of events:

1. An asset balance on the accounting books is greater than balance on its tax books. This arises when: (a) Expenses (or losses) become tax deductible *before* being expensed for accounting purposes. (An example of this is depreciation and the related PP&E accounts in the early years of the asset's life where straight-line depreciation is used for accounting purposes and MACRS for tax return purposes); and (b) Revenues (or gains) become taxable *after* they are recognized in the accounting income statement. (For example, certain types of installment sales are recognized as accounting sales immediately but on the tax books they are treated as taxable income only as payments are received.)

2. A liability balance on the accounting books is greater than its balance on the tax books. This arises when: (a) Expenses (or losses) become tax deductible *after* the recognition of the expense. (For example when a company provides warranties or guarantees on a product or service. Generally accepted accounting principles require a company to estimate the expense and liability for warranties when the revenue is recognized; tax rules permit no deductions for anticipated warranty work, only for repairs actually made); and (b) Revenue (or gains) become taxable *before* being recognized as accounting income. (Rent collected in advance is such an item and is recorded as unearned revenue (a liability) for GAAP purposes but is treated as revenue when the cash is collected for tax purposes.)

It should be noted that in the first instance, accounting income exceeds taxable income, thus giving rise to a deferred tax liability; in the latter example, the reverse is true: There is a deferred tax asset that, in simple terms, is like a prepaid income tax. (To be precise it is *not* prepaid tax. Instead, it is the income tax benefit of future deductions.) Many companies have both, perhaps a deferred tax liability because of different depreciation policies and a deferred tax asset because of the alternative treatment of warranty expenses.

Accounting for Deferred Taxes

Current accounting treatment for deferred taxes utilizes the **liability method.** Following this approach, companies must recognize both the current and future tax consequences of events that have been recognized in either the financial statements or the tax returns. A deferred tax liability (or asset) must be recognized for all tax effects due to temporary differences as alluded to in the prior section. The key to the liability method is that any temporary book-tax difference in the value of an asset or liability will result in taxable or tax-deductible amounts in future periods. Such items must be valued using the marginal tax rates expected to apply to taxable income in future periods.

A simple way to look at this is the following: If the assets and liabilities on the accounting books are always the same as on the tax books, there's no concern about interperiod tax allocation. But when book assets and tax asset values (or book liabilities and tax liabilities values) differ due to temporary differences, there is a need to recognize a deferred tax expense or a deferred tax benefit. Suppose the following: Cedar Floors, Inc. had no temporary accounting differences between its book and tax accounting for its entire history; then in 1999, the first such difference occurred. At the end of 1999, inventory on the tax books was $300,000 higher then on the accounting books. This happened because the company recorded an allowance for $300,000 for obsolete inventory. But it wasn't a tax deductible item under tax rules until the actual inventory items were scrapped or sold. Suddenly, there is book-tax difference: a book asset has a tax basis that is 300,000 *higher* than its book carrying cost. In the case of the $300,000 book-tax difference in inventory, and assuming a 34% tax rate, an entry must be made as follows:

```
Deferred tax asset (A) . . . . . . . . . . . . . . (inc) 102,000
    Deferred tax expense (E) . . . . . . . . . . . . . . . . .        (dec) 102,000
```

The effect of this entry is to *reduce* income tax expense for the year, which is appropriate because the tax return reflects lower inventory cost deductions than the accounting books. In other words, the current income tax *expense* should be adjusted down by $102,000 because of this temporary book-tax difference.

Applying the liability method to our example of Sample Company (Exhibit 13.8), recall that tax depreciation was figured on a two-year basis and accounting depreciation was taken over four years and that the asset's original cost was $1,000. The asset's account balance per the tax books and the accounting books would be as follows:

	Tax Calculations		Accounting Calculations	
Year	**Yearly Depreciation**	**End-of-Year Undepreciated Asset Cost**	**Yearly Depreciation**	**End-of-Year Undepreciated Asset Cost**
1	$500	$500	$250	$750
2	500	–0–	250	500
3		–0–	250	250
4		–0–	250	–0–

At the end of Year 1, the balance sheet of Sample Company reflects an asset valued at $750:

```
Asset (at cost)                          $1,000
Less: Accumulated depreciation             (250)
                                         _____
Asset (net)                              $  750
```

However, this asset has an undepreciated cost basis of $500 on the tax books, and the difference between the two cost bases is $250. When the accounting basis temporarily differs from the tax basis for an asset (or a liability) like this, it means that a deferred tax liability (or asset) must be recognized.

In this case, at the end of Year 1, an additional tax liability will occur in the future because of the temporary accounting-tax difference. If tax rates are expected to remain at 40 percent, there will be a $100 additional tax liability (0.40 × $250) in the future. Thus, the Deferred Tax Liability account at the end of Year 1 should be $100, and the Deferred Tax Expense amount to be recorded in Year 1 is also $100 (the beginning Deferred Tax Liability account was zero). The deferred taxes would be calculated as follows for the four years for the Sample Company:

	End of Year			
	1	**2**	**3**	**4**
Accounting asset NBV*	$750	$500	$ 250	$ –0–
Tax asset NBV	500	–0–	–0–	–0–
Difference	$250	$500	$ 250	$ –0–
Tax rate (during the year)	0.4	0.4	0.4	0.4
Deferred tax liability	$100	$200	$ 100	$ –0–
Deferred tax expense	$100	$100	$(100)	$(100)

*(NBV = net book value.)

In reviewing these figures, it is important to recall the purpose of deferred tax accounting: Deferred tax liabilities (and assets) measure the future tax expenditures (or benefits) that a company faces due only to the differences between tax accounting and financial statement accounting.

Using the above data for Sample Company, the asset's tax basis at the end of Year 1 is $250 below its accounting basis, so there should be a $100 deferred tax liability *associated with this asset* (that is, 0.40 × $250). In the following year the difference in the two cost bases is $500, so the deferred tax liability must be $200. To increase the liability requires an expense in Year 2 of $100; hence,

Years 1 and 2
Dr. Income Tax Expense (E). . . . . (inc.) 100
  Cr. Deferred Tax Liability (L) . . . .   (inc.) 100
Years 3 and 4
Dr. Deferred Tax Liability (L) . . . . (dec.) 100
  Cr. Income Tax Expense (E) . . . .   (dec.) 100

Note that at the end of Year 1, it was determined that the ending balance for the Deferred Tax Liability account should be $100. Since there was no beginning balance in this account, the deferred tax expense is also $100. At the end of Year 2, it was determined that the ending balance for the Deferred Tax Liability account should be $200. Since there was a beginning balance of $100, the account requires another $100 increase which is also Year 2's deferred tax expense.

Deferred Tax Liability

	Beginning of Year 1	$ 0
	(Plug) Deferred tax expense	100
	End of Year 1	$100
	(Plug) Deferred tax expense	100
	End of Year 2	$200

Each asset or liability that may reflect a temporary accounting-tax difference in carrying value is analyzed separately. The taxable or tax-deductible amounts in future years are projected, and the deferred tax assets or liabilities are calculated each year at the incremental tax rate *expected to apply* to taxable income in *future periods* when the deferred tax assets and liabilities are realized. The deferred tax expense for each year is then the difference in the deferred tax liability or asset from the beginning of the year to the end of the year (that is, a "plug"). In other words, the liability is calculated first and then the expense figure is derived to obtain the new balance for the deferred tax liability.

The accounting for some items, such as warranties, is the reverse of that for depreciable assets. For example, the balance sheet may show a reserve for future warranty claim or some such liability. This represents a liability with an accounting-tax difference the other way: Expensing on the accounting statements has preceded its tax deduction. A deferred tax asset must be created to reflect this difference. Consider the following warranty example:

	At the End of Year		
	1	**2**	**3**
Accounting basis of warranty liability	$(500)	$(400)	$(200)
Tax basis of warranty liability	–0–	–0–	–0–
Difference	$(500)	$(400)	$(200)
Tax rate (during the year)	0.40	0.40	0.40
Deferred tax asset	$ 200	$ 160	$ 80
Deferred tax expense (benefit) for the year	$(200)	$ 40	$ 80

Suppose that during Year 1 a liability for future warranty expense was established for the first time at $500. Because *estimated* warranty expenses cannot be deducted for tax purposes, at the end of Year 1 there is a liability with an accounting-tax difference of $500. The deferred tax asset related to this liability is $200 (0.40 × $500). The difference between the beginning and ending deferred tax assets is thus $200. As a consequence, a $200 deferred tax adjustment (or negative expense) exists. At the end of Year 2, the warranty liability is $400, indicating that the actual warranty cost recognized on the tax return exceeded the warranty expense reflected in the accounting statements by $100. Because the end of Year 2 accounting-tax difference is $400, the deferred tax asset's end of Year 2 balance should be $160 (0.40 × $400). To reduce the deferred tax asset account, a deferred tax expense of $40 will be recorded in Year 2. A similar situation occurs in Year 3.

Financial Disclosures for Deferred Taxes

U.S. GAAP requires disclosure of the primary categories of deferred tax asset and liability such as the following from the annual report of Hasbro, Inc., an international manufacturer of children's toys:

(thousands)	1994	1993
Deferred tax assets:		
Accounts receivable	$ 27,782	30,049
Inventories	12,600	12,090
Net operating loss and other loss carryovers	16,923	11,073
Operating expenses	33,948	32,393
Postretirement benefits	11,487	8,675
Other	41,223	39,554
Total gross deferred tax assets	143,963	133,834
Valuation allowance	(11,829)	(10,376)
Net deferred tax assets	132,134	123,458
Deferred tax liabilities:		
Property rights and property, plant, and equipment	64,743	68,614
Other	7,786	6,468
Total gross deferred tax liabilities	72,529	75,082
Net deferred income taxes	$ 59,605	48,376

Think about why each of the items is associated with a deferred tax asset or liability. Take accounts receivable for example: On Hasbro's balance sheet, receivables are valued at $717,890 thousand as of December 31, 1994. The $27,782 thousand deferred tax asset listed above is certainly due to the company's provision for uncollectible accounts, which gives rise to a book-tax difference in the carrying value of receivables. A good estimate of the December 31, 1994 tax basis for accounts receivable would be $797,267 ($717,890 + $27,782/0.35) assuming a 35 percent tax rate.

The classification of deferred tax assets and liabilities in the balance sheet must reflect the classification of the liabilities and assets with which they are associated. Thus, deferred tax liabilities resulting from accounting-tax depreciation differences are always classified as noncurrent because the assets associated with them, fixed assets, are always classified as noncurrent. Although it is possible to have four deferred tax items in a balance sheet—current and noncurrent liabilities, and current and noncurrent assets—current deferred tax assets must be netted against current deferred tax liabilities; the same is true for noncurrent deferred tax assets and liabilities unless the assets and liabilities are attributable to different tax-paying organizational units of the corporation.

The footnotes must also reconcile the U.S. federal **statutory tax rate** to the **effective tax rate**; the effective tax rate is defined as:

$$\text{Effective tax rate} = \frac{\text{Income tax expense}}{\text{Income before income tax}}$$

Exhibit 13.9 shows the income tax rate reconciliation from Hasbro's annual report. The company determined its effective tax rate to be 38.5 percent. The table at the top of the exhibit describes all the components of income tax expense; the total for 1994 was $112,254 thousand. The table at the very bottom of the exhibit reports that the total income before tax that year was $291,569. The ratio of the two figures is, of course, 38.5 percent.

Here is another way to understand the effective tax rate disclosures. Exhibit 13.10 contains an illustration of where the components of this calculation can be found. Total income tax expense has two parts: the current tax expense from the U.S. tax return and all the other income tax returns the company must file, and the deferred income tax expense, which is determined by an examination of all temporary book-tax differences as we have discussed previously.

EXHIBIT 13.9

Hasbro, Inc.
Income Tax Disclosures

Income Taxes

Income taxes attributable to earnings before income taxes are as follows:

	1994	1993	1992
Current			
Federal	$ 60,539	81,770	64,825
Foreign	42,543	28,614	33,147
State and local	10,417	12,541	13,012
	113,499	122,925	110,984
Deferred			
Federal	1,924	315	2,612
Foreign	(3,349)	1,817	(663)
State and local	180	149	279
	(1,245)	2,281	2,228
	$112,254	125,206	113,212

The cumulative effect of the change in accounting principles resulting from the adoption of Statement of Financial Accounting Standards No. 109, "Accounting for Income Taxes," increased 1992 net earnings by $12,349.

Certain tax benefits are not reflected in income taxes on the consolidated statements of earnings. Such benefits of $9,800 in 1994, $6,299 in 1993, and $12,583 in 1992 relate primarily to stock options and cumulative effect of changes in accounting principles.

A reconciliation of the statutory U.S. federal income tax rate to the company's effective income tax rate is as follows:

	1994	1993	1992
Statutory income tax rate	35.0%	35.0%	34.0%
State and local income taxes, net of federal income tax effect	2.4	2.6	3.0
Amortization of goodwill	1.6	1.4	1.4
Foreign earnings taxed at rates other than the U.S. statutory rate	(0.7)	—	(0.6)
Other, net	0.2	(0.5)	0.9
	38.5%	38.5%	38.7%

The components of earnings before income taxes are as follows:

	1994	1993	1992
Domestic	$177,672	243,820	190,268
Foreign	113,897	81,390	102,108
	$291,569	325,210	292,376

Calculation of Effective Income Tax Rate

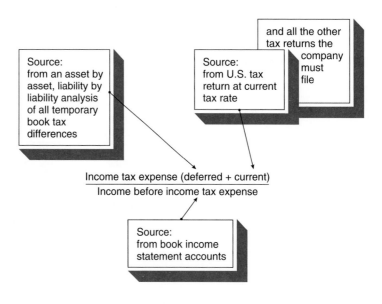

Although the International Accounting Standards Committee has proposed the adoption of the liability method to account for temporary differences, in line with U.S. GAAP, it has yet to be adopted. In the meantime, practice varies widely from country to country because some countries do not have accounting-tax differences by statute (e.g., Japan) and thus do not need deferred income-tax accounting while others have accounting-tax differences (e.g. U.K.) but are not required to adopt deferred income tax accounting.

The Boeing Company's 1997 annual report provides an excellent example of one final point we wish to make about deferred taxes. Exhibit 13.11 contains the company's footnote disclosure for income taxes. In 1997 Boeing's income tax *expense* was negative $163 million. Boeing reported a loss of $341 million before income taxes, hence net earnings (loss) was ($178) million [341 – 163]. The current tax expense was $112 million [103 + 9] and the deferred portion was ($275) million [253 + 22]. We know that for a company to report a net deferred tax expense of a certain amount, net deferred tax liabilities must have increased by that amount; and for there to be a deferred tax benefit, net deferred tax assets must have increased. Which is what happened. In 1997, net deferred tax assets increased from $1,505 million to $1,780 million or $275 million! This is how Boeing determined that the deferred tax benefit was $275 million. A word of warning—not all financial statements show this relationship so clearly. Note that for Boeing, during 1996, net deferred tax assets increased by $290 million [1,505 – 1,215], but the deferred tax benefit was only $84 million. Shouldn't these be the same? Ordinarily yes, but events like acquisitions and divestments can cloud this relationship.

EXHIBIT 13.11

Boeing Company
Income Tax Disclosures

Income Taxes

The provision for taxes on income consisted of the following:

Year ended December 31,	1997	1996	1995
U.S. Federal			
Taxes paid or currently payable	$ 103	$689	$ 379
Change in deferred taxes	(253)	(78)	(675)
	(150)	611	(296)
State			
Taxes paid or currently payable	9	57	32
Change in deferred taxes	(22)	(6)	(112)
	(13)	51	(80)
Income tax provision (benefit)	$(163)	$662	$(376)

The following is a reconciliation of the income tax provision (benefit) computed by applying the U.S. federal statutory rate of 35 percent to the recorded income tax provision:

	1997	1996	1995
U.S. federal statutory tax	$(119)	$ 868	$(144)
Foreign Sales Corporation tax benefit	(79)	(110)	(85)
Research benefit	(8)	(4)	(90)
Prior years' investment tax credit		(95)	
Prior years' tax investment	(23)	(30)	
Nondeductibility of goodwill and merger costs	71	2	
State income tax provision, net of effect on U.S. federal tax	(9)	31	(53)
Other provision adjustments	4		(4)
Income tax provision (benefit)	$(163)	$ 662	$(376)

The deferred tax assets, net of deferred tax liabilities, resulted from an alternative minimum tax credit carryforward and from temporary tax differences associated with the following:

Year ended December 31,	1997	1996	1995
Inventory and long-term contract methods of income recognition	$1,186	$ 999	$ 861
Pension benefit accruals	(1,152)	(1,026)	(684)
Retiree health care accruals	1,806	1,712	1,307
Other employee benefits accruals	318	339	291
Customer and commercial financing	(378)	(519)	(690)
Alternative minimum tax credit carryforward			130
Net deferred tax assets	$1,780	$1,505	$1,215

The temporary tax differences associated with inventory and long-term contract methods of income recognition encompass related costing differences, including timing and depreciation differences.

Valuation allowances were not required due to the nature of and circumstances associated with the temporary tax differences.

Income taxes have been settled with the Internal Revenue Service (IRS) for all years through 1978, and IRS examinations have been completed through 1987. In connection with these examinations, and the years 1979 through 1987 are in litigation. The Company has also filed refund claims for additional research and development tax credits, primarily in relation to its fixed-price government development programs. These credits have not been recorded as the claims are under review by the IRS in the context of prior years' audits. Successful resolutions will result in increased income to the Company.

The Company believes adequate provision has been made for all open years.

Income tax payments and transfers were $219, $648 and $263 in 1997, 1996 and 1995, respectively.

SUMMARY

Leases, pensions, and deferred income taxes are significant obligations that present unique valuation issues. Capital leases are reported in the balance sheet at their present value; pension obligations are disclosed in the footnotes at their present value, and, under some circumstances, a portion of this obligation may appear on the balance sheet as a liability. Deferred income taxes, on the other hand, are not reported at their present value but are reported in the balance sheet.

Many types of leases exist, but only those that meet one or more of the four tests (that is, ownership, alternative ownership, economic life, or value) are considered to be capital leases. Capital leases are recorded on the books of the lessee as both an asset and a liability at their present value at the time the lease is signed. Lease assets are amortized in a manner similar to other depreciable assets as if the asset were owned. Lease liabilities, on the other hand, are amortized using the effective interest method as one would amortize a bond.

Pensions and other retirement benefits are important because of the sheer magnitude of the dollars involved. They are complex because of the variety of estimates one must make to value an entity's retirement obligations. No matter how a pension is to be funded, whether by contributions from the employer, the employee, or both, the two basic types are defined-contribution and defined-benefit plans. The latter is more complex because accountants, actuaries, and management must estimate future benefits, employee mortality, retirement ages, and the future earnings rate of pension assets. In situations in which the accumulated benefit obligation (or ABO) is less than the plan assets, a pension liability may be created reflecting this difference.

Differences between the accounting procedures adopted for tax purposes and for financial reporting purposes may result in deferred tax liabilities and/or assets and deferred tax expenses and/or benefits. Some items result in permanent accounting-tax differences and are not subject to deferred tax accounting. Only temporary differences, such as those created by differences in depreciation, result in interperiod income tax allocations.

Three special appendices are included with this chapter. They are designed to further explain the accounting for leases, pensions, and deferred income taxes, and they contain additional examples of each.

NEW CONCEPTS AND TERMS

Accumulated benefits obligation

Capital lease

Defined-benefit plan

Defined-contribution plan

Effective tax rate

ERISA

Federal statutory tax rate

Interperiod tax allocation

Lease

Lessee

Lessor

Liability method

Off-balance-sheet financing

Operating leases

Pension

Pension expense

Permanent differences

Plan assets at fair value

Projected benefit obligation

Temporary differences

Unfunded pension cost

Leases in Detail

Chapter 13 introduced the concepts of operating and capital leases and discussed the accounting for both types of leases from the lessee's perspective. Here we will explain more fully the calculations underlying the accounting for capitalized leases for both the lessee and the lessor. The accounting and required disclosures for capitalized leases for lessors, including the *direct-financing type* and *sales-type leases,* are also described.

We will continue to use the example of the Boeing airplane leased by American Airlines from Prudential Insurance Co. Recall that the present value of the lease was $125 million and that the lease asset will be depreciated on a straight line basis and the lease liability will be amortized using the effective interest method.

Amortization of the Lease Liability

Exhibit 13A.1 presents the lease amortization schedule for the American Airlines lease liability. Column 2 is the quarterly payment due at the *beginning* of each quarter, and columns 3 and 4 identify the interest expense portion and the principal reduction portion of this payment. Thus, the first quarter's payment is all principal reduction. After this payment, the principal is then $120,520,129. Note that the lease payments are due at the beginning of the period. This is typical of a lease agreement, while mortgage and bond payments are typically due at the end of the period.

The key to Exhibit 13A.1 is the way that the interest expense and principal reduction portions of the payment are separated. We know that the interest rate per quarter is 2 percent. Thus, for the second payment, the interest expense portion must be $0.02 \times \$120,520,129$, or $2,410,403. Because the payment is always $4,479,871 per quarter for this lease, the remainder is the principal reduction, or $2,069,468 (that is, $4,479,871 − $2,410,403). Because the principal balance is reduced by this amount, the ending principal balance for Quarter 2 is $118,450,660, or $120,520,129 − $2,069,468. Each quarter's payment is separated in this manner. Note that the last payment's principal reduction, $4,392,030, is almost the same as the outstanding principal of $4,392,031. The difference is due to rounding.[1]

---

[1] One might ask why there is any interest portion at all in the last payment since the payment is made at the *beginning of the period.* The explanation is that annuities such as this lease, with 40 payments made at the beginning of the period, are really liabilities that extend over only 39 periods. It is as if one borrowed $120,520,129 and repaid it at $4,479,871 per quarter for 39 quarters, with payments made at the end of the period—when the interest expense for that period had been accrued.

EXHIBIT 13A.1

Lease Amortization Schedule:
Aircraft Financing Example
(in millions)

Quarter	Payment	Interest Portion	Principal Reduction	Ending Principal
0				$125,000,000
1	$ 4,479,871	$ —	$ 4,479,871	120,520,129
2	4,479,871	2,410,403	2,069,468	118,450,660
3	4,479,871	2,369,013	2,110,858	116,339,803
4	4,479,871	2,326,796	2,153,075	114,186,728
5	4,479,871	2,283,735	2,196,136	111,990,591
6	4,479,871	2,239,812	2,240,059	109,750,532
7	4,479,871	2,195,011	2,284,860	107,465,672
8	4,479,871	2,149,313	2,330,558	105,135,114
9	4,479,871	2,102,702	2,377,169	102,757,945
10	4,479,871	2,055,159	2,424,712	100,333,233
11	4,479,871	2,006,665	2,473,206	97,860,027
12	4,479,871	1,957,201	2,522,671	95,337,356
13	4,479,871	1,906,747	2,573,124	92,764,232
14	4,479,871	1,855,285	2,624,586	90,139,646
15	4,479,871	1,802,793	2,677,078	87,462,568
16	4,479,871	1,749,251	2,730,620	84,731,948
17	4,479,871	1,694,639	2,785,232	81,946,716
18	4,479,871	1,638,934	2,840,937	79,105,779
19	4,479,871	1,582,116	2,897,755	76,208,024
20	4,479,871	1,524,160	2,955,711	73,252,313
21	4,479,871	1,465,046	3,014,825	70,237,488
22	4,479,871	1,404,750	3,075,121	67,162,367
23	4,479,871	1,343,247	3,136,624	64,025,743
24	4,479,871	1,280,515	3,199,356	60,826,387
25	4,479,871	1,216,528	3,263,343	57,563,044
26	4,479,871	1,151,261	3,328,610	54,234,434
27	4,479,871	1,084,689	3,395,182	50,839,251
28	4,479,871	1,016,785	3,463,086	47,376,165
29	4,479,871	947,523	3,532,348	43,843,817
30	4,479,871	876,876	3,602,995	40,240,823
31	4,479,871	804,816	3,675,055	36,565,768
32	4,479,871	731,315	3,748,556	32,817,212
33	4,479,871	656,344	3,823,527	28,993,686
34	4,479,871	579,874	3,899,997	25,093,688
35	4,479,871	501,874	3,977,997	21,115,691
36	4,479,871	422,314	4,057,557	17,058,134
37	4,479,871	341,163	4,138,708	12,919,425
38	4,479,871	258,389	4,221,483	8,697,943
39	4,479,871	173,959	4,305,912	4,392,031
40	4,479,871	87,841	4,392,030	0
Totals	$179,194,842	$54,194,842	$125,000,000	

Note one more thing about Exhibit 13A.1: The total payments are $179,194,842, of which $54,194,842 is interest and the rest principal. Thus, in American Airlines' footnotes, this capital lease could be disclosed as follows:

Future minimum lease payments	$179,194,842
Less: Amount representing interest	54,194,842
Present value of minimum lease payments	$125,000,000

Depreciation of the Lease Asset

In Chapter 13 we learned that the depreciation policies for capital-lease assets are the same as those that a lessee adopts for similar owned assets. If, however, American Airlines depreciates its other aircraft over 12 years on a straight-line approach, it has an interesting problem: What time frame should it use to depreciate the leased asset when the lease runs for 10 years and the asset's normal depreciable life is 12 years?

Convention is to use the economic life of a leased asset if ownership is expected to transfer to the lessee and to use the lease lifetime only if the lease qualifies for capitalization because it meets the economic-life or valuation tests (but not one of the ownership tests). In the airline case, the asset-depreciation period should be 12 years or 48 quarters; hence, the leased asset will be depreciated at the rate of $10,416,667 per year (or $125 million divided by 12 years).

Accounting for the Lessor

If a lease meets *any* of the four capital lease tests discussed in Chapter 13, the lessor treats the agreement as a capitalized lease if it meets two *additional* tests: (1) There is reasonable assurance that the lease payments will be received and (2) there are no other major uncertainties as to costs or revenues. The need for these two additional tests is obvious: A lease asset (lease receivable) must not be recorded if collectibility is in doubt, and the value of the receivable must be known at the inception of the lease for an accounting entry to be recorded. Assuming that a lease meets these criteria, it is then necessary for the lessor to determine whether the lease is a *direct-financing-type* or a *sales-type* capital lease. This decision rests on whether or not the asset's market value is the same as the lessor's cost of the asset.

In the case of the airplane lease, the insurance company enters into a typical *direct-financing lease* arrangement because, at the lease date, the airplane's cost to the lessor (Prudential Insurance Co.) is the same as its current market value. The insurance company first buys the airplane and carries it on its books as an asset. Later, when the lease is signed, the airplane asset will be replaced by a capital-lease asset (that is, a receivable). As lease payments are received, the reported amount of the lease receivable will decline according to the amortization schedule. The insurance company's profit on the transaction does not come from "selling" the plane; instead, it will come from the interest income associated with the lease payments (that is, from financing the airline's purchase of the aircraft).

When Prudential purchases the airplane from Boeing, the transaction is recorded as follows:

Dr. Aircraft (A). . . . . (inc.) 125,000,000
  Cr. Cash (A) . . . .   (dec.) 125,000,000

When the lease agreement is signed, the asset is removed from the insurance company's books and is replaced by two accounts: Minimum Lease Payment Receivable (the total undiscounted lease receivable) and Unearned Revenues (the future interest payments to be received). Referring to Exhibit 13A.1, note that the total payments are to be $179,194,842. In the leasing industry, this figure is called the *minimum lease payment receivable*. The $54,194,842 is the unearned revenue, and the $125 million is the present value of the future lease payments (it is also the market value of the asset). Clearly,

Minimum lease payment receivable =
Unearned revenue + Present value of lease payments.

Thus, the insurance company makes the following entry when the lease is signed:

```
Dr. Minimum Lease Payment
    Receivable (A) . . . . . . . . . . . . (inc.) 179,194,842
  Cr. Unearned Revenue (L) . . . . . . . . . . . . . . . . . .        (inc.)   54,194,842
  Cr. Aircraft (A). . . . . . . . . . . . . . . . . . . . . . . . . . . .        (dec.) 125,000,000
```

Each quarter, Prudential will make entries to record the receipt of the lease payment and to recognize its portion of the revenue earned. For example, the second-quarter entries would look like this:

```
Dr. Cash (A) . . . . . . . . . . . . . . . . . . . . (inc.) 4,479,871
  Cr. Minimum Lease Payment Receivable (A) . . . . . .        (dec.) 4,479,871
Dr. Unearned Revenue (L). . . . . . . . . (dec.) 2,410,403
  Cr. Interest Revenue (R). . . . . . . . . . . . . . . . . . . .        (inc.) 2,410,403
```

At 2 percent per quarter, the quarterly interest income is 2,410,403 (0.02 × 120,520,129).

In contrast to the direct-financing lease example just described, when a manufacturing company makes a product and then leases it, it generates a *sales-type lease* (that is, the asset's market value is not the same as the lessor's cost of the asset). The accounting issues become (1) how much profit the company should show on the sale of the product itself, as opposed to the interest revenue on the lease, and (2) when it should be shown.

Let us return to the American Airlines example and suppose that the Boeing Company, instead of a third-party insurance company, was to be the lessor at the same terms as those offered by Prudential. Suppose also that Boeing's cost of manufacturing the airplane was $100 million. When the lease is signed, Boeing makes an entry for this sales-type lease that recognizes a profit (or loss) on executing the lease (thus the origin of the "sales-type" label). The following is the "sale" entry:

```
Dr. Cost of Goods Sold (E) . . . . . . . . (inc.) 100,000,000
Dr. Minimum Lease Payment
    Receivable (A) . . . . . . . . . . . . (inc.) 179,194,842
  Cr. Sales (R) . . . . . . . . . . . . . . . . . . . . . . . . . . .        (inc.) 125,000,000
  Cr. Unearned Revenue (L) . . . . . . . . . . . . . . . . . .        (inc.)   54,194,842
  Cr. Inventory (A) . . . . . . . . . . . . . . . . . . . . . . . . . .        (dec.) 100,000,000
```

Under this type of lease, Boeing will make entries each quarter to record the receipt of the lease payment and to recognize the portion of the interest revenue earned as if it were a direct-financing lease. For example, these would be the second-quarter entries:

```
Dr. Cash (A) . . . . . . . . . . . . . . . . . . . . (inc.) 4,479,871
  Cr. Minimum Lease Payment Receivable (A) . . . . . .        (dec.) 4,479,871
Dr. Unearned Revenue (L). . . . . . . . . (dec.) 2,410,403
  Cr. Interest Revenue (R). . . . . . . . . . . . . . . . . . . .        (inc.) 2,410,403
```

Boeing's profit on the sale of the airplane is the same whether it is sold to Prudential or leased directly to American Airlines. And if Boeing ends up being the lessor rather than Prudential, Boeing will recognize the same interest income each quarter as would Prudential.

EXHIBIT 13A.2

Comdisco, Inc.
Lessor's Lease Accounting Disclosures

Note 2: Lease Accounting Policies

FASB Statement of Financial Accounting Standards No. 13 requires that a lessor account for each lease by either the direct financing, sales-type or operating method.

Leased Assets:

- Direct financing and sales-type leased assets consist of the present value of the future minimum lease payments plus the present value of the residual (collectively referred to as the net investment). Residual is the estimated fair market value at lease termination.
- Operating leased assets consist of the equipment cost, less the amount depreciated to date.

Revenue, Costs and Expenses:

- Direct financing leases—Revenue consists of interest earned on the present value of the lease payments and residual. Revenue is recognized periodically over the lease term as a constant percentage return on the net investment. There are no costs and expenses related to direct financing leases since leasing revenue is recorded on a net basis.
- Sales-type leases—Revenue consists of the present value of the total contractual lease payments which is recognized at lease inception. Costs and expenses consist of the equipment's net book value at lease inception, less the present value of the residual. Interest earned on the present value of the lease payments and residual, which is recognized periodically over the lease term as a constant percentage return on the net investment, is included in direct financing lease revenue in the statement of earnings.
- Operating leases—Revenue consists of the contractual lease payments and is recognized on a straight-line basis over the lease term. Costs and expenses are principally depreciation of the equipment. Depreciation is recognized on a straight-line basis over the lease term to the company's estimate of the equipment's fair market value at lease termination, also commonly referred to as "residual" value.

- Equity transactions—The company enters into equity transactions with third-party investors who obtain ownership rights, which include tax depreciation deductions and residual interests. The company retains control and the use of the equipment generally throughout its economic life by leasing back the equipment from the third-party investor. Accordingly, the leased asset cost related to the period of control remains on the balance sheet. Revenue consists of the profit recognized on equity transactions and is included in operating lease revenue. Profit is recognized on a straight-line basis over the leaseback term (life of the transaction).
- Initial direct costs related to operating and direct financing leases, including salespersons' commissions, are capitalized and amortized over the lease term.

Note 3: Leased Assets

The components of the net investment in direct financing and sales-type leases as of September 30 are as follows:

(in millions)	1994	1993
Minimum lease payments receivable	$2,177	$2,080
Estimated residual values	260	305
Less: unearned revenue	(293)	(312)
Net investment in direct financing and sales-type leases	$2,144	$2,073

Unearned revenue is recorded as leasing revenue over the lease terms. Operating leased assets include the following as of September 30:

(in millions)	1994	1993
Operating leased assets	$3,132	$3,308
Less: accumulated depreciation and amortization	(1,436)	(1,474)
Net	$1,696	$1,834

Disclosure for Lessors

Lessors with significant leasing activities have extensive disclosure requirements for both operating and capital leases. Exhibit 13A.2 contains the leasing footnotes from Comdisco, Inc.'s 1994 annual report. This company is a major lessor of computing equipment with three kinds of leases: direct financing, sales-type, and operating leases. The company has done a careful job of explaining its accounting for each. From Note 3, the two items that will

EXHIBIT 13A.2 concluded

Note 4: Lease Portfolio Information

The size of the company's lease portfolio can be measured by the cost of leased assets at the date of lease inception. Cost at lease inception represents either the equipment's original cost or its net book value at termination of a prior lease. The following table summarizes, by year of lease commencement and by year of projected lease termination, the cost at lease inception for all leased assets recorded at September 30, 1994 (in millions):

		Projected year of lease termination				
Year lease commenced	Cost at lease inception	1995	1996	1997	1998	1999 and after
1990 and prior	$ 936	$ 659	$ 166	$ 69	$ 18	$ 24
1991	1,017	441	399	93	78	6
1992	1,514	612	387	409	53	53
1993	1,473	234	557	323	278	81
1994	1,582	83	334	662	270	233
	$6,522	$2,029	$1,843	$1,556	$697	$397

The following table summarizes the estimated net book value at lease termination for all leased assets recorded at September 30, 1994. The table is presented by year of lease commencement and by year of projected lease termination (in millions):

		Projected year of lease termination				
Year lease commenced	Net book value at lease termination	1995	1996	1997	1998	1999 and after
1990 and prior	$ 73	$ 64	$ 7	$ 1	$ 1	$—
1991	97	47	47	3	—	—
1992	179	89	41	44	—	5
1993	193	36	68	40	36	13
1994	241	20	56	101	40	24
	$783	$256	$219	$189	$77	$42

Note 5: Owned Equipment—Future Noncancelable Lease Rentals and Disaster Recovery Subscription Fees

Presented below is a summary of future noncancelable lease rentals on owned equipment and future subscription fees on noncancelable disaster recovery contracts (collectively, "cash in-flows"). The summary presents expected cash in-flows, except for cash to be received on non-owned equipment of $35 million, due in accordance with the contractual terms in existence as of September 30, 1994. The table also presents the amounts to be received by financial institutions for leases discounted on a nonrecourse basis (see Note 6 of Notes to Consolidated Financial Statements).

	Years ending September 30,					
(in millions)	95	96	97	98	99 and after	Total
Expected future cash in-flows:						
Operating leases	$ 737	$ 441	$190	$ 58	$ 22	$1,448
Direct financing and sales-type leases	912	645	361	160	99	2,177
Disaster recovery contracts	190	149	101	58	27	525
Total	1,839	1,235	652	276	148	4,150
Less: To be received by financial institutions						
Operating leases	391	234	94	19	3	741
Direct financing and sales-type leases	405	286	159	77	30	957
Total	796	520	253	96	33	1,698
To be received by the company	$1,043	$ 715	$399	$180	$115	$2,452

E X H I B I T   1 3 A . 3

The Boeing Company
Disclosure of Sales-Type Leases

Note 7: Customer and Commercial Financing

Customer and commercial financing at December 31 consisted of the following:

	1997	1996
Aircraft financing		
Notes receivable	$ 651	$ 334
Investment in sales-type/ financing leases	1,646	1,605
Operating lease equipment, at cost, less accumulated depreciation of $254 and $206	1,289	868
Commercial equipment financing		
Notes receivable	313	478
Investment in sales-type/ financing leases	407	358
Operating lease equipment, at cost, less accumulated depreciation of $96 and $106	502	395
Less valuation allowance	(208)	(150)
	$4,600	$3,888

Financing for aircraft is collateralized by security in the related asset, and historically the Company has not experienced a problem in accessing such collateral. The operating lease aircraft category includes new and used jet and commuter aircraft, spare engines and spare parts.

The components of investment in sales-type/financing leases at December 31 were as follows:

	1997	1996
Minimum lease payments receivable	$2,709	$2,735
Estimated residual value of leased assets	519	589
Unearned income	(1,220)	(1,361)
	$2,008	$1,963

Scheduled payments on customer and commercial financing are as follows:

Year	Principal Payments on Notes Receivable	Sales-type/ Financing Lease Payments Receivable	Operating Lease Payments Receivable
1998	$272	$ 312	$214
1999	91	300	164
2000	70	255	129
2001	64	246	108
2002	60	216	97
Beyond 2002	407	1,380	878

The Company has entered into interest rate swaps with third-party investors whereby the interest rate terms differ from the terms in the original receivable. These interest rate swaps related to $64 of customer financing receivables as of December 31, 1997. Interest rate swaps on financing receivables are settled on the same dates interest is due on the underlying receivables.

Interest rates on fixed-rate notes ranged from 4.00% to 15.67%, and effective interest rates on variable-rate notes ranged from 0.40% to 1.25% above the London Interbank Offered Rate (LIBOR).

Sales and other operating revenues included interest income associated with notes receivable and sales-type/financing leases of $217, $195 and $296 for 1997, 1996 and 1995, respectively.

The valuation allowance is subject to change depending on estimates of collectibility and realizability of the customer financing balances.

appear in the September 30, 1994, balance sheet are Net Investment in Direct Financing and Sales-Type Leases, $2,144 million, and Operating Leased Assets—Net, $1,696 million. Notes 4 and 5 contain a lot of interesting information not always shown by lessors. Perhaps the reason for disclosing this information is to convince the reader that the volume of leases is increasing (Note 4) even if the computer marketplace seems to be moving away from mainframes to small machines, and also that the company's projected cash flows from existing contracts (Note 5) were substantial. Comdisco had been suffering from declining revenues and low profitability, and it had cut its dividends on common stock. The last sentence in Note 6 suggests that the company has also sold its interest in some of the leases.

Exhibit 13A.3 is the Boeing Company's footnote disclosure for its customer financing, which includes leases taken from the 1997 annual report. Boeing disclosed its sales-type leases ($1,646 million as of December 31, 1997) on a net basis without bothering to break out the gross amount less the amount attributable to unearned income or future interest. It is interesting that Boeing chose to disclose its derivative activities in this same footnote, or at least that part associated with customer financing programs. A word of caution: Do not expect to find those 12 AMR jets in this list of leased aircraft from Boeing. AMR did not necessarily lease them from the Boeing Company.

Pensions in Detail

This appendix presents some basic pension terminology and illustrates the calculations necessary to determine a company's pension expense. It explains the significance of the required footnote disclosures for defined-benefit plans and interprets an actual pension footnote. Finally, an example of pension accounting is presented.

Terminology

To understand the valuation of defined-benefit pension obligations and the disclosure of pension expense, and liability and asset information reflected in corporate annual reports, one must first learn the language of pension accounting. The following concepts and definitions are essential for a complete understanding of pension accounting.

Plan assets—the market value of the assets in a pension fund under the control of a trustee. These assets are owned by the pension fund or trust, a separate legal entity, and appear on the balance sheet of the trust, not of the employer-company.

Accumulated benefit obligation (ABO)—the present value of the projected payments a company must make in the future to satisfy the retirement benefits that have already been earned by employees and retirees. Discounting of the future cash outflow is done using an interest rate termed the *settlement rate* or *discount rate,* an external market rate reflecting the return on high-quality, fixed-income investments. Projections are made using only *current* salary levels but with assumptions for such factors as mortality and retirement patterns. Conceptually, if a company were to terminate a pension agreement now and seek to settle whatever obligations it had to employees and retirees by making a single payment to an external pension administrator, the ABO would be the amount it owed. Note that an employer can cancel a pension agreement, but it is obligated to pay benefits for the accumulated years of service each employee has earned. Also note that, as each year passes, qualified employees "earn" another year of benefits.

Projected benefit obligation (PBO)—an obligation similar to the ABO except that it is based on projected or future salary levels. Consequently, the PBO is always higher than the ABO. The PBO is the present value (using the settlement rate) of the pension benefits that have been earned to date by employees and retirees. It reflects expected mortality, expected salary increases, and expectations about employee turnover.

Expected rate—the expected long-term rate of return on a pension fund's assets. This rate is used to estimate what the trustee will earn on a fund's invested assets.

Vested benefits—*vested* means that an employee has met the minimum plan length-of-service requirements and is qualified to receive pension benefits. In most corporate pension plans, employees must work full-time for a defined period of time, say two years, before they become eligible for a pension. For example, suppose that two people joined a company at the same time and that one quit after two years and the other left after four years. If the company had a three-year vesting requirement, the first person would receive no pension. The second person would be eligible for a pension based on the four years of service. A company's PBO for all employees and retirees might be $130 million, but perhaps only $110 million for vested employees and retirees—those with more than the required years of service (that is, the vesting period).

Funded status of the plan—the difference between the projected benefit obligation (PBO) and a plan's assets at market value.

Net gain or loss—the difference between the actual earnings of a plan for a year and the expected earnings (expected rate times beginning of the year value of the plan's assets). If the difference is included in pension expense, it is considered "recognized." If it is accumulated and amortized at some later date, it is termed *the accumulated, unrecognized net gain or loss.* Generally accepted accounting practice is to recognize the net gains or losses only when they exceed a threshold (10 percent of the higher of the PBO or the plan assets).

Financial Accounting Standard 87 (SFAS No. 87)—the current U.S. GAAP for pensions.

Financial Accounting Standard (SFAS No. 106)—the current U.S. GAAP for retirement benefits other than pensions.

Net obligation—the difference between the PBO and the plan assets at the time SFAS No. 87 was adopted. It is also called the *transition asset (or liability).* It is amortized or recognized in the income statement on a straight-line basis over the expected working lives of the workforce at the time SFAS No. 87 was adopted.

Accrued or prepaid pension cost—the cumulative total of the unfunded pension expense or, if funding has exceeded the cumulative expenses, the cumulative prepaid pension cost.

Service cost (or current service cost or normal cost)— the present value of the benefits earned in the current year by the existing employees in a plan. Perhaps the best way to conceptualize service cost is the following. As each year goes by, the employees should say to themselves, "I've just put in another year of service toward retirement. I'll get another X percent of my ending salary in each retirement check." The employer must predict just how many of those employees will survive to begin collecting their retirement and how long that retirement will last. The present value cost of this obligation, for just this year, is the *service cost.* Calculating the service cost requires projections of mortality and future salary levels. Discounting the future payments is done at the settlement rate.

Prior service cost—when a pension plan is first adopted, an employer often gives credit to existing employees for their years of service prior to the adoption of the plan. For example, 63-year-old employees will suddenly be treated as if they had been in the plan since they were hired. They may get 35 or 40 years of service "with the stroke of a pen." The present value of this prior (or past) service is estimated by using projected salary levels, mortality, and the settlement rate. The same thing happens when a plan's benefit levels are increased and made retroactive.

Interest cost—for the year, the beginning of the year PBO times the settlement rate. Conceptually, interest cost is like saying "At the beginning of this year, our total pension obligation (as measured by the PBO) on a discounted basis was $320 million. We are now at the end of the year, one year closer to the payouts. Hence, the value of the obligation has increased by a year's interest." Another way to say this is that at the beginning of the year the PBO was, for example, $100 million, where at the end of the year the PBO was $110 million. Ignoring all items related to new employees or retirements and terminations, the difference between the two PBO's is simply due to interest. The obligation is now one year closer.

Actual return on plan assets—the total actual earnings of the pension-fund assets for a year.

Actuarial gains and losses—a catchall category for the favorable and unfavorable adjustments arising from changes in expected mortality (and other actuarial) assumptions.

Additional minimum liability—an amount in addition to any current accrued or prepaid pension cost that may be required to be shown as a pension liability when a plan's assets are less than the ABO.

Accounting for Defined-Benefit Plans

Each year, actuaries and accountants project the number of an employer's present workforce who will survive to retirement and the life expectancies for those projected retirees. Salary levels are projected, benefits calculated, and an expected pension payout schedule is prepared as of the end of each accounting period. This payout schedule is then discounted using a *settlement rate* to derive a *projected benefit obligation* (PBO). A similar calculation, the *accumulated benefit obligation* (ABO), is prepared using only current salary levels. Thus, there are two liability figures—one assuming current salary levels and one assuming salary progression. It is important to note that these "liabilities" do not necessarily appear in the employer's balance sheet; at this stage, they are simply calculations.

Under SFAS No. 87, the *pension expense* for a given year to be reported by an employer is the net of the following four items:

1. The *service cost* for the year (that is, the present value cost of future benefits earned by employees for this year only).

2. *Plus* the *interest cost* on the PBO as of the beginning of the year, which is like the debt service cost on the total pension liability as of the beginning of the year.

3. *Less* the *actual return on plan assets* for the year (what the pension fund actually earned). In an ideal world, the pension fund's assets at the beginning of the year would equal only the PBO at the beginning of the year. During the year, the fund would earn only the year's interest cost on the PBO, so items 2 and 3 would offset one another.

4. *Plus/minus* four miscellaneous adjustments:
   a. The difference between the actual return on plan assets and the expected return on plan assets for the year. The effect is to replace the actual return on plan assets with the *expected return on plan assets*. The differences between actual and expected returns are accumulated and, if they exceed a threshold, are amortized over the expected working lifetime of the employees. This adjustment smooths the recognition of differences between the actual and expected earnings rate.
   b. Actuarial gains and losses, which are treated the same way.
   c. The difference between the PBO and the total fund assets at the time SFAS No. 87 was adopted is called the *net obligation* or *transition amount*. It too is amortized over the expected workforce service life.
   d. If the plan is modified in later years and these modifications lead to prior service costs, this cost is also amortized.

The concept underlying this complex calculation of the yearly expense is based on the following logic: In a perfect world, a company's pension expense should be only its current pension service cost. This amount would be paid to the pension trust, which would add it to the fund's assets. Each year, the fund's invested assets would earn just what was expected. In such a situation, the PBO (the present value of the total pension obligation) would always equal the fund's assets. The following exemplifies this "perfect world" situation:

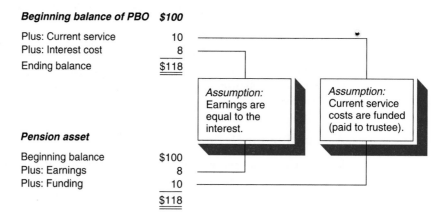

Beginning balance of PBO	*$100*
Plus: Current service	10
Plus: Interest cost	8
Ending balance	$118

Assumption: Earnings are equal to the interest.

Assumption: Current service costs are funded (paid to trustee).

Pension asset	
Beginning balance	$100
Plus: Earnings	8
Plus: Funding	10
	$118

In such a world, the pension assets would always be equal to the pension obligation. In the real world, however, many things are different:

- Actual earnings on the pension assets are rarely equal to expected earnings. The effect of SFAS No. 87 is to substitute the expected return for the actual return and then amortize the accumulated differences between the two over time if the cumulative amount gets "too big" (that is, it smooths out the effects of stock and bond market swings).

- Sometimes management increases the benefits level. This has an immediate impact on the PBO (it increases it). The new obligation created by these plan modifications (prior service costs) is amortized over time—another smoothing activity.

- Sometimes the actuaries change their mortality tables or make similar changes to their assumptions. This can immediately either raise or lower the PBO. SFAS No. 87 smooths this by amortizing the actuarial gain or loss over time.

- Finally, when SFAS No. 87 was first adopted, most companies had a PBO different from their fund assets. This difference, or transition amount, is amortized over time.

The consequence of all of these smoothings and adjustments is to ensure that for a company that funds its pension costs on a timely basis, the plan assets approximate the PBO over time without causing the annual pension expense to fluctuate widely.

Disclosure Requirements for Defined-Benefit Plans

Companies with defined-benefit pension programs must disclose the nature of their programs, types of benefits, funding policies, and actuarial methods. They must also disclose both the settlement rate and the expected earnings rate, the major elements of the actual pension expense, the ABO, and the PBO. The cumulative overfunded and underfunded status of different pension plans for a single employer cannot be netted together.

The 1998 footnote disclosure of Sysco Corporation, presented earlier in Exhibit 13.5 is typical of footnotes under the disclosure requirements of SFAS No. 87.

Sysco's 1998 pension expense for its defined benefit plans, for example, was $14.9 million, and this is the amount that is included in the income statement for that year. It consists of $23.1 million of service cost (the present value of benefits earned by employees during the year), $19.4 million of interest cost on the PBO (simply because of the passage of time), and an actual return during 1998 on the plan's assets of $48.9 million.

The fourth item, net amortization and deferral, is a composite of several items:

- deferral of the excess of the plan's earnings over the expected long-term return. The actual earnings were $48.9 million and the expected return was set at 10.5% in 1998. One could estimate the expected return to be $26.0 million (10.5% × 247.8 million) so the amount deferred was $22.9 million (48.9 − 26.0).

- amortization of the transition asset. In 1998 that amount was $1.2 million (6.777 − 5.598).

- all other adjustments, which net to be $.4 million (22.9 + (1.2) − 21.3). These could be adjustments to reflect changes in actuarial assumptions such as workforce turnover estimates.

Defined-Benefit Pension Liability on the Balance Sheet

Under certain circumstances, a pension liability other than a particular year's accrued or prepaid pension cost could appear on a company's balance sheet. SFAS No. 87 requires that, whenever total pension fund assets are less than the ABO (that is, the present value of the projected benefits *without* salary progression), a minimum liability is to be recognized in the employer's balance sheet even though the pension assets are under the control of and on the books of the pension plan.

Three situations are possible. When there is no current accrued or prepaid pension cost, the additional minimum liability is just the ABO minus the plan assets—*the unfunded ABO*. When there is a current *prepaid* pension cost, the additional liability is the unfunded ABO plus the prepaid pension cost. When there is a current accrued pension liability, the additional liability is the unfunded ABO less the accrued pension cost (except that when the unfunded liability is less than the accrued pension liability, there is no additional minimum liability).

For example, consider the following situation:

Accumulated benefit obligation (ABO)	$(3,500)
Provision for salary progression	(2,100)
Projected benefit obligation (PBO)	$(5,600)
Fair value of plan assets	3,000
Funded status of plan (underfunded)	$(2,600)
Unrecognized net gain or loss	400
Unrecognized net obligation	1,800
(Accrued) prepaid pension cost	$ (400)

The unfunded ABO is thus $500:

ABO	$(3,500)
Plan assets	3,000
	$ 500

The additional minimum liability is $100:

Unfunded ABO	$ 500
(Accrued) prepaid pension cost	(400)
	$ 100

The requirement to reflect this minimum liability on the employer's balance sheet was the result of a compromise by the FASB between the dictates of accounting theory and the realities of business practice. One might easily argue that when the pension assets are less than the PBO, the difference is an obligation of the employer that should be recognized just like any other liability. The compromise resulted in the FASB's decision that a liability must be recognized in the balance sheet only when the plan assets are less than the ABO.

In the previous example, the difference between the ABO and the plan assets is $500, but the firm already has a $400 accrued pension liability. This portion of the liability has already been recognized by being expensed, but has not yet been funded. Hence, the additional, minimum liability to be shown on the balance sheet is $100.

Conditions leading to the recognition of a minimum liability usually arise when a new plan is adopted and benefits are granted for prior service. The "goodwill" created in the workforce by the new plan is considered to be an intangible asset, and an entry would be made as follows:

Dr. Unamortized Pension Cost (A) . . . . (inc.) 100	
Cr. Pension Liability (L)	(inc.) 100

Each year the previous year's minimum liability and related asset are removed from the books, and a new liability and asset are added if conditions indicate that an unfunded ABO exists. Some critics refer to this as a "post-it" entry that appears each year as a different figure as long as the fund's assets do not exceed the value of the ABO.

If the ABO exceeds the fund's assets *by an amount in excess of the unrecognized prior period costs and the unrecognized net obligation,* the excess amount is deducted from the recorded pension asset and is shown as a contra equity account. In other words, if the ABO exceeds the fund assets for reasons other than the cost of prior service, the plan is essentially underfunded, and it should appear as a liability without any offsetting asset. In the example just discussed, this would not be the case because the unrecognized net obligation or transition amount is $1,800.

Pension accounting is complex because pensions are complex. SFAS No. 87 introduced many new and potentially confusing concepts such as the PBO and ABO, the additional minimum liability, and the unrecognized net obligation. It may be some time before readers of financial statements become thoroughly familiar with this information, but its impact on reported net income and the statement of financial position is not likely to be significant for most large publicly traded corporations because most have funded some or all of their pensions. The same cannot be said about a related issue—postretirement medical costs. These costs are predicted to rise rapidly in the next decade. Most corporations have provided no funding or reserves for such costs. SFAS No. 106 added significant liabilities to U.S.

corporate balance sheets for these future obligations.

Effective with SFAS No. 106, a company must report its annual expense for medical, life insurance, and other postretirement benefits, segmented into

- Current service cost
- Interest on the PBO
- Actual return on plan assets
- Amortization of the unrecognized transition obligation

and other adjustments. It must also disclose

- Fair value of plan assets
- ABO

and details of remaining unamortized prior service cost, transition obligation, and net gain/loss on plan assets. These disclosures closely parallel the pension disclosures.

Many companies expensed their entire PBO when they adopted SFAS No. 106, although for most it was a noncash expense because the liability was not funded. Otherwise companies would have had to amortize the transition obligation over the working lifetimes of their employees (for that portion of the PBO obligated to current employees), which would have reduced net income each year going forward. For many, the onetime, noncash catch-up charge was preferable.

A Complete Example

Exhibit 13B.1 reports the pension expense for a hypothetical company that adopted SFAS No. 87 in 1987; Exhibit 13B.2 illustrates the derivation of accrued or prepaid pension cost following the format used in most U.S. annual reports today. In this particular illustration, the company experiences five years when the expected returns exceed the actual returns on the invested plan assets. Then the reverse is true. In addition, the actuarial assumptions change in 1990 and 1993. In 1989 the plan is amended to grant retroactive (prior service) benefits to employees. The effects of these events will be reflected in the pension assets and liability.

To begin, consider the first three lines of Exhibit 13B.2. The company's pension liability (PBO) at the beginning of 1987 was $400 larger than the pension assets of $3,000. Note that in this illustration the pension liability rises steadily (in years such as 1989, it seems to jump considerably), and the plan assets lag behind for several years, resulting in a sharp increase in the unfunded PBO. Beginning in 1993, however, the fund's assets increase dramatically. In spite of these large changes in assets, the PBO, and the funded status of the plan, the pension expense (Exhibit 13B.1) reflects only gradual changes, which is exactly what SFAS No. 87 attempts to achieve.

In following the calculations, perhaps the first thing that one should note is that at the time of adoption of SFAS No. 87, the difference between the PBO and the plan assets is the unrecognized net obligation ($400). This amount is amortized over 10 years (the projected average working lifetime of the present employees) and becomes a part of the pension expense for those years. If the company funds the expense each year by giving money to the pension trust, this will add to the assets and in 10 years will close the gap between the assets and PBO if there are no other variances between what is expected and what actually happens.

EXHIBIT 13B.1

Calculation of Pension Expense

	1987	1988	1989	1990	1991	1992	1993	1994
Service cost	300	310	320	330	340	350	360	370
Interest cost	340	404	475	605	708	813	930	1,039
Actual return on plan assets	(240)	(267)	(201)	(214)	(567)	(847)	(1,103)	(1,114)
Net amortization (see below)	(20)	(17)	(141)	(193)	88	252	366	212
Pension expense	380	430	454	528	569	568	553	506
Explanation of net amortization:								
Amortization—unrecognized net (gain)/loss	–0–	–0–	–0–	–0–	2	–0–	–0–	–0–
Actual—expected earnings	(60)	(57)	(231)	(283)	(4)	162	276	122
Amortization—unrecognized net obligation	40	40	40	40	40	40	40	40
Amortization—unrecognized prior service cost	–0–	–0–	50	50	50	50	50	50
Net amortization	(20)	(17)	(141)	(193)	88	252	366	212

EXHIBIT 13B.2

Reconciliation of (Accrued) Prepaid Pension Cost

	Begin	End of Year							
	1987	1987	1988	1989	1990	1991	1992	1993	1994
Projected benefit obligation	(3,400)	(4,040)	(4,754)	(6,049)	(7,084)	(8,133)	(9,296)	(10,386)	(11,794)
Fair value of assets	3,000	3,240	4,317	4,972	5,713	6,850	8,265	9,921	11,542
Funded status of plan	(400)	(800)	(437)	(1,078)	(1,371)	(1,283)	(1,031)	(464)	(253)
Unrecognized prior service cost		–0–	–0–	450	400	350	300	250	200
Unrecognized net (gain) loss		60	117	348	731	733	571	94	(27)
Unrecognized net obligation	400	360	320	280	240	200	160	120	80
(Accrued) prepaid pension cost	–0–	(380)	–0–	–0–	–0–	–0–	–0–	–0–	–0–

One should next note Exhibit 13B.3, the calculation of the PBO. Each year, the PBO is increased by the current year's service cost and interest on the beginning of the year's PBO. The PBO is also increased when the terms of the pension plan are changed, giving additional benefits to employees based on their past years of service. This benefit increase is called *prior service cost*. Note that this is assumed to occur in 1989. Actuarial adjustments also change the PBO as depicted in 1990 and 1993. The reader should note also what does not change the PBO: actual funding by the employer and earnings on the plan assets. The PBO is reduced as retirees begin receiving their benefits (that is, when the projected payouts are actually made). To simplify matters, this example assumes that there are as yet no retirees and their expected working life continues to be 10 years.

EXHIBIT 13B.3

Calculation of Projected Benefit Obligation

	1987	1988	1989	1990	1991	1992	1993	1994
Projected benefit obligation—Beginning	(3,400)	(4,040)	(4,754)	(6,049)	(7,084)	(8,133)	(9,296)	(10,386)
Add: Service cost	(300)	(310)	(320)	(330)	(340)	(350)	(360)	(370)
Interest	(340)	(404)	(475)	(605)	(708)	(813)	(930)	(1,039)
New prior service cost	–0–	–0–	(500)	–0–	–0–	–0–	–0–	–0–
Actuarial adjustment	–0–	–0–	–0–	(100)	–0–	–0–	200	–0–
Deduct: Pension benefits paid	–0–	–0–	–0–	–0–	–0–	–0–	–0–	–0–
Projected benefit obligation—end	(4,040)	(4,754)	(6,049)	(7,084)	(8,133)	(9,296)	(10,386)	(11,794)

EXHIBIT 13B.4

Calculation of Fair Value of Assets

	1987	1988	1989	1990	1991	1992	1993	1994
Fair value of assets—beginning	3,000	3,240	4,317	4,972	5,713	6,850	8,265	9,921
Add: Actual return on plan assets	240	267	201	214	567	847	1,103	1,114
Amount funded	–0–	810	454	528	569	568	553	506
Deduct: Pension benefits paid	–0–	–0–	–0–	–0–	–0–	–0–	–0–	–0–
Fair value of assets—end	3,240	4,317	4,972	5,713	6,850	8,265	9,921	11,542

Exhibit 13B.4 illustrates the calculation of the plan assets. They are increased by company funding and the earnings on the fund. They decline when payouts are made to retirees.

Referring back to Exhibit 13B.1, the periodic pension expense is composed of service cost, interest on the PBO, actual return on the plan assets, and net amortization. (The actual derivation of service cost is not explained in this example.) Note that the interest cost is based on the beginning of the period PBO and the settlement rate, here assumed to be 10 percent. Pension expense is reduced by the actual earnings on the plan assets, or $240 in 1987.

The net amortization consists of four elements. The first is the amortization of the unrecognized net gain or loss. The logic of this adjustment is that over time most gains and losses (actual minus expected returns) should cancel one another. Only if the cumulative difference gets too large should one increase (or decrease) the level of expensing and funding. SFAS No. 87 chose the threshold of 10 percent. Hence, as long as the cumulative gain/loss on plan assets is less than 10 percent of the greater of the PBO or the plan assets, no amortization is necessary. If the net gain or loss exceeds this threshold, the amount in excess of 10 percent is amortized over the remaining working lifetime of the employees.

<u>**EXHIBIT 13B.5**</u>

Calculation of Amortization of Unrecognized Gain/Loss

	1987	1988	1989	1990	1991	1992	1993	1994
Unrecognized (gain)/loss—Beginning of year	–0–	60	117	348	731	733	571	94
10% of the greater of the PBO or fair value	340	404	475	605	708	813	930	1,039
Unrecognized (gain)/loss subject to amortization	–0–	–0–	–0–	–0–	22	–0–	–0–	–0–
Amortization of unrecognized (gain) loss	–0–	–0–	–0–	–0–	2	–0–	–0–	–0–

<u>**EXHIBIT 13B.6**</u>

Calculation of Unrecognized Gain (Loss)

	1987	1988	1989	1990	1991	1992	1993	1994
Unrecognized (gain)/loss—Beginning of year	–0–	60	117	348	731	733	571	94
Less: Amortization	–0–	–0–	–0–	–0–	2	–0–	–0–	–0–
Unrecognized (gain)/loss—before adjustment	–0–	60	117	348	729	733	571	94
Add: Actuarial net (gain) loss	–0–	–0–	–0–	100	–0–	–0–	(200)	–0–
Net asset (gain) loss (actual – expected)	60	57	231	283	4	(162)	(276)	(122)
Unrecognized (gain)/loss—end of year	60	117	348	731	733	571	94	(27)

<u>**EXHIBIT 13B.7**</u>

Calculation of Unrecognized Prior Service Cost

	1987	1988	1989	1990	1991	1992	1993	1994
Prior service cost—beginning of year		–0–	–0–	450	400	350	300	250
Add: New prior service cost	–0–	–0–	500	–0–	–0–	–0–	–0–	–0–
Less: Amortization of prior service cost	–0–	–0–	50	50	50	50	50	50
Prior service cost—end of year	–0–	–0–	450	400	350	300	250	200

As explained in Exhibit 13B.5, only in 1992 does the cumulative deficit in expected earnings exceed the 10 percent level. The calculation of the unrecognized gain/loss is explained in Exhibit 13B.6. Note that it is decreased by amortization and increased (or decreased) by the difference between the expected and actual investment performance of the plan. Note also that it is affected by actuarial gains and losses. In this illustration, the actuarial changes in 1990 increased the unrecognized loss; in 1993, the change was a gain.

Returning to Exhibit 13B.1, note that the adjustment for the actual – expected earnings, when combined with the actual return on plan assets, results in the pension expense reflecting the expected return. Only if the accumulated actual – expected earnings is outside the 10 percent corridor does it affect pension expense. The two remaining items to be amortized have already been mentioned: the $400 unrecognized net obligation (on adoption of SFAS No. 87) and the prior service cost (calculated in Exhibit 13B.7).

A final word about this example. SFAS No. 87 requires a reconciliation of PBO and plan assets back to prepaid or accrued pension cost. If the pension expense is actually funded each year (as illustrated in all years except 1987), there should be no accrued prepaid pension cost because the funded status of the plan should just be the sum of the following:

- Unamortized net obligation (transition amount to SFAS No. 87).
- Unamortized net gain or loss (cumulative actual – expected earnings).
- Unamortized prior service cost (since inception of SFAS No. 87).

Deferred Income Taxes in Detail

The concept of *interperiod tax allocation* and the recognition of deferred tax liabilities and deferred tax assets were explained in Chapter 13. This explanation did not discuss one of the most important complications arising from deferred tax accounting: What happens when tax rates change? Furthermore, it did not discuss the important limits on recognizing deferred tax assets required by SFAS No. 109. These two items are explained in this appendix.

When Tax Rates Change

Chapter 13 explained the fundamentals of deferred tax accounting by using an illustration of the calculation of deferred tax expense and the associated deferred tax liability from Sample Company:

	End of Year			
	1	**2**	**3**	**4**
Accounting asset NBV	$750	$500	$250	$–0–
Tax asset NBV	500	–0–	–0–	–0–
Difference	$250	$500	$250	$–0–
Tax rate (during the year)	0.4	0.4	0.4	0.4
Deferred tax liability	$100	$200	$100	$–0–
Deferred tax expense	$100	$100	$(100)	$(100)

We will again refer to this example to explain what happens when income tax rates change.

SFAS No. 109 requires that when tax rates change, the changes are to be reflected in the accounting for deferred taxes when the legislation is enacted. This means that if, for example, the corporate income tax rates are increased in 2000, effective 2001, the effect of the change to the deferred tax liability and deferred tax assets is to be recorded in 2000. In the case of depreciation, perhaps the single largest cause of deferred taxes, this would mean higher deferred tax liabilities and, immediately, higher deferred tax expense.

Using this same example, if at the beginning of Year 3 the income tax rates were reduced to 30 percent, the changes (called *reversals*) in the accounting-tax differences at the new tax rate would yield a revised (and lower) deferred tax liability:

Year	Accounting-Tax Difference	Tax Rate	Deferred Tax Liability
3	$250	0.3	$75
4	250	0.3	75
	$500		$150

This change in the deferred tax liability and the related deferred tax benefit of $50 would be reflected in the first quarter of Year 3. At the end of Year 3, the deferred tax liability would be $75. The *net* deferred tax benefit for Year 3 is $125: $50 is the immediate benefit reflecting the effect of the lower income tax rate, and $75 reflects the Year 3 difference between accounting and tax depreciation—at the 30 percent rate.

The four-year summary table reflects exactly what will happen to Sample Company:

Accounting asset NBV	$750	$500	$250	$-0-
Tax asset NBV	500	-0-	-0-	-0-
Difference	$250	$500	$250	$-0-
Tax rate (during the year)	0.4	0.4	0.3	0.3
Deferred tax liability	$100	$200	$ 75	$-0-
Deferred tax expense (benefit)	100	100	(125)	(75)

In Years 3 and 4, the depreciation deductions on the tax return exceed the accounting depreciation expense. The deferred tax benefit adjusts for this difference, drawing down the balance in the deferred tax liability buffer. Year 3 also reflects the catch-up or adjustment to the deferred tax liability because of the changed tax rate. The impact of this catch-up is clearly seen in the revised income statements for Sample Company:

	Year 1	Year 2	Year 3	Year 4
Sales	$1,000	$1,000	$1,000	$1,000
Depreciation	250	250	250	250
All other expenses	400	400	400	400
Taxable income	350	350	350	350
Current income tax expense	40	40	180	180
Deferred income tax expense	100	100	-125	-75
Total income tax expense	140	140	55	105
Net income	210	210	295	245

The net income in Year 4 is higher than in years 1 and 2 because tax rates are lower. The Year 3 net income is even higher, by $50, because the tax rate was lowered before the deferred tax liability was reduced by the reversal of the accounting-tax depreciation charges. In effect, in Years 1 and 2, a total of $500 of taxable income was deferred by Sample Corporation into Years 3 and 4 when the tax rates were lower by 10 percent. This immediately saved $50 (0.10 × $500), which is reflected in Year 3, the year the tax rate changes were announced.

Deferred Tax Assets

No doubt the most controversial aspect of SFAS No. 109 is the valuation of deferred tax assets; in certain circumstances, the full amount of the deferred tax assets may *not* be included in the financial statements even though a company must include all deferred tax liabilities. For example, consider an event for which the expense deduction for tax purposes lagged behind the deduction for accounting purposes, as in the provision for warranty expenses. Diagrammatically,

---

The provision for warranty expenses for accounting purposes

---

leads to

A temporary accounting-tax difference in warranty liability book values

---

that leads to

A deferred tax asset and deferred income tax benefit

---

that leads to

Lower tax expense and higher accounting net income

This is just the mirror image of the accelerated depreciation example but with the reverse effect: The income tax expense is shown at a lower amount than the current income taxes payable, and accounting net income is higher.

The logic may be consistent, but the FASB concluded that permitting deferred tax *benefits* due to accounting-tax differences on liabilities (such as warranty reserves) could violate the principal of conservatism in that a company would have to assume that it would make profits in the future and therefore have to pay taxes and consequently actually have tax liabilities against which to offset its tax benefits. SFAS No. 109 prescribes that a *valuation allowance* be established if it is "more likely than not" that all or a portion of the deferred tax assets will *not* be realized. Such a valuation allowance is to be based upon management's judgment as to the likelihood of future taxable income. A firm with continuing losses and a real issue of "going concern" might need to establish a valuation allowance up to or equal to the amount of the deferred tax asset. In practice, deferred tax assets typically relate to

- Bad debt allowances.
- Inventory reserves.
- Restructuring reserves.
- Litigation reserves.

EXHIBIT 13C.1

Amgen, Inc.
Income Taxes

The provision for income taxes includes the following (in thousands):

	Years ended December 31,		
	1994	**1993**	**1992**
Current provision:			
Federal	$231,306	$165,822	$178,609
State	34,855	25,856	34,937
Total current provision	266,161	191,678	213,546
Deferred provision (benefit):			
Federal	516	19,723	(8,012)
State	1,927	6,394	—
Total deferred provision (benefit)	2,443	26,117	(8,012)
	$268,604	$217,795	$205,534

Deferred income taxes reflect the net tax effects of net operating loss carryforwards and temporary differences between the carrying amounts of assets and liabilities for financial reporting purposes and the amounts used for income tax purposes. Significant components of the Company's deferred tax assets and liabilities as of December 31, 1994 and 1993 are as follows (in thousands):

	December 31,	
	1994	**1993**
Deferred tax assets:		
Net operating loss carryforwards	$ 89,478	$ 3,913
Expense accruals	78,481	42,834
Fixed assets	17,018	7,280
Royalty obligation buyouts	11,772	12,936
State income taxes	9,499	6,501
Research collaboration expenses	8,033	7,865
Other	7,215	6,969
Total deferred tax assets	221,496	88,298
Valuation allowance	(79,497)	(17,805)
Net deferred tax assets	141,999	70,493
Deferred tax liabilities:		
Purchase of technology rights	(25,708)	(9,608)
Other	(5,649)	(1,948)
Total deferred tax liabilities	(31,357)	(11,556)
	$110,642	$58,937

The net change in the valuation allowance for deferred tax assets during the year ended December 31, 1994 was $61,692,000. This change primarily relates to the net operating loss carryforwards acquired through the purchase of Synergen (Note 2).

- Operating loss carryforwards.

- Capital loss and tax credit carryforwards.

- Postretirement employee benefit accruals.

When companies with a history of profits record valuation allowances, they are usually associated with

- Unique sources, such as foreign tax credits that must be matched with taxable income in a particular country.

- Jurisdictional issues, such as operating loss carryforwards in a particular state.

- Unique timing issues, such as reversal patterns on pensions and other postretirement benefits that might run 30 years or more.[1]

For example, Exhibit 13C.1 is the income taxes footnote of Amgen, Inc.'s 1994 annual report. On a consolidated basis, Amgen has paid well over half a billion dollars in taxes during the 1992–1994 time period, and yet the company has a valuation allowance of $79.5 million. As the last sentence in its footnote explains, most of this valuation is associated with net operating loss carryforwards of an acquisition, Synergen. Apparently, the $61.7 million loss carryforward at Synergen is not applicable to the rest of Amgen.

ASSIGNMENTS

13.1. Accounting for leases: the lessee.* SC Company leases an asset with a market value of $200,000 under conditions by which the company agrees to pay $47,479.28 each year for five years (assume annual payments at year-end). The agreement is noncancelable; five years is the expected economic life of the asset; there is no expected residual value to the asset. (Thus, the lease is to be capitalized.) The lease is executed on January 1, 1999.

Required:

a. What entry does the lessee make on January 1, 1999?

b. What entry does the lessee make at the end of 1999 to record the cash payment of $47,479.28?

c. For 1999, what expenses will be reflected on the income statement with respect to the lease?

d. How will the lease asset and liability items appear on the books as of January 1, 1999? 2000? 2001? 2002? 2003? 2004?

e. How much of the lease liability will appear as a current item in the balance sheet as of December 31, 1999? How much of the leased asset will appear as a current item on that date?

13.2. Accounting for leases: the lessor.* SC Company leased the asset referred to in 13.1 from AC Manufacturing Company. The cost of the asset that AC Manufacturing Company leases to SC Company is $150,000. (This is a sales-type lease.)

---

[1] T. R. Petree; G. J. Gregory; and R. J. Vitray, "Evaluating Deferred Tax Assets," *Journal of Accountancy,* March 1995, pp. 71–77.

Required:

a. What entry does the lessor make on January 1, 1999?

b. What entry does it make at the end of 1999 to record the cash received of $47,479.28? What other entry is required?

c. For the year 1999, what will be reflected on the income statement with respect to the lease?

d. What items will appear on the lessor's balance sheet as of December 31, 1999? 2000? 2001? 2002? 2003?

13.3. Accounting for leases.* Kenyon Auto Company owns land on which it can build a new showroom at a cost of $60,000. As an alternative, Kenyon can have Robbin Leasing Company build the showroom and Kenyon can lease it for $7,010 a year for 15 years, which is the estimated useful life of the building. Kenyon would pay all maintenance and insurance costs. The $7,010 a year will give Robbin an 8 percent return on its investment of $60,000. Lease payments would be made at the end of each year.

Required:

a. How should a lease of this type be classified, and why?

(1) By the lessee.

(2) By the lessor.

b. If Kenyon decides to lease the showroom from Robbin, what entry(ies) will Kenyon make in its books on January 2, 1999, the date the lease would begin?

c. If Kenyon decides to lease the showroom from Robbin, what entry(ies) will Kenyon make on its books on December 31, 1999, the end of the lease year and the company's fiscal year?

13.4. Deferred income taxes. The income tax footnote contained in the 1994 annual report for Curtiss-Wright Corporation (C-W) is presented next. Based on the information contained in it, answer the following questions:

a. How much income tax expense will C-W report in its income statement for 1994?

b. How much income tax for 1994 does C-W actually owe?

c. It appears that C-W's deferred income taxes are caused by a variety of factors. Explain why environmental cleanup is one of the causes and whether it was a benefit or a detriment to C-W in 1994.

---

* Copyright © 1988 by the Darden Graduate Business School Foundation, Charlottesville, VA. All rights reserved.

Curtiss-Wright Corp. and Subsidiaries

7. Income Taxes.

Effective January 1, 1993, the Corporation adopted SFAS No. 109, "Accounting for Income Taxes." It requires an asset and liability approach for financial accounting and reporting for deferred income taxes. Pursuant to SFAS No. 109, the Corporation recognized a net tax benefit of $5,861,000 in 1993 (of which $3,764,000 or $0.74 per share was recognized as a cumulative effect of changes in accounting principles), primarily from the utilization of its capital loss carryforward, and correspondingly recorded a valuation allowance to offset this deferred tax asset, based on management's assessment of the likely realization of future capital gain income. During 1994, the Corporation realized $1,697,000 of capital gain income resulting in a reduction to the valuation allowance of $594,000. An additional valuation of $193,000 was recorded for an unrealized loss on securities. The net valuation allowance decreased by $401,000. The Corporation had available, at December 31, 1994, net capital loss carryforwards of $11,110,000 and $3,940,000 that will expire on December 31, 1995 and December 31, 1997, respectively.

Earnings (loss) before income taxes and cumulative effect of changes in accounting principles for domestic and foreign operations are:

(In thousands)	1994	1993	1992
Domestic	$24,009	$(1,639)	$28,246
Foreign	4,748	2,969	4,471
Total	$28,757	$1,330	$32,717

The provisions for taxes on earnings before cumulative effect of changes in accounting principles consist of:

(In thousands)	1994	1993	1992
Federal income taxes currently payable	$4,755	$3,100	$11,367
Foreign income taxes currently payable	1,991	1,035	1,531
State and local income taxes currently payable	668	1,411	1,925
Deferred income taxes	1,603	(5,303)	(3,130)
Adjustment for deferred tax liability rate change	—	453	(663)
Federal income tax on net capital gains	594	367	998
Utilization of capital loss carryforward	(594)	(367)	(998)
Valuation allowance	193	3,586	—
	$9,210	$4,282	$11,030

The rates used in computing the provision for federal income taxes vary from the U.S. Federal statutory tax rate principally due to the following:

	1994	1993	1992
U. S. Federal statutory tax rate	35.0%	35.0%	34.0%
Add (deduct):			
Utilization of capital loss carryforward	(2.1)	(78.8)	(3.6)
Dividends received deduction and tax-exempt dividends	(1.9)	(85.9)	(0.3)
Increase (decrease) in deferred tax liability for change in tax rate	—	34.0	(2.0)
State and local taxes	2.3	106.1	5.9
Valuation allowance	0.7	269.7	—
All other	(2.0)	41.9	(0.3)
	32.0%	322.0%	33.7%

The components of the Corporation's deferred tax assets and liabilities at December 31 are as follows:

(In thousands)	1994	1993
Deferred tax assets:		
Environmental clean-up	$ 7,323	$ 8,688
Postretirement/employment benefits	3,912	3,632
Inventories	2,032	1,665
Facility closing costs	1,081	1,290
Legal matters	1,147	1,190
Net capital losses and tax carryforward	5,460	5,861
Other	4,158	4,460
Total deferred tax assets	25,113	26,786
Deferred tax liabilities:		
Pension	9,830	8,414
Depreciation	6,600	7,733
Contracts in progress	—	1,030
Other	1,465	1,220
Total deferred tax liabilities	17,895	18,397
Deferred tax asset valuation allowance	(5,460)	(5,861)
Net deferred tax assets	$(1,758)	$(2,528)

Deferred tax assets and liabilities are reflected on the Corporation's consolidated balance sheets as follows:

(In thousands)	1994	1993
Current deferred tax assets	$(8,204)	$(8,882)
Non-current deferred tax liabilities	6,446	6,354
Net deferred tax assets	$(1,758)	$(2,528)

Income tax payments of $7,586,000 were made in 1994, $10,491,000 in 1993, $18,100,000 in 1992.

13.5. Deferred income taxes. Target Corporation is to begin its operations on January 1, 1999. Pro forma income statements for the new corporation are shown below. No provision has been made for deferred taxes, but there is a temporary book-tax difference due to depreciation.

Required:

a. Use a 35 percent tax rate and complete (and correct if necessary) the preparation of these pro forma statements.

b. What will Target show on its balance sheet each year (1999–2003) for deferred taxes?

c. Can you explain the company's calculation of current income tax expense in 2001?

Target Corporation
(millions)

	1999	2000	2001	2002	2003
Sales	3,400	3,604	3,820	4,049	4,292
less: CGS	1,598	1,712	1,834	1,964	2,103
Gross margin	1,802	1,892	1,986	2,085	2,189
Operating costs	633	681	729	777	826
Depreciation expense*	325	330	337	343	356
Income before tax	844	881	920	965	1,007
Current income tax	195	239	296	346	391
Deferred income tax	?	?	?	?	?
Income tax expense	195	239	296	346	391
Net income	649	642	624	619	616
*Note					
Book depreciation	325	330	337	343	356
Tax depreciation	612	528	411	320	245
Book value—assets	980	978	1,012	1,114	1,099
Tax value—assets	693	493	453	578	674

13.6. Deferred income taxes. Suppose that Target Corporation were to revise its pro forma statements to include an accrual for estimated warranty expense (in addition to the effects of 13.5), but the recognition of these expenses would be delayed for tax purposes as follows:

	1999	2000	2001	2002	2003
Book warranty expense	112	132	137	128	119
Tax warranty expense	13	39	78	143	141

Required:

a. How would this affect the balance sheets? The income statements?

b. Would the balance sheets still balance?

13.7. Changing income tax rates. What would happen to the pro forma statements in 13.6. if, in 2001, Congress overrode the president's veto and raised the corporate income tax rate to 38 percent effective in 2000?

13.8. Pension accounting. It was December 31, 1995 and Mr. Joe Wadkin, controller of Schroeder-Price Manufacturing (SP), was at his desk organizing a pile of papers. He had just talked to his son Earl, about the impact of SFAS No. 87 on pension accounting and reporting. SP had just gone public the first of the year and found it now necessary to prepare financial statements in total conformity with U.S. GAAP.

Mr. Wadkin had overall responsibility for managing the pension fund. He had read several articles on SFAS No. 87 and was specifically interested in what actions he should take to insure his company's accounting was in line with the new pension standard.

Earl and Mr. Wadkin had decided that the following information was important:

1. The pension plan was established on January 1, 1988 but Mr. Wadkin had declared it retroactive to the start of the company on January 1, 1986.

2. Since the company was located in a small town, all 80 of the original employees still worked at SP. The assumption was made that all 80 would stay with the company until retirement and none would leave or die prior to retirement.

3. The average age of the employees was 24 when the company opened its doors.

4. The settlement rate was 8%, the expected rate of return on plan assets was 9%, and the 1995 actual return on the beginning of the year pension balance of $149,200 was 11%.

5. Retirement was mandatory at age 65 with benefits of $35 per month for every year of service paid for a period of 16 years to the retiree or a designated beneficiary.

6. The amount funded for 1995 was to be the same as the amount expensed, and the decision was made to adopt the pension accounting and reporting standards from SFAS No. 87 as of January 1, 1995.

Mr. Wadkin spent a few hours writing down some questions for Earl to answer the following day after the family's New Year's meal. He certainly hoped that Earl would be able to answer them.

Required:

a. What does the timeline look like for the company's pension plan?

b. What was the actuarial present value of the past service cost as of January 1, 1988, the date the plan was adopted?

c. Calculate the actuarial present value of the projected benefit obligation as of January 1, 1995.

d. Calculate the amount of the 1995 pension expense as follows:

    1. Service Cost

    2. Interest Cost

    3. Actual return on plan assets

    4. Actuarial adjustment to convert actual return on plan assets to expected return on plan assets

    5. Amortization of Transition amount

e. What is the total 1995 pension expense?

f. What is the amount of pension liability to be shown in the balance sheet assuming adoption of the "minimum liability" provision of SFAS No. 87?

g. What are six actuarial assumptions that are usually needed when determining the amount of annual pension expense? Were all of them needed for this plan? Why?

13.9. Pension disclosures.   The pension disclosures from Bethlehem Steel Corporation's 1994 annual report are reported in footnote H on the following page.

Required:

a. What was the total pension expense appearing in Bethlehem's income statement for 1994?

b. What do you consider to be the pension liability for Bethlehem as of the end of 1994? Explain.

c. What are the total pension assets as of the end of 1994? Do these assets exceed the total liability?

d. How much of this, if any, appears on the corporation's balance sheet?

e. Reference is made to a "minimum liability." How was that determined? Does it appear on the balance sheet? If so, where?

Bethlehem Steel

H. Postretirement Pension Benefits

We have noncontributory defined benefit pension plans which provide benefits for substantially all employees. Defined benefits are based on years of service and the five highest consecutive years of pensionable earnings during the last ten years prior to retirement or a minimum amount

based on years of service. We fund annually the amount required under ERISA minimum funding standards plus additional amounts as appropriate.

The following sets forth the plans' actuarial assumptions used and funded status at year end together with amounts recognized in our consolidated balance sheets:

	December 31	
(Dollars in millions)	1994	1993
Assumptions:		
Discount rate	9.0%	7.5%
Average rate of compensation increase	3.1%	2.9%
Actuarial present value of benefit obligations:		
Vested benefit obligation	$4,246.9	$4,816.4
Accumulated benefit obligation	4,392.9	4,979.4
Projected benefit obligation	4,578.8	5,208.6
Plan assets at fair value:		
Fixed income securities	1,758.6	1,955.0
Equity securities	1,371.4	1,232.2
Cash and marketable securities	145.8	178.6
Total plan assets	$3,275.8	$3,365.8
Projected benefit obligation in excess of plan assets	1,303.0	1,842.8
Unrecognized net loss	(82.1)	(289.7)
Remaining unrecognized net obligation resulting from adoption of Statement No. 87	(255.2)	(293.5)
Unrecognized prior service cost from plan amendments	(275.2)	(307.1)
Adjustment required to recognize minimum liability—Intangible asset liability"]—Additional paid-in capital (pre-tax) (Note L)	426.6	600.6
	—	60.5
Pension liability	$1,117.1	$1,613.6

The assumptions used in each year and the components of our annual pension cost are as follows:

(Dollars in millions)	1994	1993	1992
Assumptions:			
Return on plan assets	8.75%	9.50%	9.50%
Discount rate	7.50%	8.50%	8.50%
Pension cost:			
Service cost—benefits earned during the period $51.9	$ 39.3	$ 45.0	
Interest on projected benefit obligation	375.7	380.4	394.2
Return on plan assets—actual	60.3	(308.8)	(250.0)
—deferred	(365.3)	4.3	(62.2)
Amortization of initial net obligation	36.7	37.7	37.8
Amortization of unrecognized prior service cost from plan amendments	32.7	19.8	18.8
Total defined benefit plans	192.0	172.7	183.6
PBGC premiums, administration fees, etc.	11.1	10.9	5.1
Total cost	$ 203.1	$ 183.6	$ 188.7

13.10.   Health care and life insurance benefits. Footnote I of Bethlehem Steel Corporation's 1994 annual report is shown below.

Required:

a. What is the difference between the "pay-as-you-go" approach and the accrual basis? Will the new treatment be better for employees? For shareholders?

b. How much of these amounts appear in the company's balance sheet? Income statement?

c. How sensitive is the company's forecast for health care cost trends?

Bethlehem Steel

I. Postretirement Benefits Other Than Pensions

In addition to providing pension benefits, we currently provide health care and life insurance benefits for most retirees and their dependents.
Information regarding our plans' actuarial assumptions, funded status, and liability follows:

(Dollars in millions)	December 31	
	1994	1993
Assumptions:		
Discount rate	9.0%	7.5%
Trend rate—beginning	9.0%	9.0%
—ending (year 2000)	4.6%	4.6%
Accumulated postretirement benefit obligation:		
Retirees	$1,427.6	$1,506.7
Fully eligible active plan participants	99.7	126.8
Other active plan participants	160.4	236.1
Total	1,687.7	1,869.6
Plan assets at fair value:		
Fixed income securities	135.5	158.5
Accumulated postretirement benefit obligation in excess of plan assets	1,552.2	1,711.1
Unrecognized net gain (loss)	27.2	(130.5)
Total obligation	1,579.4	1,580.6
Current portion	(138.0)	(132.3)
Long-term obligation	$1,441.4	$1,448.3

The assumptions used in each year and the components of our postretirement benefit cost follow:

(Dollars in millions)	1994	1993	1992
Return on plan assets	8.75%	9.50%	9.50%
Discount rate	7.50%	8.50%	8.50%
Trend rate			
—beginning	9.00%	9.50%	9.50%
—ending (2000)	4.60%	5.50%	5.50%
Service cost	$ 11.1	$ 9.0	$ 9.0
Interest on accumulated postretirement benefit obligation	138.8	144.1	139.0
Return on plan assets—actual	4.7	(17.9)	(18.4)
—deferred	(17.6)	3.8	4.5
Total cost	$137.0	$139.0	$134.1

A 1 percent increase or decrease in the assumed health care trend rate would increase or decrease the accumulated postretirement benefit obligation by about $120 million and 1994 expense by about $20 million.

13.11. Deferred income taxes. Early in 1999, Strafford Corporation acquired a $100,000 asset that was to be depreciated on a straight-line basis for accounting purposes and on an accelerated basis for taxes according to the following schedules:

	Straight-Line	Accelerated
1999	$ 8,333	$ 16,667
2000	16,666	27,778
2001	16,667	18,519
2002	16,667	12,347
2003	16,667	8,230
2004	16,667	8,230
2005	8,333	8,230
	$100,000	$100,000

Required:

Prepare a schedule illustrating the annual deferred tax entries for each year associated with this asset. Use a 35 percent tax rate. When will the deferred income tax liability begin to reverse?

13.12. Leases. On January 2, 1996, Lion Metal Forming, Inc., entered a lease for a new 50-ton hydraulic press costing $75,000 and having an estimated life of eight years. The management of Lion Metal believes the new press will be much more efficient than equipment presently in use and that it will allow Lion Metal to manufacture certain items that it previously had to subcontract out. The noncancelable term of the lease is seven years, at which time the press is returned to the lessor. The residual value is expected to be minimal. Rental payments of $16,433 are due at the *end* of each year. All executory costs are to be paid directly by Lion Metal, which depreciates its fixed assets on the straight-line basis. Its incremental borrowing rate is 15 percent.

Required:

a. Calculate the lessor's implicit interest rate in the lease.

b. Why does this lease qualify as a *capital lease* to Lion Metal for financial reporting purposes?

c. For questions (c) and (d), assume the implicit rate is 12 percent. Prepare the entry that Lion Metal should make to record the lease on January 2, 1996.

d. What amounts (properly labeled) related to the lease will appear in Lion Metal's

    (1) Balance sheet as of December 31, 1996?

    (2) Income statement for the year ending December 31, 1996?

13.13. Retirement Benefits. The 1994 annual report of Warner Lambert contained three footnotes on retirement benefits that are reproduced here. Based on the information contained in the footnotes, answer the following pension-related questions:

a. Explain what is meant by a noncontributory plan. Are these plans defined benefit or defined contribution?

b. What is the total amount of Warner Lambert's pension expense shown in the company's 1994 income statement?

c. What is meant by

    (1) Vested benefit obligation?

    (2) Accumulated benefit obligation?

(3) Projected benefit obligation?

d. Why is one of the components of the pension cost the interest cost on the projected benefit obligation? How is the amount determined?

e. The actual return on plan assets has changed considerably from 1992 to 1994. Does this result in a very volatile annual pension expense figure for the defined-benefit plans? Explain.

f. Are Warner Lambert's defined-benefit pension plans overfunded as of 1994? How do you know?

Warner-Lambert

NOTE 12—PENSIONS:

The company has various noncontributory pension plans covering substantially all of its employees in the U.S. Benefits covering most employees are based on years of service and average compensation during the last years of employment. Current policy is to fund these plans in an amount that ranges from the minimum contribution required by ERISA to the maximum tax-deductible contribution. Certain foreign subsidiaries also have various plans, which are funded in accordance with the statutory requirements of the particular countries.

Pension costs for the plans included the following components:

	Years Ended December 31,		
	1994	1993	1992
Service cost—benefits earned during the year	$ 50.9	$ 44.9	$ 42.0
Interest cost on projected benefit obligation	134.3	130.1	122.6
Return on assets	(24.2)	(199.2)	(127.2)
Net amortization and deferral	(124.5)	59.4	(5.5)
Net pension expense	$ 36.5	$ 35.2	$ 31.9

Net pension expense attributable to foreign plans and included in the above was $21.4, $17.9 and $18.2 in 1994, 1993 and 1992, respectively.

The 1993 restructuring charge, discussed in Note 3, included a $4.6 curtailment loss representing a decrease in unrecognized prior service costs resulting from a reduction in domestic plan participants.

The plans' funded status at December 31 was as follows:

	Plans in Which Assets Exceed Accumulated Benefits		Plans in Which Accumulated Benefits Exceed Assets	
	1994	1993	1994	1993
Plan assets at fair value	$1,583.9	$1,605.9	$ 70.5	$ 80.6
Actuarial present value of accumulated benefit obligation:				
Vested	1,421.5	1,464.9	140.3	141.6
Nonvested	45.4	30.3	9.4	10.4
	1,466.9	1,495.2	149.7	152.0
Estimated future salary increases	138.5	171.5	27.6	35.7
Projected benefit obligation	1,605.4	1,666.7	177.3	187.7
Excess of projected benefit obligation over plan assets	(21.5)	(60.8)	(106.8)	(107.1)
Unrecognized net (asset) obligation	(22.0)	(38.1)	7.2	7.8
Unrecognized prior service cost	36.2	41.8	2.7	3.0
Unrecognized net actuarial loss	150.8	208.5	21.5	28.7
Minimum liability adjustment	—	—	(18.6)	(19.0)
Net pension asset (liability) included in consolidated balance sheets	$ 143.5	$ 151.4	$ (94.0)	$ (86.6)

continued

Plan assets are composed primarily of investments in equities and bonds.

Foreign plan assets at fair value included in the preceding table were $570.1 in 1994 and $524.1 in 1993. The foreign plan projected benefit obligation was $596.4 in 1994 and $536.2 in 1993.

The assumptions for the U.S. plans were:

	Years Ended December 31,		
	1994	1993	1992
Expected long-term rate of return on plan assets	**10.5%**	10.5%	10.5%
Expected increase in salary levels	**4.0**	4.0	5.0
Weighted average discount rate	**8.8**	7.5	8.8

Assumptions for foreign plans did not vary significantly from the U.S. plans.

NOTE 13—POSTEMPLOYMENT BENEFITS:

The company adopted the provisions of SFAS No. 112, "Employers' Accounting for Postemployment Benefits," effective January 1, 1993. This accounting change resulted in a cumulative effect adjustment which decreased net income upon adoption by $17.0 ($27.0 pretax) or $0.13 per share. SFAS No. 112 requires employers to recognize an obligation for postemployment benefits to former or inactive employees after employment but before retirement. This one-time charge primarily represented the present value of medical and life insurance costs for employees receiving long-term disability benefits.

NOTE 14—OTHER POSTRETIREMENT BENEFITS:

The company provides other postretirement benefits, primarily health insurance, for domestic employees who retired prior to January 1, 1992 and their dependents. Although the plans are currently noncontributory, the company has implemented a cap which limits future contributions for medical and dental coverage under these plans. The company is generally self-insured for these costs and the plans are funded on a pay-as-you-go basis. Domestic employees retiring after December 31, 1991 will receive additional pension benefits based on years of service in lieu of these benefits.

The annual cost of providing other postretirement benefits for domestic retirees amounted to $15.0, $14.0 and $13.4 in 1994, 1993 and 1992, respectively. These amounts primarily represent the accrual of interest on the present value obligation.

A reconciliation from the plans' benefit obligation to the liabilities recognized in the consolidated balance sheets as of the latest actuarial valuations was as follows:

	December 31,	
	1994	1993
Accumulated postretirement benefit obligation	**$179.3**	$180.2
Unrecognized prior service cost	**1.8**	2.0
Unrecognized net actuarial loss	**(49.4)**	(45.9)
Accrued postretirement benefit cost recognized in the consolidated balance sheets	**$131.7**	$136.3

The health care cost trend rate used to develop the accumulated postretirement benefit obligation for those retirees under age 65 was 12.3 percent in 1994 declining to 6 percent over 12 years. For those 65 and over, a rate of 8 percent was used in 1994 declining to 6 percent over 7 years. A one percentage point increase in the health care cost trend rate in each year would increase the accumulated postretirement benefit obligation as of December 31, 1994 by $5.8 and the interest cost component of the postretirement benefit cost for 1994 by $0.5. The weighted average discount rate used to develop the accumulated postretirement benefit obligation was 8.8 percent, 7.5 percent and 8.8 percent for 1994, 1993, and 1992, respectively.

Other postretirement benefit costs for foreign plans expensed under the cash method in 1994, 1993 and 1992 were not material.

13.14. Pensions. Footnote 13 is taken from the 1997 annual report of Johnson & Johnson (J&J).

a. Which, if any, of these amounts would appear in J&J's:

    1. Income Statement?

    2. Balance Sheet?

    3. Statement of Cash Flows?

(Note: When we say "appear," it means that the specific item would be included in revenues or expenses (income statement); assets, liabilities or equity (balance sheet); or, sources or uses of cash (statement of cash flows) even if they have been aggregated under some other account title.)

b. What decisions does the management of J&J make concerning the accounting for pensions? What, if any, impact do these decisions have on:

    1. Income Statement?

    2. Balance Sheet?

    3. Statement of Cash Flows?

c. Are J&J's pensions "over-funded" or "underfunded"? Please explain.

d. What is the item "Book reserves (prepaids):" under the Domestic, 1997 column (the amount is $322 million). Is this the result of any management decision?

e. Why is it that in the table that explains "Net periodic pension cost" (the first table in footnote 13), the item labeled "Net amortization and deferral" is $304 million and $175 million in 1997 and 1996, but $310 million in 1995? Any guess on what it'll be in 1998?

f. Has the management of J&J been conservative or aggressive with respect to its handling of pensions? What tells you that?

13 Retirement and Pension Plans

The Company sponsors various retirement and pension plans, including defined benefit, defined contribution and termination indemnity plans, which cover most employees worldwide.

Plan benefits are primarily based on the employee's compensation during the last three to five years before retirement and the number of years of service. The Company's objective in funding its domestic plans is to accumulate funds sufficient to provide for all accrued benefits. International subsidiaries have plans under which funds are deposited with trustees, annuities are purchased under group contracts, or reserves are provided.

In certain countries other than the United States, the funding of pension plans is not a common practice as funding provides no economic benefit. Consequently, the Company has several pension plans which are not funded.

Net pension expense for the Company's defined benefit plans for 1997, 1996 and 1995 included the following components:

(Dollars in Millions)	1997	1996	1995
Service cost for benefits earned during period	$ 166	159	121
Interest cost on projected benefit obligations	239	230	207
Actual return on plan assets	(576)	(403)	(555)
Net amortization and deferral	304	175	310
Curtailment and settlement losses (gains)	1	–	25
Net periodic pension cost	$ 134	161	108

The net periodic pension cost attributable to domestic plans and included above was $50 million in 1997, $84 million in 1996 and $43 million in 1995.

The following tables provide the domestic assumptions and the range of international assumptions, which are based on the economic environment of each applicable country, used to develop net periodic pension cost and the actuarial present value of projected benefit obligations:

Domestic Pension Plans	1997	1996	1995
Expected long-term rate of return on plan assets	9.0%	9.0%	9.0%
Weighted average discount rate	7.25	7.75	7.25
Rate of increase in compensation levels	5.0	5.5	5.5

International Pension Plans	1997	1996	1995
Expected long-term rate of return on plan assets	5.0 – 9.5%	5.0 – 10.0%	5.0 – 10.0%
Weighted average discount rates	4.0 – 8.0	4.0 – 8.5	4.25 – 9.5
Rate of increase in compensation levels	3.0 – 5.5	3.0 – 6.5	3.0 – 7.0

The following table sets forth the actuarial present value of benefit obligations and funded status at year-end 1997 and 1996 for the Company's defined benefit plans:

(Dollars in Millions)	Year-end 1997 Domestic	Year-end 1997 International Over-funded	Year-end 1997 International Under-funded	Year-end 1996 Domestic	Year-end 1996 International Over-funded	Year-end 1996 International Under-funded
Plan assets at fair value, primarily stocks and bonds	$2,454	1,127	113	2,195	1,043	92
Book reserves (prepaids)	322	(58)	253	284	(82)	256
Total assets and reserves	2,776	1,069	366	2,479	961	348
Actuarial present value of benefit obligations:						
Vested benefits	1,971	703	252	1,723	666	254
Nonvested benefits	55	25	59	52	26	49
Accumulated benefit obligation	2,026	728	311	1,775	692	303
Effect of projected future salary increases	346	218	75	338	224	80
Projected benefit obligation	2,372	946	386	2,113	916	383
Assets and reserves in excess of (less than) projected benefit obligation	$ 404	123	(20)	366	45	(35)
Components of assets and reserves in excess of (less than) projected benefit obligation:						
Unrecognized prior service cost	$ (51)	(35)	(16)	(45)	(34)	(16)
Unrecognized net gain (loss)	438	99	6	387	10	(6)
Unamortized net transition assets (liabilities)	10	59	(18)	16	69	(17)
Additional minimum liability	7	—	8	8	—	4
Total	$ 404	123	(20)	366	45	(35)
Assets and reserves in excess of accumulated benefit obligation	$ 750	341	55	704	269	45

13.15. Income Taxes. IBM included the following in its 1994 annual report:

The significant components of deferred tax assets and liabilities included on the balance sheet were as follows:

	At December 31	
(Dollars in millions)	1994	1993*
Deferred Tax Assets		
Retiree medical benefits	$ 2,500	$ 1,961
Restructuring charges	2,446	5,253
Capitalized R&D	2,057	1,739
Foreign tax credits	1,380	885
Alternative minimum tax credits	738	729
Inventory	633	621
Foreign tax loss carryforwards	469	989
Doubtful accounts	453	480
General business credits	452	452
Equity alliances	445	309
State and local tax loss carryforwards	370	566
Employee benefits	363	480
Intracompany sales and services	357	440
Depreciation	249	234
U.S. federal tax loss carryforwards	230	1,093
Warranty	163	125
Retirement benefits	127	124
Software income deferred	78	186
Other	2,685	2,521
Gross deferred tax assets	16,195	19,187
Less: Valuation allowance	4,551	5,035
Total deferred tax assets	$11,644	$14,152
Deferred Tax Liabilities		
Sales-type leases	$ 2,862	$ 3,118
Depreciation	1,653	1,537
Software costs deferred	1,283	1,824
Retirement benefits	1,061	1,069
Other	823	1,379
Gross deferred tax liabilities	$ 7,682	$ 8,927

* Reclassified to conform with 1994 presentation.

The valuation allowance applies to U.S. federal tax credit and net operating loss carryforwards, state and local net deferred tax assets and net operating loss carryforwards, and net operating losses in certain foreign jurisdictions that may expire before the company can utilize them. The net change in the total valuation allowance for the year ended December 31, 1994, was a decrease of $484 million.

Explain each of the lines in this figure. What is the impact, if any, of these figures on the income, assets, owners' equity, and cash flow of the company?

Owners' Equity

─────────

It seems to me that the realities of stock options can be summarized quite simply. If options aren't a form of compensation, what are they? If compensation isn't an expense, what is it? And, if expenses shouldn't go into the calculation of earnings, where in the world should they go?[1]

─────────────── **Key Chapter Issues** ───────────────

- What is owners' equity and how does a company acquire it?
- What difference does it make if an organization is legally a proprietorship or partnership rather than a corporation?
- What happens when a company sells new shares of its common stock? What happens when it buys some of them back?
- What is par value? What happens if new shares are issued at prices that exceed par value?

- What is the difference between common stock and treasury stock? What is preferred stock?
- How do cash dividends, stock dividends, and stock splits affect owners' equity?
- What are stock options and why are they so controversial? How does the accounting for stock options affect owners' equity?
- Some corporations include a foreign currency translation adjustment in owners' equity. What is this, and why is it in owners' equity?

[1] Warren Buffett's chairman's letter from the 1992 Berkshire Hathaway Inc. annual report.

A ccording to the basic accounting equation (A = L + OE), owners' equity is simply the difference between a company's assets and its liabilities. It is the amount that would be left over if the assets were liquidated at their book values and the liabilities were then paid off. Owners' equity is also sometimes referred to as the **net worth** or the *net book value* of a company. However, owners' equity can also be considered on its own terms—as one of the three elements of the accounting equation—rather than only the residual of assets minus liabilities.

Owners' equity usually takes two principal forms: **contributed capital,** as represented by the capital stock of a company, and **retained capital,** as represented by the cumulative retained earnings of a company. For many companies, transactions involving the owners' equity accounts are simple and straightforward. In fact, some publicly held companies bypass the presentation of a formal statement of owners' equity and provide what little detail might be of interest to financial statement users as a footnote or as part of the income statement. To a very large degree, the owners' equity accounts are of more interest to attorneys than to management because the attorneys are responsible for a company's legal status and because many of the transactions in the owners' equity accounts have to do with a company's legal life. However, the owners' equity accounts are always of interest to a company's shareholders because these accounts measure the shareholders' residual interest in the net assets of the company. For this reason, owners' equity is also sometimes called *shareholders' equity.*

In the first section of this chapter we consider the various ways in which a company can be legally organized and explore some of the activities common to the corporate form of organization. In the second section we examine some of the most common transactions affecting the owners' equity accounts, the accounting entries that are required, and the financial statement presentation that is conventionally followed. In the final section we illustrate the typical owners' equity disclosures using data from IBM's annual report.

THE FORM OF A BUSINESS

Business entities are organized in different ways, and the differences are important. A business can be a proprietorship, a partnership, or a corporation, depending on the legal structure of the entity's ownership.

Many small businesses are organized as proprietorships or partnerships because both types are relatively simple and inexpensive to form. To establish a proprietorship, one simply obtains the required permits to do business from a local or state governmental agency. The same is true for a partnership except that, in addition, the partners typically execute a written contract among themselves detailing the terms of their financial arrangements. The desirability of having a written agreement is as great for a two-person partnership as it is for partnerships composed of hundreds of partners. Some of the items usually detailed in a partnership agreement include the amount of each partner's investment, the rights of partners to withdraw funds, the manner in which profits and losses are to be divided, and the procedure to be followed in admitting a new partner.

The Partnership

We can make some general statements about **partnerships** (and proprietorships) that flow in part from the legal characteristics accorded to partnerships and in part from the way businesspeople have applied these legal forms in practice:

- *Limited ownership:* As a practical matter, most partnerships have relatively few partners.

- *Owners as managers:* The partners frequently manage the business.

- *Mutual agency:* Each partner, acting within the scope of reasonable partnership activities, acts as an agent for the business entity, and any single partner may act on behalf of all the other partners.

- *Unlimited liability:* Ordinarily, each partner is personally liable for all of the debts of the partnership.

- *Division of profit and loss:* Partnership profits and losses may be divided in whatever manner the individual partners agree.

- *Withdrawal of resources:* Unless the partners agree otherwise, they may withdraw resources from the business in an amount equal to their total investment in the partnership any time they wish to do so.

- *Limited life:* Unless the partners agree otherwise, the death or withdrawal of a partner automatically dissolves a partnership.

- *Taxes:* The partnership itself is not subject to income tax. Income earned (or a loss incurred) by the partnership is taxable income for the partners, whether or not it is distributed. This requirement is sometimes an advantage (as in the early years of a real estate partnership when depreciation generates large tax losses) and sometimes a disadvantage (as in the early years of a growing company that generates earnings but must retain the operating cash flow for reinvestment).

The Corporation

The creation of a corporation is a more complex legal procedure than the creation of a partnership or a proprietorship. The incorporators (the initial shareholders) must first apply to a state commission, requesting permission to form a corporation. When a state agency grants that permission, a new entity comes into being. The newly incorporated entity's **charter of incorporation** thereby creates a legal entity that can sell shares to stockholders, own property, borrow money and incur obligations, and sue and be sued, all in its own name independently of its owners.

Again, we can make some general statements about the operations of corporations, in part because of their legal characteristics and in part because of the way corporate life has evolved in practice:

- *Diverse ownership:* The owners of a corporation are called *stockholders* or *shareholders,* and ownership in a corporation is evidenced by shares of capital stock. The number of stockholders a corporation may have is not limited. In most states, a corporation can be formed with just a few stockholders. On the other hand, a corporation may be owned by a very large number of stockholders (General Motors' shares were owned by more than a million investors in December, 1999), and the shares may be traded in a public market like the New York Stock Exchange. The stock of a corporation may be held by individuals, mutual funds, or other corporations.

- *Separation of ownership and management:* The management of public corporations often owns only a small percentage (or none) of the company.

- *Limited liability:* As a separate legal entity, a corporation is responsible for its own debts. Stockholders are not personally liable for a corporation's debts, and the maximum financial loss that stockholders can incur is the amount of their investment in the corporation.

- *Withdrawal of resources:* Stockholders are entitled to withdraw resources from a corporation only in the form of dividends and only after the board of directors has authorized a dividend payment. Dividends are paid to all stockholders in proportion to their ownership of the corporation, unless otherwise provided in the stock agreement.

- *Transferability of ownership:* Stockholders may buy and sell shares of capital stock in a corporation without interfering with the activities or the life of the corporation whose shares they are buying. Most of the millions of shares that are traded daily on stock exchanges represent private transactions between independent buyers and sellers. The activities of the corporations themselves are unaffected by such transactions.

- *Government regulation:* Although a corporation exists as a result of a charter granted by a governmental agency, no significant legal implications flow from the chartering process. For instance, no charter requires any corporation to prepare financial statements or file annual reports. A publicly held corporation—that is, one with more than 500 stockholders and more than $5 million in assets—is subject to federal securities laws by virtue of the public distribution of its stock. It must register its stock with the U.S. Securities and Exchange Commission; and the SEC's regulations *do* impose significant legal obligations on the corporation, including the periodic public distribution of financial statements.

- *Taxes:* As separate legal entities, corporations pay federal and state income taxes on their earnings. When any part of these earnings is subsequently distributed to stockholders in the form of dividends, the stockholders also pay income taxes on the amount of dividends received. This separation of entity and ownership results in double taxation.[2]

A Glimpse of Corporate Life

Typically, individual stockholders have very little say in the management of the company they own. Small stockholders "vote with their feet," selling their stock if they conclude that the company is not progressing and prospering. Major stockholders can be more assertive and use their voting rights to elect a board of directors to represent them. In most companies, the board of directors is responsible for the corporation's overall direction. The board of directors elects and oversees the corporate officers who are directly responsible for the day-to-day management of the corporation. The officers usually include a president, vice president, secretary, and treasurer.

The officers report periodically to the board of directors and at least once a year to the shareholders. The officers usually present a business plan for the board's approval and request the board's advice and concurrence regarding major decisions. The board members, on the other hand, prepare employment agreements for the officers and generally monitor their progress in moving the company forward according to the approved business plan. Board members and officers have significant legal obligations, as fiduciaries, to work in the best interests of a company's stockholders.

Corporations typically hold an annual meeting of stockholders subsequent to the end of each fiscal year. A **fiscal year** is the 12-month period a corporation selects as its accounting year; it may or may not be the calendar year. The annual meeting is held for purposes such

---

[2] Under certain conditions specified by the Internal Revenue Code, U.S. corporations with no more than 35 shareholders may elect to be treated as a partnership for tax purposes and thus pay no corporate income tax. Instead, the owners of these companies, called *S corporations,* pay personal income taxes on their respective share of the business's earnings regardless of whether the earnings are actually withdrawn from the business.

as reviewing the past year's performance; discussing business, economic, and political issues of importance to the corporation; selecting an independent auditor; electing directors; and voting on any other business that requires stockholder ratification. The board of directors also decides—depending on the corporation's earnings' history, expectations for the future, cash position and needs, and (last but not least) expectations of the stock market—how much of the corporation's earnings should be paid out as dividends.

Even though corporate stock can be bought and sold without affecting the company, corporations must keep track of stockholder transactions to know who is entitled to receive dividends and who is entitled to vote at shareholder meetings. A small corporation can keep track of its stockholders relatively easily because it has few transactions involving the stock. For a large, publicly held company, however, keeping track of its stockholders is very difficult because its shares trade in large volumes every day on the public stock exchanges. In fact, many corporations engage the services of a transfer agent and registrar to record stockholder transactions, cancel old stock certificates, issue new ones, and maintain a current record of stockholders and the number of shares each owns. Transfer agents and registrars are usually banks or trust companies.

Publicly held companies whose stock is registered with the SEC must publish quarterly and annual reports for use by stockholders and other interested parties. These reports generally include status reports on a company's progress, from both the chairperson of the board and the president, and financial statements for the period. The financial statements in the annual report are accompanied by a report from an independent accounting firm, stating the accountants' opinion as to whether the financial statements are presented fairly, in all material respects, in conformity with generally accepted accounting principles. Similar, but not identical, requirements exist in other countries where, for example, Japanese public corporations must file financial statements with the Ministry of Finance and Brazilian corporations must file with the Comissao de Valores Mobiliários.

OWNERS' EQUITY TRANSACTIONS

The most common transactions affecting the owners' equity accounts include the recognition of revenue and expenses for the year (which result in net income), the payment of dividends, and the sale or repurchase of capital stock.

Sales of Stock

A corporation may sell stock to new stockholders or to its existing stockholders. Those stock sales are recorded in the owners' equity account at the net cash (or other consideration) that the company receives for the stock sold. For example, the journal entry might appear as:

```
Dr. Cash (A) . . . . . . . . . . . . . . . . . . . . . . (inc.) 50,000
    Cr. Capital Stock, at Par Value (OE) . . . . . . . . . . .      (inc.)  1,000
    Cr. Paid-In-Capital in Excess of Par Value (OE) . . . .      (inc.) 49,000
```

Note that if the sale price of the stock exceeds the *par* (or *stated*) value of the purchased shares, the excess is recorded in the Paid-In-Capital in Excess of Par Value account. Thus, the sum of the Capital Stock account and the Paid-In-Capital in Excess of Par Value account represents the aggregate contributed capital of a company.

As noted earlier in this text, par value (and stated value) is a legal value required by some state incorporation commissions. Originally, it was meant to be the minimum capital required to be contributed to, and maintained in, a company by the stockholders. That concept has eroded in practice, however, and today the concept has very little practical significance. Nonetheless, most financial statements continue to distinguish between par value and paid-in capital in excess of par value.

Most often, stock is issued for cash and so the value received in the exchange for the shares of stock is easy to determine. However, companies sometimes exchange their stock for other forms of assets, including the stock or bonds of another corporation. In these exchanges, the total capital received (and, in turn, the assets received) are valued at the market value of the stock issued or the asset received, whichever provides the most reliable measure of value. When shares of stock are actively traded, the per share market price from those trades is usually considered the most reliable measure of the value involved in a swap of stock for other forms of assets. When the stock is not actively traded, the transaction may have to be valued at the value of the assets exchanged.

Every corporation issues **common stock** as its basic equity security. But it is also possible to raise capital by selling other equity securities with special terms. **Preferred stock,** for example, is an equity security with some of the characteristics of a bond. Preferred stocks usually carry a specific dividend rate, stated as an amount per share or as a percentage of its par value. A preferred stock is "preferred" in that its dividend requirements have a first claim on a company's earnings before any claims of the common shareholders. Thus, in the event that earnings are limited, the preferred shareholders must receive their full dividend before common shareholders receive any. Should a company be liquidated, the preferred stockholders are entitled to secure the par value of their shares before any distribution is made to the common stockholders.

A preferred stock may also be **cumulative;** that is, its dividend preferences accumulate year to year even if the company has not earned enough to pay the dividend in any one year.[3] Preferred stock may be **participating** in that it may share in a company's earnings in excess of its stated dividend requirements, along with the common stock. It may also be **convertible** into a stated number of common shares. Finally, it may be **callable** in that a company may have the right to call the security for redemption, usually at a premium above the stated or par value of the stock.

Class B common stock usually has the same provisions as a company's regular common stock regarding liquidation and dividend rights, but it may have disproportionate (usually lower) voting rights. For example, in some companies, the class B stock carries only one-tenth the voting power of a company's class A common stock. In many cases the class B stock is traded publicly, but the class A stock can be exchanged only between members of the company's founding family. Class B stocks are very popular with European companies who do not want to dilute home-country ownership and thus the Class B stock is used in the foreign equity markets where they seek to raise capital. Class B stocks have also become popular in the U.S. as a defense mechanism against hostile takeovers.

---

[3] Unpaid accumulated dividends are called **dividends in arrears,** and although not representing a liability of a company until the dividends are declared, they must be disclosed in the footnotes to the financial statements.

The terminology used to describe equity accounts in other countries is somewhat different. In the United Kingdom and other Commonwealth nations (such as Canada and Australia), the terms are as follows:

United States	Commonwealth Nations
Common Stock	Ordinary Share or Called-up Share Capital
Preferred Stock	Preference Share
Paid-in Capital in Excess of Par Value	Share Premium
Retained Earnings	Profit and Loss Account

It is also not uncommon to find accounts termed "reserves" in the equity sections in the United Kingdom, Japan, Sweden, Germany, and other countries. Typically these reserves pertain to foreign currency translation adjustments, provisions for goodwill, legal reserves required by law, accruals for future expected expenses, and/or asset write-up revaluations.

For example, the equity section of the balance sheet in Carlton Communications' annual report is as follows:

£M	19X1	19X2
Capital and reserves		
Called-up share capital	18,190	18,143
Share premium account	7,880	3,228
Revaluation reserve	2,346	11,977
Other reserves	30,659	40,214
Profit and loss account	365,658	309,730
Total	424,733	383,292

Carlton Communications is a U.K.-based telecommunications company. The "other reserves" item for this company is primarily related to requirements under the Companies Act of 1985 and the former British practice of charging goodwill, in total, to owners' equity.

Retained Earnings Transactions: Net Income

As we saw in Chapter 3, revenue and expense-producing transactions affect many balance sheet accounts—cash, accounts receivable, inventory, fixed assets, liabilities—but ultimately, the effects of these transactions are recorded in the Retained Earnings account. It may be useful at this point to recall the relationship between the balance sheet and the income statement. As the following chart (from Chapter 2) depicts, these two statements are linked by the Retained Earnings account:

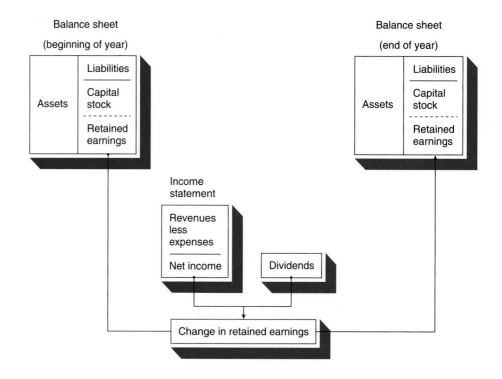

The net income for the period, less any dividends declared, is added to the Retained Earnings account on the balance sheet. This addition reflects the shareholders' increasing ownership interest in the net worth of the company.

Retained Earnings Transactions: Dividends

After net income, the second most common entry to the Retained Earnings account is the payment of dividends. We have said this several times, but it is worth repeating—dividends are a distribution of a company's income to its shareholders but are not an expense of the business. The accounting entry to record a $5,000 cash dividend on the **date of declaration** by the board of directors looks like this:

Dr. Retained Earnings (OE) . . . . (dec.) 5,000
    Cr. Dividends Payable (L) . . . .   (inc.) 5,000

and on the **date of payment**,[4] it looks like this:

Dr. Dividends Payable (L) . . . . (dec.) 5,000
    Cr. Cash (A) . . . .   (dec.) 5,000

---

[4] Technically, the entry recording the declaration of a $5,000 cash dividend is

Dr. Dividends Declared (COE) . . . . (inc.) 5,000
    Cr. Dividends Payable (L) . . . .   (inc.) 5,000

and at the end of the accounting period, before preparation of the financial statements, Dividends Declared is then closed against the Retained Earnings account.

To be entitled to receive a dividend, a shareholder must own the stock on the **date of record,** which is set by the board of directors. For example, on January 29, 1999 Exxon Corp. declared a $0.75 quarterly dividend payable March 12, 1999 to shareholders *of record* as of February 12, 1999.

Typically, dividends are paid in cash. Growth-oriented companies that have strategically important places to invest their cash, however, may pay a **stock dividend** instead. The shareholders—who now own a few more shares than they did before the stock dividend—can then ride along with a company's expected growth, or they can liquidate part of their shareholdings by selling the stock dividend and converting it to cash. The accounting entry for a stock dividend is conceptually the same as for a cash dividend, except that the credit portion of the entry is an increase in common stock rather than a decrease in cash. The dollar value of the entry is measured by the fair market price of the stock issued at the date the dividend was declared:

```
Dr. Stock Dividends Declared (OE). . . . . . . (dec.) 5,000
    Cr. Capital Stock, at Par Value (OE) . . . . . . . . . . . .     (inc.)   500
    Cr. Paid-in-Capital in Excess of Par Value (OE)  . . . .     (inc.) 4,500
```

(This entry assumes that the fair market value of the shares issued was $5,000 and that the par value was $500.) As with a cash dividend, the Stock Dividend Declared account must be closed to Retained Earnings at the end of the accounting period and thus has the effect of transferring a portion of retained earnings to the capital stock accounts.

Stock Splits versus Stock Dividends

A company may "split" its stock for any number of reasons, but most often it is to reduce the market value of each share. The theory supporting a stock split is that investors will be more interested in a stock with a current market value of $25 than in one with a current market value of $100. Ordinarily, no journal entry is required for a stock split, although the number of shares outstanding increases and the par value (or stated value) of each share decreases proportionately. In a 2-for-1 stock split, for example, the number of shares outstanding doubles and the par value is halved, leaving the aggregate value of owners' equity unchanged. A **stock split** is, quite simply, a pro rata issuance of new shares to all existing shareholders.[5]

Sometimes a stock split is accounted for without changing a stock's par value. For example, in 1990, PepsiCo declared a 3-for-1 stock split. PepsiCo did not change the par value ($0.0167) of its capital stock but transferred an amount equal to the total par value of the new shares from the Capital in Excess of Par Value account to the Capital Stock account.

The economic substance of a stock split is not very different from that of a stock dividend; however, the accounting implications are quite different. Note that a stock dividend transfers some part of a company's retained earnings to the capital stock accounts whereas (usually) the accounting for a split simply reallocates the paid-in capital over a larger number of shares. That theoretical accounting difference is perhaps justifiable when a split is large—2 for 1 or 4 for 1. That difference is less justifiable, however, with a smaller split. In fact, the American and New York Stock exchanges have adopted reporting rules that have become general practice. They have said that a stock split is any distribution of stock in *excess* of 25 percent of the previously outstanding shares, whereas a distribution of *less* than 25 percent is always considered a stock dividend. Thus, for example, under these stock

---

[5] A stock split may be either a *forward* split or a *reverse* split. A forward split increases the number of shares outstanding; a reverse split reduces the number of shares outstanding.

exchange rules, a stock distribution equal to 10 percent of the previously outstanding shares must be accounted for as a stock dividend even if it is legally described as a stock split. In that situation, the fair market value of the newly distributed shares is transferred from retained earnings to the capital accounts.

Microsoft Corporation presents a good example of the effect of a stock split. In its 1997 annual report, the company reported the following:

Shares of common stock outstanding were as follows (in millions):

Year ending June 30	1996	1997
Balance, beginning of year	1,176	1,194
Issued	44	47
Repurchased	(26)	(37)
Balance, end of year	1,194	1,204

Microsoft claimed that 1,204 million common shares were outstanding as of the end of their fiscal year, June 30, 1997. In the 1998 annual report, however, the company reported:

Shares of common stock outstanding were as follows:

Year ending June 30	1997	1998
Balance, beginning of year	2,388	2,408
Issued	94	101
Repurchased	(74)	(39)
Balance, end of year	2,408	2,470

Note that the company now claimed that the number of shares outstanding at June 30, 1997 was 2,408 million.

How can this be? The answer is a two-for -one stock split, announced in February, 1998. The effect was to double the number of shares outstanding and probably halve the stock price. To insure that the company's financial data is presented on a comparable basis across time, the previous 1997 statements were recast to reflect the effect of the split.

Many countries make no distinction between stock splits and stock dividends. They simply appear under a heading such as "free share distribution" or a similar title. For example, ISCOR, the South African Steel Company, reported the following in its 1994 annual report:

> As was the case at the interim when a capitalisation share award was declared in the ratio of 1,2 new fully paid ordinary shares of R1 each in Iscor for every 100 ordinary shares, the directors again elected the allocation of a final capitalisation share award, in order to preserve cash resources.

Essentially, the company declared a 1.2 percent stock dividend on their one Rand par value common stock. (Note that in many countries the use of the comma and the decimal point to delineate thousands and fractional amounts is reversed. While we might write 132,843.12 in the United States, the same amount might appear as 132.843,12 in many other countries. That is one reason why Americans are often confused when they see a tag reading 73.035,50 hanging on a T-shirt in Florence.)

Treasury Stock Transactions

In the United States, companies may, at the discretion of management, buy back a proportion of their own outstanding stock. A company may, for example, repurchase its own stock because it has commitments for future issuances of stock to satisfy various stock options, stock warrants, or convertible securities (to be discussed shortly). Or a company may reacquire some of its own shares because it has excess cash and because the board of directors believes that the company's own stock represents the best investment opportunity for that cash. A company may also buy some of its outstanding shares because management believes that the current market price of the stock is too low, and it hopes to bolster that price by reducing the supply of available shares.

If the reacquired shares are to be held and reissued sometime in the future, they are accounted for in a contra-owners' equity account titled **Treasury Stock.** The reacquired shares are usually recorded in the Treasury Stock account at the cost paid to repurchase the shares:

> Dr. Treasury Stock (COE) . . . . (inc.) 15,000
>   Cr. Cash (A) . . . .   (dec.) 15,000

Under U.S. GAAP, a company's investment in its own stock is not considered to be an asset; instead, it is treated as a reduction in owners' equity. Note however, that practice varies from country to country. Many countries forbid companies from buying and then reissuing their own stock. In other countries, such as Italy and France, treasury stock is carried as an asset, often in the Long-Term Investments account.

When treasury stock is reissued as a result of a sale, to satisfy stock options or for the conversion of convertible bonds, the cost of the reissued shares is removed from the Treasury Stock account. If the proceeds related to that reissuance differ from the cost of the treasury shares issued, that difference is added to (or subtracted from) the Paid-in Capital in Excess of Par Value account. For example, suppose that Smith Company purchased 100 shares of its own stock at $12 a share. The shares will be used to satisfy employee stock options with an exercise price of $10 per share. The entry to record that purchase is an increase in its Treasury Stock account (a contra owners' equity account) for $1,200 and a decrease in the Cash account of the same amount. Assuming that options for 100 shares are exercised, the following accounting entry is made:

> Dr. Cash (A) . . . . (inc.) 1,000
> Dr. Paid-in Capital in Excess of Par Value (OE) . . . . . . (dec.)   200
>   Cr. Treasury Stock (COE) . . . .   (dec.) 1,200

If a company reacquires its own shares with no intention of reissuing them, it formally, legally retires them. Instead of a debit entry to the Treasury Stock account, the company debits the cost of the stock acquired to the Common Stock (at Par) account and the Paid-in Capital account for any difference. If the difference between the par value and the per-share cost of the reacquired shares is more than the average per-share paid-in capital from prior issuances of stock, that difference may have to be charged against retained earnings.

Other Stock Transactions

Stock options. Many companies maintain **stock option plans** for their employees, and issuances of stock in satisfaction of those commitments are frequent owners' equity transactions. A stock option plan might work this way: Assume that Smith Company is on the verge of a new business cycle and that its board of directors concludes that management motivation will be a major factor in the company's success. At the present time, the company's $1 par value stock is selling at $10 a share. The board might agree to grant 100 options to key management people entitling them to purchase shares of the company's stock at $10 a share (the market price of a share at date of grant) any time after five years from today (the vesting period), thereby creating a financial incentive for the executives to manage the company over the next several years so that its stock price appreciates.

Under most stock option plans, no accounting entry is necessary when such an option is granted. The entry to record the issuance of those shares when the employees ultimately exercise their options assumes that the transaction is simply a sale of stock at $10 a share—even if the stock price is $20 a share on the exercise date:

```
Dr. Cash (A) . . . . . . . . . . . . . . . . . . . . . . . . . . . . . . . (inc.) 1,000
    Cr. Common Stock, at Par Value (OE) . . . . . . . . . . . . . . . . . .        (inc.) 100
    Cr. Paid-in Capital in Excess of Par Value (OE). . . . . . . . . . . .        (inc.) 900
```

Some stock option plans produce no tax deductions for a corporation; similarly, the employee has no taxable income as a result of the award of the option or the exercise of the option. The most common situation, however, is that the corporation is able to deduct, for tax purposes, the difference between the fair value of the stock and the exercise price at the time the options are exercised and the employee also experiences a commensurate taxable gain at exercise date. The employee will experience another taxable gain when the stock is sold, with that gain based on the difference between the ultimate sale price of the stock and the fair value of the stock at the time of the option exercise.

In recent years, a great variety of stock option plans have come into use, some of which do require the company to recognize an option expense, for financial statement purposes, over the option period and do require the employee to recognize taxable income. Companies establish one plan or another (sometimes a combinations of plans) depending on the impact of the plans on their earnings and their tax position, as well as the needs of their employees.

For many years there has been controversy about accounting for stock options because they are used so often by corporations and the values associated with them are clearly material in many instances. Warren Buffett's quote at the beginning of this chapter illustrates one position in the debate. In 1993, the FASB issued an exposure draft titled *Accounting for Stock-Based Compensation.* It would have required the *fair-value based method* of valuation for all options at the time of their grant. The previous approach was termed the *intrinsic-value based method* because only the excess of the market value of the stock over the exercise price, the intrinsic value, is recognized as expense when the options are *granted.* Under the proposed standard, the *value of the options* granted would be amortized to earnings as a compensation expense over the vesting period and the credit would be to owners' equity. The value of options granted without any vesting period would immediately be recognized as an expense.

Let's look at the fair-value based method in more depth. Companies can select one of several binomial option pricing models to value the options at the grant date. One of the most popular of these is the Black-Scholes model, which is widely used in the financial community and frequently studied in business schools. These models are sensitive to the current stock price, the exercise price, the expected dividend yield, stock price volatility, the option exercise term, and the prevailing interest rate.[6] The models do not depend upon earnings growth or forecasts of future market prices.

For example, assume a company grants 900,000 options to employees as of January 1, 2000, when the company's stock price was $50, and the exercise price is also $50. The options vest after three years; the expected life of the options is six years; and the maximum term of the options is 10 years. Expected dividend yield is 2.5 percent; the risk-free rate of interest is 7.5 percent; and the volatility is 30 percent. Volatility is the standard derivation of the continuously compounded rates of return of the stock over a specified period. Finally, assume that each year during the vesting period, 3 percent of the options are canceled because of employee attrition. These are the assumptions necessary to value a stock option using one of the binomial models.

Using these assumptions and the Black-Scholes option pricing model modified for dividends, the value of each option at the grant date is $17.15. (The Black-Scholes calculations are not shown here, but they are discussed in Appendix 14A.) Thus, the value of the options at the grant date is

$$\$17.15 \times 900,000 \times 0.97 \times 0.97 \times 0.97 = \$14,087,108$$

Under the fair value accounting rules proposed by the FASB, the value of the options granted would be amortized over the service period. Typically this means the vesting period; consequently, at the end of years 2000, 2001, and 2002, the following entry would have been recorded:

Dr. Compensation Expense (E)....... (inc.) 4,695,703
    Cr. Additional Paid-in Capital—Options (OE).......   (inc.) 4,695,703

A deferred tax asset would also be established for the temporary difference related to compensation expense.

If the options are all exercised in 2005, when the stock price is 70, the entry to record the sale of stock, assuming 821,406 shares are issued, looks like this:

Dr. Cash (A) .... (inc.) 41,070,300
Dr. Additional Paid-in Capital— Options (OE) ..... (dec.) 14,087,108
    Cr. Capital Stock (OE)................................   (inc.) 55,157,408
    (divided appropriately between common stock and other paid-in capital)

Entries would also erase any accumulated deferred tax asset and record the income tax benefit of the options when exercised if the options produce a tax deduction to the issuer. The effect of this approach to valuing options is to increase the capital stock accounts by the sum of the exercise price (what the grantees actually paid in cash for their stock) and the value of the options at the grant date (valued using Black-Scholes or another option pricing model), which was earlier charged to compensation expense. The market value of the shares at the exercise date is ignored. The intrinsic-value based method, in contrast, values stock issued via options at the exercise price only.

In summary, fair value accounting for stock options would result in charges to net income for the cost of options granted based on a valuation model. These expenses are recognized

[6] F. Black and M. Scholes, "The Pricing of Options and Corporate Liabilities," *Journal of Political Economy* 81 (May–June 1973), pp. 637–54. See also R. C. Merton, "Theory of Rational Option Pricing," *Bell Journal of Economics and Management Science* 4 (Spring 1973), pp. 141–83.

over the vesting period. When the options are exercised, the value of the options exercised plus the proceeds from the issuance of the new shares are recorded as an increase in capital stock. If the options are tax-deductible compensation, the actual tax consequences of the stock option are based on the difference between the exercise price and the market value of the shares at the exercise date. This is explained more fully in Appendix 14A.

The impact of the FASB proposed stock option accounting could have been significant, particularly for start-up companies. In the end, the FASB backed down. Effective for fiscal years beginning after December 31, 1995, companies must describe the general characteristics of any option plan and they must disclose the number and weighted-average exercise prices of options in each of the following categories, together with the weighted-average grant-date fair value of options granted during the year and the methods and assumptions employed to establish these valuations:

- Outstanding at the beginning of the year.
- Outstanding at the end of the year.
- Exercisable at the end of the year.
- Granted during the year.
- Exercised during the year.
- Forfeited during the year.
- Expired during the year.

Under current U.S. GAAP, companies may elect to recognize the value of options granted as compensation expense or merely footnote the pro forma net income and earnings per share effect of the options vested using the fair value method. In essence, companies were left to choose whether to bring the cost of options granted to their balance sheets and income statements. The intention of many companies on this point was clear: They had no intention of booking the value of options granted as a compensation expense.

To illustrate the financial disclosures associated with stock options, consider Exhibit 14.1 which presents Microsoft Corporation's 1998 annual report footnote disclosure pertaining to its stock option plans. Note that Microsoft has chosen to follow the older accounting practice wherein no compensation cost is accounted for at the time the stock options are granted. As of June 30, 1998, the company had 446 million options outstanding, equivalent to 18.5% of its total shares outstanding.

Although Microsoft chose to follow APB No.25, the company is required under SFAS No. 123 to show the proforma impact of its options on earnings and earnings per share. Note that in 1996 the impact on EPS is 14% ($.86 vs. .74) but only 12% by 1998 ($1.67 vs $1.47). Twelve percent is a big difference, especially on a figure as sensitive as EPS. The decline from 14% to 12% is due to the interaction of four factors:

- the number of options granted declined substantially during 1998
- the value of the options granted during 1998 increased substantially from $8.86 to $23.62
- earnings before considering stock option costs doubled from 1996 to 1998
- the proforma calculations began in 1996 and used a five year amortization period so the proformas have only one year of amortization in the 1996 figures; but for 1998, the proformas reflect amortization of stock option costs from all three years

EXHIBIT 14.1

Microsoft Corporation
Financial Disclosures for Stock Option Plan

Stock option plans

The Company has stock option plans for directors, officers, and employees, which provide for nonqualified and incentive stock options. The option exercise price is the fair market value at the date of grant. Options granted prior to 1995 generally vest over four and one-half years and expire 10 years from the date of grant. Options granted during and after 1995 generally vest over four and one-half years and expire seven years from the date of grant, while certain options vest over seven and one-half years and expire after 10 years. At June 30, 1998, options for 222 million shares were vested and 523 million shares were available for future grants under the plans.

Stock options outstanding were as follows:

	Shares	Price per share Range	Weighted average
Balance, June 30, 1995	456	$ 0.39 – $20.79	$ 7.28
Granted	114	20.05 – 29.47	22.50
Exercised	(80)	0.39 – 22.63	5.38
Canceled	(14)	1.30 – 27.72	13.93
Balance, June 30, 1996	476	0.55 – 29.47	$11.04
Granted	110	27.66 – 59.60	29.15
Exercised	(90)	0.55 – 29.47	6.64
Canceled	(18)	8.50 – 48.57	19.42
Balance, June 30, 1997	478	1.12 – 59.60	15.72
Granted	69	33.12 – 87.25	62.56
Exercised	(88)	1.12 – 62.47	9.27
Canceled	(13)	1.32 – 83.88	29.37
Balance, June 30, 1998	446	1.12 – 87.25	23.87

For various price ranges, weighted average characteristics of outstanding stock options at June 30, 1998 were as follows:

Range of exercise prices	Outstanding options Shares	Remaining life (years)	Weighted average price	Exercisable options Shares	Weighted average price
$ 1.12 – $ 8.50	85	2.7	$ 5.06	84	$ 5.07
8.51 – 11.94	100	4.4	10.47	83	10.19
11.95 – 27.25	97	4.9	21.62	38	21.14
27.26 – 59.60	100	5.6	29.81	17	28.99
59.61 – 87.25	64	6.5	64.00	–	–

The Company follows Accounting Principles Board Opinion 25, *Accounting for Stock Issued to Employees,* to account for stock options and the employee stock purchase plan. No compensation cost is recognized because the option exercise price is equal to the market price of the underlying stock on the date of grant.

An alternative method of accounting for stock options is SFAS 123, *Accounting for Stock-Based Compensation.* Under SFAS 123, employee stock options are valued at grant date using the Black-Scholes valuation model and compensation cost is recognized ratably over the vesting period. Had compensation cost for the Company's stock option and employee stock purchase plans been determined based on the Black-Scholes value at the grant dates for awards as prescribed by SFAS 123, pro forma income statements for 1996, 1997, and 1998 would have been as follows:

EXHIBIT 14.1 concluded

Year Ended June 30	1996		1997		1998	
	Reported	Pro forma	Reported	Pro forma	Reported	Pro forma
Revenue	$8,671	$8,671	$11,358	$11,358	$14,484	$14,484
Operating expenses:						
Cost of revenue	1,188	1,204	1,085	1,107	1,197	1,227
Research and development	1,432	1,655	1,925	2,230	2,502	2,924
Acquired in-process technology	—	—	—	—	296	296
Sales and marketing	2,657	2,823	2,856	3,082	3,412	3,725
General and administrative	316	362	362	424	433	520
Other expenses	19	19	259	259	230	230
Total operating expenses	5,612	6,063	6,487	7,102	8,070	8,922
Operating income	3,059	2,608	4,871	4,256	6,414	5,562
Interest income	320	320	443	443	703	703
Income before income taxes	3,379	2,928	5,314	4,699	7,117	6,265
Provision for income taxes	1,184	1,026	1,860	1,646	2,627	2,325
Net income	2,195	1,902	3,454	3,053	4,490	3,940
Preferred stock dividends	—	—	15	15	28	28
Net income available for common shareholders	$2,195	$1,902	$ 3,439	$ 3,038	$ 4,462	$ 3,912
Diluted earnings per share	$ 0.86	$ 0.74	$ 1.32	$ 1.16	$ 1.67	$ 1.47

The pro forma disclosures in the previous table include the amortization of the fair value of *all* options vested during 1996, 1997, and 1998, regardless of the grant date. If only options granted after 1996 were valued, as prescribed by SFAS 123, pro forma net income would have been $2,073 million, $3,179 million, and $4,019 million, and earnings per share would have been $0.81, $1.21, and $1.50 for 1996, 1997, and 1998.

The weighted average Black-Scholes value of options granted under the stock option plans during 1996, 1997, and 1998 was $8.86, $11.72, and $23.62. Value was estimated using an expected life of five years, no dividends, volatility of .32 in 1998 and .30 in prior years, and risk-free interest rates of 6.0%, 6.5%, and 5.7% in 1996, 1997, and 1998.

In other countries, stock options outstanding are frequently disclosed in a footnote similar to that of Microsoft. In some countries they are not disclosed at all; in others, only the awards to officers and directors are disclosed. Exhibit 14.2, from the annual report of Reckitt & Colman, a U.K. consumer goods firm, illustrates the type of disclosure typical in Commonwealth countries.

Stock warrants. A cash-short firm that is going through a difficult period may find that it is unable to sell new shares of stock at a price it believes is reasonable. In lieu of a stock sale, a company may sell **stock warrants,** which enable the holder to purchase shares of stock at a fixed price at some time in the future. The proceeds from the sale of warrants are simply added to the Paid-in Capital in Excess of Par Value account:

```
Dr. Cash (A) . . . . . . . . . . . . . . . . . . . . . . . . (inc.) 5,000
   Cr. Paid-in Capital in Excess of Par Value (OE). . . . .    (inc.) 5,000
```

EXHIBIT 14.2

Reckitt & Colman Plc
British Stock Option Disclosures

Called-up Share Capital

Options unexercised at 31 December:

Executive Share Option Schemes			Savings-Related Share Option Scheme		
Number of shares	**Price to be paid**	**Exercisable by**	**Number of shares**	**Price to be paid**	**Exercisable by**
32,498	376.9p	April 1997	34,209	379.7p	June 1995
76,018	323.6p	April 1998	90,838	386.0p	July 1995
279,842	420.8p	April 1999	30,949	308.2p	June 1996
169,671	442.9p	April 2000	78,500	385.2p	June 1996
45,826	481.6p	Oct 2000	131,884	548.2p	June 1997
253,402	578.4p	April 2001	52,807	386.0p	July 1997
91,544	685.5p	Oct 2001	50,815	385.2p	June 1998
363,670	628.2p	April 2002	329,869	426.7p	June 1998
282,413	532.4p	Sept 2002	72,069	548.2p	June 1999
247,079	594.6p	April 2003	125,381	489.9p	June 1999
323,334	612.4p	Sept 2003	171,158	426.7p	June 2000
281,459	602.5p	April 2004	199,738	477.1p	July 2000
			42,175	489.9p	June 2001
			61,227	477.1p	July 2002

Shares to be Issued (Including Premium)	**Number of Shares**	**£m**
Share capital—ordinary shares of 10p each	46,983,898	4.70
Share premium account (after costs of issue)		224.60
		229.30

When a warrant is exercised, the proceeds are added to the common stock account using the same theory followed for the exercise of stock options. Sometimes warrants for the purchase of common stock are issued in connection with the sale of a bond to make the bonds more attractive to potential purchasers. In those situations, some portion of the proceeds of the bond sale are allocated to the Paid-in Capital in Excess account, just as though the company had sold the bonds and the warrants separately.

Convertible securities. Many companies sell **convertible bonds** that enable the holder to exchange a bond for shares of common stock at a predetermined ratio (the conversion ratio). Convertible bonds are usually less expensive for the issuing corporation because they can be sold with a lower interest rate than would otherwise be required (because the conversion feature itself has value). Convertible bonds are attractive to the holder because they ensure a steady stream of interest income for a certain number of years, as well as the possibility of sharing in any potential appreciation of the common stock. The proceeds from the sale of a convertible bond increase the cash account and increase the bond account. If some of the bonds are subsequently converted, a pro rata share of the bond's carrying value is transferred from the Bond Payable account (a decrease) to the Common Stock and Paid-in Capital accounts (increases). Similar accounting is followed for convertible preferred stock.

Hybrid Transactions

Earlier we indicated that all transactions involving the owners' equity accounts that relate to stock issuances are reported in the statement of owners' equity and that all owners' equity transactions that involve revenue and expenses are reported in the income statement. For many years, the dividing line between the two types of transactions was clearly defined and stoutly defended. The accounting profession argued that it was important to include *all* income and expense items (and *only* those items) in the determination of income for the period. With the introduction of the concept of Comprehensive Income, however, the line between income and equity transactions has become blurred. Today, several nonstock events may be reported in both the statement of owners' equity and the income statement. The two nonstock events are (1) the residual that results from translating the foreign currency value of assets and liabilities held outside the United States into U.S. dollars and (2) the residual that results from adjusting the carrying value of available-for-sale investments to their current market value. Under current U.S. GAAP, these two accounts (and sometimes others) are aggregated to form **other comprehensive income,** which appears as a component of owners' equity on the balance sheet. Other comprehensive income thus reflects those wealth changes for a company that are unrelated to its regular daily operations.

To describe the **currency translation adjustment,** it may be easiest if we use an example. Assume that a U.S.-based company has a subsidiary in Germany with receivables, inventory, equipment, and payables denominated in German marks. Obviously, adding together the company's dollar-stated accounts and its mark-stated accounts would not be appropriate. If the exchange rate stayed the same from one year to the next (for example, 1 mark = $0.50 or $1 = 2 marks), it would be easy to convert the mark-stated accounts into their U.S. dollar equivalents and then to add those dollar-equivalent accounts to the U.S. dollar-stated accounts.

Exchange rates fluctuate, however, and sometimes they change dramatically. In previous years, the exchange rate between the U.S. dollar and the German mark has been 1 to 4, with a mark being equal to $0.25 U.S. Hence, a piece of equipment purchased for a company's German operations at that time might have cost 1 million marks and would therefore have had a U.S. dollar cost of only $250,000. With an exchange rate of $1 to 2 marks, the translated dollar cost for that piece of equipment would be $500,000. Accountants and businesspeople have been concerned about the appropriate accounting for that extra $250,000. No one wanted to include the apparent increase in asset value in the income statement because it did not seem to be a revenue item. In addition, the exchange rates might reverse in a subsequent period, and consequently companies would report fluctuations in earnings induced by the exchange markets rather than due to operations. Instead, it was agreed (in SFAS No. 52) that all such translation adjustments be included as a unique element of owners' equity until those assets or liabilities were liquidated, converted to U.S. dollars, and repatriated. Only after those non-U.S. assets (or liabilities) are realized in dollars is the resulting gain or loss recognized in the income statement.

The second unique element of owners' equity builds on the same logic as the translation adjustment. A company that owns less than 20 percent of the stock of another company, and whose intent is that such shares are available for sale if the right circumstances come along, must report that investment at its market value in the balance sheet. As elaborated on more fully in Chapter 8, if the market value of the available-for-sale shares held has changed since the last balance sheet report date, the Investment asset account must be adjusted, and the resultant unrealized holding gain or loss carried to an account in the owners' equity section of the balance sheet. In essence, this owners' equity account acts as a holding account for the shares' market appreciation or diminution until such time that the shares are actually sold and the realized gain or loss, based on original cost, is then recognized in that period's income statement. Once the shares have been sold, the owners' equity holding gain or loss account pertaining to the shares would no longer be needed and thus would be zeroed out.

OWNERS' EQUITY DISCLOSURES

To illustrate the typical annual report disclosures involving owners' equity, we refer to the 1997 IBM annual report. Exhibit 14.3 presents the shareholders' equity section of the IBM consolidated balance sheet. This exhibit presents summary information concerning IBM's shareholder equity accounts, whereas detailed information is presented in Exhibit 14.4 in the consolidated statement of shareholders' equity.

From these two exhibits, the following observations can be made:

- IBM has two classes of capital stock outstanding—the $.01 par value per share Preferred Stock and the $.50 par value per share Common Stock. Although the company was authorized to issue 150 million of the preferred stock, as of year end 1997, there were only 1.73% of those shares issued and outstanding. The company had 1,875 million authorized shares of common stock, of which 969 million shares were issued and outstanding as of December 31, 1997.

- The aggregate contributed capital at year end 1997 was $8,853 million (252 + 8,601), whereas total shareholders' equity was $19,816 million.

- Retained earnings *decreased* from 1996 to 1997 by $179 million. The explanation of this is found in the statement of shareholders' equity: Although the company earned $6,093 million in 1997, it paid out $783 million of dividends, purchased and retired $6,020 million of common stock in the open market ($5,455 million of which was debited to retained earnings), and there were $34 million of miscellaneous adjustments. It is interesting to note that in 1997, IBM repurchased and retired more than $6 billion of treasury shares, almost equal to the $8.6 billion book value of common stock outstanding. The company attributed part of the cost of the retirement to common stock ($565 million) and the remainder to retained earnings.

- In 1997 IBM created an employee benefits trust by contributing 10 million shares of treasury stock. These shares are to be used by the trustees to satisfy certain compensation and benefit obligations, but according to the footnote disclosure were not to be considered outstanding for purposes of earnings per share calculations.

- The cumulative foreign currency translation account totaled $791 million — a decrease of $1,610 million from 1996, reflecting a strengthening of foreign currencies relative to the U.S. dollar in those areas where IBM maintains operations.

E X H I B I T   1 4 . 3

IBM Corporation
Shareholders' Equity Section
As of December 31, 1997, and December 31, 1996
(in millions)

	1997	1996
Shareholders' equity		
Preferred stock, par value $.01 per share—		
shares authorized: 150,000,000		
shares issued: 1997 — 2,597,261; 1996 — 2,610,711	252	253
Common stock, par value $.50* per share—		
shares authorized: 1,875,000,000*		
shares issued: 1997 — 969,015,351; 1996 — 1,018,141,084*	8,601	7,752
Retained earnings	11,010	11,189
Translation adjustments	791	2,401
Treasury stock, at cost (shares: 1997 — 923,955;		
1996 — 2,179,066*)	(86)	(135)
Employee benefits trust, at cost (10,000,000 shares)	(860)	—
Net unrealized gain on marketable securities	108	168
Total stockholders' equity	19,816	21,628
Total liabilities and stockholders' equity	$81,499	$81,132

* Adjusted to reflect a two-for-one stock split on May 9, 1997.

Because of the importance of employee stock option and stock compensation plans, the principal features of these plans are detailed in the footnotes to the financial statements. Exhibit 14.5 presents the footnote disclosure for IBM's employee incentive plan. Also included are footnotes discussing the stock repurchases and the employee benefit trust.

Management Issues

Most of the decisions that managers are called upon to make concerning the accounting for owners' equity issues are episodic—such as a new issue of common stock, a new preferred stock, stock splits, acquisitions paid for with common stock, and the decision to repurchase common stock. Managers give a good deal of attention to these decisions because they can have an immediate impact on a firm's stock price—usually the single most important measure of how well management is performing its job. Because they are infrequent and of a critical importance, companies often bring in experts to help with the decisions. Investment bankers, public accountants, and lawyers are almost always present when these big equity events are being considered. The overriding issue is typically: "What's this going to do to our stock price? What signal will be given to the market? What will the analysts say about this?" Because of the direct and immediate link between these equity decisions and the share price, most executives have a detailed knowledge of the implications of each alternative being considered. As more public attention is brought to bear on stock options, this too will become a priority concern for senior executives.

EXHIBIT 14.4

IBM Corporation
Consolidated Statement of Stockholders' Equity (in millions except per share amounts)

	Preferred Stock	Common Stock	Retained Earnings	Translation Adjustments	Treasury Stock	Employee Benefits Trust	Net Unrealized Gain on Marketable Securities	Total
1995								
Shareholders' Equity, January 1, 1995	$1,081	$7,342	$12,352	$ 2,672	$ (34)	$ —	$ —	$23,413
Net earnings			4,178					4,178
Cash dividends declared – common stock			(572)					(572)
Cash dividends declared – preferred stock			(20)					(20)
Common stock purchased and retired (101,812,600* shares)		(655)	(4,209)					(4,864)
Preferred stock purchased and retired (8,534,289 shares)	(828)		(42)					(870)
Common stock issued under employee plans (8,543,896* shares)		279						279
Purchases (9,324,094* shares) and sales (9,413,928* shares) of treasury stock under employee plans — net			(57)		(7)			(64)
Conversion of debentures (13,306,242* shares)		471						471
Tax effect — stock transactions		51						51
Other				364			57	421
Stockholders' equity, December 31, 1995	253	7,488	11,630	3,036	(41)	—	57	22,423
1996								
Net earnings			5,429					5,429
Cash dividends declared — common stock			(686)					(686)
Cash dividends declared – preferred stock			(20)					(20)
Common stock purchased and retired (97,951,400* shares)		(710)	(5,046)					(5,756)
Common stock issued under employee plans (19,694,458* shares)		811	(13)					798
Purchases (8,914,332* shares) and sales (7,584,432* shares) of treasury stock under employee plans — net			(105)		(94)			(199)
Tax effect — stock transactions		163						163
Other				(635)			111	(524)
Stockholders' equity, December 31, 1996	253	7,752	11,189	2,401	(135)	—	168	21,628
1997								
Net earnings			6,093					6,093
Cash dividends declared — common stock			(763)					(763)
Cash dividends declared – preferred stock			(20)					(20)
Common stock purchased and retired (68,777,336 shares)		(565)	(5,455)					(6,020)
Preferred stock purchased and retired (13,450 shares)	(1)							(1)
Common stock issued under employee plans (19,651,603 shares)		985	(2)					983
Purchases (3,850,643shares) and sales (5,105,754 shares) of treasury stock under employee plans — net			(32)		49			17
Employee benefits trust (10,000,000 shares)						(860)		(860)
Tax effect — stock transactions		429						429
Other				(1,610)			(60)	(1,670)
Shareholders' Equity, December 31, 1997	$252	$8,601	$11,010	$ 791	$ (86)	$(860)	$ 180	$19,816

* Adjusted to reflect a two-for-one stock split on May 9, 1997.

EXHIBIT 14.5

IBM Corporation
Selected Footnote Disclosures:
Employee Incentive Plans

Stock-Based Compensation Plans

The company applies Accounting Principles Board (APB) Opinion 25 and related Interpretations in accounting for its stock-based compensation plans. A description of the terms of the company's stock-based compensation plans follows:

Long-Term Performance Plan

Incentive awards are provided to officers and other key employees under the terms of the IBM 1997 Long-Term Performance Plan, which was approved by the stockholders in April 1997, and its predecessor plan, the 1994 Long-Term Performance Plan ("the Plans"). The Plans are administered by the Executive Compensation and Management Resources Committee of the Board of Directors. The committee determines the type and terms of the awards to be granted, including vesting provisions.

Awards may include stock options, stock appreciation rights (SARs), restricted stock, cash or stock awards, or any combination thereof. The number of shares that may be issued under the IBM 1997 Long-Term Performance Plan for awards is 50.3 million, which was 5 percent of the outstanding common stock at February 10, 1997. There were 46.4 million unused shares available for granting under the 1994 Long-Term Performance Plan at December 31, 1997.

Awards under the Plans resulted in compensation expense of $214.1 million, $203.9 million and $106.3 million that were included in net earnings before income taxes in 1997, 1996 and 1995, respectively. Such awards include those that settle in cash, such as SARs, and restricted stock grants.

Stock Option Grants

Stock options granted under the Plan allow the purchase of IBM's common stock at 100 percent of the market price on the date of grant and generally expire 10 years from the date of grant. The following table summarizes option activity of the Plans during 1997, 1996 and 1995:

	1997		1996		1995	
	Wtd. Avg. Exercise Price	No. of Shares under Option	Wtd. Avg. Exercise Price	No. of Shares under Option	Wtd. Avg. Exercise Price	No. of Shares under Option
Balance at January 1	$44	61,435,322	$39	68,565,806	$34	68,126,634
Options granted	71	21,471,228	63	15,359,058	39	12,937,404
Options exercised	42	(19,360,005)	36	(19,302,622)	26	(7,391,578)
Options terminated	56	(1,548,184)	61	(3,186,920)	52	(5,106,654)
Balance at December 31	54	61,728,361	44	61,435,322	39	68,565,806
Exercisable at December 31	38	26,619,548	41	30,603,845	46	38,352,820

The shares under option at December 31, 1997, were in the following exercise price ranger:

	Options Outstanding			Options currently Exercisable	
Exercise Price Range	No. of Options	Wtd. Avg. Exercise Price	Wtd. Avg. Contractual Life (in years)	No. of Options	Wtd. Avg. Exercise Price
$21 – 50	25,762,003	$32	6	20,646,476	$31
$51 – 69	16,880,188	62	7	5,959,624	61
$70 and over	19,086,170	76	9	13,448	74
	61,728,361			26,619,548	

EXHIBIT 14.5 continued

IBM Employees Stock Purchase Plan

The IBM Employees Stock Purchase Plan (ESPP) enables substantially all regular employees to purchase full or fractional shares of IBM common stock through payroll deductions of up to 10 percent of eligible compensation. The price an employee pays is 85 percent of the average market price on the last day of an applicable pay period.

During 1997, 1996 and 1995, employees purchased 4,676,980; 6,461,856 and 8,958,680 shares, all of which were treasury shares, for which $354 million, $324 million and $344 million were paid to IBM, respectively.

There were approximately 35.5 million, 40.2 million and 46.6 million reserved unissued shares available for purchase under the ESPP, as previously approved by stockholders, at December 31, 1997, 1996 and 1995, respectively.

Pro Forma Disclosure

In applying APB Opinion 25, no expense was recognized for stock options granted under the Plan and for employee stock purchases under the ESPP. SFAS 123 requires that a fair market value of all awards of stock-based compensation be determined using standard techniques and that pro forma net earnings and earnings per share be disclosed as if the resulting stock-based compensation amounts were recorded in the Consolidated Statement of Earnings as follows:

(Dollars in millions except per share amounts)

	1997		1996		1995	
	As reported	Pro forma	As reported	Pro forma	As reported	Pro forma
Net earnings applicable to common shareholders	$6,073	$5,866	$5,409	$5,267	$4,116	$4,020
Net earnings per share of common stock	$ 6.18	$ 5.97	$ 5.12	$ 4.98	$ 3.61	$ 3.53
Net earnings per share of common stock—assuming dilution	$ 6.01	$ 5.82	$ 5.01	$ 4.89	$ 3.53	$ 3.45

The above pro forma amounts, for purposes of SFAS 123, reflect the portion of the estimated fair value of awards earned in 1997, 1996 and 1995. The aggregate fair value of awards granted is earned ratably over the vesting or service period and is greater than that included in the pro forma amounts.

The company used the Black-Scholes model to value the stock options granted in 1997, 1996 and 1995. The weighted average assumptions used to estimate the value of the options included in the pro forma amounts, and the weighted average estimated fair value of an option granted are as follows:

	1997	1996	1995
Term (years)*	5/6	5/6	5/6
Volatility**	23.0%	22.0%	21.0%
Risk-free interest rate (zero coupon U.S. Treasury note)	6.2%	6.0%	7.0%
Dividend yield	1.0%	1.2%	2.0%
Weighted average fair value	$ 25	$ 20	$ 12

* Option term is based on tax incentive options (5 years) and non-tax incentive options (6 years).

** To determine volatility, the company measured the daily price changes of the stock over the most recent 5 and 6 year periods.

EXHIBIT 14.5 concluded

Stock Repurchases

The Board of Directors has authorized the company to repurchase IBM common stock. The company repurchased 81,505,200 common shares at a cost of $7,128 million and 98,930,400 common shares at a cost of $5,810 million in 1997 and 1996, respectively. The repurchases resulted in a reduction of $34,338,668 and $61,831,500 in the stated capital (par value) associated with common stock in 1997 and 1996, respectively. In 1997, 10 million repurchased shares were used to establish the Employee Benefits Trust, while 2,727,864 and 979,000 in 1997 and 1996, respectively, were used to fund new acquisitions. The rest of the repurchased shares were retired and restored to the status of authorized but unissued shares. At December 31, 1997, approximately $2.7 billion of Board authorized repurchases remained. The company plans to purchase shares on the open market from time to time, depending on market conditions.

During 1995, the IBM Board of Directors authorized the company to purchase all its outstanding Series A 7½ percent preferred stock. The company repurchased 13,450 shares at a cost of $1.4 million during 1997, which resulted in a $134.50 ($.01 par value per share) reduction in the stated capital associated with preferred stock. The repurchased shares were retired and restored to the status of authorized but unissued shares. No shares were repurchased in 1996. The company plans to purchase remaining shares on the open market and in private transactions from time to time, depending on market conditions.

Employee Benefits Trust

Effective November 1, 1997, the company created an employee benefits trust to which the company contributed 10 million shares of treasury stock. The company is authorized to instruct the trustee to sell shares from time to time and to use proceeds from such sales, and any dividends paid on such contributed stock, toward the partial satisfaction of the company's future obligations under certain of its compensation and benefits plans, including its retiree medical plans. The shares held in trust are not considered outstanding for earnings per share purposes until they are committed to be released, and the shares will be voted by the trustee in accordance with its fiduciary duties. As of December 31, 1997, no shares have been committed to be released.

SUMMARY

The owners' or shareholders' equity represents the residual value of a company, or its assets minus its liabilities. The transactions affecting the shareholder equity accounts are summarized in the statement of owners' equity. The principal owners' equity transactions include the sale of capital stock, the results of operations (that is, the net income or net loss resulting from a company's principal business activity), the payment of dividends (either cash or stock), the exercise of stock options or warrants, the conversion of convertible preferred stock or debentures, and the purchase or reissuance of treasury stock. In addition to these transactions involving individuals or organizations outside the company, the statement of owners' equity also depicts two hybrid transactions: (1) the adjustment for foreign currency changes when consolidating the results of foreign operations and (2) the adjustment for valuation changes in the long-term investment portfolio.

The owners' equity of a company is also referred to as its *net worth or book value.* In many cases the market value of a company, as defined by the market price of its capital stock, far exceeds the company's net worth or book value. Why this may be the case was the focus of Chapter 7.

NEW CONCEPTS AND TERMS

Callable preferred stock	Fiscal year
Charter of incorporation	Net worth
Common stock	Other comprehensive income
Convertible bonds	Participating preferred stock
Contributed capital	Partnership
Convertible preferred stock	Preferred stock
Cumulative preferred stock	Retained capital
Currency translation adjustment	Stock dividend
Date of declaration	Stock options plans
Date of payment	Stock split
Date of record	Stock warrant
Dividends in arrears	Treasury stock

Stock Options in Detail

In its simplest form, a stock option is a right to purchase a certain number of shares of company stock at a set price during some future period of time beyond the grant date. Typically, the shares are the common stock of the corporation and the exercise price is the market price of the stock on the grant day so as to avoid any income tax issues. Options typically have vesting restrictions; that is, one must be employed for so many months in order to exercise the first block of options, so many months for the next block, and so on. With what are called *American options,* owners may exercise their options at any time beyond the vesting date up to the expiration date. *European options* can be exercised only on the expiration date. Options are used as a type of incentive compensation, and it is common for directors, officers, and managers (and sometimes all employees) to receive stock options. Some companies have promised to sell millions of shares of stock under these option agreements. As of June 30, 1998, Microsoft Corporation, for example, had 446 million options outstanding at a weighted average exercise price of $23.87. The average stock price during the fourth quarter ranged from $81.88 to $108.56. This means Microsoft was prepared to sell shares with a market value of $42 billion for $10.6 billion.

The Debate over Accounting for Stock Options

Between 1993 and 1995, while the proposed accounting standard that would require companies to book a compensation expense for the value of stock options at their granting date was being discussed by the FASB, the debate about its merits raged throughout the financial community. For example, under a headline of "FASB's Folly," Malcolm S. Forbes Jr., Editor-in-Chief of *Forbes* magazine wrote the following in an editorial:

> The Financial Accounting Standards Board will soon hold pro forma hearings on one of its most asinine, destructive proposals ever. It wants to force companies to put a value on grants of stock options and expense them against profits.
>
> The idea is utterly illogical. How can a company know what its stock will be worth several years down the road? By definition the valuation is totally arbitrary, no matter how highfalutin the computer models used to come up with the numbers.
>
> The ruling will severely impact new companies. Many start-ups depend heavily on stock options to attract top-rate people. Coercing these outfits to penalize what are already anemic earnings with a capricious charge for options will make it even more difficult for them to attract good talent and fresh capital.[1]

[1] *Forbes,* Jan. 31, 1994, p. 25.

A *Harvard Business Review* editorial countered with the following:

But that's precisely the point, the FASB says. Since stock options make up the difference between a market-level salary at an established company and a below-market salary at a start-up, options have a calculable value. If you can calculate them, and they have an effect on your financial condition and the condition of your stock, then you must count them as an expense.[2]

Actually the debate began much earlier; the issue had been on the FASB agenda for 10 years. One of the sharpest criticisms of the old accounting came from Warren Buffett in his chairman's letter in the 1992 Berkshire Hathaway Inc. annual report:

Shareholders should understand that companies incur costs when they deliver something of value to another party and not just when cash changes hands. Moreover, it is both silly and cynical to say that an important item of cost should not be recognized simply because it can't be quantified with pinpoint precision. Right now, accounting abounds with imprecision. After all, no manager or auditor knows how long a 747 is going to last, which means he also does not know what the yearly depreciation charge for the plane should be. No one knows with any certainty what a bank's annual loan loss charge ought to be. And the estimates of losses that property-casualty companies make are notoriously inaccurate.

Does this mean that these important items of cost should be ignored simply because they can't be quantified with absolute accuracy? Of course not. Rather, these costs should be estimated by honest and experienced people and then recorded. When you get right down to it, what other item of major but hard-to-precisely-calculate cost—other, that is, than stock options—does the accounting profession say should be ignored in the calculation of earnings?

Moreover, options are just not that difficult to value. Admittedly, the difficulty is increased by the fact that the options given to executives are restricted in various ways. These restrictions affect value. They do not, however, eliminate it. In fact, since I'm in the mood for offers, I'll make one to any executive who is granted a restricted option, even though it may be out of the money: On the day of issue, Berkshire will pay him or her a substantial sum for the right to any future gain he or she realizes on the option. So if you find a CEO who says his newly issued options have little or no value, tell him to try us out. In truth, we have far more confidence in our ability to determine an appropriate price to pay for an option than we have in our ability to determine the proper depreciation rate for our corporate jet.

Mr. Buffett, one of America's best-known investors, prided himself on being able to "look through" GAAP accounting to see the reality of an economic situation.

Almost as if in answer to Mr. Buffett's charge, Microsoft Corporation published the following statement and table in their 1994 annual report:

At Microsoft, every employee is eligible to become a stockholder in the company through the company's employee stock purchase and stock option plans. Management believes stock options have made a major contribution to the success of

---

[2] "Taking Account of Stock Options," *Harvard Business Review,* January–February 1994.

the company by aligning employee interests with those of other stockholders. Stock options are in widespread use today, and many of the company's competitors have similar programs. During the last several years there has been considerable debate about the appropriate accounting for stock options. Questions in this ongoing discussion include how stock options should be measured; whether they should be recorded in traditional financial statements, subject to already complex and increasingly difficult rules; whether they should be highlighted in a separate new financial statement or table; or whether further information concerning stock options should be disclosed in footnotes to financial statements. Pending resolution of these outstanding issues, on the accompanying page [see below] we have provided a table of outstanding common shares and net options and changes in their computed values based on quoted prices for the company's stock. It provides a clear understanding of the company's equity, its equity holders, and the value or possible value of their vested and unvested holdings.

In this table, common shares are those outstanding. Net vested and unvested options represent the number of common shares issuable upon exercise of such stock options less the number of common shares that could be repurchased with proceeds from their exercise. Computed values are calculated based on the closing price of the company's common stock on the Nasdaq National Market System on the dates indicated.

(In millions)			June 30		
	1992	Change	1993	Change	1994
Outstanding Common Shares and Options					
Directors' and officers' common shares	273	(13)	260	(21)	239
Employees' and directors' net vested and unvested stock options	78	(11)	67	(5)	62
Employees' and directors' shares and options	351	(24)	327	(26)	301
Other investors' common shares	271	34	305	37	342
Total	622	10	632	11	643
Nasdaq closing price per share	$35		$44		$51½
Computed Values					
Directors' and officers' common shares	$ 9,579	$1,886	$11,465	$ 845	$12,310
Employees' and directors' net vested and unvested stock options	2,714	245	2,959	269	3,228
Employees' and directors' shares and options	12,293	2,131	14,424	1,114	15,538
Other investors' common shares	9,486	3,930	13,416	4,259	17,675
Total	$21,779	$6,061	$27,840	$5,373	$33,213

To compute what Microsoft calls "net vested and unvested stock options" the company subtracted the amount to be paid on the option from the market value to get a net figure, then divided this by the market value of the shares to calculate the number of option shares outstanding.

SFAS No. 123

The FASB decision on the matter, announced in October of 1995, was presented in Chapter 14 of the text. Essentially, the FASB urged the adoption of the fair value method of accounting for options granted, but stopped short of making it mandatory. If a company does not adopt SFAS No. 123, it must report the pro forma impact on net income and EPS in the footnotes. Whatever election is made, the footnotes must also disclose the details of the company's options programs and must show fair values for all options granted.

Let's use the example from Chapter 14 to look more closely at fair value accounting for stock options.[3] Recall the details of the example:

Stock price at grant date	$50
Exercise price	$50
Vesting	January 1, 2003
Expected life of options	6 years
Maximum term of options	10 years
Expected dividend yield	2.5%
Risk-free rate of interest	7.5%
Expected volatility	30%
Expected cancellation rate	3%/year
Black-Scholes valuation	$17.15/share

For simplicity, the Black-Scholes valuation used in this example is actually based on the assumption that all options are exercised in six years, as if they were European options. Black-Scholes itself is particularly sensitive to the expected life of the option and the volatility. For example, the following table shows the Black-Scholes valuation for different combinations of volatility and expected life.

Black-Scholes Valuations of the $50, January 1, 2003, Options

		Expected life of options (in years)							
		1	2	3	4	5	6	7	8
Volatility	0.20	5.10	7.67	9.71	11.41	12.86	14.11	15.18	16.11
	0.23	5.56	8.27	10.38	12.12	13.59	14.85	15.92	16.84
	0.25	6.02	8.87	11.06	12.85	14.34	15.60	16.68	17.58
	0.28	6.48	9.47	11.75	13.58	15.10	16.38	17.45	18.35
	0.30	6.94	10.08	12.43	14.32	15.87	17.15	18.22	19.12
	0.33	7.40	10.69	13.12	15.06	16.63	17.93	19.00	19.89
	0.35	7.87	11.29	13.81	15.80	17.40	18.71	19.78	20.66
	0.38	8.33	11.90	14.50	16.53	18.16	19.48	20.56	21.43

Thus, if the volatility is only 0.25 (about the average for New York Stock Exchange stocks) and the life is just two years, the options are valued at only $8.87 over a $50 exercise price. The assumptions used in the example were for a volatility of 0.3 and a life of six years, thus the value of $17.15.

Returning to the example begun in Chapter 14, the yearly compensation expense over the vesting period would be net of applicable income taxes. U.S. income tax regulations permit deductions for stock options, generally the excess of the market price at the time of exercise over the exercise price. Following fair value accounting rules, the compensation expense is

---

[3] This example is taken from SFAS No. 123.

based on the option pricing model's valuation of the option at the grant date. Thus, the tax deductions are at different amounts and at different times than the financial statement compensation expense.

The process is illustrated below. Recall the transaction to record the compensation expense in year 2000, 2001 and 2002 was:

```
Dr. Compensation Expense (E). . . . . . . (inc.) 4,695,703
    Cr. Additional Paid-in Capital-Options (OE) . . . . . . . .      (inc.) 4,695,703
```

Assuming a 35 percent federal tax rate, the entry to establish the deferred tax asset each year over the vesting period would look like this:

```
Dr. Deferred tax asset (A). . . . . . . . . . (inc.) 1,643,496
    Cr. Deferred tax expense (E) . . . . . . . . . . . . . . . . .       (dec.) 1,643,496
```

The net aftertax effect on net income is thus $3,052,207 per year ($4,695,703 – $1,643,496).

If the options are all exercised in 2005, when the stock price is 70, the entry based upon 821,406 shares will be as follows:

```
Dr. Cash (A). . . . . . . . . . . . . . . . . . . (inc.) 41,070,300
Dr. Additional Paid-in Capital—
    Options (OE). . . . . . . . . . . . . . . . (dec.) 14,087,108
        Cr. Capital Stock* (OE). . . . . . . . . . . . . . . . . . .       (inc.) 55,157,408
```

*(divided appropriately between common stock and other paid-in capital)

The difference between the market price of the stock on the exercise date and the exercise price is deductible for tax purposes. Thus ($70 × $50) × 821,406 or $16,428,120 is deductible; therefore, the tax benefit realized on the tax return is $16,428,120 × 0.35, or $5,749,842. The accounting entries are

```
Dr. Deferred tax expense (E) . . . . . . . . (inc.) 4,930,488
    Cr. Deferred tax asset (A). . . . . . . . . . . . . . . . . . . .       (dec.) 4,930,488
```

to reverse the cumulative effect of the three years of deferred tax entries in years 2000, 2001, and 2002 and:

```
Dr. Current taxes payable (L). . . . . . . . (dec.) 5,749,842
    Cr. Current tax expense (E) . . . . . . . . . . . . . . . . . .       (dec.) 4,930,488
    Cr. Additional paid-in capital—Stock options (OE) . . .       (inc.)   819,354
```

to recognize the tax benefit of the options that are deductible when the options are exercised.

Options that vest partially over time—for example, 25 percent the first year, 25 percent the second year, and 50 percent the third year—are simply treated as if they were three different options. Each would have its own vesting and exercise periods and its own option valuation.

Some stock option plans are based upon performance measures such as revenues, profits, or share of market. The maximum number of options is specified at the grant date and then a schedule is established specifying how many options vest by Year 1 if various performance targets are met, how many options vest by Year 2, and so on. For such performance-based stock options, the application of the fair-value based method of accounting requires an assumption of expected performance. Adjustments to these estimates would be made over the life of the performance period (which corresponds to the vesting period). Thus, the

EXHIBIT 14A.1

Stock Option Plan Disclosure

At December 31, 2006, the Company has four stock-based compensation plans, which are described below. The Company applies APB Opinion 25 and related Interpretations in accounting for its plans. Accordingly, no compensation cost has been recognized for its fixed stock option plans and its stock purchase plan. The compensation cost that has been charged against income for its performance-based plan was $6.7 million, $9.4 million, and $0.7 million for 2004, 2005, and 2006, respectively. Had compensation cost for the Company's four stock-based compensation plans been determined based on the fair value at the grant dates for awards under those plans consistent with the method of FASB Statement No. 123, the Company's net income and earnings per share would have been reduced to the pro forma amounts indicated below:

		2004	2005	2006
Net income	As reported	$347,790	$407,300	$479,300
	Pro forma	$336,828	$394,553	$460,398
Primary earnings per share	As reported	$1.97	$2.29	$2.66
	Pro forma	$1.91	$2.22	$2.56
Fully diluted earnings per share	As reported	$1.49	$1.73	$2.02
	Pro forma	$1.44	$1.68	$1.94

Source: *FASB Statement of Financial Accounting Standards No. 123, Accounting for Stock-Based Compensation* is copyrighted by the Financial Accounting Standards Board, 401 Merritt 7, P.O. Box 5116, Norwalk, CT 06856-5116, U.S.A. Portions are reprinted with permission. Copies of the complete document are available from the Financial Accounting Standards Board.

compensation costs of performance-based stock options are based on valuations using appropriate option pricing models and at performance levels estimated by management on a prospective basis. Employee stock purchase rights are also included in SFAS No. 123. An example of such a disclosure, taken from Appendix B of SFAS No. 123, is presented in Exhibit 14A.2, together with disclosures of simple stock option plans and a performance-based plan.

Let's step through the disclosure. The first paragraph is key. If the company adopts the fair-value based method of accounting for stock options, the compensation cost will include the amortized portion of stock options granted, including options granted in an earlier period. If the company had elected not to follow the fair value method, then the first paragraph would be replaced with one like that shown in Exhibit 14A.1 (the reference to APB Opinion No. 25 is to the earlier accounting standard employing the intrinsic-value based method). It is here that the company would disclose the pro forma impact of SFAS No. 123 on net income and EPS.

The disclosure in Exhibit 14A.2 describes each of the company's stock-based plans. Note that the level of detail is such that any reader equipped with their own Black-Scholes valuation model could test the sensitivity of the valuations, although they could not recreate the actual compensation expenses because some of the other assumptions made by management, such as projected forfeiture rates, have not been disclosed. Note that the fair value of the options granted under the Fixed Stock Option Plan was $15.90 in 2004 and $16.25 under the Performance-Based Stock Option Plan:

Fiscal Year 2004

	Shares	Value	Total
Fixed stock options	900,000	$15.90	$14,310,000
Performance-based options	850,000	16.25	13,812,500
			$28,122,500

This $28.1 million is not the same as the $23.3 million compensation expense in 2004 (see next page) for the stock-based plan for several reasons:

- The 2004 awards vest over time, not immediately on the award date.

- Awards from earlier years may have vesting periods that span 2004.

- Management has made certain assumptions about forfeitures that reduce the estimated cost.

EXHIBIT 14A.2

Stock Option Plan Disclosures: Fair-Value Method

Stock Compensation Plans

At December 31, 2006, the Company has four stock-based compensation plans, which are described below. The Company accounts for the fair value of its grants under those plans in accordance with FASB Statement 123. The compensation cost that has been charged against income for those plans was $23.3 million, $28.7 million, and $29.4 million for 2004, 2005, and 2006, respectively.

Fixed Stock Option Plans

The Company has two fixed option plans. Under the 1999 Employee Stock Option Plan, the Company may grant options to its employees for up to 8 million shares of common stock. Under the 2004 Managers' Incentive Stock Option Plan, the Company may grant options to its management personnel for up to 5 million shares of common stock. Under both plans, the exercise price of each

option equals the market price of the Company's stock on the date of grant and an option's maximum term is 10 years. Options are granted on January 1 and vest at the end of the third year under the 1999 Plan and at the end of the second year under the 2004 Plan.

The fair value of each option grant is estimated on the date of grant using the Black-Scholes option-pricing model with the following weighted-average assumptions used for grants in 2004, 2005, and 2006, respectively: dividend yield of 1.5 percent for all years; expected volatility of 24, 26, and 29 percent, risk-free interest rates of 6.5, 7.5, and 7 percent for the 1999 Plan options and 6.4, 7.4, and 6.8 percent for the 2004 Plan options; and expected lives of 6, 5, and 5 years for the 1999 Plan options and 5, 4, and 4 years for the 2004 Plan options.

A summary of the status of the Company's two fixed stock option plans as of December 31, 2004, 2005, and 2006, and changes during the years ending on those dates is presented below:

Fixed Options	2004 Shares (000)	2004 Weighted-Average Exercise Price	2005 Shares (000)	2005 Weighted-Average Exercise Price	2006 Shares (000)	2006 Weighted-Average Exercise Price
Outstanding at beginning of year	4,500	$34	4,600	$38	4,660	$42
Granted	900	50	1,000	55	950	60
Exercised	(700)	27	(850)	34	(800)	36
Forfeited	(100)	46	(90)	51	(80)	59
Outstanding at end of year	4,600	38	4,660	42	4,730	47
Options exercisable at year-end	2,924		2,873		3,159	
Weighted-average fair value of options granted during the year	$15.90		$17.46		$19.57	

The following table summarizes information about fixed stock options outstanding at December 31, 2006:

Range of Exercise Prices	Options Outstanding Number Outstanding at 12/31/06	Options Outstanding Weighted-Average Remaining Contractual Life	Options Outstanding Weighted-Average Exercise Price	Options Exercisable Number Exercisable at 12/31/06	Options Exercisable Weighted-Average Exercise Price
$25 to 33	1,107,000	3.6 years	$29	1,107,000	$29
39 to 41	467,000	5.0	40	467,000	40
46 to 50	1,326,000	6.6	48	1,326,000	48
55 to 60	1,830,000	8.5	57	259,000	55
$25 to 60	4,730,000	6.5	47	3,159,000	41

continued

EXHIBIT 14A.2 concluded

Performance-Based Stock Option Plan

Under its Goals 2010 Stock Option Plan adopted in 2002, each January 1 the Company grants selected executives and other key employees stock option awards whose vesting is contingent upon increases in the Company's market share for its principal product. If at the end of 3 years market share has increased by at least 5 percentage points from the date of grant, one-third of the options under the award vest to active employees. However, if at that date market share has increased by at least 10 percentage points, two-thirds of the options under the award vest, and if market share has increased by 20 percentage points or more, all of the options under the award vest. The number of shares subject to options under this plan cannot exceed

5 million. The exercise price of each option, which has a 10-year life, is equal to the market price of the Company's stock on the date of grant.

The fair value of each option grant was estimated on the date of grant using the Black-Scholes option-pricing model with the following assumptions for 2004, 2005, and 2006, respectively: risk-free interest rates of 6.5, 7.6, and 7.4 percent; dividend yield of 1.5 percent for all years; expected lives of 6, 6, and 7 years; and volatility of 24, 26, and 29 percent.

A summary of the status of the Company's performance-based stock option plan as of December 31, 2004, 2005, and 2006, and changes during the years ending on those dates is presented below:

Fixed Options	2004		2005		2006	
	Shares (000)	Weighted-Average Exercise Price	Shares (000)	Weighted-Average Exercise Price	Shares (000)	Weighted-Average Exercise Price
Outstanding at beginning of year	830	$46	1,635	$48	2,533	$51
Granted	850	50	980	55	995	60
Exercised	0		0		(100)	46
Forfeited	(45)	48	(82)	50	(604)	51
Outstanding at end of year	1,635	48	2,533	51	2,824	55
Options exercisable at year-end	0		780	46	936	47
Weighted-average fair value of options granted during the year	$16.25		$19.97		$24.32	

As of December 31, 2006, the 2.8 million performance options outstanding under the Plan have exercise prices between $46 and $60 and a weighted-average remaining contractual life of 7.7 years. The Company expects that approximately one-third of the nonvested awards at December 31, 2006, will eventually vest based on projected market share.

Employee Stock Purchase Plan

Under the 1987 Employee Stock Purchase Plan, the Company is authorized to issue up to 10 million shares of common stock to its full-time employees, nearly all of whom are eligible to participate. Under the terms of the Plan, employees can choose each year to have up to 6 percent of their annual base earnings withheld to purchase the

Company's common stock. The purchase price of the stock is 85 percent of the lower of its beginning-of-year or end-of-year market price. Approximately 75 to 80 percent of eligible employees have participated in the Plan in the last 3 years. Under the Plan, the Company sold 456,000 shares, 481,000 shares, and 503,000 shares to employees in 2004, 2005, and 2006, respectively. Compensation cost is recognized for the fair value of the employees' purchase rights, which was estimated using the Black-Scholes model with the following assumptions for 2004, 2005, and 2006, respectively: dividend yield of 1.5 percent for all years; an expected life of 1 year for all years; expected volatility of 22, 24, and 26 percent; and risk-free interest rates of 5.9, 6.9, and 6.7 percent. The weighted-average fair value of those purchase rights granted in 2004, 2005, and 2006 was $11.95, $13.73, and $15.30, respectively.

ASSIGNMENTS

14.1. Stock issuances and dividend payments. Mesa Corporation was incorporated on January 1, 1997, and issued the following stock, for cash:

> 1,000,000 shares of no-par common stock were authorized; 100,000 shares were issued on January 1 at $18 per share.

> 200,000 shares of $1 par value, 10 percent cumulative preferred stock were authorized, and 50,000 shares were issued on January 1, 1999, at $14 per share.

The year 1999 went relatively well. Net income was $700,000, and the board of directors declared dividends of $200,000 and paid them by year end.

Required:

Prepare the entries required to record the issuances of the shares of stock and the payment of the dividends.

14.2. Preferred stock characteristics. Netway Corporation has four issues of preferred stock outstanding in addition to its common stock. All of these issues are detailed in the following footnote. Describe in your own words the characteristics of each of these preferred stock issues.

Netway Corporation and Subsidiaries

Capital Stock
The number of shares of capital stock outstanding is as follows:

	December 31	
	1998	**1997**
5% Cumulative preferred—$50 par value. Authorized, 585,730.	**407,718(a)**	407,718(a)
$5.50 Dividend cumulative convertible preferred— no par value—$20 stated value (each share convertible into 4.5 shares of common; maximum liquidation value, $3,252,900 and $3,476,800). Authorized, 1,164,077.	**32,529**	34,768
$4.50 Dividend cumulative preferred—$100 par value. Authorized, 103,976.	**103,976**	103,976
$4.30 Dividend cumulative preferred—no par value— $100 stated value. Authorized, 1,069,204.	**836,585**	836,585
Common—$1 par value. Authorized, 60,000,000.	**22,414,564(b)**	22,404,494(b)
After deducting treasury shares		
(a) 5% cumulative preferred	**178,012**	178,012
(b) Common	**4,822,088**	4,822,066

14.3. Treasury stock transactions. Smith Company has sold stock to its employees and to outsiders at various times during its life, as follows:

1994	100,000 shares originally sold at par value for $100,000 in cash.
1994	10,000 shares issued to an employee as an inducement to sign an employment contract; no cash exchanged.
1995	25,000 shares sold to an independent investor for $50,000 in cash.
1996	100,000 shares sold to a group of 25 investors at $30 a share.
1997	A 2-for-1 stock split declared.
1998	500,000 shares sold in a public offering through Merrill Lynch at $25 a share.
1999	100,000 shares given to the top management as a bonus. The market price was then $20.

In 2000 the company purchased 50,000 shares on the open market at $12 a share.

Required:

a. Prepare the entry required to record the 50,000 share purchase, assuming the company plans to reissue the shares as a bonus to its employees at a future date.

b. Prepare the entry required to record the share purchase, assuming the company plans to retire the reacquired shares.

14.4. Convertible preferred stock. In 1998 Clever Corp. raised $1,000,000 in capital by the sale of 10,000 shares of convertible preferred stock, par value $100. The preferred stock required an annual dividend of only $4 a share even though the prime rate at the time was 8 percent. Each share of preferred stock was convertible into five shares of Clever common stock, which had a market value of $10 at the time of the preferred stock issuance.

Required:

a. Prepare the entry to record the sale of the preferred stock. How would you propose to recognize the value of the conversion feature in the financial statements? Please provide the rationale for your answer.

b. Why would Clever want to issue convertible preferred instead of regular preferred or additional common stock?

c. Why would an investor buy the Clever convertible preferred when it pays only a $4 dividend?

14.5. Convertible preferred, revisited. In 1999 all of the holders of Clever Corp. convertible preferred stock (discussed in 14.4) turned in their shares for conversion and were given five shares of common stock for each share of preferred stock.

Required:

a. Why would the holders of the preferred stock turn their shares in for redemption at this time?

b. What entry would Clever Corp. make at the time of the conversion?

14.6. Stock options. Aggressive Corporation was doing very well with its new product line, and it seemed as though the company could double in size over the next three years. It was a tense time for the management people, however, and the good fortune brought its own questions. Do we have enough inventory to meet demand? Should we expand the plant to accommodate one more assembly line? If we encourage sales by granting extended credit terms, how will we pay our own bills? Nonetheless, management had worked very hard for a long time with very little reward, and members were delighted to bask in the prospects of the future. The board of directors was pleased, too, and at the end of the year awarded the top five people stock options, which would enable each of them to buy 10,000 shares of the company's stock at $9, the current market price. It was indeed a happy new year.

Required:

a. Why might Aggressive's board of directors have believed it appropriate to issue the stock options to the top management people at this time at $9 a share?

b. How might you feel about the stock options if you were one of the top management people? Why? How might you feel if you were a nonmanagement shareholder in the company?

c. Assuming SFAS No. 123 is not yet applicable, prepare the entry required to recognize the issuance of the options at the issue date. Explain the reasons for your entry.

d. Now assume that SFAS No. 123 is applicable and that the value of the options is calculated to be $2.15. What accounting would be required?

14.7. Stock options exercised. Three years after Aggressive's board of directors issued the stock options to its top five employees (see 14.6) the company's sales had grown nearly three times and profits were up 250 percent. The stock market had recognized the company's success, and the shares regularly traded at $32. Three of the top five employees exercised their options in full, but the other two had not as yet done so.

Required:

a. Prepare the entries required under both the intrinsic-value based method and the fair value method of accounting to recognize the exercise of the options for 30,000 shares. Explain the rationale for your entry and then explain the source of your numbers.

b. What factors might have motivated the three management people to have exercised their stock options? What factors might have motivated the other two to hold on to the options, at least for the time being?

14.8. Describing stock options. The status of Procter & Gamble's stock option program, as of the end of each of the last three years, is described in footnote 6 to the company's 1998 report to stockholders as follows:

Stock option activity was as follows:

	Options in Thousands		
	1998	**1997**	**1996**
Outstanding, July 1	68,514	66,657	63,384
Granted	20,315	10,409	9,605
Exercised	(8,477)	(8,357)	(6,110)
Canceled	(434)	(195)	(222)
Outstanding, June 30	79,918	68,514	66,657
Exercisable	59,610	58,098	57,048
Available for grant	31,558	28,538	24,418
Average price			
Outstanding,			
beginning of year	$ 31.00	$ 24.79	$ 21.36
Granted	83.26	58.72	40.87
Exercised	18.57	16.02	14.52
Outstanding, end of year	45.58	31.00	24.79
Exercisable, end of year	32.74	26.03	22.09
Weighted average grant			
date fair value of options	24.56	17.14	10.88

Required:

In your own words, describe the events depicted by each of the line items in the table from the footnote. What do the numbers in the table mean? What might the sources of those numbers be?

14.9. Stock compensation programs. Footnote 10 from the annual report to shareholders from the Snap-On Tools Corporation reads as follows:

Note 10 Corporation Stock Option and Purchase Plans

The corporation has a stock option plan for directors, officers, and key employees with expiration dates on the options ranging from 1996 to 2004. The plan provides that options be granted at exercise prices equal to market value on the date the option is granted.

	Number of Shares	Option Price Per Share
Options outstanding at		
December 28, 1991	1,890,032	$20.56–38.13
Granted	150,025	33.75–34.75
Exercised	(151,116)	20.56–35.50
Surrendered	(54,934)	20.56–38.13
Options outstanding at		
January 2, 1993	1,834,007	20.56–38.13
Granted	532,619	31.75–35.00
Exercised	(361,057)	20.56–35.50
Surrendered	(106,905)	20.56–35.50
Options outstanding at		
January 1, 1994	1,898,664	20.56–38.13
Granted	40,500	36.75–37.25
Exercised	(203,445)	20.56–35.00
Surrendered	(182,502)	20.56–31.75
Options outstanding at		
December 31, 1994	**1,553,217**	**$20.56–38.73**
Shares reserved for		
future grants	**1,738,093**	
Shares exercisable at		
December 31, 1994	**1,498,004**	

The corporation offers shareholders a convenient way to increase their investment in the corporation through a no-commission dividend reinvestment and stock purchase plan. Participating shareholders may invest the cash dividends from all or a portion of their common stock to buy additional shares. The program also permits shareholders to invest cash for additional shares that are purchased for them each month. For 1994, 1993, and 1992, shares issued under the dividend reinvestment and stock purchase plan totaled 17,991, 15,485, and 17,587. At December 31, 1994, 933,501 shares were reserved for issuance to shareholders under this plan.

Employees of the corporation are entitled to participate in an employee stock purchase plan and are entitled to purchase shares up to the maximum allowed by the Internal Revenue Code. The purchase price of the common stock is the lesser of the closing market price of the stock on the beginning date (May 15th) or ending date (May 14th) of each plan year. The board of directors may terminate this plan at any time. For 1994, 1993, and 1992, shares issued under the employee stock purchase plan totaled 43,205, 44,563, and 66,554. At December 31, 1994, shares totaling 94,282 were reserved for issuance to employees under this plan, and the corporation held contributions of approximately $1.3 million for the purchase of common stock.

Franchised dealers are entitled to participate in a dealer stock purchase plan. The purchase price of the common stock is the lesser of the closing market price of the stock on the beginning date (May 15th) or ending date (May 14th) of each plan year. For 1994, 1993, and 1992, shares issued under the dealer stock purchase plan totaled 50,126, 4,683, and 348. At December 31, 1994, 144,843 shares were reserved for issuance to franchised dealers under this plan, and the corporation held contributions of approximately $1.5 million for the purchase of common stock.

In 1993, shareholders approved the Directors' 1993 Fee Plan. Under this plan, nonemployee directors receive a mandatory minimum of 25 percent and an elective maximum of up to 100 percent of their fees and retainer in shares of corporation stock. Directors may elect to defer receipt of all or part of these shares. For 1994 and 1993, shares issued under the Directors' Fee Plan totaled 1,545 and 184. Additionally, receipt of 602 and 1,004 shares were deferred in 1994 and 1993. At December 31, 1994, 196,665 shares were reserved for issuance to directors under this plan.

Required:

Comment on each of the following:

a. From the company's perspective, what is the purpose of each of these five stock plans?

b. How do the programs differ in terms of impact on the participants and on the company?

c. What accounting is afforded each of the programs?

14.10. Shareholder transactions.   Wal-Mart's 1995 annual report contained the following statement of consolidated changes in shareholders' investment:

(Amounts in millions except per share data)	Number of Shares	Common Stock	Capital in Excess of Par Value	Retained Earnings	Foreign Currency Translation Adjustment	Total
Balance — January 31, 1992	1,149	$115	$626	$6,249	$—	$6,990
Net Income				1,995		1,995
Cash dividends ($0.11 per share)				(241)		(241)
Two-for-one stock split	1,150	115	(115)			—
Other	1		16			16
Balance — January 31, 1993	2,300	230	527	8,003	—	8,760
Net Income				2,333		2,333
Cash dividends ($0.13 per share)				(299)		(299)
Other	(1)		9	(50)		(41)
Balance — January 31, 1994	2,299	230	536	9,987	—	10,753
Net Income				2,681		2,681
Cash dividends ($0.17 per share)				(391)		(391)
Foreign currency translation adjustment					(256)	(256)
Other	(2)		3	(64)		(61)
Balance — January 31, 1995	2,297	$230	$539	$12,213	$(256)	$12,726

Required:

a. Is Wal-Mart's common stock no par or par? Explain.

b. Explain to a stockholder owning 100 shares of stock just what happened in the two-for-one stock split in 1992.

14.11. Shareholders' transactions with treasury stock. Footnote 5 from the 1989 annual report of the H. J. Heinz Company follows:

(In thousands)	Cumulative Preferred Stock — Third, $1.70 First Series $10 par — Amount	Common Stock — Issued — Amount	Issued — Shares	In Treasury — Amount	In Treasury — Shares	Additional Capital — Amount
Balance April 30, 1986	$1,141	$71,850	143,700	$227,374	10,283	$ 85,882
Reacquired	—	—	—	236,165	5,471	—
Conversion of preferred into common stock	(171)	—	—	(1,295)	(77)	(1,124)
Stock options exercised	—	—	—	(10,430)	(619)	4,763
Reduction in par value of common stock	—	(35,925)	—	—	—	35,925
Other, net	—	—	—	166	3	—
Balance April 29, 1987	$970	$35,925	143,700	$451,980	15,061	$125,446
Reacquired	—	—	—	123,519	2,703	—
Conversion of preferred into common stock	(128)	—	—	(972)	(58)	(843)
Stock options exercised	—	—	—	(27,598)	(1,638)	11,013
Other, net	—	—	—	809	14	269
Balance April 27, 1988	$ 842	$35,925	143,700	$547,738	16,082	$135,885
Reacquired	—	—	—	97,508	2,056	—
Conversion of preferred into common stock	(85)	—	—	(693)	(38)	(608)
Conversion of subordinated debentures	—	—	—	(30,906)	(1,150)	3,784
Stock options exercised	—	—	—	(35,379)	(1,756)	6,293
Other, net	—	—	—	1,390	25	236
Balance May 3, 1989	$ 757	$35,925	143,700	$579,658	15,219	$145,590
Authorized Shares—May 3, 1989	76	—	600,000	—	—	—

Capital Stock: The preferred stock outstanding is convertible at a rate of one share of preferred stock into 4.5 shares of common stock. The company can redeem the stock at $25.50 per share.

In September 1986 the shareholders approved an increase to the authorized common stock of the company from 300,000,000 shares to 600,000,000 shares and changed the par value of the common stock from 50 cents per share to 25 cents per share.

On May 3, 1989, there were authorized, but unissued, 2,200,000 shares of third cumulative preferred stock for which the series had not been designated.

Required:

For each of the five transactions highlighted above:

a. Describe in your own words the underlying event, explaining in particular (1) the factor(s) that triggered the event and (2) the probable source of the numbers used.

b. Prepare the probable entry(ies) that were required.

14.12. Stock for debt exchange. In 1989 RJR Nabisco, Inc., was taken private by Kohlberg Kravis Roberts & Co. in a leveraged buyout. As part of the buyout, RJR Nabisco issued large amounts of high-yield "junk bonds." For example, one part of the leveraged buyout involved the issuance of $2.86 billion of 17 percent bonds due in 2007.

Beginning in late 1990, KKR & Co. began efforts to reduce the level of debt carried on the books of RJR Nabisco. One such proposal involved the issuance of 82.8 million shares of RJR stock and $350 million of cash in exchange for $753 million (face value) of the 17 percent bonds.

Assume that the RJR Nabisco stock has a par value of $1; the stock, being privately held, has no readily determined market value; and the bonds are trading at their face value.

Required:

a. Why would the company make that exchange at this time?

b. What entry would the company make at the time of the exchange?

c. What entry would be made if the bonds were trading at $830 rather than $1,000 face value?

14.13. Convertible preferred stock. On August 16 *The Wall Street Journal* carried an advertisement concerning Baker Hughes. The following is from that advertisement: "Baker Hughes Incorporated has called for redemption of all its $3.50 Convertible Preferred Stock."

According to the advertisement, Baker Hughes had decided to exercise the redemption feature on its outstanding preferred stock and to redeem the stock at a price of $52.45 per share plus accrued dividends of $0.16, for a total of $52.61, on August 31. The preferred stock also carried a conversion feature that would permit the owner to convert the preferred stock into 1.9608 shares of common stock (par value of $1). The market price of the common stock on August 13 was $32.625 per share. The advertisement emphasized that the conversion feature of the preferred stock expired on August 27.

Required:

a. Assume that Baker Hughes has 1 million shares of preferred stock outstanding and that its par value is $5. How would the company account for (1) the redemption of all shares and (2) the conversion of all shares?

b. If you held 100 shares of Baker Hughes preferred stock, which alternative (conversion or redemption) would you choose, and why?

c. If you were the CEO of Baker Hughes, which alternative would you prefer, and why?

14.14. Translation of foreign financial statements. Graham International, Inc., is a subsidiary of a U.S.-based corporation, The Graham Group. Graham International is headquartered in Mexico City, Mexico, although it represents the parent company worldwide.

Presented below are Graham International's income statement for 19X9, expressed in pesos, and its balance sheets as of December 31, 19X8, and December 31, 19X9, also expressed in pesos. Assume the exchange rate between the Mexican peso and the U.S. dollar was as follows:

12/31/X8	$0.0004 (1 peso = $0.0004 U.S.)
12/31/X9	$0.00036 (1 peso = $0.00036 U.S.)
19X9 average	$0.00038

Graham International had been in existence since 19X2, when it was capitalized with an investment of 3,000,000 pesos. At that time, the exchange rate was 1,800 pesos to the U.S. dollar. Since then, the company has earned (after taxes and dividends) 15,000,000 pesos, with a translation value of $7,500 U.S.

Required:

a. Prepare the translated (in U.S. dollar equivalents) financial statements of Graham International, Inc., at December 31, 19X9.

b. Determine the balance (if any) required in the Translation Adjustment account for the equity section of The Graham Group's 19X9 balance sheet.

Graham International, Inc.
Statement of Income
For the Year Ended December 31, 19X9
(in thousands of pesos)

Sales	82,000
Less: Costs and expenses	
Costs of sales	42,000
Depreciation	4,050
Selling, general, and administrative expenses	7,250
Interest	2,500
	55,800
Net income before taxes	26,200
Less: Income taxes	13,300
Net income	12,900
Dividends paid to parent (12/31/X5)	1,500

Graham International, Inc.
Balance Sheet
As of December 31
(in thousands of pesos)

	19X8	19X9
Assets:		
Cash	2,000	3,000
Accounts receivable	6,000	7,400
Inventory	7,000	10,000
Total current assets	15,000	20,400
Plant and equipment	39,000	42,000
Less: Accumulated depreciation	(4,950)	(9,000)
Net plant and equipment	34,050	33,000
Total assets	49,050	53,400
Equities:		
Liabilities		
Accounts payable	6,050	4,000
Long-term debt	25,000	20,000
Total	31,050	24,000
Owners' equity:		
Capital stock	3,000	3,000
Retained earnings	15,000	26,400
Total	18,000	29,400
Total equities	49,050	53,400

14.15. Stock options. On January 1, 1997, Biotrack, Inc., planned to announce a new employee stock option program under which certain officers, directors, and employees would be eligible to purchase the company's $1 par value common shares. The details were as follows:

Required:

1. A total of 900,000 options to be awarded

2. Market price of shares at grant date: $60.00

3. Option price: $60.00

4. Expiration date: January 1, 2005

5. Expected exercise date: 3 years after vesting

6. Vesting: 1/3 on January 1, 1998
   1/3 on January 1, 1999
   1/3 on January 1, 2000

7. Estimated forfeitures: 2%/year

8. Volatility on company shares: 20%

9. Risk free borrowing rate: 5%

10. Dividend rate: 3%

Assume that Biotrack has opted to adopt the fair-value based method of accounting for stock options. Ignore income taxes.

(The following table may be used in this problem. It is based on a Black-Scholes option pricing model adapted for dividends, and it assumes a 5 percent borrowing rate and a 3 percent dividend payout rate.)

Black-Scholes Options Pricing Model
Adapted for Dividends
Assumptions: 5% Borrowing Rate, 3% Dividend Payout

		Expected Lifetime in Years							
		1	2	3	4	5	6	7	8
	0.15	3.38	4.89	6.04	6.97	7.74	8.40	8.97	9.45
	0.18	3.85	5.53	6.78	7.78	8.61	9.30	9.89	10.39
	0.20	4.33	6.17	7.52	8.60	9.48	10.21	10.82	11.33
Volatility	0.23	4.80	6.80	8.26	9.41	10.35	11.11	11.75	12.28
	0.25	5.27	7.44	9.01	10.23	11.21	12.01	12.67	13.22
	0.28	5.75	8.08	9.75	11.04	12.07	12.91	13.59	14.15
	0.30	6.22	8.71	10.48	11.85	12.93	13.80	14.51	15.08
	0.33	6.69	9.35	11.22	12.65	13.78	14.68	15.41	15.99

Required:

a. What entry should the company make on January 1, 1997, when the options are granted? What entry is made at year-end 1997?

b. What entry is made to record the compensation expense associated with these options for the fiscal year 1998?

c. Suppose that the assumption as to forfeiture was reduced on January 1, 1999. It now appeared that there would be 290,000 options vesting as of December 31, 1999. What entry is made to record the compensation expense associated with these options for the fiscal year 1999?

d. Suppose that 400,000 options were exercised during December 2000, when the average market price was $80.00. What entry would the company make?

e. Suppose that 400,000 options were exercised during December 2001, when the average market price was $90.00. What entry should the company make?

f. Suppose that the last of the options to be exercised, 55,000, were exercised during December 2002, when the average market price was $100.00. What entry would the company make?

g. Over the whole program, how many options were exercised? How many were canceled or lapsed? What was the overall effect on owner's equity? What other entries would be necessary?

PART IV

Special Considerations in Preparing and Using Accounting Data

CHAPTER 15

Communicating Corporate Value

Communicating
Corporate Value[1]

We all want, above all, to be heard—but not merely to be heard. We want to be understood—heard for what we think we are saying, for what we know we meant. With increased understanding of the ways [we] use language should come a decrease in frequency of the complaint "You just don't understand." [2]

Key Chapter Issues

- What is the role of financial reporting in communicating corporate value?
- What factors inhibit the communication of corporate value?
- How does the efficient market hypothesis help us understand the role of financial communications in establishing security market prices?

- How might a business report differ from a financial report?
- As the economy evolves to more service industries, what implications does that have for financial reporting and the communication of corporate value?

---

[1] Earlier versions of this chapter were presented during the Ira Shapiro/Beta Alpha Psi Distinguished Lecture Series at The University of Maryland at College Park, and as part of the 1992 Price Waterhouse Speaker Series at Miami University, Oxford, Ohio. We want to thank both universities for their support and encouragement.

[2] D. Tannen, *You Just Don't Understand: Women and Men in Conversation* (New York: Ballantine, 1990), p. 48.

P rofessor Tannen's words seem particularly appropriate as the introduction to the capstone chapter for this text. Her thought-provoking book helped many understand the enormously complex process of interpersonal communication. Indeed, she illustrated how the effectiveness of communication depends on the background of the speaker and of the listener; on the way language is used; on what the parties expect from the conversation; and on the context of the discussion. We believe all of these factors apply in business communication as well as in interpersonal communication. Moreover, we believe business communication is inhibited by a set of additional factors that include the use of specialized language, the intensity of commercial competition, and the existence of legal restraints.

The focus of this chapter is on the communications between a company and its financial stakeholders. It is very different from the previous 14 chapters in that it seeks to highlight the critical thinking applicable to today's accounting debates. It should be read not with the idea that you will find resolutions for those debates here, but rather that you will join the search for more effective business and financial communications. Indeed, this search is one that engages most financial managers at some time in their career. For example, managers of growing but cash-hungry companies often complain that despite their hard work to create a flourishing business, no one outside the management team really understands how truly wonderful their company is.[3] Clearly, part of their frustration is an outgrowth of their natural bias about their company, but very often their frustration is based in fact. With but a moment's reflection, it should be obvious that it is an impossible task to set forth the total essence of a complex company in a set of numbers or even in a verbal description. If management does find a way to tell the company's story somewhat effectively, telling that story in a way that then attracts the interest of potential stakeholders is still difficult. To the extent that the communication between the company and its financial stakeholders fails to fully inform, there is a real cost to the company. At best, the company's stock may be underpriced and its capital costs excessive. At worst, the company is vulnerable to a hostile takeover or a forced restructuring.

Communicating to outsiders the real value inherent in a company is subject to a number of natural impediments:

- Management will always have a better understanding of their company than will ever be possible for an outside financial stakeholder.

- In financial communications, the speaker and the listener will almost always have dramatically different contexts.

- Outside stakeholders will have many other companies clamoring for their attention (there are more than 12,000 companies registered with the U.S. Securities and Exchange Commission), and the attention those stakeholders can allocate to any particular company's story is, of necessity, limited.

- All financial communication is subject to antifraud statutes, and all managers understand the risk of being subjected to that legal web. A manager with good news to report is faced with a difficult trade-off: There is a natural temptation to announce the news quickly so as to impound that information into the stock price; but caution suggests delaying that announcement until the facts are ironclad and there is little possibility of a subsequent disappointment likely to spawn a follow-on lawsuit.

- The language used in communications with financial stakeholders is primarily accounting-based, and for many reasons the language of accounting is an imperfect communication device. In particular, financial reporting is an imperfect communication vehicle (1) because of the estimates that are required in preparing a financial report, (2) because of the politics and personalities that shape accounting rules, and (3) because reporting conventions represent compromises aimed to meet the needs of those who want accounting to measure the past and those who want it to predict the future.

---

[3] A poll by Louis Harris and Associates found that 60 percent of executives surveyed believed that the shares of their companies were undervalued. See "Companies Feel Underrated by the Street," *Business Week*, February 20, 1984, p. 14.

AN ACCOUNTING PERSPECTIVE ON COMMUNICATING
WITH FINANCIAL STAKEHOLDERS

The 1960s generated a good deal of concern about accounting in general and about the accounting standard-setting process in particular. The decade came to be characterized as the "Go-Go Years," and many of the excesses that plagued the financial marketplace during those years were attributed to accounting and the accountants. In response to such criticisms, the financial community in the early 1970s established two task forces. The first was to explore alternative ways of establishing timely accounting standards and to make sure that the resultant standards met the needs of the financial community as a whole. The second was to rethink the role of accounting and to set a conceptual course for the future of accounting standard setting. The deliberations of the first task force resulted in the dismantling of the Accounting Principles Board (APB) and the formation of the Financial Accounting Standards Board (FASB). The deliberations of the second task force resulted in the publication of an important report titled "The Objectives of Financial Statements." Here are perhaps the most important assertions of that report:

- The basic **objective of financial statements** is to provide information useful for making economic decisions.

- An objective of financial statements is to provide information useful to investors and creditors for predicting, comparing, and evaluating potential cash flows to them in terms of timing and related uncertainty.

- An objective of financial statements is to serve primarily those users who have limited authority, ability, or resources to obtain information and who rely on financial statements as their principal source of information about an enterprise's economic activities.[4]

These conclusions may seem elemental, but like all fundamental statements, they communicate important truths. In essence, the conclusions of the report challenged the accounting profession to work to meet the needs of users. The report also concluded that users needed to have information to help them make investment decisions. Finally, the report concluded that the users to be served were those who depended on the financial reporting process as their primary source for investment information. Thus, the report informed the accounting profession what their real mandate was, what their customers wanted, and who their customers were.

After many years of study—while dealing concurrently with many specific accounting issues—the FASB issued a series of releases referred to as its **conceptual framework** that attempted to codify and clearly state the primary underpinnings of the financial reporting process. The first of those releases built on the work of the earlier "Objectives" task force; here are two of the key points from *Concepts Statement No. 1:*

- Financial reporting should provide information that is useful to present and potential investors and creditors and other users in making rational investment, credit, and similar decisions.

- Financial reporting should provide information to help present and potential investors and creditors and other users in assessing the amounts, timing, and uncertainty of

[4] *Report of the Study Group on the Objectives of Financial Statements (The Trueblood Report),* (New York: American Institute of Certified Public Accountants, 1973), pp. 13, 17, 20.

prospective cash receipts from dividends, interest, and the proceeds from the sale, redemption, or maturity of securities or loans.[5]

Hindsight might suggest that the FASB has at times lost sight of those objectives and has failed to focus on the user. For example, in the late 1980s the FASB devoted substantial efforts to the accounting for income taxes and the accounting for pensions and health benefits. During those two major efforts, the FASB frequently found itself caught up in the same kinds of conceptual preoccupations and politicking that its predecessor the APB had found so unproductive. Indeed, the impetus for the new income tax accounting was a concern that the prior approach resulted in balance sheet numbers (deferred tax assets and liabilities) that did not meet the conceptual definition of either assets or liabilities. However, some critics have argued that the end result of the FASB's eight years of work on income taxes (SFAS No. 109) still failed to meet the objective of providing information to help assess the "amounts, timing, and uncertainty of prospective cash receipts."[6] Similarly, the accounting community became concerned about the growing obligation companies had as a result of their commitment to employees and retirees for health care benefits. As a result of that concern, the FASB published a complex standard (SFAS No. 106) that requires the accrual of very large liabilities to recognize those commitments. However, in a subsequent article on the editorial page of *The Wall Street Journal,* an actuary suggested that the actual benefits to be paid were subject to so many variables as to make such accounting accruals meaningless. He concluded, "Information about the future is useful only when it allows us to make better decisions today. Unless a 50-year commitment to retiree health benefits has been made, the best thing a manager can do with the FASB rule is to do what the financial analysts have done so far—ignore it..."[7]

While the FASB was devoting incredible time and effort toward these specific issues, several important environmental shifts were under way, suggesting that all was not well with the overall financial reporting process:

- The proportion of shares owned by individual investors in the U.S. shrank, and the proportion owned by institutional investors grew. According to a report by the Securities Industry Association (SIA), the percentage of stocks held by individuals fell to 49.7 percent in the second quarter of 1992, down from 71 percent in 1980 and 84 percent in 1965.[8] The New York Stock Exchange reported the proportion of individuals owning shares directly declined from 29.2 million in 1992 to 27.4 million in 1995. It was estimated that individuals accounted for less than 40% of all stockholders. Further, institutional investors came to dominate the activity in the market, accounting for more than two-thirds of the trading volume of common stocks on United States' markets. There are many explanations for the rise of the institutions and the relative decline in the role of individual investors; unfortunately, it is very likely that one explanation is that individuals have decided that corporate communications are too complex. It may very well be that the average individual investor has been forced to conclude that only a full-time professional can discern the value of a company's stock by interpreting the bewildering display of corporate financial information included in published annual reports.

---

[5] "Objectives of Financial Reporting by Business Enterprises" FASB Statement of Concepts No. 1, para. 34 and 37, The Financial Accounting Standards Board, November 1978.

[6] See, for example, several articles and an editorial in the June 1989 issue of *Accounting Horizons,* published by the American Accounting Association.

[7] Jeffery Peteril, "Ignore the Retiree Health Benefits Rule," *The Wall Street Journal,* February 21, 1992, p. 14.

[8] The SIA study was reported in an article by Michael Siconolfi in *The Wall Street Journal,* November 13, 1992, page C1.

- In the 1980s, a large number of savings and loan associations collapsed, shortly after issuing an apparently healthy balance sheet supported by an unqualified opinion from a CPA firm. Some argued that Congress was at fault because of the industry-specific accounting rules they had set for the S&Ls, and that the accountants were simply following those rules. That argument, however, was counterproductive: It only served to reinforce the notion that accounting and accountants had become so rule-oriented that the financial reporting system was unable to communicate financial reality.

- During the 1980s, while the accounting standard setters were debating how to measure assets and liabilities, the major CPA firms were facing unprecedented litigation.[9] The most notorious lawsuits charged CPAs with failure to find management fraud at such companies as Lincoln Savings, Phar Mor, MiniScribe, and Regina. There was also a related concern that financial reporting (and the audit of those financials) had become so mechanical that it did not communicate the real risks and opportunities in a business. In response, CPA firms expressed concern that the public had unrealistic expectations for the financial reporting process.

These trends and events suggested that there had been a basic change in the environment for accounting. In response, the American Institute of Certified Public Accountants (AICPA) commissioned another introspective endeavor, establishing a special committee to look into the future of financial reporting. The special committee's report, often referred to as the Jenkins Committee Report, reiterated the primary role of accounting as a vehicle to communicate information. The report concluded, however, that the information to be communicated for effective decision making was much broader than that encompassed by existing notions of corporate accounting systems. The report suggested that **business reporting** take the place of **financial reporting.** Here are some of the key suggestions contained in the report:

- Business reporting serves a critical role in supporting effective capital allocation. In many respects, it serves that role well, providing those who use it with essential information. However, profound, accelerating changes affecting business threaten the continued relevance of business reporting. To stay relevant, it must change in response to users' evolving needs for information.

- To meet users' changing needs, business reporting must
  - Provide more information about plans, opportunities, risks, and uncertainties.
  - Focus more on the factors that create longer-term value, including nonfinancial measures indicating how key business processes are performing.
  - Better align information reported externally with the information reported internally to senior management to manage the business.[10]

The committee's focus on "business reporting" rather than on "financial reporting" is particularly relevant to us in this chapter as we focus on communicating corporate value. For example, the call for increased emphasis on reporting those "factors that create long-term

---

[9] In 1992, *Business Week* reported that insurance premiums for the Big 6 CPA firms had increased tenfold since 1985, and that for some firms premiums and legal fees consume up to 25 percent of what would otherwise go to partners. See, "The Big 6 Are in Trouble," *Business Week,* April 6, 1992, pp. 78–79.

[10] *Improving Business Reporting—A Customer Focus (The Jenkins Committee Report),* American Institute of Certified Public Accountants, New York, 1994, p. 3.

value" in the business might suggest that accounting step away from the traditional concern for the reliability of the numbers and focus more on the usefulness of the information presented. That might suggest, for instance, that a "business report" for General Mills should report the market share trend of its various cereals—certainly the value of General Mills is not in its plant and equipment but in its presence on the supermarket shelves. Further, a frank discussion of "plans, opportunities, risks, and uncertainties" that was set forth in a way to help the user see the company as management sees it might help users understand the potential value in a biotech firm that consistently reports losses under GAAP accounting but is on the verge of introducing a dramatic new cancer drug. Today's accounting for R&D prevents any attempt to measure the potential in that new product, yet that is clearly where the value of a biotech company lies. The direction suggested by the Jenkins Committee report is exciting because it urges a focus on the communication of value-creating factors. To do that, however—to move toward business reporting—the accounting profession and the FASB must find a way to avoid the conceptual debates and the details that have plagued it in the past. And corporate financial management must find a way to avoid knee-jerk rejections of calls for more disclosure. Toward that end, some have argued that the legal climate must be eased to encourage more open disclosure and to discourage punitive lawsuits.[11] In any event, it will take a communitywide effort if we are to realize the promise in the Jenkins Committee report.[12]

A FINANCE PERSPECTIVE ON COMMUNICATING WITH FINANCIAL STAKEHOLDERS

Researchers in accounting and finance have devoted considerable effort over the years to studying the relationship between a company's financial information and the market price for its stock. The result of that research has been the development (and at least partial support) of an idea called the **efficient market hypothesis** (EMH). The EMH argues that where there are enough players in an active auction-type market, the price paid for a security in that market will reflect its real value.

Some theorists argue a **strong form of the EMH,** claiming that the market price for a security at any time must reflect all information that pertains to that security whether the information has been publicly disseminated or not. The strong form of the EMH is based on the assumption that the market is composed of a great many curious and motivated players who will search for, find, and obtain *all relevant* information about a company whether or not that information is publicly available. Once they have the information they will act on it, and their actions will be reflected in the market price of the security. That understanding

---

[11] In December 1995 Congress did pass a litigation reform bill that contains a more effective safe harbor for disclosure of forward-looking information, restrictions on class action suits, and a change in the way damages are assessed from the prior joint-and-several approach to a contributory-share approach.

[12] It is interesting that the two study groups, 20 years apart, both argued for a focus on the needs of the user. But it is especially significant that the Jenkins Committee redefined the users not as those who depend on financial reporting for their information but as the financial analysts who presumably have the power and the tools to get the information they need in other ways. That definition of the user of financial reporting—as a professional analyst—recognizes the increased influence and power of institutional investors and their professional advisers. It has obvious implications for communication: On the positive side, it will be easier for corporate management to tell their story to and through a professional analyst because the analysts can be located more easily than a diverse group of individual shareholders, and because they will usually be better-informed listeners. But conversely, because of the concentration of ownership in the institutions, the analysts have a concentrated power. If they do not understand or do not believe the company's story, there is no one else to whom management can appeal.

of the marketplace assumes the total interest and dedicated ingenuity of the players in the market, and that degree of assumed interest and ingenuity is a bit too hypothetical for most of us to accept. Most theorists argue a **semistrong form of the EMH:** They argue that the players in an active market will be motivated to analyze information that is available to them and to act on opportunities that information illuminates. As a consequence, *all available* information will be incorporated in the trading price for a security, and no one can expect to profit from information once it is in the public domain. However, the semistrong form of the EMH also acknowledges that there will be information about a company that has not been discovered and cannot be deduced, and that the market price of that company's securities can reflect only the information that is publicly available. The semistrong form of the EMH has gained fairly wide acceptance, in part because research has demonstrated its validity and in part because it seems consistent with the day-to-day observations that the market price of a stock reacts to new information and that once that new information has been digested, a new equilibrium price is established.

The following quotation succinctly captures the essence of the semistrong form of the EMH and introduces some questions that are important to our study here:

> A securities market is defined as efficient if (1) the prices of the securities traded in that market act as though they fully reflect all available information and (2) these prices react instantaneously or nearly so, in an unbiased fashion, to new information. We note in passing that even if the view of a sophisticated market embedded in the EMH is valid, individual investors may still make wrong decisions. Hence the hypothesis requires "experts" (or arbitragers) of significant numbers or wealth to produce an efficient market. Furthermore, the hypothesis refers to the total market. It is quite possible that for a particular stock at a particular time the hypothesis may not be true. As with all hypotheses, the EMH is an approximation of the world, and those who hold this idea believe it to be substantially accurate and operationally useful.[13]

Most financial people would agree with the semistrong form of the EMH, but most would also agree with the penultimate sentence in the quotation: "It is quite possible that for a particular stock at a particular time, the hypothesis may not be true." Certainly the EMH has some applicability to the market as a whole and to a security over time. But those involved in the financial markets also know from experience that at various times there will be information about a company that has not yet been digested in the public marketplace. Moreover, where an equilibrium price seems to have been established, prices for a security may fluctuate around that equilibrium, occasionally quite widely. In this chapter's discussion of the role of corporate communication in setting stock prices, we believe that as long as there is an interested, inquiring, liquid market for a company's security, the prices established in an auction for that security will, over the long term, reflect the value of all of the information regarding that company that is publicly available and has been absorbed by the key stakeholders in the market.

Note the three important caveats imbedded in our notion of the EMH:

1. There must be a significant number of players in the market, and they must be interested in and curious about a particular company and objective and unbiased in their valuation judgments.

[13] T. Dyckman, D. Downes, and R. Magee, *Efficient Capital Markets and Accounting: A Critical Analysis.* (Englewood Cliffs, N.J.: Prentice Hall, 1975), p. 4. This booklet, one in a series titled Contemporary Topics in Accounting, provides both a useful introduction and a more exhaustive exploration of the EMH and its implication for accounting.

2. Over some period of time, the average market prices will reflect the reality of the information available for the market as a whole and—given enough time—for a particular company's security.

3. To have an impact on a security's price, information must be available to and understood by the participants in the public financial marketplace.

We now will explore each of these three EMH caveats and their implications for financial managers. A popular finance text states, "For the corporate treasurer who is concerned with issuing or purchasing securities, the efficient market theory has obvious implications. In one sense, however, it raises more questions than it answers. The existence of efficient markets does not mean that the financial manager can let financing take care of itself."[14] The EMH caveats that we have just outlined suggest some important challenges for financial managers—in particular, communication challenges.

Caveat Number One: The marketplace for a particular company's stock is composed of a sufficient number of interested and curious players who are unbiased and objective in their judgments. Although there is strong empirical evidence to support the semistrong form of the EMH as it applies to the securities markets in the United States, there is also anecdotal evidence that raises continuing doubts. For example, the financial market has invented a name for companies whose stock is publicly held but that are not followed by a research analyst. Such available but professionally ignored companies are referred to as **wallflowers.** There are 12,000 companies whose securities trade publicly in the United States, but the most popular investment advisory service, Value Line, reports on about 2,000 companies. How important is it for a company to have the attention of an investment advisory service? How much does it cost the company if its shares are relegated to wallflower status? In theory, the EMH would argue that arbitragers would see the value in a wallflower company and keep its price in a fair range. However, a *New York Times* article dealing with the wallflower phenomenon said, "for these neglected stocks, the question of efficient market prices is more problematic. Is all 'available information' about them reaching the buyers and sellers whose daily decisions are determining the stock's price? Of course not, say the experts. And the result is an inefficient market, one in which investors who do extensive homework can often find bargains—and those who do not are vulnerable to some very nasty surprises."[15]

The fact that an independent investment analyst follows a company helps that company's stock price move toward its real value in part because the analyst's report provides one more vehicle for the dissemination of the company's story, in part because the analyst's report provides some assurance that the company's message is understood, and in part because the attention provided by an analyst's coverage attracts the attention of busy market participants. And, of course, the converse is true—the lack of analyst coverage can cost the company in terms of reduced share prices.

While there are a great many potential buyers in an equity market as large as that of the United States, there are also a great many investment opportunities, and more arrive every day.[16] The size of the marketplace in the United States adds to its overall efficiency, but it can also bury a company that is unable to attract enough attention. Individual investors have

---

[14] R. Brealey and S. Myers, *Principles of Corporate Finance,* 4th ed. (New York: McGraw Hill, 1991), p. 310.

[15] Diana B. Henriques, "The Wallflowers of Wall Street," *The New York Times,* April 14, 1991, section 3, page 12.

[16] According to A. Raghavan in "Underwriters Revel in a Robust Year as Interest Rates Drop," *The Wall Street Journal,* January 2, 1996, p. R38, 572 companies went through an initial public offering in the United States in 1995, raising more than $30 billion.

little chance to identify prospective investments on their own and so depend upon the advice of brokers or investment advisory services in making their selection. If a company is not on the screen of an advisory firm, few individual investors will know about it or take the chance of investing in it. We might expect the larger, institutional investors to be more interested in searching out investment opportunities and to be less dependent on reports from advisory services for their initial introduction to a company. Still, why should the manager of an institution such as a state pension fund make the effort to look for values in an unknown stock when there are enough other well-analyzed investments to pick from? Why should the financial analyst take the risk of investing the pension fund's assets in such an unknown company when there are plenty of other companies where other analysts have already digested the most important data? In fact, to protect themselves from charges of recklessness, some fiduciarily-minded institutional investors have a policy to not invest in a company's securities unless it is covered by at least two independent advisory services. Corporate financial officers do have an obligation to tell their company story, but first they have to have someone to tell the story to. Therefore, one of the first obligations of a corporate financial officer, in addition to merely crafting the company's financial story, is to develop and cultivate a cadre of investment advisors who will follow the company's stock.

Another Wall Street saying that informs this inquiry is a movement called the "herd mentality." The EMH assumes a group of players each independent of the other, each free from any bias or influence. But there is no line of human endeavor where that is true. Most of us would agree that a national election in the United States is a reasonably efficient marketplace because it involves the votes of tens of millions of individuals. We recognize that human emotion and a herd mentality enter into those election results, but we take comfort in the fact that those human factors are lost in the grand total of the participants and that the end result is reasonably efficient in reflecting the true sentiment of the populace. That overall perspective may be true for an election of a president, but the analogy fails when it is compared to a stock market. In a stock market there is no voting as to whether a security is good or bad; rather, an attempt is being made to determine the fair value of a security at a particular time. As much as management may wish to have the market's approval of their company, they want even more to have the market price of the stock fairly valued.[17]

The emotions of the time, good or bad, will drive the values established for a company's stock, and those emotion-driven values may or may not reflect the real value in the company. What proportion of a stock's value (or its shortfall from its value) is due to the herd mentality on the street? No one knows the answer to that question, but the reality of this phenomenon was demonstrated in the incredible growth in prices that were accorded any

---

[17] In 1988, an important case in this area was decided by the U.S. Supreme Court. The officers and directors of Basic Inc., together with the company itself, were sued in an action alleging that the officers had misled the market. It had been rumored that the company was about to be acquired by Combustion Engineering, but each time they were asked about those rumors the officers denied that any merger negotiations were under way; they were evidently trying to protect the negotiations and wanted to control the timing of the announcement according to their own schedule. Eventually the merger was completed and announced, and the shareholders who had bought on the strength of the rumor but sold on the strength of the denials sued. The Court, relying on the EMH, ruled in favor of the suing shareholders, saying that the officers' denials had misled the market and therefore had misled the suing shareholders; the Supreme Court sent the case back to a lower court for determination of damages. Two justices dissented to that decision, arguing against the strong forms of the EMH and providing backhanded confirmation of the semistrong form by saying, "We note that there may be a certain incongruity between the assumption that Basic shares are traded on a well-developed, efficient, and information-hungry market, and the allegation that such a market could remain misinformed, and its valuation of Basic shares depressed, for 14 months, on the basis of the three public statements." But even as they affirmed the semistrong form of the EMH, the dissenting justices raised the question of valuation, saying, "the fraud-on-the-market theory produces the "economically correct result"…but…the question of damages under the theory is quite problematic. Not surprisingly, the difficult damages question is one that the Court expressly declines to address today."

company having to do with the Internet in the late 1990s,[18] or the variations that were accorded the "technology stocks" as one or another of the companies in that group reported good news or bad news during the late 1990s. There were plenty of players in those markets, but given the movements in the stock prices, it would be hard to argue that they all were objective and unbiased.

Finally, an efficient market says that a security's fair value is its equilibrium value—that is, the value at which there are an equal number of interested sellers and interested buyers. It may be true that such a balancing of supply and demand produces an equilibrium price, but the extension of that thesis, which then says that the equilibrium price is the fair price, is not necessarily true. Consider the phenomenon of discounts and premiums on closed-end mutual funds. A closed-end fund is a mutual fund that owns stocks, bonds, and cash just as traditional mutual funds do. However, the common stock of a closed-end fund is traded between individual shareholders just as the stock of a commercial company might be. At the end of each accounting period, management of the closed-end fund values the securities in the fund's portfolio and reports the fund's net assets on a market value basis. It is a simple matter to take that aggregate net asset value and divide it by the number of shares outstanding to determine a net asset value per share. Because the fund's assets consist solely of marketable securities—each of which have a value determined in an efficient market— we might expect that the fund's own shares would trade at a price exactly equal to the inherent value of the securities in the fund. But that is almost never true. Unlike the shares of traditional mutual funds, which can be redeemed at their net asset value at any time, the shares of closed-end funds almost always trade at a premium or discount to their net asset values—usually a discount of from 5 to 10 percent.[19]

Why should that be? Why should a seller be willing to sell a share in a fund at a price that is less than the fundamental values of the securities in that fund? The answer is that there are not enough buyers who will pay a higher price. And it follows that we ought to ask why open-end funds trade exactly at their net asset value. The answer is that the fund itself stands ready to buy its shares from anyone who wants to sell. In effect, a traditional open-end fund makes a market in its own shares, and because it is willing to redeem its shares at their net asset value, the market value of those shares is equal to the market value of the securities it holds. On the other hand, a closed-end fund depends on the players in the auction market to buy and sell its shares and to establish the equilibrium price, regardless of the underlying value of the assets. The phenomenon of the closed-end fund illustrates that the market price for securities is influenced in part by the underlying value of the entity and in part by factors of supply and demand. That understanding can be applied to the stock of a commercial company as well: There is more to the pricing of a company's shares than the underlying value in the company, and more even than the full and fair telling of the company's story.

---

[18] For example, Netscape Communications Corp. came to the market in 1995 at a time when there was a great deal of enthusiasm for anything having to do with the Internet. At the time of the offering, Netscape reported a loss for the nine months ended September 30, 1995, and earnings of only $0.04 for the latest quarter. However, the company did have an intriguing product that promised to become the industry standard for surfing the net. The stock that was to be issued in the IPO was valued by the underwriters at $28 a share, but trading opened at $71. The shares closed the year at $139.

[19] In 1995, The Global Privatization Fund, Inc., a closed-end fund investing in large-scale privatization projects throughout the world, was merged into the Worldwide Privatization Fund, an open-end fund. Both were operated by Alliance Capital Management, and both had similar objectives—in fact, the two funds held many of the same securities. Because it was a closed-end fund, Global had traded at discounts of between 6 percent and 19 percent since its public offering, whereas the Worldwide fund had sold and redeemed its shares at their net asset value. The board of directors of Global concluded that it would be in the best interests of its shareholders to be merged with the Worldwide Fund so as to eliminate the discount and provide for greater liquidity for the shareholders. The shares of Global were exchanged share for share with Worldwide, and the shareholders of Global found themselves with an immediate increase in share value.

The pricing of a company's securities will depend on the development of an adequate demand.

Caveat Number Two: The market prices of well-followed stocks will average out to reflect aggregate fair values over a period of time, but those average, aggregate market prices will not necessarily be the fair price for a particular security at a particular time. Some have suggested that companies should consider a program to manage their stock prices on a day-to-day basis. For example, C. Callard observes: "Unlike the CEO, who attempts to achieve longer-term value, the security analyst makes judgments about the margin of short-term change, which may or may not become permanent."[20] Mr. Callard also suggests that management has a responsibility to manage the company's cost of capital by managing both the long-term growth of the company *and* by buying and selling the company's stock when the short-term trading price of the stock deviates significantly from its "warranted value." Warranted value is a calculated value for the stock, given the company's steady-state asset growth, its current earnings, and the prevailing cost of capital and management should look for opportunities to buy or sell the company's stock when the current price is outside a range based on the warranted value. The notion of managing a company's stock price in this way is oddly controversial. Consider the following:

- Few managers will publicly acknowledge that they have a **target** (or **warranted**) **price** for their company's stock because they understand that they might then be expected to take action to achieve that price. However, we know that managers *do* watch their company's stock price—they trade in their company's stock for their personal accounts, and they manage the timing and the amounts of shares to be purchased under the company's share repurchase programs.

- Some managers will argue that the stock market decides its own value for the stock and that the value of the stock can only be the current trading price. They argue that they cannot develop a value that is more accurate than the market does itself. And yet those managers develop capital expenditure budgets that are based on hurdle rates, which in turn are designed to earn a return to support or increase a targeted stock value.

- Some managers argue that their job is to manage the company and not the stock price. They argue that the market ought to be left to its own devices and to value their management efforts as the market players see fit. And yet, the fact is that shareholders are interested in the operations of the company only as those operations can be converted into an increased stock price. A shareholder might well argue that management's ultimate job is not the management of the company but is instead the management of the value of the stock.

It is impossible to know how many companies actively manage their day-to-day stock prices by buying into and selling out of price opportunities. It is well known, however, that many companies have authorized share repurchase plans that are implicitly designed to support a stock price floor.

---

[20] The ideas outlined here are more fully explained by C. G. Callard in "Managing Today's Stock Price," *Planning Review* (March/April 1988), pp. 34–39. The contents of Exhibits 16.1 and 16.2 are reprinted from *Strategy & Leadership* (formerly *Planning Review*), (March/April 1988) with permission from the Strategic Leadership Forum (formerly The Planning Forum), The International Society for Strategic Management.

EXHIBIT 15.1

Abbott Laboratories: Shareholder's Wealth Relative to S&P 500

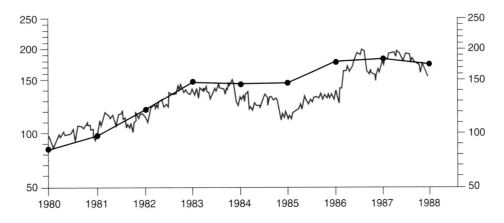

Note: The weekly values compare shareholder wealth (price appreciation plus dividends) relative to a corresponding calculation for the S&P 500. The annual values are the stock's warranted value for the beginning of each fiscal year, but plotted relative to the beginning year Abbott/S&P price ratio. Because cost of capital (COC) changes during the year, it is necessary to focus on the longer-term asset growth strategy and the earnings factor without being disturbed by short-term changes in COC. Hence, the objective is to fix a beginning year COC and let price reflect changing expectations for asset growth and earnings. The bullets (•) above reflect such a calculation. See footnote 20.

Mr. Callard illustrates his main thesis by determining a warranted price for the stock of Abbott Laboratories over a period of years and plotting those prices to the S&P 500 as shown in Exhibit 15.1.

The results do suggest that the short-term swings in the market price of a company's stock move in a random fashion around some norm. But what is particularly interesting for the discussion in this chapter is the set of explanations offered by the author for the short-term declines in the stock price, which are presented in Exhibit 15.2.

Note, for instance, the gap in 1979 and 1980, which is explained as "relative overvaluation," and the gap in 1984, which is described as "momentum error." Abbott Labs may have been fortunate that the momentum atrophied and that the stock price recovered to its norm without incident. Similarly, Abbott was probably fortunate that the relative overvaluation in the early 1980s was not followed by a shareholder suit as the correction worked its way out. This case example illustrates that the stock market may be efficient, but, if so, it achieves that efficiency only over a long period of time. That understanding has significant implications for the manager who has the obligation to assure a fair valuation of the company's stock and the power—through communications—to help the market correct over and under valuations. Although the market on its own might come to see the value in the company's stock over time, in the interval the company will be forced to pay higher capital costs and will be at risk for a stock market raid or forced restructuring. In less dynamic times than today, it may have been possible for a company to wait out the market and hope that the real value in the company would be discovered. Today, however, with the concentration of marketplace power in institutional hands, the enormous liquidity created by the bull market, and the relatively relaxed attitude toward take-overs that prevails in

EXHIBIT 15.2

Short-Term Relative Declines Exceeding 10 Percent

Peak Date	Price		Length of Decline (Weeks)	% Change		Net	Classification
	Abbott	S&P		Abbott	S&P 500		
12/28/79	10.25	107.84	9	−8.9%	6.7%	−14.6%	Relative overvaluation
9/19/80	13.69	129.25	10	−7.3	7.6	−13.9	" "
6/26/81	15.81	132.56	11	−24.1	−9.4	−16.2	" "
9/24/82	18.44	123.32	21	2.4	19.7	−14.5	Relative earnings decline
10/28/83	25.32	163.37	6	−14.1	1.3	−15.2	" "
2/17/84	22.50	155.74	3	−10.3	2.2	−12.2	Momentum error
8/31/84	23.63	166.68	6	−18.0	−2.4	−16.0	" "
8/01/86	51.50	234.91	13	−16.5	3.9	−19.6	Relative overvaluation
6/05/87	62.38	293.45	17	−2.4	11.8	−12.7	Relative earnings decline
Average			11	−11.0%	4.6%	−15.0%	

Note: See footnote 20.

Washington, a takeover or a stockholder rebellion can come with lightning swiftness. Every financial executive has an obligation to monitor the company's stock price against a target and—based on the length of *time* the values are out of line or the *degree* to which the values are skewed—take action to protect the company and its shareholders.

Another provocative article on this subject outlines a number of important levers that managements can control to enhance the value of their company's shares.[21] Increasing the dividend payout is the first obvious answer, but it is important to note that one can increase shareholder value by reducing the perceived risk attributed to the company and by increasing the perceived value of future cash flows by better communication of future prospects. This particular article concludes that long-term market values are not driven by quarterly earnings or other short-term events but are more heavily influenced by "the market's perception of the present value of the stock in the future." To support that point, an interesting experiment is described wherein the author looked at the stock market's valuation for the companies that make up the Dow Jones Industrials. The dividend payout from each of those firms was aggregated over a 10-year period, 1975–1984, and added to the actual stock price at the end of 1984. Those actual numbers were then discounted back to the beginning of 1975 using discount rates that recognized each company's risk profile. Finally, that aggregate present value was compared with the market price for those stocks at the beginning of 1975. The results of that experiment demonstrated several things:

1. On average, only 42 percent of the value of a stock is in its dividend payout, with the rest coming from the expected terminal value.
2. The market is generally optimistic—that is, almost all of the beginning-of-period stock prices were higher than would have been justified by the results during the following period. On average, the market overvalued the Dow Jones Industrials by about 33 percent.

---

[21] A. H. Seed, "Winning Strategies for Shareholder Value Creation," *Journal of Business Strategy* (Fall 1985), pp. 44–51.

EXHIBIT 15.3

Comparison of Expected Stock Values
(as Reflected in Beginning-of-Period Quoted Prices)
with Actual Cash Returns from the
Dow Jones Industrials for 1981–1991

	Present Value of Actual Cash			Expected Cash (Beginning-of-period Value)	Expected Cash as a Percentage of Actual Value
Company*	Dividends	End-of-period Value	Total		
Alcoa	5.83	9.65	15.49	25.625	165.43%
American Brands	4.58	8.63	13.21	9.470	71.69%
American Express	2.46	2.52	4.97	10.590	213.08%
Chevron	10.09	11.95	22.04	38.625	175.25%
DuPont	3.99	7.11	11.10	12.625	113.73%
Eastman Kodak	6.64	9.33	15.97	28.890	180.90%
Exxon	8.04	12.86	20.90	15.380	73.59%
General Electric	4.85	10.25	15.10	14.090	93.31%
General Motors	8.31	10.40	18.71	22.250	118.92%
Goodyear	6.08	8.57	14.65	17.625	120.31%
IBM	16.96	15.90	32.86	54.000	164.33%
International Paper	4.89	10.23	15.13	19.875	131.36%
Merck	3.53	32.24	35.77	14.130	39.50%
3M	7.77	16.20	23.97	27.250	113.68%
Procter & Gamble	6.58	19.38	25.96	18.530	71.38%
Sears	6.78	5.86	12.64	16.125	127.57%
Texaco	13.76	12.73	26.49	33.750	127.41%
Union Carbide	4.57	2.90	7.47	16.120	215.80%
US Steel	5.20	5.12	10.32	32.000	310.08%
United Tech	5.36	8.05	13.41	22.630	168.75%
Westinghouse	2.47	2.44	4.91	6.250	127.29%
Woolworth	2.42	4.25	6.67	4.750	71.21%
Average excess expected					136.12%
Standard deviation					59.63%

*The original experiment we describe in the chapter omitted those companies that were not included in the Dow Jones Industrials throughout the entire period. Our repeat of his experiment also left those companies out of the database, and it also omitted Bethlehem Steel, which went into and came out of bankruptcy in the 1981–1991 time period.

3. Within that average, several companies were considerably overvalued, and several were considerably undervalued. The standard deviation of the averages in that sample was 65 percent.

We replicated that experiment using the 10-year period 1981 through 1991. The results of that experiment are reflected in Exhibit 15.3.

As is apparent from Exhibit 15.3, the use of more current data produced results that were very close to the original study: the average excess was around 36 percent and the standard deviation of the average results was around 60 percent. Rerunning the experiment using shorter, different time periods produced the following results:

- Using the data for the first five years of the period produced an average excess of 9 percent and a standard deviation of 46 percent.

- Using the data for the last five years of the period produced an average excess of 42 percent and a standard deviation of 59 percent.

- Using the data for the last three years of the period produced an average excess of 28 percent and a standard deviation of 41 percent.

Interestingly, the average excess varied considerably as shorter, different time periods were used. Nonetheless, the standard deviation remained quite high. That continued variability in the ability of the market to predict the results that an investment will produce suggests an enormous opportunity for management. Because management understands the company and its prospects better than any outside member of the market ever will, and because that understanding of the future is so important to the valuation of the stock price, it is incumbent on the management team to explain that future as effectively as it can. Looking again at the results in Exhibit 15.3, we have to feel sympathy for the managers at Merck, at American Brands, at Procter & Gamble, and at Woolworth as they saw the market's consistent undervaluation of their efforts. It may be that it was difficult to value those companies because the key valuation information was not disseminated in any organized way: Merck's assets are in its product pipeline, the value of which has been expensed as R&D costs; the real assets that Procter & Gamble and American Brands bring to bear are their important product franchises, the value of which is expensed as advertising and promotion costs; Woolworth has a consumer franchise too, but its value has deteriorated as the retail market has changed. In the case of Woolworth, the market may have been correct in its long-term valuation of the company's prospects, but it misvalued the cash flow potential from the company in the interim.

There is no reason to think that the results of this experiment would be any different if we used a set of companies other than the Dow Jones Industrials; in fact, it would be reasonable to conclude that the results would be more extreme for companies that have less of a following on Wall Street. The results of this experiment provide a solid argument for a proactive movement on the part of financial managers to communicate the values that are inherent but latent in their companies.

Caveat Number Three: To have an impact on a security's price, information must be available to and understood by the players in the public financial marketplace. The accounting and finance literature provide a number of illustrations of the ability of the marketplace to react to information when it first becomes available. One of the most interesting looked at stock price values before and after 1970, when the SEC first required presentation of revenue and earnings data by business segment.[22] The research had the benefit of business segment data for the current year as well as retrospective disclosures of segment data for the two prior years. The research found that the stock prices in 1970 were closer to a target value than they had been in the earlier years when the segment data had not been publicly available.

But it is not just that the data must be available to the market; it must be interpreted by the players in the market, and that fact makes the job of the financial manager much more difficult. One other Wall Street phenomenon often heard discussed is the "conglomerate discount." At one time conglomerates were greatly in favor because it was felt that a company could assure its shareholders more stable returns if it developed a portfolio of

---

[22] D. Collins, "SEC Product Line Reporting and Market Efficiency," *Journal of Financial Economics,* 1975. Cited in *Efficient Capital Markets and Accounting* by T. Dyckman, D. Downes and R. Magee (Englewood Cliffs, N.J.: Prentice Hall, 1975).

businesses whose business cycles might smooth each other out. In recent years, however, the financial markets have penalized conglomerates, and managements of those companies have been under pressure to break them up. Often, in those disputes, it is reported that the breakup value of the conglomerate is 5 to 10 percent more than the quoted stock price.

Why should that be? So long as the company provides good business segment information, should not the market be able to value the company as a whole by simply valuing its individual components? A number of explanations are offered for the conglomerate discount including (1) the concern that management cannot manage a diverse group of companies and that its attention will therefore be diluted or (2) that the market focuses only on the most obvious of the components and values the income stream from the entire entity at the earnings multiple applicable to that business, so that the more valuable entities in the company are undervalued. All such explanations may be true, but other nagging concerns suggest that the problem is more complex. The process of investment analysis is multifaceted because the investment advisor must understand the company's industry. Very few analysts focus on individual companies, but most do focus on individual industries. If it makes sense to concentrate your analytical expertise on an industry-by-industry basis (and it seems intuitively logical to do so), how would you field a team to prepare an investment analysis of a company like USX, with its very different steel and oil operations? If you were developing an expertise in the oil industry, why would you devote your time to USX? Would you not prefer to concentrate your analysis effort on a relatively "pure play" like Shell or Exxon? It is entirely likely that some portion of the conglomerate discount is attributable to the structural weakness inherent in the conglomerate form. But it is also very likely that some part of the conglomerate discount can be traced to the market. If so, one of the key tasks of the financial executive is to ensure that the players in the market understand the company's various businesses and have reason to be interested in their results.

A CASE STUDY

J. Walter Thompson (JWT) was one of the premier advertising agencies in the world, with a consistent record of award-winning advertising campaigns and a loyal following from a blue-ribbon clientele. The company began operations in 1864, selling advertising space in religious magazines. By 1986, more than 120 years later, JWT had revenues in excess of $650 million and employed more than 10,000 people in 200 offices around the world.

An advertising agency is different from a merchandising or manufacturing company in that an advertising company's assets are almost exclusively its people. Those people will stay with an agency as long as they feel challenged and rewarded. In turn, clients are drawn to an agency because of its creative people, and they will stay with an agency only as long as the creative people stay. Advertising is unique in other, more prosaic ways, as well: Advertising is a surprisingly seasonal business, with peak revenues in the second and fourth quarter of the calendar year, and it is very vulnerable to the ups and downs of the business cycles. For example, in the mid 1980s a combination of declining advertising volume and pressure on fees depressed the financial results of almost every agency in the industry. However, there was a good bit of hope in the international sector as the European countries moved toward commercial television; it was expected that the need for advertising services in that market would grow enough to offset any decline in the U.S. market.

JWT had been through a particularly difficult period in the 1970s but had been rescued by the creative energies of Don Johnston, who had become chairman in 1975. In the years from 1975 to 1986, JWT made a number of important acquisitions and grew its volume substantially. Unfortunately, profits were erratic: The company earned $16 to $29 million in each of the years 1980, 1983, 1984, and 1985. However, in 1982 the company took a substantial earnings hit as a result of a fraud reported in its overseas operations and only broke even for the year. The company's strong earnings in 1985 were surprising, given the general problems of the industry. But then, in 1986, earnings dropped to approximately $6 million as a result of a number of factors—including the costs of an expanded staff (anticipating the overseas expansion of TV advertising), the costs of absorbing a complex merger (it was a pooling and so the costs the two companies incurred in closing duplicate facilities all were charged to reported income for the year), and a very high effective tax rate (the company had losses overseas that it could not offset against its earnings at home).

The stock market had rewarded the company for its rather extraordinary results in 1985 (earnings in the fourth quarter of 1985 set a record), and the stock closed the year at $41 a share. But when the 1986 results began to be apparent, quarter by quarter, the stock sank to $30. The analysts who followed JWT concluded that the company's abilities and its people should enable it to grow revenues by 10 to 15 percent a year. It was also felt that with a cost containment program, the company could grow its earnings by 25 percent a year. When the 1986 financial statements showed the expected increase in revenues but also showed costs that had grown even faster, the analysts became discouraged. One analyst said, "He [Johnston] has not been willing to accept a partner in running the agency in those areas—financial controls and business organization—where he is weak." It was true—between 1979 and 1986 there had been four different CFOs at JWT.

All of that might have been simply one more episode in a history of boom and bust years. However, while all of this was going on at JWT, the world was changing: The British pound strengthened against the dollar, and the fiscal conservatism of Prime Minister Thatcher in the U.K. was in full swing. On June 10, 1987, when JWT's stock was trading at $30, WWP Ltd., a newly formed company in the United Kingdom, bid $45 a share for all of JWT's shares. After a brief struggle (which resulted in an increase in the bid to $55 a share) the board of directors of JWT was forced to agree to the tender. JWT and its component parts were absorbed into WWP, and the 120-year-old company disappeared.

PULLING IT ALL TOGETHER

The financial market's response to a particular company's stock will be in part a reaction to its industry and the overall economy. The market's response will also be in part a reaction to the company's actual results, its expected results, the strategy it has outlined, and its demonstrated ability to execute that strategy. Finally, the reaction of the market to a company's stock will be in part a reaction to the way the company tells its story and the trust earned by the management team. This chapter has been devoted to an exploration of these latter factors, which are most clearly the purview of the financial executive. The discussion in this chapter and the experiences of companies such as JWT suggest a few observations for your consideration and debate:

- We must move accounting standards toward presentations that will help users see the inherent values in the company. For example, the FASB has just issued a new statement on "Comprehensive Income." We might have hoped that such a statement would have given us a defined approach to measuring and reporting the components of net income, with a focus on defining "Core Income." A more consistent definition of core income would help analysts and others deconstruct this year's income and develop better forecasts for the following years. Unfortunately, the new FASB standard on comprehensive income deals only with a narrow accounting issue—the non-income items that flow through equity. While we wait for the FASB to deal with core income, chief financial officers can use the SEC's required management discussion and analysis (MD&A) to help the reader isolate the effects of unusual or nonrecurring items that might be buried in the current year's income.

- Now that Congress has established a more effective safe harbor for forward-looking information,[23] companies might experiment with supplemental presentations in their financial reports, including such things as fair-value presentations and forecasts. In our financial society, forecasts of company operations are provided by the investment analysts who follow the company; those forecasts are based on data developed by the analysts, but also on data provided by the company. Some companies have provided data willingly, while some have left the analysts to develop information on their own; some managers have ignored the analysts' forecasts, and some have commented on forecasts that seem out of line. Now that the new safe harbor is in place, we might expect that companies will be more open with the analysts working on a forecast and might be more outgoing in their comments on the forecasts, which have heretofore been prohibited. Still, given the new safe harbor, why should analysts be the purveyors of financial forecasts? Why shouldn't management provide forecasts of their companies' future results, directly? Again, the MD&A required by the SEC provides a vehicle for companies to provide that information, now in a more protected forum.

- Our traditional accounting system and conventions are designed for merchandising and manufacturing companies and do not lend themselves to communicating the value of service companies, whose assets are talented people. Managers of those companies must be permitted to report new ways of explaining their results (such as revenues per employee, growth in number of employees, average tenure of employees, and so on), and it will be especially important for them to find ways to describe the investment they make in employees and productivity each year. Given the time lag between an investment in people and the return that might be expected, disclosure of forecasts and plans will be important. It may even be that because of the financial communication difficulties inherent in these companies (consider JWT), they ought not depend on the stock market for their capital.

- Top managers must focus on the quality of the product or service that the company produces, but they cannot ignore the expectations and needs of the capital market. Today every public company is vulnerable to a takeover raid. It will be important for managers to have a target price in mind for their stock and to take action when the trading price falls too far below that target. One manager explained that his company talked about things as being "BT and AT," referring to a takeover raid on the company by a well-established financier, and events or decisions as being before or after that takeover raid. The manager explained that in the past, management had not worried much about the potential reaction of the financial market as they made various decisions on running the company. But as a result of the takeover raid they learned to anticipate the market's reaction as they considered every decision, from strategic actions to accounting choices. (As you mull the JWT case, you might reflect on these questions: Would the company have been vulnerable to a raid and a takeover at $55 a share if the

---

[23] See footnote 10.

stock had been at $40 rather than $30? How far away from a targeted price can the market be before the company is vulnerable? Would management have been so hopeful in their hiring of people for Europe if they had considered the impact of those hirings on the current financial results and on the stock price? Would the market have reacted so dramatically to the 1986 results if the CFO had been in place for a number of years and had been able to demonstrate that investments in people in one year had paid off in the future? Would the market have reacted so negatively to the 1986 results if the acquisition had been a purchase rather than a pooling, and if the merger expenses been allocated to goodwill rather than to the operations of the year?)

- The top officers of the company must be prepared to go before the financial analyst community and communicate personally. In a large company it may be possible to delegate some part of that contact to a stockholder relations person, but in most firms the analysts will insist on a personal contact with a senior executive. One senior financial manager explained that 40 percent of his time was devoted to making analyst presentations and answering analyst phone calls. A CEO explained to us that he devoted several days each quarter to visits with the top people in the institutions that owned the majority of his company's shares. He was careful to explain that he told each investor team the same story so as to avoid any suggestion of favoritism or charges of revealing inside information. But if that is the case, why is it necessary for him to visit each of those major investors personally? Why not invite them to a central location and tell his story to the group? He explained that it is important for him to be seen personally because only in a personal interview can those major investors make an assessment of his management abilities. They want to assess his candor, his grasp of the facts, and frankly, his health. They want to be assured that he is in charge of the company and managing their investment.

- A company that operates in a seasonal business must have a store of credibility built up with the financial community. Managers must be able to say (and demonstrate) that any slowdown is due to outside forces, the effects of which they can manage. It will be important for them to be able to say (and demonstrate) that they are in control of the company during good times and bad. One financial manager explained that his company had carefully studied the expectations for raw material prices and had decided that they would not need to hedge against cost increases. Results proved them wrong, and earnings for that next year were significantly depressed. The manager said that he met the analysts who followed the company and explained that the extra-high raw material costs were not due to a management error but were due to a conscious decision that in hindsight turned out to be wrong. The market accepted his explanation—because of the reputation for integrity that he had developed with the analyst group over many prior years—and the price of the stock stayed steady even after the dramatic drop in earnings. He had demonstrated that the company was under control, and the blip in the earnings stream created by the high material costs was an aberration not likely to be repeated.

One of the more practical ways to make such personal contact is to establish a conference call linkup the day after an important announcement is made, as, for instance, after quarterly results are released. In establishing such conference calls, any analyst who has expressed an interest in the company is usually invited to join in to hear the CFO (and often the CEO) discuss the results for the period and outline the directions of the company's future. Those presentations are important because they give the company a chance to explain the numbers and to humanize those numbers. One analyst explained that he often participates in such calls not to ask questions himself but to hear what questions others ask and to listen to the way management responds. One senior manager explained that he conducts those calls in a conference room lined with chalkboards: When questions are asked, staff people write the answers on the board or refer him to an answer in a preprepared briefing book. His goal is to provide honest answers to questions posed but also to demonstrate his command of the company's operations. If managers do their job well in these conference calls—answering questions forthrightly and with a minimum of hype—they will build trust in the company and reduce the market's level of uncertainty about the company's future prospects.

- Corporate management should seek regular criticism of its relationships with the financial community and its communications program and should be prepared to take action necessary to rectify identified problems. These steps might include, for instance, a stock buyback program to increase the cash flow to the shareholders and to demonstrate the company's confidence in its own future. If the company does not have an adequate following in the analyst community, it may be necessary to do some institutional advertising or to make some dramatic reporting moves to attract some attention. Or a company might engineer a stock sale to a major supplier or customer whose participation will attract one or more large institutions. Of course, any such challenge ought to include a careful scrutiny of the financial reporting practices followed by the company to assure that they tell the company's story as fully as possible and that they are perceived as honest and straightforward.

- All of the prior discussion has assumed a chief financial officer in the United States interfacing with the United States' financial market. But think about the role of business reporting in a different market setting, such as Germany, where equity investments are largely held by banks. In those countries, where the equity market is more of a closed system, the communication of value-creating factors ought to be easier. Very often the banks who hold a strong equity position in a company have representation on the company's board of directors, and so the communication can be immediate and in as much detail as is necessary. Even if there are no representatives on the board, the CFO will surely know the bank people personally, and the legal environment will make it possible to talk to those primary equity holders one-on-one. The reverse is also true, however; as those companies come to the United States and the United Kingdom, with their more egalitarian marketplaces, their managers will have to rethink their financial communications because the same norms, rules, and expectations cannot be presumed to apply.[24]

[24] See for example, "Planes, Trains and Automobiles," a *Financial Times* interview with Jurgen Schrempp, the newly appointed chairman of Daimler-Benz. The company had recently listed its equity securities on the New York Stock Exchange; it was the first German company to do so. In the interview, the author reported, "he peppered his rapid-fire conversation with talk of shareholder value" and quoted Mr. Schrempp as saying, "I introduced the notion in this company; now everybody talks about it." *Financial Times,* November 7, 1995, p. 15.

SUMMARY

Accounting and financial reporting are complex and interesting subjects that warrant the attention of every manager and therefore every student of business. This text is an attempt to help you master the language of accounting. It is important, however, to keep things in perspective: The real goal of all of accounting is to help owners understand the real value in a company. Financial reporting plays a critically important part in the communication process between managers and owners. We believe that traditional accounting reports are only a tool in the communications process and only one of the many tools available. Managers understand that their communication program must be a comprehensive program, integrating such components as the financial statements, the MD&A, the annual report, quarterly reports, meetings with analysts, news releases, and conference calls. Such a communications program must be driven toward one goal—a full understanding of the company by the marketplace and a fair value for the stock.

NEW CONCEPTS AND TERMS

Business reporting	**Semistrong form of the EMH**
Conceptual framework	**Strong form of the EMH**
Efficient market hypothesis (EMH)	**Target price**
Financial reporting	**Wallflowers**
Objectives of financial statements	**Warranted price**

ASSIGNMENTS

15.1. Pick one publicly held company that interests you, and find several magazine and newspaper articles that discuss the company and its prospects. Make some notes from that reading, outlining things about the company that you like and things that might worry you as a stockholder. Then read the company's annual report (the president's letter, the MD&A, and the financial statements). Look for amplification of the positive things you highlighted, and look for reassurance about the things you were concerned about. Prepare a short essay on your findings, and come to class prepared to talk about them.

15.2. Select one industry that interests you, and think about the factors that drive the value of the companies in that industry. Identify three companies in that industry and study their annual reports (the president's letter, the MD&A, and the financial statements) to see how each company reports on those value drivers. Prepare a short essay describing your findings and offering suggestions to the companies themselves, and to the standard setters, suggesting how the accounting policies and rules for that industry might be modified to focus on those value drivers.

15.3. Select a company that interests you, and find an analyst's report on the company that includes an estimate of the company's earnings and its future stock price. What factors did the analyst consider in the development of the forecast earnings and forecast stock price? Read the company's annual report and quarterly reports, looking to see how the company reports on those factors that were evidently important to the analyst. To what degree is the information used by the analyst provided by the company in its formal reports? If it is not available in the annual report, why is it not? Where might the analyst find that information if it is not readily available in public reports?

15.4. Study two Statements of Financial Accounting Standards issued by the FASB in the last five years (other than No. 106 and No. 109) and prepare an essay, critiquing the accounting that results from those standards against a goal that says that the accounting is to "provide information to help present and potential investors and creditors…in assessing the amounts, timing and uncertainties of prospective cash receipts"

15.5. Study the report from the AICPA, "Improving Business Reporting—A Customer Focus" (the Jenkins Committee Report), and make some notes about the kinds of information that might be provided in a "business report" that are not likely to be included in a traditional "financial report." Select a company that interests you and read the annual report provided by the company. To what degree would the annual report have to change if it was to be a "business report" as contemplated by the Jenkins Committee? Would those changes be made in the chairman's letter section of the annual report? In management's discussion and analysis? In the formal financial statements? How would you feel about making those changes if you were the CFO? How would you feel about making those changes if you were the CPA?

15.6. As part of its deliberative process, the FASB issued an invitation to comment on the recommendations in the Jenkins Committee Report. Study the Jenkins Report and prepare your own letter to the FASB suggesting specific projects that the Board ought to add to its agenda to implement the report's recommendations. Be sure that your letter provides a solid rationale for your recommendations.

15.7. Obtain a copy of the annual report of a major company whose securities are not registered for sale in the United States, and compare the discussions and communications contained in that report with the presentation in the annual report of a United States company in the same industry (for example, Bayer/Dow or Toyota/Ford).

15.8. The SEC requires each company to include in its annual report a quarterly summary of its stock price movement. Prepare an essay arguing for and against this statement:

The inclusion of stock price information in the annual report, along with the audited financial statements and the other required disclosures, directs the stockholders to short-term thinking about their company. There is no need to include that stock price information in the annual report, inasmuch as it is available from other sources. More importantly, its inclusion carries an implication suggesting that the shareholder has invested in a stock, when we should be encouraging the understanding that the shareholder has invested in a company.

15.9. Select a company that interests you, and study its annual report from a year ago and an analyst's report from the same period. Think about the factors that might influence the company's stock price, including, for example, its earnings and its P/E ratio, its net assets, and its ratio of net assets to market value. Using those characteristics and others that seem appropriate to you, develop a target price for the stock. Then chart the actual movement of the stock, month by month, over the next year. Read the president's letter and the MD&A from the current year's annual report and a current analyst's report on the company. Prepare a short essay explaining how the stock price moved compared to your target, and outline some of the factors that might have caused that movement. Comment on what the company (and the analyst) had to say about the movement of the stock during the year and the factors that might have caused that movement.

GLOSSARY

Accelerated Cost Recovery System (ACRS) A method to depreciate tangible assets placed in service between 1981 and 1986 for U.S. income tax purposes.

Accelerated depreciation A cost allocation method in which depreciation deductions are largest in an asset's earlier years but decrease over time.

Account (T-account) An accounting information file usually associated with the general ledger, which appears as follows:

Account

Debit side	Credit side

Accounting A language used by businesspeople to communicate the financial status of their enterprise to interested parties.

Accounting cycle The process of analyzing a transaction and then journalizing it, followed by posting it to the ledger accounts, and then preparing a trial balance, any necessary adjusting entries, financial statements, and closing entries.

Accounting equation Assets = Equities; Assets = Liabilities + Owners' equity. An equation depicting the balance sheet or statement of financial position.

Accounting exposure (risk) The hazard of recognizing and reporting foreign exchange gains (losses) in the income statement for a given period.

Accounting period The time period, usually a quarter or one year, to which accounting reports are related.

Accounting policies The specific accounting principles and practices adopted by a company to report its financial results.

Accounting Principles Board (APB) An organization of the AICPA that established GAAP during the 1957–1973 period; some of the APB's opinions remain in force today.

Accounting Standards Committee (ASC) The principal accounting standards-setting organization in the United Kingdom until 1990; issued statements of standard accounting practice or SSAPs.

Accounts payable (trade payable) Amounts owed to suppliers for merchandise purchased on credit but not yet paid for; normally classified as a current liability.

Accounts receivable (trade receivable) Amounts due to a company from customers who purchased goods or services on credit; payment is normally expected in 30, 60, or 90 days.

Accounts receivable turnover ratio A measure of the effectiveness of receivable management calculated as net credit sales for the period divided by the average balance in accounts receivable.

Accrual method (accrual basis of accounting) An accounting measurement system that records the financial effects of transactions when a business transaction occurs without regard to the timing of the cash effects of the transaction.

Accumulated depreciation (allowance for depreciation) A contra asset account deducted from the acquisition cost of property, plant, and equipment that represents the portion of the original cost of an asset that has been allocated to prior accounting periods.

Active investment An intercorporate investment by an investor-company that allows the investor to exercise influence or control over the operations of the investee-company.

Additional paid-in-capital Amounts paid by shareholders in excess of the minimum amount required for the shares to be fully paid (that is, par or stated value); also known as paid-in capital in excess of par value and share premium reserve.

Adjusting entries Journal entries recorded to update or correct the accounts in the general ledger.

Administrative expense A general operating expense, such as depreciation on a company's headquarters building, associated with the overall management of the company; a period expense.

Advance Corporation Tax (ACT) A British tax set at 25 percent in 1995 and paid by corporations based on the level of dividends expected to be distributed to shareholders.

Affiliated company A company in which an investor-company holds an equity investment in excess of 20 percent of the voting capital stock.

Aging of accounts receivables A method of accounting for uncollectible trade receivables in which an estimate of the bad debts expense is determined by classifying the specific receivable balances into age categories and then applying probability estimates of noncollection.

Aktiebolag (AB) A limited liability company in Sweden.

Aktiengesellschaft (AG) A publicly held corporation in Germany.

Allocation principle An accounting principle that permits the financial effects of business transactions to be assigned to or spread over multiple accounting periods.

Allowance for Decline in Value of Inventory A contra asset account deducted from the cost basis of ending inventory to reflect the write-down of inventory to its replacement value under the lower-of-cost-or-market method.

Allowance for Change in Value of Marketable Securities A contra asset (addendum) account deducted from (added to) the cost basis of marketable securities; represents the unrealized change in a portfolio of securities resulting from the application of the mark-to-market method.

Allowance for Uncollectible Accounts (allowance for bad debts) A contra asset account deducted from accounts or notes receivable; represents the portion of the outstanding receivables balance whose collection is doubtful.

American depositary receipt (ADR) A security issued by a bank or other recognized trustee representing an actual shareholding in a foreign company; these beneficial ownership shares are issued to avoid problems relating to the collection of dividends denominated in a foreign currency and to facilitate rapid ownership transfer; also referred to as stock depositary receipts.

American Institute of Certified Public Accountants (AICPA) The national professional association of certified public accountants (CPAs) in the United States.

Amortization A cost allocation process that spreads the cost of an intangible asset over the asset's expected useful life.

Annual report The report prepared by a company at year end for its stockholders and other interested parties. It frequently includes a letter to the shareholders from the chairperson of the board, management's discussion and analysis of financial performance, and a variety of financial highlights in addition to the basic financial statements. It also includes the auditor's report in which the independent accountants express an opinion as to the fairness of the financial data presented in the financial statements.

Annuity A payment, or a receipt, occurring every period for a set number of periods (for example, interest expense or interest income on a debt instrument).

Antidilutive security A security that, if converted or assumed to be converted into common stock, causes the level of earnings per share to increase.

Asset management The effective utilization of a company's revenue-producing assets; a measure of management's ability to effectively utilize a company's assets to produce income.

Asset turnover The rate at which sales (or revenues) are generated from a given level of assets; a measure of a company's effectiveness in generating revenues from the assets at its disposal, calculated as net sales divided by average total assets.

Assets Tangible and intangible resources of an enterprise that are expected to provide it future economic benefits.

Associated company One that is not a legal subsidiary of another company (control is less than 50+ percent) but in which the other company exercises significant influence (presumably at least a 20 percent shareholding).

Audit A process of investigating the adequacy of a company's system of internal controls, the company's consistent use of generally accepted accounting principles, and the presence of material errors or mistakes in the company's accounting data.

Auditor's opinion A report to a company's shareholders and the board of directors issued by an independent auditor summarizing his or her findings with regard to the company's financial statements. The four types of opinions that may be issued are clean or unqualified, qualified, adverse, and disclaimer.

Authorized shares The total number of shares of capital stock that are authorized to be sold under a company's charter of incorporation.

Available-for-sale investments Securities owned by a company where management's intent is not to trade them on a frequent basis but to sell if and when they deem best.

Average cost method An inventory cost-flow method that assigns the average cost of available finished goods to units sold and, thus, to cost of goods sold.

Average days'-inventory-on-hand ratio A measure of the effectiveness of inventory management calculated as 365 days divided by the inventory turnover ratio; a measure of the appropriateness of current inventory levels given current sales volume.

Average receivable collection period A measure of the effectiveness of accounts receivable management calculated by dividing the receivable turnover ratio into 365 days.

Bad debt An account receivable considered to be uncollectible.

Bad debt expense An estimate (under the allowance method) of the dollar amount of accounts receivable that will eventually prove to be uncollectible; the actual bad debts that are written off if the direct write-off method is used.

Balance The difference between the total left-side (debit) entries and the total right-side (credit) entries made in an account.

Balance sheet (statement of financial position) An accounting statement describing, as of a specific date, the assets, liabilities, and owners' equity of an enterprise.

Betterment An expenditure that extends the useful life or productive capability of an asset and that is capitalized to the balance sheet as an asset.

Blocked funds risk The hazard that a government will restrict the flow of funds either into or out of a given locale.

Board of directors A group of individuals elected by a company's shareholders to oversee the overall management of the company (that is, a board of advisers for the company's managers).

Bond (debenture) An interest-bearing obligation issued by a company to various creditors, usually in amounts of $1,000 or $5,000 and payable at some future maturity date.

Bond discount The amount by which the net proceeds of a bond issue are less than the amount of the principal that must be repaid at maturity date. The amount of the bond discount must be amortized over the life of the bond, thereby making the bond's effective rate of interest greater than its coupon rate of interest.

Bond indenture The document in which the details associated with a bond issue are specified.

Bond payable A financial instrument sold in the capital markets, carrying a specified rate of interest (coupon rate) and a specified repayment date (maturity date); usually classified as a long-term liability.

Bond premium The amount by which the net proceeds of a bond issue exceed the amount of the bond principal that must be repaid at maturity date. The amount of the bond premium that must be amortized over the life of the bond, thereby making its effective rate of interest less than its coupon rate of interest.

Book value (per share) The dollar amount of the net assets of a company on a per share of common stock basis; calculated as (total assets minus total liabilities) divided by the number of outstanding shares of class A common stock.

Book value (of an asset) The original cost of an asset less any accumulated depreciation (depletion or amortization) taken to date; also known as carrying value.

Borsa Valori di Milano The Italian stock exchange in Milan, Italy.

Bovespa The São Paulo stock exchange, the largest stock exchange in Brazil (Bolsa de Valores de São Paulo).

Brazilian commercial code A principal source of accounting and auditing standards in Brazil along with income tax laws and the CVM.

Business combination When one or more businesses are brought together into one accounting entity but not necessarily into one legal entity.

Callable debt Bonds or other obligations that may be legally retired before maturity at the discretion of the debtor-company.

Capital Another term for owners' equity; also used to mean the total assets of an organization.

Capital budgeting The process of proposing and selecting from among a variety of investment proposals or certain long-lived assets to be acquired. This process frequently considers the net present value of projected cash flows for proposed investments.

Capital expenditure An expenditure for the purchase of a noncurrent asset, usually property, plant, or equipment.

Capital intensity ratio A measure of a company's operating leverage, calculated as fixed assets divided by total assets.

Capitalization (of an expenditure) The process of assigning value to a balance sheet account—for example a capitalized asset (that is, a leased asset) or a capitalized liability (such as a lease liability).

Capitalization (of a company) The composition of a company's long-term financing, specifically, owners' equity and long-term debt.

Capital lease A noncancelable lease obligation accounted for as a liability on the balance sheet; a lease agreement in which the risks and rewards of asset ownership are passed (either formally or informally) to the lessee.

Capital stock A certificate representing an ownership interest in an enterprise. See also common stock and preferred stock.

Cash A current asset account representing the amount of money on hand or in the bank.

Cash basis of accounting An accounting measurement system that records the financial effects of business transactions when the underlying event has a cash effect.

Cash discount An amount, usually 2 percent of the gross purchase price, that a buyer may deduct from the final price of an asset if cash is remitted within the discount period, usually 10 days of purchase.

Cash dividend payout A measure of the cash return to common shareholders, calculated as cash dividend per common share divided by the basic earnings per share.

Cash dividend yield A measure of the cash return to common shareholders, calculated as the cash dividend per common share divided by the average market price per common share.

Cash equivalents Bank deposits, usually in the form of certificates of deposit, whose withdrawal may be restricted but whose maturity is expected in the current accounting period.

Cash flow adequacy ratio A cash flow ratio calculated as the cash flow from operations divided by the sum of capital expenditures, dividends paid, and long-term debt repayment; indicates the extent to which cash flows from operations are sufficient to cover asset replacement and capital carrying costs.

Cash flow from operations (CFFO) A measure of the net cash flows from transactions involving sales of goods or services and the acquisition of inputs used to provide the goods or services sold; the excess of cash receipts over cash disbursements relating to the operations of a company for a given period; net income calculated on a cash basis.

CFFO to current liabilities ratio A measure of firm liquidity, calculated as the cash flow from operations (CFFO) divided by average current liabilities; reflects the short-term debt coverage provided by current cash flows from operations.

CFFO to interest charges ratio A measure of solvency, calculated as the cash flow from operations divided by interest charges; reflects the extent to which interest charges are covered by current cash flows from operations.

CFFO to total liabilities ratio A measure of solvency, calculated as the cash flow from operations divided by average total liabilities; reflects the extent to which current cash flow from operations is sufficient to satisfy both long-term and short-term obligations.

Certified public accountant (CPA) An accountant who has passed the Uniform CPA Examination prepared by the American Institute of CPAs and who has met prescribed requirements of the state issuing the CPA certificate.

Chaebol Korean business conglomerates (similar to Japan's keiretsu), numbering approximately 30, that dominate that country's economy (such as Samsung, Hyundai, Lucky Goldstar, and Daewoo).

Chartered accountant (CA) A certified public accountant in the U.K.

Charter of incorporation A legal document creating a corporate entity; specifies (among other things) the number and type of shares of capital stock that the corporate entity can sell.

Chart of accounts A list of the general ledger accounts used by an enterprise in its accounting system.

Chusik Hoesa A Korean joint-stock company formed by seven or more investors with a minimum capitalization of W50 million (approximately $62,000).

Class B common stock A form of common stock that usually carries a lower voting power and lower dividend return than Class A common stock.

Classified balance sheet A balance sheet that delineates the assets and liabilities as current and noncurrent.

Closing entries Accounting data entries prepared at the end of an accounting period; designed to close or set equal to zero the temporary accounts.

Collateral The value of various assets used as security for various debts, usually bank borrowings, that will be transferred to a creditor if the obligation is not fully paid.

Comissao de Valores Mobiliários (CVM) The securities and exchange commission of Brazil.

Commercial Code of Japan Dates to 1899; provides general rules for the valuation of assets and liabilities, provision of reserves, and the accounting for legal and capital reserves.

Commissione Nazionale per le Societa e la Borsa (CONSOB) The Italian equivalent of the U.S. Securities and Exchange Commission; regulates listing requirements and accounting disclosures for publicly held Italian companies.

Commitment A type of contingent liability in which the value of the future obligation is known but that is not currently an obligation because various future events or conditions have not transpired or are currently satisfied.

Common equity share of operating earnings (CSOE) A measure of the proportion of a company's operating earnings allocable to common shareholders.

Common shareholders' capital structure leverage ratio (CSL) A measure of a company's financial leverage, calculated as average total assets divided by average common equity.

Common-size balance sheet A balance sheet in which all account balances are expressed as a percentage of total assets or total equities.

Common-size financial statement Financial statements in which the dollar amounts are expressed as a percentage of some common statement item (for example, a common-size income statement might express all items as a percentage of sales).

Common-size income statements An income statement in which all revenue and expense items are expressed as a percentage of net sales.

Common stock A form of capital stock that usually carries the right to vote on corporate issues; a senior equity security.

Common stock equivalent A security that is not a common stock but that contains provisions to enable its holder to become a common stockholder.

Companies Act of 1985 Current British regulation governing the formation of corporations in that country.

Compensating balances The percentage of a line of credit or of a loan that a bank requires a borrower to keep on deposit at the bank. Its amount has the effect of increasing the effective interest rate of any amount borrowed.

Completed contract A revenue recognition method in which project or contract revenues are unrecognized until the project or contract is substantially completed.

Compound interest A method of calculating interest by which interest is figured on both the principal of a loan and any interest previously earned but not distributed.

Conservatism principle An accounting principle that stipulates that when there is a choice between two approaches to record an economic event, the one that produces the least favorable yet realistic effect on net income or assets should be adopted.

Consignment Inventory placed with a retailer for sale to a final consumer but not sold to the retailer; title to the inventory is retained by the manufacturer until a final sale occurs.

Consistency principle An accounting principle underlying the preparation of financial statements that stipulates that an enterprise should, when possible, use the same set of GAAP from one accounting period to the next.

Consolidated financial statements Financial statements prepared to reflect the operations and financial condition of a parent company and its wholly or majority-owned subsidiaries.

Consolidated reporting A reporting approach in which the financial statements of the parent and subsidiary companies are combined to form one set of financial statements.

Contingent asset An asset that may arise in the future if certain events occur.

Contingent liability A liability that may arise in the future if certain events occur.

Contra account (contra asset, contra liability, contra owners' equity) An account that is subtracted from a related account; for example, accumulated depreciation is subtracted from the Building or Equipment account; other examples include the Allowance for Uncollectible accounts, the Bond Discount account, and the Treasury Stock account.

Contributed capital The sum of the capital stock accounts and the capital in excess of par (or stated) value accounts. Also called paid-in capital.

Convenience statement A set of foreign financial statements translated into the language and the currency of another country.

Convenience translation A set of foreign financial statements translated into the language (not currency) of another country.

Conversion The exchange of convertible bonds or convertible preferred stock for a predetermined quantity of common stock.

Conversion ratio The exchange ratio used to determine the number of common shares that will be issued on conversion of a convertible bond or a convertible preferred stock.

Convertible debt (bond) An obligation or debt security exchangeable, or convertible, into the common stock of a company at a prespecified conversion (or exchange) rate.

Convertible preferred stock A preferred stock that is exchangeable or convertible into the common stock of a company at a prespecified conversion (or exchange) rate.

Corporation A business enterprise owned by one or more owners, called stockholders, that has a legal identity separate and distinct from that of its owners.

Correçao monetaria A system of monetary correction in Brazil designed to reflect the hyperinflationary effects of that country in reported financial statements.

Cost The total acquisition value of an asset; the value of resources given up to acquire an asset.

Cost of goods manufactured The total cost of goods manufactured in an accounting period; the sum of all product costs (such as direct materials, direct labor, and manufacturing overhead).

Cost of goods sold The value assigned to inventory units actually sold in a given accounting period.

Coupon interest rate (face rate) The rate of interest stated on the face of a debt instrument.

Countertrade A trade practice equivalent to barter or the exchange of goods and/or services for other goods and services (that is, no currency is exchanged); typically occurs as a consequence of restrictive currency laws.

Country risk analysis A process of identifying the various types of risks associated with investing or doing business in a given country.

Credit An entry on the right side of an account; credits increase liability, owners' equity, and revenue accounts but decrease asset and expense accounts.

Creditor An individual or company that loans cash or other assets to another person or company.

Cross-sectional analysis A process of analyzing financial data between or among firms in the same industry, or between a firm and industry averages, to identify comparative financial strengths and weaknesses.

Cruzada Plan Instituted in 1986; an attempt to rectify the hyperinflationary environment of Brazil. The heavily devalued cruzeiro was replaced by the cruzado as the primary monetary unit of Brazil.

Cumulative preferred stock A preferred stock in which any unpaid prior dividends accumulate year to year (called dividends in arrears) and must be paid in full before any current period dividends may be paid to either preferred or common shareholders.

Currency risk See foreign exchange risk.

Current asset Those resources of an enterprise, such as cash, inventory, or prepaid expenses, whose consumption or use is expected to occur within the current operating cycle.

Current cost accounting A method of accounting in which financial data are expressed in terms of current rather than historical cost.

Current liability An obligation of an enterprise whose settlement requires the use of current assets or the creation of other current liabilities and occurs within one year.

Current maturity of long-term debt That portion of a long-term obligation that is payable within the next operating cycle or one year.

Current rate method A method of restating foreign financial statements using the current exchange rate.

Current ratio A measure of liquidity and short-term solvency calculated as current assets divided by current liabilities.

Date of declaration The calendar date on which the payment of a cash or stock dividend is officially declared by a company's board of directors.

Date of payment The calendar date on which a cash or stock dividend is actually paid or distributed.

Date of record The calendar date on which a shareholder must own a company's stock to be entitled to receive a declared dividend.

Debenture A general obligation bond of a company.

Debit An entry on the left side of an account; debits increase asset and expense accounts but decrease liability, owners' equity, and revenue accounts.

Debt-to-equity ratio A measure of solvency, calculated as long-term debt divided by total shareholders' equity.

Debt-to-total assets ratio A measure of solvency or long-term liquidity calculated as total debt divided by total assets.

Debt-to-total capitalization ratio A measure of solvency, calculated as long-term debt divided by the sum of total shareholders' equity and long-term debt.

Debtors An alternative designation for accounts and notes receivables, principally used in the financial statements of Great Britain and other Commonwealth companies.

Declining balance method A method to depreciate the cost of a tangible asset in which the allocated cost is greater in the early periods of the asset's life (that is, an accelerated method).

Default risk The probability (or risk) that a company will be unable to meet its short-term or long-term obligations.

Defeasance A method of early retirement of debt in which U.S. Treasury notes are purchased and then placed in a trust account to be used to retire the outstanding debt at its maturity.

Deferral A postponement in the recognition of an expense (such as Prepaid Insurance) or a revenue (such as Unearned Rent) account.

Deferred charge An asset that represents an expenditure whose related expense will not be recognized in the income statement until a future period. Prepaid rent is an example.

Deferred income taxes The portion of a company's income tax expense not currently payable that is postponed because of differences in the accounting policies adopted for financial statement purposes versus those policies used for tax reporting purposes.

Deferred revenue Revenue received as cash but not yet earned.

Deficit An accumulated loss in the retained earnings account; a debit balance in retained earnings.

Defined benefit plan A pension plan in which an employer promises to pay certain levels of future benefits to employees on their retirement from the company.

Defined contribution plan A pension plan in which an employer promises to make periodic payments to the plan on behalf of its employees.

Demand deposit A bank account that may be drawn against on demand.

Depletion A cost allocation method for natural resources.

Depreciation A systematic allocation process that allocates the acquisition cost of a long-lived asset over the expected productive life of the asset.

Devaluation A material downward adjustment of the exchange rate between two currencies.

Diluted earnings per share A standardized measure of performance calculated as net income applicable to common stock divided by the weighted-average number of common shares outstanding plus common stock equivalents and any other potentially dilutive securities.

Direct-financing-type lease A capital lease in which the lessor receives income only from financing the "purchase" of the leased asset.

Direct write-off method A method of accounting for uncollectible trade receivables in which no bad debt expense is recorded until specific receivables prove to be uncollectible.

Discount A reduction in the price paid for a security or a debt instrument below the security's face value.

Discount rate The rate of interest used to discount a future cash flow stream when calculating its present value.

Discounted cash flows The present value of a future stream of cash flows.

Discounting receivables The process of selling accounts or notes receivables to a bank or other financial company at a discount from the maturity value of the account or note.

Discretionary cash flows A measure of a company's cash flows from operations that are available to finance such discretionary corporate activities as the acquisition of another company, the early retirement of debt or equity, or some form of capital asset expansion; also referred to as free cash flows.

Dividend A distribution of the earned income of an enterprise to its owners.

Dividend payout ratio A measure of the percentage of net income (or cash flows from operations) paid out to shareholders as dividends; calculated as cash dividends divided by net income (or cash dividends divided by the cash flow from operations).

Dividends in arrears The dividends on a cumulative preferred stock that have been neither declared nor paid; not a legal liability of a company until declared.

Dividend yield A measure of the level of cash actually distributed to common stockholders, calculated as the cash divided per common share divided by the market price per common share.

Donated capital The increase in owners' equity resulting from a donation of an asset to a company.

Double-declining-balance depreciation A method of calculating depreciation by which a percentage equal to twice the straight-line percentage is multiplied by the declining book value to determine the depreciation expense for the period. Salvage value is ignored when calculating it.

Double-entry system An accounting record-keeping system that records all financial transactions in the accounting system using (at least) two data entries.

Double taxation The taxation of income at the company level plus the taxation of dividends declared and paid to investors from the company earnings.

Doubtful account An account receivable thought to be uncollectible.

Du Pont formula An overall indicator of corporate performance obtained by multiplying a company's asset turnover by its profit margin; equivalent to ROA or ROI.

Early retirement The process of prepaying, or retiring, outstanding debt before its stated maturity.

Earned surplus A term synonymous with retained earnings.

Earnings Income or profit.

Earnings per share A standardized measure of performance calculated as net income divided by the weighted-average number of common shares outstanding during an accounting period. Also known as basic earnings per share.

Economic exposure (risk) The risk of experiencing a real gain (loss) in purchasing power as a consequence of foreign exchange rate fluctuations.

Economic income The excess or additional resources of an enterprise resulting from its primary business activity and measured relative to the beginning level of resources.

Effective interest method A method to amortize a discount or a premium on a debt instrument based on the time value of money.

Effective interest rate The real rate of interest paid (or earned) on a debt instrument.

Efficient market hypothesis A theory to explain the functioning of capital markets in which stock and bond prices always reflect all publicly available information, and any new information is quickly impounded in security prices.

Emerging Issues Task Force (EITF) An affiliate organization of the FASB whose purpose is to address new accounting and reporting issues before divergent practice can become widely adopted.

Employee Retirement Income and Security Act (ERISA) Legislation passed by the U.S. Congress in 1974 to govern the funding of private pension plans.

Entity principle An accounting convention that views a corporate enterprise as separate and distinct from its owners; thus, the financial statements of the corporation describe only the financial condition of the enterprise itself, not that of its shareholders.

Equity A claim against the assets of a company by creditors or the owners.

Equity in earnings of investee An income statement account representing an investor-company's percentage ownership of an investee's (or subsidiary's) net earnings.

Equity method A method to value intercorporate equity investments by adjusting the investor's cost basis for the percentage ownership in the investee's earnings (or losses) and for any dividends paid by the investee.

European currency unit (ECU) A currency intended to be used by all European Union members in conducting trade.

European exchange rate mechanism (ERM) A system created by the EU to stabilize the rate of exchange of currency between EU member nations.

European Union (EU) An organization of politically independent European nations (currently numbering 15), united to act as a single economic (trading) entity (or bloc); includes three cooperative alliances intended to improve the efficiency and competitive ability of its member nations: the European Coal and Steel Community, the European Atomic Energy Commission, and the European Economic Community.

Exchange Currency or legal tender used to facilitate trade between parties.

Exchange rate The rate at which one unit of currency may be purchased by another unit of currency.

Ex-dividend A condition of capital stock if sold (or purchased) after the date of record; that is, the purchaser of an ex-dividend stock is not entitled to receive the most recently declared dividend.

Executory contracts A category of legal agreements requiring some type of future performance.

Expenditure An outflow of cash, usually representing the acquisition of an asset or the incurring of an expense.

Expense An outflow of assets, an increase in liabilities, or both, from transactions involving an enterprise's principal business activity (such as sales of products or services).

Expropriation exposure (risk) The likelihood that a company's assets located in a foreign domain will be involuntarily appropriated by the local government, with or without compensation.

External reporting Financial reporting to stockholders and others outside an enterprise.

Extraordinary item A loss or gain that is both unusual in nature and infrequent in occurrence.

Face amount (maturity value) The value of a security as stated on the instrument itself.

Factor A financial corporation, bank, or other financial institution that buys accounts and notes receivables from companies; receivables may be purchased with or without recourse.

Factory overhead Another name for manufacturing overhead. For inventory valuation purposes, it is allocated to units of production by some type of rational systematic method.

Federal income tax The tax levied by the federal government on corporate and individual earnings.

Financial accounting The accounting rules and conventions used in preparing external accounting reports.

Financial Accounting Standards Board (FASB) An independent, private sector organization responsible for establishing generally accepted accounting principles.

Financial Reporting Council (FRC) An accounting standard-setting organization in the United Kingdom founded in 1990 that succeeded the Accounting Standards Committee; issues financial reporting standards.

Financial reporting standard (FRS) An official accounting pronouncement issued by the Financial Reporting Council of the United Kingdom.

Financial statements The basic accounting reports issued by a company, including the balance sheet, the income statement, and the statement of cash flows.

Financial statement analysis The process of reviewing, analyzing, and interpreting the basic financial statements to assess a company's operating performance and/or financial health.

Finished goods Inventory having completed the manufacturing process and ready for sale.

Finished goods inventory Fully assembled or manufactured goods available for sale and classified as a current asset on the balance sheet.

First-in, first-out (FIFO) An inventory cost-flow method that assigns the first cost value in finished goods inventory to the first unit sold and thus to cost of goods sold.

Fiscal year Any continuous 12-month period, usually beginning after a natural business peak.

Fixed assets A subcategory of noncurrent assets; usually represented by property, plant, and equipment.

FOB Free-on-board, some location. Examples are FOB shipping point and FOB destination. The location denotes the point at which title passes from the seller to the buyer.

Footnotes Written information by management designed to supplement the numerical data presented in a company's financial statement.

Foreign currency option contract A contract providing the right to buy or sell a set quantity of foreign currency at a present exchange rate within a specified future time frame; typically used to hedge foreign exchange risk exposure, and often thought of as currency insurance.

Foreign currency translation adjustment An owners' equity account measuring the change in value of a company's net assets held in a foreign country, attributable to changes in the exchange rate of a foreign currency as compared to the U.S. dollar.

Foreign exchange Any currency other than the one in which a company prepares its basic financial statements.

Foreign exchange risk The risk associated with changes in exchange rates between the U.S. dollar and foreign currencies when a company maintains operations in a foreign country.

Form 8-K A special SEC filing required when a material event or transaction occurs between Form 10-Q filing dates. Events that usually necessitate the filing of Form 8-K include a change in control or ownership of an enterprise, the acquisition or disposition of a significant amount of assets, a bankruptcy declaration, the resignation of an executive or director of an enterprise, or a change in the independent external auditor.

Form 10-K The annual financial report filing with the SEC required of all publicly held enterprises.

Form 10-Q The quarterly financial report filing with the SEC required of all publicly held enterprises; it is filed only for the first three quarters of a fiscal year.

Form 20-F The annual financial report filing with the SEC required of all foreign companies whose debt or equity capital is available for purchase/sale on a U.S. exchange.

Forward exchange contract A contract providing for the payment (receipt) of a foreign currency at a future date at a specified exchange rate; typically used to hedge foreign exchange risk exposure.

Forward exchange rate An exchange rate between two currencies quoted for 30, 60, 90, or 180 days in the future; a rate quoted currently for the exchange of currency at some future specified date.

Fourth Directive A European Union agreement, adopted in 1978, to (1) eliminate legal and bureaucratic obstacles to economic activity between EU member nations and (2) establish the basic reporting requirements and financial statement formats (that is, comparability) for companies operating in EU member nations.

Free cash flows See discretionary cash flows.

Freight-in Freight costs associated with the purchase and receipt of inventory.

Freight-out Freight costs associated with the sale and delivery of inventory.

Front-end loading An accounting process by which revenues (expenses) are recognized for income statement purposes before they have been earned (incurred).

Functional currency The currency of the primary business environment (country) of a company's operations.

Gain An increase in asset values, usually involving a sale (realized) or revaluation (unrealized), unrelated to the principal revenue-producing activity of a business.

General journal An accounting data file containing a chronological listing of financial transactions affecting an enterprise.

General ledger An accounting data file containing aggregate account information for all accounts listed in an enterprise's chart of accounts.

Generally accepted accounting principles (GAAP) Those methods identified by authoritative bodies (APB, FASB, SEC) as being acceptable for use in the preparation of external accounting reports.

Generally accepted auditing standards (GAAS) Those auditing practices and procedures established by the AICPA that are used by CPAs to evaluate a company's accounting system and financial results.

Gesellschaft mit beschränkter Haftung (GmbH) A privately held corporation in Germany.

Going-concern concept An accounting concept underlying the preparation of financial statements that assumes that the enterprise will continue its operations for the foreseeable future.

Goodwill An intangible asset representing the excess of the purchase price of acquired net assets over their fair market value.

Gross profit (gross margin) A measure of a company's profit on sales calculated as net sales minus the cost of goods or services sold.

Gross profit margin ratio A measure of profitability that assesses the percentage of each sales dollar that is recognized as gross profit (after deducting the cost of goods sold) and that is available to cover other operating expenses (such as selling, administrative, interest, and taxes).

Harmonization The attempt by various organizations (such as the IASC, the EU, and IOSCO) to establish a common set of international accounting and reporting standards.

Hedge A process of buying or selling commodities, forward contracts, or options for the explicit purpose of reducing or eliminating foreign exchange risk.

Hedged items Those accounts (assets, liabilities, revenues) or contracts for which an artificial or natural hedge exists.

Hedging instrument A forward exchange contract or option contract acquired to hedge some type of exposure (such as currency risk, expropriation risk, political risk).

Highest-in, first-out (HIFO) An inventory cost-flow method that assigns the highest cost value available in finished goods inventory to the first unit sold and thus cost of goods sold.

Historical cost principle An accounting principle that stipulates that all economic transactions should be recorded using the dollar value incurred at the time of the transaction.

Hold-to-maturity investments Securities, usually debt securities, owned by a company where management's intent is to hold them until the securities' stipulated maturity date.

Holding company (parent company) A company that owns a majority of the voting capital stock of another company.

Impairment A temporary or permanent reduction in asset value; usually necessitates a write-down in the asset's balance sheet value.

Income A generic term that may be used to indicate revenue from miscellaneous sources (such as interest income or rent income) or the excess of revenue over expenses for product sales or services.

Income and Loss Summary A temporary account used to transfer the net income or loss of an enterprise from the income statement to the retained earnings account on the balance sheet.

Income smoothing An accounting practice that implicitly or explicitly attempts to present a stable (but growing) measure of net income (such as straight-line depreciation).

Income statement (statement of earnings) An accounting statement describing the revenues earned and expenses incurred by an enterprise for a given period.

Independent auditor A professionally trained individual whose responsibilities include the objective review of a company's financial statements prepared for external distribution.

Inflation A phenomenon of generally rising prices.

Initial public offering (IPO) The first or initial sale of voting stock to the general market by a previously privately held concern.

Insolvent (bankrupt) A condition in which a company is unable to pay its current obligations as they come due.

Installment basis A method of recognizing revenue that parallels the receipt of cash.

Installment sale A credit sale in which the buyer agrees to make periodic payments, or installments, on the amount owed.

Instituto Brasileiro de Contadores (IBC) The professional society of certified public accountants in Brazil.

Intangible assets Those resources of an enterprise, such as goodwill, trademarks, or tradenames, that lack an identifiable physical presence.

Intercompany profit The profit resulting when one related company sells to another related company; intercompany profits are removed from the financial statements when consolidated financial statements are prepared.

Intercorporate investments Investments in the stocks and bonds of one company by another.

Interest coverage ratio See times-interest-earned ratio.

Interest expense The cost of borrowing funds.

Interim financial statements Financial statements prepared on a monthly or quarterly basis; usually unaudited.

Internal control structure The policies and procedures implemented by management to safeguard a company's assets and its accounting system against misapplication or misuse.

International accounting standards (IAS) The accounting and reporting standards adopted and promulgated by the IASC.

International Accounting Standards Committee (IASC) An association of professional accounting bodies formed in 1973 to develop and issue international accounting and reporting standards.

International Federation of Accountants (IFAC) An association of professional accounting organizations from more than 70 nations founded in 1977; largely concerned with developing international guidelines for the accounting profession in the areas of auditing, ethics, and education.

International Organization of Securities Commissions and Similar Organizations (IOSCO) An organization of securities regulatory agencies representing various member countries, whose goal is to assist in the creation and regulation of orderly international capital markets.

International Stock Exchange (ISE) The largest securities exchange in the United Kingdom.

Interperiod tax allocation The process of allocating the actual taxes paid by a company over the periods in which the taxes are recognized for accounting purposes.

Inventory The aggregate cost of salable goods and merchandise available to meet customer sales.

Inventory turnover A measure of the rate of inventory sales.

Inventory turnover ratio A measure of the effectiveness of inventory management calculated as the cost of goods sold for a period divided by the average inventory held during that period.

Investment ratio A cash flow ratio calculated as capital expenditures divided by the sum of depreciation and proceeds from the sale of assets; indicates the relative change in a company's investment in productive assets.

Investment tax credit A reduction in the current income taxes payable earned through the purchase of various applicable assets.

Investor company A company that holds an equity investment in another company (the investee company).

Issued shares The number of authorized shares of capital stock sold to shareholders less any shares repurchased and retired.

Japanese Securities and Exchange Law of 1948 Based largely on the U.S. securities laws of 1933 and 1934; requires companies issuing securities to the public to file financial statements (zaimushohyo) audited by an independent auditor with the Ministry of Finance; also known as shokentorihikiho.

Journal A chronological record of events and transactions affecting the accounts of a company recorded by means of debits and credits; a financial diary of a company.

Journal entry A data entry into a company's journal system.

Journalize The process of recording data in the journal system of a company by means of debits and credits.

Keiretsu An association of Japanese companies with interlocking shareholdings that provide economic support to one another; literally interpreted as "headless combines."

Last-in, first-out (LIFO) An inventory cost-flow method that assigns the last cost value in finished goods inventory to the first unit sold and thus to cost of goods sold.

Lease An agreement to buy or rent an asset.

Leasehold improvement Expenditures made by a lessee to improve or change a leased asset.

Lessee An individual or company who leases an asset.

Lessor The maker of a lease agreement; an individual or company who leases an asset to another individual or company.

Leverage The extent to which a company's long-term capital structure includes debt financing; a measure of a company's dependency on debt. A company with large quantities of debt is said to be highly leveraged.

Liabilities The dollar value of an enterprise's obligations to repay monies loaned to it, to pay for goods or services received by it, or to fulfill commitments made by it.

LIFO liquidation The sale of inventory units acquired or manufactured in a prior period at a lower cost; results when the level of LIFO inventory is reduced below its beginning-of-period level.

LIFO reserve An amount presented in the footnotes to the financial statements of companies employing the LIFO method of inventory valuation; calculated as the current cost of ending inventory minus the LIFO cost of ending inventory.

Limited company (Ltd) A limited liability but privately held company in the United Kingdom having no minimum capital requirement.

Limited liability The concept that shareholders in a corporation are not held personally liable for its losses and debts.

Limited partnership A partnership composed of at least one general partner and at least one limited partner, in which the general partner(s) assumes responsibility for all debts and losses of the partnership.

Line of credit An agreement with a bank by which an organization obtains authorization for short-term borrowings up to a specified amount.

Liquid assets Those current assets, such as cash, cash equivalents, or short-term investments, that either are in cash form or can be readily converted to cash.

Liquidating dividend A cash dividend representing a return of invested capital and, hence, a liquidation of a previous investment.

Liquidation The process of selling off the assets of a business, paying any outstanding debts, and then distributing any remaining cash to the owners.

Liquidity The short-term debt repayment ability of a company; a measure of a company's cash position relative to currently maturing obligations.

Listed company A company whose shares or bonds have been accepted for trading on a recognized securities exchange (such as the NYSE).

Long-term liabilities (noncurrent liabilities) The obligations of a company payable after more than one year.

Loss The excess of expenses over revenues for a single transaction.

Lower of cost or market A method to value inventories; the lower of an asset's cost basis or current market value is used to value the asset account for balance sheet purposes.

Machine-hour method A method to depreciate the cost of a machine or other equipment based on its actual usage.

Maintenance expenditure An expenditure to maintain the original productive capacity of an asset; deducted as an expense.

Managerial accounting The accounting rules and conventions used in the preparation of internal accounting reports.

Manufacturing overhead The factory-related costs indirectly associated with the manufacture or production of a good; for example, the costs of production-line supervision, maintenance of the production equipment, and depreciation of the factory building.

Market price The current fair value of an asset as established by an arm's length transaction between a buyer and a seller.

Marketable securities Short- or long-term investments in the stocks or bonds of other corporations.

Mark-to-market A method to value investments in trading or available-for-sale securities wherein they are reported on corporate balance sheets at their fair market value, not at cost.

Matching principle An accounting principle that stipulates that when revenues are reported, the expenses incurred to generate those revenues should be reported in the same accounting period.

Materiality principle An accounting principle underlying the preparation of financial statements; stipulates that only those transactions that might influence the decisions of a reasonable person should be disclosed in detail in the financial statements; all other information may be presented in summary format.

Maturity date The principal repayment date for a bond or debenture, specified as part of the indenture agreement.

Maturity value (face amount) The amount of cash required to satisfy an obligation at the date of its maturity.

Merger A combination of one or more companies into a single corporate entity.

Minority interest The percentage ownership in the net assets of a subsidiary held by investors other than the parent company.

Modified Accelerated Cost Recovery System (MACRS) A method to depreciate tangible assets placed in service after 1986 for U.S. income tax purposes.

Monetary assets Resources of an enterprise, such as cash and marketable securities, whose principal characteristic is monetary denomination.

Mortgage An agreement in which a lender (the mortgagee) agrees to loan money to a borrower (the mortgagor) to be repaid over a specified period of time and at a specified rate of interest.

Mortgage bond A bond secured or collateralized by a company's noncurrent assets, usually its property, plant, and equipment.

Multinational corporation (MNC) A for-profit organization with operations in two or more countries.

Multinational enterprise (MNE) A for-profit or not-for-profit organization with operations in two or more countries (such as a multinational corporation).

Multiple reporting Reporting by a company that requires the preparation of multiple sets of financial statements in the language and currency of another country.

Natural hedge A hedging instrument that exists as a consequence of the normal course of business.

Natural resources Noncurrent, nonrenewable resources such as oil and gas, coal, ore, and uranium.

Negative goodwill The excess of the net book value of an acquired company over the consideration paid for it.

Negotiable instruments Receivables, payables, or securities that can be bought and sold (that is, negotiated) between companies.

Net assets Total assets minus total liabilities; equal total owners' equity.

Net current assets Current assets minus current liabilities; working capital.

Net income (net earnings) The difference between the aggregate revenues and aggregate expenses of an enterprise for a given accounting period; when aggregate expenses exceed aggregate revenues, the term net loss is used.

Net realizable value The amount of funds expected to be received upon the sale or liquidation of an asset.

Net sales Total sales less sales returns and allowances and sales discounts.

Net worth (of an enterprise) Total assets minus total liabilities, or the value of owners' equity; also known as the book value of an enterprise.

Nonclassified balance sheet A balance sheet in which the assets and liabilities are not classified as current or noncurrent; in nonclassified balance sheets, assets and liabilities are considered to be noncurrent.

Noncurrent assets The long-lived resources of an enterprise, such as property, plant, and equipment, whose consumption or use is not expected to be completed within the current operating cycle.

Noncurrent asset turnover ratio A measure of the effectiveness of noncurrent asset management calculated as net sales for the period divided by the average balance of noncurrent assets.

Noncurrent liability An obligation of an enterprise whose settlement is not expected within one year.

Nondiversifiable risk Unique, nonsystematic risk associated with an investment that cannot be effectively hedged (through, for example, portfolio diversification).

Nonmonetary assets Those resources of an enterprise, such as inventory or equipment, whose principal characteristic is other than its monetary denomination or value.

Notes payable An obligation to repay money or other assets in the future evidenced by a signed contractual agreement or note.

Notes receivable Amounts due a company from customers who purchased goods or services on credit; the obligation is evidenced by a legal document called a note.

Off-balance-sheet debt Economic obligations that are not reported on the face of the balance sheet (such as operating leases).

Operating cycle The average length of time between the investment in inventory and the subsequent collection of cash from the sale of that inventory.

Operating expenses Expenses incurred in carrying out the operations of a business, for example, selling expenses.

Operating funds index A cash flow ratio calculated as net income divided by cash flow from operations that indicates the portion of operating cash flow provided by net income.

Operating lease A lease agreement in which the risks and rewards of asset ownership are retained by the lessor.

Operating leverage The extent to which a company operates with a high proportion of fixed costs.

Operational risk The probability that unforeseen or unexpected events will occur and consequently reduce or impair the revenue, earnings, and cash flow streams of a company.

Option A contract in which a buyer receives the right to buy inventory or stock in the future at a prespecified price.

Option contract Usually used for hedging purposes to grant one party the right to choose whether (and sometimes when) a currency exchange will actually take place.

Organization costs The expenditures associated with starting a new business venture, including legal fees and incorporation fees; frequently accounted for as an intangible asset of a company.

Outstanding shares The number of authorized shares of capital stock that have been sold to shareholders and are currently in the possession of shareholders; the number of issued shares less the shares held in treasury.

Owners' equity (shareholders' equity) The dollar value of the owners' (or shareholders') investment in an enterprise; may take two forms—the purchase of shares of stock or the retention of earnings in the enterprise for future use.

Paid-in-Capital in Excess of Par Value (Contributed Capital in Excess of Par Value) An owners' equity account reflecting the proceeds from the sale of capital stock in excess of the par value (or stated value) of the capital stock.

Participating preferred stock A preferred stock that entitles shareholders to share in any "excess dividend payments" (that is, after the common shareholders have received a fair dividend return).

Partnership A business enterprise jointly owned by two or more persons.

Par value A legal value assigned to a share of capital stock that must be considered in recording the proceeds received from the sale of the stock. See also stated value.

Passive investment An intercorporate investment in which the investor cannot (or does not) attempt to influence the operations of the investee-company.

Past service cost The cost of committed pension benefits earned by employees for periods of work prior to the adoption of a formal pension plan.

Payback period The period of time required to recover the cash outlay for an asset or other investment.

Pension A retirement plan for employees that will provide income to the employee upon retirement.

Percentage of completion A revenue recognition method in which total project or contract revenues are allocated between several accounting periods on the basis of the actual work completed in those periods.

Percentage of credit sales method A method of accounting for uncollectible trade receivables in which an estimate of the bad debts expense is recorded each period on the basis of the credit sales for the period.

Period costs Costs, such as administrative and selling expenses, associated with the accounting period in which they were incurred.

Periodic inventory system An inventory record-keeping system that determines the quantity of inventory on hand by a physical count.

Permanent accounts Those accounts, principally the balance sheet accounts, that are not closed at the end of an accounting period and that carry accounting information forward from one period to the next.

Permanent difference A difference in reported income or expenses between a company's tax return and its financial statements that will never reverse (that is, the difference is permanent).

Permanent earnings (cash flows) The recurring earnings (cash flows) of a company; earnings (cash flows) expected to recur in future periods.

Perpetual inventory system An inventory record-keeping system that continuously (or perpetually) updates the quantity of inventory on hand on the basis of units purchased, manufactured, and sold.

Pledging When assets are used as collateral for a bank loan, the assets are said to have been pledged.

Political exposure (risk) The degree of stability (or lack thereof) among political groups and the established government in a given country.

Pooling-of-interests A consolidation method that combines the financial results of a parent company and its subsidiary on the basis of existing book values.

Posting An accounting process involving the transfer of financial data from the general journal to the general ledger.

Preemptive right The privilege of a shareholder to maintain his or her proportionate ownership in a corporation by being able to purchase an equivalent percentage of all new capital stock offered for sale.

Preferred stock A (usually) nonvoting form of capital stock whose claims to the dividends and assets of a company precede those of common stockholders.

Premium An amount paid in excess of the face value of a security or debt instrument.

Prepaid expenses A current asset that represents prior expenditures and whose consumption is expected to occur in the next accounting period.

Present value The value today of a future stream of cash flows calculated by discounting the cash flows at a given rate of interest.

Price-earnings (P/E) ratio A market-based measure of the investment potential of a security, calculated as the market price per share divided by the earnings per share; also known as P/E multiple.

Price-level-adjusted financial statements Financial statements in which the account balances have been restated to reflect changes in price levels due to inflation.

Prime rate The interest rate charged by banks on borrowings by preferred customers.

Principal The remaining balance of an outstanding obligation to be paid in the future.

Prior period adjustment An accounting event or transaction that does not affect the current period's earnings but instead is reflected as an adjustment to retained earnings.

Private placement The sale, or "placement," of a significant number of stocks or bonds to a limited group of buyers; the securities are not offered for sale to the general marketplace.

Privatization The sale of all or part of a previously state-controlled entity to the general public.

Product cost A cost directly related to the production of a good or service—for example, the cost of goods sold.

Productivity index A cash flow ratio calculated as the cash flow from operations divided by the capital investment; indicates the relative cash productivity of a company's capital investments.

Profit The excess of revenues over expenses for a single transaction.

Profit and loss reserve The amount of retained earnings of a company; see retained earnings.

Profit margin The excess (or insufficiency) of operating revenues over operating expenses; a measure of a company's ability to generate profits from a given level of revenues; calculated as net income after tax divided by net sales; also known as the return on sales ratio.

Profitability The relative success of a company's operations; a measure of the extent to which accomplishment exceeded effort.

Pro forma (financial statement) A forecast or projected financial statement for a future accounting period.

Promissory note A written promise to pay a specific sum of money at a specific date; a liability.

Property, plant, and equipment The noncurrent assets of a company, principally used in the revenue-producing operations of the enterprise.

Proportionate consolidation A method of consolidating the financial results of a parent company and its subsidiary, in which only the proportion of net assets owned by the parent are consolidated; as a consequence there is no need for a minority interest account.

Proprietary company A label used in some countries to describe a privately held (or nonpublic) company.

Prospectus A document describing the nature of a business and its recent financial history, usually prepared in conjunction with an offer to sell capital stock or bonds by a company.

Proxy A legal document granting another person or company the right to vote for a shareholder on matters involving a shareholder vote.

Prudence The criterion used under German GAAP to establish the appropriateness and necessity of recognizing a loss contingency.

Public company One whose voting shares are listed for trading on a recognized securities exchange or are otherwise available for purchase (sale) by public investors.

Public limited company (Plc) A limited liability publicly held company in the United Kingdom; must have share capital of at least £50,000.

Purchase accounting A consolidation method in which the financial results of a parent-company and its subsidiary are combined using the fair market value of the subsidiary's net worth.

Purchase discount A cash discount (usually 2 percent) given to a buyer if the buyer pays for the purchases within the discount period (usually 10 days after purchase).

Purchase Discounts Lost An expense account representing the finance or interest costs incurred as a consequence of not paying for goods purchased on credit on a timely basis (such as 2/10, net 30).

Purchases Goods or inventory acquired for sale or manufacture.

Qualified opinion An opinion issued by an independent auditor indicating that the financial statements of a company are fairly presented on a consistent basis and use generally accepted accounting principles, but for which some concern or exception has been noted.

Quick assets Highly liquid, short-term assets such as cash, cash equivalents, short-term investments, and receivables.

Quick ratio (acid test ratio) A measure of liquidity and short-term solvency calculated as quick assets divided by current liabilities.

Ratio A financial indicator (such as the current ratio) formed by comparing two account balances (such as current assets and current liabilities).

Ratio analysis The process of analyzing and interpreting the ratios formed from two or more financial statement numbers.

Raw (basic) earnings per share (EPS) A measure of EPS, calculated as net income after taxes minus preferred dividends, divided by the weighted average number of common (or ordinary) shares outstanding.

Raw material inventory Materials and purchased parts awaiting assembly or manufacture; classified as a current asset on the balance sheet.

Realized loss (gain) A loss (gain) that is recognized in the financial statements, usually due to the sale of an asset.

Rear-end loading An accounting process by which expenses (revenues) are deferred for income statement purposes despite being incurred (earned).

Receivable turnover A measure of the rate of collections on sales.

Receivable turnover ratio A measure of the rate of collections on sales, calculated as net sales divided by the average receivable balance: the rate at which a company's receivables are converted to cash.

Recognition principle An accounting principle that stipulates that revenues should not be recorded in the accounting records until earned and that expenses should not be recorded until incurred.

Reconciliation report A statement or report reconciling the financial statements of a foreign entity to the accepted or prevailing accounting practice of another country.

Redeemable (callable) preferred stock A preferred stock that may be retired (redeemed or called) at the discretion of the issuing company, usually after a specified date and usually at a premium above the stated (or par) value of the preferred stock.

Redemption The retirement of preferred stock or bonds before a specified maturity date.

Registrar An independent agent, normally a bank or a trust company, that maintains a record of the number of shares of capital stock of a company that have been issued and to whom.

Relevance principle An accounting principle used to select which accounting information should be presented in a company's financial statements.

Reliability principle An accounting principle that stipulates that accounting information, and hence accounting reports, must be reliable to be useful to financial statement users.

Reorganization (quasi-reorganization) A process of changing the ownership structure of a company, usually as a direct result of a deficit in retained earnings.

Replacement cost The cost to reproduce or repurchase a given asset (such as a unit of inventory).

Reporting currency The currency used to measure and report a company's net assets (that is, the "local" currency).

Reserve An owners' equity account including the profit and loss reserve (retained earnings), revaluation reserve, capital reserve or share premium reserve (paid-in-capital in excess of par value), and legal reserves (those mandated by a given country's laws of incorporation).

Retained earnings Those earnings of an enterprise that have been retained in the enterprise (have not been paid out as dividends) for future corporate use.

Retained earnings—appropriated The amount of total retained earnings that has been allocated for specific corporate objectives, such as the redemption of debt or capital stock.

Retained earnings—restricted The amount of total retained earnings that is legally restricted from being paid out as dividends to shareholders; the restriction usually results from a borrowing agreement with a bank or other financial institution.

Return on common equity (ROCE) ratio A measure of profitability, calculated as the net income available to common shareholders divided by the average total common equity for the period.

Return on owners' equity (ROE) A measure of profitability; a measure of the relative effectiveness of a company in using the assets provided by the owners to generate net income; calculated as net income divided by average owners' equity.

Return on sales ratio (net profit margin ratio) A measure of profitability, calculated as the percentage of each sales dollar that is earned as net income; may be either retained in the company or paid out as a dividend.

Return on total assets (ROA) A measure of profitability that assesses the relative effectiveness of a company in using available resources to generate net income; also called the return on investment, or ROI; calculated as net income divided by average total assets.

Revaluation A material upward adjustment of the exchange rate between two currencies; an upward adjustment in asset value, usually undertaken to reflect the economic effects of inflation.

Revenue bond A bond secured or collateralized by a revenue stream from a particular group of assets.

Revenues The inflow of assets, the reduction in liabilities, or both, from transactions involving an enterprise's principal business activity (for example, sales of products or services).

Sale A legal term suggesting that the title to an asset has passed from a seller to a buyer.

Sale/Leaseback An accounting transaction in which an asset is first sold and then immediately leased back by the selling entity; a financing transaction.

Sales-type lease A capital lease that generates two income streams: (1) from the "sale" of the asset and (2) from financing the "purchase" of the asset.

Salvage value (residual value) The amount that is expected to be recovered when an asset is retired, removed from active use, and sold.

Securities Act of 1933 A 1933 legislative act of the U.S. Congress that requires certain disclosures by enterprises issuing (or desiring to issue) shares of capital stock.

Securities and Exchange Commission (SEC) A government agency responsible for the oversight of U.S. securities markets; this agency also specifies the form and content of all financial reports by companies issuing securities to the public.

Securities Exchange Act of 1934 A 1934 legislative act of the U.S. Congress that created the Securities and Exchange Commission.

Self-sustaining foreign operation A foreign entity financially and operationally independent of its parent company.

Selling expense Expenses incurred directly as a consequence of selling and delivering a product to customers.

Sensitivity analysis A process by which the effect of a change in a given assumption is assessed (as in a pro forma analysis).

Seventh Directive A European Union agreement adopted in 1983, governing the preparation of consolidated financial statements for companies operating in EU member nations.

Sinking fund A trust account established in conjunction with the issuance of bonds into which funds are paid periodically to be used to retire the debt at maturity; an asset account.

Società a Responsibilità Limitada (S.r.l.) A closely held, limited liability entity in Italy.

Società per Azioni (S.p.A.) A publicly held (joint stock) company in Italy.

Sole proprietorship A business enterprise owned by one person.

Solvency The long-term debt repayment ability of a company; a measure of a company's long-term liquidity.

Special journal An accounting data file containing a chronological listing of special financial transactions (for example, cash purchases or cash receipts) affecting an enterprise.

Specific identification An inventory cost-flow method that assigns the actual cost of producing a specific unit to that unit; the only inventory method that matches exactly the cost flow and physical flow.

Spot rate The prevailing exchange rate between two currencies on a given date.

Standard product cost An inventory valuation method that uses estimated or projected costs of producing a product rather than actual costs.

Stated value The recorded accounting value of capital stock. See also par value.

Statement of cash flows An accounting statement describing the sources and uses of cash flows for an enterprise for a given period.

Statement of fund flows An accounting statement describing a company's inflows and outflows of funds over a given period; funds defined with reference to a company's cash, liquid assets, or working capital.

Statement of owners' equity (statement of shareholders' equity) An accounting statement describing the principal transactions affecting the owners' (or shareholders') interests in an enterprise for a given period.

Statement of retained earnings An accounting statement describing the beginning and ending balances in retained earnings and the major changes to the retained earnings account (for example, dividends and net income).

Statements of financial accounting standards (SFAS) The official pronouncements of the FASB.

Stewardship The management and supervision of enterprise resources.

Stock certificate A legal document evidencing the purchase of capital stock in a company.

Stock depositary receipt (SDR) A beneficial ownership share in a foreign entity held by a trustee (such as a bank or brokerage firm) on behalf of the investor; see American depositary receipt.

Stock dividend A distribution of additional shares of capital stock to a company's stockholders.

Stockholders' equity The owners' equity of a corporation; comprises paid-in capital and retained earnings.

Stock option A right issued by a company to its employees entitling an employee to buy a set quantity of capital stock in the future at a prespecified price.

Stock split An increase (a forward split) or a decrease (a reverse split) in the number of shares issued by a company; equivalent to a large stock dividend.

Stock warrant (stock right) A certificate issued by a company that carries the right or privilege to buy a set quantity of capital stock in the future at a prespecified price.

Straight-line method A method to depreciate the cost of a tangible asset or to amortize the cost of an intangible asset in which the allocated cost is constant over the life of the asset.

Subchapter S corporation A small corporation that pays no corporate taxes; all earnings are divided among the owners and are taxed at the individual level.

Subsidiary A company in which an investor company (the parent) holds an equity investment in excess of 50 percent of the voting stock of the investee company.

Subsidiary ledger An accounting data file containing detailed account information to supplement or explain the aggregate account balance contained in the general ledger.

Sum-of-the-years' digits method A method to depreciate the cost of a tangible asset in which the allocated cost is greater in the early periods of the asset's life (that is, an accelerated method).

Take-or-pay contract An executory contract by which one party agrees to pay for certain inventory (or other products) regardless of whether the inventory is physically received or not.

Tangible asset Those resources of an enterprise, such as property, plant, and equipment, that possess physical characteristics or have a physical presence.

Temporal method A method of translating foreign financial statements in which cash, receivables, and payables are translated at the exchange rate in effect at the balance sheet date; other assets and liabilities translated at historical rates; revenues and expenses translated at the weighted-average rate for the period.

Temporary accounts Those accounts that are closed at the end of each accounting period—for example, the income statement accounts, dividends, and the income and loss summary.

Temporary difference A difference in reported income or expenses between a company's tax return and its financial statements that will reverse out in some future period.

Times-interest-earned ratio A measure of solvency and leverage calculated as net income plus interest and income taxes divided by interest charges; a measure of the extent to which current interest payments are covered by current earnings.

Time value of money Because money can always be invested at a bank to earn interest for the period it is on deposit, money is said to have a "time value."

Timing differences Differences in the timing of the reporting of certain revenues and expenses for tax purposes and for external financial reporting purposes.

Total asset turnover ratio A measure of asset management effectiveness reflecting the rate at which sales are generated from a company's investment in assets; calculated as net sales divided by average total assets.

Total debt-to-total assets ratio A measure of solvency or long-term liquidity, calculated as total debt divided by total assets.

Trade payables See accounts payable and notes payable.

Trade receivables See accounts receivable.

Trading investment A security owned by a company where management's intent is to sell it in the very near term.

Transaction exposure (risk) A source of foreign exchange risk resulting from exchange rate fluctuations between the date on which a contract is signed or goods delivered and the date of payment.

Transaction principle A concept underlying the preparation of financial statements that requires that the source of all accounting information be economic transactions affecting an enterprise and its resources.

Transfer agent An independent agent, usually a bank or a trust company, that maintains a record of, and executes all, capital stock transfers and sales, as well as the payment of dividends on those shares.

Transitory earnings (cash flows) The nonrecurring earnings (cash flows) of a company; earnings (cash flows) that are not expected to reoccur in future periods.

Translation exposure (risk) A source of foreign exchange risk resulting from the restatement of foreign financial statements denominated in a foreign currency into U.S. dollar-equivalents; also known as accounting exposure.

Treasury stock Outstanding capital stock that has been repurchased but not retired and is usually held to be reissued at some future date.

Trend analysis The analysis of ratios or absolute account balances over one or more accounting periods to identify the direction or trend of a company's financial health.

Trial balance A listing of the preadjusted, preclosing account balances from the general ledger designed to verify that the sum of the accounts with debit balances equals the sum of the accounts with credit balances.

True and fair view The current standard of precision required of all audited financial data in the EU; analogous to the "fairly presented" standard used in the United States.

Turnover A measure of the rate of sales of goods or services; in the United Kingdom, a measure of net sales or net revenues.

Uncollectible account An account receivable that a company expects not to be able to collect.

Underwriter A brokerage house or investment banker hired by a company to help sell a bond or stock offering.

Unearned revenue Revenue that is received as cash but that has not yet been earned.

Unit-of-production method A method to depreciate the cost of a tangible asset or to deplete the cost of a natural resource; the allocated cost is based on the actual production by the asset.

Unleveraged ROA (UROA) A refinement of the return on assets (ROA) ratio, obtained by restating net income to include interest charges on an aftertax basis (that is, net income plus interest expense net of tax benefits).

Unrealized change in value of available-for-sale investment portfolio A contra owners' equity (addendum) account representing a write-down (write-up) in the available-for-sale portfolio for temporary market fluctuations, as a consequence of the mark-to-market method.

Unrealized loss (gain) A loss (gain) that is recognized in the financial statements but is not associated with an asset sale; usually involves a revaluation of an asset value.

Useful life The estimated productive life of a noncurrent asset.

Value-added statement A financial statement prepared by some foreign companies reflecting a measure of the wealth created by the operations of the company and the distribution of that wealth among its major constituents (for example, employees, investors, and the government).

Value-added tax A tax levied at each stage in the production and distribution chain on the basis of the value that is added to a product as it passes through a given stage.

Vendor A company selling goods or services.

Vested benefits Pension benefits owed to employees at retirement regardless of whether they continue to be employed by the company until they reach retirement age.

Warrant A legal document enabling the holder to buy a set number of shares of capital stock at a prespecified price within a set period of time.

Warranty obligation An obligation for future costs to maintain a product sold in good working condition.

Wasting assets Noncurrent assets, such as natural resources, that decrease in value as a result of depletion or consumption of the asset.

Weighted-average cost method An inventory cost-flow method that assigns the average cost of available finished goods, weighted by the number of units available at each price, to a unit sold and thus cost of goods sold, and to ending inventory.

Wirtschaftsprüfer (WP) A certified public accountant in Germany.

With (without) recourse Terms of the sale of an account or note receivable. A sale with recourse obligates the selling company to "make good" the receivable in the event that the factor is unable to collect on the receivable; a sale without recourse obligates the factor to assume all liability for noncollectibility.

Work in process inventory Partially completed goods or products; classified as a current asset on the balance sheet.

Working capital A measure of liquidity or short-term solvency, calculated as total current assets minus total current liabilities.

Working capital maintenance agreement An executory contract by which one entity guarantees to maintain the level of working capital of a second entity; usually arises as a consequence of a borrowing agreement by the second entity for which the first party becomes a guarantor.

World standards report A set of financial statements prepared according to IASC accounting standards.

Zaibatsu Japanese industrial conglomerates that existed prior to World War II but were disbanded and have been subsequently replaced by keiretsu.

INDEX